Principles of Macroeconomics

PEARSON CUSTOM PUBLISHING

Principles of Macroeconomics

Compiled from:

Economics
Eighth Edition
by Michael Parkin, Melanie Powell and Kent Matthews

PEARSON

Harlow, England • London • New York • Boston • San Francisco • Toronto • Sydney • Auckland • Singapore • Hong Kong
Tokyo • Seoul • Taipei • New Delhi • Cape Town • Sao Paulo • Mexico City • Madrid • Amsterdam • Munich • Paris • Milan

Pearson Education Limited
Edinburgh Gate
Harlow
Essex CM20 2JE

And associated companies throughout the world

Visit us on the World Wide Web at:
www.pearsoned.co.uk

Compiled from:

Economics
Eighth Edition
by Michael Parkin, Melanie Powell and Kent Matthews
ISBN 978 0 273 73575 5

ISBN 978 1 78134 208 4

Printed and bound by 4edge, Hockley. www.4edge.co.uk. FSC Certified

Contents

PART 6

Monitoring Macroeconomic Performance

The Big Picture

Macroeconomics is a large and controversial subject that is interlaced with political ideological disputes. And it is a field in which charlatans as well as serious thinkers have much to say.

The subject seeks to understand the causes of economic growth, business cycles (booms and busts), unemployment, inflation, exchange rate and interest rate fluctuations, government budget surpluses and deficits, and international payments surpluses and deficits.

Macroeconomics is data-driven. In governments and international organizations, economic statisticians measure and record the performance of the economy.

The two chapters in this part (20 and 21) explain how two main macroeconomic variables, GDP and unemployment, are monitored and measured. You will learn how we use GDP to assess the standard of living and how we use the unemployment rate to assess the overall state of health of the economy.

Understanding Macroeconomic Performance

The first step towards the scientific study of macroeconomics was a reaction against a popular belief, known as *Mercantilism*, that a nation's wealth depends on the amount of gold (or more generally money) that it possesses. Mercantilists said that by imposing tariffs to discourage imports and by increasing its exports, a nation could earn more than it spends and become more wealthy.

Writing in the early 1740s, David Hume (who can lay claim to being the first macroeconomist though the term wasn't coined until well into the twentieth century) explained why the quantity of money (gold in his day) has no effect on a nation's wealth and only affects the general level of prices and the value of money. You will learn about Hume's 'quantity theory of money' later in this book.

In the 1740s, data were scarce and Hume was not able to confirm his theories by checking them against facts. Instead, he conducted thought experiments. He imagined how things would change as the quantity of money increased. Today, macroeconomics is a ruthlessly empirical discipline. It uses data, both historical and current, to probe the causes of economic growth and its fluctuations, and inflation and deflation.

The very idea of making a graph of time-series data arose in a macroeconomic context. In 1776, coincidentally the year in which David Hume died and Adam Smith published his *Wealth of Nations*, yet another Scot, William Playfair, created the first time-series graph. His graph showed the exports, imports and balance of trade between England and a number of other countries. Graphs that you can make with a click of a mouse took hours of painstaking pen and ink drawing at that time and the data on which they were based were extremely scarce.

Today the Office of National Statistics, the OECD, the International Monetary Fund and the statistical departments of every major government and central bank pump out macroeconomic data every day.

It is a good idea to get into the habit of doing your own macroeconomic monitoring. Make a start by visiting www.statistics.gov.uk and dig around.

David Hume, a Scot who lived from 1711 to 1776, did not call himself an economist. 'Philosophy and general learning' is how he described the subject of his life's work. Hume was an extraordinary thinker and writer. Published in 1742, his *Essays, Moral and Political*, range across economics, political science, moral philosophy, history, literature, ethics and religion, and explore such topics as love, marriage, divorce, suicide, death and the immortality of the soul!

His economic essays provide astonishing insights into the forces that cause inflation, business cycle fluctuations, balance of payments deficits and interest rate fluctuations; and they explain the effects of taxes and government deficits and debts.

Data were scarce in Hume's day, so he was not able to draw on detailed evidence to support his analysis. But he was empirical. He repeatedly appealed to experience and evidence as the ultimate judge of the validity of an argument. Hume's fundamentally empirical approach dominates macroeconomics today.

'. . . in every kingdom into which money begins to flow in greater abundance than formerly, everything takes a new face: labour and industry gain life; the merchant becomes more enterprising, the manufacturer more diligent and skilful, and even the farmer follows his plough with greater alacrity and attention.'

DAVID HUME
Essays, Moral and Political

CHAPTER 20

Measuring GDP and Economic Growth

After studying this chapter you will be able to:

- Define GDP and explain why it equals aggregate expenditure and aggregate income
- Explain how the Office for National Statistics measures UK GDP
- Describe how GDP is used and explain its limitations

The recent recession in the UK has been described as the worst since the 1930s. To assess the state of the economy, economists, commentators and politicians turn to the measure of GDP and the growth of GDP. What exactly is GDP and what does it tell us about the state of the economy? And how can we compare economic growth in the 2000s with that in the 1930s?

This chapter explains how the economic statisticians at the Office for National Statistics measure GDP. *Reading Between the Lines* at the end of the chapter, looks at the recession of 2008–2009 and compares it with the recession during the 1930s.

Gross Domestic Product

What exactly is GDP, how is it calculated, what does it mean and why do we care about it? You are going to discover the answers to these questions in this chapter. First, what is GDP?

GDP Defined

GDP or **gross domestic product** is the market value of all the final goods and services produced within a country in a given time period – usually a year. This definition has four parts:

- Market value
- Final goods and services
- Produced within a country
- In a given time period

We examine each in turn.

Market Value

To measure total production, we must add together the production of apples and oranges, computers and popcorn. Just counting the items doesn't get us very far. For example, which is the greater total production: 100 apples and 50 oranges, or 50 apples and 100 oranges?

GDP answers this question by valuing items at their *market values* – the prices at which items are traded in markets. If the price of an apple is 10 pence, the market value of 50 apples is £5. If the price of an orange is 20 pence, the market value of 100 oranges is £20. By valuing production at market prices, we can add the apples and oranges together. The market value of 50 apples and 100 oranges is £5 plus £20, or £25.

Final Goods and Services

To calculate GDP, we value the *final goods and services* produced. A **final good** (or service) is an item that is bought by its final user during a specified time period. It contrasts with an **intermediate good** (or service), which is an item that is produced by one firm, bought by another firm and used as a component of a final good or service.

For example, a Ford Focus is a final good, but a tyre on the Ford Focus is an intermediate good. A Dell computer is a final good, but an Intel Pentium chip inside it is an intermediate good.

If we were to add the value of intermediate goods and services produced to the value of final goods and services, we would count the same thing many times – a problem called *double counting*. The value of a Ford Focus already includes the value of the tyres, and the value of a Dell PC already includes the value of the Pentium chip inside it.

Some goods can be an intermediate good in some situations and a final good in other situations. For example, the ice cream that you buy on a hot summer day is a final good, but the ice cream that a café buys and uses to make sundaes is an intermediate good. The sundae is the final good. So whether a good is an intermediate good or a final good depends on what it is used for, not on what it is.

Some items that people buy are neither final goods nor intermediate goods and they are not part of GDP. Examples of such items include financial assets – stocks and bonds – and secondhand goods – used cars or existing homes. A secondhand good was part of GDP in the year in which it was produced, but not in GDP this year.

Produced Within a Country

Only goods and services that are produced *within a country* count as part of that country's GDP. When James Dyson, a British entrepreneur who makes vacuum cleaners, produces them in Malaysia, the market value of those cleaners is part of Malaysia's GDP, not part of the UK's GDP. Toyota, a Japanese firm, produces cars in Deeside, Wales, and the value of this production is part of UK GDP, not part of Japan's GDP.

In a Given Time Period

GDP measures the value of production *in a given time period* – normally either a quarter of a year (called the quarterly GDP data) or a year (called the annual GDP data).

GDP measures not only the value of total production but also total income and total expenditure. The equality between the value of total production and total income is important because it shows the direct link between productivity and living standards. Our standard of living rises when our incomes rise and we can afford to buy more goods and services. But we must produce more goods and services if we are to be able to buy more goods and services.

Rising incomes and a rising value of production go together. They are two aspects of the same phenomenon: increasing production. To see why, we study the circular flow of expenditure and income.

GDP and the Circular Flow of Expenditure and Income

Figure 20.1 illustrates the circular flow of expenditure and income. The economy consists of households, firms, governments and the rest of the world (the rectangles), which trade in factor markets and goods (and services) markets. Let's focus first on households and firms.

Households and Firms

Households sell and firms buy the services of labour, capital and land in factor markets. For these factor services, firms pay income to households: wages for labour services, interest for the use of capital and rent for the use of land. A fourth factor of production, entrepreneurship, receives profit.

Firms' retained earnings – profits that are not distributed to households – are also part of the household sector's income. You can think of retained earnings as being income that households save and lend back to firms. Figure 20.1 shows the *aggregate income* received by all households, including retained earnings, as the blue flow labelled Y.

Households buy and firms sell consumption goods and services – such as beer, pizzas and dry cleaning services – in goods markets. Total payment for these goods and services is **consumption expenditure**, shown by the red flow labelled C.

Firms buy and sell new capital equipment – such as computer systems, aeroplanes, trucks, trains and assembly line equipment – in goods markets.

Some of what firms produce is not sold but is added to their stocks (or inventories). For example, if Ford produces 1,000 cars and sells 950 of them, the other 50 cars remain unsold and the firm's stock of cars increases by 50. When a firm adds unsold output to its stocks, we can think of the firm as buying goods from itself. The purchase of new plant, equipment and buildings, and the additions to stocks, are **investment**, shown by the red flow labelled I.

Figure 20.1 The Circular Flow of Expenditure and Income

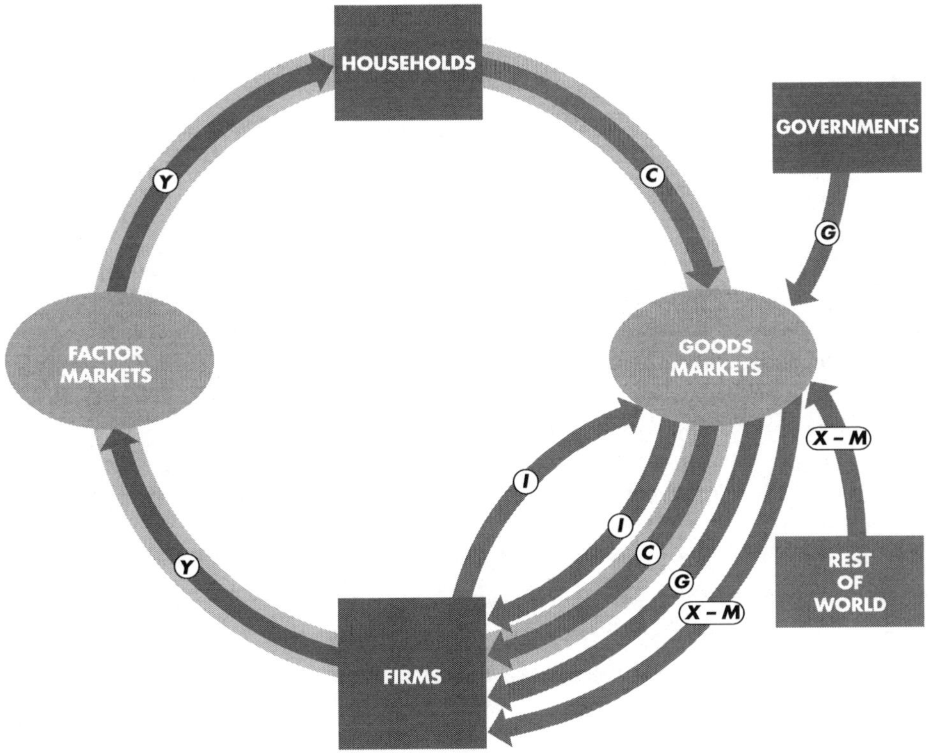

Households make consumption expenditures (C); firms make investments (I); the government purchases goods and services (G); the rest of the world buys net exports ($X - M$). Firms pay incomes (Y) to households.

Aggregate income (blue flow) equals aggregate expenditure (red flows).

Billions of pounds in 2010	
C =	948
I =	208
G =	338
$X - M$ =	–46
Y =	1,448

myeconlab Animation

Governments

Governments buy goods and services from firms and their expenditure on goods and services is called **government expenditure**. In Figure 20.1, government expenditure on goods and services is shown as the red flow *G*.

Governments finance their expenditure with taxes, but taxes are not part of the circular flow of expenditure and income. Governments also make financial transfers to households, such as unemployment benefits and subsidies to firms. These financial transfers, like taxes, are not part of the circular flow of expenditure and income. Financial transfers and taxes are neither expenditures on goods and services nor income from the services of factors of production.

Rest of World

Firms in the UK sell goods and services to the rest of the world, **exports**, and buy goods and services from the rest of the world, **imports**. The value of exports (X) minus the value of imports (M) is called **net exports**. Figure 20.1 shows net exports by the red flow $X - M$.

If net exports are positive, the net flow of goods and services is from the rest of the world to UK firms. If net exports are negative, the net flow of goods and services is from UK firms to the rest of the world.

GDP Equals Expenditure Equals Income

GDP can be measured in two ways: by the total expenditure on goods and services (called the expenditure approach) or by the total income earned by producing goods and services (called the income approach).

The total expenditure – *aggregate expenditure* – is the sum of the red flows in Figure 20.1. Aggregate expenditure equals consumption expenditure plus investment plus government expenditure plus net exports.

Aggregate income earned by producing goods and services is equal to the total amount paid for the factors used – wages, interest, rent and profit. The blue flow in Figure 20.1 shows aggregate income. Because firms pay out as incomes (including retained profits) everything they receive from the sale of their output, aggregate income (the blue flow) equals aggregate expenditure (the sum of the red flows). That is:

$$Y = C + I + G + X - M$$

The table in Figure 20.1 shows the UK numbers for 2010. You can see that the sum of the expenditures is £1,448 billion, which also equals aggregate income.

Because aggregate expenditure equals aggregate income, these two methods of valuing GDP give the same answer. So:

GDP equals aggregate expenditure and equals aggregate income.

The circular flow model is the foundation on which the national economic accounts are built.

Why Is Domestic Product 'Gross'?

What does the 'gross' in GDP mean? *Gross* means before deducting the depreciation of capital. The opposite of 'gross' is net, which means after deducting the depreciation of capital.

Depreciation is the decrease in the value of a firm's capital that results from wear and tear and obsolescence. The total amount spent on purchases of new capital and on replacing depreciated capital is called **gross investment**. The amount by which the value of the firm's capital increases is called **net investment**.

Net investment = Gross investment – Depreciation

For example, if easyJet buys 5 new aeroplanes and retires 2 old aeroplanes from service, its gross investment is the value of the 5 new aeroplanes, depreciation is the value of the 2 old aeroplanes retired, and net investment is the value of 3 new aeroplanes.

Gross investment is one of the expenditures included in the expenditure approach to measuring GDP. So the resulting value of total product is a gross measure.

Gross profit, which is a firm's profit before subtracting depreciation, is one of the incomes included in the income approach to measuring GDP. So again, the resulting value of total product is a gross measure.

Review Quiz

1 Define GDP and distinguish between a final good and an intermediate good. Provide examples.
2 Why does GDP equal aggregate income and also equal aggregate expenditure?
3 What is the distinction between gross and net?

You can work these questions in Study Plan 20.1 and get instant feedback. myeconlab

Let's now see how the ideas that you have just studied can be used in practice. We'll see how GDP and its components are measured in the UK today.

Measuring UK GDP

The Office for National Statistics uses the concepts that you met in the circular flow model to measure GDP and its components, which it publishes in the *United Kingdom National Accounts – The Blue Book*.

Because the value of aggregate output equals aggregate expenditure and aggregate income, there are two approaches available for measuring GDP, and both are used. They are:

- The expenditure approach
- The income approach

The Expenditure Approach

The *expenditure approach* measures GDP as the sum of consumption expenditure (*C*), investment (*I*), government expenditure on goods and services (*G*) and net exports of goods and services (*X* – *M*), corresponding to the red flows in the circular flow model in Figure 20.2. Table 20.1 shows the results of this approach for 2010. The table also shows the terms used in the *United Kingdom National Accounts – The Blue Book*.

Consumption expenditure is the expenditure by households on goods and services produced in the UK and the rest of the world. It includes goods such as beer, CDs, books and magazines; and services such as insurance, banking and legal advice. It includes the purchases of consumer durable goods such as cars and washing machines, but it does *not* include the purchase of new houses, which is counted as part of investment.

Investment is expenditure on capital equipment and buildings by firms and expenditure on new residential houses by households. It also includes the change in firms' stocks or inventories.

Government expenditure is the expenditure on goods and services by all levels of government – from Westminster to the local town hall. This item includes expenditure on national defence, law and order, street lighting and refuse collection. It does *not* include unemployment benefits because they are not purchases of goods and services.

Net exports are the value of UK exports minus the value of UK imports. When a UK company sells a car to a buyer in the US, the value of that car is part of UK exports. When your local Skoda dealer stocks up on the latest model, its expenditure is part of UK imports.

Table 20.1 shows the relative magnitudes of the four items of aggregate expenditure.

Table 20.1

GDP: The Expenditure Approach

Item	Symbol	Amount in 2010 (billions of pounds)	Percentage of GDP
Consumption expenditure (Final consumption expenditure: personal)	*C*	948	65.5
Investment (Gross capital formation)	*I*	208	14.4
Government expenditure (Final consumption expenditure: governments)	*G*	338	23.3
Net exports (External balance of goods and services)	*X* – *M*	–46	–3.2
Gross domestic product	*Y*	1,448	100.0

The expenditure approach measures GDP as the sum of consumption expenditure (*C*), investment (*I*) government expenditure (*G*) and net exports (*X* – *M*). In 2010, GDP as measured by the expenditure approach was £1,448 billion. Almost two-thirds of aggregate expenditure is consump-tion expenditure.

Source of data: Office for National Statistics, *Statistical Bulletin*, 28 September 2010.

Figure 20.2 Aggregate Expenditure

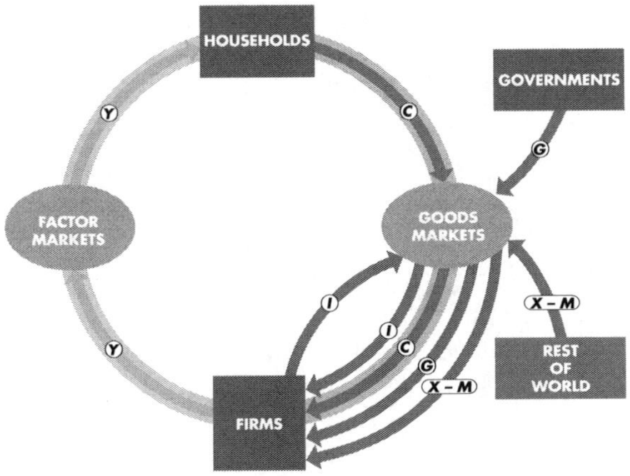

Aggregate expenditure is the sum of the red flows.

myeconlab Animation

The Income Approach

The *income approach* measures GDP by summing the incomes paid by firms to households for the services of the factors of production they hire – wages for labour, interest for capital, rent for land and profit for entrepreneurship. Let's see how the income approach works.

In the *United Kingdom National Accounts – The Blue Book*, incomes are grouped into three components:

1 Compensation of employees
2 Gross operating surplus
3 Mixed income

Compensation of employees is the total payments by firms for labour services. This item includes gross wages and benefits, such as pension contributions and is shown by the blue flow *W* in Figure 20.3.

Gross operating surplus is the total profit made by companies and the surpluses generated by publicly owned enterprises. Some of the profits are paid to households in the form of dividends, and some are retained by companies as undistributed profits. The surpluses from publicly owned enterprises are either retained by the enterprises or paid to the government as part of its general revenue. They are all income and are shown by the blue flow *P* in Figure 20.3.

Mixed income is a combination of rental income and income from self-employment. Rental income is the payment for the use of land and other rented inputs. It includes payments for rented housing and imputed rent for owner-occupied housing. (Imputed rent is an estimate of what homeowners would pay to rent the housing they own and use themselves. By including this item in the national accounts, we measure the total value of housing services, whether they are owned or rented.) Income from self-employment is a mixture of the factor incomes that we have just reviewed. The proprietor of an owner-operated business supplies labour, capital and perhaps land and buildings to the business.

Table 20.2

GDP: The Income Approach

Item	Amount in 2010 (billions of pounds)	Percentage of GDP
Compensation of employees	788	54.4
Gross operating surplus	308	21.3
Mixed income	170	11.7
Gross domestic income at factor cost	1,266	87.4
Indirect taxes less subsidies	182	12.6
Gross domestic product	1,448	100.0

The sum of all factor incomes equals gross domestic income at factor cost. GDP equals net domestic income at factor cost plus indirect taxes less subsidies. In 2010, GDP measured by the factor incomes approach was £1,448 billion. Compensation of employees was by far the largest part of total factor income.

Source of data: Office for National Statistics, *Statistical Bulletin*, 28 September 2010.

Figure 20.3 Aggregate Income

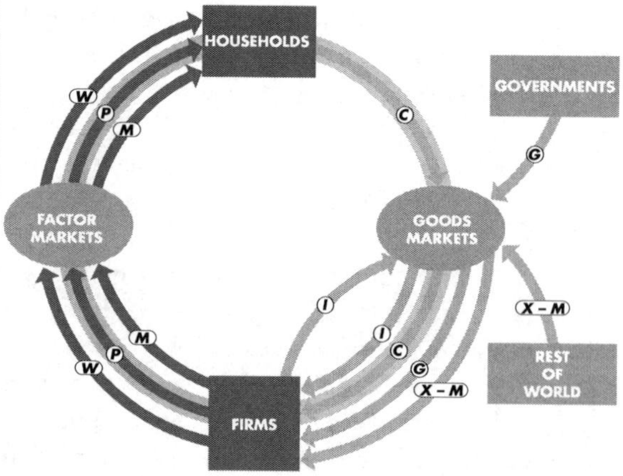

Aggregate income is the sum of the components of the blue flows.

myeconlab Animation

Table 20.2 shows these three components of aggregate income and their relative magnitudes.

The sum of the incomes is called *gross domestic income at factor cost*. The term *factor cost* is used because it is the cost of the *factors of production* used to produce final goods and services. When we sum all the expenditures on final goods and services, we arrive at a total called *domestic product at market prices*. Market prices and factor cost would be the same except for indirect taxes and subsidies.

An *indirect tax* is a tax paid by consumers when they buy goods and services, such as VAT. An indirect tax makes the market price exceed the factor cost. A *subsidy* is a payment by the government to a producer. With a subsidy, the factor cost exceeds the market price. To get from factor cost to market price, we add indirect taxes and subtract subsidies.

Nominal GDP and Real GDP

Often, we want to compare GDP in two periods, say 2000 and 2010. In 2000, GDP was £977 billion and in 2010 it was £1,448 billion – 48 per cent higher than in 2000. This increase in GDP is a combination of an increase in production and a rise in prices. To isolate the increase in production from the rise in prices, we distinguish between *real* GDP and *nominal* GDP.

Real GDP is the value of final goods and services produced in a given year when valued at the *prices of a reference base year*. By comparing the value of production in the two years at the same prices, we reveal the change in production.

Currently, the reference base year is 2006 and we describe real GDP as measured in 2006 pounds – in terms of what the pound would buy in 2006.

Nominal GDP is the value of final goods and services produced in a given year when valued at the prices of that year. Nominal GDP is just a more precise name for GDP.

Economic statisticians at the Office for National Statistics calculate real GDP using the method described in the Mathematical Note on pp. 476–477. Here, we'll explain the basic idea but not the technical details.

Table 20.3

Calculating Nominal GDP and Real GDP

Item	Quantity (millions)	Price (pounds)	Expenditure (millions of pounds)
(a) In 2006			
C Shirts	10	5	50
I Computer chips	3	10	30
G Security services	1	20	20
Y Real and Nominal GDP in 2006			100
(b) In 2010			
C Shirts	4	5	20
I Computer chips	2	20	40
G Security services	6	40	240
Y Nominal GDP in 2010			300
(c) Quantities of 2010 valued at prices of 2006			
C Shirts	4	5	20
I Computer chips	2	10	20
G Security services	6	20	120
Y Real GDP in 2010			160

In 2006, the reference base year, real GDP equals nominal GDP and was £100 million. In 2010, nominal GDP increased to £300 million. But real GDP in 2010 in part (c), which is calculated by using the quantities of 2010 in part (b) and the prices of 2006 in part (a), was only £160 million – a 60 per cent increase from 2006.

Calculating Real GDP

We'll calculate real GDP for an economy that produces one consumption good, one capital good and one government service. Net exports are zero.

Table 20.3 shows the quantities produced and the prices in 2006 (the base year) and in 2010. In part (a), we calculate nominal GDP in 2006. For each item, we multiply the quantity produced in 2006 by its price in 2006 to find the total expenditure on the item. We sum the expenditures to find nominal GDP, which in 2006 is £100 million. Because 2006 is the base year, both real GDP and nominal GDP equal £100 million.

In Table 20.3(b), we calculate nominal GDP in 2010, which is £300 million. Nominal GDP in 2010 is three times its value in 2006. But by how much has production increased? Real GDP will tell us.

In Table 20.3(c), we calculate real GDP in 2010. The quantities of the goods and services produced are those of 2010, as in part (b). The prices are those in the reference base year – 2006, as in part (a).

For each item, we multiply the quantity produced in 2010 by its price in 2006. We then sum these expenditures to find real GDP in 2010, which is £160 million. This number is what total expenditure would have been in 2010 if prices had remained the same as they were in 2006.

Nominal GDP in 2010 is three times its value in 2006, but real GDP in 2010 is only 1.6 times its 2006 value – a 60 per cent increase in production.

Review Quiz

1. What is the expenditure approach to measuring GDP?
2. What is the income approach to measuring GDP?
3. What adjustment must be made to total income to make it equal to GDP?
4. What is the distinction between nominal GDP and real GDP?
5. How is real GDP calculated?

You can work these questions in Study Plan 20.2 and get instant feedback. myeconlab

The Uses and Limitations of Real GDP

We use estimates of real GDP for two main purposes. They are:

- To compare the standard of living over time
- To compare the standard of living across countries

The Standard of Living Over Time

One method of comparing the standard of living over time is to calculate real GDP per person in different years. **Real GDP per person** is real GDP divided by the population. Real GDP per person tells us the value of goods and services that the average person can enjoy. By using *real* GDP, we remove any influence that rising prices and a rising cost of living might have had on our comparison.

We're interested in both the long-term trends and the shorter-term cycles in the standard of living.

Figure 20.4 Rising UK Standard of Living

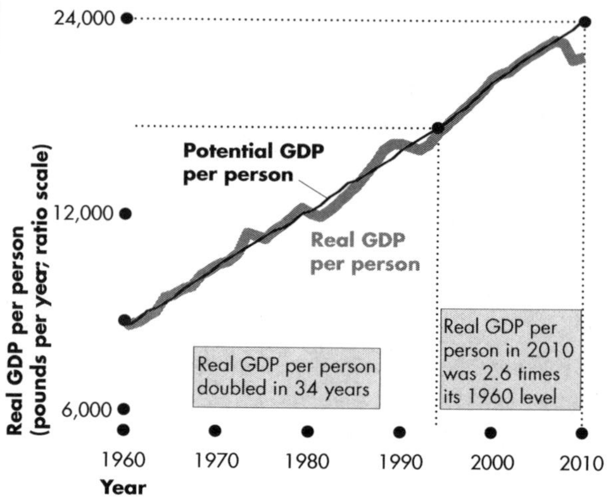

Real GDP per person in the UK doubled between 1960 and 1994. In 2010, real GDP per person was 2.6 times its 1960 level. Real GDP per person, the red line, fluctuates around potential GDP per person, the black line. (The *y*-axis is a ratio scale – see the Appendix, pp. 474–475.)

Source of data: Office for National Statistics, *Statistical Bulletin*. 28 September 2010.

myeconlab Animation

Long-term Trend

A handy way of comparing real GDP per person over time is to express it as a ratio of some reference year. For example, in 1960 real GDP per person was £8,070 and in 2010 it was £21,216. So real GDP per person in 2010 was 2.6 times its 1960 level – that is, £21,216 divided by £8,070. To the extent that real GDP per person measures the standard of living, people were 2.6 times as well off in 2010 as their grandparents had been in 1960.

Figure 20.4 shows the path of UK real GDP per person for the 50 years from 1960 to 2010 and highlights two features of our expanding living standard:

- The growth of potential GDP per person
- Fluctuations of real GDP per person

The Growth of Potential GDP

Potential GDP is the value of production when all the economy's labour, capital, land and entrepreneurial ability are fully employed. Potential GDP per person, the smoother black line in Figure 20.4, grows at a steady pace because the quantities of the factors of production and their productivities grow at a steady pace.

But potential GDP per person doesn't grow at a constant pace. During the 1960s, it grew at 2.8 per cent per year but slowed to only 2.1 per cent per year during the 1970s. This slowdown might seem small, but it had big consequences, as you'll soon see.

Fluctuations of Real GDP

You can see that real GDP per person, shown by the red line in Figure 20.4, fluctuates around potential GDP per person, and sometimes real GDP per person shrinks.

Let's take a closer look at the two features of our expanding living standard that we've just outlined.

Productivity Growth Slowdown

How costly was the slowdown in productivity growth after 1970? The answer is provided by the *Lucas wedge*, which is the pound value of the accumulated gap between what real GDP per person would have been if the 1960s growth rate had persisted and what real GDP per person turned out to be. (Nobel Laureate Robert E. Lucas Jr. drew attention to this gap.)

Figure 20.5 illustrates the Lucas wedge. The wedge started out small during the 1970s, but by 2010 real GDP per person was £5,962 per year lower than it would have been with no growth slowdown and the accumulated gap was £88,000 per person.

Figure 20.5 The Cost of Slower Growth

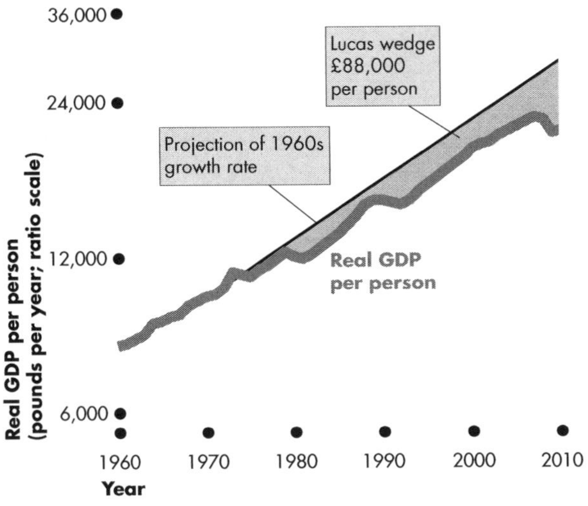

The black line projects the 1960s growth rate of real GDP per person to 2010. The Lucas wedge arises from the slowdown of productivity growth that began during the 1970s. The cost of the slowdown is £88,000 per person.

Source of data: Office for National Statistics, *Statistical Bulletin*. 28 September 2010.

myeconlab Animation

Real GDP Fluctuations – The Business Cycle

We call the fluctuations in the pace of expansion of real GDP the business cycle. The **business cycle** is a periodic but irregular up-and-down movement of total production and other measures of economic activity. The business cycle isn't a regular predictable cycle like the phases of the moon, but every cycle has two phases:

1 Expansion
2 Recession

and two turning points:

1 Peak
2 Trough

Figure 20.6 shows these features of the most recent UK business cycle.

An **expansion** is a period during which real GDP increases. In the early stage of an expansion real GDP returns to potential GDP and as the expansion progresses, potential GDP grows and real GDP eventually exceeds potential GDP.

A common definition of **recession** is a period during which real GDP decreases – its growth rate is negative – for at least two successive quarters. The definition used by the National Bureau of Economic Research, which dates the US business cycle phases and turning points, is 'a period of significant decline in total output, income, employment and trade, usually lasting from six months to a year, and marked by contractions in many sectors of the economy'.

An expansion ends and a recession begins at a business cycle peak, which is the highest level that real GDP has attained up to that time. A recession ends at a trough, when real GDP reaches a temporary low point and from which the next expansion begins.

In the second quarter of 2008 the UK economy went into recession. From a long way below potential GDP, a recovery began at the end of 2009. The recovery looked strong in the first half of 2010, but doubts are beginning to emerge about whether the pace of the recovery will be sustained. *Reading Between the Lines* on pp. 472–473 discusses why.

Figure 20.6 The Most Recent UK Business Cycle

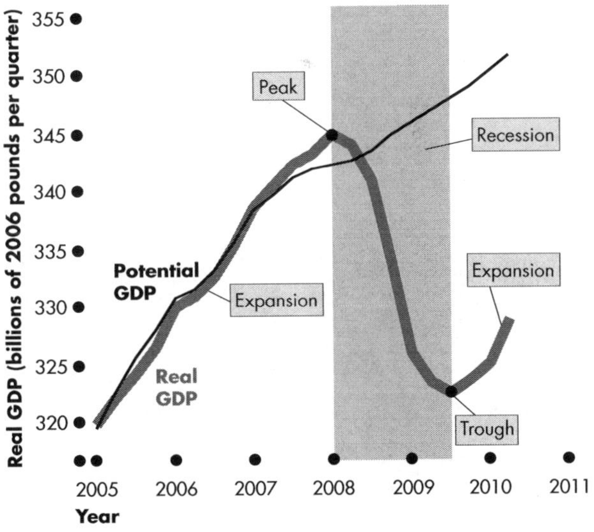

A business cycle expansion, which began in the fourth quarter of 2001, ended at a peak in the second quarter of 2008. A deep and long recession followed the 2008 peak and ended in a trough at the end of 2009 when an expansion began.

Source of data: Office for National Statistics, *Statistical Bulletin*. 28 September 2010.

myeconlab Animation

The Standard of Living Across Countries

Two problems arise in using real GDP to compare living standards across countries. First, the real GDP of one country must be converted into the same currency units as the real GDP of the other country. Second, the goods and services in both countries must be valued at the same prices. Comparing the US and China provides a striking example of these two problems.

China and the US in US Dollars

In 2010, real GDP per person in the US was $42,800 and in China it was 23,400 yuan. The yuan is the currency of China and the price at which the dollar and the yuan exchanged, the market exchange rate, was 8.2 yuan per US$1. Using this exchange rate, 23,400 yuan converts to $2,850. These numbers tell us that real GDP per person in the US was 15 times that in China.

The red line in Figure 20.7 shows real GDP per person in China from 1980 to 2010 when the market exchange rate is used to convert yuan to US dollars.

China and the US at PPP

Figure 20.7 shows a second estimate of China's real GDP per person that values China's production on the same terms as US production. It uses *purchasing power parity* or *PPP* prices, which are the *same prices* for both countries.

Figure 20.7 Two Views of Real GDP in China

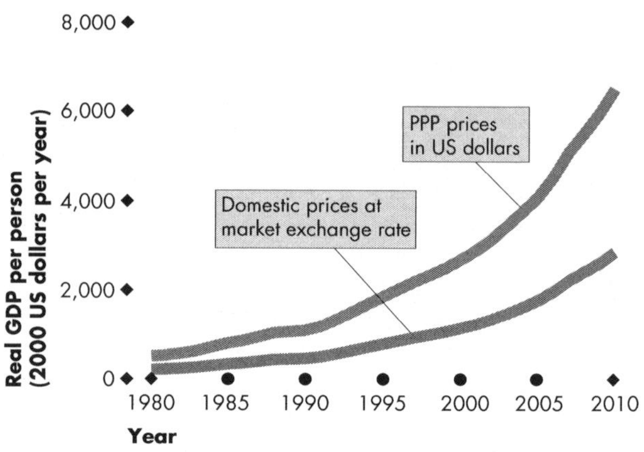

Real GDP per person in China has grown rapidly. But how rapidly it has grown and to what level depends on how real GDP is valued. When GDP in 2010 is valued at the market exchange rate, US income per person is 15 times that in China. China looks like a poor developing country. But the comparison is misleading. When GDP is valued at purchasing power parity prices, US income per person is only 6.5 times that in China.

Source of data: International Monetary Fund, World Economic Outlook database, April 2010.

myeconlab Animation

The price of a Big Mac is $3.75 in Chicago and 13.25 yuan or $1.62 in Shanghai. To compare real GDP in China and the US, we must value China's Big Macs at the $3.75 US price – the PPP price.

The prices of some goods are higher in the US than in China, so these items get a smaller weight in China's real GDP than they get in US real GDP. An example is a Big Mac that costs $3.75 in Chicago. In Shanghai, a Big Mac costs 13.25 yuan which is the equivalent of $1.62. So in China's real GDP, a Big Mac gets less than half the weight that it gets in US real GDP.

Some prices in China are higher than in the US but more prices are lower, so Chinese prices put a lower value on China's production than do US prices.

According to the PPP comparisons, real GDP per person in the US in 2010 was 6.5 times that of China, not 15 times.

You've seen how real GDP is used to make standard of living comparisons over time and across countries. But real GDP isn't a perfect measure of the standard of living and we'll now examine its limitations.

Limitations of Real GDP

Real GDP measures the value of goods and services that are bought in markets. Some of the factors that influence the standard of living and that are not part of GDP are:

- Household production
- Underground economic activity
- Health and life expectancy
- Leisure time
- Environmental quality
- Political freedom and social justice

Household Production

An enormous amount of production takes place every day in our homes. Changing a light bulb, cutting the grass, washing the car and growing vegetables are all examples of household production. Because these productive activities are not traded in markets, they are not included in GDP.

The omission of household production from GDP means that GDP *underestimates* total production. But it also means that the growth rate of GDP *overestimates* the growth rate of total production. The reason is that some of the growth rate of market production (included in GDP) is a replacement for home production. So part of the increase in GDP arises from a decrease in home production.

Two trends point in this direction. One is the trend in the number of women who have jobs, which increased from 52.7 per cent of the female population of working age in 1971 to 56.7 per cent in 2010. The other is the trend in the purchase of traditionally home-produced goods and services in the market. For example, more households now buy takeaways, eat in restaurants and use childcare services. This trend means that increasing proportions of food preparation and childcare that used to be part of household production are now measured as part of GDP. So real GDP grows more rapidly than does real GDP plus home production.

Underground Economic Activity

The *underground economy* is the part of the economy purposely hidden from view by the people operating in it to avoid taxes and regulations or because the goods and services they are producing are illegal. Because underground economic activity is unreported, it is omitted from GDP.

The underground economy is easy to describe, even if it is hard to measure. It includes the production and distribution of illegal drugs, prostitution, production that uses illegal labour that is paid less than the minimum wage, and jobs done for cash to avoid paying income taxes. This last category might be quite large and includes tips earned by taxi drivers, hairdressers and hotel and restaurant workers.

Estimates of the scale of the underground economy range between 3.5 and 13.5 per cent of GDP (£51 billion to £195 billion) in the UK and much more in some countries, particularly in Eastern European countries that are making the transition from centrally planned economies to market economies.

If the underground economy is a constant proportion of the total economy, the growth rate of real GDP provides a useful estimate of *changes* in economic welfare and the standard of living. But sometimes production shifts from the underground economy to the rest of the economy, and sometimes it shifts the other way. The underground economy expands relative to the rest of the economy if taxes rise sharply or if regulations become especially restrictive. And the underground economy shrinks relative to the rest of the economy if the burdens of taxes and regulations ease.

Whose production is more valuable: the chef's whose work gets counted in GDP . . .

. . . or the busy mother's whose dinner preparations and child minding don't get counted?

During the 1980s, when tax rates were cut, there was an increase in the reporting of previously hidden income and tax revenues increased. So some part (but probably a very small part) of the expansion of real GDP during the 1980s represented a shift from the underground economy rather than an increase in production.

Health and Life Expectancy

Good health and a long life – the hopes of everyone – do not show up in real GDP, at least not directly. A higher real GDP does enable us to spend more on medical research, healthcare, healthy food and exercise equipment. As real GDP has increased, our life expectancy has lengthened – from 70 years at the end of the Second World War to approaching 80 years today.

But we face new health and life expectancy problems every year. AIDS, drug abuse, suicide and murder are taking young lives at a rate that causes serious concern. When we take these negative influences into account, we see that real GDP growth overstates the improvements in the standard of living.

Leisure Time

Leisure time is an economic good that adds to our standard of living. Other things remaining the same, the more leisure we have, the better off we are. Our time spent working is valued as part of GDP, but our leisure time is not. Yet that leisure time must be at least as valuable to us as the wage that we earn for the last hour worked. If it were not, we would work instead of taking the leisure. Over the years, leisure time has steadily increased. The working week has become shorter and the number and length of holidays have increased. These improvements in economic well-being are not reflected in GDP.

Environmental Quality

Economic activity directly influences the quality of the environment. The burning of hydrocarbon fuels is the most visible activity that damages our environment. But it is not the only example. The depletion of non-renewable resources, the mass clearing of forests, and the pollution of lakes and rivers are other major environmental consequences of industrial production.

Resources used to protect the environment are valued as part of GDP. For example, the value of catalytic converters that help to protect the atmosphere from vehicle emissions is part of GDP. But if we did not use such pieces of equipment and instead polluted the atmosphere, we would not count the deteriorating air that we were breathing as a negative part of GDP.

An industrial society possibly produces more atmospheric pollution than does an agricultural society. But pollution does not always increase as we become wealthier. Wealthy people value a clean environment and are willing to pay for one. Compare the pollution in China today with pollution in the UK. China, a poor country, pollutes its rivers, lakes and atmosphere in a way that is unimaginable in the UK.

Political Freedom and Social Justice

Most people value political freedoms such as those provided by the western democracies. They also value social justice or fairness – equality of opportunity and of access to social security safety nets that protect people from the extremes of misfortune.

A country might have a very large real GDP per person but have limited political freedom and equity. For example, a small elite might enjoy political liberty and extreme wealth, while the vast majority are effectively enslaved and live in abject poverty. Such an economy would generally be regarded as having less economic welfare than one that had the same amount of real GDP but in which political freedoms were enjoyed by everyone. Today, China is the world's fastest-growing economy but the Chinese people have limited political freedoms. India's economy is growing less quickly than China's but the people of India enjoy a democratic political system. Economists have no easy way to determine which of these two countries is better off.

The Bottom Line

Do we get the wrong message about the growth in economic welfare by looking at the growth of real GDP? The influences that are omitted from real GDP are probably important and could be large.

Developing countries have more household production and a larger underground economy than do developed countries, so the gap between their living standards is exaggerated. Also, as real GDP grows, part of the measured growth might reflect a switch from home production to market production and from underground to regular production. This measurement error overstates the growth in economic well-being and the improvement in the standard of living.

ECONOMICS IN ACTION

A Broader Indicator of Economic Well-being

The limitations of real GDP reviewed in this chapter affect the standard of living and general well-being of every country. So to make international comparisons of the general state of economic well-being, we must look at real GDP and other indicators.

The United Nations has constructed a broader measure called the Human Development Index (HDI), which combines real GDP, life expectancy and health and education. Real GDP per person (measured on the PPP basis) is a major component of the HDI.

The dots in the figure show the relationship between real GDP per person and the HDI. The United Arab Emirates (UAE) has one of the highest real GDP per person, but it ranks 35th on the HDI. Norway has the highest HDI, and the UK, Australia and Japan have a higher HDI than the UAE. The HDI of the UAE is lower than that of 34 other countries because the people of those countries live longer and have better access to healthcare and education than do citizens of the UAE.

African nations have the lowest levels of economic well-being. The Democratic Republic of Congo has the lowest real GDP per person and Niger has the lowest HDI. But real GDP per person in South Africa is in the middle of the range and its HDI is also in the middle of the range.

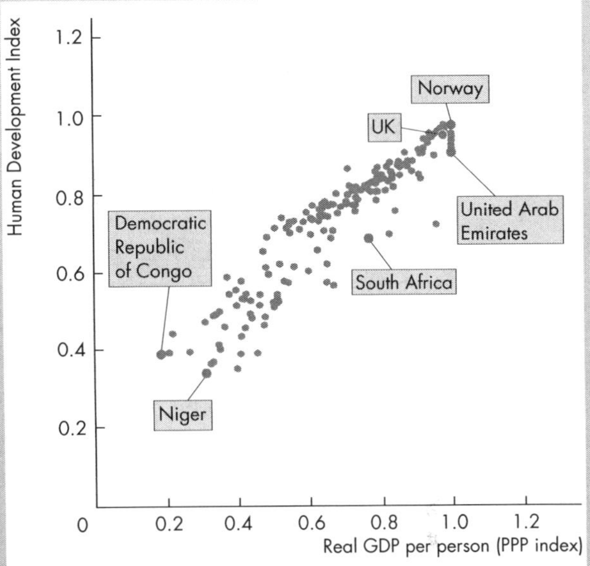

Figure 1 The Human Development Index

Source of data: United Nations, hdr.undp.org/en/statistics/data

Other influences on the standard of living include the amount of leisure time available, the quality of the environment, the security of jobs and homes and the safety of city streets.

It is possible to construct broader measures that combine the many influences that contribute to human happiness. Real GDP will be one element in those broader measures, but it will by no means be the whole of those measures. The United Nation's Human Development Index (HDI) is one example of attempts to provide broader measures of economic well-being and the standard of living. This measure places a good deal of weight on real GDP. Dozens of other measures have been proposed. One includes resource depletion and emissions in a Green GDP measure. Another emphasizes the enjoyment of life rather than the production of goods in a 'genuine progress index' or GPI.

Despite all the alternatives, real GDP per person remains the most widely used indicator of economic well-being and the standard of living.

Review Quiz

1. Distinguish between real GDP and potential GDP and describe how each grows over time.
2. How does the growth rate of real GDP contribute to an improved standard of living?
3. What is a business cycle and what are its phases and turning points?
4. What is PPP and how does it help us to make valid international comparisons of real GDP?
5. Explain why real GDP might be an unreliable indicator of the standard of living.

You can work these questions in Study Plan 20.3 and get instant feedback. myeconlab

You now know how economists measure GDP and what the GDP data tell us. In *Reading Between the Lines* on pp. 472–473, we examine the path of GDP as we emerge from recession during 2010. Your task in the next chapter is to learn how we monitor employment and unemployment and retail prices.

Reading Between the Lines

The Fragile UK Recovery

The Financial Times, 6 October 2010

Employers Fear Recovery is in Peril from Spending Cuts

Daniel Pimlotte

The economy grew at a reasonable pace in the third quarter but businesses are increasingly alarmed about the prospects for another recession or much weaker growth, according to a closely watched survey. Growth between July and September looks likely to have been 0.4 to 0.5 per cent, according to polling company Markit, an estimate based on its surveys of purchasing managers in the service, manufacturing and building sectors.

That is not far from the 0.6 per cent long-run average pace at which the UK has grown but much slower than the 1.2 per cent growth in the second quarter. Markit warned that many companies were worried about spending cuts, with greater detail on the austerity measures due this month in the government's spending review.

'Orders are not coming through at anything like the pace before the public sector contracts are being cut. Businesses believe these cuts are arriving at the wrong time.'

The evidence of business fears came as Markit published its combined index of activity in services, manufacturing and construction.

Services sector data published on Tuesday showed weak business confidence and new orders rising at the slowest pace in 15 months.

The Essence of the Story

- A poll of purchasing managers suggest that growth in the third quarter of 2010 could be between 0.4 and 0.5 per cent.
- This quarterly growth rate translates into an annual growth rate of 2 per cent, which is not far from the UK long-term growth rate of 2.4 to 2.5 per cent a year.
- Many businesses are worried about cuts in government spending that might depress demand and stall the recovery.
- The fragility of demand and the growth of GDP have raised the prospect that the economy may recover very slowly or even turn down into a double-dip recession.

Economic Analysis

- The 2008–2009 recession was an unusually deep one and although the second quarter of 2010 showed a strong recovery, predictions for subsequent quarters were for weak growth.
- Figure 1 illustrates the severity of the 2008–2009 recession using the concepts of potential GDP and real GDP that you learned about in this chapter.
- At the trough in the third quarter of 2009, real GDP was about £25 billion below potential GDP or 7 per cent of potential GDP.
- To put the magnitude of the gap between potential GDP and real GDP into perspective, each person's share (your share) of the lost production for the whole of 2009 was about £1,667.
- The prediction from the Markit survey is that the economy will grow by only 0.5 per cent in the third quarter of 2010, which shows the fragility of the recovery and possibly a second downturn.
- However, a slowdown in the growth rate does not necessarily mean that the economy will slip back into recession.
- The 2008–2009 recession has been described as the worst recession since the 1930s. Figure 2 shows the quarterly profile of the 1930s recession plotted alongside the 2008–2009 recession.
- The similarity of the downturn and the recovery between the two periods is striking. It is also the case that just when the economy came out of deep recession in 1931 the economy slipped back into recession in 1932.
- While the recession and recovery during the 1930s looks similar to the quarterly profile of 2008–2009 there are many differences in policy that do not make it obvious that the economy will turn downwards in 2011, as it did in 1932.

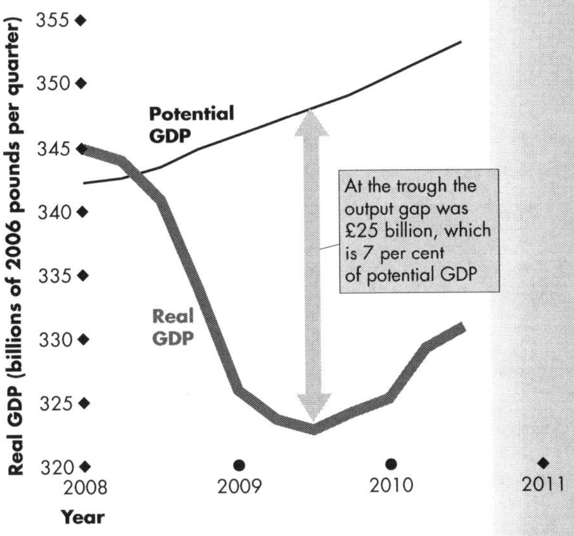

Figure 1 The deep 2008–2009 recession

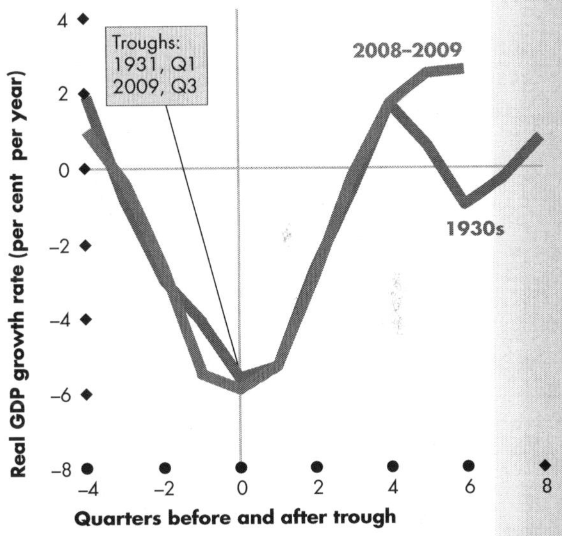

Figure 2 The 1930s versus 2008–2009

- *The Economist* magazine publishes the results of a weekly poll of forecasters and on 9 October 2010 the range of forecasts for UK GDP growth in 2011 was from a low of 0.6 per cent a year to a high of 2.4 per cent a year.

Chapter 20 Appendix

Graphs in Macroeconomics

After studying this appendix, you will be able to:

- Make and interpret a time-series graph
- Make and interpret a graph that uses a ratio scale

The Time-series Graph

In macroeconomics we study the fluctuations and trends in the key variables that describe macroeconomic performance and policy. These variables include GDP and its expenditure and income components that you've learned about in this chapter. They also include variables that describe the labour market and consumer prices that you study in Chapter 22.

Regardless of the variable of interest, we want to be able to compare its value today with that in the past; and we want to describe how the variable has changed over time. The most effective way to do these things is to make a time-series graph.

Figure A20.1 A Time-series Graph

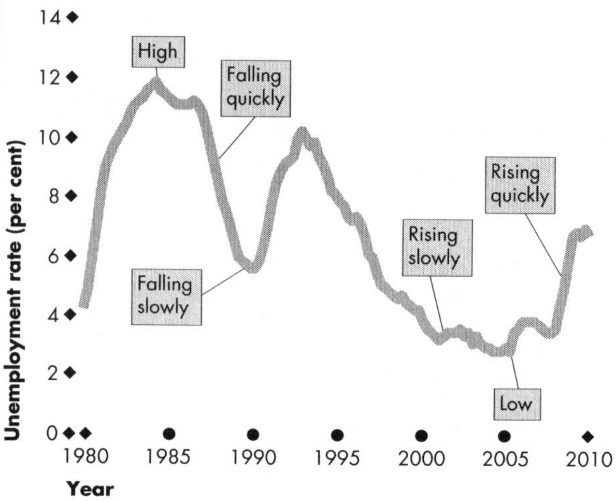

A time-series graph plots the level of a variable on the *y*-axis against time (here measured in years) on the *x*-axis. This graph shows the unemployment rate each year from 1980 to 2010. It shows when unemployment was high, when it was low, when it increased, when it decreased and when it changed quickly and changed slowly.

myeconlab Animation

Making a Time-series Graph

A **time-series graph** measures time (for example, years, quarters or months) on the *x*-axis and the variable or variables in which we are interested on the *y*-axis. Figure A20.1 is an example of a time-series graph. It provides some information about unemployment in the UK since 1980. In this figure, we measure time in years starting in 1980. We measure the unemployment rate (the variable that we are interested in) on the *y*-axis.

A time-series graph enables us to visualize how a variable has changed over time and how its value in one period relates to its value in another period. It conveys an enormous amount of information quickly and easily.

Let's see how to 'read' a time-series graph.

Reading a Time-series Graph

To practise reading a time-series graph, take a close look at Figure A20.1. The graph shows the level, change and speed of change of the variable.

- The *level* of the variable: it tells us when unemployment is high and low. When the line is a long distance above the *x*-axis, the unemployment rate is high, as it was, for example, in 1983 and again in 2009. When the line is close to the *x*-axis, the unemployment rate is low, as it was, for example, in 2001.
- The *change* in the variable: it tells us how unemployment changes – whether it increases or decreases. When the line slopes upward, as it did in 2008 and 2009, the unemployment rate is rising. When the line slopes downward, as it did in 1984 and 1997, the unemployment rate is falling.
- The *speed* of change in the variable: it tells us whether the unemployment rate is rising or falling quickly or slowly. If the line is very steep, then the unemployment rate increases or decreases quickly. If the line is not steep, the unemployment rate increases or decreases slowly. For example, the unemployment rate rose quickly in 2008 and slowly in 2003 and it fell quickly in 1987 and slowly in 1989.

Ratio Scale Reveals Trend

A time-series graph also reveals whether a variable has a **cycle**, which is a tendency for a variable to alternate between upward and downward movements, or a **trend**, which is a tendency for a variable to move in one general direction.

The unemployment rate in Figure A20.1 has a cycle but no strongly visible trend. When a trend is present, a special kind of time-series graph, one that uses a ratio scale on the *y*-axis, reveals the trend.

A Time-series with a Trend

Many macroeconomics variables, among them GDP and the average level of prices, have an upward trend. Figure A20.2 shows an example of such a variable: the average prices paid by consumers.

In Figure A20.2(a), consumer prices since 1970 are graphed on a normal scale. In 1970 the level is 100. In other years, the average level of prices is measured as a percentage of the 1970 level.

The graph clearly shows the upward trend of prices. But it doesn't tell us when prices were rising fastest or whether there was any change in the trend. Just looking at the upward-sloping line in Figure A20.2(a) gives the impression that the pace of growth of consumer prices was constant.

Using a Ratio Scale

On a graph axis with a normal scale, the gap between 1 and 2 is the same as that between 3 and 4. On a graph axis with a ratio scale, the gap between 1 and 2 is the same as that between 2 and 4. The ratio 2 to 1 equals the ratio 4 to 2. By using a ratio scale, we can 'see' when the growth rate (the percentage change per unit of time) changes.

Figure A20.2(b) shows an example of a ratio scale. Notice that the values on the *y*-axis get closer together but the gap between 400 and 200 equals the gap between 200 and 100. The ratio gaps are equal.

Graphing the data on a ratio scale reveals the trends. In the case of consumer prices, the trend is much steeper during the 1970s and early 1980s than in the later years. The steeper the line in the ratio-scale graph in part (b), the faster are prices rising. Prices rose rapidly during the 1970s and early 1980s and more slowly in the later 1980s and 1990s. The ratio-scale graph reveals this fact. We use ratio-scale graphs extensively in macroeconomics.

Figure A20.2 Ratio Scale Reveals Trend

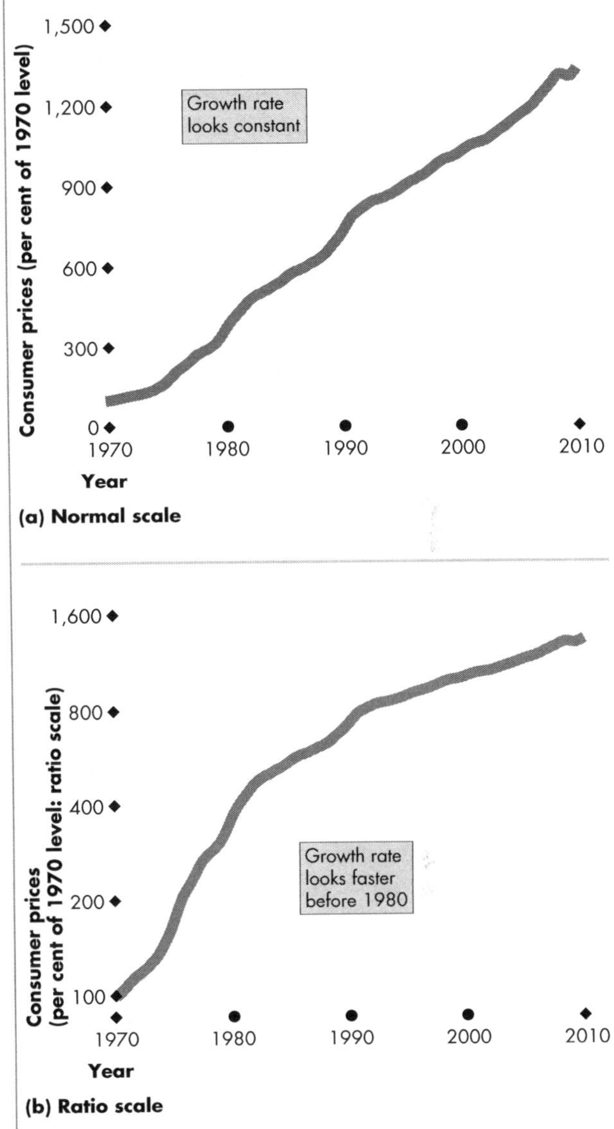

The graph shows the average of consumer prices from 1970 to 2010. The level is 100 in 1970 and the value in other years is a percentage of the 1970 level. Consumer prices normally rise each year so the line slopes upward. In part (a), where the *y*-axis scale is normal, the rate of increase appears to be constant.

In part (b), where the *y*-axis is a ratio scale (the ratio of 400 to 200 equals the ratio 200 to 100), prices rose faster in the 1970s and early 1980s and slower in the later years. The ratio scale reveals this trend.

myeconlab Animation

MATHEMATICAL NOTE

Chain Volume Measure of Real GDP

In the real GDP calculation on p. 465, real GDP in 2010 is 1.6 times its value in 2006. But suppose that we use 2010 as the reference base year and value real GDP in 2006 at 2010 prices. If you do the mathematics, you will see that real GDP in 2006 is £150 million at 2010 prices. GDP in 2010 is £300 million (in 2010 prices), so now the numbers say that real GDP has doubled. Which is correct? Did real GDP increase 1.6 times or double? Should we use the prices of 2006 or 2010? The answer is that we need to use both sets of prices.

The Office for National Statistics uses a measure of real GDP called the **chain volume measure** of real GDP. Three steps are needed to calculate this measure:

- Value production in the prices of adjacent years
- Find the average of two percentage changes
- Link (chain) back to the reference base year

Value Production in Prices of Adjacent Years

The first step is to value production in adjacent years at the prices of both years. We'll make these calculations for 2010 and its preceding year, 2009.

Table 1 shows the quantities produced and prices in the two years. Part (a) shows the nominal GDP calculation for 2009 – the quantities produced in 2009 valued at the prices of 2009. Nominal GDP in 2009 is £145 million. Part (b) shows the nominal GDP calculation for 2010 – the quantities produced in 2010 valued at the prices of 2010. Nominal GDP in 2010 is £300 million. Part (c) shows the value of the quantities produced in 2010 at the prices of 2009 – a total of £160 million. And part (d) shows the value of the quantities produced in 2009 at the prices of 2010 – a total of £275 million.

Table 1

Real GDP Calculation Step 1: Value Production in Adjacent Years at Prices in Both Years

Item	Quantity (millions)	Price (pounds)	Expenditure (millions of pounds)
(a) In 2009			
C Shirts	3	5	15
I Computer chips	3	10	30
G Security services	5	20	100
Y Real and Nominal GDP in 2009			**145**
(b) In 2010			
C Shirts	4	5	20
I Computer chips	2	20	40
G Security services	6	40	240
Y Nominal GDP in 2010			**300**
(c) Quantities of 2010 valued at prices of 2009			
C Shirts	4	5	20
I Computer chips	2	10	20
G Security services	6	20	120
Y 2010 production at 2009 prices			**160**
(d) Quantities of 2009 valued at prices of 2010			
C Shirts	3	5	15
I Computer chips	3	20	60
G Security services	5	40	200
Y 2009 production at 2010 prices			**275**

Step 1 is to value the production of adjacent years at the prices of both years. Here, we value the production of 2009 and 2010 at the prices of both 2009 and 2010. The value of 2009 production at 2009 prices, in part (a), is nominal GDP in 2009. The value of 2010 production at 2010 prices, in part (b), is nominal GDP in 2010. Part (c) calculates the value of 2010 production at 2009 prices, and part (d) calculates the value of 2009 production at 2010 prices. We use these numbers in Step 2.

Find the Average of Two Percentage Changes

The second step is to find the percentage change in the value of production based on the prices in the two adjacent years. Table 2 summarizes these calculations.

Part (a) shows that, valued at the prices of 2009, production increased from £145 million in 2009 to £160 million in 2010, an increase of 10.3 per cent.

Part (b) shows that, valued at the prices of 2010, production increased from £275 million in 2009 to £300 million in 2010, an increase of 9.1 per cent. Part (c) shows that the average of these two percentage changes in the value of production is 9.7. That is, $(10.3 + 9.1) \div 2 = 9.7$.

By applying this average percentage change to real GDP, we can find the value of real GDP in 2010. Real GDP in 2009 is £145 million, so a 9.7 per cent increase

Table 2

Real GDP Calculation Step 2: Find Average of Two Percentage Changes

Value of Production	Millions of pounds	
(a) At 2009 prices		
Nominal GDP in 2009	145	
2010 production at 2009 prices	160	
Percentage change in production at 2009 prices		**10.3**
(b) At 2010 prices		
2009 production at 2010 prices	275	
Nominal GDP in 2010	300	
Percentage change in production at 2010 prices		**9.1**
(c) Average percentage change in 2010		**9.7**

Using the numbers in Step 1, the percentage change in production from 2009 to 2010 valued at 2009 prices is 10.3 per cent, in part (a). The percentage change in production from 2009 to 2010 valued at 2010 prices is 9.1 per cent, in part (b). The average of these two percentage changes is 9.7 per cent, in part (c).

is £14 million. Then real GDP in 2010 is £145 million plus £14 million, which equals £159 million. Because real GDP in 2009 is in 2009 pounds, real GDP in 2010 is also in 2009 pounds.

Although the real GDP of £159 million is expressed in 2009 pounds, the calculation uses the average of the prices of the final goods and services that make up GDP in 2009 and 2010.

Link (Chain) Back to the Base Year

The third step is to express GDP in the prices of the reference base year. To do this, the Office for National Statistics performs calculations like the ones that you've just worked through to find the percentage change in real GDP in each pair of years. It then selects a base year (currently 2006) in which, by definition, real GDP equals nominal GDP. Finally, it uses the percentage changes to calculate real GDP in 2006 prices starting from real GDP in 2006.

To illustrate this third step, we'll assume that the Office for National Statistics has calculated the growth rates since 2006 shown in Table 3. The 2010 growth rate that we've just calculated is highlighted in the table. The other (assumed) growth rates are calculated in exactly the same way as that for 2010.

Table 3

Real GDP Calculation Step 3: Repeat Growth Rate Calculations

Year	2006	2007	2008	2009	**2010**
Growth rate	8.0	6.0	7.0	8.0	**9.7**

Figure 1 illustrates the chain link calculations. In the reference base year, 2006, real GDP equals nominal GDP, which we'll assume is £135 million. Table 3 tells us that the growth rate in 2006 was 8 per cent, so real GDP in 2006 is 8 per cent higher than it was in 2005, which means that real GDP in 2005 is £125 million ($125 \times 1.08 = 135$).

Table 3 also tells us that the growth rate in 2007 was 6 per cent, so real GDP in 2007 is 6 per cent higher than it was in 2006, which means that real GDP in 2007 is £143 million ($135 \times 1.06 = 143$).

By repeating these calculations for each year, we obtain the chain volume measure of real GDP in 2006 pounds for each year. In 2009, chain volume measure of real GDP in 2006 pounds is £165 million. So the 9.7 per cent growth rate in 2010 that we calculated in Table 2 means that real GDP in 2010 is £181 million.

Notice that the growth rates are independent of the reference base year, so changing the reference base year does not change the growth rates.

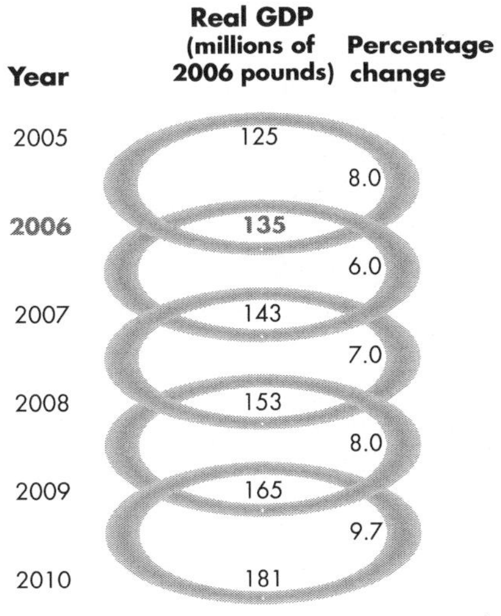

Figure 1 Real GDP calculation step 3: link (chain) back to base year

SUMMARY

Key Points

Gross Domestic Product

- GDP, or gross domestic product, is the market value of all the final goods and services produced in a country during a given period.
- A final good is an item that is bought by its final user and it contrasts with an intermediate good, which is a component of a final good.
- GDP is calculated by using the expenditure or income totals in the circular flow model of expenditure and income.
- Aggregate expenditure on goods and services equals aggregate income and GDP.

Working Problems 1 to 7 will give you a better understanding of gross domestic product.

Measuring UK GDP

- Because aggregate expenditure, aggregate income and the value of aggregate output are equal, we can measure GDP by either the expenditure approach or the income approach.
- The expenditure approach adds together consumption expenditure, investment, government expenditure on goods and services and net exports.
- The income approach adds together the incomes paid to the factors of production – wages, interest, rent and profit – and indirect taxes less subsidies.
- Real GDP is measured using a common set of prices to remove the effects of inflation from GDP.

Working Problems 8 to 15 will give you a better understanding of measuring UK GDP.

The Uses and Limitations of Real GDP

- Real GDP is used to compare the standard of living over time and across countries.
- Real GDP per person grows and fluctuates around the more smoothly growing potential GDP.
- A slowing of the growth rate of real GDP per person during the 1970s has lowered incomes by a large amount.
- International real GDP comparisons use PPP prices.
- Real GDP is not a perfect measure of economic welfare because it excludes household production, the underground economy, health and life expectancy, leisure time, environmental quality and political freedom and social justice.

Working Problem 16 will give you a better understanding of the uses and limitations of real GDP.

Key Terms

Business cycle
Chain volume measure
Consumption expenditure
Cycle
Depreciation
Expansion
Exports
Final good
Government expenditure
Gross domestic product (GDP)
Gross investment
Imports
Intermediate good
Investment
Net exports
Net investment
Nominal GDP
Potential GDP
Real GDP
Real GDP per person
Recession
Time-series graph
Trend

STUDY PLAN PROBLEMS AND APPLICATIONS

myeconlab You can work Problems 1 to 17 in MyEconLab Chapter 20 Study Plan and get instant feedback.

Gross Domestic Product (Study Plan 20.1)

1 Classify each of the following items as a final good or service or an intermediate good or service and identify which is a component of consumption expenditure, investment, or government expenditure on goods and services:

- ◆ Banking services bought by a student.
- ◆ New cars bought by Hertz, the car rental firm.
- ◆ Newsprint bought by *The Times* newspaper.
- ◆ The purchase of a new limo for the prime minister.
- ◆ New house bought by Wayne Rooney.

2 The firm that printed this textbook bought the paper from XYZ Paper Mills. Was this purchase of paper part of GDP? If not, how does the value of the paper get counted in GDP?

Use the following figure, which illustrates the circular flow model, to work Problems 3 and 4.

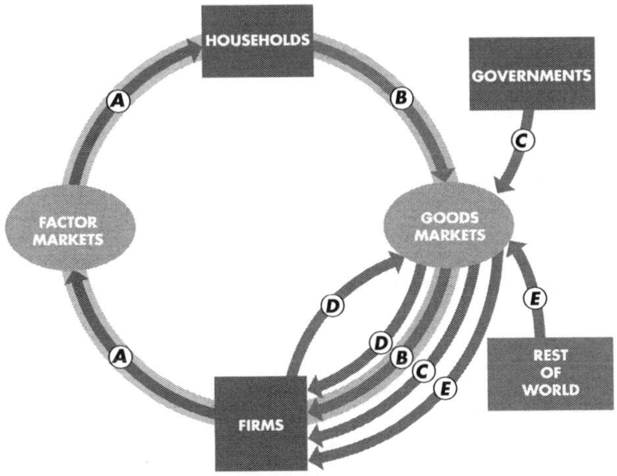

3 During 2008, in an economy:

- ◆ Flow *B* was £90 billion.
- ◆ Flow *C* was £20 billion.
- ◆ Flow *D* was £30 billion.
- ◆ Flow *E* was –£7 billion.

Name the flows and calculate the value of:

a Aggregate income.

b GDP.

4 During 2009, flow A was £130 billion, flow B was £91 billion, flow D was £33 billion, and flow E was –£8 billion.

Calculate the 2009 values of

a GDP.

b Government expenditure.

5 Use the following data to calculate aggregate expenditure and imports of goods and services.

- ◆ Government expenditure: £20 billion.
- ◆ Aggregate income: £100 billion.
- ◆ Consumption expenditure: £67 billion.
- ◆ Investment: £21 billion.
- ◆ Exports of goods and services: £30 billion.

6 **US Economy Shrinks Modestly**

GDP fell 1 per cent as businesses cut investment by 8.9 per cent, consumers cut spending by 1.2 per cent, purchases of new houses fell 38 per cent, and exports fell 29.9 per cent.

Source: Reuters, 31 July 2009

Use the letters on the figure in Problem 3 to indicate the flow in which each item in the news clip occurs. How can GDP have fallen by only 1.0 per cent with the big expenditure cuts reported?

7 A market research firm deconstructed an Apple iPod and studied the manufacturers' costs and profits of each of the parts and components. The final results are:

- ◆ An Apple iPod sells in the US for $299.
- ◆ A Japanese firm, Toshiba, makes the hard disk and display screen, which cost $93.
- ◆ Other components produced in South Korea cost $25.
- ◆ Other components produced in the US cost $21.
- ◆ The iPod is assembled in China at a cost of $5.
- ◆ The costs and profits of retailers, advertisers and transportation firms in the US are $75.

a What is Apple's profit?

b Where in the national accounts of the US, Japan, South Korea and China are these transactions recorded.

c What contribution does one iPod make to world GDP?

Measuring UK GDP (Study Plan 20.2)

Use the following table, which lists some macroeconomic data for the UK, to work Problems 8 and 9.

Item	Billions of pounds
Compensation of employees	750
Consumption expenditure	900
Gross operating surplus	300
Investment	250
Government expenditure	300
Net exports	–40
Mixed income	150

8 Calculate UK GDP.

9 Given the data supplied, which approach (expenditure or income) to measuring GDP can you use to calculate UK GDP? Explain your answer.

Use the following data to work Problems 10 and 11.

The national accounts of Parchment Paradise are kept on (you guessed it) parchment. A fire destroys the statistics office. The accounts are now incomplete but they contain the following data:

- Consumption expenditure: £2,000.
- Indirect taxes less subsidies: £100.
- Gross operating surplus: £500.
- Investment: £800.
- Government expenditure: £400.
- Compensation of employees: £2,000.
- Net exports: –£200.

10 Calculate GDP.

11 Calculate gross domestic income at factor cost.

Use the following data to work Problems 12 and 13.

Tropical Republic produces only bananas and coconuts. The base year is 2009. The table gives the quantities produced and the prices.

Quantities	2009	2010
Bananas	800 kilograms	900 kilograms
Coconuts	400	500
Prices	**2008**	**2009**
Bananas	£2 per kilogram	£4 per kilogram
Coconuts	£10 each	£5 each

12 Calculate nominal GDP in 2009 and 2010.

13 Calculate real GDP in 2010 expressed in base-year prices.

Use the following news clip to work Problems 14 and 15.

Toyota to Shift US Manufacturing Efforts

Toyota plans to adjust its US manufacturing operations to meet customer demands for smaller, more fuel-efficient vehicles. In 2008, Toyota started building a plant to produce the 2010 Prius for the US market in Blue Springs, Mississippi. Earlier models of the Prius were produced in Asia.

Source: CNN, 10 July 2008

14 Explain how this change by Toyota will influence US GDP and the components of aggregate expenditure.

15 Explain how this change by Toyota will influence the factor incomes that make up US GDP.

The Uses and Limitations of Real GDP (Study Plan 20.3)

16 Based on the following data in which year did the US standard of living (i) increase and (ii) decrease. Explain your answer.

Year	Real GDP	Population
2006	$13.0 trillion	300 million
2007	$13.2 trillion	302 million
2008	$13.2 trillion	304 million
2009	$12.8 trillion	307 million

Mathematical Note (Study Plan 20.MN)

17 The table provides data on the economy of Maritime Republic that produces only fish and crabs.

Quantities	2009	2010
Fish	1,000 tonnes	1,100 tonnes
Crabs	500 tonnes	525 tonnes
Prices	**2009**	**2010**
Fish	£20 per tonne	£30 per tonne
Crabs	£10 per tonne	£8 per tonne

a Calculate Maritime Republic's nominal GDP in 2009 and 2010.

b Calculate Maritime Republic's chain volume measure of real GDP in 2010 expressed in 2009 pounds.

Data Graphing

Use the Data Grapher in MyEconLab to work Problems 18 and 19.

18 In which country in 2009 was the growth rate of real GDP per person highest: Canada, Japan or the US?

19 In which country in 2009 was the growth rate of real GDP per person lowest: France, China or the US?

ADDITIONAL PROBLEMS AND APPLICATIONS

myeconlab You can work these problems in MyEconLab if assigned by your lecturer.

Gross Domestic Product

20 Classify each of the following items as a final good or service or an intermediate good or service and identify which is a component of consumption expenditure, investment, or government expenditure on goods and services:

- Banking services bought Google.
- Security system bought by Barclays.
- Coffee beans bought by Starbucks.
- New coffee grinders bought by Starbucks.
- Starbuck's grande mocha frappuccino bought by a student.
- An aircraft carrier bought by the Royal Navy.

Use the figure in Problem 3 on p. 479 to work Problems 21 and 22.

21 In 2009, flow *A* was £1,000 billion, flow *C* was £250 billion, flow *B* was £650 billion, and flow *E* was £50 billion. Calculate investment.

22 In 2010, flow *D* was £2 trillion, flow *E* was –£1 trillion, flow *A* was £10 trillion, and flow *C* was £4 trillion. Calculate consumption expenditure.

Use the following information to work Problems 23 and 24.

Mitsubishi Heavy Industries makes the wings of the new Boeing 787 Dreamliner in Japan. Toyota assembles cars for the US market in Kentucky.

23 Explain where these activities appear in the US national accounts.

24 Explain where these activities appear in Japan's national accounts.

Use the following news clip to work Problems 25 and 26, and use the circular flow model to illustrate your answers.

Boeing Bets the House

Boeing is producing some components of its new 787 Dreamliner in Japan and is assembling it in the US. Much of the first year's production will be sold to ANA (All Nippon Airways), a Japanese airline.

Source: *The New York Times*, 7 May 2006

25 Explain how Boeing's activities and its transactions affect US and Japanese GDP.

26 Explain how ANA's activities and its transactions affect US and Japanese GDP.

Measuring UK GDP

Use the following data to work Problems 27 and 28.

The table lists some macroeconomic data for the UK.

Item	Billions of pounds
Compensation of employees	770
Consumption expenditure	900
Gross operating surplus	300
Investment	200
Government expenditure	2,900
Net exports	–30

27 Calculate UK GDP.

28 Given the data supplied, which approach (expenditure or income) to measuring GDP can you use to calculate UK GDP? Explain your answer.

Use the following data to work Problems 29 to 31.

An economy produces only apples and oranges. The base year is 2009, and the table gives the quantities produced and the prices.

Quantities	2009	2010
Apples	60	160
Oranges	80	220
Prices	**2009**	**2010**
Apples	£0.50 each	£1 each
Oranges	£0.25 each	£2 each

29 Calculate nominal GDP in 2009 and 2010.

30 Calculate real GDP in 2009 and 2010 expressed in base-year prices.

31 **GDP Expands 11.4 per cent, Fastest in 13 Years**

China's gross domestic product grew 11.4 per cent last year and marked a fifth year of double-digit growth. The increase was especially remarkable given that the US is experiencing a slowdown due to the sub-prime crisis and housing slump. Citigroup estimates that each 1 per cent drop in the US economy will shave 1.3 per cent off China's growth, because Americans are heavy users of Chinese products. In spite of the uncertainties, China is expected to post its sixth year of double-digit growth next year.

Source: *The China Daily*, 24 January 2008

Use the expenditure approach for measuring China's GDP to explain why 'each 1 per cent drop in the US economy will shave 1.3 per cent off China's growth'.

The Uses and Limitations of Real GDP

32 The United Nations' Human Development Index (HDI) is based on real GDP per person, life expectancy at birth, and indicators of the quality and quantity of education.

a Explain why the HDI might be better than real GDP as a measure of economic welfare.

b Which items in the HDI are part of real GDP and which items are not in real GDP?

c Do you think the HDI should be expanded to include items such as pollution, resource depletion, and political freedom? Explain.

d What other influences on economic welfare should be included in a comprehensive measure?

33 UK Living Standards Outstrip US

Oxford analysts report that living standards in Britain are set to rise above those in America for the first time since the nineteenth century. Real GDP per person in Britain will be £23,500 this year, compared with £23,250 in America, reflecting not only the strength of the pound against the dollar but also the UK economy's record run of growth since 2001. But the Oxford analysts also point out that Americans benefit from lower prices than those in Britain.

Source: *The Sunday Times*, 6 January 2008

If real GDP per person is more in the UK than in the US but Americans benefit from lower prices, does this comparison of real GDP per person really tell us which country has the higher standard of living?

34 Use the news clip in Problem 31.

a Why might China's recent GDP growth rates overstate the actual increase in the level of production taking place in China?

b Explain the complications involved with attempting to compare economic welfare in China and the US by using the GDP for each country.

35 Poor India Makes Millionaires at Fastest Pace

India, with the world's largest population of poor people created millionaires at the fastest pace in the world in 2007. India added another 23,000 more millionaires in 2007 to its 2006 tally of 100,000 millionaires measured in euros. That is 1 millionaire for about 7,000 people living on less than €2 a day.

Source: *The Times of India*, 25 June 2008

a Why might real GDP per person misrepresent the standard of living of the average Indian?

b Why might €2 a day underestimate the standard of living of the poorest Indians?

Economics in the News

36 After you have studied *Reading Between the Lines* on pp. 472–473 answer the following questions.

a Which measure of GDP would you use to describe the shape of the recovery from recession: real GDP or nominal GDP? Explain your answer.

b Which measure of GDP would you use to describe the rate of growth of the standard of living: real GDP or nominal GDP? Explain your answer.

c If the growth rate of potential GDP is 2.5 per cent a year, how fast must the UK economy grow to close the gap between actual GDP and potential GDP: less than 2.5 per cent a year, more than 2.5 per cent a year or 2.5 per cent a year?

d Why might the news article be wrong about the economy sliding into a double-dip recession?

37 Totally Gross

GDP has proved useful in tracking both short-term fluctuations and long-run growth. Which isn't to say GDP doesn't miss some things. Amartya Sen, at Harvard, helped create the UN Human Development Index, which combines health and education data with per capita GDP to give a better measure of the wealth of nations. Joseph Stiglitz, at Columbia, advocates a 'green net national product' that takes into account the depletion of natural resources. Others want to include happiness in the measure. These alternative benchmarks have merit but can they be measured with anything like the frequency, reliability and impartiality of GDP?

Source: *Time*, 21 April 2008

a Explain the factors that the news clip identifies as limiting the usefulness of GDP as a measure of economic welfare.

b What are the challenges involved in trying to incorporate measurements of those factors in an effort to better measure economic welfare?

c What does the ranking of the UK in the Human Development Index imply about the levels of health and education relative to other nations?

Mathematical Note

38 Use the information in Problem 29 to calculate the chain volume measure of real GDP in 2010 expressed in 2009 pounds.

Data Graphing

Use the Data Grapher in MyEconLab to work Problems 39 and 40.

39 In which country in 2009 was the growth rate of real GDP per person highest: UK, Japan or France?

40 In which country in 2009 was the growth rate of real GDP per person lowest: China, the US or Australia?

CHAPTER 21

Monitoring Jobs and Inflation

After studying this chapter you will be able to:

- Explain why unemployment is a problem and describe the trends and cycles in labour market indicators
- Explain why unemployment is an imperfect measure of underutilized labour and why it is present even at full employment
- Explain why inflation is a problem, how we measure it and why the official measures might be biased

Each month, we track the course of employment and unemployment as measures of economic health. How do we measure the unemployment rate? Is it a reliable vital sign for the economy?

Having a good job that pays a decent wage is only one half of the equation that translates into a good standard of living. The other half is the cost of living. We track the cost of the items we buy with two other numbers that are published every month: the CPI and RPI. How are these numbers calculated and do they provide a good guide to the changes in our cost of living?

These are the questions we study in this chapter. In *Reading Between the Lines* at the end of the chapter, we put the spotlight on the CPI and RPI.

Employment and Unemployment

The state of the labour market has a big impact on our incomes and our lives. In a few years you will be entering the labour market. What kind of market will you enter? Will there be plenty of good jobs to choose among, or will jobs be so hard to find that you end up taking one that doesn't use your education and pays a low wage? The answer depends, to a large degree, on the total number of jobs available and on the number of people competing for them.

Those leaving university in 2010 had an unusually tough time in the jobs market. As recession deepened, the number of unemployed steadily increased until, in May 2009, it passed the 2.4 million mark. Unemployment remained above that level for the rest of 2009 and the whole of 2010. In a normal year, unemployment is less than half that level. And in normal times, the UK economy is an incredible job-creating machine. Even in 2009, 26 million people had jobs. But in recent years, population growth has outstripped jobs growth, so unemployment has become a major problem.

Why Unemployment is a Problem

Unemployment is a serious personal, social and economic problem for two main reasons. It results in:

- Lost incomes and production
- Lost human capital

Lost Incomes and Production

The loss of a job brings with it a loss of income and lost production. These losses are devastating for the people who have to bear them. Unemployment benefits create a safety net and cushion the blow of loss of earnings, but they do not replace lost earnings.

Lost production means lower income and lower consumption. It also means lower investment in capital, which lowers the standard of living both in the present and the future.

Lost Human Capital

Prolonged unemployment permanently damages a person's job prospects by destroying human capital.

ECONOMICS IN ACTION

What Kept John Maynard Keynes Awake at Night

In 1921, the UK unemployment rate shot up to 15 per cent. It remained between 10 and 15 per cent until the early 1930s when it jumped yet higher to almost 25 per cent. Unemployment wouldn't return to below 5 per cent until the first years of World War II in the 1940s.

Puzzled by persistently high unemployment, economist John Maynard Keynes set to work trying to understand how it could happen and what might be done about it. He published his answers in 1936 in the *General Theory of Employment, Interest, and Money*, a book that created what we now call macroeconomics.

Many economists have studied this period of economic history and a shorter yet equally severe Great Depression that occurred in the US and many other economies. Among them are the current chairman of the US Federal Reserve System, Ben Bernanke.

A key reason why the Federal Reserve and the Bank of England were so aggressive in cutting interest rates and injecting money to save banks like Bear Stearns in the US and Northern Rock and the Royal Bank of Scotland in the UK during the recent recession is that economists today are keenly aware of the horrors of total economic collapse. Both the Federal Reserve and the Bank of England were determined to avoid what they see as the mistakes of the 1920s and 1930s that brought Britain's interwar depression and the Great Depression in the US.

Think about a manager who loses his job when his employer downsizes. He takes work as a taxi driver. After a year he finds out that he can't compete with fresh graduates. Eventually he gets a management job but in a small firm at a lower salary than he was earning before. He has lost some of his human capital.

The cost of unemployment is spread unequally and is one of the most important causes of poverty and social deprivation.

Governments try to measure unemployment accurately and adopt policies to ease its pain. Let's see how the UK government measures unemployment.

Labour Force Survey

Every working day, interviewers of the Social and Vital Statistics Division of the Office for National Statistics (the ONS) contact close to 1,000 households (60,000 in a three-month period) and ask them questions about the age and labour market status of the household's members. This survey is called the Labour Force Survey (or LFS). The ONS uses the information obtained to describe the changing anatomy of the labour market.

Figure 21.1 shows the population categories used by the ONS and the relationships among them. The population divides into two groups: the working-age population and others. The **working-age population** is the total number of men aged 16 to 64 and women aged 16 to 59 who are not in prison, hospital or some other form of institutional care.

Members of the working-age population are either economically active or economically inactive. The **economically active** – also called the **workforce** – are people who have a job or are willing and able to take a job. The **economically inactive** are people who don't want a job. Most of the economically inactive are in full-time education or have retired.

The economically active are either employed or unemployed. To be counted as employed, a person must have either a full-time job or a part-time job. A student who does part-time work is counted as employed. To be counted as *un*employed, people must be available for work within the two weeks following their interview and must be in one of three categories:

1 Without work, but having made specific efforts to find a job within the previous four weeks.

2 Waiting to be called back to a job from which they have been laid off.

3 Waiting to start a new job within 30 days.

Figure 21.1 Population Workforce Categories

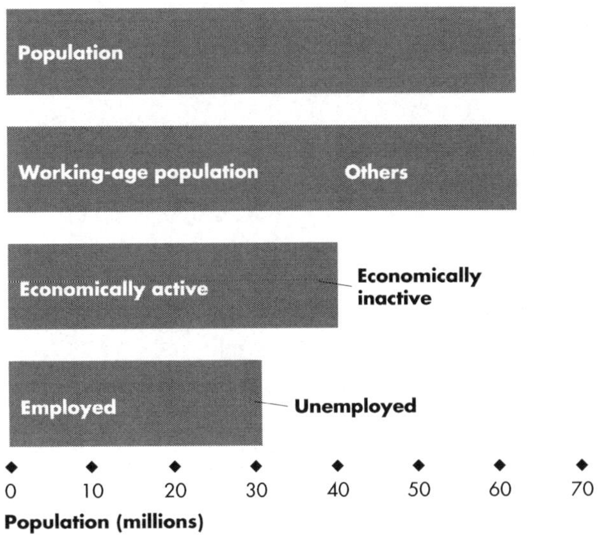

The population is divided into the working-age population and others (the young, the retired and institutionalized). The working-age population is divided into those who are economically active (in the workforce) and those who are economically inactive. The economically active are either employed or unemployed.

Source of data: Office for National Statistics.

myeconlab Animation

People in the working-age population who are neither employed nor unemployed are classified as economically inactive.

In 2010, the population of the UK was 62.1 million. There were 22.1 million below or above working age or living in institutions. So the working-age population in 2010 was 40 million. Of this number, 9.3 million were economically inactive (not in the workforce). The remaining 30.7 million were economically active. Of the economically active, 28.3 million were employed and 2.4 million were unemployed.

Three Labour Market Indicators

The Office for National Statistics calculates three indicators of the state of the labour market. They are:

- The unemployment rate
- The employment rate
- The economic activity rate

The Unemployment Rate

The amount of unemployment is an indicator of the extent to which people who want jobs can't find them. The **unemployment rate** is the percentage of economically active people who are unemployed.

$$\text{Unemployment rate} = \frac{\text{Number of people unemployed}}{\text{Workforce}} \times 100$$

and

$$\text{Workforce} = \text{Number employed} + \text{Number unemployed}$$

In the UK in 2010, the number of people employed was 28.3 million and the number unemployed was 2.4 million. By using the above equations, the workforce was 30.7 million (28.3 million plus 2.4 million) and the unemployment rate was 7.8 per cent (2.4 million divided by 30.7 million, multiplied by 100).

Figure 21.2 shows the unemployment rate between 1980 and 2010. The average unemployment rate was 10 per cent during the decade of the 1980s and 8.3 per cent during the 1990s, but during the 2000s it was 5.5 per cent. The unemployment rate fluctuates and reached peak values at the end of recessions in 1980–1982 and 1990–1992. In 2010, it was not possible to say if the unemployment rate had reached a peak.

The Employment Rate

The number of people of working age who have jobs is an indicator of the availability of jobs and the degree of match between people's skills and jobs. The **employment rate** is the percentage of the people of working age who have jobs. That is:

$$\text{Employment rate} = \frac{\text{Number of people employed}}{\text{Working-age population}} \times 100$$

In 2010, the number of people employed in the UK was 28.3 million and the working-age population was 40 million. By using the above equation, you can calculate the employment rate. It was 70.8 per cent (28.3 million divided by 40 million, multiplied by 100).

Figure 21.3 shows the UK employment rate. It has followed a gently rising trend through the period since 1980. This upward trend means that the economy has created jobs at a faster rate than the working-age population has grown.

Figure 21.2 The Unemployment Rate: 1980–2010

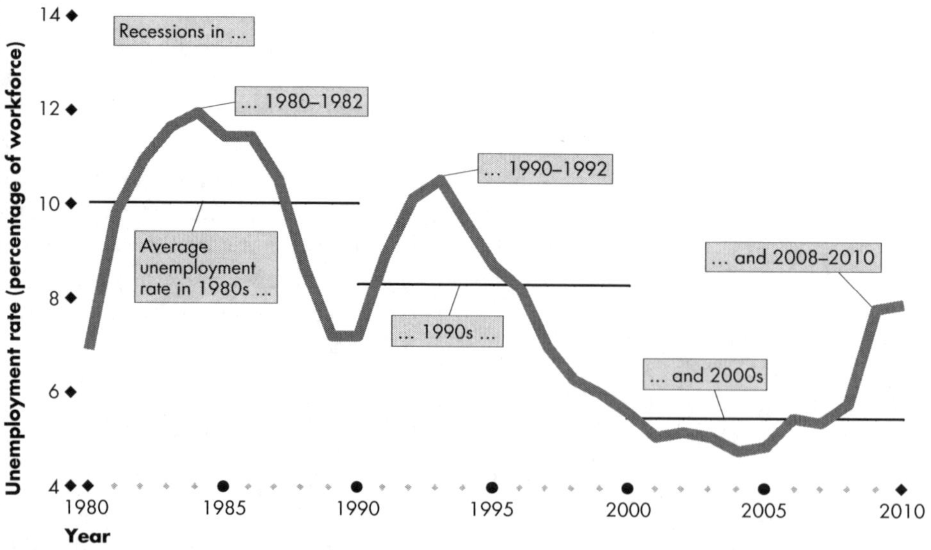

The average unemployment rate was 10 per cent during the 1980s, 8.3 per cent during the 1990s and 5.5 per cent during the 2000s.

The unemployment rate increases in recessions and decreases in expansions.

In 2010, it was unclear whether the unemployment rate had peaked.

Source of data: Office for National Statistics.

myeconlab Animation

Figure 21.3 Economic Activity Rate and Employment Rate: 1980–2010

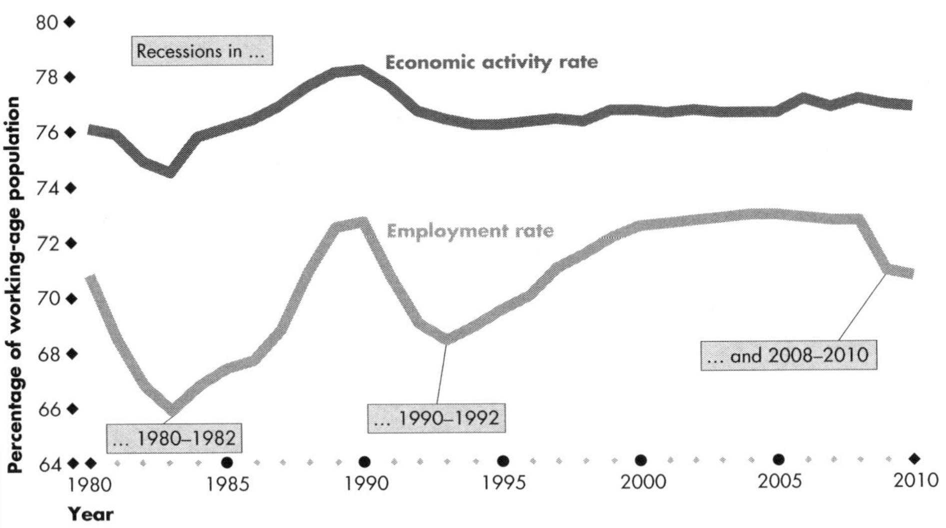

The employment rate decreases in recessions and increases in expansions. It has a slight upward trend. The economic activity rate has no trend The employment rate fluctuates more than the economic activity rate and reflects cyclical fluctuations in the unemployment rate. Fluctuations in the economic activity rate arise from fluctuations in the number of workers who want a job.

Source of data: Office for National Statistics.

myeconlab Animation

This labour market indicator also fluctuates over the business cycle. It reached a trough of 65.9 per cent in 1983, and its fluctuations coincide with, but are opposite to, those in the unemployment rate.

The Economic Activity Rate

The number of people in the workforce is an indicator of the willingness of the people of working age to take jobs. The **economic activity rate** is the percentage of the working-age population who are economically active. They are the members of the workforce.

$$\text{Economic activity rate} = \frac{\text{Workforce}}{\text{Working-age population}} \times 100$$

In 2010, the workforce was 30.7 million and the working-age population was 40 million. By using the above equation, you can calculate the economic activity rate. It was 76.8 per cent (30.7 million divided by 40 million, multiplied by 100).

Figure 21.3 shows the economic activity rate. It rose slightly from 76.1 per cent in 1980 to 76.8 per cent in 2010. It also had some mild fluctuations, which result from unsuccessful job seekers leaving the workforce during a recession and re-entering during an expansion.

Other Definitions of Economic Inactivity and Unemployment

Do fluctuations in the economic activity rate over the business cycle mean that people who leave the workforce during a recession should be counted as unemployed? Or are they correctly counted as economically inactive?

The ONS believes that the official unemployment definition gives the correct measure of the unemployment rate. But the ONS provides data on the reasons for economic inactivity. These data provide information on two relevant groups of people:

- Discouraged workers
- Others who want a job

Discouraged Workers

A **discouraged worker** is someone who is available and willing to work but who has stopped actively looking for a job because he or she believes that no jobs are available. These workers often temporarily leave the workforce during a recession and re-enter during an expansion.

The distinction between an unemployed person and a discouraged worker turns on whether there has been recent job search activity. Both are available for work and want work but the unemployed person has looked for a job while the discouraged worker has given up looking.

Figure 21.4 shows the percentage of economically inactive people who are discouraged workers from 1993 (when the ONS started measuring this number) to 2010.

You can see that discouraged workers are a tiny percentage of the economically inactive and have become less important during the 2000s. The number did, though, increase during the recent recession.

Others Who Want a Job

Others who want a job are people who are economically inactive and are willing to work but who have stopped actively looking for a job and who are not available to start a job in the next two weeks.

Like the discouraged workers, many of these people temporarily leave the workforce during a recession and re-enter during an expansion.

Figure 21.4 shows the percentage of economically inactive people who say they want a job (excluding discouraged workers) from 1993 to 2010.

You can see that this category of people is large. On average, about 25 per cent of the economically inactive say they want a job. This percentage fluctuates between a low of 22 per cent and a high of more than 27 per cent. The correlation between these fluctuations and the business cycle is not strong.

The official unemployment measure excludes economically inactive people because they haven't made specific efforts to find a job within the past four weeks and they are not available for work in the next two weeks. In other respects, they are unemployed.

Most Costly Unemployment

All unemployment is costly, but the most costly is long-term unemployment that results from job loss. People who are unemployed for a few weeks and then find another job bear some costs of unemployment. But these costs are low compared to the costs borne by people who remain unemployed for many weeks.

Also, people who are unemployed because they voluntarily leave their jobs to find better ones or because they have just entered or re-entered the labour market bear some costs of unemployment. But these costs are lower than those borne by people who lose their job and are forced back into the job market.

Figure 21.4 Discouraged Workers and Others Who Want a Job: 1993–2010

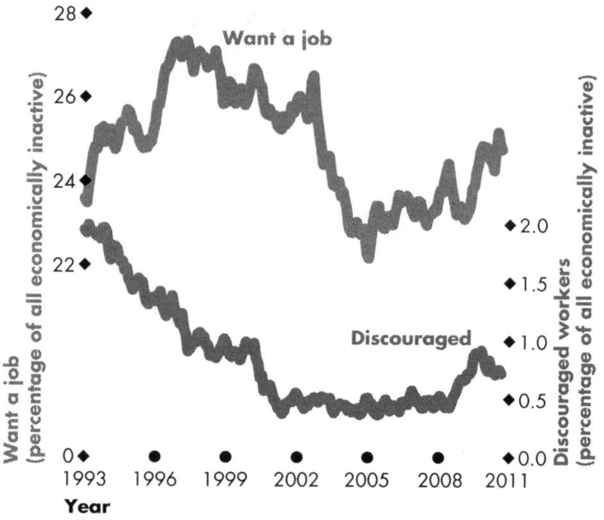

Discouraged workers make up a very small percentage of the economically inactive. They fell from 2 per cent in 1993 to about 0.5 per cent during most of the 2000s. In the 2009 recession, they increased to almost 1 per cent. Others who want a job average about 25 per cent of the economically inactive and this percentage fluctuates but does not correlate closely with the business cycle.

Source of data: Office for National Statistics.

myeconlab Animation

Review Quiz

1. What determines if a person is economically active?
2. What distinguishes an unemployed person from one who is economically inactive?
3. Describe the trends and fluctuations in the UK unemployment rate from 1980 to 2010.
4. Describe the trends and fluctuations in the UK employment rate and economic activity rate from 1980 to 2010.
5. Describe the types of economic inactivity that might be considered to be underutilized labour resources.

You can work these questions in Study Plan 21.1 and get instant feedback. myeconlab

You've now seen how we measure employment and unemployment. Your next task is to see what we mean by full employment and how unemployment and real GDP fluctuate over the business cycle.

Unemployment and Full Employment

There is always someone without a job who is searching for one, so there is always some unemployment. The key reason is that the economy is a complex mechanism that is always changing – it experiences frictions, structural change and cycles.

Frictional Unemployment

There is an unending flow of people into and out of the workforce as people move through the stages of life – from being in school to finding a job, to working, perhaps to becoming unhappy with a job and looking for a new one and, finally, to retiring from full-time work.

There is also an unending process of job creation and job destruction as new firms are born, firms expand or contract and some firms fail and go out of business.

The flows into and out of the workforce and the processes of job creation and job destruction create the need for people to search for jobs and for businesses to search for workers. Businesses don't usually hire the first person who applies for a job, and unemployed people don't usually take the first job that comes their way. Instead, both firms and workers spend time searching for what they believe will be the best available match. By this process of search, people can match their own skills and interests with the available jobs and find a satisfying job and a good income.

The unemployment that arises from the normal labour turnover we've just described – from people entering and leaving the workforce and from the ongoing creation and destruction of jobs – is called **frictional unemployment**. Frictional unemployment is a permanent and healthy phenomenon in a dynamic growing economy.

Structural Unemployment

The unemployment that arises when changes in technology or international competition change the skills needed to perform jobs or change the location of jobs is called **structural unemployment**. Structural unemployment usually lasts longer than frictional unemployment because workers must usually retrain and possibly relocate to find a job. For example, on the day the shipyards in the Upper Clyde announced the loss of 600 jobs, a computer chip company in Gwent announced the creation of 750 new jobs. The unemployed former shipyard workers remained unemployed for several months until they moved home, retrained and got one of the new jobs created in other parts of the country.

Structural unemployment is painful, especially for older workers for whom the best available option might be to retire early or to take a lower-skilled, lower-paid job.

Cyclical Unemployment

The higher than normal unemployment at a business cycle trough and the lower than normal unemployment at a business cycle peak is called **cyclical unemployment**. A worker who is laid off because the economy is in a recession and who gets rehired some months later when the expansion begins has experienced cyclical unemployment.

'Natural' Unemployment

Natural unemployment is the unemployment that arises from frictions and structural change when there is no cyclical unemployment – when all the unemployment is frictional and structural. Natural unemployment as a percentage of the workforce is called the **natural unemployment rate**.

Full employment is defined as a situation in which the unemployment rate equals the natural unemployment rate.

What determines the natural unemployment rate? Is it constant or does it change over time?

The natural unemployment rate is influenced by many factors but the most important ones are:

- The age distribution of the population
- The scale of structural change
- The real wage rate
- Unemployment benefits

The Age Distribution of the Population

An economy with a young population has a large number of new job seekers every year and has a high level of frictional unemployment. An economy with an ageing population has fewer new job seekers and a low level of frictional unemployment.

The Scale of Structual Change

The scale of structural change is sometimes small. The same jobs using the same machines remain in place for many years. But sometimes there is a technological upheaval. The old ways are swept aside: millions of jobs are lost and the skill to perform them loses value. The amount of structural unemployment fluctuates with the pace and volume of technological change and the change driven by fierce international competition, especially from fast-changing Asian economies. A high level of structural unemployment is present in many parts of the UK today.

The Real Wage Rate

The natural unemployment rate is influenced by the level of the real wage rate. Real wage rates that bring unemployment are a minimum wage and an efficiency wage. Chapter 6 (see pp. 131–132) explains how the minimum wage creates unemployment. An *efficiency wage* is a wage set above the going market wage to enable firms to attract the most productive workers, get them to work hard and discourage them from leaving.

Unemployment Benefits

Unemployment benefits increase the natural unemployment rate by lowering the opportunity cost of job search. European countries have more generous unemployment benefits and higher natural unemployment rates than the US. Extending unemployment benefits increases the natural unemployment rate.

There is no controversy about the existence of a natural unemployment rate. Nor is there disagreement that the natural unemployment rate changes. But economists don't know its exact size or the extent to which it fluctuates.

There is no official estimate of the natural unemployment rate for the UK. The one in Figure 21.5 is our own estimate. In 2010 our estimate of the natural unemployment rate was 4.8 per cent – about a half of the unemployment in that year.

Real GDP and Unemployment Over the Business Cycle

The quantity of real GDP at full employment is potential GDP (p. 466). Over the business cycle, real GDP fluctuates around potential GDP. The gap between real GDP and potential GDP is called the **output gap**. As the output gap fluctuates over the business cycle, the unemployment rate fluctuates around the natural unemployment rate.

Figure 21.5 The Output Gap and the Unemployment Rate

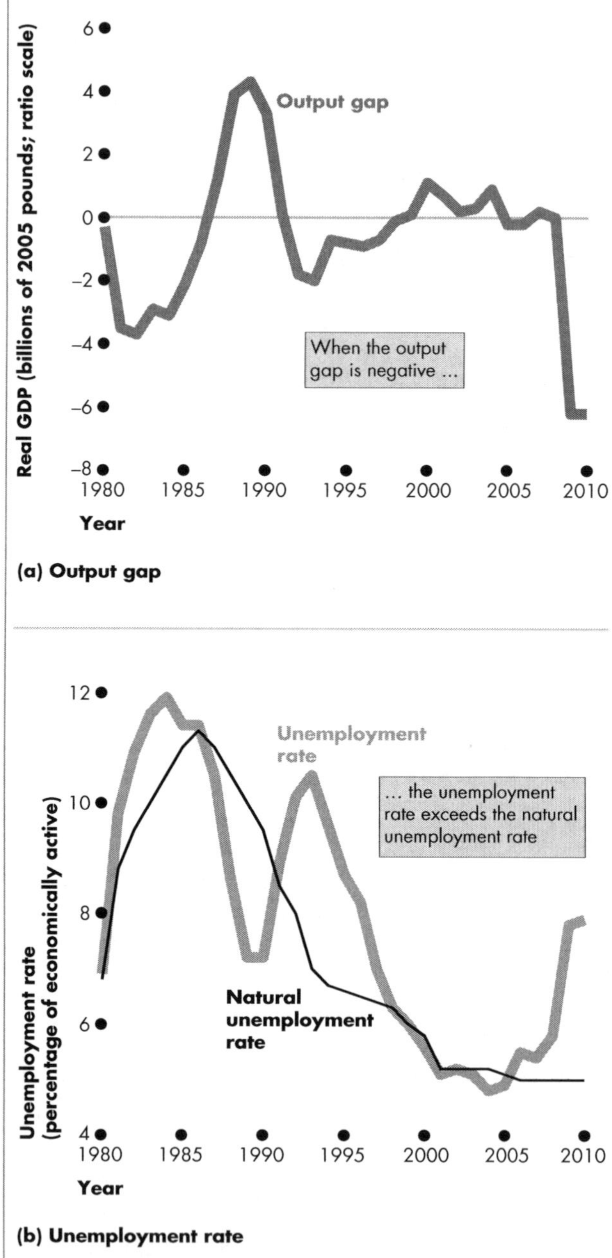

As real GDP fluctuates around potential GDP in part (a), the unemployment rate fluctuates around the natural unemployment rate in part (b). During the recession in the early 1990s, the output gap became negative and the unemployment rate increased to 10 per cent. During the 1980s the natural unemployment rate fell. The graph shows our estimate of how far it fell.

Sources of data: Office for National Statistics; and authors' assumptions and calculations.

myeconlab Animation

ECONOMICS IN ACTION

Jobs in Recession and Recovery

You've seen in Figure 21.5 how fluctuations in the output gap line up with fluctuations in the unemployment rate around the natural unemployment rate.

Here, we are looking at the relationship between real GDP and employment. When real GDP falls during a recession, employment falls too; when real GDP rises in an expansion, employment rises. But there is a delay in the response of employment that is visible in high frequency quarterly data.

The figure shows the changes in real GDP and employment during the recession and expansion during 2008 to 2010. Real GDP shrank until the third quarter of 2009 and then started to expand. Total employment shrank with real GDP, but kept on shrinking until the first quarter of 2010. Only in the second quarter of 2010 did total employment begin to increase.

There is an interesting difference in the way that part-time and full-time employment change during recession and expansion. Part-time employment increases right through the recession. Full-time employment falls until the expansion has been running for six months.

In a recession firms are reluctant to take on new full-time workers. Hiring part-time workers gives them greater flexibility to respond in either direction to changes in production.

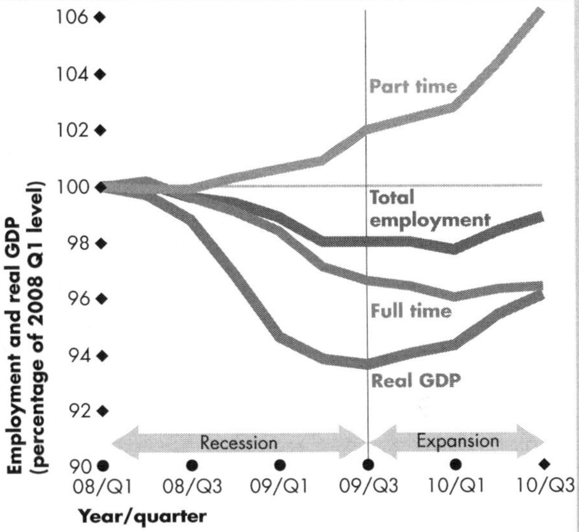

Figure 1 Real GDP and Employment in Recession and Recovery

Source of data: Office for National Statistics.

Figure 21.5 illustrates these fluctuations in the UK between 1980 and 2010 – the output gap in part (a) and the unemployment rate and natural unemployment rate in part (b).

When the economy is at full employment, the unemployment rate equals the natural unemployment rate and real GDP equals potential GDP so the output gap is zero. When the unemployment rate is less than the natural unemployment rate, real GDP is greater than potential GDP and the output gap is positive. And when the unemployment rate is greater than the natural unemployment rate, real GDP is less than potential GDP and the output gap is negative.

Figure 22.5(b) shows an estimate of the natural unemployment rate that is consistent with the estimate of the output gap in part (a). While we have a good estimate of real GDP and unemployment, we must use assumptions to estimate potential GDP, the output gap and the natural unemployment rate. So the picture presented in the figure is just one estimate. In the figure, the natural unemployment rate is high during the 1980s but falls steadily through the 1980s and 1990s to 5 per cent by 2006. This estimate of the natural unemployment rate in the UK is one that many, but not all, economists would accept.

Review Quiz

1. Define frictional, structural and cyclical unemployment and provide an example of each type of unemployment.
2. What is the natural unemployment rate?
3. What factors might make the natural unemployment rate change?
4. How does the unemployment rate fluctuate over the business cycle?

You can work these questions in Study Plan 21.2 and get instant feedback. myeconlab

Your final task in this chapter is to learn about another vital sign that gets monitored every month, the Retail Prices Index (RPI) and the Consumer Prices Index (CPI). What are the RPI and CPI, how do we measure them and what do they mean?

The Price Level, Inflation and Deflation

What will it *really* cost you to pay off your student loan? What will your parents' life savings buy when they retire? The answers depend on what happens to the **price level**, the average level of prices and the value of money. A persistently rising price level is called **inflation**; a persistently falling price level is called **deflation**.

We are interested in the price level, inflation and deflation for two main reasons. First, we want to measure the price level and the inflation rate or deflation rate. Second, we want to distinguish between the money values and real values of economic variables such as your student loan and your parent's savings.

We begin by explaining why inflation and deflation are problems, then we look at how we measure the price level and the inflation rate and finally, we return to the task of distinguishing real values from money values.

Why Inflation and Deflation are Problems

Low, steady and anticipated inflation or deflation isn't a problem, but an unexpected burst of inflation or period of deflation brings four big problems and costs:

- Redistributes income
- Redistributes wealth
- Lowers real GDP and employment
- Diverts resources from production

Redistributes Income

Workers and employers sign wage contracts that last for a year or more. An unexpected burst of inflation raises prices but doesn't immediately raise wages. Workers are worse off because their wages buy less than they bargained for and employers are better off because their profits rise.

An unexpected deflation has the opposite effect. With a fall in prices, workers are better off because their fixed wages buy more than they bargained for and employers are worse off with lower profits.

Redistributes Wealth

People enter into loan contracts that are fixed in money terms and that pay an interest rate agreed as a percentage of the money borrowed and lent. With an unexpected burst of inflation, the money that the borrower repays to the lender buys less than the money originally loaned. The borrower wins and the lender loses. The interest paid on the loan doesn't compensate the lender for the loss in the value of the money loaned. With an unexpected deflation, the money that the borrower repays to the lender buys more than the money originally loaned. The borrower loses and the lender wins.

Lowers Real GDP and Employment

Unexpected inflation that raises firms' profits brings a rise in investment and a boom in production and employment. Real GDP rises above potential GDP and the unemployment rate falls below the natural rate. But this situation is temporary. Profitable investment dries up, spending falls, real GDP falls below potential GDP and the unemployment rate rises. Avoiding these swings in production and jobs means avoiding unexpected swings in the inflation rate.

An unexpected deflation has even greater consequences for real GDP and jobs. Businesses and households that are in debt (borrowers) are worse off and they cut their spending. A fall in total spending brings a recession and rising unemployment.

Diverts Resources from Production

Unpredictable inflation or deflation turns the economy into a casino and diverts resources from productive activities to forecasting inflation. It can become more profitable to forecast the inflation rate or deflation rate correctly than to invent a new product. Doctors, lawyers, accountants, farmers – just about everyone – can make themselves better off, not by specializing in the profession for which they have been trained but by spending more of their time dabbling as amateur economists and inflation forecasters and managing their investments.

From a social perspective, the diversion of talent that results from unpredictable inflation is like throwing scarce resources into a landfill. This waste of resources is a cost of inflation.

At its worst, inflation becomes **hyperinflation** – an inflation rate of 50 per cent a month or higher that grinds the economy to a halt and society to a collapse. Hyperinflation is rare, but Zimbabwe has experienced it in recent years.

The ONS monitors the price level every month and devotes considerable resources to measuring it accurately. You're now going to see how the ONS does this.

The Price Indexes

The ONS calculates two price indexes every month. They are the **Retail Prices Index (RPI)** and the **Consumer Prices Index (CPI)** and both measure an average of the prices paid by consumers for a fixed 'basket' of goods and services. What you learn in this section will help you to interpret the RPI and the CPI and see how they tell you what has happened to the value of your money.

Reading the RPI and CPI

The RPI is defined to equal 100 for a period called the **reference base period**. Currently, the reference base period is January 1987. That is, for January 1987, the RPI equals 100. In January 2010, the RPI was 217.9. This number tells us that the average of the prices paid by households for a particular basket of consumer goods and services was 117.9 per cent higher in January 2010 than it was in January 1987.

The reference base period for the CPI is June 2005 and in June 2010, the CPI was 114.6. We read the CPI and calculate the percentage change since the base period in the same way as you've just seen for the RPI. The CPI in June 2010 was 14.6 per cent higher than in June 2005.

Constructing the RPI and CPI

Constructing the RPI and the CPI is a huge operation that costs millions of pounds and involves three stages:

- Selecting the basket
- Conducting a monthly price survey
- Calculating the price index

Selecting the Basket

The first stage in constructing a price index is to select the 'basket' of goods and services that the index will cover. The RPI basket contains the goods and services bought by an average household in the UK. The idea is to make the relative importance of the items in the RPI basket the same as that in the budget of an average household. For example, because people spend more on housing than on bus rides, the RPI places more weight on the price of housing than on the price of a bus ride.

The CPI basket is a bit different from the RPI basket and covers *all* expenditure on consumer goods and services made in the UK by private households, residents of institutions and tourists.

To determine the spending patterns of households and to select the RPI and CPI baskets, the ONS conducts periodic expenditure surveys. These surveys are costly and so are undertaken infrequently. Figure 21.6 shows the RPI and CPI baskets in 2010.

Figure 21.6 The RPI and CPI Baskets

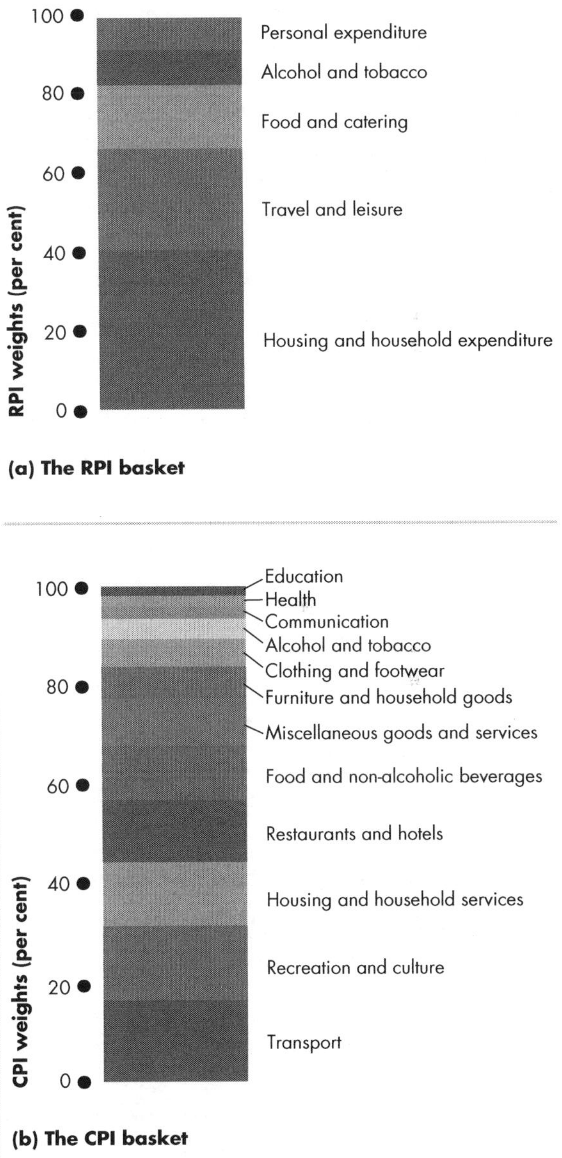

The RPI basket contains items that a typical household buys. The CPI basket is broader and contains all the goods and services bought by households in the UK.

Source of data: Office for National Statistics.

myeconlab Animation

For the RPI, there are five major categories of which by far the largest is housing and household expenditure. Travel and leisure comes next and is larger than food, alcoholic drinks and tobacco combined.

The ONS breaks down each of these categories into ever smaller ones, right down to distinguishing between packaged and loose new potatoes!

The CPI basket contains 12 major categories of which transport and recreation and culture are the largest.

As you look at the relative importance of the items in the RPI and CPI baskets, remember that they apply to an *average* household. *Individual* households are spread around the average. Think about your own expenditure and compare the basket of goods and services you buy with the RPI and CPI baskets.

Conducting a Monthly Price Survey

Each month, ONS employees check 110,000 prices of more than 550 types of goods and services. They visit shops in about 150 places throughout the UK to see the goods and the prices to ensure accuracy. Because the RPI and CPI aim to measure price *changes*, it is important that the prices recorded each month refer to exactly the same item. For example, suppose the price of a packet of biscuits has decreased but a packet now contains fewer biscuits. Has the price of biscuits decreased, remained the same or increased? The ONS price checker must record the details of changes in quality or packaging so that price changes can be isolated from other changes.

Calculating the Price Index

The RPI and CPI calculations have three steps:

1 Find the cost of the basket at base-period prices.
2 Find the cost of the basket at current-period prices.
3 Calculate the index for the base period and the current period.

We'll work through these three steps for a simple example of an RPI calculation. Suppose the RPI basket contains only two goods and services: oranges and haircuts. We'll construct an annual price index rather than a monthly index with the reference base period 2010 and the current period 2011.

Table 21.1 shows the quantities in the RPI basket and the prices in the base period and current period. Part (a) contains the data for the base period. In that period, consumers bought 10 oranges at £1 each and 5 haircuts at £8 each. To find the cost of the RPI basket in the base-period prices, multiply the quantities in the basket by the base-period prices. The cost of oranges is £10 (10 at £1 each), and the cost of haircuts is £40 (5 at £8 each). So total cost of the RPI basket in the base period is £50 (£10 + £40).

Table 21.1

The RPI: A Simplified Calculation

(a) The cost of the RPI basket at base-period prices: 2010

RPI basket			
Item	**Quantity**	**Price**	**Cost of basket**
Oranges	10	£1	£10
Haircuts	5	£8	£40
Cost of the RPI basket at base-period prices			£50

(b) The cost of the RPI basket at current-period prices: 2011

RPI basket			
Item	**Quantity**	**Price**	**Cost of basket**
Oranges	10	£2	£20
Haircuts	5	£10	£50
Cost of the RPI basket at current-period prices			£70

Part (b) contains the price data for the current period. The price of an orange increased from £1 to £2, which is a 100 per cent increase ($£1 \div £1 \times 100 = 100$). The price of a haircut increased from £8 to £10, which is a 25 per cent increase ($£2 \div £8 \times 100 = 25$).

A price index provides a way of averaging these price increases by comparing the cost of the basket rather than the price of each item. To find the cost of the RPI basket in the current period, 2011, multiply the quantities in the basket by their 2011 prices. The cost of oranges is £20 (10 at £2 each), and the cost of haircuts is £50 (5 at £10 each). So total cost of the basket at current-period prices is £70 (£20 + £50).

You've now taken the first two steps towards calculating a RPI: calculating the cost of the RPI basket in the base period and the current period. The third step uses the numbers you've just calculated to find the value of the RPI in 2010 and 2011.

To calculate the RPI, we use the formula:

$$\text{RPI} = \frac{\text{Cost of basket at current-period prices}}{\text{Cost of basket at base-period prices}} \times 100$$

In Table 21.1 you have established that in 2010 the cost of the RPI basket was £50 and in 2011 it was £70. You also know that the base period is 2010. So the cost of the RPI basket at base-period prices is £50. If we use these numbers in the formula above, we can find the RPI for 2010 and 2011. For 2010:

$$\text{RPI in 2010} = \frac{\text{£}50}{\text{£}50} \times 100 = 100$$

For 2011:

$$\text{RPI in 2011} = \frac{\text{£}70}{\text{£}50} \times 100 = 140$$

The principles that you've applied in this simplified RPI calculation apply to the more complex calculations performed every month by the ONS.

Measuring the Inflation Rate

A major purpose of the RPI is to measure *changes* in the cost of living and in the value of money. To measure these changes, we calculate the **inflation rate**, which is the percentage change in the price level from one year to the next. To calculate the inflation rate, we use the formula:

$$\text{Inflation rate} = \frac{(\text{RPI this year} - \text{RPI last year})}{\text{RPI last year}} \times 100$$

We can use this formula to calculate the inflation rate in 2010. The RPI in September 2009 was 215.3, and the RPI in September 2010 was 225.3. So the inflation rate during the year ended September 2010 was:

$$\text{Inflation rate} = \frac{(225.3 - 215.3)}{215.3} \times 100$$

$$= 4.6 \text{ per cent}$$

Distinguishing High Inflation from a High Price Level

Figure 21.7 shows the RPI and the inflation rate from 1970 to 2010. The two parts of the figure are related and emphasize the distinction between high inflation and high prices.

Figure 21.7 The RPI and the Inflation Rate

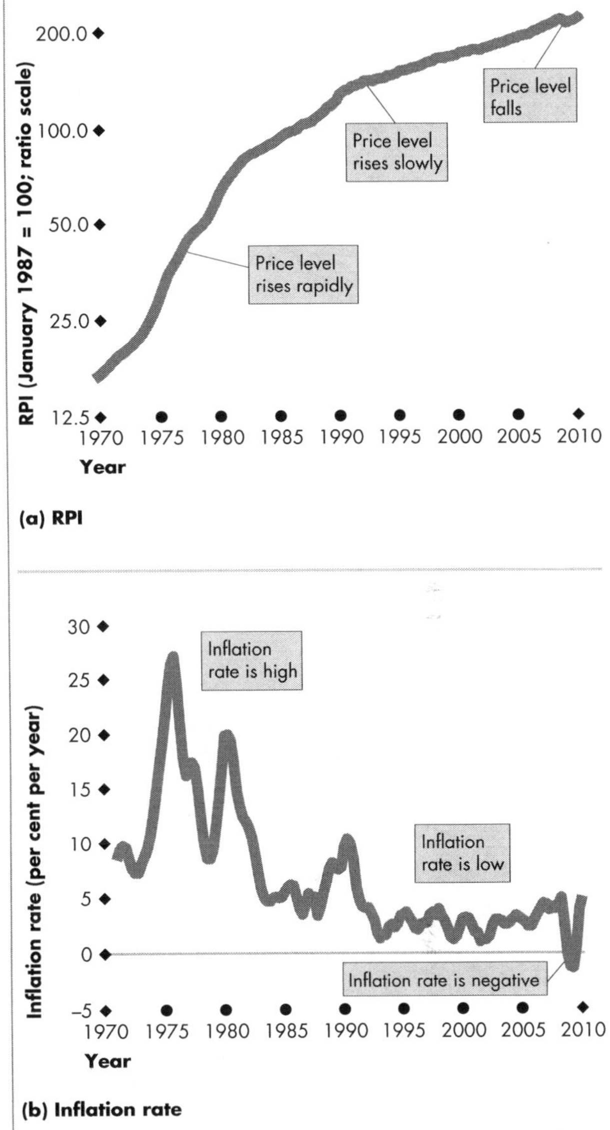

During the 1970s and early 1980s, the price level in part (a) increased rapidly and the inflation rate in part (b) was high. After 1985, the price level increased more slowly and the inflation rate was lower. In 2009, the price level fell and inflation was negative – there was deflation.

Source of data: Office for National Statistics.

myeconlab Animation

When the price *level* in part (a) *rises rapidly*, the inflation rate in part (b) is *high*. When the price level in part (a) *rises slowly*, the inflation rate in part (b) is *low*.

A high inflation rate means that the price level is rising rapidly, while a high price level means that there has been a sustained period of inflation.

When the price level in part (a) falls, as it did in 2009, the inflation rate in part (b) is negative – *deflation*.

The RPI is not a perfect measure of the price level, and changes in the RPI can overstate the inflation rate. Let's look at the sources of bias in price indexes such as the RPI and CPI against which the ONS must guard.

Biased Price Indexes

The main sources of bias in a price index are:

- New goods bias
- Quality change bias
- Substitution bias

New Goods Bias

New goods keep replacing old goods. For example, CDs have replaced LP records and PCs have replaced typewriters. If you want to compare the price level in 2005 with that in 1975, you somehow have to compare the price of a CD and a computer today with that of an LP and typewriter in 1975. Because CDs and PCs are more expensive today than LPs and typewriters, the arrival of these new goods puts an upward bias into the estimate of the price level.

Quality Change Bias

Most goods undergo constant quality improvement. Cars, computers, CD players and even textbooks get better year after year. Quality improvements often increase the price, but such price increases are not inflation. For example, suppose that a 1999 car is 5 per cent better and costs 5 per cent more than a 1995 car. Adjusted for the quality change, the price of the car has not changed. But in calculating the RPI, the price of the car will have increased by 5 per cent.

Estimates have been made of the quality change bias, especially for obvious changes such as those in cars and computers. Allowing for quality improvements changes the inflation picture by 1 percentage point a year, on average, according to some economists. That is, correctly measured, the inflation rate might be as much as 1 percentage point a year less than the published numbers.

Substitution Bias

A change in the price index measures the percentage change in the price of a *fixed* basket of goods and services. But changes in relative prices lead consumers to seek less costly items. For example, by shopping more frequently at discount shops and less frequently at corner shops, consumers can cut the prices they pay. By using discount fares on airlines, they can cut the cost of travel. This kind of substitution of cheaper items for more costly items is not picked up by the price index. Because consumers make such substitutions, a price index based on a fixed basket overstates the effects of a given price change on the inflation rate.

Some Consequences of Bias in the RPI and CPI

The RPI is also used to calculate increases in pensions and other government outlays. So a bias in the RPI could end up swelling government expenditure (and taxes). The CPI is used by the Bank of England to determine whether the interest rate needs to be raised or lowered. So a bias in the CPI could lead to an inappropriate policy decision.

Mindful of these potentially harmful effects, our price indexes are constructed with the greatest possible care to minimize the biases we've just examined.

An Alternative Price Index: The GDP Deflator

The RPI and the CPI are just two of many alternative price level index numbers. Because of the bias in the price indexes, other measures are used for some purposes. One of these alternative price indexes is the **GDP deflator**, which is an index of the prices of all the items in GDP. These items are consumption expenditure, investment, government expenditure and net exports.

The RPI and CPI measure only the prices of consumption goods and services, so they cover a narrower range of items than does the GDP deflator.

The GDP deflator is calculated using two numbers that you have already met: GDP and real GDP and the formula for the GDP deflator is:

$$\text{GDP deflator} = (\text{Nominal GDP} \div \text{Real GDP}) \times 100$$

This broader price index is appropriate for macroeconomics because it is a comprehensive measure of the cost of the real GDP basket of goods and services.

Another difference between the GDP deflator and the other two indexes is the dating of the expenditure basket. Because real GDP is a *chained volume measure* (see pp. 476–477), it is based on expenditures in the two adjacent years that are being compared and then 'chained' back to the reference base year. This procedure means that the weights in the GDP deflator are current weights so they avoid some of the sources of bias that we described above.

The main disadvantage of the GDP deflator is that it is calculated only every quarter and with a time lag and is subject to ongoing revisions. These features make it unsuitable for timely and firm estimation of the inflation rate. But it is a good measure for macroeconomic analysis and our efforts to understand economic performance.

The Alternatives Compared

No matter whether we calculate the inflation rate using the RPI, the CPI or the GDP deflator, the number bounces around a good deal from quarter to quarter. How do the alternative measures compare? How different are the inflation stories they tell?

The three measures give different average inflation rates and different inflation fluctuations. Since 2000, the RPI has increased at an average rate of 2.7 per cent per year, the CPI at an average rate of 1.9 per cent per year and the GDP deflator at 2.5 per cent per year.

Figure 21.8 shows the path of each measure of inflation since 2000. You can see that the RPI is much more variable than the other two measures and it is the only one to show deflation in 2009. The CPI has a mild upward trend and the GDP deflator has no trend.

The key conclusion is that there is no unique measure of inflation and we must carefully determine which measure is most useful for the purpose at hand.

Real Variables in Macroeconomics

One major purpose of price index numbers is to measure and distinguish nominal variables and real variables. You saw in Chapter 20 how we measure real GDP. And you've seen in this chapter how we can use nominal GDP and real GDP to calculate the GDP deflator measure of the price level.

Viewing real GDP as nominal GDP deflated, opens up the idea of other real variables. By using the GDP deflator, we can deflate other nominal variables such as the nominal wage rate to find their real values.

There is one variable that is a bit different – an interest rate. A real interest rate is not a nominal interest rate divided by the price level. You'll learn how to adjust the nominal interest rate for inflation to find the real interest rate in Chapter 23. But all the other real variables of macroeconomics are calculated by dividing a nominal variable by the price level.

Figure 21.8 Comparing Three Measures of Inflation

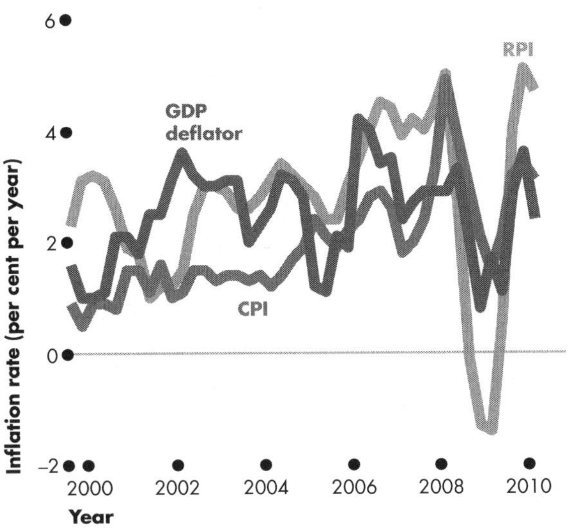

The three measures of the inflation rate give different average rates and different fluctuations. The RPI and CPI measures tend to increase and decrease together, but the RPI measure fluctuates more. The GDP deflator measure is the least volatile.

Source of data: Office for National Statistics.

myeconlab Animation

Review Quiz

1. What is the price level?
2. What are the RPI and CPI and how are they calculated?
3. How do we calculate the inflation rate and what is the relationship between the price index and the inflation rate?
4. How might a price index be biased?
5. What problems arise from the biased RPI and CPI?
6. What is the GDP deflator and what are its advantages and disadvantages?

You can work these questions in Study Plan 21.3 and get instant feedback. myeconlab

You've now completed your study of the measurement of macroeconomic performance. Your task in the following chapters is to learn what determines that performance. But first, take a look at the differences in the CPI and the RPI in the period 2008 to 2010 in *Reading Between the Lines* on pp. 498–499.

Reading Between the Lines

Measuring Inflation

The Financial Times, 14 September 2010

Measuring up with a Tale of Two Indices

Chris Giles

What measure of inflation should trade unionists, meeting in Manchester this week, use for pay bargaining this autumn? The answer is likely to lead to much dispute.

Inflation, according to the retail prices index, was 4.6 per cent in August, while it was 3.1 per cent if measured by the newer consumer price index.

These debates are both unfortunate and bogus, argues Stephen Nickell, Warden of Nuffield College, Oxford, and a former member of the monetary policy committee.

The average British household faces only one inflation rate, and . . . [w]hat matters is that there is a reliable, single inflation statistic that measures the changing cost of consumption.

Some of the differences between the RPI and CPI are well known, such as the historic inclusion of mortgage interest payments in the RPI and the exclusion of owner-occupied housing costs in the CPI. . . . In August these housing differences contributed 0.72 percentage points of the difference between the indices. . . .

Much less well-known, however, is that another important discrepancy between the two inflation measures has emerged this year. . . . This relates to different techniques for averaging prices in shops.

In August, clothing and footwear inflation measured by the RPI stood at 6.3 per cent, while the CPI inflation for the same goods was –1.7 per cent – a total difference of 8 percentage points. . . .

The upshot for union wage bargainers is that, unless they are sure their members need to wear Nicole Farhi, the RPI is probably overstating the inflation rate they experience. 'Put simply, the CPI is the better guide,' says Allan Monks of JP Morgan.

The measure of inflation most used for wage settlements is the Retail Price Index, . . . which . . . climbed in the 12 months to November by 3.9 per cent, . . . the highest reading since May 1998.

The Essence of the Story

- In August 2010, the annual inflation rate was 4.6 per cent according to the RPI and 3.1 per cent according to the CPI.
- Among many differences in coverage of the two indexes, the RPI includes mortgage interest payments but the CPI excludes them.
- The two indexes use different price sampling methods.
- A consequence of these differences is that the RPI said clothing and footwear prices increased 6.3 per cent in August while the CPI said they *decreased* 1.7 per cent.

Economic Analysis

- The CPI and the RPI give conflicting accounts of UK inflation.
- Figure 1 shows the CPI inflation rate minus the RPI inflation rate for each month from January 2009 to September 2010. The CPI inflation rate was higher in 2009 and the RPI inflation rate was higher in 2010.
- The actual items included in the baskets of the two price indexes are different even when the category has the same name.
- For example, clothing and footwear, noted in the news article, includes different items in the two baskets.
- Even for goods that are common, such as alcohol and tobacco, the two inflation measures differ.
- Figure 2 shows the inflation rate of alcohol and tobacco measured by the CPI and the RPI. Sampling bias makes the CPI alcohol and tobacco inflation rate higher than the RPI inflation rate.
- Trades unions may want to use the RPI rate of inflation as the basis for wage bargaining because the RPI measure of inflation is higher than the CPI measure. But Figure 3 shows that earnings growth has followed neither measure of inflation.
- Real wage rates are determined in the market for labour. To translate real wage rates into money wage rates, unions and employers need a good measure of inflation.
- While the ONS tries to measure inflation so that there is a minimum of bias, both the CPI and the RPI remain imperfect measures of inflation.
- Unions and employers find it necessary to look at both measures of inflation in seeking what Stephen Nickell calls a 'reliable, single inflation statistic that measures the changing cost of consumption'.

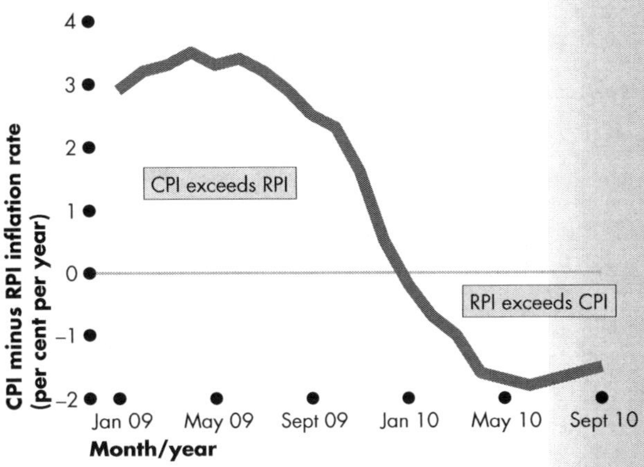

Figure 1 The difference between the CPI and RPI inflation rates

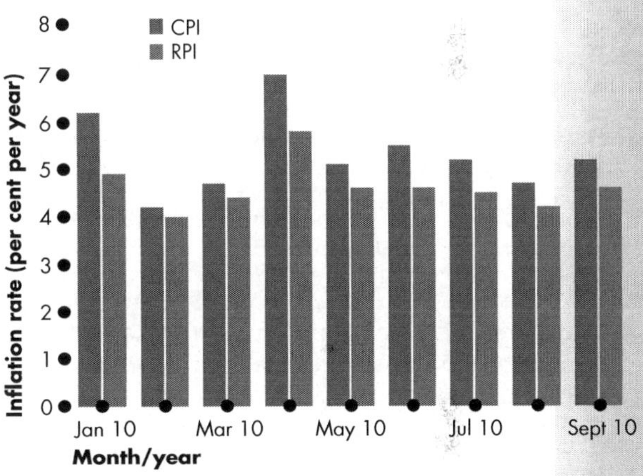

Figure 2 Inflation rates of alcohol and tobacco in two indexes

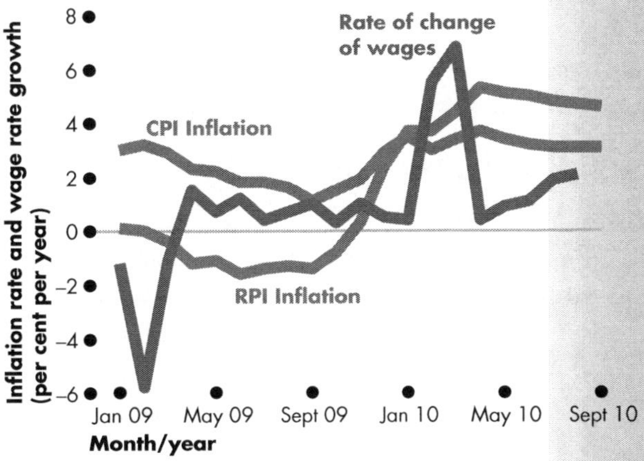

Figure 3 Inflation and wage rate

SUMMARY

Key Points

Employment and Unemployment

- Unemployment is a serious personal, social and economic problem because it results in lost output and income and human capital.
- The unemployment rate averaged 10 per cent during the 1980s, 8.3 per cent during the 1990s and 5.5 per cent during the 2000s.
- The unemployment rate, the economic activity rate and the employment rate fluctuate with the business cycle.

Working Problems 1 to 7 will give you a better understanding of employment and unemployment.

Unemployment and Full Employment

- People are constantly entering and leaving the state of unemployment.
- Three types of unemployment are frictional, structural and cyclical.
- When all the unemployment is frictional and structural, the unemployment rate equals the natural unemployment rate, the economy is at full employment and real GDP equals potential GDP.
- Over the business cycle, real GDP fluctuates around potential GDP and the unemployment rate fluctuates around the natural unemployment rate.

Working Problems 8 to 13 will give you a better understanding of unemployment and full employment.

The Price Level, Inflation and Deflation

- Inflation and deflation that are unexpected redistribute income and wealth and divert resources from production.
- The Retail Prices Index (RPI) and the Consumer Prices Index (CPI) measure the average prices paid by consumers for a specified basket of goods and services.
- The inflation rate is the percentage change in the RPI (or CPI) from one year to the next.
- The RPI and CPI probably overstate the inflation rate because of the bias that arises from new goods, quality changes and substitutions between goods and services.
- The RPI bias increases government outlays and the CPI bias might lead to inappropriate interest rate policy.

Working Problems 14 to 27 will give you a better understanding of the price level, inflation and deflation.

Key Terms

Consumer Prices Index (CPI)
Cyclical unemployment
Deflation
Discouraged worker
Economic activity rate
Economically active
Economically inactive
Employment rate
Frictional unemployment
Full employment
GDP deflator
Hyperinflation
Inflation
Inflation rate
Natural unemployment rate
Output gap
Price level
Reference base period
Retail Prices Index (RPI)
Structural unemployment
Unemployment rate
Workforce
Working-age population

STUDY PLAN PROBLEMS AND APPLICATIONS

myeconlab You can work Problems 1 to 27 in MyEconLab Chapter 21 Study Plan and get instant feedback.

Employment and Unemployment
(Study Plan 21.1)

1 In 2008, the Labour Force Survey measured the economically active at 30,512,000, employment at 28,771,000 and the working-age population at 39,575,000. Calculate for 2008:

a The unemployment rate.

b The economic activity rate.

c The employment rate.

2 During 2009, the working-age population increased by 230,000, employment fell by 549,000 and the number of economically active people increased by 98,000. Use this information along with the data in Problem 1 to calculate the change in unemployment during 2009.

Use the following information to work Problems 3 and 4.

In July 2009, in the economy of Sandy Island, 10,000 people were employed, 1,000 were unemployed and 5,000 were economically inactive.

3 Calculate the unemployment rate and the employment rate in July 2009.

4 During August 2009, 80 people lost their jobs and didn't look for new ones, 20 people quit their jobs and retired, 150 unemployed people were hired, 50 people quit the workforce and became economically inactive and 40 people entered the workforce to look for work.

Calculate the number of people unemployed, the number of people employed and the unemployment rate at the end of August 2009.

Use the following information to work Problems 5 and 6.

The UK unemployment rate was 6.9 per cent in January 2009 and 8.1 per cent in January 2010.

5 Predict what happened to unemployment between January 2009 and January 2010 if the economically active population remained the same.

6 Predict what happened to the economically active population if the number of people unemployed remained the same.

7 **Shrinking US Workforce Keeps Unemployment Rate From Rising**

An exodus of discouraged workers from the US job market has kept the unemployment rate from climbing to 10 per cent. Had the workforce not decreased by 661,000, the unemployment rate would have been 10.4 per cent. The number of discouraged workers rose to 929,000 last month.

Source: Bloomberg, 9 January 2010

What is a discouraged worker? Explain how an increase in discouraged workers influences the official unemployment rate.

Unemployment and Full Employment
(Study Plan 21.2)

Use the following news clip to work Problems 8 to 10.

Jobs Market is on the 'Road to Recovery'

A new study suggests the job market is on the 'road to recovery', despite 2.5 million people unemployed. With a strong rise in demand for permanent staff in the past four months and with the rise in demand for temporary staff in December the biggest in six months, the recovery looks strong. But KPMG warns the future of the recovery is uncertain, as the government's austerity measures take effect.

Source: BBC News, 12 January 2011

8 With the demand for permanent and temporary workers rising strongly, explain which type of unemployment is most likely to fall if the recovery continues.

9 As the government's austerity measures take effect, explain which type of unemployment might increase.

10 Why might the government's cutbacks in the public service (part of the austerity measures) change the natural unemployment rate in the UK?

Use the following news clip to work Problems 11 to 13.

US Economic Pain Deepens

A spike in the unemployment rate – the biggest in more than two decades – raised new concerns that the US economy is heading into a recession. The unemployment rate soared to 5.5 per cent in May from 5 per cent in April – much higher than forecasted. The surge marked the biggest one-month jump in unemployment since February 1986, and the 5.5 per cent rate is the highest seen since October 2004.

Source: CNN, 6 June 2008

11 Based on information in the news clip, how does the US unemployment rate in May 2008 compare to that in earlier recessions?

12 Why might the unemployment rate tend to actually underestimate the unemployment problem, especially during a recession?

13 Given the information in the news clip, does the jump in the US unemployment rate in May 2008 look like an increase in the natural unemployment rate or an increase in the cyclical unemployment rate? What information would you need on the output gap to confirm your answer?

The Price Level, Inflation and Deflation (Study Plan 21.3)

Use the following information to work Problems 14 and 15.

The people on Coral Island buy only juice and cloth. The RPI basket contains the quantities bought in 2009. The average household spent €60 on juice and €30 on cloth in 2009 when the price of juice was €2 a bottle and the price of cloth was €5 a metre. In the current year, 2010, juice is €4 a bottle and cloth is €6 a metre.

14 Calculate the RPI basket and the percentage of the household's budget spent on juice in 2009.

15 Calculate the RPI and the inflation rate in 2010.

Use the following data to work Problems 16 to 18.

The Office for National Statistics reported the following RPI data:

June 2008: 216.8

June 2009: 213.4

June 2010: 221.1

16 Calculate the inflation rates for the years ended June 2009 and June 2010. How did the inflation rate change in 2010?

17 Why might these RPI numbers be biased?

18 Does the GDP deflator help to avoid some of the bias in the RPI numbers?

19 **Inflation Can Act as a Safety Valve**

Workers will more readily accept a real wage cut that arises from an increase in the price level than a cut in their nominal wage rate.

Source: FT.com, 28 May 2009

How does inflation influence the real wage rate?

20 The IMF *World Economic Outlook* reports the following price level data (2000 = 100):

Region	2006	2007	2008
US	117.1	120.4	124.0
Eurozone	113.6	117.1	119.6
Japan	98.1	98.1	98.8

a In which region was inflation the highest in 2007 and 2008?

b Describe the path of the price level in Japan.

21 **We are Heading Back to Massive Inflation**

Inflation is an arbitrary tax that falls hardest on those who have done the right thing: it penalises thrift, disadvantages businesses and weakens competitiveness.

Source: *The Telegraph*, 13 January 2011

a Explain why unexpected inflation 'penalizes thrift'.

b Explain why unexpected inflation 'disadvantages businesses'.

c Explain why unexpected inflation 'weakens competitiveness'.

Use the following data to work Problems 22 to 24.

The Office for National Statistics reported that the annual CPI inflation rate in November 2010 was 3.3 per cent and the annual RPI inflation rate was 4.7 per cent.

Food and non-alcoholic drink prices rose by 1.6 per cent, compared to a 0.6 per cent rise a year earlier. Bread and cereal prices rose by 1.9 per cent and meat prices rose by 1.0 per cent.

Clothing and footwear prices rose by 2.0 per cent, compared with 0.6 per cent a year earlier, while furniture and household equipment rose 1.6 per cent.

Air transport fares fell by 6.4 per cent, compared with a fall of 2.6 per cent a year earlier. Fuel and lubricant prices rose by 1.6 per cent, compared with 2.8 per cent a year earlier. Recreation and culture prices fell by 0.2 per cent this year but rose by 0.2 per cent a year earlier.

22 Which components of the CPI basket experienced price increases (i) faster than the average and (ii) slower than the average?

23 The change in which price contributed most to the 3.3 per cent increase in the CPI?

24 Distinguish between the CPI and RPI. Why might the RPI inflation rate be higher than the CPI inflation rate?

25 What is the GDP deflator and what are the main differences between it and the RPI and CPI?

26 Why might the GDP deflator provide a more reliable indicator of the inflation rate than the CPI and RPI?

27 If the GDP deflator does provide a more reliable indicator of the inflation rate than the CPI and RPI, why might we nevertheless use the CPI and RPI?

ADDITIONAL PROBLEMS AND APPLICATIONS

myeconlab You can work these problems in MyEconLab if assigned by your lecturer.

Employment and Unemployment

28 What is the unemployment rate supposed to measure and why is it an imperfect measure?

29 The Office for National Statistics reported the following data for 2010:

Economic activity rate: 76.6 per cent

Working-age population: 40.01 million

Employment rate: 70.7 per cent

Calculate the

a Workforce.

b The number of people employed

c Unemployment rate.

30 In 2009, the Labour Force Survey measured the economically active at 30.6 million, employment at 28.2 million and the working-age population at 39.8 million. Calculate for 2009:

a The unemployment rate.

b The economic activity rate.

c The employment rate.

31 The ONS reported the following reasons for economic inactivity in August to October 2010 (the numbers are thousands):

Students	2,209
Looking after family at home	2,265
Temporarily sick	175
Long-term sick	2,216
Discouraged workers	67
Retired	1,530
Other	823
Do not want a job	6,969
Want a job	2,367

a Which of the above categories were counted in the official unemployment rate? Explain your answer.

b Which of the above categories of reasons for economic inactivity would you expect to fluctuate with real GDP over the business cycle?

c What are the implications of your answer to part (b) for the mismeasurement of the unemployment rate?

32 A high unemployment rate tells us that a large percentage of the workforce is unemployed, but it doesn't tell us why the unemployment rate is high. What other information would be useful to tell us why the unemployment rate is high?

33 Why might the official unemployment rate underestimate the underutilization of labour resources?

34 Some Firms Struggle to Hire Despite High Unemployment

With about 15 million Americans looking for work, some employers are swamped with job applicants, but many employers can't hire enough workers. During the recession, millions of middle-skill, middle-wage jobs disappeared. Now with the recovery, these people can't find the skilled jobs that they seek and have a hard time adjusting to lower-skilled work with less pay.

Source: *The Wall Street Journal*, 9 August 2010

a What has changed in the jobs market?

b If the government decided to extend the period over which a worker can claim unemployment benefits, how will the cost of unemployment change?

Unemployment and Full Employment

Use the following data to work Problems 35 to 37.

The IMF *World Economic Outlook* reports the following unemployment rates:

Region	2007	2008
US	4.6	5.4
Eurozone	7.4	7.3
Japan	3.9	3.9

35 What do these numbers tell you about the phase of the business cycle in the three regions in 2008?

36 What do these numbers tell us about the relative size of the natural unemployment rates in the three regions?

37 Do these numbers tell us anything about the relative size of the economic activity rate and the employment rate in the three regions?

38 A Half-Year of Job Losses

Employers trimmed jobs in June for the sixth straight month, with the total for the first six months at 438,000 jobs lost by the US economy.

The job losses in June were concentrated in manufacturing and construction, two sectors that have been badly battered in the recession.

Source: CNN, 3 July 2008

a Based on the news clip, what might be the main source of increased unemployment?

b Based on the news clip, what might be the main type of unemployment that increased?

The Price Level, Inflation and Deflation

39 A typical family on Sandy Island consumes only juice and cloth. Last year, which was the reference base year, the family spent €40 on juice and €25 on cloth. Last year, juice was €4 a bottle and cloth was €5 a metre. This year, juice is €4 a bottle and cloth is €6 a metre. Calculate:

a The RPI basket.

b The RPI in the current year.

c The inflation rate in the current year.

40 Amazon.com agreed to pay its workers $20 an hour in 1999 and $22 an hour in 2001. The price level for these years was 166 in 1999 and 180 in 2001. Calculate the real wage rate in each year. Did these workers really get a pay raise between 1999 and 2001?

41 In the third quarter of 2010, UK real GDP was £331.2 billion and nominal GDP was £365.9 billion. In the third quarter of 2009, real GDP was £322.7 billion and nominal GDP was £348.1 billion. Calculate the GDP deflator in these two quarters and the inflation rate over the year.

Economics in the News

42 After you have studied *Reading Between the Lines* on pp. 498–499 answer the following questions.

a What was the inflation rate as measured by the CPI and the RPI in August 2010?

b Explain why the two measures of inflation deliver different inflation rates.

c If you were the wage negotiator for your local union, explain which of these two measures of inflation you would use as your basis of negotiation.

d If you were an entrepreneur and your workers asked for an increase in their wage to keep their real wage constant, which measure of inflation would you use to calculate the increase in the real wage? Explain.

43 **Out of a Job and Out of Luck at 54**

Too young to retire, too old to get a new job. That's how many older workers feel after getting the sack and spending time on the unemployment line. Many lack the skills to craft resumes and search online, experts say. Older workers took an average of 21.1 weeks to get a new job in 2007, about 5 weeks longer than younger people. 'Older workers will be more adversely affected because of the time it takes to transition into another job', said Deborah Russell, AARP's director of workforce issues.

Source: CNN, 21 May 2008

a What type of unemployment might older workers be more prone to experience?

b Explain how the unemployment rate of older workers is influenced by the business cycle.

c Why might older unemployed workers become discouraged workers during a recession?

44 **Land Rover Jaguar Job Applications 'Overwhelm' Halewood**

More than 14,000 people applied for 1,500 new jobs at a new Jaguar Land Rover car plant at Halewood on Merseyside. The jobs have been created by the decision to produce a new Range Rover at this plant.

Source: BBC, 15 January 2010

a What does this news clip suggest about unemployment on Merseyside?

b How will this new car plant change the economic activity rate, the employment rate and the working age population on Merseyside?

c How will this new car plant change the natural unemployment rate and the cyclical unemployment rate on Merseyside?

Data Graphing

Use the Data Grapher in MyEconLab to work Problems 45 to 47.

45 In which country in 2009 was the unemployment rate highest and in which was it lowest: Canada, Japan, France or the UK?

46 In which country in 2009 was the inflation rate highest and in which was it lowest: Australia, the UK, France or the US?

47 Make a scatter diagram of UK inflation and unemployment. Describe the relationship.

PART 7

Macroeconomic Trends

Expanding the Frontier

Economic growth maintained at a steady pace over a number of decades is the single most powerful influence on any society. It brings a transformation that continues to amaze thoughtful people. Maintained at a rapid rate, economic growth transforms a society in years, not decades. Such transformations are taking place right now in many Asian countries. These transformations are economic miracles.

The first two chapters in this part deal with the standard of living and the miracle of rapid economic growth. Chapter 22 explains how potential GDP and full employment are determined and what makes potential GDP grow. The key to economic growth is labour productivity growth and the chapter explains the sources of this growth. Chapter 23 looks at the financial markets that channel the funds that enable businesses and governments to invest in capital.

Money that makes possible specialization and exchange in markets is a huge contributor to economic growth. But too much money brings a rising cost of living with no improvement in the standard of living. Chapters 24 and 25 explain what money is and how central banks regulate its quantity to determine inflation and exchange rate movements.

Understanding Macroeconomic Trends

Economics is about how we cope with scarcity. We cope as individuals by making choices that balance marginal benefits and marginal costs so that we use our scarce resources efficiently. We cope as societies by creating incentive systems and social institutions that encourage specialization and exchange.

These choices and the incentive systems that guide them determine what we specialize in; how much work we do; how hard we work at school to learn the mental skills that form our human capital and that determine the kinds of jobs we get and the incomes we earn; how much we save for future big-ticket expenditures; how much businesses and governments spend on new capital – on satellites, car assembly lines, computers and fibre cables, shopping malls, roads, bridges and tunnels and the problems that scientists, engineers and other inventors work on to develop new technologies.

Rapid and sustained growth of incomes require rapid and sustained productivity growth. Can we count on that happening? Thomas Robert Malthus thought that we could not. He believed that population, unchecked, would grow at a geometric rate – 1, 2, 4, 8, 16, . . . – while food supply would grow at an arithmetic rate – 1, 2, 3, 4, 5, ... To prevent the population from outstripping the available food supply, there would be periodic wars, famines and plagues. As industrialization proceeded through the nineteenth century, Malthus's idea came to be applied not only to food but also to all natural resources, especially those that are non-renewable. Modern day Malthusians believe that his idea is correct and that if we continue to increase our use of energy we will eventually run out of resources and be doomed to a return of subsistence and poverty.

Some economists argue that Malthus was wrong and that human creativity and ingenuity is the ultimate natural resource. They believe that increasing population lessens the pressure on other natural resources as more creative thinkers find more efficient ways of using our resources. Joseph Schumpeter was the unwitting founder of this modern growth theory. But he didn't see the process as plain sailing through tranquil waters.

Joseph Schumpeter (1883–1950), the son of a textile factory owner, was born in Austria. He moved to Germany during the tumultuous 1920s when both countries experienced hyperinflation. In 1932, in the depths of the Great Depression, he went to the US and became a professor of economics at Harvard University.

This creative economic thinker wrote about economic growth and development, business cycles, political systems and economic biography. He was a person of strong opinions who expressed them forcefully and delighted in verbal battles.

Schumpeter saw the development and diffusion of new technologies by profit-seeking entrepreneurs as the source of economic progress. But he saw economic progress as a process of creative destruction – the creation of new profit opportunities and the destruction of currently profitable businesses. For Schumpeter, economic growth and the business cycle were a single phenomenon.

'Economic progress, in capitalist society, means turmoil.'

JOSEPH SCHUMPETER
Capitalism, Socialism, and Democracy

CHAPTER 22

Economic Growth

After studying this chapter you will be able to:

- Define economic growth and explain the implications of sustained growth
- Describe the economic growth trends in the UK and other countries and regions
- Explain how population growth and labour productivity growth make potential GDP grow
- Explain the sources of labour productivity growth
- Explain the theories of economic growth, the empirical evidence on its causes and policies to increase its rate

In China, India and some other Asian economies, real GDP doubles in seven years. In the UK, it doubles every 25 years or so. In many African economies, real GDP barely changes from one year to the next. Why?

What makes an economic miracle like the ones we see in East Asia today? Can China and India continue to expand at the current dizzying rate? Or will this growth come to an end? And if so, what kind of end: abrupt or gradual? And why do some countries stagnate?

You'll find some answers in this chapter. And in *Reading Between the Lines* at the end of the chapter, we'll speculate about the future economic growth rates of China and its Asian neighbours.

The Basics of Economic Growth

Economic growth is a sustained expansion of production possibilities measured as the increase in real GDP over a given period.

Even slow economic growth maintained over many centuries brings great wealth. That is the story of human economic growth up to the Industrial Revolution that began around 1760.

Rapid economic growth maintained over only a small number of years can transform a poor nation into a rich one. That has been the story of Hong Kong, South Korea and Taiwan, and it is the story of China, India and some other Asian economies today.

The absence of growth can condemn a nation to devastating poverty. Such has been the fate of Sierra Leone, Somalia, Zambia and much of the rest of Africa.

The goal of this chapter is to help you to understand why some economies expand rapidly and others stagnate. We'll begin by learning how to calculate the economic growth rate and by discovering the magic of sustained growth.

Calculating Growth Rates

We express the **economic growth rate** as the annual percentage change of real GDP. To calculate this growth rate, we use the formula:

$$\text{Real GDP growth rate} = \frac{\text{Real GDP in current year} - \text{Real GDP in previous year}}{\text{Real GDP in previous year}} \times 100$$

For example, if real GDP in the current year is £1,320 billion and if real GDP in the previous year was £1,200 billion, then the economic growth rate is 10 per cent.

The growth rate of real GDP tells us how rapidly the *total* economy is expanding. This measure is useful for telling us about potential changes in the balance of economic power among nations. But it does not tell us about changes in the standard of living.

The standard of living depends on **real GDP per person** (also called *per capita* real GDP), which is real GDP divided by the population. So the contribution of real GDP growth to the change in the standard of living depends on the growth rate of real GDP per person. We use the above formula to calculate this growth rate, replacing real GDP with real GDP per person.

Suppose, for example, that in the current year, when real GDP is £1,320 billion, the population is 60.6 million. Then real GDP per person is £1,320 billion divided by 60.6 million, which equals £21,782. And suppose that in the previous year, when real GDP was £1,200 billion, the population was 60 million. Then real GDP per person in that year was £1,200 billion divided by 60 million, which equals £20,000. Use these two real GDP per person values with the growth formula above to calculate the growth rate of real GDP per person. That is,

$$\text{Real GDP per person growth rate} = \frac{£21{,}782 - £20{,}000}{£20{,}000} \times 100 = 8.9 \text{ per cent}$$

The growth rate of real GDP per person can also be calculated (approximately) by subtracting the population growth rate from the real GDP growth rate. In the example you've just worked through, the growth rate of real GDP is 10 per cent. The population changes from 60 million to 60.6 million, so the population growth rate is 1 per cent. The growth rate of real GDP per person is approximately equal to 10 per cent minus 1 per cent, which equals 9 per cent.

Real GDP per person grows only if real GDP grows faster than the population grows. If the growth rate of the population exceeds the growth of real GDP, real GDP per person falls.

The Magic of Sustained Growth

Sustained growth of real GDP per person can transform a poor society into a wealthy one. The reason is that economic growth is like compound interest.

Compound Interest

Suppose that you put £100 in the bank and earn 5 per cent a year interest on it. After one year, you have £105. If you leave that £105 in the bank for another year, you earn 5 per cent interest on the original £100 and on the £5 interest that you earned last year. You are now earning interest on interest! The next year, things get even better. Then you earn 5 per cent on the original £100 and on the interest earned in the first year and the second year. You are even earning interest on the interest that you earned on the interest of the first year.

Your money in the bank is growing at a rate of 5 per cent a year. Before too many years have passed, your initial deposit of £100 will have grown to £200. But after how many years?

The answer is provided by a formula called the **Rule of 70**, which states that the number of years it takes for

Figure 22.1 The Rule of 70

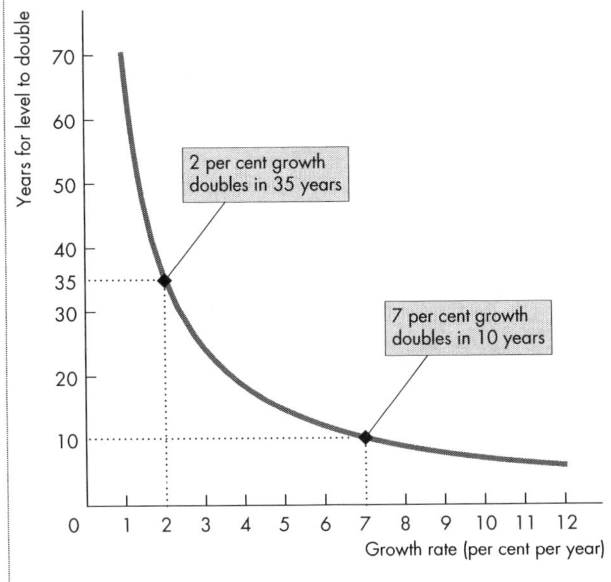

Growth rate (per cent per year)	Years for level to double
1	70.0
2	35.0
3	23.3
4	17.5
5	14.0
6	11.7
7	10.0
8	8.8
9	7.8
10	7.0
11	6.4
12	5.8

The number of years it takes for the level of a variable to double is approximately 70 divided by the annual percentage growth rate.

myeconlab Animation

the level of any variable to double is approximately 70 divided by the annual percentage growth rate of the variable. Using the Rule of 70, you can now calculate how many years it takes your £100 to become £200. It is 70 divided by 5, which is 14 years.

Applying the Rule of 70

The Rule of 70 applies to any variable, so it applies to real GDP per person. Figure 22.1 shows the doubling time for growth rates of 1 per cent per year to 12 per cent per year.

You can see that real GDP per person doubles in 70 years (70 divided by 1) – an average human life span – if the growth rate is 1 per cent a year. It doubles in 35 years if the growth rate is 2 per cent a year and in just 10 years if the growth rate is 7 per cent a year.

We can use the Rule of 70 to answer other questions about economic growth. For example, in 2000, US real GDP per person was approximately 8 times that of China. China's recent growth rate of real GDP per person was 7 per cent a year. If this growth rate were maintained, how long would it take China's real GDP per person to reach that of the US in 2000?

The answer, provided by the Rule of 70, is 30 years. China's real GDP per person doubles in 10 (70 divided by 7) years. It doubles again to 4 times its current level in another 10 years. And it doubles yet again to 8 times its current level in another 10 years. So after 30 years of growth at 7 per cent a year, China's real GDP per person will be 8 times its current level and equal that of the US in 2000. Of course, after 30 years, US real GDP per person would have increased, so China would still not have caught up to the US.

Review Quiz

1. What is economic growth and how do we calculate its rate?
2. What is the relationship between the growth rate of real GDP and the growth rate of real GDP per person?
3. Use the Rule of 70 to calculate the growth rate that leads to a doubling of real GDP per person in 20 years.

You can work these questions in Study Plan 22.1 and get instant feedback. myeconlab

You now know the basics of economic growth. Let's next review the trends in economic growth in the UK and around the world.

Economic Growth Trends

You've seen the power of economic growth to increase incomes. At a 1 per cent growth rate, it takes a human life span to double the standard of living. But at a 7 per cent growth rate, the standard of living doubles every decade. How fast is our economy growing? How fast are other economies growing? Are poor countries catching up to rich ones, or do the gaps between the rich and poor persist or even widen? Let's answer these questions.

Growth in the UK Economy

Figure 22.2 shows real GDP per person in the UK for the 100 years from 1910 to 2010. The red line is the path of real GDP and the black line is potential GDP. The trend in potential GDP per person tells us about economic growth. Fluctuations around potential GDP tell us about the business cycle.

Some extraordinary events dominate the first 50 years in this graph: two World Wars and two periods, the 1920s and the 1930s, of extreme recession and depression. The recession of 2008–2009 is clearly visible in the graph as a serious event but it is not on the scale of severity of those interwar depressions.

For the century as a whole, the average growth rate was 1.6 per cent a year, which represents a doubling of real GDP per person every 44 years.

But the economic growth rate has varied. During the years to 1950, it was 1.2 per cent per year – too slow to double real GDP per person in the 50-year period. In the 50 years to 2010, the growth rate was 2.1 per cent per year – doubling the level in 33 years.

Growth was most rapid during the 1960s at 2.2 per cent per year and the 1980s at 2.8 per cent per year.

A major goal of this chapter is to explain why our economy grows and why the long-term growth rate varies. Another goal is to explain variations in the economic growth rate across countries. Let's look at some facts about other countries' growth rates.

Figure 22.2 One Hundred Years of Economic Growth in the UK

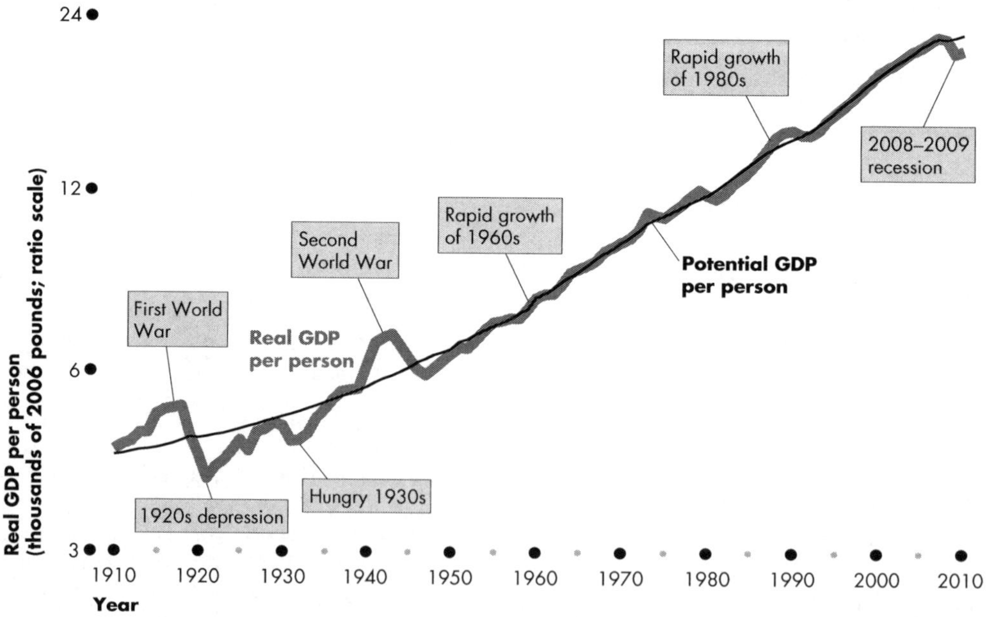

During the 100 years from 1910 to 2010, real GDP per person in the UK grew by 1.6 per cent a year, on average. The growth rate was slower during the first 50 years, at 1.2 per cent (58 years to double) than in the second 50 years at 2.1 per cent (33 years to double). Growth was fastest during the 1960s and the 1980s.

Sources of data: Charles Feinstein, *National Income Expenditure and Output of the United Kingdom 1855–1965*, Cambridge, Cambridge University Press, 1972; Office for National Statistics.

myeconlab Animation

Real GDP Growth in the World Economy

Figure 22.3 shows real GDP per person in the US and in other countries between 1960 and 2010. Part (a) looks at the seven richest countries – known as the G7 nations. Among these nations, the US has the highest real GDP per person. In 2010, Canada had the second-highest real GDP per person, ahead of Japan and France, Germany, Italy and the UK (collectively the Europe Big 4).

During the 50 years shown here, the gaps between the US, Canada and the Europe Big 4 have been almost constant. But starting from a long way below, Japan grew fastest. It caught up to Europe in 1982 and to Canada in 1990. But during the 1990s, Japan's economy stagnated.

Many other countries are growing more slowly than, and falling farther behind, the US. Figure 22.3(b) looks at some of these countries.

In Central and South America, real GDP per person was 28 per cent of the US level in 1960 and reached 30 per cent of the US level by 1980, but then growth slowed and by 2010, real GDP per person in these countries was 23 per cent of the US level.

In Eastern Europe, real GDP per person has grown more slowly than anywhere except Africa, and fell from 32 per cent of the US level in 1980 to 19 per cent in 2003 and then increased again to 22 per cent in 2010.

Real GDP per person in Africa, the world's poorest continent, fell from 10 per cent of the US level in 1960 to 5 per cent in 2007 and then increased slightly to 6 per cent in 2010.

Figure 22.3 Economic Growth Around the World: Catch-up or Not?

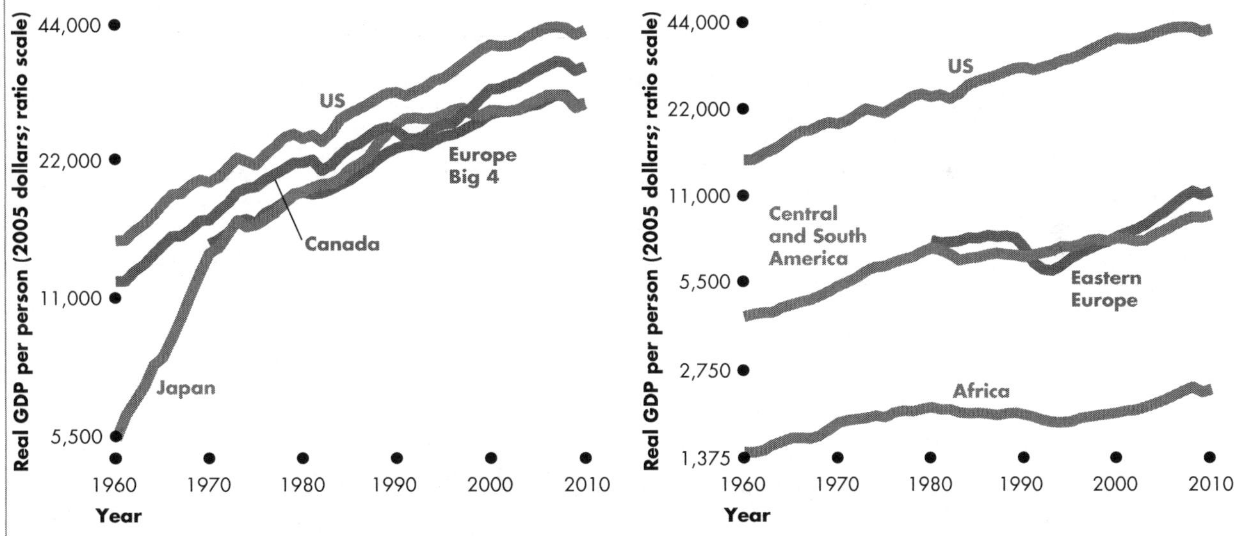

(a) Catch-up?

Real GDP per person has grown throughout the world. Among the rich industrial countries in part (a), real GDP per person has grown slightly faster in the US than in Canada and the four big countries of Europe (France, Germany, Italy, and the UK). Japan had the fastest growth rate before 1973 but then growth slowed and Japan's economy stagnated during the 1990s.

(b) No catch-up?

Among a wider range of countries shown in part (b), growth rates have been lower than that of the US. The gaps between the real GDP per person in the US and in these countries have widened. The gaps between the real GDP per person in the US and Africa and in the US and Eastern Europe have widened.

Sources of data: (1960–2007) Alan Heston, Robert Summers and Bettina Aten, Penn World Table Version 6.3, Center for International Comparisons at the University of Pennsylvania (CICUP), August 2009; and (2008–2010) International Monetary Fund, World Economic Outlook, April 2010.

myeconlab Animation

ECONOMICS IN ACTION

Fast Trains on the Same Track

Four Asian economies, Hong Kong, Korea, Singapore and China, have experienced spectacular growth, which you can see in Figure 1. During the 1960s, real GDP per person in these economies ranged from 3 to 28 per cent of that in the US. But by 2010, real GDP per person in Singapore and Hong Kong had surpassed that of the US.

The figure also shows that China is catching up rapidly but from a long way behind. China's real GDP per person increased from 3 per cent of the US level in 1960 to 26 per cent in 2010.

The Asian economies shown here are like fast trains running on the same track at similar speeds and with a roughly constant gap between them. Singapore and Hong Kong are hooked together as the lead train, which runs about 20 years in front of Korea and about 34 years in front of China.

Real GDP per person in Korea in 2010 was similar to that in Hong Kong in 1988, and real GDP in China in 2010 was similar to that of Hong Kong in 1976. Between 1976 and 2010, Hong Kong transformed itself from a poor developing economy into one of the richest economies in the world.

The rest of China is now doing what Hong Kong has done. China has a population 200 times that of Hong Kong and more than 4 times that of the US. So if China continues its rapid growth, the world economy will change dramatically.

As these fast-growing Asian economies catch up with the US, we can expect their growth rates to slow. But it will be surprising if China's growth rate slows much before it has closed the gap on the US.

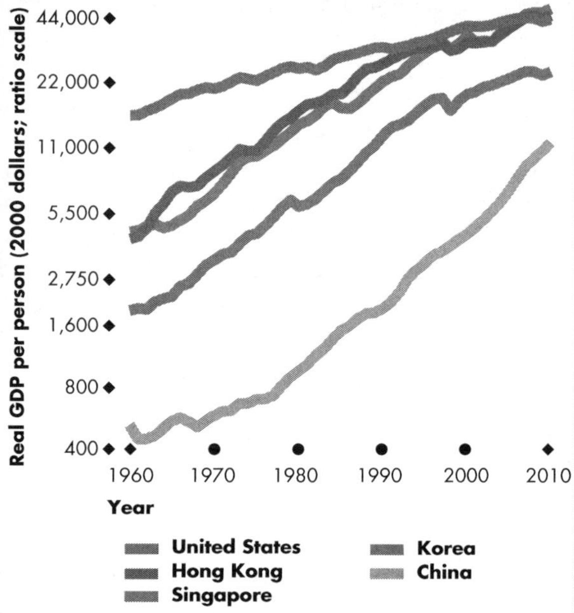

Figure 1 Closing the Gap

Sources of data: (1960–2007) Alan Heston, Robert Summers, and Bettina Aten, Penn World Table Version 6.3, Center for International Comparisons at the University of Pennsylvania (CICUP), August 2009; and (2008–2010) International Monetary Fund, *World Economic Outlook*, April 2010.

Even modest differences in economic growth rates sustained over a number of years bring enormous differences in the standard of living. So the facts about economic growth in the UK and around the world raise some big questions.

What are the preconditions for economic growth and what sustains it? How can we identify the sources of economic growth and measure the contribution that each source makes? What can we do to increase the sustainable rate of economic growth?

We're now going to address these questions. We start by seeing how potential GDP is determined and what makes it grow. You will see that labour productivity growth is the key to rising living standards and go on to explore the sources of this growth.

Review Quiz

1. What has been the average growth rate in the UK over the past 100 years? In which period was growth most rapid and in which was it slowest?
2. Describe the gaps between the levels of real GDP per person in the US and other countries. For which countries are the gaps narrowing? For which countries are the gaps widening? For which countries are the gaps remaining unchanged?
3. Compare the growth rates and levels of real GDP per person in Hong Kong, Singapore, South Korea, China and the US. How far is China behind the other Asian economies?

You can work these questions in Study Plan 22.2 and get instant feedback. myeconlab

How Potential GDP Grows

Economic growth occurs when real GDP increases. But a one-shot rise in real GDP or a recovery from recession isn't economic growth. Economic growth is a sustained, year-after-year increase in potential GDP.

So what determines potential GDP and what are the forces that make it grow?

What Determines Potential GDP?

Labour, capital, land and entrepreneurship produce real GDP, and the productivity of the factors of production determines the quantity of real GDP that can be produced.

The quantity of land is fixed and on any given day, the quantities of entrepreneurial ability and capital are also fixed and their productivities are given. The quantity of labour employed is the only variable factor of production. Potential GDP is the level of real GDP when the quantity of labour employed is the full-employment quantity.

To determine potential GDP, we use a model with two components:

- An aggregate production function
- An aggregate labour market

Aggregate Production Function

When you studied the limits to production in Chapter 2 (see p. 32), you learned that the production possibilities frontier is the boundary between the combinations of goods and services that can be produced and those that cannot. We're now going to think about the production possibilities frontier for two special 'goods': real GDP and the quantity of leisure time.

Think of real GDP as a number of big shopping carts. Each cart contains some of each kind of different goods and services produced, and one cartload of items costs £1 billion. To say that real GDP is £1.3 trillion (or £1,300 billion) means that it is 1,300 very big shopping carts of goods and services.

The quantity of leisure time is the number of hours spent not working. Each leisure hour could be spent working. If we spent all our time taking leisure, we would do no work and produce nothing. Real GDP would be zero. The more leisure we forgo, the greater is the quantity of labour we supply and the greater is the quantity of real GDP produced.

But labour hours are not all equally productive. We use our most productive hours first and as more hours are worked, less and less productive hours are used. So for each additional hour of leisure forgone (each additional hour of labour), real GDP increases by successively smaller amounts.

The **aggregate production function** is the relationship that tells us how real GDP changes as the quantity of labour changes when all other influences on production remain the same. Figure 22.4 shows this relationship – the curve labelled *PF*. An increase in the quantity of labour (and a corresponding decrease in leisure hours) brings a movement along the production function and an increase in real GDP.

Aggregate Labour Market

In macroeconomics, we pretend that there is one large labour market that determines the quantity of labour employed and the quantity of real GDP produced. To see how this aggregate labour market works, we study the demand for labour, the supply of labour and labour market equilibrium.

The Demand for Labour

The demand for labour is the relationship between the quantity of labour demanded and the real wage rate. The

Figure 22.4 The Aggregate Production Function

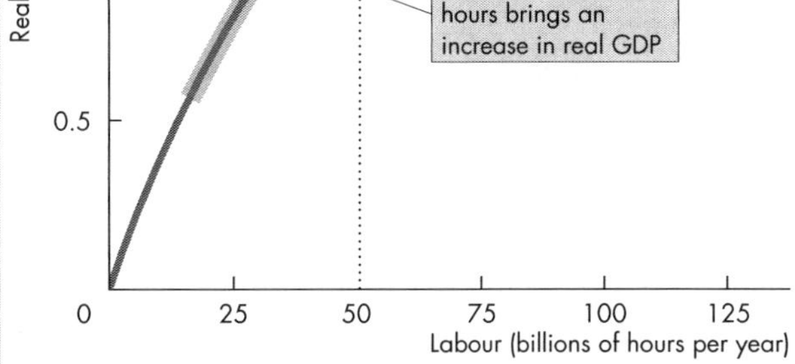

At point A on the aggregate production function *PF*, 50 billion hours of labour produce £1.3 trillion of real GDP.

myeconlab Animation

quantity of labour demanded is the number of labour hours hired by all the firms in the economy during a given period. This quantity depends on the price of labour, which is the real wage rate.

The **real wage rate** is the quantity of goods and services that an hour of labour earns. It contrasts with the money wage rate, which is the number of pounds that an hour of labour earns. The real wage rate is calculated by dividing the money wage rate by the price level.

The *real* wage rate influences the quantity of labour demanded because what matters to firms is not the number of pounds they pay (money wage rate) but how much output they must sell to earn those pounds.

The quantity of labour demanded *increases* as the real wage rate *decreases* – the demand for labour curve slopes downward. Why? The answer lies in the shape of the production function.

You've seen that along the production function, each additional hour of labour increases real GDP by successively smaller amounts. This tendency has a name: *the law of diminishing returns*. Because of diminishing returns, firms will hire more labour only if the real wage rate falls to match the fall in the extra output produced by that labour.

The Supply of Labour

The *supply of labour* is the relationship between the quantity of labour supplied and the real wage rate. The quantity of labour supplied is the number of labour hours that all the households in the economy plan to work during a given period. This quantity depends on the real wage rate.

The *real* wage rate influences the quantity of labour supplied because what matters to households is not the number of pounds they earn (money wage rate) but what they can buy with those pounds.

The quantity of labour supplied *increases* as the real wage rate *increases* – the supply of labour curve slopes upward. At a higher real wage rate, more people choose to work and more people choose to work longer hours if they can earn more per hour.

Labour Market Equilibrium

The price of labour is the real wage rate. The forces of supply and demand operate in labour markets to eliminate a shortage or a surplus but a shortage or a surplus of labour brings only a gradual change in the real wage rate. If there is a shortage of labour, the real wage rate rises to eliminate it; and if there is a surplus of labour, the real wage rate eventually falls to eliminate it. When there is neither a shortage nor a surplus, the labour market is in equilibrium – a full-employment equilibrium.

Figure 22.5 illustrates labour market equilibrium. The demand for labour curve is *LD* and the supply of labour curve is *LS*. This labour market is in equilibrium at a real wage rate of £15 an hour and 50 billion hours a year are employed.

If the real wage rate exceeds £15 an hour, the quantity of labour supplied exceeds the quantity demanded and there is a surplus of labour. When there is a surplus of labour, the real wage rate falls towards the equilibrium real wage rate where the surplus is eliminated.

If the real wage rate is less than £15 an hour, the quantity of labour demanded exceeds the quantity supplied and there is a shortage of labour. When there is a shortage of labour, the real wage rate rises towards the equilibrium real wage rate where the shortage is eliminated.

If the real wage rate is £15 an hour, the quantity of labour demanded equals the quantity supplied and there is neither a shortage nor a surplus of labour. In this

Figure 22.5 Labour Market Equilibrium

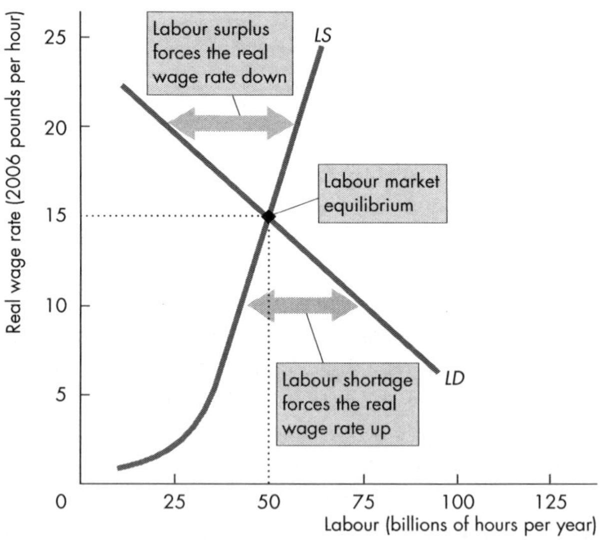

Labour market equilibrium occurs when the quantity of labour demanded equals the quantity of labour supplied. The equilibrium real wage rate is £15 per hour and equilibrium employment is 50 billion hours per year.

At a wage rate above £15 an hour, there is a surplus of labour and the real wage rate falls to eliminate the surplus. At a wage rate below £15 an hour, there is a shortage of labour and the real wage rate rises to eliminate the shortage.

myeconlab Animation

situation, there is no pressure in either direction on the real wage rate. So the real wage rate remains constant and the market is in equilibrium. At this equilibrium real wage rate and level of employment, the economy is at full employment.

Potential GDP

You've seen that the production function tells us the quantity of real GDP that a given amount of labour can produce – see Figure 22.4. The quantity of real GDP produced increases as the quantity of labour increases. At the equilibrium quantity of labour, the economy is at full employment and the quantity of real GDP at full employment is potential GDP. So the full-employment quantity of labour produces potential GDP.

Figure 22.6 illustrates the determination of potential GDP. Part (a) shows the labour market. At the equilibrium real wage rate, equilibrium employment is 50 billion hours. Part(b) shows the production function. With 50 billion hours of labour, the economy can produce a real GDP of £1.3 trillion. This amount is potential GDP.

What Makes Potential GDP Grow?

We can divide all the forces that make potential GDP grow into two categories:

- Growth of the supply of labour
- Growth of labour productivity

Growth of the Supply of Labour

When the supply of labour grows, the supply of labour curve shifts rightward. The quantity of labour at a given real wage rate increases.

The quantity of labour is the number of workers employed multiplied by average hours per worker; and the number employed equals the employment rate multiplied by the working-age population (see Chapter 21, pp. 486–487). So the quantity of labour changes as a result of changes in

1 Average hours per worker
2 The employment rate
3 The working-age population

Average hours per worker have decreased as the workweek has become shorter and the employment rate has increased as more women have entered the labour force. The combined effects of these factors have kept average hours per working-age person (approximately) constant.

Figure 22.6 The Labour Market and Potential GDP

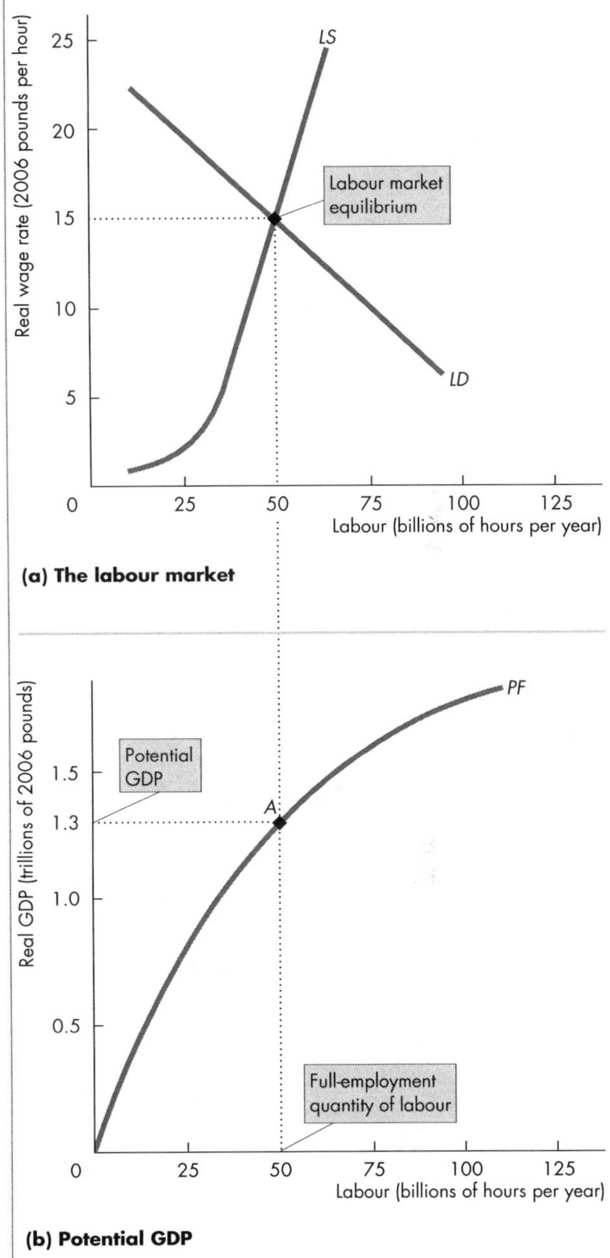

The economy is at full employment when the quantity of labour demanded equals the quantity of labour supplied, in part (a). The real wage rate is £15 an hour and employment is 50 billion hours per year. In part (b), potential GDP is determined by the production function and the full-employment quantity of labour.

myeconlab Animation

Growth in the supply of labour has come from growth in the working-age population. In the long run, the working-age population grows at the same rate as the total population.

The Effects of Population Growth

Population growth brings growth in the supply of labour, but it does not change the demand for labour or the production function. The economy can produce more output by using more labour, but there is no change in the quantity of real GDP that a given quantity of labour can produce.

With an increase in the supply of labour and no change in the demand for labour, the real wage rate falls and the equilibrium quantity of labour increases. The increased quantity of labour produces more output and potential GDP increases.

Illustrating the Effects of Population Growth

Figure 22.7 illustrates the effects of an increase in the population. In Figure 22.7(a), the demand for labour curve is *LD* and initially the supply of labour curve is LS_0. The equilibrium real wage rate is £15 an hour and the quantity of labour is 50 billion hours a year. In Figure 22.7(b), the production function, *PF*, shows that with 50 billion hours of labour employed, potential GDP is £1.3 trillion at point *A*.

An increase in the population increases the supply of labour and the supply of labour curve shifts rightward to LS_1. At a real wage rate of £15 an hour, there is now a surplus of labour. So the real wage rate falls. In this example, the real wage rate will fall until it reaches £10 an hour. At £10 an hour, the quantity of labour demanded equals the quantity of labour supplied. The equilibrium quantity of labour increases to 75 billion hours a year.

Figure 22.7(b) shows the effect on real GDP. As the equilibrium quantity of labour increases from 50 billion to 75 billion hours, potential GDP increases along the production function from £1.3 trillion to £1.6 trillion at point *B*.

So an increase in the population increases the full-employment quantity of labour, increases potential GDP and lowers the real wage rate. But the population increase decreases potential GDP per hour of labour. Initially, it was £26 (£1.3 trillion divided by 50 billion). With the population increase, potential GDP per hour of labour is £21.33 (£1.6 trillion divided by 75 billion).

Diminishing returns are the source of the decrease in potential GDP per hour of labour.

Figure 22.7 The Effects of an Increase in Population

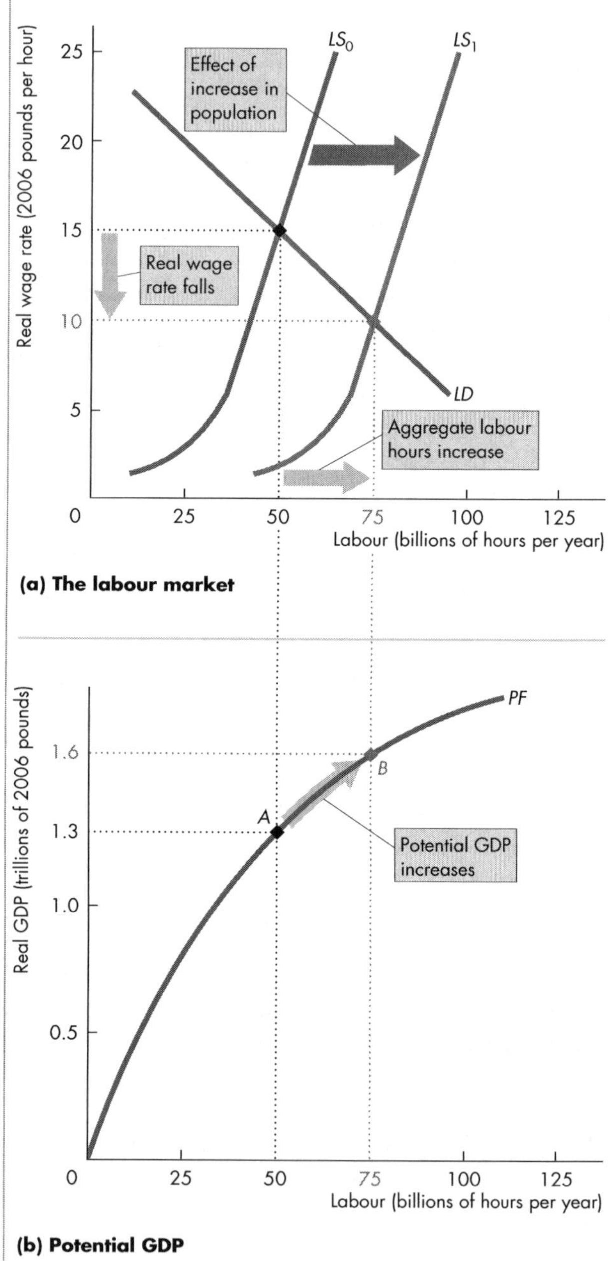

In part (a) an increase in the population increases the supply of labour and shifts the supply of labour curve rightward. The real wage rate falls and the full-employment quantity of labour increases. In part (b), the increase in aggregate labour hours brings an increase in potential GDP. But diminishing returns bring a decrease in potential GDP per hour of labour.

myeconlab Animation

Growth of Labour Productivity

Labour productivity is the quantity of real GDP produced by an hour of labour. It is calculated by dividing real GDP by aggregate labour hours. For example, if real GDP is £1.3 trillion and aggregate hours are 50 billion, labour productivity is £26 per hour.

When labour productivity grows, real GDP per person grows and brings a rising standard of living. Let's see how an increase in labour productivity changes potential GDP.

Effects of an Increase in Labour Productivity

If labour productivity increases, production possibilities expand. The quantity of real GDP that any given quantity of labour can produce increases. If labour is more productive, firms are willing to pay more for a given number of hours of labour so the demand for labour also increases.

With an increase in the demand for labour and *no change in the supply of labour*, the real wage rate rises and the quantity of labour supplied increases. The equilibrium quantity of labour also increases.

So an increase in labour productivity increases potential GDP for two reasons: labour is more productive and more labour is employed.

Illustrating the Effects of an Increase in Labour Productivity

Figure 22.8 illustrates an increase in labour productivity. In part (a), the production function initially is PF_0. With 50 billion hours of labour employed, potential GDP is £1.3 trillion at point *A*. In part (b), the demand for labour curve is LD_0 and the supply of labour curve is *LS*. The real wage rate is £15 an hour and the equilibrium quantity of labour is 50 billion hours a year.

Now labour productivity increases. In Figure 22.8(a), the increase in labour productivity shifts the production function upward to PF_1. At each quantity of labour, more real GDP can be produced. For example, at 50 billion hours, the economy can now produce £1.8 trillion of real GDP at point *B*.

In Figure 22.8(b), the increase in labour productivity increases the demand for labour and the demand for labour curve shifts rightward to LD_1. At the initial real wage rate of £15 an hour, there is now a shortage of labour. The real wage rate rises. In this example, the real wage rate will rise until it reaches £20 an hour. At £20 an hour, the quantity of labour demanded equals the quantity of labour supplied and the equilibrium quantity of labour is 55 billion hours a year.

Figure 22.8 The Effects of an Increase in Labour Productivity

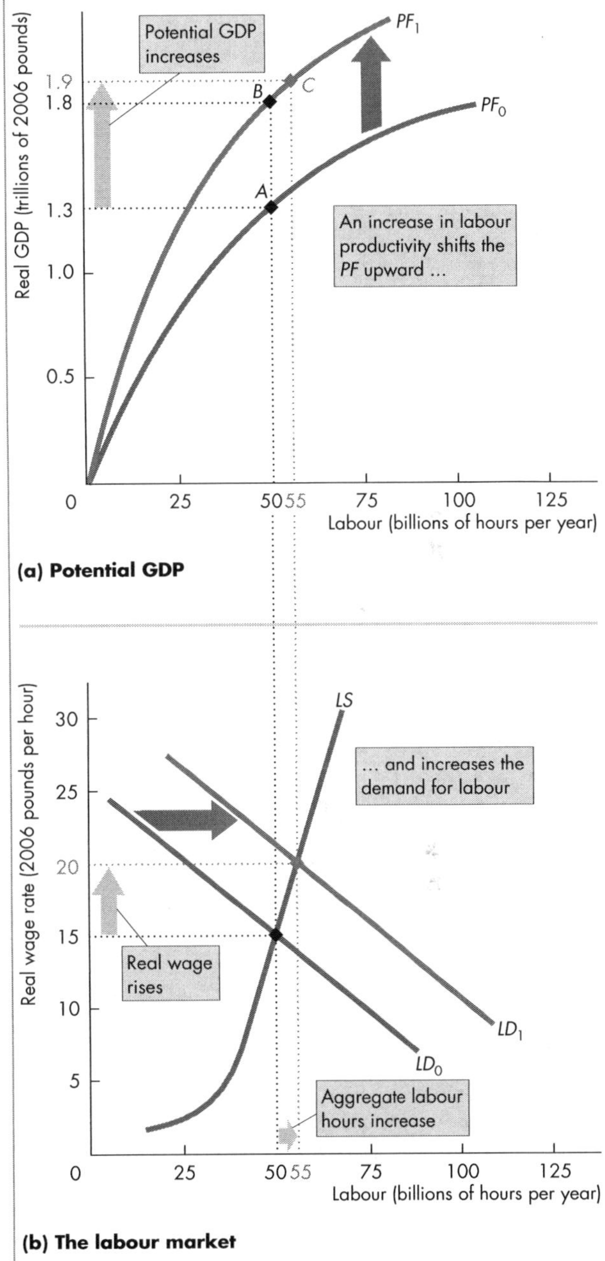

An increase in labour productivity shifts the production function upward from PF_0 to PF_1 in part (a) and shifts the demand for labour curve rightward from LD_0 to LD_1 in part (b). The real wage rate rises to £20 an hour, and aggregate labour hours increase from 50 billion to 55 billion. Potential GDP increases from £1.3 trillion to £1.9 trillion.

myeconlab Animation

Figure 22.8(a) shows the effects of the increase in labour productivity on potential GDP. There are two effects. At the initial quantity of labour, real GDP increases to point *B* on the new production function. But as the equilibrium quantity of labour increases from 50 billion to 55 billion hours, potential GDP increases to £1.9 trillion at point *C*.

Potential GDP per hour of labour also increases. Initially, it was £26 (£1.3 trillion divided by 50 billion). With the increase in labour productivity, potential GDP per hour of labour is £34.55 (£1.9 trillion divided by 55 billion).

The increase in aggregate labour hours that you have just seen is a consequence of an increase in labour productivity. This increase in aggregate labour hours and labour productivity is an example of the interaction effects that economists seek to identify in their search for the ultimate causes of economic growth.

In the case that we've just studied, aggregate labour hours increase but that increase is a *consequence*, not a *cause*, of the growth of potential GDP. The source of the increase in potential GDP is an increase in labour productivity.

Labour productivity is the key to increasing output per hour of labour and rising living standards. But what brings an increase in labour productivity? The next section answers this question.

Review Quiz

1. What is the aggregate production function?
2. What determines the demand for labour, the supply of labour, and labour market equilibrium?
3. What determines potential GDP?
4. What are the two broad sources of potential GDP growth?
5. What are the effects of an increase in the population on potential GDP, the quantity of labour employed, the real wage rate and potential GDP per hour of labour?
6. What are the effects of an increase in labour productivity on potential GDP, the quantity of labour employed, the real wage rate and potential GDP per hour of labour?

You can work these questions in Study Plan 22.3 and get instant feedback. myeconlab

Why Labour Productivity Grows

You've seen that labour productivity growth makes potential GDP grow; and you've seen that labour productivity growth is essential if real GDP per person and the standard of living are to grow. But why does labour productivity grow? What are the preconditions that make labour productivity growth possible and what are the forces that make it grow? Why does labour productivity grow faster at some times and in some places than others?

Preconditions for Labour Productivity Growth

The fundamental precondition for labour productivity growth is the *incentive* system created by firms, markets, property rights and money. These four social institutions are the same as those described in Chapter 2 (see pp. 43–44) that enable people to gain by specializing and trading.

ECONOMICS IN ACTION

Intellectual Property Rights Propel Economic Growth

In 1760, when the states that 16 years later would become the United States of America were developing agricultural economies, England was on the cusp of an economic revolution, the Industrial Revolution.

For 70 dazzling years, technological advances in the use of steam power, the manufacture of cotton, wool, iron and steel, and in transport, accompanied by massive capital investment associated with these technologies, transformed the economy of England. Incomes rose and brought an explosion in an increasingly urbanized population.

By 1825, advances in steam technology had reached a level of sophistication that enabled Robert Stephenson to build the world's first steam-powered rail engine (the Rocket pictured here) and the birth of the world's first railroad.

Why did the Industrial Revolution happen? Why did it start in 1760? And why in England?

Economic historians say that intellectual property rights – England's patent system – provides the answer.

England's patent system began with the Statute of Monopolies of 1624, which gave inventors a monopoly to use their idea for a term of 14 years. For about 100 years,

It was the presence of secure property rights in Britain in the middle 1700s that got the Industrial Revolution going (see Economics in Action below). And it is their absence in some parts of Africa today that is keeping labour productivity stagnant.

With the preconditions for labour productivity growth in place, three things influence its pace:

- Physical capital growth
- Human capital growth
- Technological advances

Physical Capital Growth

As the amount of capital per worker increases, labour productivity also increases. Production processes that use hand tools can create beautiful objects, but production methods that use large amounts of capital per worker are much more productive. The accumulation of capital on farms, in textile factories, in iron foundries and steel mills, in coal mines, on building sites, in chemical plants, in car plants, in banks and insurance companies and in shopping malls has added incredibly to our labour productivity.

the system was used to reward friends of the royal court rather than true inventors. But from around 1720 onward, the system started to work well. To be granted a 14-year monopoly, an inventor only had to pay the required £100 fee (about £14,000 in today's money) and register his or her invention. The inventor was not required to describe the invention in too much detail, so registering and getting a patent didn't mean sharing the invention with competitors.

This patent system, which is in all essentials the same as today's, aligned the self-interest of entrepreneurial inventors with the social interest and unleashed a flood of inventions, the most transformative of which was steam power and, by 1825, the steam locomotive.

Human Capital Growth

Human capital – the accumulated skill and knowledge of human beings – is the fundamental source of labour productivity growth. Human capital grows when a new discovery is made and it grows as more and more people learn how to use past discoveries.

The development of one of the most basic human skills – writing – was the source of some of the earliest major gains in productivity. The ability to keep written records made it possible to reap ever-larger gains from specialization and trade.

Later, the development of mathematics laid the foundation for the eventual extension of knowledge about physical forces and chemical and biological processes. This base of scientific knowledge was the foundation for the technological advances of the Industrial Revolution and of today's information revolution.

But a lot of human capital that is extremely productive is much more humble. It takes the form of millions of individuals learning and becoming remarkably more productive by repetitively doing simple production tasks. One much-studied example of this type of human capital growth occurred in the Second World War. With no change in physical capital, thousands of workers and managers in US shipyards learned from experience and accumulated human capital that more than doubled their productivity in less than two years.

Technological Advances

The accumulation of physical capital and human capital have made a large contribution to labour productivity growth. But technological change – the discovery and the application of new technologies – has made an even greater contribution.

Labour is many times more productive today than it was a hundred years ago but not because we have more steam engines and more horse-drawn carriages per person. Rather, it is because we have transport equipment that uses technologies that were unknown a hundred years ago and that are more productive than the old technologies were.

To reap the benefits of technological change, capital must increase. Some of the most powerful and far-reaching fundamental technologies are embodied in human capital – for example, language, writing and mathematics. But most technologies are embodied in physical capital. For example, to reap the benefits of the internal combustion engine, millions of horse-drawn carriages had to be replaced with cars; and to reap the benefits of digital music, millions of Discmans had to be replaced by iPods and giant server farms had to be built to operate iTunes and other online shops.

A Crucial Distinction

Although all three influences on labour productivity – physical capital, human capital and technological change – contribute to productivity growth, there is a crucial distinction between their contributions: physical capital is subject to diminishing returns while the other two are not.

The *law of diminishing returns* states that as the quantity of one factor of production increases with the quantities of all other factors remaining the same, output increases but by ever smaller increments.

You've seen how the law of diminishing returns applies to labour (p. 514). With a given amount of capital, each additional hour of labour produces less additional output than the previous hour. Sharing one computer, two typists produce fewer than twice as many pages per day as one typist produces.

The law of diminishing returns also applies to physical capital. If a given number of hours of labour use more capital (with the same human capital and technology), the additional output that results from the additional capital gets smaller as the amount of capital increases. A typist working with two computers can't produce twice as much as a typist working with one computer. The second computer increases productivity much less than the first computer does.

We can illustrate the diminishing marginal product of physical capital with a **productivity curve**, which is a relationship between labour productivity and physical capital per hour of labour when the amount of human capital and the state of technology are fixed.

Figure 22.9 shows the productivity curve. Its shape reflects the law of diminishing returns. On productivity curve PC_0, one hour of labour working with £40 of capital can't produce twice as much as one hour of labour working with £20 of capital.

An increase in human capital or an advance in technology increases the real GDP per hour of labour that can be produced by a given amount of capital per hour of labour and shifts the productivity curve upward. For example, if capital per hour of labour is £20 and a technological change increases labour productivity from £7 to £10, the productivity curve shifts upward from PC_0 to PC_1.

Figure 22.9 How Labour Productivity Grows

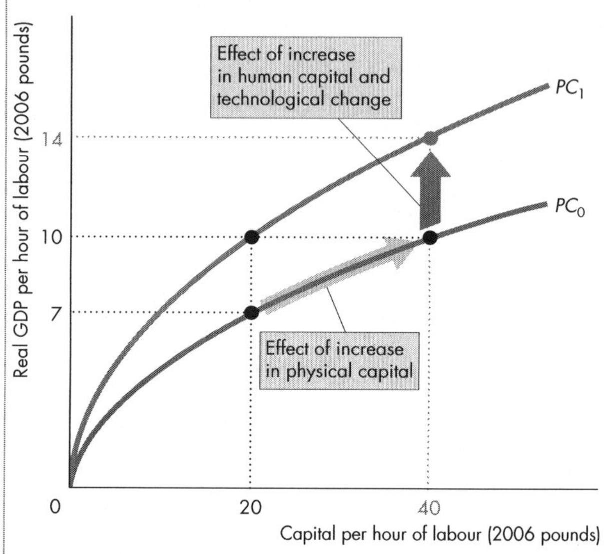

The productivity curve, *PC*, shows the effects of an increase in capital per hour of labour on productivity. Here, when capital per hour of labour increases from £20 to £40, labour productivity increases from £7 to £10 along the productivity curve PC_0.

Technological advance shifts the productivity curve upward. Here, the advance in technology shifts the productivity curve from PC_0 to PC_1. When capital per hour of labour is £40, the advance in technology increases labour productivity from £10 to £14.

myeconlab Animation

The productivity curve illustrates a fundamental fact about productivity growth; growth of physical capital alone brings a slowing rate of productivity growth. To sustain a high growth rate, it is vital to accumulate human capital and make technology advance.

Review Quiz

1. What are the preconditions for labour productivity growth?
2. What are the three influences on the pace of labour productivity growth?
3. What is the crucial distinction between the influences on labour productivity growth?
4. What is the productivity curve and how does it illustrate the crucial distinction between the influences on labour productivity growth?

You can work these questions in Study Plan 22.4 and get instant feedback. myeconlab

Growth Theories, Evidence and Policies

You've seen how the growth of population and labour productivity make potential GDP grow. You've also seen that the growth of physical capital and human capital and technological advances make labour productivity grow. How do these factors interact? What is cause and what is effect? Growth theories address these questions.

Alternative theories of economic growth provide insights into the process of economic growth, but none provides a complete and definite answer to the basic questions: What causes economic growth and why do growth rates vary? Economics has some way to go before it can provide definite answers to these questions. We look at the current state of the empirical evidence. Finally, we'll look at the policies that might achieve faster growth.

Let's start by studying the three main theories of economic growth:

- Classical growth theory
- Neoclassical growth theory
- New growth theory

Classical Growth Theory

Classical growth theory is the view that the growth of real GDP per person is temporary and that when it rises above the subsistence level, a population explosion eventually brings it back to the subsistence level. Adam Smith, Thomas Robert Malthus and David Ricardo – the leading economists of the late eighteenth century and early nineteenth century – proposed this theory, but the view is most closely associated with the name of Malthus and is sometimes called the *Malthusian theory*. Charles Darwin's ideas about evolution by natural selection were inspired by the insights of Malthus.

Modern-day Malthusians

Many people today are Malthusians. They say that if today's global population of 6.9 billion explodes to 11 billion by 2050 and perhaps 35 billion by 2300, we will run out of resources, real GDP per person will decline and we will return to a primitive standard of living. We must, say Malthusians, contain population growth.

Modern-day Malthusians also point to global warming and climate change as reasons to believe that eventually, real GDP per person will decrease.

Neoclassical Growth Theory

Neoclassical growth theory is the proposition that real GDP per person grows because technological change induces saving and investment that make physical capital grow. Diminishing returns end growth if technological change stops. Robert Solow of MIT suggested the most popular version of this growth theory in the 1950s.

Neoclassical growth theory's big break with its classical predecessor is its view about population growth.

The Neoclassical Theory of Population Growth

The population explosion of eighteenth century Europe that created the classical theory of population eventually ended. The birth rate fell, and while the population continued to increase, its rate of increase moderated.

The opportunity cost of a woman's time is the key influence that slowed the population growth rate. As women's wage rates increase and their job opportunities expand, the opportunity cost of having children increases. Faced with a higher opportunity cost, families choose to have fewer children and the birth rate falls.

Technological advances that bring higher incomes also bring advances in healthcare that extends lives. So as incomes increase, both the birth rate and the death rate decrease. These opposing forces offset each other and result in a slowly rising population.

This modern view of population growth and the historical trends that support it contradict the views of the classical economists. They also call into question the modern doomsday view that the planet will be swamped with more people than it can support.

Technological Change and Diminishing Returns

In neoclassical growth theory, the pace of technological change influences the economic growth rate but economic growth does not influence the pace of technological change. It is assumed that technological change results from chance. When we're lucky, we have rapid technological change, and when bad luck strikes, the pace of technological advance slows.

To understand neoclassical growth theory, imagine the world of the mid-1950s, when Robert Solow is explaining his idea. Income per person is around $12,000 a year in today's money. The population is growing at about 1 per cent a year. Saving and investment are about 20 per cent of GDP, enough to keep the quantity of capital per hour of labour constant. Income per person is growing but not very fast.

Then technology begins to advance at a more rapid pace across a range of activities. The transistor revolutionizes an emerging electronics industry. New plastics revolutionize the manufacture of household appliances. The interstate highway system revolutionizes road transportation. Jet airliners start to replace piston-engine airplanes and speed air transportation.

These technological advances bring new profit opportunities. Businesses expand, and new businesses are created to exploit the newly available profitable technologies. Investment and saving increase. The economy enjoys new levels of prosperity and growth. But will the prosperity last? And will the growth last? Neoclassical growth theory says that the prosperity will last but the growth will not last unless technology keeps advancing.

According to neoclassical growth theory, the prosperity will persist because there is no classical population growth to induce the wage rate to fall. So the gains in income per person are permanent.

Growth Stops Without Technological Change

Growth will eventually stop if technology stops advancing because of diminishing returns to capital. The high profit rates that result from technological change bring increased saving and capital accumulation. But as more capital is accumulated, more and more projects are undertaken that have lower rates of return – diminishing returns. As the return on capital falls, the incentive to invest weakens. With weaker incentives to save and invest, saving decreases and the rate of capital accumulation slows. Eventually, the pace of capital accumulation slows so that it is only keeping up with population growth. Capital per worker remains constant.

A Problem with Neoclassical Growth Theory

All economies have access to the same technologies and capital is free to roam the globe, seeking the highest available real interest rate. Capital will flow until rates of return are equal, and rates of return will be equal when capital per hour of labour are equal. Real GDP growth rates and income levels per person around the world will converge. Figure 22.3 on p. 511 shows that while there is some sign of convergence among the rich countries in part (a), convergence is slow, and part (b) shows that it does not appear to be imminent for all countries. New growth theory overcomes this shortcoming of neoclassical growth theory. It also explains what determines the pace of technological change.

New Growth Theory

New growth theory holds that real GDP per person grows because of the choices people make in the pursuit of profit and that growth will persist indefinitely. Paul Romer of Stanford University developed this theory during the 1980s, based on ideas of Joseph Schumpeter during the 1930s and 1940s.

According to the new growth theory, the pace at which new discoveries are made – and at which technology advances – is not determined by chance. It depends on how many people are looking for a new technology and how intensively they are looking. The search for new technologies is driven by incentives.

Profit is the spur to technological change. The forces of competition squeeze profits, so to increase profit, people constantly seek either lower-cost methods of production or new and better products for which people are willing to pay a higher price. Inventors can maintain a profit for several years by taking out a patent or a copyright, but eventually, a new discovery is copied and profits disappear. So more research and development is undertaken in the hope of creating a new burst of profitable investment and growth.

A Public Good and No Diminishing Returns

Two facts about discoveries and technological knowledge play a key role in the new growth theory: discoveries are (at least eventually) a public capital good; and knowledge is capital that is not subject to diminishing returns.

Economists call a good a public good when no one can be excluded from using it and when one person's use does not prevent others from using it. National defence is the classic example of a public good. The programming language used to write apps for the iPhone is another.

Because knowledge is a *public good*, as the benefits of a new discovery spread, free resources become available. Nothing is given up when they are used: they have a zero opportunity cost. When a student in York writes a new iPhone app, his use of the programming language doesn't prevent another student in Leeds from using it.

Knowledge is even more special because it is not subject to diminishing returns. But increasing the stock of knowledge makes both labour and machines more productive. Knowledge capital does not bring diminishing returns. Biotech knowledge illustrates this idea well. Biologists have spent a lot of time developing DNA sequencing technology. As more has been discovered, the productivity of this knowledge capital has relentlessly increased. In 1990, it cost about £50 to sequence one DNA base pair. That cost had fallen to £1 by 2000 and to 1/10,000th of a penny by 2010.

The implication of this simple and appealing observation is astonishing. Unlike the other two theories, new growth theory has no growth-stopping mechanism. As physical capital accumulates, the return to capital – the real interest rate – falls. But the incentive to innovate and earn a higher profit becomes stronger. So innovation occurs, capital becomes more productive, the demand for capital increases, and the real interest rate rises again.

Labour productivity grows indefinitely as people discover new technologies that yield a higher real interest rate. The growth rate depends only on people's incentives and ability to innovate.

A Perpetual Motion Economy

New growth theory sees the economy as a perpetual motion machine, which Figure 22.10 illustrates.

No matter how rich we become, our wants exceed our ability to satisfy them. We always want a higher standard of living. In the pursuit of a higher standard of living, human societies have developed incentive systems – markets, property rights and money – that enable people to profit from innovation. Innovation leads to the development of new and better techniques of production and new and better products. To take advantage of new techniques and to produce new products, new firms start up and old firms go out of business – firms are born and die. As old firms die and new firms are born, some jobs are destroyed and others are created. The new jobs created are better than the old ones and they pay higher real wage rates. Also, with higher wage rates and more productive techniques, leisure increases. New and better jobs and new and better products lead to more consumption goods and services and, combined with increased leisure, bring a higher standard of living.

But our insatiable wants are still there, so the process continues: wants and incentives create innovation, new and better products, and a yet higher standard of living.

Figure 22.10 A Perpetual Motion Machine

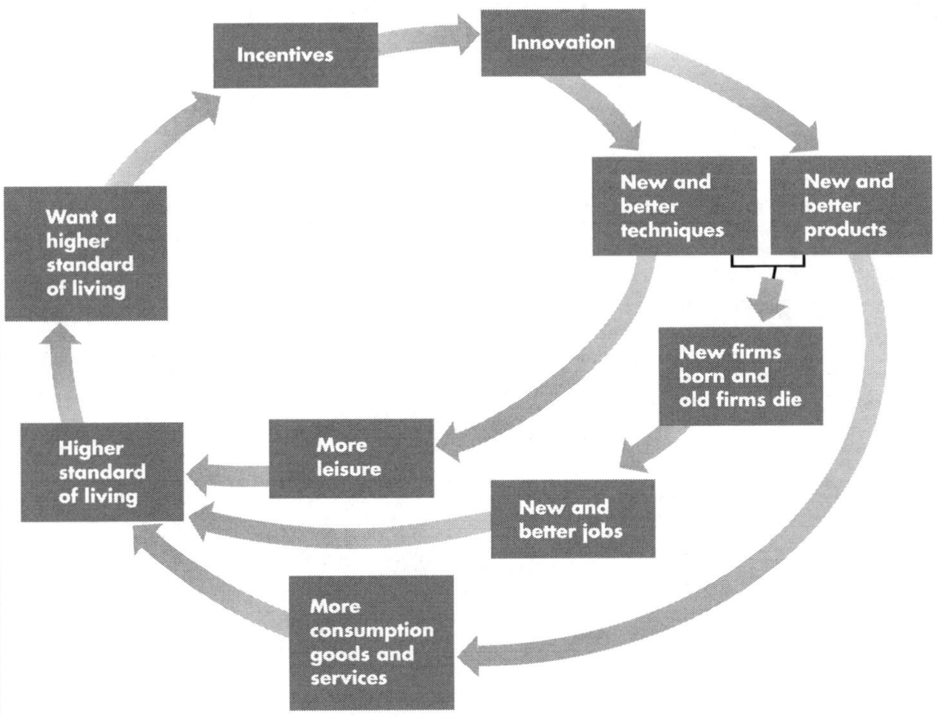

People want a higher standard of living and are spurred by profit incentives to make the innovations that lead to new and better techniques and new and better products, which in turn lead to the birth of new firms and the death of some old firms, new and better jobs, more leisure and more consumption of goods and services. The result is a higher standard of living. But people want a still higher standard of living and the growth process continues.

Source: Based on a similar figure in *These Are the Good Old Days: A Report on United States Living Standards*, Federal Reserve Bank of Dallas 1993 Annual Report.

myeconlab Animation

New Growth Theory versus Malthusian Theory

The contrast between the Malthusian theory and new growth theory couldn't be more sharp. Malthusians see the end of prosperity as we know it today and new growth theorists see unending plenty. The contrast becomes clearest by thinking about the differing views about population growth.

To a Malthusian, population growth is part of the problem. To a new growth theorist, population growth is part of the solution. People are the ultimate economic resource. A larger population brings forth more wants, but it also brings a greater amount of scientific discovery and technological advance. So rather than being the source of falling real GDP per person, population growth generates faster labour productivity growth and rising real GDP per person. Resources are limited, but the human imagination and ability to increase productivity are unlimited.

Sorting Out the Theories

Which theory is correct? None of them tells us the whole story, but each teaches us something of value.

Classical growth theory reminds us that our physical resources are limited and that without advances in technology, we must eventually hit diminishing returns.

Neoclassical growth theory reaches the same conclusion but not because of a population explosion. Instead, it emphasizes diminishing returns to capital and reminds us that we cannot keep growth going just by accumulating physical capital. We must also advance technology and accumulate human capital. We must become more creative in our use of scarce resources.

New growth theory emphasizes the capacity of human resources to innovate at a pace that offsets diminishing returns. New growth theory fits the facts of today's world more closely than do either of the other two theories, but that doesn't make it correct.

The Empirical Evidence on the Causes of Economic Growth

Economics makes progress by the interplay between theory and empirical evidence. A theory makes predictions about what we will observe if the theory is correct. Empirical evidence, the data generated by history and the natural experiments that it performs, provide the data for testing the theory.

Economists have done an enormous amount of research confronting theories of growth with the empirical evidence. The way in which this research has been conducted has changed over the years.

In 1776, when Adam Smith wrote about 'the nature and causes of the Wealth of Nations' in his celebrated book, empirical evidence took the form of carefully selected facts described in words and stories. Today, large databases, sophisticated statistical methods, and fast computers provide numerical measurements of the causes of economic growth.

Economists have looked at the growth rate data for more than 100 countries for the period since 1960 and explored the correlations between the growth rate and more than 60 possible influences on it. The conclusion of this data crunching is that most of these possible influences have variable and unpredictable effects, but a few of them have strong and clear effects. Table 22.1 summarizes these more robust influences. They are arranged in order of difficulty (or in the case of region, the impossibility) of changing. Political and economic systems are hard to change, but market distortions, investment and openness to international trade are features of a nation's economy that can be influenced by policy.

Let's now look at growth policies.

Policies for Achieving Faster Growth

Growth theory supported by empirical evidence tells us that to achieve faster economic growth, we must increase the growth rate of physical capital, the pace of technological advance, or the growth rate of human capital and openness to international trade.

The main suggestions for achieving these objectives are:

- Stimulate saving
- Stimulate research and development
- Improve the quality of education
- Provide international aid to developing nations
- Encourage international trade

Stimulate Saving

Saving finances investment, so stimulating saving increases economic growth. The East Asian economies have the highest growth rates and the highest saving rates. Some African economies have the lowest growth rates and the lowest saving rates.

Table 22.1

The Influences on Economic Growth

Influence	Good for Economic Growth	Bad for Economic Growth
Region	◆ Far from equator	◆ Sub-Sahara Africa
Politics	◆ Rule of law ◆ Civil liberties	◆ Revolutions ◆ Military coups ◆ Wars
Economic system	◆ Capitalist	
Market distortions		◆ Exchange rate distortions ◆ Price controls and black markets
Investment	◆ Human capital ◆ Physical capital	
International trade	◆ Open to trade	

Source of information: Xavier Sala-i-Martin, 'I Just Ran Two Million Regressions', *The American Economic Review*, Vol. 87, No 2 (May 1997), pp. 178–183.

Tax incentives can increase saving. Economists claim that a tax on consumption rather than income provides the best saving incentive.

Stimulate Research and Development

Everyone can use the fruits of basic research and development efforts. For example, all biotechnology firms can use advances in gene-splicing technology. Because basic inventions can be copied, the inventor's profit is limited and the market allocates too few resources to this activity. Governments can direct public funds towards financing basic research, but this solution is not foolproof. It requires a mechanism for allocating the public funds to their highest-valued use.

Improve the Quality of Education

The free market produces too little education because it brings benefits beyond those valued by the people who receive the education. By funding basic education and by ensuring high standards in basic skills such as language, mathematics and science, governments can contribute to a nation's growth potential. Education can also be stimulated and improved by using tax incentives to encourage improved private provision.

Provide International Aid to Developing Nations

It seems obvious that if rich countries give financial aid to developing countries, investment and growth will increase in the recipient countries. Unfortunately, the obvious does not routinely happen. A large amount of data-driven research on the effects of aid on growth has turned up a zero and even negative effect. Aid often gets diverted and spent on consumption.

Encourage International Trade

Trade, not aid, stimulates economic growth. It works by extracting the available gains from specialization and trade. The fastest-growing nations are those most open to trade. If the rich nations truly want to aid economic development, they will lower their trade barriers against developing nations, especially in farm products. The World Trade Organization's efforts to achieve more open trade are being resisted by the richer nations.

Review Quiz

1. What is the central idea of classical growth theory that leads to the dismal outcome?
2. What, according to the neoclassical growth theory, is the fundamental cause of economic growth?
3. What is the key proposition of the new growth theory that makes growth persist?

You can work these questions in Study Plan 22.5 and get instant feedback. myeconlab

To complete your study of economic growth, take a look at *Reading Between the Lines* on pp. 526–527 and see why China's spectacular economic growth might slow in the coming years.

Reading Between the Lines

China's Long-term Growth

The Financial Times, 28 September 2010

ADB Warns on China's Long-term Growth

Kevin Brown

China's average annual rate of economic growth over the next two decades will fall to little more than half the current level as its ability to sustain huge investment declines, according to the Asian Development Bank. . . .

In its first official attempt to quantify China's long-term growth prospects, the ADB said on Tuesday that its baseline projection was just 5.5 per cent on average for the 20 years to 2030, compared with 9.4 per cent between 1981 and 2007 and a forecast 9.6 per cent this year.

Growth could average 6.6 per cent if China implemented reforms to reduce its dependence on investment and increase productivity through improvements in education, property rights and research and development, the ADB said.

Jong-Wha Lee, ADB chief economist, said many other countries in Asia would face the same growth problem because their rapid rates of economic growth over the past three decades had been underpinned by unsustainable levels of investment. . . .

The ADB report forecasts that South Korea's long-term economic growth will fall from an average of 6.3 per cent to a baseline projection of 3.9 per cent, Taiwan's from 6.1 per cent to 3.1 per cent, Indonesia's from 4.8 per cent to 4.4 per cent and India's from 5.5 per cent to 4.5 per cent. . . .

Countries that have invested less in the past three decades are forecast to increase average growth rates, with Pakistan moving from 5.1 per cent a year to a baseline 6.5 per cent and the Philippines from 3.4 per cent to 5.7 per cent.

The Essence of the Story

- The Asian Development Bank (ADB) predicts that China's real GDP growth rate will slow from 9.4 per cent per year during the past 16 years to 5.5 per cent per year.
- The ADB also predicts that the real GDP growth rates will slow in South Korea, Taiwan and Indonesia.
- The ADB says that China has had an excessive dependence on physical capital accumulation and it needs to invest more in human capital, property rights and technological change.
- Pakistan and the Philippines, countries that have accumulated a smaller amount of physical capital, will have higher future growth rates.

Economic Analysis

- Figure 1 shows the growth rates for six Asian economies for 1981–2007 and the ADB's projected growth rates for 2011–2030.
- The ADB says China, South Korea and Taiwan will grow at a slower rate while Pakistan and the Philippines will grow at a faster rate.
- Figure 2 illustrates the reasoning behind the ADB forecasts. In 1981, China had a small amount of capital per hour of labour and capital accumulation brought rapid real GDP growth.
- But 30 years of high investment has brought diminishing returns to capital and over the coming years will bring even stronger diminishing returns shown by the falling slope of the productivity curve.
- Figure 3 shows the ADB's decomposition of the sources of China's real GDP growth rate both in the past and the future.
- Capital growth will still contribute the most to overall growth in 2011–2030. The next most important contributor is education and technological change. The shift in the productivity curve from PC_0 to PC_1 in Figure 2 illustrates this influence on real GDP per hour of labour.
- Capital growth is projected to contribute less to real GDP in the future than it did in the past because of diminishing returns to capital.
- It is hard to predict what the contribution of technological advance will be in the future.
- China might be at the same stage of economic development as Japan was in the decade after the Second World War.
- By copying Western technology, Japan learned to innovate and experienced rapid technological change. The same could happen in China and its fast growth would be sustained despite diminishing returns to capital.

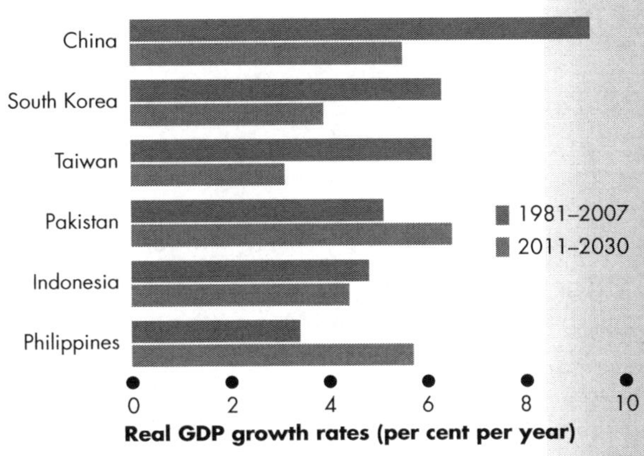

Figure 1 Real GDP growth in six Asian economies

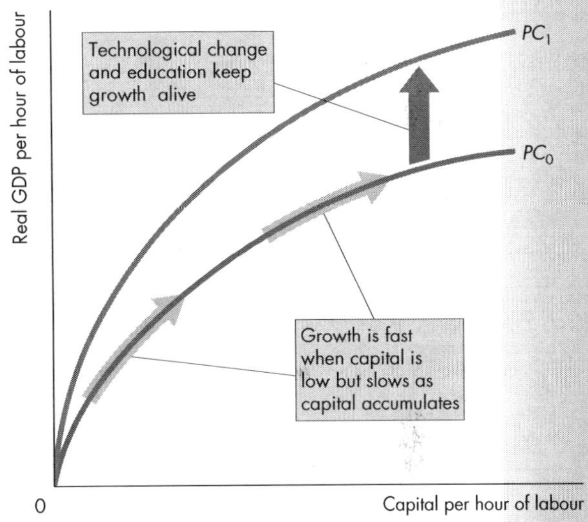

Figure 2 The sources of real GDP growth

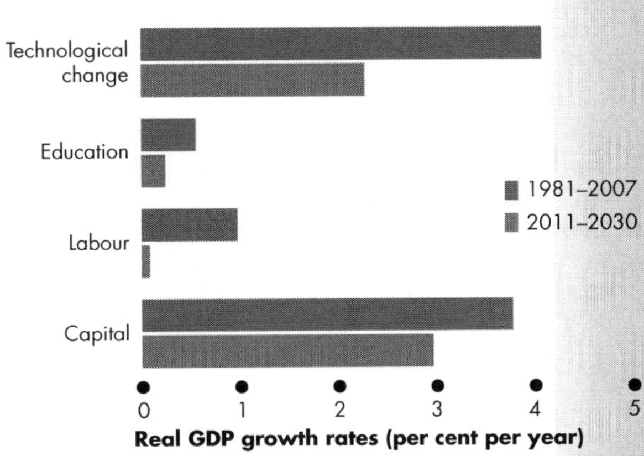

Figure 3 The changing sources of China's real GDP growth

SUMMARY

Key Points

The Basics of Economic Growth

- Economic growth is the sustained expansion of production possibilities and is measured as the annual percentage growth rate of real GDP.
- The Rule of 70 tells us the number of years in which real GDP doubles – 70 divided by the annual percentage growth rate.

Working Problems 1 to 5 will give you a better understanding of the basics of economic growth.

Economic Growth Trends

- Real GDP per person in the UK has grown at an average rate of 1.6 per cent per year. Growth was more rapid during the 1960s and the 1980s.
- The gap in real GDP per person between the US and Central and South America has persisted. The gaps between the US and Hong Kong, Korea and China have narrowed. The gaps between the US and Africa and Central Europe have widened.

Working Problem 6 will give you a better understanding of economic growth trends.

How Potential GDP Grows

- Potential GDP grows if the labour supply grows or if labour productivity grows.
- Only labour productivity growth makes real GDP per person and the standard of living grow.

Working Problems 7 to 14 will give you a better understanding of how potential GDP grows.

Why Labour Productivity Grows

- Labour productivity growth requires an incentive system created by firms, markets, property rights and money.
- The sources of labour productivity growth are growth of physical capital and human capital and advances in technology.
- Physical capital growth has diminishing returns but human capital growth and advances in technology don't have diminishing returns.

Working Problems 15 and 16 will give you a better understanding of why labour productivity grows.

Growth Theories, Evidence and Policies

- In classical theory, real GDP per person keeps returning to the subsistence level.
- In neoclassical growth theory, diminishing returns to capital limit economic growth.
- In new growth theory, economic growth persists indefinitely at a rate determined by decisions that lead to innovation and technological change.
- Policies for achieving faster growth include stimulating saving and research and development, encouraging international trade and improving the quality of education.

Working Problems 17 and 18 will give you a better understanding of growth theories, evidence and policies.

Key Terms

Aggregate production function
Classical growth theory
Economic growth
Economic growth rate
Labour productivity
Neoclassical growth theory
New growth theory
Productivity curve
Real GDP per person
Real wage rate
Rule of 70

STUDY PLAN PROBLEMS AND APPLICATIONS

myeconlab You can work Problems 1 to 18 in MyEconLab Chapter 22 Study Plan and get instant feedback.

The Basics of Economic Growth

(Study Plan 22.1)

1 Brazil's real GDP was 1,360 trillion reais in 2009 and 1,434 trillion reais in 2010. Brazil's population was 191.5 million in 2009 and 193.3 million in 2010. Calculate:

a The economic growth rate.

b The growth rate of real GDP per person.

c The approximate number of years it takes for real GDP per person in Brazil to double if the 2010 economic growth rate and population growth rate are maintained.

2 Japan's real GDP was 525 trillion yen in 2009 and 535 trillion yen in 2010. Japan's population was 127.6 million in 2009 and 127.5 million in 2010. Calculate:

a The economic growth rate.

b The growth rate of real GDP per person.

c The approximate number of years it takes for real GDP per person in Japan to double if the real GDP economic growth rate returns to 3 per cent a year and the population growth rate is maintained.

Use the following data to work Problems 3 and 4.

China's real GDP per person was 9,280 yuan in 2009 and 10,110 yuan in 2010. India's real GDP per person was 30,880 rupees in 2009 and 32,160 rupees in 2010.

3 By maintaining their current growth rates, which country will double its 2010 standard of living first?

4 The population of China is growing at 1 per cent a year and the population of India is growing at 1.4 per cent a year. Calculate the growth rate of real GDP in each country.

5 **China's Economy Picks Up Speed**

China's trend growth rate of real GDP per person was 2.2 per cent a year before 1980 and 8.7 per cent a year after 1980. In the year to August 2009, China's output increased by 11.3 per cent.

Source: World Economic Outlook and FT.com, 14 September 2009

a Distinguish between a rise in China's economic growth rate and a temporary cyclical expansion.

b How long, at the current growth rate, will it take for China to double its real GDP per person?

Economic Growth Trends (Study Plan 22.2)

6 China was the largest economy for centuries because everyone had the same type of economy – subsistence – and so the country with the most people would be economically biggest. Then the Industrial Revolution sent the West on a more prosperous path. Now the world is returning to a common economy, this time technology- and information-based, so once again population triumphs.

a Why was China the world's largest economy until 1890?

b Why did the US surpass China in 1890 to become the world's largest economy?

How Potential GDP Grows

(Study Plan 22.3)

Use the following information to work Problems 7 and 8.

Suppose that France cracks down on illegal immigrants and returns millions of workers to their home countries.

7 Explain what will happen to potential GDP, employment and the real wage rate in France.

8 Explain what will happen to potential GDP, employment and the real wage rate in the countries to which the immigrants return.

Use the following news clip to work Problems 9 to 11.

US Workers World's Most Productive

Americans work longer hours than those in other rich nations. Americans also produce more per person but only part of US productivity growth can be explained by the longer hours they work. Americans also create more wealth per hour of work. US employees worked an average of 1,804 hours in 2006, compared to 1,564.4 for the French, but far less than the 2,200 hours that Asians worked. But in Asian countries, average labour productivity is lower.

Source: CBS News, 3 September 2007

9 What is the difference between productivity in this news clip and real GDP per person?

10 Identify and correct a confusion in the news clip between levels and growth rates of labour productivity.

11 If workers in developing Asian economies work more hours than Americans, why are they not the world's most productive?

Use the following tables to work Problems 12 to 14.

The tables describe an economy's labour market and its production function in 2010.

Real wage rate (euros per hour)	Labour hours supplied	Labour hours demanded
80	45	5
70	40	10
60	35	15
50	30	20
40	25	25
30	20	30
20	15	35

Labour (hours)	Real GDP (2005 euros)
5	425
10	800
15	1,125
20	1,400
25	1,625
30	1,800
35	1,925
40	2,000

12 What are the equilibrium real wage rate, the quantity of labour employed in 2010, labour productivity and potential GDP in 2010?

13 In 2011, the population increases and labour hours supplied increase by 10 at each real wage rate. What are the equilibrium real wage rate, labour productivity and potential GDP in 2011?

14 In 2011, the population increases and labour hours supplied increase by 10 at each real wage rate. Does the standard of living in this economy increase in 2011? Explain why or why not.

Why Labour Productivity Grows (Study Plan 22.4)

15 **Labour Productivity on the Rise**

During the year ended June 2009, US non-farm sector output fell 5.5 per cent as labour productivity increased 1.9 per cent – the largest increase since 2003. But in the manufacturing sector, output fell 9.8 per cent as labour productivity increased by 4.9 per cent – the largest increase since the first quarter of 2005.

Source: bls.gov/news.release, 11 August 2009

In both sectors, output fell while labour productivity increased. Did the quantity of labour (aggregate hours) increase or decrease? In which sector was the change in the quantity of labour larger?

16 For three years, there was no technological change in Longland but capital per hour of labour increased from €10 to €20 to €30 and real GDP per hour of labour increased from €3.80 to €5.70 to €7.13. Then, in the fourth year, capital per hour of labour remained constant, but real GDP per hour of labour increased to €10. Does Longland experience diminishing returns? Explain why or why not.

Growth Theories, Evidence and Policies (Study Plan 22.5)

17 Explain the processes that will bring the growth of real GDP per person to a stop according to:

a Classical growth theory.

b Neoclassical growth theory.

c New growth theory.

18 In the economy of Cape Despair, the subsistence real wage rate is €15 an hour. Whenever real GDP per hour rises above €15, the population grows, and whenever real GDP per hour of labour falls below this level, the population falls. The table shows Cape Despair's production function:

Labour (billions of hours per year)	Real GDP (billions of 2005 euros)
0.5	8
1.0	15
1.5	21
2.0	26
2.5	30
3.0	33
3.5	35

Initially, the population of Cape Despair is constant and real GDP per hour of labour is at the subsistence level of €15. Then a technological advance shifts the production function upward by 50 per cent at each level of labour.

a What are the initial levels of real GDP and labour productivity?

b What happens to labour productivity immediately following the technological advance?

ADDITIONAL PROBLEMS AND APPLICATIONS

myeconlab You can work these problems in MyEconLab if assigned by your lecturer.

The Basics of Economic Growth

19 If in 2012 China's real GDP is growing at 9 per cent a year, its population is growing at 1 per cent a year, and these growth rates continue, in what year will China's real GDP per person be twice what it is in 2012?

20 South Africa's real GDP was 1,782 billion rand in 2009 and 1,835 billion rand in 2010. South Africa's population was 49.3 million in 2009 and 49.9 million in 2010. Calculate:

a The economic growth rate.

b The growth rate of real GDP per person.

c The approximate number of years it takes for real GDP per person in South Africa to double if the 2010 economic growth rate and population growth rate are maintained.

21 Turkey's real GDP was 97.1 billion Turkish lira in 2009 and 104.7 billion Turkish lira in 2010. Turkey's population was 70.5 million in 2009 and 71.4 million in 2010. Calculate:

a The economic growth rate.

b The growth rate of real GDP per person.

c The approximate number of years it takes for real GDP per person in Turkey to double if economic growth returns to its average since 2009 of 3.6 per cent a year and is maintained.

Economic Growth Trends

22 **The New World Order**

While gross domestic product growth is cooling a bit in emerging market economies, the results are still tremendous compared with the US and much of Western Europe. The emerging market economies posted a 6.7 per cent jump in real GDP in 2008, down from 7.5 per cent in 2007. The advanced economies grew an estimated 1.6 per cent in 2008. The difference in growth rates represents the largest spread between emerging market economies and advanced economies in the 37-year history of the survey.

Source: *Fortune*, 14 July 2008

Do growth rates over the past few decades indicate that gaps in real GDP per person around the world are shrinking, growing or staying the same? Explain.

How Potential GDP Grows

23 If a large increase in investment increases labour productivity, explain what happens to:

a Potential GDP.

b Employment.

c The real wage rate.

24 If a severe drought decreases labour productivity, explain what happens to:

a Potential GDP.

b Employment.

c The real wage rate.

Use the following tables to work Problems 25 to 27.

The first table describes an economy's labour market and the second table describes its production function in 2010.

Real wage rate (euros per hour)	Labour hours supplied	Labour hours demanded
80	55	15
70	50	20
60	45	25
50	40	30
40	35	35
30	30	40
20	25	45

Labour (hours)	Real GDP (2005 euros)
15	1,425
20	1,800
25	2,125
30	2,400
35	2,625
40	2,800
45	2,925
50	3,000

25 What are the equilibrium real wage rate and the quantity of labour employed in 2010?

26 What are labour productivity and potential GDP in 2010?

27 Suppose that labour productivity increases in 2010. What effect does the increased labour productivity have on the demand for labour, the supply of labour, potential GDP and real GDP per person?

Why Labour Productivity Grows

28 India's Economy Hits the Wall

Just six months ago, India was looking good. Annual growth was 9 per cent, consumer demand was huge, and foreign investment was growing. But now most economic forecasts expect growth to slow to 7 per cent – a big drop for a country that needs to accelerate growth. India needs urgently to upgrade its infrastructure and education and healthcare facilities. Agriculture is unproductive and needs better technology. The legal system needs to be strengthened with more judges and courtrooms.

Source: *Business Week*,1 July 2008

Explain five potential sources for faster economic growth in India suggested in this news clip.

Growth Theories, Evidence and Policies

29 The Productivity Watch

According to former Federal Reserve chairman Alan Greenspan, IT investments in the 1990s boosted productivity, which boosted corporate profits, which led to more IT investments, and so on, leading to a nirvana of high growth.

Source: *Fortune*, 4 September 2006

Which of the growth theories that you've studied in this chapter best corresponds to the explanation given by Mr Greenspan?

30 Is faster economic growth always a good thing? Argue the case for faster growth and the case for slower growth. Then reach a conclusion on whether growth should be increased or slowed.

31 Makani Power: A Mighty Wind

Makani Power aims to generate energy from what are known as high-altitude wind-extraction technologies. And that's about all its 34-year-old Aussie founder, Saul Griffith, wants to say about it. But Makani can't hide entirely, not when its marquee investor is Google.org, the tech company's philanthropic arm. Makani's plan is to capture that high-altitude wind with a very old tool: kites. Harnessing higher-altitude wind, at least in theory, has greater potential than the existing wind industry because at a thousand feet above the ground, the wind is stronger and more consistent.

Source: *Fortune*, 28 April 2008

Explain which growth theory best describes the news clip.

Economics in the News

32 After you have studied *Reading Between the Lines* on pp. 526–527 answer the following questions:

- **a** What does the Asia Development Bank expect will happen to the economic growth rate of China over the next two decades?
- **b** What is the reasoning behind the ADB's expectation?
- **c** On which growth theory have the ADB economists based their forecast? Explain your answer.
- **d** What policy does the ADB suggest will sustain China's high economic growth rate of the recent past? Explain your answer.

33 Make Way for India – The Next China

China grows at around 9 per cent a year, but its one-child policy will start to reduce the size of China's working population within the next 10 years. India, by contrast, will have an increasing working population for another generation at least.

Source: *The Independent*, 1 March 2006

- **a** Given the expected population changes, do you think China or India will have the greater economic growth rate? Why?
- **b** Would China's growth rate remain at 9 per cent a year without the restriction on its population growth rate?
- **c** India's population growth rate is 1.6 per cent a year, and in 2005 its economic growth rate was 8 per cent a year. China's population growth rate is 0.6 per cent a year and in 2005 its economic growth rate was 9 per cent a year. In what year will real GDP per person double in each country?

Data Graphing

34 Use the Data Grapher to create a graph of the growth rate of real GDP per person in the US, Canada, Germany and the UK.

- **a** Which country had the fastest growth of real GDP per person since 1980 and which had the slowest?
- **b** In which country has real GDP per person fluctuated most?

CHAPTER 23

Finance, Saving and Investment

After studying this chapter you will be able to:

- Describe the flows of funds through financial markets and institutions
- Explain how investment and saving along with borrowing and lending decisions are made and interact in the loanable funds market
- Explain how a government deficit (or surplus) influences the real interest rate, saving and investment
- Explain how international borrowing and lending influence the real interest rate, saving and investment

On 17 September 2007, long queues of depositors wanting to withdraw their funds formed outside the branches of the mortgage lender Northern Rock. On that same day in Detroit, Michigan, a distraught family loaded its pick-up truck, locked the door of its mortgaged home and drove away from its debt. How are these two events connected? They are connected through the global financial market that you study in this chapter. You will learn how financial markets work – mostly very well but sometimes badly.

In *Reading Between the Lines* at the end of the chapter, you will apply what you've learned to understand the influence on financial markets of large government budget deficits in the UK, Portugal, Ireland, Greece and Spain.

Financial Institutions and Financial Markets

The financial institutions and markets that we study in this chapter play a crucial role in the economy. They provide the channels through which saving flows to finance the investment in new capital that makes the economy grow. In studying the economics of financial institutions and markets, we distinguish between:

- Finance and money
- Physical capital and financial capital

Finance and Money

In economics, we use the term *finance* to describe the activity of borrowing and lending. Borrowing and lending provides the funds that finance expenditures on capital that make productivity grow.

The study of finance examines how households, firms and governments obtain and use financial resources and how they cope with the risks that arise in this activity.

We use the term *money* to describe the stuff that we use to make payments for goods and services, for factors of production including expenditures on new capital and to make financial transactions – to receive and repay loans.

The study of money looks at how households and firms use it, how much of it they hold, how banks create and manage it, and how its quantity influences the economy.

In the economic lives of individuals, businesses and governments, finance and money are closely interrelated. Money is what you get when you borrow from a bank. Money is what you use when you finance the purchase of a new car. And banks and other financial institutions provide both financial services and monetary services. Nevertheless, by distinguishing between *finance* and *money* and studying them separately, we will better understand our financial and monetary markets and institutions.

For the rest of this chapter, we study finance. Money is the topic of the next chapter.

Physical Capital and Financial Capital

Economists distinguish between physical capital and financial capital. *Physical capital* is the tools, instruments, machines, buildings and other items that have been produced in the past and that are used today to produce goods and services. Inventories of raw materials, semifinished goods, and components are part of physical capital. When economists use the term capital, they mean physical capital. The funds that firms use to buy physical capital are called **financial capital**.

Along the *aggregate production function* in Chapter 22 (see p. 513), the quantity of capital is fixed. An increase in the quantity of capital increases production possibilities and shifts the aggregate production function upward. You're going to see, in this chapter, how investment, saving, borrowing and lending decisions influence the quantity of capital and make it grow, and, as a consequence, make real GDP grow. We begin by describing the links between capital and investment and between wealth and saving.

Capital and Investment

The quantity of capital changes because of investment and depreciation. *Investment* increases the quantity of capital and *depreciation* decreases it (see Chapter 20, p. 462). The total amount spent on new capital is called **gross investment**. The change in the value of capital is called **net investment**. Net investment equals gross investment minus depreciation. Figure 23.1 illustrates these terms. On 1 January 2011, Ace Bottling Inc. had machines worth €30,000 – Ace's initial capital. During 2011, the market value of Ace's machines fell by 67 per cent – €20,000. After this depreciation, Ace's machines were valued at €10,000. During 2011, Ace spent €30,000 on new machines. This amount is Ace's gross investment. By 31 December 2011, Ace Bottling had capital valued at €40,000, so its capital had increased by €10,000. This amount is Ace's net investment. Ace's net investment equals its gross investment of €30,000 minus depreciation of its initial capital of €20,000.

Wealth and Saving

Wealth is the value of all the things that people own. What people own is related to what they earn, but it is not the same thing. People earn an income, which is the amount they receive during a given time period from supplying the services of the resources they own. **Saving** is the amount of income that is not paid in taxes or spent on consumption goods and services.

Saving increases wealth. Wealth also increases when the market value of assets rises – called capital gains – and decreases when the market value of assets falls – called capital losses.

Figure 23.1 Capital and Investment

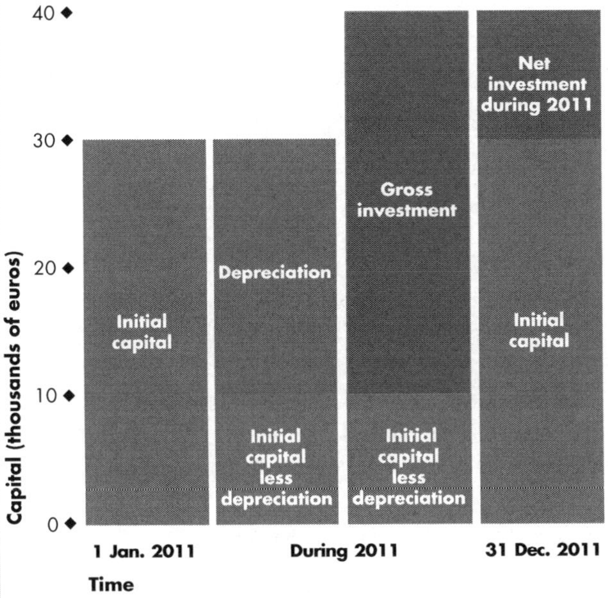

On 1 January 2011, Ace Bottling had capital worth €30,000. During the year, the value of Ace's capital fell by €20,000 – depreciation – and it spent €30,000 on new capital – gross investment. Ace's net investment was €10,000 (€30,000 gross investment minus €20,000 depreciation) so that at the end of 2011, Ace had capital worth €40,000.

myeconlab Animation

For example, at the end of term you have €250 in the bank and a coin collection worth €300, so your wealth is €550. During the summer, you earn €5,000 (net of taxes) and spend €1,000 on consumption goods and services, so your saving is €4,000. Your bank account increases to €4,250 and your wealth becomes €4,550. The €4,000 increase in wealth equals saving. If coins rise in value and your coin collection is now worth €500, you have a capital gain of €200, which is also added to your wealth.

National wealth and national saving work like this personal example. The wealth of a nation at the end of a year equals its wealth at the start of the year plus its saving during the year, which equals income minus consumption expenditure.

To make real GDP grow, saving and wealth must be transformed into investment and capital. This transformation takes place in the markets for financial capital and through the activities of financial institutions. We're now going to describe these markets and institutions.

Financial Capital Markets

Saving is the source of the funds that are used to finance investment, and these funds are supplied and demanded in three types of financial markets:

- Loan markets
- Bond markets
- Stock markets

Loan Markets

Businesses often want short-term finance to buy inventories or to extend credit to their customers. Sometimes they get this finance in the form of a loan from a bank. Households often want finance to purchase a high expenditure item, such as a car or household furnishings and appliances. They get this finance as bank loans, often in the form of outstanding credit card balances. Households also get finance to buy new homes. (Expenditure on new homes is counted as part of investment.) These funds are usually obtained as a loan that is secured by a **mortgage** – a legal contract that gives ownership of a home to the lender in the event that the borrower fails to meet the agreed loan payments (repayments and interest). Mortgage loans were at the centre of the sub-prime loans crisis of 2007–2008. All of these types of financing take place in loan markets.

Bond Markets

When Wal-Mart (the largest retailer in the world) expands its business into China, it gets the finance it needs by selling bonds. National and local governments also raise finance by issuing bonds.

A **bond** is a promise to make specified payments on specified dates. For example, you can buy a Wal-Mart bond that promises to pay $5.00 every year until 2024 and then to make a final payment of $100 in 2025.

The buyer of a bond from Wal-Mart makes a loan to the company and is entitled to the payments promised by the bond. When a person buys a newly issued bond, he or she may hold the bond until the borrower has repaid the amount borrowed or sell it to someone else. Bonds issued by firms and governments are traded in the **bond market**.

The term of a bond might be long (decades) or short (just a month or two). Firms often issue very short-term bonds as a way of getting paid for their sales before the buyer is able to pay. These short-term bonds are called commercial paper. For example, when Rolls Royce sells

£100 million of aero engines to Qantas, Rolls Royce wants to be paid when the items are shipped. But Qantas doesn't want to pay until the engines are installed and the engines are earning an income. In this situation, Qantas might promise to pay GM £101 million three months in the future. A bank would be willing to buy this promise for (say) £100 million. Rolls Royce gets £100 million immediately and the bank gets £101 million in three months when Qantas honours its promise. The UK Treasury issues promises of this type, called Treasury bills.

Another type of bond is a **mortgage-backed security**, which entitles its holder to the income from a package of mortgages. Mortgage lenders create mortgage-backed securities. They make mortgage loans to homebuyers and then create securities that they sell to obtain more funds to make more mortgage loans. The holder of a mortgage-backed security is entitled to receive payments that derive from the payments received by the mortgage lender from the homebuyer–borrower.

Mortgage-backed securities were at the centre of the storm in the financial markets in 2007–2008.

Stock Markets

When Boeing wants finance to expand its aeroplane building business, it issues stock. A **stock** is a certificate of ownership and claim to the firm's profits. Boeing has issued about 900 million shares of its stock. So if you owned 900 Boeing shares, you would own one millionth of Boeing and be entitled to receive one millionth of its profits. Unlike a stockholder, a bondholder does not own part of the firm that issued the bond.

A **stock market** is a financial market in which shares of stocks of corporations are traded. The London Stock Exchange, the Frankfurt Stock Exchange, the New York Stock Exchange and the Tokyo Stock Exchange are all examples of stock markets.

Financial Institutions

Financial markets are highly competitive because of the role played by financial institutions in those markets. A **financial institution** is a firm that operates on both sides of the markets for financial capital. The financial institution is a borrower in one market and a lender in another.

Financial institutions also stand ready to trade so that households with funds to lend and firms or households seeking funds can always find someone on the other side of the market with whom to trade.

The key financial institutions are:

- Commercial banks
- Mortgage companies (building societies)
- Pension funds
- Insurance companies

Commercial Banks

Commercial banks are financial institutions that accept deposits, provide payment services and make loans to firms and households. The bank that you use for your own banking services and that issues your debit card is a commercial bank. These institutions play a central role in the monetary system and we study them in detail in Chapter 24.

Mortgage Companies (Building Societies)

Mortgage companies are financial institutions that specialise in making loans for property purchases. In the UK these companies are called building societies. Traditionally building societies took deposits and made loans from the deposit funds they held. Since the 1990s, the building societies began to borrow funds from other financial institutions to make mortgage loans. Many building societies became banks so that they could fund their mortgage business by borrowing from the global interbank market.

In the US, two large financial institutions that specialize in mortgages, the Federal National Mortgage Association, or Fannie Mae, and the Federal Home Loan Mortgage Corporation, or Freddie Mac, were at the epicentre of the global financial crisis (see *Economics in Action* opposite). These financial institutions bought mortgages from banks, packaged them into mortgage-backed securities, and sold them to financial institutions all over the world.

In September 2008, Fannie and Freddie owned or guaranteed $6 trillion worth of mortgages (half of the US$12 trillion of mortgages) and were taken over by the US federal government.

Many former UK building societies followed the model of Fannie Mae and Freddie Mac. They borrowed funds in the global interbank loans market and loaned them to house buyers. They then packaged the mortgage loans into mortgage-backed securities and sold them to other financial institutions. Often the buyers of these securities would be the lenders of the funds that were used to make the loans to house buyers.

Pension Funds

Pension funds are financial institutions that use the pension contributions of firms and workers to buy bonds and stocks. The mortgage backed securities of Fannie Mae and Freddie Mac and specialized mortgage lenders in the UK are among the assets of pension funds. Some pension funds are very large and play an active role in the firms whose stock they hold.

Insurance Companies

Insurance companies enable households and firms to cope with risks such as accident, theft, fire, ill-health and a host of other misfortunes. They receive premiums from their customers and pay claims. Insurance companies use the funds they have received but not paid out as claims to buy bonds and stocks on which they earn interest income.

In normal times, insurance companies have a steady inflow of funds from premiums and interest and a steady, but smaller, outflow of funds paying claims. Their profit is the gap between the two flows.

In unusual times, when large and widespread losses are being incurred, insurance companies can run into difficulty in meeting their obligations.

Insolvency and Illiquidity

A financial institution's **net worth** is the market value of what it has lent minus the market value of what it has borrowed. If net worth is positive, the institution is solvent. But if net worth is negative, the institution is insolvent and must go out of business. The owners of an insolvent financial institution – usually its stockholders – bear the loss.

A financial institution both borrows and lends, so it is exposed to the risk that its net worth might become negative. To limit that risk, financial institutions are regulated and a minimum amount of their lending must be backed by their net worth.

Sometimes, a financial institution is solvent but illiquid. A firm is *illiquid* if it has made long-term loans with borrowed funds and is faced with a sudden demand to repay more of what it has borrowed than its available cash.

In normal times, a financial institution that is illiquid can borrow from another institution. But if all the financial institutions are short of cash, the market for loans among financial institutions dries up. In such a situation, the central bank can provide funds.

Insolvency and illiquidity were at the core of the financial meltdown of 2007–2008.

ECONOMICS IN ACTION

The 2008 Financial Crisis

Bear Stearns: absorbed by JPMorgan Chase with help from the US Federal Reserve. Lehman Brothers: gone. Fannie Mae and Freddie Mac: taken into government oversight. Merrill Lynch: absorbed by Bank of America. AIG: given an $85 billion lifeline by the Federal Reserve and sold off in parcels to financial institutions around the world. Wachovia: taken over by Wells Fargo. Washington Mutual: taken over by JPMorgan Chase. Morgan Stanley: 20 per cent bought by Mitsubishi, a large Japanese bank. These are some of the events in the financial crisis of 2008. What was going on?

Between 2002 and 2005, mortgage lending exploded and home prices rocketed. Mortgage lenders bundled their loans into mortgage-backed securities and sold them to eager buyers around the world. When interest rates began to rise in 2006 and asset prices fell, financial institutions took big losses. Some losses were too big to bear and big-name institutions failed.

Interest Rates and Asset Prices

Stocks, bonds, short-term securities and loans are collectively called financial assets. The interest rate on a financial asset is the interest received expressed as a percentage of the price of the asset.

Because the interest rate is a percentage of the price of an asset, if the asset price rises, other things remaining the same, the interest rate falls. Conversely, if the asset price falls, other things remaining the same, the interest rate rises.

To see this inverse relationship between an asset price and the interest rate, let's look at an example. We'll consider a bond that promises to pay its holder €5 a year forever. What is the rate of return – the interest rate – on this bond? The answer depends on the price of the bond. If you could buy this bond for €50, the interest rate would be 10 per cent per year:

$$\text{Interest rate} = (€5 \div €50) \times 100 = 10 \text{ per cent.}$$

But if the price of this bond increased to €200, its rate of return or interest rate would be only 2.5 per cent per year. That is,

$$\text{Interest rate} = (€5 \div €200) \times 100 = 2.5 \text{ per cent.}$$

This relationship means that the price of an asset and the interest rate on that asset are determined simultaneously – one implies the other.

This relationship also means that if the interest rate on the asset rises, the price of the asset falls, debts become harder to pay and the net worth of the financial institution falls. Insolvency can arise from a previously unexpected large rise in the interest rate. In the next part of this chapter, we learn how interest rates and asset prices are determined in the financial markets.

Review Quiz

1. Distinguish between physical capital and financial capital and give two examples of each.
2. What is the distinction between gross investment and net investment?
3. What are the three main types of markets for financial capital and what makes them different?
4. What are the main types of financial institutions and how do they differ?
5. Explain the connection between the price of a financial asset and its interest rate.

You can work these questions in Study Plan 23.1 and get instant feedback. myeconlab

The Loanable Funds Market

In macroeconomics, we group all the financial markets that we described in the previous section into a single loanable funds market. The **loanable funds market** is the aggregate of all the individual financial markets.

The circular flow model of Chapter 20 (see p. 461) can be extended to include flows in the loanable funds market that finance investment.

Funds that Finance Investment

Figure 23.2 shows the flows of funds that finance investment. They come from three sources:

1. Household saving
2. Government budget surplus
3. Borrowing from the rest of the world

Households' income, Y, is spent on consumption goods and services, C, saved, S, or paid in net taxes, T. **Net taxes** are the taxes paid to governments minus the cash transfers received from governments (such as Social Security and unemployment benefits). So income is equal to the sum of consumption expenditure, saving and net taxes:

$$Y = C + S + T$$

You saw in Chapter 20 (p. 462) that Y also equals the sum of the items of aggregate expenditure: consumption expenditure, C, investment, I, government expenditure, G, and exports, X, minus imports, M. That is:

$$Y = C + I + G + X - M$$

By using these two equations, you can see that

$$I + G + X = M + S + T$$

Subtract G and X from both sides of the last equation to obtain

$$I = S + (T - G) + (M - X)$$

This equation tells us that investment, I, is financed by household saving, S, the government budget surplus, $(T - G)$, and borrowing from the rest of the world, $(M - X)$.

A government budget surplus $(T > G)$ contributes funds to finance investment, but a government budget deficit $(T < G)$, competes with investment for funds and decreases the amount available to invest.

Figure 23.2 Financial Flows and the Circular Flow of Expenditure and Income

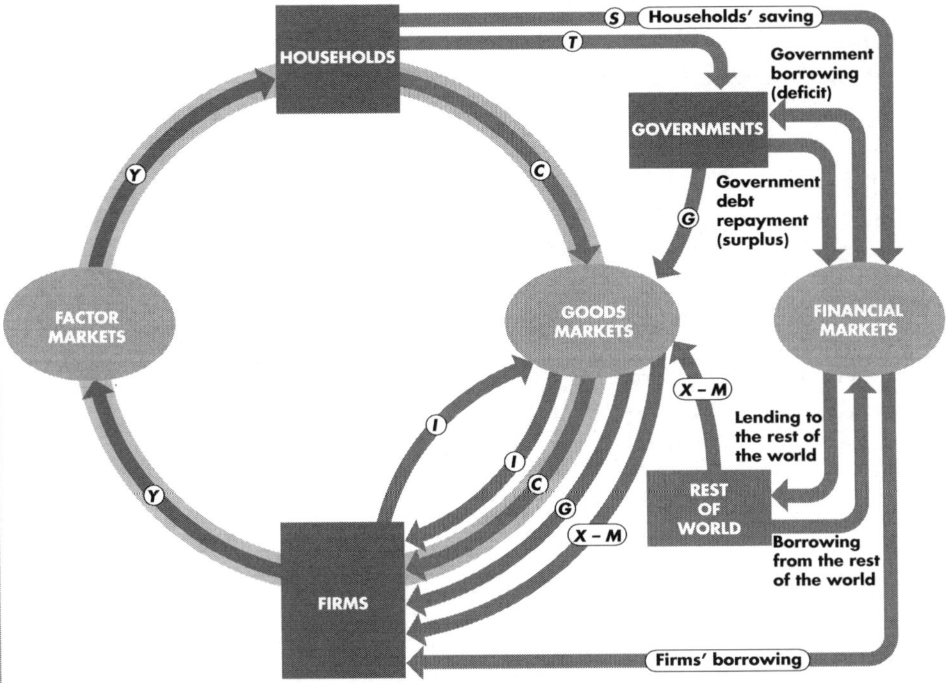

Households use their income for consumption expenditure (C), saving (S) and net taxes (T). Firms borrow to finance their investment expenditure.

Governments borrow to finance a budget deficit or repay debt if they have a budget surplus. The rest of the world borrows to finance its deficit or lends its surplus.

myeconlab Animation

If we export less than we import, we borrow $(M - X)$ from the rest of the world to finance some of our investment. If we export more than we import, we lend $(X - M)$ to the rest of the world and part of US saving finances investment in other countries.

The sum of private saving, S, and government saving, $(T - G)$, is called **national saving**. National saving and foreign borrowing finance investment.

In 2010, total investment in the UK was £208 billion. The government (national and local combined) had a deficit of £144 billion. This total of £352 billion was financed by private saving of £306 billion and borrowing from the rest of the world (negative net exports) of £46 billion.

You're going to see how investment and saving and the flows of loanable funds – all measured in constant 2005 euros – are determined. The price in the loanable funds market that achieves equilibrium is an interest rate, which we also measure in real terms as the real interest rate. In the loanable funds market, there is just one interest rate, which is an average of the interest rates on all the different types of financial securities that we described earlier. Let's see what we mean by the real interest rate.

The Real Interest Rate

The **nominal interest rate** is the number of pounds or euros that a borrower pays and a lender receives in interest in a year expressed as a percentage of the number of pounds or euros borrowed and lent. For example, if the annual interest paid on a €500 loan is €25, the nominal interest rate is 5 per cent per year: €25 ÷ €500 × 100 or 5 per cent.

The **real interest rate** is the additional goods and services that the lender can buy with the interest received. It is the nominal interest rate adjusted to remove the effects of inflation on the buying power of money. The real interest rate is approximately equal to the nominal interest rate minus the inflation rate.

You can see why if you suppose that you have put €500 in a savings account that earns 5 per cent a year. At the end of a year, you have €525 in your savings account. Suppose that the inflation rate is 2 per cent per year – during the year, all prices increased by 2 per cent. Now, at the end of the year, it costs €510 to buy what €500 would have bought one year ago. Your money in the bank has really only increased by €15, from €510 to €525. That €15 is equivalent to a real interest rate of

3 per cent a year on your original €500. So the real interest rate is the 5 per cent nominal interest rate minus the 2 per cent inflation rate.[1]

The real interest rate is the opportunity cost of loanable funds. The real interest paid on borrowed funds is the opportunity cost of borrowing. And the real interest rate forgone when funds are used either to buy consumption goods and services or to invest in new capital goods is the opportunity cost of not saving or not lending those funds.

We're now going to see how the loanable funds market determines the real interest rate, the quantity of funds loaned, saving and investment. In the rest of this section, we will ignore the government and the rest of the world and focus on households and firms in the loanable funds market. We will study:

- The demand for loanable funds
- The supply of loanable funds
- Equilibrium in the loanable funds market

The Demand for Loanable Funds

The *quantity of loanable funds demanded* is the total quantity of funds demanded to finance investment, the government budget deficit and international investment or lending during a given period. Our focus here is on investment. We'll bring the other two items into the picture in later sections of this chapter.

What determines investment and the demand for loanable funds to finance it? Many details influence this decision, but we can summarize them in two factors:

1 The real interest rate

2 Expected profit

Firms invest in capital only if they expect to earn a profit and fewer projects are profitable at a high real interest rate than at a low real interest rate, so:

Other things remaining the same, the higher the real interest rate, the smaller is the quantity of loanable funds demanded; and the lower the real interest rate, the greater is the quantity of loanable funds demanded.

Figure 23.3 The Demand for Loanable Funds

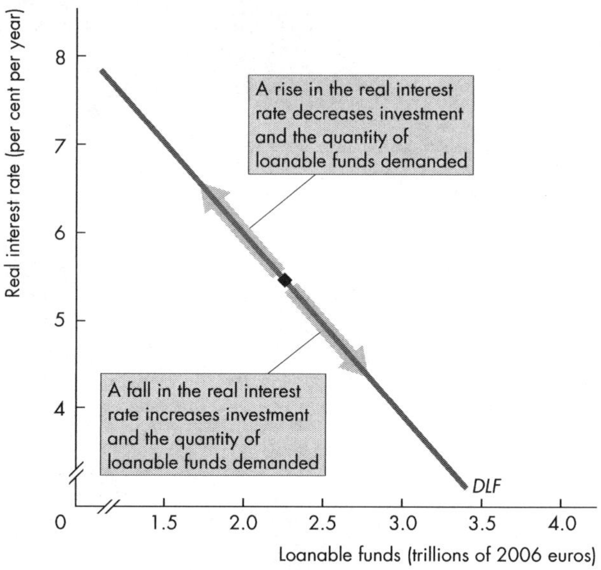

A change in the real interest rate changes the quantity of loanable funds demanded and brings a movement along the demand for loanable funds curve.

myeconlab Animation

Demand for Loanable Funds Curve

The **demand for loanable funds** is the relationship between the quantity of loanable funds demanded and the real interest rate, when all other influences on borrowing plans remain the same. The demand curve *DLF* in Figure 23.3 is a demand for loanable funds curve.

To understand the demand for loanable funds, think about Amazon.com's decision to borrow €100 million to build a new warehouse. If Amazon expects a return of €5 million a year from this investment before paying interest costs and the interest rate is less than 5 per cent a year, Amazon would make a profit, so it builds the warehouses. But if the interest rate is more than 5 per cent a year, Amazon would incur a loss, so it doesn't build the warehouses. The quantity of loanable funds demanded is greater the lower is the real interest rate.

Changes in the Demand for Loanable Funds

When the expected profit changes, the demand for loanable funds changes. Other things remaining the same, the greater the expected profit from new capital, the greater is the amount of investment and the greater the demand for loanable funds.

[1] The exact real interest rate formula, which allows for the change in the purchasing power of both the interest and the loan is:
Real interest rate = (Nominal interest rate – Inflation rate) ÷ (1 + Inflation rate/100). If the nominal interest rate is 5 per cent a year and the inflation rate is 2 per cent a year, the real interest rate is: (5 – 2) ÷ (1 + 0.02) = 2.94 per cent a year.

Expected profit rises during a business cycle expansion and falls during a recession; rises when technological change creates profitable new products; rises as a growing population brings increased demand for goods and services; and fluctuates with contagious swings of optimism and pessimism, called 'animal spirits' by Keynes and 'irrational exuberance' by Alan Greenspan.

When expected profit changes, the demand for loanable funds curve shifts.

The Supply of Loanable Funds

The *quantity of loanable funds supplied* is the total funds available from private saving, the government budget surplus and international borrowing during a given period. Our focus here is on saving. We'll bring the other two items into the picture later.

How do you decide how much of your income to save and supply in the loanable funds market? Your decision is influenced by many factors, but chief among them are:

1. The real interest rate
2. Disposable income
3. Expected future income
4. Wealth
5. Default risk

We begin by focusing on the real interest rate.

Other things remaining the same, the higher the real interest rate, the greater is the quantity of loanable funds supplied; and the lower the real interest rate, the smaller is the quantity of loanable funds supplied.

The Supply of Loanable Funds Curve

The **supply of loanable funds** is the relationship between the quantity of loanable funds supplied and the real interest rate when all other influences on lending plans remain the same. The curve *SLF* in Figure 23.4 is a supply of loanable funds curve.

Think about a student's decision to save some of what she earns from her summer job. With a real interest rate of 2 per cent a year, she decides that it is not worth saving much – better to spend the income and take a student loan if funds run out during the semester. But if the real interest rate jumped to 10 per cent a year, the payoff from saving would be high enough to encourage her to cut back on spending and increase the amount she saves.

Figure 23.4 The Supply of Loanable Funds

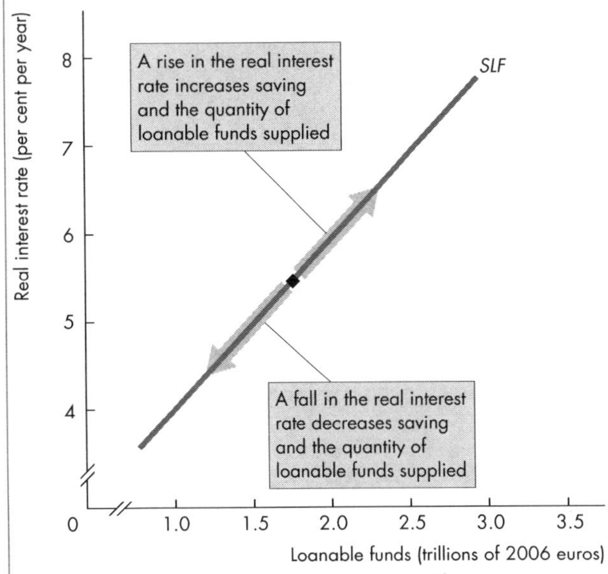

A change in the real interest rate changes the quantity of loanable funds supplied and brings a movement along the supply of loanable funds curve.

myeconlab Animation

Changes in the Supply of Loanable Funds

The supply of loanable funds changes if disposable income, expected future income, wealth or default risk changes.

Disposable Income

A household's *disposable income* is the income minus net taxes. When disposable income increases, both saving and consumption expenditure increase. So the greater a household's disposable income, other things remaining the same, the greater is its saving.

Expected Future Income

The higher a household's expected future income, the smaller is its saving today.

Wealth

The higher a household's wealth, other things remaining the same, the smaller is its saving. If a person's wealth increases because of a capital gain, the person sees less need to save.

For example, during 2007 when house prices were still rising, wealth increased despite the fact that personal saving dropped close to zero.

Default Risk

Default risk is the risk that a loan will not be repaid. The greater that risk, the higher is the interest rate needed to induce a person to lend and the smaller is the supply of loanable funds.

Shifts of the Supply of Loanable Funds Curve

When any of the four influences on the supply of loanable funds changes, the supply of loanable funds changes and the supply curve shifts. An increase in disposable income, a decrease in expected future income, a decrease in wealth, or a fall in default risk increases saving and increases the supply of loanable funds.

Equilibrium in the Loanable Funds Market

You've seen that other things remaining the same, the higher the real interest rate, the greater is the quantity of loanable funds supplied and the smaller is the quantity of loanable funds demanded. There is one real interest rate at which the quantities of loanable funds demanded and supplied are equal, and that interest rate is the equilibrium real interest rate.

Figure 23.5 shows how the demand for and supply of loanable funds determine the real interest rate. The *DLF* curve is the demand curve and the *SLF* curve is the supply curve. If the real interest rate exceeds 6 per cent a year, the quantity of loanable funds supplied exceeds the quantity demanded – a surplus of funds. Borrowers find it easy to get funds, but lenders are unable to lend all their funds. The real interest rate falls until the quantity of funds supplied equals the quantity demanded.

If the real interest rate is less than 6 per cent a year, the quantity of loanable funds supplied is less than the quantity demanded – a shortage of funds. Borrowers can't get the funds they want, but lenders are able to lend all the funds they have available. So the real interest rate rises and continues to rise until the quantity of funds supplied equals the quantity demanded.

Regardless of whether there is a surplus or a shortage of loanable funds, the real interest rate changes and is pulled towards an equilibrium level. In Figure 23.5, the equilibrium real interest rate is 6 per cent a year. At this interest rate there is neither a surplus nor a shortage of loanable funds. Borrowers can get the funds they want, and lenders can lend all the funds they have available. The investment plans of borrowers and the saving plans of lenders are consistent with each other.

Figure 23.5 Loanable Funds Market Equilibrium

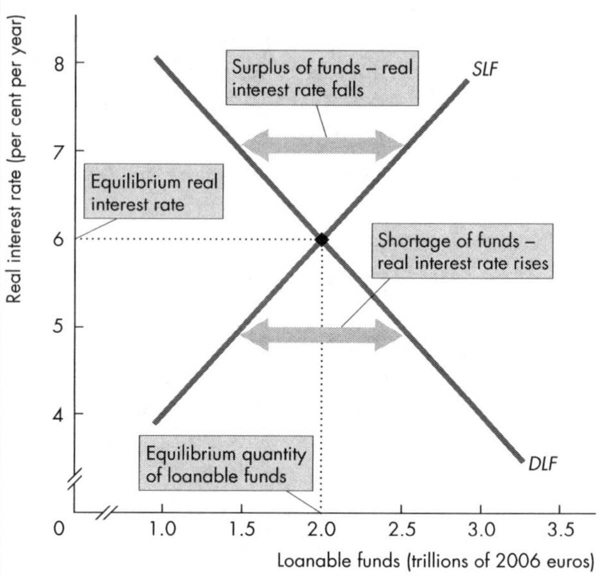

A surplus of funds lowers the real interest rate and a shortage of funds raises it. At an interest rate of 6 per cent a year, the quantity of funds demanded equals the quantity supplied and the market is in equilibrium.

myeconlab Animation

Changes in Demand and Supply

Financial markets are highly volatile in the short run but remarkably stable in the long run. Volatility in the market comes from fluctuations in either the demand for loanable funds or the supply of loanable funds. These fluctuations bring fluctuations in the real interest rate and in the equilibrium quantity of funds lent and borrowed. They also bring fluctuations in asset prices.

Here we'll illustrate the effects of increases in demand and supply in the loanable funds market.

An Increase in Demand

If the profits that firms expect to earn increase, they increase their planned investment and increase their demand for loanable funds to finance that investment. With an increase in the demand for loanable funds, but no change in the supply of loanable funds, there is a shortage of funds. As borrowers compete for funds, the interest rate rises and lenders increase the quantity of funds supplied.

Figure 23.6(a) illustrates these changes. An increase in the demand for loanable funds shifts the demand curve rightward from DLF_0 to DLF_1. With no change in

Figure 23.6 Changes in Demand and Supply

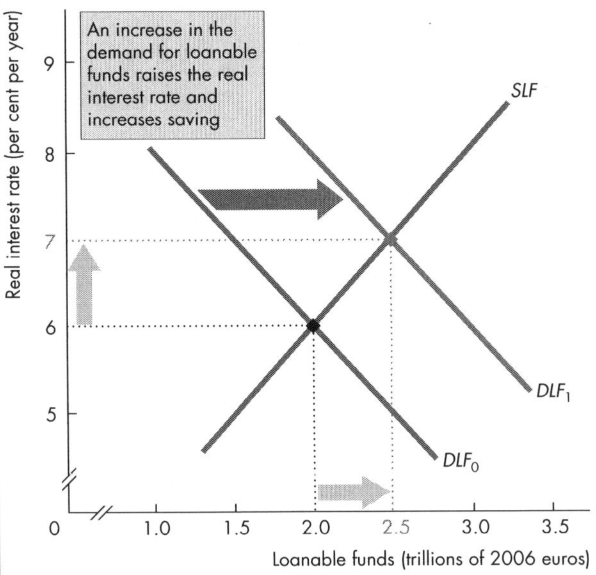

(a) An increase in demand

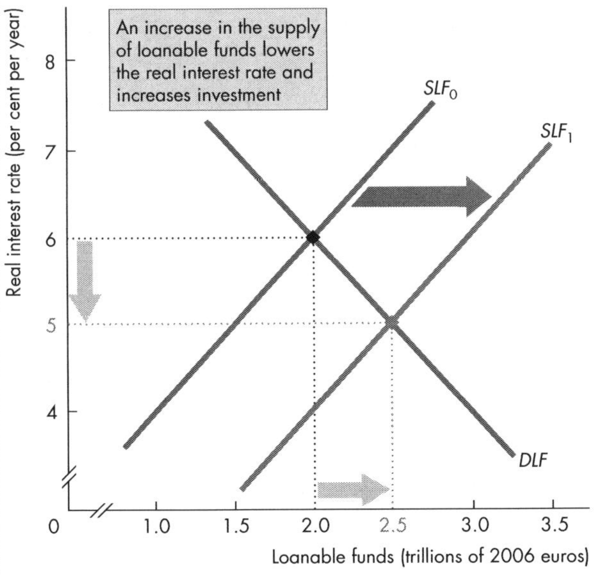

(b) An increase in supply

In part (a), the demand for loanable funds increases and supply doesn't change. The real interest rate rises (financial asset prices fall) and the quantity of funds increases.

In part (b), the supply of loanable funds increases and demand doesn't change. The real interest rate falls (financial asset prices rise) and the quantity of funds increases.

myeconlab Animation

the supply of loanable funds, there is a shortage of funds at a real interest rate of 6 per cent a year. The real interest rate rises until it is 7 per cent a year. Equilibrium is restored and the equilibrium quantity of funds has increased.

An Increase in Supply

If one of the influences on saving plans changes and increases saving, the supply of loanable funds increases. With no change in the demand for loanable funds, the market is flush with loanable funds. Borrowers find bargains and lenders find themselves accepting a lower interest rate. At the lower interest rate, borrowers find additional investment projects profitable and increase the quantity of loanable funds that they borrow.

Figure 23.6(b) illustrates these changes. An increase in supply shifts the supply curve rightward from SLF_0 to SLF_1. With no change in demand, there is a surplus of funds at a real interest rate of 6 per cent a year. The real interest rate falls until it is 5 per cent a year. Equilibrium is restored and the equilibrium quantity of funds has increased.

Long-run Growth of Demand and Supply

Over time, both demand and supply in the loanable funds market fluctuate and the real interest rate rises and falls. Both the supply of loanable funds and the demand for loanable funds tend to increase over time. On the average, they increase at a similar pace, so although demand and supply trend upward, the real interest rate has no trend. It fluctuates around a constant average level.

Review Quiz

1. What is the loanable funds market?
2. Why is the real interest rate the opportunity cost of loanable funds?
3. How do firms make investment decisions?
4. What determines the demand for loanable funds and what makes it change?
5. How do households make saving decisions?
6. What determines the supply of loanable funds and what makes it change?
7. How do changes in the demand for and supply of loanable funds change the real interest rate and quantity of loanable funds?

You can work these questions in Study Plan 23.2 and get instant feedback. myeconlab

ECONOMICS IN ACTION

Loanable Funds Fuel the US Home Price Bubble

The financial crisis that gripped the US and global economies in 2007 and cascaded through the financial markets in 2008 had its origins much earlier in events taking place in the loanable funds market.

Between 2001 and 2005, a massive injection of loanable funds occurred. Some funds came from the rest of the world, but that source of supply has been stable. The Federal Reserve (the US central bank) provided funds to keep interest rates low and that was a major source of the increase in the supply of funds. (The next chapter explains how a central bank does this.)

Figure 1 illustrates the loanable funds market starting in 2001. In that year, the demand for loanable funds was DLF_{01} and the supply of loanable funds was SLF_{01}. The equilibrium real interest rate was 4 per cent a year and the equilibrium quantity of loanable funds was $29 trillion (in 2005 dollars).

During the ensuing four years, a massive increase in the supply of loanable funds shifted the supply curve rightward to SLF_{05}. A smaller increase in demand shifted the demand for loanable funds curve to DLF_{05}. The real interest rate fell to 1 per cent a year and the quantity of loanable funds increased to $36 trillion – a 24 per cent increase in just four years.

With this large increase in available funds, much of it in the form of mortgage loans to home buyers, the demand for homes increased by more than the increase in the supply of homes. Home prices rose and the expectation of further increases fuelled the demand for loanable funds.

By 2006, the expectation of continued rapidly rising home prices brought a very large increase in the demand for loanable funds. At the same time, the Federal Reserve began to tighten credit. The result of the Fed's tighter credit policy was a slowdown in the pace of increase in the supply of loanable funds.

Figure 2 illustrates these events. In 2006, the demand for loanable funds increased from DLF_{05} to DLF_{06} and the supply of loanable funds increased by a smaller amount from SLF_{05} to SLF_{06}. The real interest rate increased to 3 per cent a year.

The rise in the real interest rate (and a much higher rise in the nominal interest rate) put many home owners in financial difficulty. Mortgage repayments increased and some borrowers stopped repaying their loans.

By August 2007, the damage from mortgage default and foreclosure was so large that the credit market began to dry up. A large decrease in both demand and supply kept interest rates roughly constant but decreased the quantity of new business.

The total quantity of loanable funds didn't decrease, but the rate of increase slowed to a snail's pace and financial institutions most exposed to the bad mortgage debts and the securities that they backed (described on p. 536) began to fail.

These events illustrate the crucial role played by the loanable funds market.

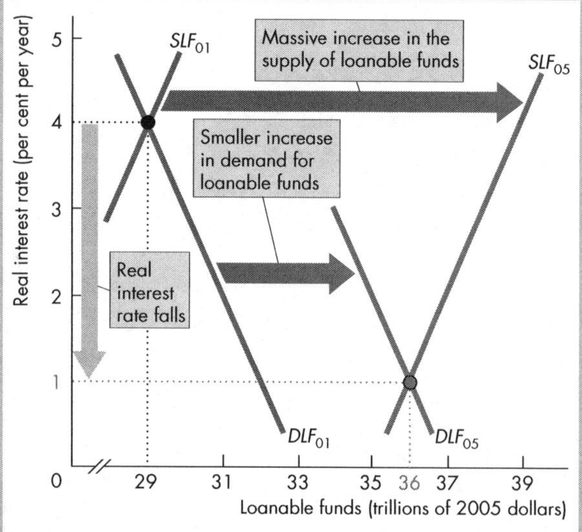

Figure 1 The Foundation of the Crisis: 2001–2005

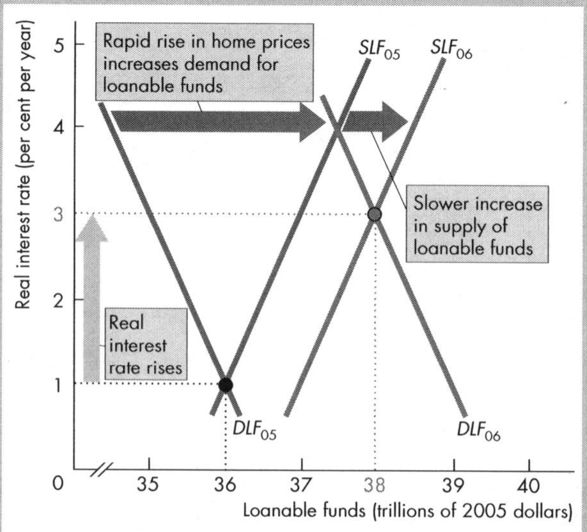

Figure 2 The Start of the Crisis: 2005–2006

Government in the Loanable Funds Market

Government enters the loanable funds market when it has a budget surplus or budget deficit. A government budget surplus increases the supply of loanable funds and contributes to financing investment; a government budget deficit increases the demand for loanable funds and competes with businesses for funds. Let's study the effects of government on the loanable funds market.

A Government Budget Surplus

A government budget surplus increases the supply of loanable funds. The real interest rate falls, which decreases household saving and decreases the quantity of private funds supplied. The lower real interest rate increases the quantity of loanable funds demanded and increases investment.

Figure 23.7 shows these effects of a government budget surplus. The private supply of loanable funds curve is *PSLF*. The supply of loanable funds curve, *SLF*, shows the sum of private supply and the government budget surplus. Here, the government budget surplus is €1 trillion, so at each real interest rate the *SLF* curve lies €1 trillion to the right of the *PSLF* curve. That is, the horizontal distance between the *PSLF* curve and the *SLF* curve equals the government budget surplus.

With no government surplus, the real interest rate is 6 per cent a year, the quantity of loanable funds is €2 trillion a year and investment is €2 trillion a year. But with the government surplus of €1 trillion a year, the equilibrium real interest rate falls to 5 per cent a year and the equilibrium quantity of loanable funds increases to €2.5 trillion a year.

The fall in the interest rate decreases private saving to €1.5 trillion, but investment increases to €2.5 trillion, which is financed by private saving plus the government budget surplus (government saving).

Government budget surpluses are rare today. Most governments including the UK, US and most in the EU, have deficits and some of them very large ones.

Let's see how a government budget deficit influences the loanable funds market.

Figure 23.7 A Government Budget Surplus

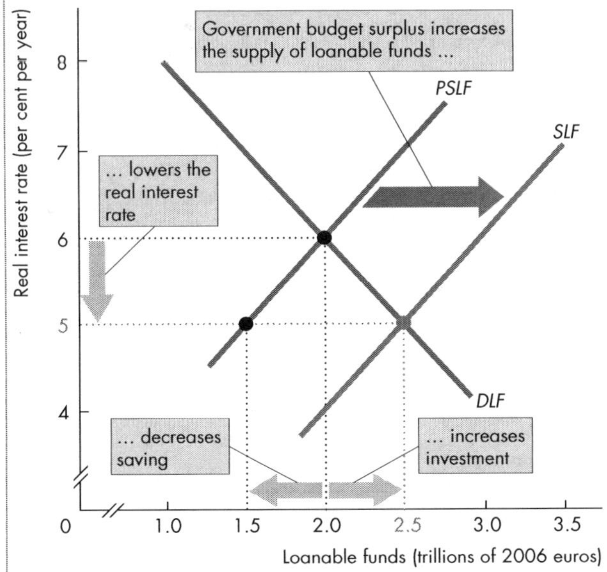

A government budget surplus of €1 trillion is added to private saving and the private supply of loanable funds (*PSLF*) to determine the supply of loanable funds, *SLF*. The real interest rate falls to 5 per cent a year, private saving decreases, but investment increases to €2.5 trillion.

myeconlab Animation

A Government Budget Deficit

A government budget deficit increases the demand for loanable funds. The real interest rate rises, which increases household saving and increases the quantity of private funds supplied. But the higher real interest rate decreases investment and the quantity of loanable funds demanded by firms to finance investment.

Figure 23.8 shows these effects of a government budget deficit. The private demand for loanable funds curve is *PDLF*. The demand for loanable funds curve, *DLF*, shows the sum of private demand and the government budget deficit. Here, the government budget deficit is €1 trillion, so at each real interest rate the *DLF* curve lies €1 trillion to the right of the *PDLF* curve. That is, the horizontal distance between the *PDLF* curve and the *DLF* curve equals the government budget deficit.

With no government deficit, the real interest rate is 6 per cent a year, the quantity of loanable funds is €2 trillion a year and investment is €2 trillion a year. But with the government budget deficit of €1 trillion a year, the equilibrium real interest rate rises to 7 per cent a year and the equilibrium quantity of loanable funds increases to €2.5 trillion a year.

The rise in the real interest rate increases private saving to €2.5 trillion, but investment decreases to €1.5 trillion because €1 trillion of private saving must finance the government budget deficit.

Figure 23.8 A Government Budget Deficit

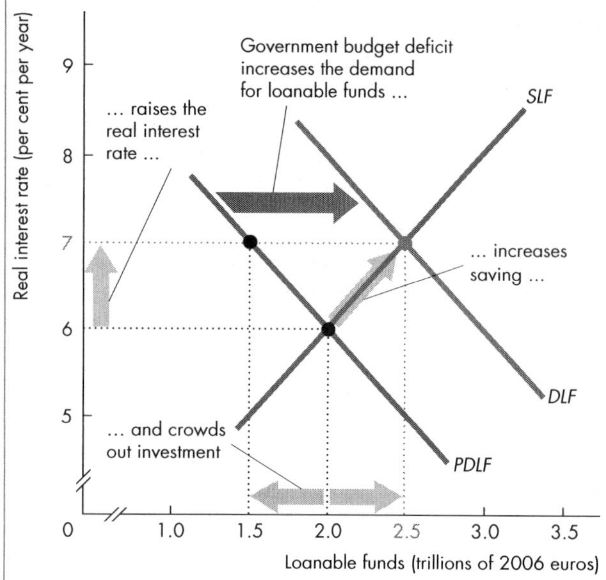

A government budget deficit adds to the private demand for loanable funds curve (*PDLF*) to determine the demand for loanable funds curve, *DLF*. The real interest rate rises, saving increases, but investment decreases – a crowding-out effect.

myeconlab Animation

Figure 23.9 The Ricardo–Barro Effect

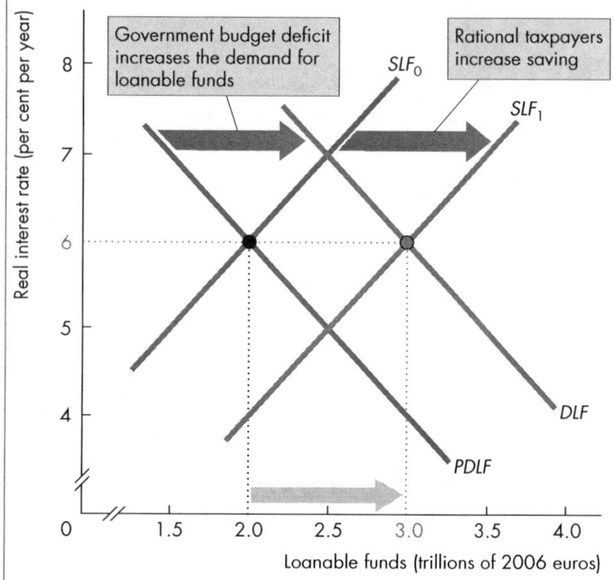

A budget deficit increases the demand for loanable funds. Rational taxpayers increase saving, which increases the supply of loanable funds curve from SLF_0 to SLF_1. Crowding out is avoided: increased saving finances the budget deficit.

myeconlab Animation

The Crowding-out Effect

The tendency for a government budget deficit to raise the real interest rate and decrease investment is called the **crowding-out effect**. The budget deficit crowds out investment by competing with businesses for scarce financial capital.

The crowding-out effect does not decrease investment by the full amount of the government budget deficit because the higher real interest rate induces an increase in private saving that partly contributes toward financing the deficit.

The Ricardo–Barro Effect

First suggested by the English economist David Ricardo in the eighteenth century and refined by Robert J. Barro of Harvard University, the Ricardo–Barro effect holds that both of the effects we've just shown are wrong and the government budget, whether in surplus or deficit, has no effect on either the real interest rate or investment.

Barro says that taxpayers are rational. They can see that a budget deficit today means that future taxes will be higher and future disposable incomes will be smaller. With smaller expected future disposable incomes, saving increases today. Private saving and the private supply of loanable funds increase to match the quantity of loanable funds demanded by the government. So the budget deficit has no effect on either the real interest rate or investment. Figure 23.9 shows this outcome.

Most economists regard the Ricardo–Barro view as extreme. But there might be some change in private saving that goes in the direction suggested by the Ricardo–Barro effect that lessens the crowding-out effect.

Review Quiz

1 How does a government budget surplus or deficit influence the loanable funds market?
2 What is the crowding-out effect and how does it work?
3 What is the Ricardo–Barro effect and how does it modify the crowding-out effect?

You can work these questions in Study Plan 23.3 and get instant feedback. myeconlab

The Global Loanable Funds Market

The loanable funds market is global, not national. Lenders on the supply side of the market want to earn the highest possible real interest rate and they will seek it by looking everywhere in the world. Borrowers on the demand side of the market want to pay the lowest possible real interest rate and they will seek it by looking everywhere in the world. Financial capital is mobile: it moves to the best advantage of lenders and borrowers.

International Capital Mobility

If a US supplier of loanable funds can earn a higher interest rate in Tokyo than in New York, funds supplied in Japan will increase and funds supplied in the US will decrease – funds will flow from the US to Japan.

If a US demander of loanable funds can pay a lower interest rate in Paris than in New York, the demand for funds in France will increase and the demand for funds in the US will decrease – funds will flow from France to the US.

Because lenders are free to seek the highest real interest rate and borrowers are free to seek the lowest real interest rate, the loanable funds market is a single, integrated, global market. Funds flow into the country in which the interest rate is highest and out of the country in which the interest rate is lowest.

When funds leave the country with the lowest interest rate, a shortage of funds raises the real interest rate. When funds move into the country with the highest interest rate, a surplus of funds lowers the real interest rate. The free international mobility of financial capital pulls real interest rates around the world toward equality.

Only when the real interest rates in New York, Tokyo and Paris are equal does the incentive to move funds from one country to another stop.

Equality of real interest rates does not mean that if you calculate the average real interest rate in New York, Tokyo and Paris, you'll get the same number. To compare real interest rates, we must compare financial assets of equal risk.

Lending is risky. A loan might not be repaid. Or the price of a stock or bond might fall. Interest rates include a risk premium – the riskier the loan, other things remaining the same, the higher is the interest rate. The interest rate on a risky loan minus that on a safe loan is called the *risk premium* and the gaps between interest rates are called *interest rate spreads*.

International capital mobility brings real interest rates in all parts of the world to equality except for differences that reflect differences in risk – differences in the risk premium.

International Borrowing and Lending

A country's loanable funds market connects with the global market through net exports. If a country's net exports are negative ($X < M$), the rest of the world supplies funds to that country and the quantity of loanable funds in that country is greater than national saving. If a country's net exports are positive ($X > M$), the country is a net supplier of funds to the rest of the world and the quantity of loanable funds in that country is less than national saving.

Demand and Supply in the Global and National Markets

The demand for and supply of funds in the global loanable funds market determines the world equilibrium real interest rate. This interest rate makes the quantity of loanable funds demanded equal the quantity supplied in the world economy. But it does not make the quantity of funds demanded and supplied equal in each national economy. The demand for and supply of funds in a national economy determine whether the country is a lender to or a borrower from the rest of the world.

The Global Loanable Funds Market

Figure 23.10(a) illustrates the global market. The demand for loanable funds curve, DLF_W is the sum of the demands in all countries. Similarly, the supply of loanable funds curve, SLF_W is the sum of the supplies in all countries. The world equilibrium real interest rate makes the quantity of funds supplied in the world as a whole equal to the quantity demanded. In this example, the equilibrium real interest rate is 5 per cent a year and the equilibrium quantity of funds is €10 trillion.

An International Borrower

Figure 23.10(b) shows the loanable funds market in a country that borrows from the rest of the world. The country's demand for loanable funds curve, *DLF*, is part of the world demand in Figure 23.10(a). The country's supply of loanable funds curve, SLF_D, is part of the world supply.

Figure 23.10 Borrowing and Lending in the Global Loanable Funds Market

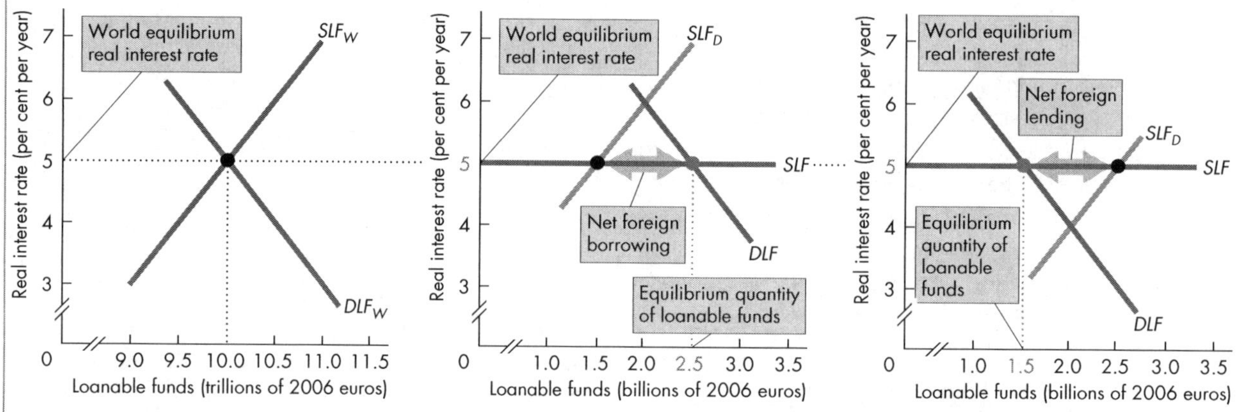

(a) The global market **(b) An international borrower** **(c) An international lender**

In the global loanable funds market in part (a), the demand for loanable funds curve, DLF_W, and the supply of funds curve, SLF_W, determine the world real interest rate. Each country can get funds at the world real interest rate and faces the (horizontal) supply curve *SLF* in parts (b) and (c).

At the world real interest rate, borrowers in part (b) want more funds than the quantity supplied by domestic lenders (SLF_D). The shortage is made up by international borrowing.

At the world real interest rate, domestic lenders in part (c) want to lend more than domestic borrowers demand. The excess quantity supplied goes to foreign borrowers.

myeconlab Animation

If this country were isolated from the global market, the real interest rate would be 6 per cent a year (where the *DLF* and SLF_D curves intersect). But if the country is integrated into the global economy, with an interest rate of 6 per cent a year, funds would *flood into* it. With a real interest rate of 5 per cent a year in the rest of the world, suppliers of loanable funds would seek the higher return in this country. In effect, the country faces the supply of loanable funds curve *SLF*, which is horizontal at the world equilibrium real interest rate.

The country's demand for loanable funds and the world interest rate determine the equilibrium quantity of loanable funds – €2.5 billion in Figure 23.10(b).

An International Lender

Figure 23.10(c) shows the situation in a country that lends to the rest of the world. As before, the country's demand for loanable funds curve, *DLF*, is part of the world demand and the country's supply of loanable funds curve, SLF_D, is part of the world supply in Figure 23.10(a).

If this country were isolated from the global economy, the real interest rate would be 4 per cent a year (where the *DLF* and SLF_D curves intersect). But if this country is integrated into the global economy, with an interest rate of 4 per cent a year, funds would quickly *flow out* of it. With a real interest rate of 5 per cent a year in the rest of the world, domestic suppliers of loanable funds would seek the higher return in other countries. Again, the country faces the supply of loanable funds curve *SLF*, which is horizontal at the world equilibrium real interest rate.

The country's demand for loanable funds and the world interest rate determine the equilibrium quantity of loanable funds – €1.5 billion in Figure 23.10(c).

Changes in Demand and Supply

A change in the demand or supply in the global loanable funds market changes the real interest rate in the way shown in Figure 23.6 (see p. 543). The effect of a change in demand or supply in a national market depends on the size of the country. A change in demand or supply in a small country has no significant effect on global demand or supply, so it leaves the world real interest rate unchanged and changes only the country's net exports and international borrowing or lending. A change in demand or supply in a large country has a significant effect on global demand or supply, so it changes the world real interest rate as well as the country's net exports and international borrowing or lending. Every country feels some of the effect of a large country's change in demand or supply.

ECONOMICS IN ACTION

Greenspan's Interest Rate Puzzle

The real interest rate paid by big corporations in the US fell from 5.5 per cent a year in 2001 to 2.5 per cent a year in 2005. Alan Greenspan, then the Chairman of the Federal Reserve, said he was puzzled that the real interest rate was falling at a time when the US government budget deficit was increasing.

Why did the real interest rate fall?

The answer lies in the global loanable funds market. Rapid economic growth in Asia and Europe brought a large increase in global saving, which in turn increased the global supply of loanable funds. The supply of loanable funds increased because Asian and European saving increased strongly.

The US government budget deficit increased the US and global demand for loanable funds. But this increase was very small compared to the increase in the global supply of loanable funds.

The result of a large increase in supply and a small increase in demand was a fall in the world equilibrium real interest rate and an increase in the equilibrium quantity of loanable funds.

Figure 1 illustrates these events. The supply of loanable funds increased from SLF_{01} in 2001 to SLF_{05} in 2005. (In the figure, we ignore the change in the global demand for loanable funds because it was small relative to the increase in supply.)

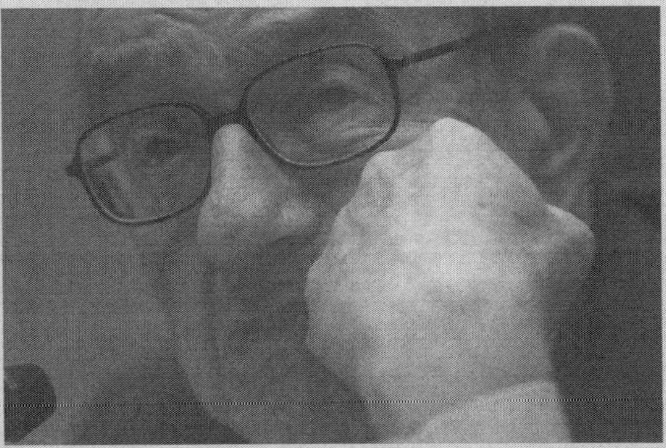

With the increase in supply, the real interest rate fell from 5.5 per cent to 2.5 per cent a year and the quantity of loanable funds increased.

In the US, borrowing from the rest of the world increased to finance the increased government budget deficit.

The interest rate puzzle illustrates the important fact that the loanable funds market is a global market, not a national market.

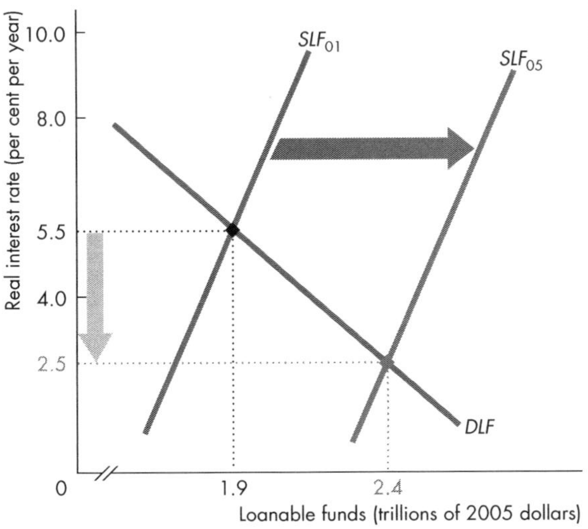

Figure 1 The Global Loanable Funds Market

Review Quiz

1 Why do loanable funds flow among countries?
2 What determines the demand for and supply of loanable funds in an individual economy?
3 What happens if a country has a shortage of loanable funds at the world real interest rate?
4 What happens if a country has a surplus of loanable funds at the world real interest rate?
5 How is a government budget deficit financed in an open economy?

You can work these questions in Study Plan 23.4 and get instant feedback. myeconlab

To complete your study of financial markets, take a look at *Reading Between the Lines* on pp. 550–551 and see how you can use the model of the loanable funds market to understand the events in the EU financial market crisis of 2010.

Reading Between the Lines

Budget Deficits in Europe

The Financial Times, 25 October 2010

Eurozone Nations are Prepared to Slash Spending

FT

Daniel Pimlott

The UK is far from alone within Europe in moving rapidly to curtail government borrowing. Greece, Ireland, Spain and Portugal are already committed to swinging the axe; all are still struggling to escape recession.

The coalition's deficit policies are almost as radical as those pursued by some of Britain's struggling neighbours in the EU, in spite of much more favourable borrowing conditions for the UK.

The Greek deficit was more than 15 per cent of GDP in 2009, in Spain it was 11.2 per cent and 9.4 per cent in Portugal. This year Ireland's is set to hit a staggering 32 per cent if the costs of its bank bail-out are factored in.

By comparison, Britain's deficit was 11 per cent of GDP in the last financial year.

If all goes to plan, Greece and Ireland should bring their deficits below the 3 per cent limit set in the Maastricht Treaty by 2014, Spain by 2013 and Portugal by 2012. Britain appears a relative laggard, dropping below the 3 per cent threshold only in 2014–15. . . .

Greece is cutting public sector salaries and pensions by 15 to 20 per cent, Portugal has warned of pay cuts of up to 10 per cent and Ireland and Spain have also pared back pay and reduced pension costs. Ireland and Portugal have both cut child benefits and other programmes.

In Britain, public sector pay freezes will last for two years, and there will be an average rise in pension contributions of about 3 percentage points; the benefits bill will be cut by about 10 per cent. . . .

The Essence of the Story

- Many governments are cutting spending to reduce their budget deficits.
- The UK is facing severe cuts in government spending although the government faces more favourable borrowing conditions than some other EU countries.
- Greece, Ireland, Spain and Portugal are projected to bring their budgets down to 3 per cent of GDP in the period 2012–2014.
- The UK is not expected to bring the budget deficit down to below 3 per cent of GDP until 2014–2015.

Economic Analysis

- A budget deficit increases the demand for loanable funds and, other things being equal, raises the real rate of interest, which raises the cost of government borrowing.
- Governments in some countries face a cost of borrowing that makes their budget unsustainable.
- A high cost of borrowing means that a government uses its budget to pay higher interest charges, which diverts resources from public services.
- A cut in public services can put political pressure on governments to default on their debt. When this happens, default risk rises, and this brings a decrease in the supply of loanable funds, which raises the real interest rate (and cost of borrowing) even further.
- Figure 1 illustrates this effect of a budget deficit. The deficit increases the demand for loanable funds and shifts the *DLF* curve rightward and the increase in default risk decreases the supply of loanable funds, which shifts the *SLF* curve leftward. The real interest rate rises.
- Figure 2 shows the sources of increased default risk: the government deficits and debts as percentages of GDP for the UK, Ireland, Spain, Portugal and Greece in 2009–2010.
- Figure 3 shows the interest rate spreads on the five governments' bonds relative to German government bond rate, which is considered to have a low (zero) risk of default.
- The global loanable funds market puts a high risk premium on Greece's debt.

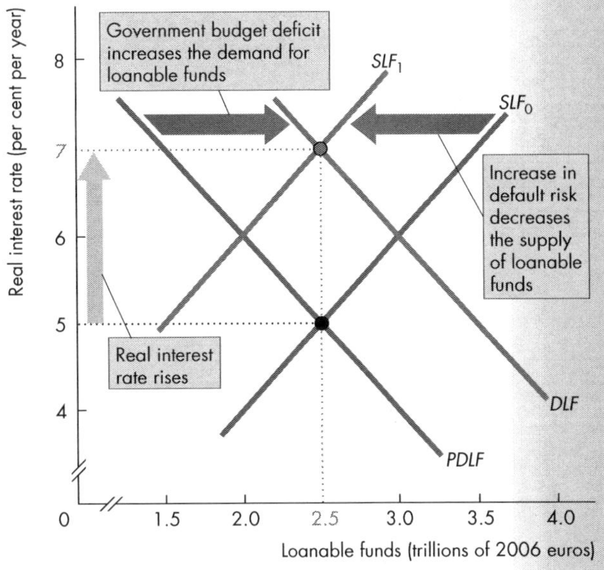

Figure 1 The market for loanable funds

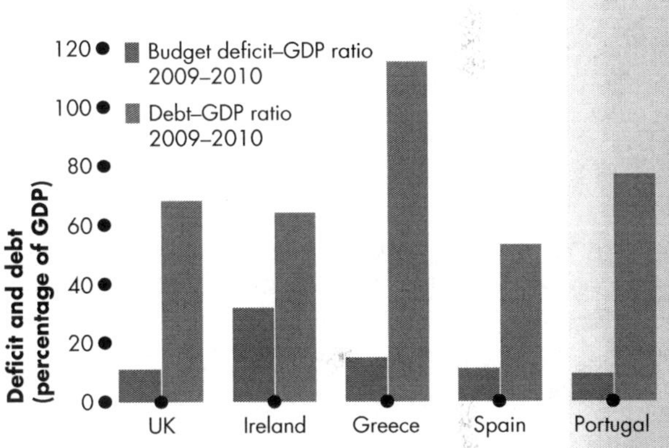

Figure 2 Budget deficits and debts

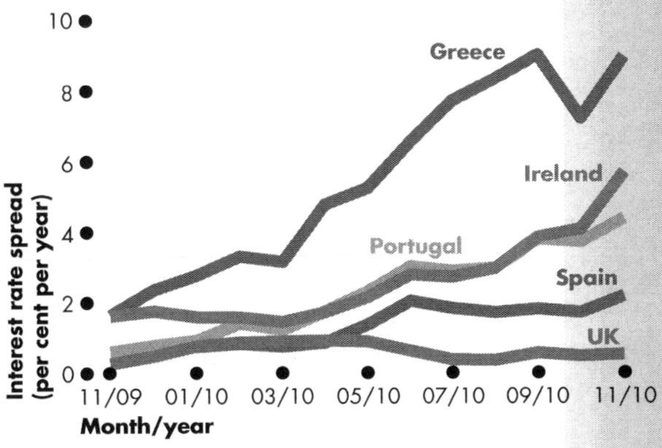

Figure 3 Bond interest rate spreads

SUMMARY

Key Points

Financial Institutions and Financial Markets

- Capital (*physical capital*) is a real productive resource; financial capital is the funds used to buy capital.
- Gross investment increases the quantity of capital and depreciation decreases it. Saving increases wealth.
- The markets for financial capital are the markets for loans, bonds and stocks.
- Financial institutions ensure that borrowers and lenders can always find someone with whom to trade.

Working Study Plan Problems 1 to 5 will give you a better understanding of financial institutions and markets.

The Loanable Funds Market

- Investment in capital is financed by household saving, a government budget surplus and funds from the rest of the world.
- The quantity of loanable funds demanded depends negatively on the real interest rate and the demand for loanable funds changes when profit expectations change.
- The quantity of loanable funds supplied depends positively on the real interest rate and the supply of loanable funds changes when disposable income, expected future income, wealth and default risk change.
- Equilibrium in the loanable funds market determines the real interest rate and quantity of funds.

Working Study Plan Problems 6 to 9 will give you a better understanding of the loanable funds market.

Government in the Loanable Funds Market

- A government budget surplus increases the supply of loanable funds, lowers the real interest rate and increases investment and the equilibrium quantity of loanable funds.
- A government budget deficit increases the demand for loanable funds, raises the real interest rate and increases the equilibrium quantity of loanable funds, but decreases investment in a crowding-out effect.
- The Ricardo–Barro effect is the response of rational taxpayers to a budget deficit: private saving increases to finance the budget deficit. The real interest rate remains constant and the crowding-out effect is avoided.

Working Study Plan Problems 10 to 15 will give you a better understanding of government in the loanable funds market.

The Global Loanable Funds Market

- The loanable funds market is a global market.
- The equilibrium real interest rate is determined in the global loanable funds market and national demand and supply determine the quantity of international borrowing or lending.

Working Study Plan Problems 16 to 18 will give you a better understanding of the global loanable funds market.

Key Terms

Bond
Bond market
Crowding-out effect
Demand for loanable funds
Financial capital
Financial institution
Gross investment
Loanable funds market
Mortgage
Mortgage-backed security
National saving
Net investment
Net taxes
Net worth
Nominal interest rate
Real interest rate
Saving
Stock
Stock market
Supply of loanable funds
Wealth

STUDY PLAN PROBLEMS AND APPLICATIONS

myeconlab You can work Problems 1 to 18 in MyEconLab Chapter 23 Study Plan and get instant feedback.

Financial Institutions and Financial Markets (Study Plan 23.1)

Use the following information to work Problems 1 and 2.

Michael is an Internet service provider. On 31 December 2009, he bought an existing business with servers and a building worth €400,000. During his first year of operation, his business grew and he bought new servers for €500,000. The market value of some of his older servers fell by €100,000.

1 What was Michael's gross investment, depreciation, and net investment during 2010?

2 What is the value of Michael's capital at the end of 2010?

3 Lori is a student who teaches golf on the weekend and in a year earns €20,000 after paying her taxes. At the beginning of 2010, Lori owned €1,000 worth of books, CDs, and golf clubs and she had €5,000 in a savings account at the bank. During 2010, the interest on her savings account was €300 and she spent a total of €15,300 on consumption goods and services. There was no change in the market values of her books, CDs and golf clubs.

a How much did Lori save in 2010?

b What was her wealth at the end of 2010?

4 In a speech at the CFA Society of Nebraska in February 2007, William Poole, former Chairman of the St Louis Federal Reserve Bank said:

Over most of the post–Second World War period, the personal saving rate averaged about 6 per cent, with some higher years from the mid-1970s to mid-1980s.

The negative trend in the saving rate started in the mid-1990s, about the same time the stock market boom started. Thus it is hard to dismiss the hypothesis that the decline in the measured saving rate in the late 1990s reflected the response of consumption to large capital gains from corporate equity stock.

Evidence from panel data of households also supports the conclusion that the decline in the personal saving rate since 1984 is largely a consequence of capital gains on corporate equities.

a Is the purchase of corporate equities part of household consumption or saving? Explain your answer.

b Equities reap a capital gain in the same way that houses reap a capital gain. Does this mean that the purchase of equities is investment? If not, explain why it is not.

5 **G-20 Leaders Look to Shake off Lingering Economic Troubles**

The G-20 aims to take stock of the economic recovery. One achievement of the G-20 in Pittsburgh could be a deal to require that financial institutions hold more capital.

Source: *USA Today*, 24 September 2009

What are the financial institutions that the G-20 might require to hold more capital? What exactly is the 'capital' referred to in the news clip? How might the requirement to hold more capital make financial institutions safer?

The Loanable Funds Markets (Study Plan 23.2)

Use the following information to work Problems 6 and 7.

First Call, plc, is a mobile phone company. It plans to build an assembly plant that costs £10 million if the real interest rate is 6 per cent a year. If the real interest rate is 5 per cent a year, First Call will build a larger plant that costs £12 million. And if the real interest rate is 7 per cent a year, First Call will build a smaller plant that costs £8 million.

6 Draw a graph of First Call's demand for loanable funds curve.

7 First Call expects its profit from the sale of mobile phones to double next year. If other things remain the same, explain how this increase in expected profit influences First Call's demand for loanable funds.

8 Draw a graph to illustrate how an increase in the supply of loanable funds and a decrease in the demand for loanable funds can lower the real interest rate and leave the equilibrium quantity of loanable funds unchanged.

9 Use the information in Problem 4.

a US household income has grown considerably since 1984. Has US saving been on a downward trend because Americans feel wealthier?

b Explain why households preferred to buy corporate equities rather than bonds.

Government in the Loanable Funds Market (Study Plan 23.3)

Use the following table to work Problems 10 to 12.

The table shows an economy's demand for loanable funds and the supply of loanable funds schedules, when the government's budget is balanced.

Real interest rate (per cent per year)	Loanable funds demanded (billions of 2006 euros)	Loanable funds supplied
4	850	550
5	800	600
6	750	650
7	700	700
8	650	750
9	600	800
10	550	850

10 Suppose that the government has a budget surplus of €100 billion. What are the real interest rate, the quantity of investment, and the quantity of private saving? Is there any crowding out in this situation?

11 Suppose that the government has a budget deficit of €100 billion. What are the real interest rate, the quantity of investment, and the quantity of private saving? Is there any crowding out in this situation?

12 Suppose that the government has a budget deficit of €100 billion and the Ricardo–Barro effect occurs. What are the real interest rate and the quantity of investment?

Use the table in Problem 10 to work Problems 13 to 15.

Suppose that the quantity of loanable funds demanded increases by €100 billion at each real interest rate and the quantity of loanable funds supplied increases by €200 billion at each interest rate.

13 If the government budget is balanced, what are the real interest rate, the quantity of loanable funds, investment, and private saving? Does any crowding out occur?

14 If the government budget becomes a deficit of €100 billion, what are the real interest rate, the quantity of loanable funds, investment, and private saving? Does any crowding out occur?

15 If the government wants to stimulate investment and increase it to €900 billion, what must it do?

The Global Loanable Funds Market (Study Plan 23.4)

Use the following information to work Problems 16 and 17.

Global Saving Glut and US Current Account, remarks by Ben Bernanke (when a governor of the Federal Reserve) on 10 March 2005:

The US economy appears to be performing well: output growth has returned to healthy levels, the labor market is firming, and inflation appears to be under control. But, one aspect of US economic performance still evokes concern: the nation's large and growing current account deficit (negative net exports). Most forecasters expect the nation's current account imbalance to decline slowly at best, implying a continued need for foreign credit and a concomitant decline in the US net foreign asset position.

16 Why is the US, with the world's largest economy, borrowing heavily on international capital markets – rather than lending, as would seem more natural?

17 **a** What implications do the US current account deficit (negative net exports) and our reliance on foreign credit have for economic performance in the US?

b What policies, if any, should be used to address this situation?

18 **IMF Says It Battled Crisis Well**

The International Monetary Fund (IMF) reported that it acted effectively in combating the global recession. Since September 2008, the IMF made $163 billion available to developing countries. While the IMF urged developed countries and China to run deficits to stimulate their economies, the IMF required developing countries with large deficits to cut spending and not increase spending.

Source: *The Wall Street Journal*, 29 September 2009

a Explain how increased government budget deficits change the loanable funds market.

b Would the global recession have been less severe had the IMF made larger loans to developing countries?

ADDITIONAL PROBLEMS AND APPLICATIONS

myeconlab You can work these problems in MyEconLab if assigned by your lecturer.

Financial Institutions and Financial Markets

19 On 1 January 2009, Terry's Towing Service owned 4 tow trucks valued at €300,000. During 2009, Terry's bought 2 new trucks for a total of €180,000. At the end of 2009, the market value of all of the firm's trucks was €400,000. What was Terry's gross investment? Calculate Terry's depreciation and net investment.

Use the following information to work Problems 20 and 21.

The Office for National Statistics reported that the UK capital stock was £4689.2 billion at the end of 2007, £4816.8 billion at the end of 2008, and £4908.6 billion at the end of 2009. Depreciation in 2008 was £105 billion, and gross investment during 2009 was £197 billion (all in 2006 pounds).

20 Calculate UK net investment and gross investment during 2008.

21 Calculate UK depreciation and net investment during 2009.

22 Annie runs a fitness centre. On 31 December 2009, she bought an existing business with exercise equipment and a building worth €300,000. During 2010, business improved and she bought some new equipment for €50,000. At the end of 2010, her equipment and buildings were worth €325,000. Calculate Annie's gross investment, depreciation and net investment during 2010.

23 Karrie is a golf pro, and after she paid taxes, her income from golf and interest from financial assets was €1,500,000 in 2010. At the beginning of 2010, she owned €900,000 worth of financial assets. At the end of 2010, Karrie's financial assets were worth €1,900,000.

a How much did Karrie save during 2010?

b How much did she spend on consumption goods and services?

The Loanable Funds Markets

Use the following information to work Problems 24 and 25.

In 2010, the Lee family had disposable income of £80,000, wealth of £140,000, and an expected future income of £80,000 a year. At a real interest rate of 4 per cent a year, the Lee family saves £15,000 a year; at a real interest rate of 6 per cent a year, they save £20,000 a year; and at a real interest rate of 8 per cent, they save £25,000 a year.

24 Draw a graph of the Lee family's supply of loanable funds curve.

25 In 2011, suppose that the stock market crashes and the default risk increases. Explain how this increase in default risk influences the Lee family's supply of loanable funds curve.

26 Draw a graph to illustrate the effect of an increase in the demand for loanable funds and an even larger increase in the supply of loanable funds on the real interest rate and the equilibrium quantity of loanable funds.

27 **Greenspan's Conundrum Spells Confusion for Us All**

In January 2005, the interest rate on bonds was 4 per cent a year and it was expected to rise to 5 per cent a year by the end of 2005. As the rate rose to 4.3 per cent a year during February, most commentators focused, not on why the interest rate rose, but on why it was so low before. Explanations of this 'conundrum' included that unusual buying and expectations for an economic slowdown were keeping the interest rate low.

Source: *Financial Times*, 26 February 2005

a Explain how 'unusual buying' might lead to a low real interest rate.

b Explain how investors' 'expectations for an economic slowdown' might lead to a lower real interest rate.

Government in the Loanable Funds Market

Use the following news clip to work Problems 28 and 29.

India's Economy Hits the Wall

At the start of 2008, India had an annual growth of 9 per cent, huge consumer demand, and increasing foreign investment. But by July 2008, India had 11.4 per cent a year inflation, large government deficits, and rising interest rates. Economic growth is expected to fall to 7 per cent a year by the end of 2008. A Goldman Sachs report suggests that India needs to lower the government's deficit, raise educational achievement, control inflation and liberalize its financial markets.

Source: *Business Week*, 1 July 2008

28 If the Indian government reduces its deficit and returns to a balanced budget, how will the demand or supply of loanable funds in India change?

29 With economic growth forecasted to slow, future incomes are expected to fall. If other things remain the same, how will the demand or supply of loanable funds in India change?

30 **Federal Deficit Surges to $1.38 trillion in August**

US House Republican Leader John Boehner of Ohio asks: when will the White House tackle these jaw-dropping deficits that pile more and more debt on future generations while it massively increases federal spending?

Source: *USA Today*, 11 September 2009

Explain the effect of the federal deficit and the mounting debt on US economic growth.

The Global Loanable Funds Market

31 **The Global Savings Glut and Its Consequences**

Several developing countries are running large current account surpluses (representing an excess of savings over investment) and rapid growth has led to high saving rates as people save a large fraction of additional income. In India, the saving rate has risen from 23 per cent a decade ago to 33 per cent today. China's saving rate is 55 per cent. The glut of saving in Asia is being put into US bonds. When a poor country buys US bonds, it is in effect lending to the US.

Source: The Cato Institute, 8 June 2007

a Graphically illustrate and explain the impact of the 'glut of savings' on the real interest rate and the quantity of loanable funds.

b How do the high saving rates in Asia influence investment in the US?

Use the following information to work Problems 32 to 35.

Most economists agree that the problems we are witnessing today developed over a long period of time. For more than a decade, a massive amount of money flowed into the US from investors abroad because the US is an attractive and secure place to do business. This large influx of money to US financial institutions – along with low interest rates – made it easier for Americans to get credit. These developments allowed more families to borrow money for cars and homes and college tuition – some for the first time. They allowed more entrepreneurs to get loans to start new businesses and create jobs.

President George W. Bush, *Address to the Nation*, 24 September 2008

32 Explain why, for more than a decade, a massive amount of money flowed into the US. Compare and contrast your explanation with that of the President.

33 Provide a graphical analysis of the reasons why the interest rate was low.

34 Funds have been flowing into the US since the early 1980s. Why might they have created problems in 2008 but not earlier?

35 Could the US stop funds from flowing in from other countries? How?

Economics in the News

36 After you have studied *Reading Between the Lines* on pp. 550–551 answer the following questions.

a Why are governments in the Eurozone and the UK taking actions aimed at cutting their budget deficits?

b In what ways might it be argued that the UK has a less acute budget problem than Ireland, Greece, Spain and Portugal?

c Why are borrowing costs for Greece, Ireland, Spain and Portugal so high compared to those for the UK and Germany?

d Draw a graph of the loanable funds market for Greece to illustrate your answer to part (c).

CHAPTER 24

Money, the Price Level and Inflation

After studying this chapter you will be able to:

- Define money and describe its functions
- Explain what banks are and do
- Describe the functions of a central bank
- Explain how the banking system creates money
- Explain how the demand for and supply of money determine the nominal interest rate
- Explain how the quantity of money influences the price level and the inflation rate

When you want to buy something, you use coins, notes, write a cheque, or present a debit or credit card. Are all these things money? When you deposit some coins or notes in the bank, is it still money? What happens when the bank lends your money to someone else? How can you still get it back if it's been lent out? Why does the amount of money in the economy matter? How does it affect the interest rate? You can find the answers in this chapter. And in *Reading Between the Lines* at the end of the chapter, you can see how the quantity of money changed in the Eurozone in 2010.

What Is Money?

What do cowrie shells, wampum, whales' teeth, tobacco, cattle and pennies have in common? The answer is that all of them are (or have been) forms of money. **Money** is any commodity or token that is generally acceptable as a means of payment. A **means of payment** is a method of settling a debt. When a payment has been made there is no remaining obligation between the parties to a transaction. So what cowrie shells, wampum, whales' teeth, cattle and pennies have in common is that they have served (or still do serve) as the means of payment. But money has three other functions:

- A medium of exchange
- A unit of account
- A store of value

Medium of Exchange

A *medium of exchange* is an object that is generally accepted in exchange for goods and services. Money acts as such a medium. Without money, it would be necessary to exchange goods and services directly for other goods and services – an exchange called *barter*. Barter requires a double coincidence of wants, a situation that rarely occurs. For example, if you want a pizza, you might offer a CD in exchange for it. But you must find someone who is selling pizza and who wants your CD.

A medium of exchange overcomes the need for a double coincidence of wants. And money acts as a medium of exchange because people with something to sell will always accept money in exchange for it. But money isn't the only medium of exchange. You can buy with a credit card. But a credit card isn't money. It doesn't make a final payment and the debt it creates must eventually be settled by using money.

Unit of Account

A *unit of account* is an agreed measure for stating the prices of goods and services. To get the most out of your budget you have to work out, among other things, whether seeing one more film is worth the price you have to pay, not in pounds and pence, but in terms of the number of ice creams, beers or cups of tea that you have to give up. It's easy to do such calculations when all these goods have prices in terms of pounds and pence (see Table 24.1). If the price of a cinema ticket is £4 and a pint of beer in the Students' Union costs £1, you know straight away that seeing one more film costs you 4 pints of beer. If the price of a cup of tea is 50 pence, one more cinema ticket costs 8 cups of tea. You need only one calculation to work out the opportunity cost of any pair of goods and services.

But imagine how troublesome it would be if your local cinema posted its price as 4 pints of beer; and if the Students' Union announced that the price of a pint of beer was 2 ice creams; and if the corner shop posted the price of an ice cream as 1 cup of tea; and if the café priced a cup of tea as 5 rolls of mints!

Now how much running around and calculating do you have to do to work out how much that film is going to cost you in terms of the beer, ice cream, tea or mints that you must give up to see it? You get the answer for beer from the sign posted at the cinema, but for all the other goods you're going to have to visit many different shops to establish the prices you need to work out the opportunity costs you face.

Cover up the column labelled 'price in money units' in Table 24.1 and see how hard it is to work out the number of local telephone calls it costs to see one film.

It is much simpler for everyone to express their prices in terms of pounds and pence.

Table 24.1

The Unit of Account Function of Money Simplifies Price Comparisons

Good	Price in money units	Price in units of another good
Cinema ticket	£4.00 each	4 pints of beer
Beer	£1.00 per pint	2 ice creams
Ice cream	£0.50 per cone	1 cup of tea
Tea	£0.50 per cup	5 rolls of mints
Mints	£0.10 per roll	1 local phone call

Money as a unit of account. The price of a cinema ticket is £4 and the price of a cup of tea is 50 pence, so a cinema ticket costs 8 cups of tea (£4.00/£0.50 = 8).

No unit of account. You go to a cinema and learn that the price of a ticket is 4 pints of beer. You go to a café and learn that a cup of tea costs 5 rolls of mints. But how many rolls of mints does it cost you to see a film? To answer that question, you go to the Students' Union bar and find that a pint of beer costs 2 ice creams. Now you head for the ice cream shop, where an ice cream costs 1 cup of tea. Now you get out your pocket calculator: 1 cinema ticket costs 4 pints of beer, or 8 ice creams, or 8 cups of tea, or 40 rolls of mints!

Sometimes we use a unit of account that is not money. An example is the European Currency Unit that preceded the euro. Also, the euro existed as a unit of account before it became money – a means of payment – on 1 January 2002.

Store of Value

Money is a *store of value* in the sense that it can be held and exchanged later for goods and services. If money were not a store of value, it could not serve as a means of payment.

Money is not alone in acting as a store of value. A physical object such as a house, a car, a work of art or a computer can act as a store of value. The most reliable and useful stores of value are items that have a stable value. The more stable the value of a commodity or token, the better it can act as a store of value and the more useful it is as money. No store of value has a completely stable value. The value of a house, a car or a work of art fluctuates over time. The value of the commodities and tokens that are used as money also fluctuate over time. And when there is inflation, their values persistently fall.

Because inflation brings a falling value of money, a low inflation rate is needed to make money as useful as possible as a store of value.

Money in the UK Today

In the UK today, money consists of:

- Currency
- Deposits at banks and building societies

Currency

The notes and coins held by individuals and businesses are known as **currency**. These notes and coins are money because the government declares them to be so. The Royal Mint maintains the inventory of coins in circulation and the Bank of England issues notes. (In Scotland and Northern Ireland, private banks also issue notes, but they must hold £1 of Bank of England notes for every £1 they issue.)

Deposits at Banks and Building Societies

Deposits at banks and building societies are also money. This type of money is an accounting entry in an electronic database in the banks' and building societies' computers. They are money because they can be converted instantly into currency and because they are used directly to settle debts. In fact, deposits are the main means of settling debts in modern societies. The owner of a deposit transfers ownership to another person simply by writing a cheque – an instruction to a bank – that tells the bank to change its database, debiting the account of one depositor and crediting the account of another.

The Official UK Measure of Money

The official measure of money in the UK today is known as M4. **M4** consists of currency held by the public plus bank deposits and building society deposits. M4 does *not* include currency held by banks and building societies and it does *not* include currency or bank deposits owned by the UK government. Figure 24.1 shows the components that make up M4.

Figure 24.1 The Official UK Measure of Money

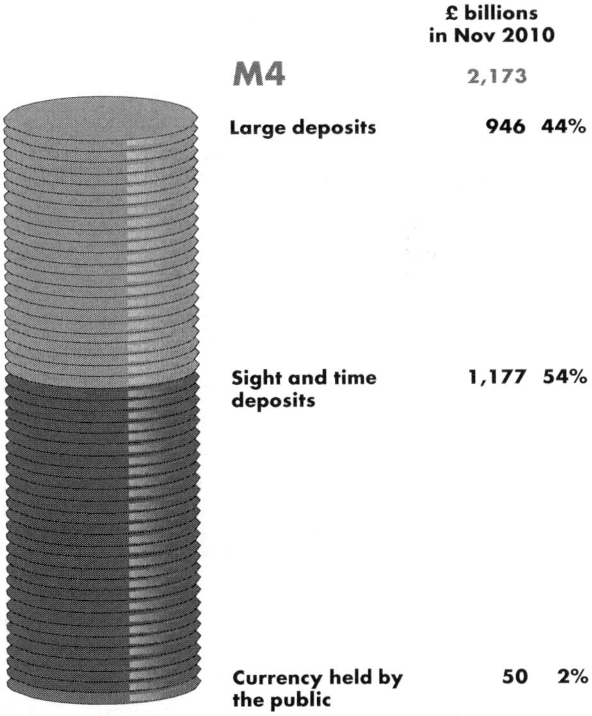

M4 is the official measure of money in the UK. It is the sum of currency held by the public, bank deposits and building society deposits. Currency represents only 2 per cent of the money in the UK economy.

Source of data: Bank of England.

myeconlab Animation

Are All the Components of M4 Really Money?

Money is the means of payment. So the test of whether something is money is whether it serves as a means of payment. Currency passes the test.

Deposits are divided into two types: sight deposits and time deposits. A *sight deposit* (sometimes called a chequeable deposit) can be transferred from one person to another by writing a cheque or using a debit card. So a sight deposit is clearly money. A *time deposit* is a deposit that has a fixed term to maturity. Although not usually a chequeable deposit, technological advances in the banking industry have made it easy to switch funds from a time deposit to a sight deposit. Because of the ease with which funds in a time deposit can be switched into a sight deposit, time deposits are included in the definition of money.

Cheques, Debit Cards and Credit Cards Are Not Money

The funds you've got in the bank are your money. When you write a cheque, you are telling your bank to move some funds from your account to the account of the person to whom you've given the cheque. Writing a cheque doesn't create more money. The money existed before you wrote the cheque. When your cheque is paid, the money is still there but it moves from you to the person to whom you wrote the cheque.

Using a debit card is just like writing a cheque except that the transaction takes place in an instant. The funds are electronically transferred from your account to that of the person you are paying the moment your card is read.

A credit card is just an ID card, but one that lets you take a loan at the instant you buy something. When you sign a credit card sales slip, you are saying: "I agree to pay for these goods when the credit card company bills me." Once you get your statement from the credit card company, you must make the minimum payment due (or clear your balance). To make that payment you need money – currency or a bank deposit. So although you use a credit card when you buy something, the credit card is not the *means of payment* and it is not money. The currency or the bank deposit that you use is money.

We've seen that the main component of money is deposits at banks and building societies. These institutions play a crucial role in our economic life and we're now going to examine that role.

ECONOMICS IN ACTION

Money in the Eurozone

The official Eurozone measure of money is called M3, but the items included in the Eurozone M3 are very similar to those in M4 in the UK. Figure 1 shows the numbers. The most interesting feature of euro money is the large amount of currency held by the public, 8 per cent of the total, compared with 2 per cent in the UK. Think about the reasons for this huge difference!

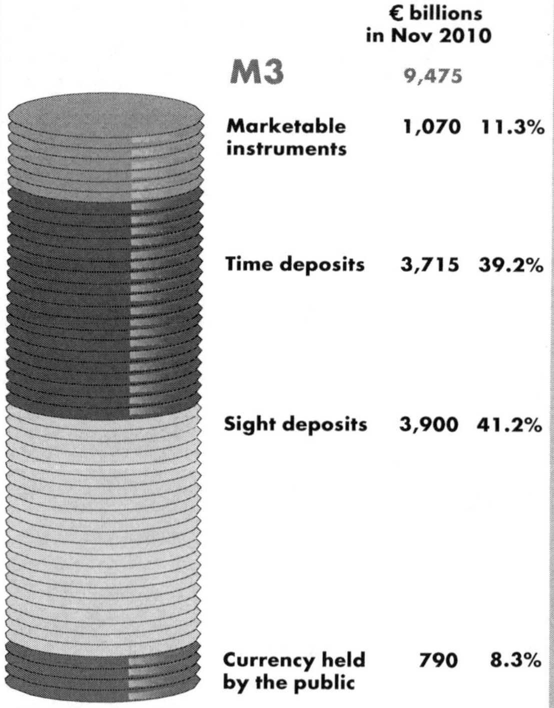

Figure 1 Official Eurozone Measure of Money

Source of data: European Central Bank.

Review Quiz

1. What makes something money? What functions does money perform? Why do you think Polo mints don't serve as money?
2. What are the largest components of money in the UK and in the Eurozone today?
3. Are all the components of M4 really money?
4. Why are cheques, debit cards and credit cards not money?

You can work these questions in Study Plan 24.1 and get instant feedback. myeconlab

Monetary Financial Institutions

A **monetary financial institution** is a financial firm that takes deposits from households and firms. These deposits are components of M4. You will learn what these institutions are, what they do, the economic benefits they bring, how they are regulated and how they have innovated to create new financial products.

Types of Monetary Financial Institutions

The deposits of two types of financial firms make up the UK's money. They are

- Commercial banks
- Building Societies

Commercial Banks

A *commercial bank* is a private firm, licensed by the Bank of England under the Banking Act 1987 to take deposits and make loans.

UK commercial banks are very large and five firms dominate the banking markets: Barclays, HSBC, Lloyds Banking Group, Royal Bank of Scotland Group and Standard Chartered. The assets of the largest commercial banks exceed £2 trillion.

These very large firms offer a wide range of banking services and have extensive international operations. The deposits of commercial banks represent the bulk of the deposits in the M4 definition of money.

Building Societies

A *building society* is a private firm licensed under the Building Societies Act 1986 to accept deposits and make loans mostly to mortgage borrowers.

Building societies are much smaller than commercial banks and most of them serve their local communities. The largest, Nationwide, has assets of £150 billion. Size falls steeply with the assets of the next largest, Britannia, at £32 billion and the third largest, Yorkshire at £16 billion.

Unlike a bank, a building society is owned by its depositors, obtains its funds in the form of savings accounts and keeps its reserves not at the Bank of England but as a deposit in a commercial bank.

The combined deposits of the largest 50 Building Societies in November 2010 was £290 billion.

What Monetary Financial Institutions Do

Monetary financial institutions provide services such as cheque clearing, account management, credit cards and Internet banking, all of which provide an income from service fees. But they earn most of their income by using the funds they receive from depositors to make loans and to buy securities that earn a higher interest rate than that paid to depositors. In this activity, they must perform a balancing act, weighing return against risk. To see this balancing act, we'll focus on the commercial banks.

A commercial bank puts the funds it receives from depositors and other funds that it borrows into four types of assets:

1. A bank's **reserves** are notes and coins in the bank's vault or in a deposit account at the Bank of England. (We'll study the Bank of England later in this chapter.) These funds are used to meet depositors' currency withdrawals and to make payments to other banks. In normal times, a bank keeps about one per cent of deposits as reserves.
2. *Liquid assets* are overnight loans to other banks and institutions, UK government Treasury bills and commercial bills. These assets are the banks' first line of defence if they need reserves. Liquid assets can be sold and instantly converted into reserves with virtually no risk of loss. Because they have a low risk, they earn a low interest rate.

   The interest rate on overnight loans is closely linked to the interest rate set by the Bank of England as its main policy interest rate (see p. 565).
3. *Investment securities* are UK government bonds and other bonds such as mortgage-backed securities. These assets can be sold and converted into reserves but at prices that fluctuate, so they are riskier than liquid assets and have a higher interest rate.
4. *Loans and advances* are funds committed for an agreed-upon period of time to corporations to finance investment and to households to finance the purchase of homes, cars and other durable goods. The outstanding balances on credit card accounts are also bank loans. Loans are a bank's riskiest and highest-earning assets: They can't be converted into reserves until they are due to be repaid, and some borrowers default and never repay.

Table 24.2 provides a snapshot of the sources and uses of funds of all the monetary financial institutions in the UK in November 2010.

Economic Benefits Provided by Monetary Financial Institutions

You've seen that a monetary financial institution earns part of its profit because it pays a lower interest rate on deposits than it earns on loans. What benefits do these institutions provide that make this outcome occur? Monetary financial institutions provide four benefits:

- Create liquidity
- Pool risk
- Lower the cost of borrowing
- Lower the cost of monitoring borrowers

Create Liquidity

Monetary financial institutions create liquidity by *borrowing short and lending long* – taking deposits and standing ready to repay them on short notice or on demand and making loan commitments that run for terms of many years.

Table 24.2

Monetary Financial Institutions: Sources and Uses of Funds

	Funds (billions of pounds)	Percentage of deposits
Total funds	3,759	132
Sources		
Deposits	2,837	100
Borrowing	520	18
Own capital and other sources	402	14
Uses		
Reserves	158	6
Liquid assets	336	12
Investment securities*	669	24
Loans and advances	2,596	92

Commercial banks get most of their funds from depositors and use most of them to make loans and advances. In normal times banks hold about 1 per cent of deposits as reserves but in 2010 they held an unusually large 6 per cent as reserves.

Source of data: The Bank of England. The data are for November, 2010. *Investment securities includes other assets.

Pool Risk

A loan might not be repaid – a default. If you lend to one person who defaults, you lose the entire amount loaned. If you lend to 1,000 people (through a bank) and one person defaults, you lose almost nothing. Monetary financial institutions pool risk.

Lower the Cost of Borrowing

Imagine there are no monetary financial institutions and a firm is looking for £1 million to buy a new factory. It hunts around for several dozen people from whom to borrow the funds. Monetary financial institutions lower the cost of this search. The firm gets its £1 million from a single institution that gets deposits from a large number of people but spreads the cost of this activity over many borrowers.

Lower the Cost of Monitoring Borrowers

By monitoring borrowers, a lender can encourage good decisions that prevent defaults. But this activity is costly. Imagine how costly it would be if each household that lent money to a firm incurred the costs of monitoring that firm directly. Monetary financial institutions can perform this task at a much lower cost.

How Monetary Financial Institutions Are Regulated

The collapse of a large bank would have damaging effects on the entire financial system and economy. Regulation seeks to lower the risk of collapse and lessen the damage if it occurs.

To lower the risk of bank failure, commercial banks are required to hold levels of reserves and owners' capital that equal or surpass ratios laid down by regulation.

The **required reserve ratio** is the minimum percentage of deposits that a bank is required to hold in reserves. This minimum is designed to ensure that a bank does not run out of cash. The *required capital ratio* is the minimum percentage of assets that must be financed by the bank's owners. This ratio is designed to ensure that a bank's assets will never be worth less than its deposits.

A new Banking Act of 2009 seeks to lessen the damage if failure occurs. It gives powers to the so-called *Tripartite Authorities* (HM Treasury, the Financial Services Authority and the Bank of England) to intervene in a distressed bank or building society to reduce the effects of failure on overall economic stability.

ECONOMICS IN ACTION

Northern Rock and the Sub-prime Loans Crisis

Northern Rock plc is a UK bank that was taken into public ownership at the height of the financial crisis caused by the problems created by US sub-prime loans.

Formerly a building society that converted to a bank in 1997, Northern Rock continued to specialize in mortgage lending. During the 2000s the bank expanded its deposits and borrowing from £22 billion in 2000 to £109 billion in 2007. Its profit rose from £149 million in 1997 to a peak of £557 million in 2006.

Northern Rock's business model was 'originate' and 'distribute'. The bank borrowed on the interbank loans market and used the funds to make mortgage loans to its customers (originate). By 2006, some of its lending was in the form of sub-prime (high-risk) mortgages. It then created mortgage-backed securities, which it sold on the global capital market (distribute).

The interest the bank received on its mortgage loans was paid to the holders of the mortgage-backed securities and the funds raised by selling these securities was used to pay back lenders in the interbank loans market.

This part of Northern Rock's business was kept separate from its normal banking business and no required capital ratio applied to it, so the bank was able to expand its borrowing and lending without having to use any of its own funds.

Figure 1 shows how the bank's balance sheet expanded and the bank's growing dependence on borrowing (the red bars) rather than on customers' deposits (the blue bars).

When the sub-prime loans crisis hit the world economy, Northern Rock was unable to raise funds in the interbank market, and as customers queued to withdraw their deposits, the bank faced a liquidity crisis. In February 2008 the bank was taken into public ownership.

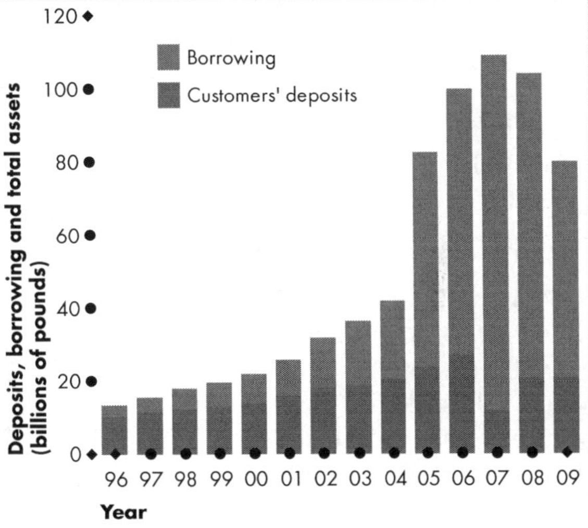

Figure 1 Northern Rock's Spectacular Rise and Fall

Source of data: Bureau van dijk Bankscope.

Financial Innovation

In the pursuit of larger profit, banks and building societies are constantly seeking ways to improve their products in a process called financial innovation. The major financial innovations included the introduction of credit cards, debit cards, automatic teller machines, interest-bearing sight deposits and automatic transfers between sight and time deposits. These innovations occurred because the development of computing power lowered the cost of calculations and record keeping.

During the 2000s, when interest rates were low and banks were flush with funds, sub-prime mortgages were developed in the US. To avoid the risk of carrying these mortgages, mortgage-backed securities were developed. The original lending institution sold these securities, lowered their own exposure to risk and obtained funds to make more loans. The model of originating mortgage loans and selling them as mortgage backed securities to other financial institutions was copied by a number of UK banks – the most notorious being Northern Rock.

Review Quiz

1 What is a monetary financial institution?
2 What are the main economic functions of a monetary financial institution?
3 What are the four types of assets held by banks?
4 How do monetary financial institutions create liquidity, pool risk, and lower borrowing costs?

You can work these questions in Study Plan 24.2 and get instant feedback. myeconlab

You now know what money is. Your next task is to learn about central banking and the ways in which a central bank can influence the quantity of money.

Central Banking

A central bank is a public authority that provides banking services to governments and commercial banks, supervises and regulates financial institutions and markets and conducts monetary policy. *Monetary policy* is the attempt to control inflation, moderate the business cycle and provide the foundation for sustained economic growth by influencing the quantity of money, interest rates and the exchange rate. We study monetary policy in Chapter 30. Our aim in this chapter is to learn about the role of a central bank in the process of creating and influencing the quantity of money and the interest rate. We'll briefly describe two central banks:

- The European Central Bank
- The Bank of England

The European Central Bank

The **European Central Bank (ECB)** is the central bank of the Eurozone – the members of the European Union that use the euro as their currency. The ECB was established on 1 June 1998.

National central banks, the largest of which are the Banque de France, Deutsche Bundesbank and Banca d'Italia, provide banking services to their governments and commercial banks and supervise and regulate their national financial institutions and markets. The Executive Board of the ECB together with the Governors of the national central banks of the Eurozone constitute the Governing Council, which is the highest decision-making body in the ECB. Through this membership of the Governing Council, national central banks play a role in setting Eurozone monetary policy.

The Bank of England

The **Bank of England** is the central bank of the UK. It was established by Parliament in 1694 in a deal between a syndicate of wealthy individuals and the government of King William and Queen Mary. The syndicate lent the government £1.2 million in return for the right to issue bank notes. And so the Bank of England notes we use today were born.

The Bank of England was first formally recognized as the central bank with the passage of the Bank of England Act of 1946, which took the Bank into public ownership.

For the next 50 years, the Bank of England was under the firm day-to-day control of the Treasury (the government) and its role was simply to implement the government's decisions. But in 1997, a major change occurred and the Bank was given independence to determine monetary policy, subject to objectives set by the government. The centrepiece of the new arrangement, which remains in place today, was the creation of the Monetary Policy Committee.

Monetary Policy Committee

The Bank of England's **Monetary Policy Committee (MPC)** formulates the UK's monetary policy. Its members are the Governor and two Deputy Governors of the Bank, two members appointed by the Governor of the Bank after consultation with the Chancellor of the Exchequer and four members appointed by the Chancellor of the Exchequer. The persons appointed by the Chancellor must have 'knowledge or experience which is likely to be relevant to the Committee's functions' – which in practice means that they are academic economists.

To appreciate the monetary policy tools available to a central bank, we must first learn about its financial structure, summarized in its balance sheet. We'll focus here on the Bank of England but the principles apply to all central banks.

The Bank of England's Balance Sheet

The Bank of England influences the economy through the size and composition of it balance sheet – the assets that it owns and the liabilities that it owes.

The Bank's Assets

The Bank of England has two main assets:

1. UK government securities
2. Loans to monetary financial institutions

The Bank holds UK government securities – Treasury bills and longer term government bonds – that it buys in the bond market. When the Bank buys or sells bonds, it participates in the *loanable funds market* (see pp. 538–543).

The Bank makes loans to monetary financial institutions. These loans are made using *repurchase agreements*. Under a repurchase agreement – called a **repo** – a commercial bank sells a government bond to the Bank of England and simultaneously agrees to *repurchase* it (buy it back) usually two weeks later. In normal times, this item is small but during the global financial crisis, the Bank provided loans on an unprecedented scale.

The Bank's Liabilities

The Bank has two liabilities:

1 Notes in circulation
2 Deposits of commercial banks

Bank of England notes are the £5, £10, £20 and £50 notes that we use in our cash transactions. Some of these notes are part of *currency* – a component of the M4 definition of money (see p. 559). And some of them are in the tills and vaults of the commercial banks – part of the banks' reserves.

The Bank of England's other liability is the deposits of commercial banks, which are part of these institutions' reserves.

The Monetary Base

The Bank of England's liabilities plus the coins issued by the Royal Mint make up the **monetary base**. Coins are part of the monetary base but do not appear in the Bank of England balance sheet because the Royal Mint, which issues coins, is a branch of the government and not a part of the Bank of England.

The Bank's assets are the sources of the monetary base. They are also called the backing for the monetary base. The Bank's liabilities are the uses of the monetary base as currency held by the public and bank reserves (notes and coins in the bank's vault or in a deposit account at the Bank of England). Table 24.3 provides a snapshot of the sources and uses of the monetary base in December 2010.

We'll next look at the Bank's tool kit.

Table 24.3

The Sources and Uses of the Monetary Base

Sources (billions of pounds)		Uses (billions of pounds)	
Government bonds	14	Notes held by the public	53
Loans to banks	181	Bank reserves	142
Monetary base	**195**	**Monetary base**	**195**

Source of data: Bank of England. The data are for 15 December 2010.

The Bank of England's Policy Tools

The Bank of England has four policy tools to influence the quantity of money and the interest rate. They are:

- Bank Rate
- Open market operations
- Lender of last resort
- Required reserve ratio

Bank Rate

Bank Rate is the interest rate that the Bank of England charges on secured overnight loans to commercial banks. It is the official policy interest rate to which many other interest rates are linked. Among them are the interest rate that the Bank pays to commercial banks on their reserve deposits and the interest rates the commercial banks pay on deposits and charge on loans.

Open Market Operations

An **open market operation** is the purchase or sale of securities by the central bank in the *loanable funds market*. The term 'open market' refers to commercial banks and the general public but not the government. The Bank of England does not transact with the government.

When the Bank buys government bonds, it pays for them with newly created bank reserves. When the Bank sells government bonds, the Bank is paid with reserves held by the commercial banks. So open market operations directly influence the reserves of banks. By changing the quantity of bank reserves, the Bank of England changes the amount of bank lending, which influences the quantity of money and the economy more broadly.

An Open Market Purchase

To see how an open market operation changes bank reserves, suppose the Bank of England buys £100 million of government securities from HSBC. When the Bank of England makes this transaction, two things happen:

1 HSBC has £100 million less securities, and the Bank has £100 million more securities.
2 The Bank places £100 million in HSBC's deposit account at the Bank of England (bank reserves in Table 24.3) to pay for the securities.

Figure 24.2 shows the effects of these actions on the balance sheets of the Bank and HSBC. Ownership of the securities passes from HSBC to the Bank of England, so

Figure 24.2 The Bank of England Buys Securities in the Open Market

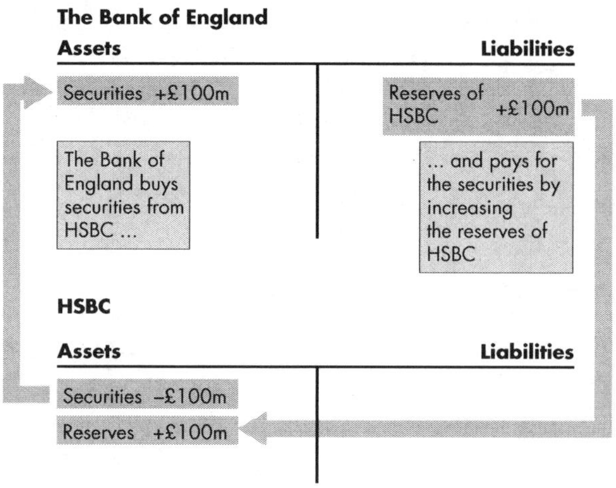

When the Bank of England buys securities in the open market, it increases bank reserves. The Bank of England's assets and liabilities increase and the selling bank's reserves increase and securities decrease.

myeconlab Animation

HSBC's assets decrease by £100 million and the Bank's assets increase by £100 million, as shown by the blue arrow running from HSBC to the Bank. The Bank pays for the securities by placing £100 million in HSBC's reserve account at the Bank, as shown by the green arrow running from the Bank to HSBC. The Bank's assets and liabilities increase by £100 million. HSBC's total assets are unchanged: it sold securities to increase its reserves.

An Open Market Sale

If the Bank of England sells £100 million of government securities to HSBC in the open market:

1. HSBC has £100 million more securities, and the Bank has £100 million less securities.
2. HSBC pays for the securities by using £100 million of its reserve deposit at the Bank.

You can follow the effects of these actions by reversing the arrows and the plus and minus signs in Figure 24.2. Ownership of the securities passes from the Bank to HSBC, so the Bank's assets decrease by £100 million and HSBC's assets increase by £100 million. HSBC uses £100 million of its reserves to pay for the securities. Both the Bank's assets and liabilities decrease by £100 million. HSBC's total assets are unchanged: it has used reserves to buy securities.

ECONOMICS IN ACTION

The Bank of England's Balance Sheet Explodes

The Bank of England's balance sheet underwent some remarkable changes during the financial crisis of 2007–2008 and the recession that the crisis triggered.

The figure shows the effects of these changes on the size and composition of the monetary base by comparing the situation in December 2010 with that before the financial crisis began in January 2007.

In 2007, a normal year, the monetary base was £58 billion and more than half of the base was currency. But between 2007 and 2010 the Bank made huge repo loans to commercial banks that more than tripled the monetary base to £194 billion. Almost all of this increase was composed of bank reserves, which increased from £20 billion in 2007 to a staggering £142 billion in 2010.

Left unchecked, this huge volume of reserves would eventually be loaned by the banks and create an explosion in the quantity of money.

When, and how quickly, to unwind the large increase in the monetary base and bank reserves is a source of much disagreement and debate.

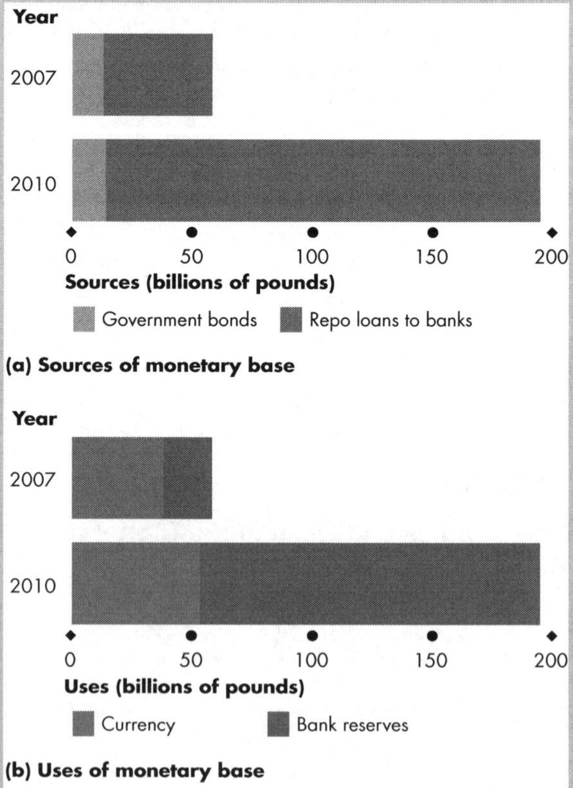

Figure 1 Changes in the Sources and Uses of Monetary Base

Source of data: Bank of England.

Lender of Last Resort

The Bank of England is the **lender of last resort**, which means that if all the banks are short of reserves, they can borrow from the central bank. Normally, last-resort loans are made overnight and secured with a repurchase agreement (a *repo*).

In recent years the Bank of England has lent on repurchase agreements for longer periods and boosted the reserves of the commercial banks massively. This form of injection of reserves is called **quantitative easing**. The reserves made available by quantitative easing are indicated in Table 24.3 as 'Loans to banks'.

In September 2007 the Bank of England made a large last-resort loan facility available to the bank Northern Rock when it was unable to obtain funds from the wholesale interbank market.

Required Reserve Ratio

The *required reserve ratio* (the minimum percentage of deposits that a bank is required to hold as reserves) can be varied to make banks hold more reserves. The Bank of England doesn't vary this percentage very often. But some central banks (the People's Bank of China is one) frequently use this tool and it is available to the Bank of England if it should choose to use it.

Review Quiz

1. What is a central bank?
2. What are the central banks of the Eurozone and the UK and what functions do they perform?
3. What are the main items in the balance sheet of a central bank?
4. What is the monetary base and how does it relate to the items in the Bank of England's balance sheet?
5. What are a central bank's policy tools?
6. How does an open market operation change the monetary base?
7. What is quantitative easing and how does it change the monetary base?

You can work these questions in Study Plan 24.3 and get instant feedback. myeconlab

Next, we're going to see how the banking system – the commercial banks and the Bank of England – creates money and how the quantity of money changes when the Bank of England changes the monetary base.

How Banks Create Money

Banks* create money. But this doesn't mean that they have smoke-filled back rooms in which counterfeiters are busily working. Remember that most money is in the form of deposits, not currency. What banks create is deposits and they do so by making loans.

Creating Deposits by Making Loans

The easiest way to see that banks create deposits is to think about what happens when Helen fills up her car with petrol at a BP service station and pays using her Visa credit card issued by Barclays. When Helen keys in her PIN, she takes a loan from Barclays and obligates herself to repay the loan at a later date. The electronic transfer of funds from Helen's Barclays Visa account to BP's bank is instantaneous. Barclays credits BP's bank account with the value of the sale (less the commission).

You can see that these transactions have created a bank deposit and a loan. Helen has increased the size of her loan (her credit card balance), and BP has increased the size of its bank deposit (minus the bank's commission). And because deposits are money, this transaction has created money.

If Helen and BP use the same bank, no further transactions take place. But the outcome is essentially the same when two banks are involved. If BP's bank is the Royal Bank of Scotland, then Barclays uses its reserves to pay the Royal Bank.

Barclays still has an increase in loans but now it has a decrease in its reserves at the Bank of England; the Royal Bank of Scotland has an increase in its reserves at the Bank of England and an increase in deposits.

The banking system as a whole has an increase in loans and deposits and no change in reserves.

You know that the interest rate that banks pay on deposits is much less than what they receive on loans. So creating deposits by making loans is a profitable business. What keeps this business in check?

The quantity of loans and deposits that the banking system can create is limited by three factors:

- The monetary base
- Desired reserves
- Desired currency holding

* In this section, we'll use the term banks to refer to commercial banks and building societies – the monetary financial institutions whose deposits are money.

The Monetary Base

You've seen that the *monetary base* is the sum of Bank of England notes and banks' deposits at the Bank of England – the Bank of England's liabilities – plus coins issued by the Royal Mint. The size of the monetary base limits the total quantity of money that the banking system can create because banks have a desired level of reserves, households and firms have a desired level of currency holding and both of these desired holdings of the monetary base depend on the quantity of deposits.

Desired Reserves

A bank's *desired reserves* – the reserves that it *plans* to hold – contrast with its *required reserves*, which is the minimum quantity of reserves that a bank must hold.

The quantity of desired reserves depends on the level of deposits and is determined by the **desired reserve ratio** – the ratio of reserves to deposits that the banks plan to hold. The desired reserve ratio exceeds the required reserve ratio by an amount that the banks determine to be prudent on the basis of their daily requirements and in the light of the current situation.

Desired Currency Holding

The ratio of money held as currency to money held as bank deposits depends on how households and firms choose to make payments: whether they plan to use currency or debit cards and cheques. These plans change slowly so the desired ratio of currency to deposits also changes slowly. If bank deposits increase, desired currency holding also increases. For this reason, when banks make loans that increase deposits, some currency leaves the banks – the banking system leaks reserves. We call the leakage of reserves into currency the *currency drain* and we call the ratio of currency to deposits the **currency drain ratio**.

We've sketched the way that a loan creates a deposit and described the three factors that limit the amount of loans and deposits that can be created. We're now going to examine the money creation process more closely and discover a money multiplier.

The Money Creation Process

The money creation process begins with an increase in the monetary base, which occurs if the Bank of England buys securities. The Bank pays for the securities it buys with newly created bank reserves.

When the Bank of England buys securities from a bank, the bank's reserves increase but its deposits don't change. So the bank has excess reserves. A bank's **excess reserves** are its actual reserves minus its desired reserves.

When a bank has excess reserves, it makes loans and creates deposits and money in a process like the one we described on the previous page when Helen buys petrol with her credit card.

When the entire banking system has excess reserves, total loans and deposits increase. One bank can make a loan and get rid of excess reserves. But the banking system as a whole can't get rid of excess reserves so easily. When the banks make loans and create deposits, the extra deposits lower excess reserves for two reasons:

1 The increase in deposits increases desired reserves.
2 A currency drain decreases total reserves.

But excess reserves don't completely disappear, so the banks lend some more and the process repeats.

As the process of making loans and increasing deposits repeats, desired reserves increase, total reserves decrease through the currency drain and eventually, enough new deposits have been created to use all the new monetary base.

Figure 24.3 summarizes one round in the process we've just described. The sequence, which repeats until excess reserves are eliminated, has the following eight steps:

1 Banks have excess reserves.
2 Banks lend excess reserves.
3 The quantity of money increases.
4 New money is used to make payments.
5 Some of the new money remains on deposit.
6 Some of the new money is a *currency drain.*
7 Desired reserves increase because deposits have increased.
8 Excess reserves decrease.

If the Bank of England sells securities, then banks have negative excess reserves – they are short of reserves. When the banks are short of reserves, loans and deposits decrease and the process we've described above works in a downward direction until desired reserves plus desired currency holdings have decreased by an amount equal to the decrease in monetary base.

A money multiplier determines the change in the quantity of money that results from a change in the monetary base.

Figure 24.3 How the Banking System Creates Money by Making Loans

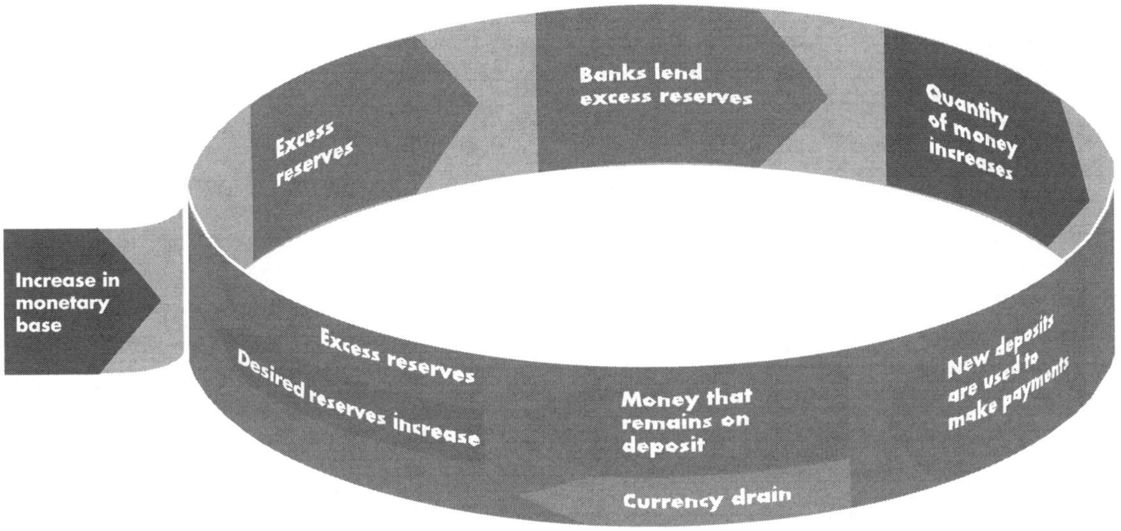

The Bank of England increases the monetary base, which increases bank reserves and creates excess reserves. Banks lend the excess reserves, new bank deposits are created and the quantity of money increases. New money is used to make payments. Some of the new money remains on deposit at banks and some leaves the banks in a currency drain. The increase in bank deposits increases banks' desired reserves. But the banks still have excess reserves, though less than before. The process repeats until excess reserves have been eliminated.

myeconlab Animation

The Money Multiplier

The **money multiplier** is the ratio of the change in the quantity of money to the change in monetary base. For example, if a £1 million increase in the monetary base increases the quantity of money by £2.5 million, then the money multiplier is 2.5.

The smaller the banks' desired reserve ratio and the smaller the currency drain ratio, the larger is the money multiplier. (See the Mathematical Note on pp. 578–579 for details on the money multiplier.)

Review Quiz

1. How do banks create money?
2. What factors limit the quantity of money that the banking system can create?
3. A bank manager tells you that she doesn't create money. She just lends the money that people deposit in the bank. Explain to her why she's wrong.

You can work these questions in Study Plan 24.4 and get instant feedback. myeconlab

ECONOMICS IN ACTION

The Variable Money Multiplier

We can measure the money multiplier, other things remaining the same, as the ratio of the quantity of money to the monetary base.

In the UK in 2007, the monetary base (in round numbers) was £60 billion and M4 was £1,500 billion, so M4 was 25 times the monetary base. The money multiplier was 25: a £1 million change in the monetary base would bring a £25 million change in M4.

The situation in 2010 was very different from that in 2007. In 2010, the monetary base was £200 billion and M4 was £2,200 billion, so M4 was only 11 times the monetary base. The money multiplier was 11: a £1 million change in the monetary base would bring an £11 million change in M4.

What happened to make the money multiplier fall so much? The answer is a global financial crisis and a very large increase in the commercial banks' desired reserve ratio. The currency drain ratio actually increased slightly.

The Money Market

There is no limit to the amount of money we would like to *receive* in payment for our labour or as interest on our savings. But there is a limit to how big an inventory of money we would like to *hold* and neither spend nor use to buy assets that generate an income. The *quantity of money demanded* is the inventory of money that people plan to hold on any given day. It is the quantity of money in our wallets and in our deposit accounts at banks. The quantity of money held must equal the quantity supplied, and the forces that bring about this equality in the money market have powerful effects on the economy, as you will see in the rest of this chapter.

But first, we need to explain what determines the amount of money that people plan to hold.

The Influences on Money Holding

The quantity of money that people choose to hold depends on four main factors. They are:

- The price level
- The *nominal* interest rate
- Real GDP
- Financial innovation

Let's look at each of them.

The Price Level

The quantity of money measured in pounds is *nominal money*. The quantity of nominal money demanded is proportional to the price level, other things remaining the same: if the price level rises by 10 per cent, people hold 10 per cent more nominal money. If you hold £20 to buy your weekly movies and coffee, you will increase your money holding to £22 if the prices of movies and coffee – and your wage rate – increase by 10 per cent.

The quantity of money measured in constant pounds (for example, in 2006 pounds) is real money. *Real money* is equal to nominal money divided by the price level and is the quantity of money measured in terms of what it will buy.

In the above example, when the price level rises by 10 per cent and you increase your money holding by 10 per cent, your real money holding is constant. Your £22 at the new price level buys the same quantity of goods and is the same quantity of real money as your £20 at the original price level. *The quantity of real money demanded is independent of the price level.*

The *Nominal* Interest Rate

A fundamental principle of economics is that as the opportunity cost of something increases, people try to find substitutes for it. Money is no exception. The higher the opportunity cost of holding money, other things remaining the same, the smaller is the quantity of real money demanded.

The interest rate is the opportunity cost of holding money. To see why, recall that the opportunity cost of any activity is the value of the best alternative forgone. The alternative to holding money is holding a savings bond or a Treasury bill that earns interest. By holding money instead, you forgo the interest that you otherwise would have received. This forgone interest is the opportunity cost of holding money.

Money loses value because of inflation. Shouldn't the inflation rate be part of the cost of holding money? It is. Other things remaining the same, the higher the expected inflation rate, the higher is the interest rate and so the higher is the opportunity cost of holding money.

Real GDP

The quantity of money that households and firms plan to hold depends on the amount they spend, and the quantity of money demanded in the economy as a whole depends on aggregate expenditure – real GDP.

Again, suppose that you hold an average of £50 to finance your weekly purchases of goods. Now imagine that the prices of these goods and of all other goods remain constant, but that your income increases. As a consequence, you now spend more and you also keep a larger amount of money on hand to finance your higher volume of expenditure.

Financial Innovation

Technological change and the arrival of new financial products – called *financial innovation* – change the quantity of money held. The major financial innovations are the widespread use of:

1. Interest-bearing sight deposits
2. Automatic transfers between sight and time deposits
3. Automatic teller machines
4. Credit cards and debit cards

These innovations have occurred because of the development of computing power that has lowered the cost of calculations and record keeping.

The Demand for Money Curve

We summarize the effects of the influences on money holding by using the demand for money curve. The **demand for money** is the relationship between the quantity of real money demanded and the interest rate – the opportunity cost of holding money – all other influences on the amount of money that people wish to hold remaining the same.

Figure 24.4 shows a demand for money curve, *MD*. When the interest rate rises, everything else remaining the same, the opportunity cost of holding money rises and the quantity of money demanded decreases – there is a movement along the demand for money curve. Similarly, when the interest rate falls, the opportunity cost of holding money falls and the quantity of money demanded increases – there is a downward movement along the demand for money curve.

When any influence on the amount of money that people plan to hold changes, there is a change in the demand for money and the demand for money curve shifts. Let's look at these shifts.

Shifts in the Demand for Money Curve

A change in real GDP or a financial innovation changes the demand for money and shifts the demand for money curve.

Figure 24.5 illustrates the changes in the demand for money. A decrease in real GDP decreases the demand for money and shifts the demand for money curve leftward from MD_0 to MD_1. An increase in real GDP has the opposite effect: it increases the demand for money and shifts the demand for money curve rightward from MD_0 to MD_2.

The influence of financial innovation on the demand for money curve is more complicated. Financial innovation decreases the demand for currency and might increase the demand for some types of deposits and decrease the demand for others. But generally financial innovation decreases the demand for money.

Changes in real GDP and financial innovation have brought large shifts in the UK demand for money curve.

Figure 24.4 The Demand for Money

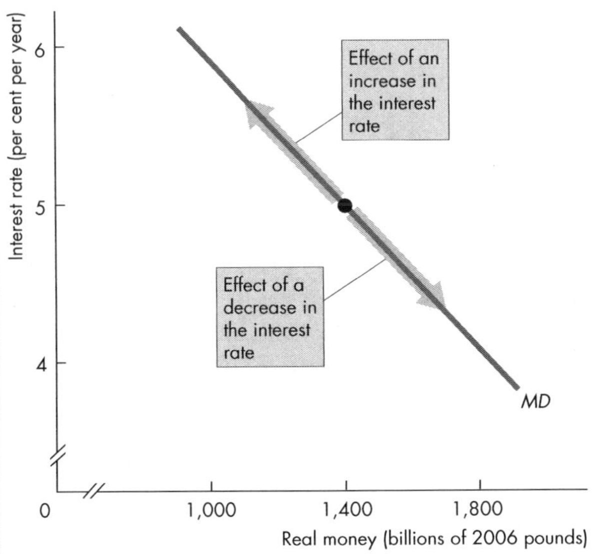

The demand for money curve, *MD*, shows the relationship between the quantity of real money that people plan to hold and the interest rate, other things remaining the same. The interest rate is the opportunity cost of holding money. A change in the interest rate leads to a movement along the demand for money curve.

myeconlab Animation

Figure 24.5 Changes in the Demand for Money

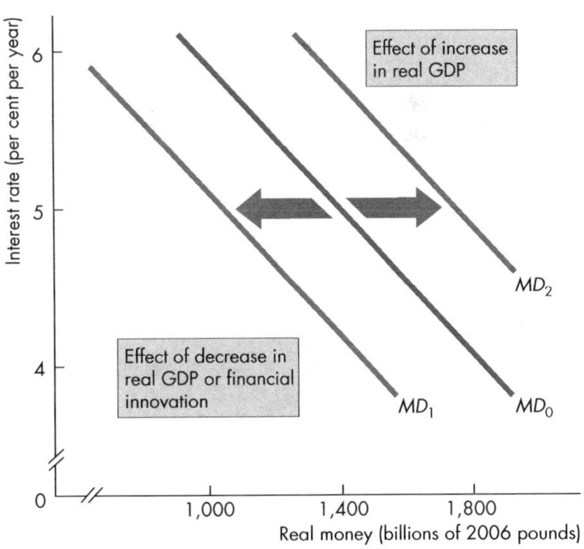

A decrease in real GDP decreases the demand for money and shifts the demand curve leftward from MD_0 to MD_1. An increase in real GDP increases the demand for money and shifts the demand curve rightward from MD_0 to MD_2. Financial innovation can either increase or decrease the demand for money depending on the specific innovation.

myeconlab Animation

Money Market Equilibrium

You now know what determines the demand for money, and you've seen how the banking system creates money. Let's now see how the money market reaches equilibrium.

Money market equilibrium occurs when the quantity of money demanded equals the quantity of money supplied. The adjustments that occur to bring money market equilibrium are fundamentally different in the short run and the long run.

Short-run Equilibrium

The quantity of money supplied is determined by the actions of the banks and the Bank of England. A change in the quantity of money brings a change in the interest rate.

In Figure 24.6, the Bank uses open market operations to make the quantity of real money supplied £1,400 billion and the supply of money curve *MS*. With the demand for money curve *MD*, the equilibrium interest rate is 5 per cent a year.

Figure 24.6 Money Market Equilibrium

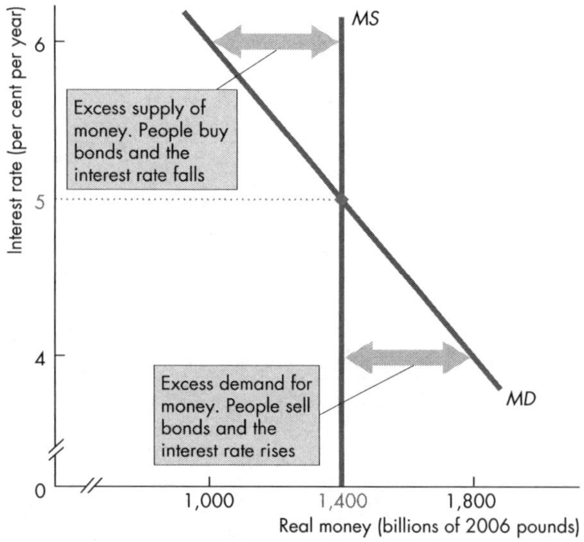

Money market equilibrium occurs when the quantity of money demanded equals the quantity supplied. In the short run, real GDP determines the demand for money curve, *MD*, and the Bank of England determines the quantity of real money supplied and the supply of money curve, *MS*. The interest rate adjusts to achieve equilibrium, here 5 per cent a year.

myeconlab Animation

If the interest rate were 4 per cent a year, people would want to hold more money than is available. They would sell bonds, bid down their price and the interest rate would rise. If the interest rate were 6 per cent a year, people would want to hold less money than is available. They would buy bonds, bid up their price and the interest rate would fall.

The Short-run Effect of a Change in the Supply of Money

Starting from a short-run equilibrium, if the Bank of England increases the quantity of money, people find themselves holding more money than the quantity demanded. With a surplus of money holding, people enter the loanable funds market and buy bonds. The increase in demand for bonds raises the price of a bond and lowers the interest rate (refresh your memory by looking at p. 538).

If the Bank of England decreases the quantity of money, people find themselves holding less money than the quantity demanded. They enter the loanable funds market and sell bonds. The increase in the supply of bonds lowers the price of a bond and raises the interest rate.

Figure 24.7 illustrates the effects of the changes in the quantity of money that we've just described. When the supply of money curve shifts rightward from MS_0 to MS_1, the interest rate falls to 4 per cent a year; when the supply of money curve shifts leftward to MS_2, the interest rate rises to 6 per cent a year.

Long-run Equilibrium

You've just seen how the nominal interest rate is determined in the money market at the level that makes the quantity of money demanded equal the quantity supplied. You learned in Chapter 23 (on p. 542) that the real interest rate is determined in the loanable funds market at the level that makes the quantity of loanable funds demanded equal the quantity of loanable funds supplied. You also learned in Chapter 23 (on p. 539) that the real interest rate equals the nominal interest rate minus the inflation rate.

When the inflation rate equals the expected (or forecast) inflation rate and when real GDP equals potential GDP, the money market, the loanable funds market, the goods market and the labour market are in long-run equilibrium – the economy is in long-run equilibrium.

If in long-run equilibrium, the quantity of money increases, eventually a new long-run equilibrium is

Figure 24.7 A Change in the Supply of Money

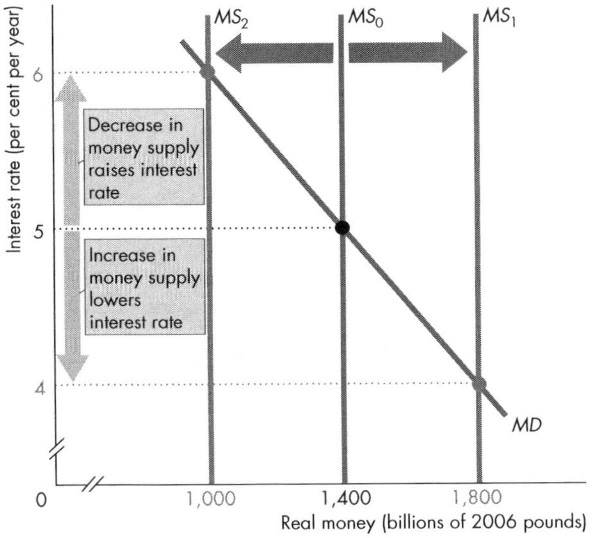

An increase in the supply of money shifts the supply of money curve from MS_0 to MS_1 and the interest rate falls. A decrease in the supply of money shifts the supply of money curve from MS_0 to MS_2 and the interest rate rises.

myeconlab Animation

reached in which nothing real has changed. Real GDP, employment, the real quantity of money and the real interest rate all return to their original levels. But something does change: the price level. The price level rises by the same percentage as the rise in the quantity of money. Why does this outcome occur in the long run?

The reason is that real GDP and employment are determined by the demand for labour, the supply of labour and the production function – the real forces described in Chapter 22 (pp. 513–515); and the real interest rate is determined by the demand for and supply of (real) loanable funds – the real forces described in Chapter 23 (pp. 540–542). The only variable that is free to respond to a change in the supply of money in the long run is the price level. The price level adjusts to make the quantity of real money supplied equal to the quantity demanded.

So when the nominal quantity of money changes, in the long run the price level changes by a percentage equal to the percentage change in the quantity of nominal money. In the long run, the change in the price level is proportional to the change in the quantity of money.

The Transition from the Short Run to the Long Run

How does the economy move from the first short-run response to an increase in the quantity of money to the long-run response?

The adjustment process is lengthy and complex. Here, we'll only provide a sketch of the process. A more thorough account must wait until you get to Chapter 26.

We start out in long-run equilibrium and the Bank of England increases the quantity of money by 10 per cent. There is an excess demand for money and the nominal interest rate falls (just like you saw in Figure 24.6). The real interest rate falls too.

With a lower real interest rate, people want to borrow and spend more. Firms want to borrow to invest and households want to borrow to invest in bigger homes or to buy more consumer goods.

The increase in the demand for goods cannot be met by an increase in supply because the economy is already at full employment. So there is a general shortage of all kinds of goods and services, which makes the price level rise. As the price level rises, the real quantity of money decreases. The decrease in the quantity of real money raises the nominal interest rate and the real interest rate. As the interest rate rises, spending plans are cut back, and eventually, the original full-employment equilibrium is restored. At the new long-run equilibrium, the price level has risen by 10 per cent and nothing real has changed.

Review Quiz

1. What are the main influences on the quantity of real money that people and businesses plan to hold?
2. Show the effects of a change in the nominal interest rate and a change in real GDP using the demand for money curve.
3. How is money market equilibrium determined in the short run?
4. How does a change in the supply of money change the interest rate in the short run?
5. How does a change in the supply of money change the interest rate in the long run?

You can work these questions in Study Plan 24.5 and get instant feedback. myeconlab

We explore the long-run link between money and the price level on the next two pages, where we study the quantity theory of money.

The Quantity Theory of Money

In the long run, the price level adjusts to make the quantity of real money demanded equal the quantity supplied. A special theory of the price level and inflation – the quantity theory of money – explains this long-run adjustment of the price level.

The **quantity theory of money** is the proposition that in the long run, an increase in the quantity of money brings an equal percentage increase in the price level. To explain the quantity theory of money, we first need to define the velocity of circulation.

The **velocity of circulation** is the average number of times a pound of money is used annually to buy the goods and services that make up GDP. But GDP equals the price level (P) multiplied by real GDP (Y). That is:

$$GDP = PY$$

Call the quantity of money M. The velocity of circulation, V, is determined by the equation:

$$V = PY/M$$

For example, if GDP is £1,000 billion (PY = £1,000 billion) and the quantity of money is £250 billion, then the velocity of circulation is 4.

From the definition of the velocity of circulation, the *equation of exchange* tells us how M, V, P and Y are connected. This equation is:

$$MV = PY$$

Given the definition of the velocity of circulation, the equation of exchange is always true – it is true by definition. It becomes the quantity theory of money if the quantity of money does not influence the velocity of circulation or real GDP. In this case, the equation of exchange tells us that the price level in the long run is determined by the quantity of money. That is:

$$P = M(V/Y)$$

where (V/Y) is independent of M. So a change in M brings a proportional change in P.

We can also express the equation of exchange in growth rates,[1] in which form it states that:

$$\text{Money growth rate} + \text{Rate of velocity change} = \text{Inflation rate} + \text{Real GDP growth rate}$$

Solving this equation for the inflation rate gives:

$$\text{Inflation rate} = \text{Money growth rate} + \text{Rate of velocity change} - \text{Real GDP growth rate}$$

ECONOMICS IN ACTION

Does the Quantity Theory Work?

On average, as predicted by the quantity theory of money, the inflation rate fluctuates in line with fluctuations in the money growth rate plus the velocity growth rate minus the real GDP growth rate. Figure 1 shows the relationship between money growth (M4 definition) and inflation in the UK. You can see a clear relationship between the two variables.

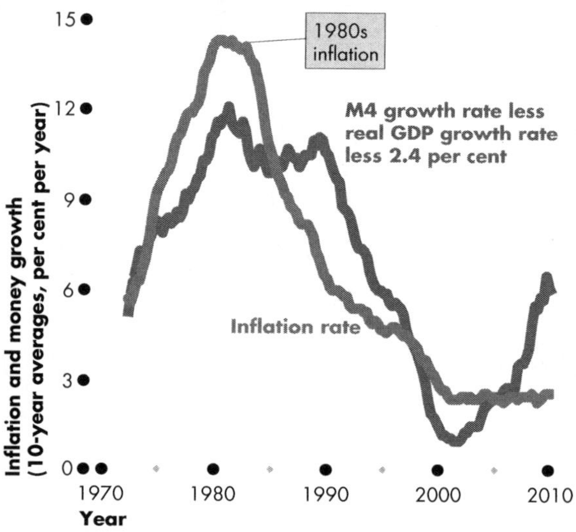

Figure 1 UK Money Growth and Inflation

Source of data: Bank of England.

In the long run, the rate of velocity change is not influenced by the money growth rate. More strongly, in the long run, the rate of velocity change is approximately zero. With this assumption, the inflation rate in the long run is determined as

---

[1] To obtain this equation, begin with

$$MV = PY$$

and then changes in these variables are related by the equation

$$\Delta MV + M\Delta V = \Delta PY + P\Delta Y$$

Divide this equation by the equation of exchange to obtain

$$\Delta M/M + \Delta V/V = \Delta P/P + \Delta Y/Y$$

The term $\Delta M/M$ is the money growth rate, $\Delta V/V$ is the rate of velocity change, $\Delta P/P$ is the inflation rate and $\Delta Y/Y$ is the real GDP growth rate.

Over the period since 1973, velocity has steadily decreased at an average annual rate of 2.5 per cent and we have subtracted that constant from the growth rate of M4 minus the growth rate of real GDP. These data are 10-year averages to reflect the long-run nature of the quantity theory.

International data also support the quantity theory. Figure 2 shows a scatter diagram of the inflation rate and the money growth rate in 134 countries and Figure 3 shows the inflation rate and money growth rate in countries with inflation rates below 20 per cent a year. You can see a general tendency for money growth and inflation to be correlated, but the quantity theory (the red line) does not predict inflation precisely.

The correlation between money growth and inflation isn't perfect, and the correlation does *not* tell us that money growth *causes* inflation.

Money growth might cause inflation; inflation might cause money growth; or some third variable might cause both inflation and money growth. Other evidence does confirm, though, that *causation runs from money growth to inflation.*

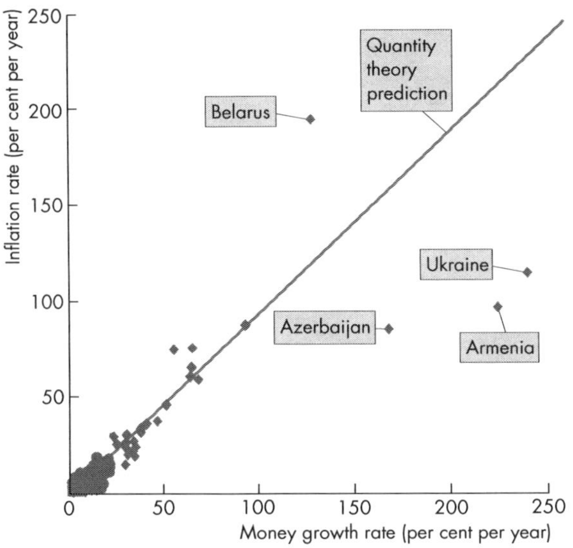

Figure 2 134 Countries: 1990–2005

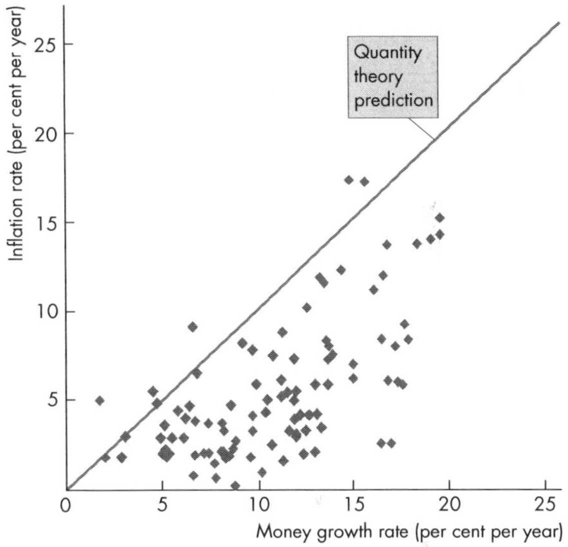

Figure 3 Lower-inflation Countries: 1990–2005

Sources of data: International Financial Statistics Yearbook, 2008 and International Monetary Fund, World Economic Outlook, October, 2008.

$$\text{Inflation rate} = \text{Money growth rate} - \text{Real GDP growth rate}$$

In the long run, fluctuations in the money growth rate minus the real GDP growth rate bring equal fluctuations in the inflation rate.

Also, in the long run, with the economy at full employment, real GDP equals potential GDP, so the real GDP growth rate equals the potential GDP growth rate. This growth rate might be influenced by inflation, but the influence is most likely small and the quantity theory assumes that it is zero. So the real GDP growth rate is given and doesn't change when the money growth rate changes – inflation is correlated with money growth.

Review Quiz

1. What is the quantity theory of money?
2. How is the velocity of circulation calculated?
3. What is the equation of exchange?
4. Does the quantity theory accurately predict the effects of money growth on inflation?

You can work these questions in Study Plan 24.6 and get instant feedback. myeconlab

You now know what money is, how the banks create it and how the quantity of money influences the nominal interest rate in the short run and the price level in the long run. *Reading Between the Lines* on pp. 576–577 looks at the actions taken by the ECB to increase the quantity of money and lower interest rates.

Reading Between the Lines

ECB Conducts Expansionary Monetary Policy

The Financial Times, 8 November 2010

ECB Forced to Act as Crisis Fears Rise

Ralph Atkins, David Oakley and Peter Wise

The European Central Bank has been forced to intervene in government bond markets for the first time in almost a month, as financial markets fret that the escalating Eurozone crisis is moving into a new and more dangerous phase.

The ECB said it spent €711m buying government debt last week, [but that] almost certainly understated significantly the scale of its actions. . . .

Bond yields in the so called Eurozone 'peripheral' economies rose to record levels on Monday. . . .

Irish 10-year bond yields rose to 7.75 per cent, the highest since the launch of the euro, while Portuguese yields increased to 6.67 per cent, close to a level the government has indicated as being the limit of what Lisbon can sustain.

Its latest intervention pointed to mounting ECB concern, but last week's bond purchases were still small in comparison with the €64bn spent since May. . . .

The ECB has so far refused to embark on asset purchases on the scale seen at the US Federal Reserve, which last week announced it was pumping $600bn into the financial system. Jean Claude Trichet, [ECB] president, has said the ECB programme was aimed simply at ensuring the correct functioning of markets.

Axel Weber, Germany's Bundesbank president, has voiced public opposition to even the current programme, which he fears is creating inflation risks. Last month, Mr Weber called for the programme to be phased out. . . .

The Essence of the Story

- The ECB conducted a €711 million open market purchase of government bonds in the first week of November 2010.
- The move was prompted by a sharp rise in the interest rate on Ireland's and Portugal's government bonds arising from concerns that these countries might default on their debt.
- The ECB has injected €64 billion of monetary base during 2010 and the German central bank warned that the increase in the quantity of money brought the risk of a rise in the inflation rate.
- The ECB bond purchases are much smaller than those of the US Federal Reserve.

Economic Analysis

- The ECB conducted a €711million open market purchase of government bonds in the first week of November 2010.
- As Figure 1 shows, this purchase was tiny compared with the €65 billion accumulated purchases of bonds since May 2010.
- Bond purchases are open market operations that increase the monetary base. Bond sales decrease the monetary base.
- From May to November 2010, the Eurozone monetary base increased by €27 billion, an increase of 3.5 per cent.
- During the same seven months, the Eurozone quantity of M3 money increased by €146 billion, an increase of 1.6 per cent.
- Figure 2 shows the *changes* in the monetary base and M3 from May to November 2010. The €27 billion increase in the monetary base brought a €146 billion increase in M3 money: a money multiplier of 5.4.
- In 2010, the *level* of M3 was €9,452 billion and the *level* of the monetary base was €786 billion: a money multiplier of 12.
- The multiplier effect of a *change* in the monetary base was smaller than the ratio of the *level* of M3 to the monetary base because the banks desired reserve ratios increased.
- Figure 3 shows that the Eurozone M3 multiplier fell from 12.2 in April to less than 12 in November.
- Banks have a larger desired reserve ratio because the global financial crisis made them less willing to lend to each other.
- As long as the banks hold the additional monetary base as reserves, the inflation risk noted by the German central bank is small.
- If inflation does appear on the horizon, the ECB can sell bonds and decrease the monetary base to prevent the quantity of M3 from growing too quickly.

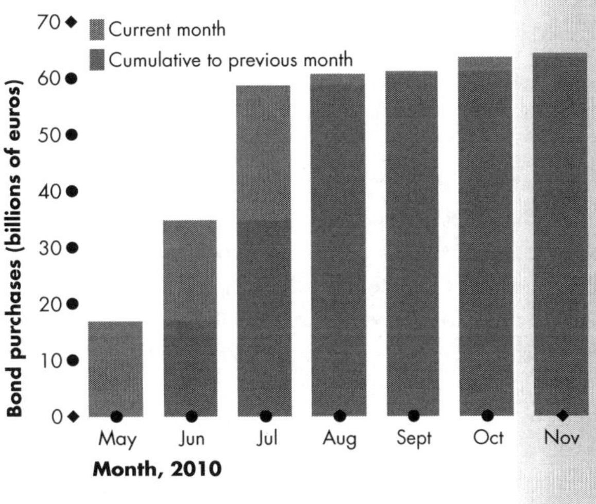

Figure 1 ECB bond purchases in 2010: May to November

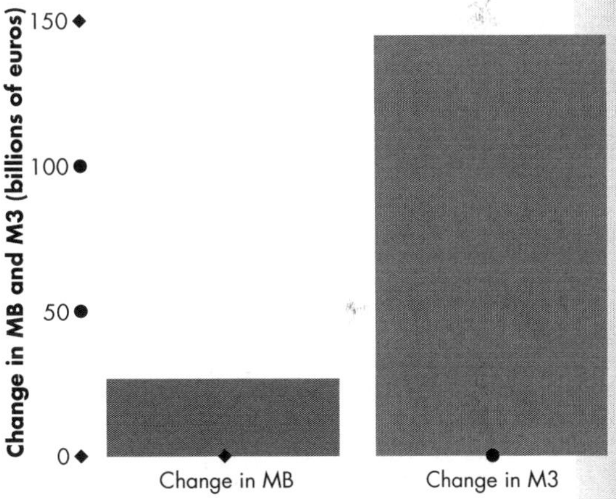

Figure 2 Changes in monetary base and M3: May to November 2010

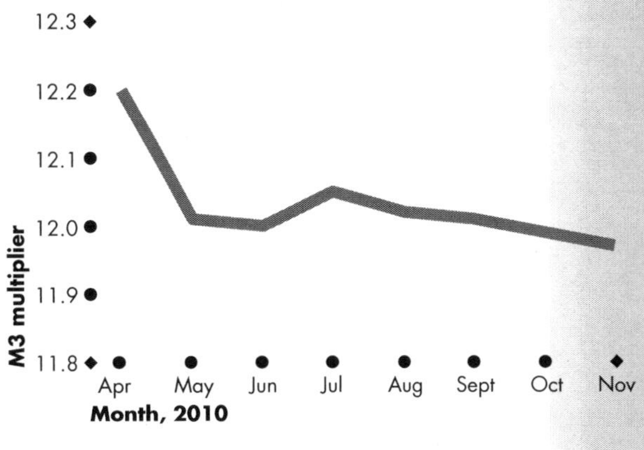

Figure 3 The M3 money multiplier in 2010

MATHEMATICAL NOTE

The Money Multiplier

This note explains the basic maths of the money multiplier and shows how the value of the multiplier depends on the banks' desired reserve ratio and the currency drain ratio.

To make the process of money creation concrete, we work through an example for a banking system in which each bank has a desired reserve ratio of 10 per cent of deposits and the currency drain ratio is 50 per cent of deposits. (Although these ratios are larger than the ones in the UK economy, they make the process end more quickly and enable you to see more clearly the principles at work.)

Figure 1 keeps track of the numbers. Before the process begins, all the banks have no excess reserves. Then the monetary base increases by £100,000 and one bank has excess reserves of this amount.

The bank lends the £100,000 of excess reserves. When this loan is made, new money increases by £100,000.

Some of the new money will be held as currency and some as deposits. With a currency drain ratio of 50 per cent of deposits, one-third of the new money will be held as currency and two-thirds will be held as deposits. That is, £33,333 drains out of the banks as currency and £66,667 remains in the banks as deposits. The increase in the quantity of money of £100,000 equals the increase in deposits plus the increase in currency holdings.

The increased bank deposits of £66,667 generate an increase in desired reserves of 10 per cent of that amount, which is £6,667. Actual reserves have increased by the same amount as the increase in deposits: £66,667. So the banks now have excess reserves of £60,000.

The process we've just described repeats but begins with excess reserves of £60,000. The figure shows the next two rounds. At the end of the process, the quantity of money has increased by a multiple of the increase in the monetary base. In this case, the increase is £250,000, which is 2.5 times the increase in the monetary base.

The sequence in the figure shows the first stages of the process that finally reaches the total shown in the final row of the 'money' column.

To calculate what happens at the later stages in the process and the final increase in the quantity of money,

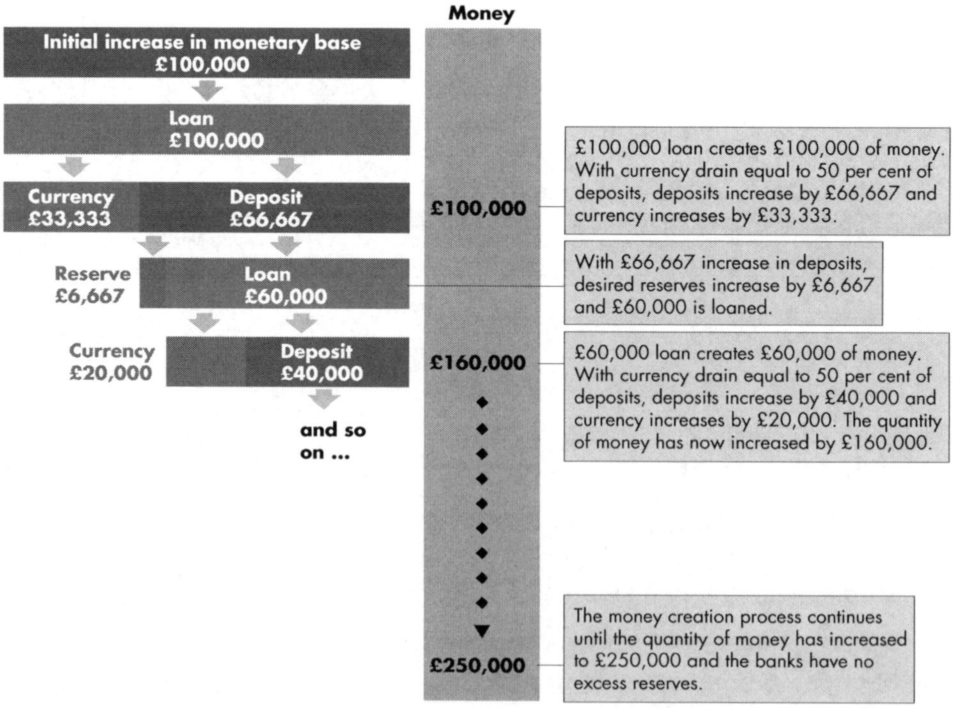

Figure 1 The money creation process

look closely at the numbers in the figure. The initial increase in reserves is £100,000 (call it A). At each stage, the loan is 60 per cent (0.6) of the previous loan and the quantity of money increases by 0.6 of the previous increase. Call that proportion L ($L = 0.6$). We can write down the complete sequence for the increase in the quantity of money as:

$$A + AL + AL^2 + AL^3 + AL^4 + AL^5 + \ldots$$

Remember, L is a fraction, so at each stage in this sequence, the amount of new loans and new money gets smaller. The total value of loans made and money created at the end of the process is the sum of the sequence,[1] which is:

$$A/(1 - L)$$

If we use the numbers from the example, the total increase in the quantity of money is:

$$£100{,}000 + 60{,}000 + 36{,}000 + \ldots$$

$$= £100{,}000\ (1 + 0.6 + 0.36 + \ldots)$$

$$= £100{,}000\ (1 + 0.6 + 0.6^2 + \ldots)$$

$$= £100{,}000 \times 1/(1 - 0.6)$$

$$= £100{,}000 \times 1/(0.4)$$

$$= £100{,}000 \times 2.5$$

$$= £250{,}000$$

The magnitude of the money multiplier depends on the banks' desired reserve ratio and the currency drain ratio. Let's explore this relationship.

The money multiplier is the ratio of money to the monetary base. Call the money multiplier *mm*, the quantity of money M, and the monetary base MB. Then:

$$mm = M/MB$$

Next recall that money, M, is the sum of deposits and currency. Call deposits D and currency C. Then:

$$M = D + C$$

Finally, recall that the monetary base, MB, is the sum of banks' reserves and currency. Call banks' reserves R. Then:

$$MB = R + C$$

Use the equations for M and MB in the *mm* equation to give:

$$mm = M/MB = (D + C)/(R + C)$$

Now divide all the variables on the right-hand side of the equation by D to give:

$$mm = M/MB = (1 + C/D)/(R/D + C/D)$$

In this equation, C/D is the *currency drain ratio* and R/D is the banks' reserve ratio. If we use the values of the example on the previous page, $C/D = 0.5$ and $R/D = 0.1$, and:

$$mm = (1 + 0.5)/(0.1 + 0.5)$$

$$= 1.5/0.6 = 2.5$$

The UK Money Multiplier

The money multiplier in the UK can be found by using the formula above along with the values of C/D and R/D in the UK economy.

Using the M4 definition of money to measure deposits, D, the numbers for December 2010 are:

$$C = £50 \text{ billion}$$

$$R = £150 \text{ billion}$$

$$MB = £200 \text{ billion}$$

$$D = £2{,}150 \text{ billion}$$

$$C/D = 0.023$$

$$R/D = 0.070$$

So

$$mm = (1 + 0.023)/(0.023 + 0.070) = 11$$

[1] The sequence of values is called a convergent geometric series. To find the sum of a series such as this, begin by calling the sum S. Then write the sum as

$$S = A + AL + AL^2 + AL^3 + AL^4 + AL^5 + \ldots$$

Multiply by L to get

$$LS = AL + AL^2 + AL^3 + AL^4 + AL^5 + AL^6 + \ldots$$

and then subtract the second equation from the first to get

$$S(1 - L) = A$$

or

$$S = A/(1 - L)$$

SUMMARY

Key Points

What is Money?

- Money is the means of payment and it functions as a medium of exchange, unit of account and store of value.
- M4 – currency held by the public and bank and building society deposits – is the main measure of money in the UK today.

Working Problems 1 to 4 will give you a better understanding of what money is.

Monetary Financial Institutions

- Commercial banks and building societies are monetary financial institutions: their liabilities are money.
- Monetary financial institutions create liquidity, minimize the cost of borrowing, minimize the cost of monitoring borrowers and pool risk.

Working Problems 5 and 6 will give you a better understanding of monetary financial institutions.

Central Banking

- A central bank is a public authority that provides banking services to banks and governments and manages the nation's financial system.
- The liabilities of the central bank are bank notes and bank reserves. These items plus coins are the monetary base.

Working Problems 7 to 9 will give you a better understanding of central banks.

How Banks Create Money

- Banks create money by making loans.
- The total quantity of money that can be created is limited by the monetary base, the banks' desired reserve ratio and the currency drain ratio.

Working Problems 10 to 14 will give you a better understanding of how banks create money.

The Money Market

- The quantity of money demanded is the amount of money that people plan to hold.
- The quantity of real money equals the quantity of nominal money divided by the price level.
- The quantity of real money demanded depends on the nominal interest rate, real GDP and financial innovation.
- The nominal interest rate makes the quantity of money demanded equal the quantity supplied.
- When the quantity of money increases, the nominal interest rate falls (the short-run effect).
- In the long run, when the quantity of money increases, the price level rises and the nominal interest rate returns to its initial level.

Working Problems 15 and 16 will give you a better understanding of the money market.

The Quantity Theory of Money

- The quantity theory of money is the proposition that money growth and inflation move up and down together in the long run.

Working Problem 17 will give you a better understanding of the quantity theory of money.

Key Terms

Bank of England
Bank Rate
Currency
Currency drain ratio
Demand for money
Desired reserve ratio
European Central Bank (ECB)
Excess reserves
Lender of last resort
M4
Means of payment
Monetary base
Monetary financial institution
Monetary Policy Committee (MPC)
Money
Money multiplier
Open market operation
Quantitative easing
Quantity theory of money
Repo
Required reserve ratio
Reserves
Velocity of circulation

STUDY PLAN PROBLEMS AND APPLICATIONS

myeconlab You can work Problems 1 to 19 in MyEconLab Chapter 24 Study Plan and get instant feedback.

What is Money? (Study Plan 24.1)

1 In the UK today, money includes which of the following items?

- **a** Bank of England bank notes in Barclay's cash machines
- **b** Your bank debit card
- **c** Coins inside a vending machine
- **d** A £10 bank note in your wallet
- **e** The cheque you've just written to pay for your rent
- **f** The loan you took out last August to pay for your university fees

2 Suppose that in June, currency held by individuals and businesses was £400 billion; sight deposits were £4,800 billion; time deposits were £2,000 billion; M4 was £9,000 billion. What is the other item that makes up M4 and what is its value?

3 Suppose that in July, the public held £1,500 billion in currency, £5,000 billion in bank deposits and £7,000 billion in building societies. Banks held £10,000 billion in currency and building societies held £2,000 billion in currency. Calculate M4.

4 **One More Thing Cell Phones Could Do: Replace Wallets**

Soon you'll be able to pull out your cell phone and wave it over a scanner to make a payment. The convenience of whipping out your phone as a payment mechanism is driving the transition.

Source: *USA Today*, 21 November 2007

If people can use their cell phones to make payments, will currency disappear? How will the components of M4 change?

Monetary Financial Institutions

(Study Plan 24.2)

Use the following news clip to work Problems 5 and 6.

Basel Committee Unveils Bank Capital Buffer Plan

Regulators want banks to hold a 'counter-cyclical capital buffer' – a required capital ratio that fluctuates with the state of the economy. The idea is to strengthen the global banking industry by putting the brakes on lending when a bubble emerges and provide a cushion to protect the banks from falling into financial difficulty.

Source: *Financial Times*, 17 July 2010

5 Explain a bank's 'balancing act' and how the required capital ratio makes bank failure less likely.

6 During the time of an emerging credit bubble, why might it be beneficial for the banks to be required to have a larger capital ratio?

Central Banking (Study Plan 24.3)

7 Suppose that at the end of December 2009, the monetary base was €700 billion, euro bank notes were €650 billion, and banks' reserves at the ECB were €20 billion. Calculate the quantity of coins.

8 **Fast Growth in 'Broad' Money**

The Bank of England's quantitative easing programme may be having an increasing effect. Holdings of M4 'broad' money were up from 6.2 per cent in the three months to April. The Bank of England pumped £200bn in newly created cash into the economy between February 2009 and early 2010.

Source: *Financial Times*, 30 June 2010

What are the Bank of England's policy tools and which policy tool did it use when it 'pumped £200bn in newly created cash into the economy'?

9 The Bank of England sells £20 million of securities to HSBC. Enter the transactions that take place to show the changes in the following balance sheets.

Bank of England

Assets (millions)	Liabilities (millions)

HSBC

Assets (millions)	Liabilities (millions)

How Banks Create Money (Study Plan 24.4)

10 The commercial banks in Zap have

Reserves €250 million

Loans €1,000 million

Deposits €2,000 million

Total assets €2,500 million

If the banks hold no excess reserves, calculate their desired reserve ratio.

Use the following information to work Problems 11 and 12.

In the economy of Nocoin, banks have deposits of €300 billion. Their reserves are €15 billion, two-thirds of which is in deposits with the central bank. Households and businesses hold €30 billion in bank notes. There are no coins!

11 Calculate the monetary base and the quantity of money.

12 Calculate the banks' desired reserve ratio and the currency drain ratio (as percentages).

Use the following news clip to work Problems 13 and 14.

Banks Drop on Higher Reserve Requirement

China's central bank will raise its reserve ratio requirement by a percentage point to a record 17.5 per cent, stepping up a battle to contain lending growth. Banks' ratio of excess reserves to deposits was 2 per cent. Every half-point increase in the required reserve ratio cuts banks' profits by 1.5 per cent.

Source: *People's Daily Online*, 11 June 2008

13 Explain how increasing the required reserve ratio influences the banks' money creation process.

14 Why might a higher required reserve ratio decrease bank profits?

The Money Market (Study Plan 24.5)

15 The spreadsheet provides information about the demand for and supply of money in Minland. Column A is the nominal interest rate, *r*. Columns B and C show the quantity of money demanded at two different levels of real GDP: Y_0 is £10 billion and Y_1 is £20 billion. The quantity of money supplied is £3 billion. Initially, real GDP is £20 billion. What happens in Minland if the interest rate:

	A	B	C
1	r	Y_0	Y_1
2	7	1.0	1.5
3	6	1.5	2.0
4	5	2.0	2.5
5	4	2.5	3.0
6	3	3.0	3.5
7	2	3.5	4.0
8	1	4.0	4.5

a Exceeds 4 per cent a year.

b Is less than 4 per cent a year.

16 The figure shows the demand for money curve.

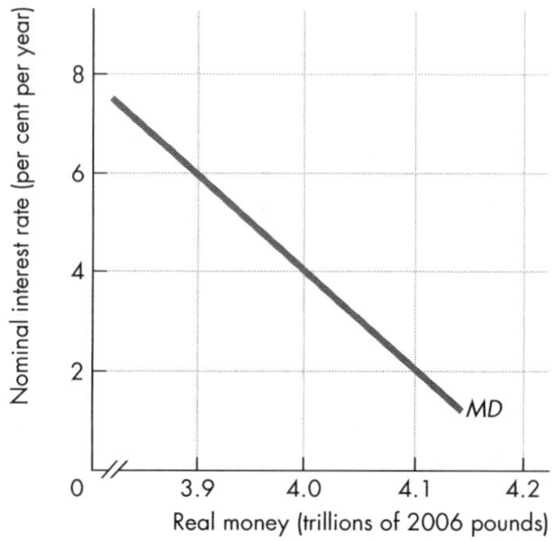

If the central bank decreases the quantity of real money supplied from £4 trillion to £3.9 trillion, explain how the price of a bond will change.

The Quantity Theory of Money (Study Plan 24.6)

17 Quantecon is a country in which the quantity theory of money operates. In year 1, the economy is at full employment and real GDP is £400 million, the price level is 200, and the velocity of circulation is 20. In year 2, the quantity of money increases by 20 per cent. Calculate the quantity of money, the price level, real GDP, and the velocity of circulation in year 2.

Mathematical Note (Study Plan 24.MN)

18 In Problem 11, the banks have no excess reserves. Suppose that the Bank of Nocoin, the central bank, increases bank reserves by €0.5 billion.

a What happens to the quantity of money?

b Explain why the change in the quantity of money is not equal to the change in the monetary base.

c Calculate the money multiplier.

19 In Problem 11, the banks have no excess reserves. Suppose that the Bank of Nocoin, the central bank, decreases bank reserves by €0.5 billion.

a Calculate the money multiplier.

b What happens to the quantity of money, deposits and currency?

ADDITIONAL PROBLEMS AND APPLICATIONS

myeconlab You can work these problems in MyEconLab if assigned by your lecturer.

What is Money?

20 Sara withdraws £1,000 from her savings account at the Lucky Building Society, keeps £50 in cash, and deposits the balance in her chequing account at HSBC. What is the immediate change in currency and in M4?

21 Rapid inflation in Brazil in the early 1990s caused the cruzeiro to lose its ability to function as money. Which of the following commodities would most likely have taken the place of the cruzeiro in the Brazilian economy? Explain why.

a Tractor parts

b Packs of cigarettes

c Loaves of bread

d Impressionist paintings

22 **From Paper-Clip to House, in 14 Trades**

A 26-year-old Montreal man appears to have succeeded in his quest to barter a single, red paperclip all the way up to a house. It took almost a year and 14 trades.

Source: CBC News, 7 July 2006

Is barter a means of payment? Is it just as efficient as money when trading on e-Bay? Explain.

Monetary Financial Institutions

Use the following news clip to work Problems 23 and 24.

The War on Moral Hazard Begins at Home

Northern Rock was a narrow bank, with only retail customers, and Northern Rock failed; Lehman Brothers was a pure investment bank, but Lehman too failed. The issues in financial reform are to do with the behaviour of businesses, not the structure of their industry. Wrong. The point of structural reform of the banking system is not to prevent banks from failing. It is to allow them to fail without imposing large costs on taxpayers, their customers and the global economy.

Source: *Financial Times*, 26 January 2011

23 Explain why attempts by banks to maximize profits can sometimes lead to bank failures.

24 Explain the effects of higher required capital ratios, higher required reserve ratios and restrictions on the types of investments banks are permitted to make. What types of structural reforms might allow banks to fail without imposing large costs on taxpayers and bank customers?

Central Banking

25 Explain the distinction between a central bank and a commercial bank.

26 If the Bank of England makes an open market sale of £1 million of securities to a bank, what initial changes occur in the economy?

27 Set out the transactions that the Bank of England undertakes to increase the quantity of money.

28 Describe the Bank of England's assets and liabilities. What is the monetary base and how does it relate to the Bank of England's balance sheet?

29 **Eurozone Banks Reluctant to Return ECB's Funds**

The European Central Bank (ECB) injected €73.5 billion into the region's banks to combat the Irish debt crisis by buying government bonds. The banks are reluctant to return these funds and offered the ECB just over €60 billion. They want to keep the extra liquidity.

Source: *Financial Times*, 29 December 2010

What is the rationale behind the ECB injecting funds into the region's banks and why might the banks be reluctant to repay the funds?

How Banks Create Money

30 Banks in New Transylvania have a desired reserve ratio of 10 per cent and no excess reserves. The currency drain ratio is 50 per cent. Then the central bank increases the monetary base by €1,200 billion.

a How much do the banks lend in the first round of the money creation process?

b How much of the initial amount lent flows back to the banking system as new deposits?

c How much of the initial amount lent does not return to the banks but is held as currency?

d Why does a second round of lending occur?

The Money Market

31 Explain the change in the nominal interest rate in the short run if

a Real GDP increases.

b The money supply increases.

c The price level rises.

32 In Minland in Problem 15, the interest rate is 4 per cent a year. Suppose that real GDP decreases to $10 billion and the quantity of money supplied remains unchanged. Do people buy bonds or sell bonds? Explain how the interest rate changes.

The Quantity Theory of Money

33 The table provides some data for the US in the first decade following the Civil War.

Item	1869	1879
Quantity of money	$1.3 billion	$1.7 billion
Real GDP (1929 dollars)	$7.4 billion	*Z*
Price level (1929 = 100)	*X*	54
Velocity of circulation	4.50	4.61

Source of data: Milton Friedman and Anna J. Schwartz, *A Monetary History of the United States 1867–1960*

a Calculate the value of X in 1869.

b Calculate the value of Z in 1879.

c Are the data consistent with the quantity theory of money? Explain your answer.

Mathematical Note

34 In the UK, the currency drain ratio is 0.38 of deposits and the reserve ratio is 0.002. In Australia, the quantity of money is $150 billion, the currency drain ratio is 33 per cent of deposits, and the reserve ratio is 8 per cent.

a Calculate the UK money multiplier.

b Calculate the monetary base in Australia.

Economics in the News

35 After you have studied *Reading Between the Lines* on pp. 576–577 answer the following questions.

a By how much did the monetary base of the Eurozone increase between May 2010 and November 2010?

b How did the ECB increase the monetary base?

c How did the increase in the monetary base increase M3?

d Was the percentage increase in the money base the same as that predicted by the money multiplier?

e Why did M3 not grow by a larger percentage than the monetary base?

f If when the monetary base increased, the banks had not increased their excess reserves, what does the quantity theory predict would have happened to the inflation rate?

36 **US Federal Reserve at Odds with ECB over Value of Policy Tool**

Many central banks use monetary aggregates as a guide to policy decision, but Bernanke believes US reliance on monetary aggregates would be unwise because the empirical relationship between US money growth, inflation and output growth is unstable. Bernanke said that the Federal Reserve had 'philosophical' and economic differences with the European Central Bank and the Bank of England regarding the role of money and that debate between institutions is healthy. 'Unfortunately, forecast errors for money growth are often significant', reducing their effectiveness as a tool for policy, Bernanke said. 'There are differences between the US and Europe in terms of the stability of money demand', Bernanke said. Ultimately, the risk of bad policy arising from a devoted following of money growth led the Federal Reserve to downgrade the importance of money measures.

Source: *International Herald Tribune*, 10 November 2006

a Explain how the debate surrounding the quantity theory of money could make monetary aggregates a less useful tool for policy makers.

b What do Bernanke's statements reveal about his stance on the accuracy of the quantity theory of money?

CHAPTER 25

International Finance

After studying this chapter you will be able to:

- Describe the foreign exchange market
- Explain the fluctuations in the exchange rate
- Describe the alternative exchange rate regimes
- Explain the benefits and costs of the euro
- Describe the balance of payments accounts and explain what causes international deficits and surpluses

The pound, the euro, the yen and the US dollar are the world's four most widely used currencies. The prices of these currencies fluctuate every day. Why? Why don't they have stable prices? What causes the value of currencies to rise and fall?

Many famous British companies have been bought by foreigners: Rover by BMW (German); MG by Nanjing Automobiles (China); Cadbury by Kraft (US). Why? What makes it possible for people to buy assets and businesses in other countries?

In *Reading Between the Lines* at the end of the chapter, you will see how some countries manipulate their currencies in an attempt to boost exports.

The Foreign Exchange Market

When Tesco imports DVD players from Japan, it pays for them using Japanese yen. And when China Airlines buys aircraft engines from Rolls Royce, it pays using pounds sterling. Whenever people buy things from another country, they use the currency of that country to make the transaction. It doesn't make any difference what the item is that is being traded internationally. It might be a DVD player, a jet engine, insurance or banking services, property, the stocks and bonds of a government or corporation, or even an entire business.

Foreign Currencies

Foreign money is just like money in the UK. It consists of notes and coins issued by a central bank and mint and deposits in banks and other monetary financial institutions. When we described UK and EU money in Chapter 24, we distinguished between currency (notes and coins) and deposits. But when we talk about foreign money, we refer to it as foreign currency. **Foreign currency** is the money of other countries regardless of whether that money is in the form of notes, coins, or bank deposits.

UK pounds are called *pounds sterling*. We buy foreign currencies in exchange for pounds sterling and foreigners buy pounds sterling in exchange for their own currencies in the foreign exchange market.

Trading Currencies

The currency of one country is exchanged for the currency of another in the **foreign exchange market**. The foreign exchange market consists of thousands of buyers and sellers. Some of these people are importers and exporters of goods and services; some are banks and other financial institutions; and some are specialist traders called *foreign exchange brokers*.

The foreign exchange market opens on Monday morning in Hong Kong. As the day advances, the foreign exchange markets in Singapore, Tokyo, Bahrain, Frankfurt, London, New York, Chicago and San Francisco open for trade. As the US West Coast markets close, Hong Kong is only an hour away from opening for the next day of business. The sun barely sets on the foreign exchange market. Dealers around the world are continually in contact by telephone and on a typical day in 2010, around $3 trillion (of all currencies) were traded in the foreign exchange market – or more than $600 trillion in a year.

Exchange Rates

An **exchange rate** is the price at which one currency exchanges for another currency in the foreign exchange market. For example, on 4 January 2011, £1 would buy 1.56 US dollars, 127 Japanese yen or 1.17 euros. So the exchange rate was 1.56 dollars per pound, or equivalently, 127 yen and 117 euro cents per pound.

The exchange rate fluctuates. Sometimes it rises and sometimes it falls. A rise in the exchange rate is called an *appreciation* of the pound, and a fall in the exchange rate is called a *depreciation* of the pound. For example, when the exchange rate rises from 1.60 dollars to 2.00 dollars per pound, the pound appreciates, and when the exchange rate falls from 2.00 dollars to 1.50 dollars per pound, the pound depreciates.

Economics in Action on the next page shows the fluctuations in the pound sterling against three currencies since 2000. Two important questions arise from an examination of the movements of the exchange rate. First, how is the exchange rate determined? Second, how do exchange rate fluctuations influence our international trade and international payments? We begin by learning how trading in the foreign exchange market determines the exchange rate.

An Exchange Rate is a Price

An exchange rate is a price and like all prices an exchange rate is determined in a market – the *foreign exchange market*.

The pound sterling trades in the foreign exchange market and is supplied and demanded by tens of thousands of traders every hour of every business day.

Because it has many traders and no restrictions on who may trade, the foreign exchange market is a *competitive market*.

In a competitive market, demand and supply determine the price. So to understand the forces that determine the exchange rate, we need to study the factors that influence demand and supply in the foreign exchange market. But there is a feature of the foreign exchange market that makes it special.

The Demand for One Money Is the Supply of Another Money

When people who are holding the money of some other country want to exchange it for pounds sterling, they demand pounds sterling and supply that other country's money. And when people who are holding pounds

ECONOMICS IN ACTION

The Pound Sterling Against the Euro, the Dollar and the Yen

The figure shows the pound sterling exchange rate against the three big currencies – the euro, the US dollar and the Japanese yen – since January 2000.

Against the euro, the pound has been on a one-way track – downward. In January 2000, you would have needed €1.60 to buy £1.00. In December 2010, €1.15 would buy £1.00. The fall has come in three stages: a drop of about 20 euro cents in 2003, a drop of another 20 euro cents in 2007 and the first quarter of 2008 and another drop of 10 euro cents in the last quarter of 2008.

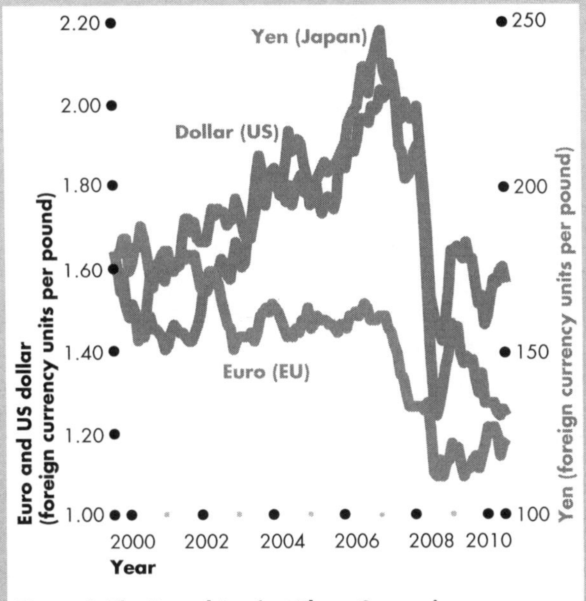

Figure 1 The Pound Against Three Currencies

Against the US dollar and the yen, the pound has moved in both directions. From January 2000 to 2007, the pound appreciated. It rose from $1.60 to more than $2.00 and from ¥180 to ¥240.

But through the global financial crisis and the following recession, the pound crashed against these two big currencies.

The fall was most spectacular against the yen – a *depreciation* of almost 50 per cent from ¥247 per pound to ¥130 per pound.

The fall against the US dollar was from $2.02 down to $1.56 per pound, a depreciation of 23 per cent – about the same as the appreciation from 2000 to 2007.

Notice that the exchange rates display high-frequency fluctuations (rapid brief up and down movements) around the broad trends that we've just described.

sterling want to exchange them for the money of some other country, they supply pounds sterling and demand that other country's money.

So the factors that influence the demand for pounds sterling also influence the supply of US dollars, or EU euros, or Japanese yen. And the factors that influence the demand for that other country's money also influence the supply of pounds sterling.

We'll first look at the influences on the demand for pounds sterling in the foreign exchange market.

Demand in the Foreign Exchange Market

People buy pounds sterling in the foreign exchange market so that they can buy UK-produced goods and services – UK exports. They also buy pounds sterling so that they can buy UK assets such as bonds, stocks, businesses and property or so that they can keep part of their money holding in a UK bank account.

The quantity of pounds demanded in the foreign exchange market is the amount that traders plan to buy during a given time period at a given exchange rate. This quantity depends on many factors, but the main ones are:

1 The exchange rate
2 World demand for UK exports
3 Interest rates in the UK and other countries
4 The expected future exchange rate

We look first at the relationship between the quantity of pounds sterling demanded in the foreign exchange market and the exchange rate when the other three influences remain the same.

The Law of Demand for Foreign Exchange

The law of demand applies to pounds sterling just as it does to anything else that people value. Other things remaining the same, the higher the exchange rate, the smaller is the quantity of pounds demanded in the foreign exchange market. The exchange rate influences the quantity of pounds demanded for two reasons:

- Exports effect
- Expected profit effect

Exports Effect

The larger the value of UK exports, the larger is the quantity of pounds demanded in the foreign exchange market. But the value of UK exports depends on the prices of UK-produced goods and services *expressed in the currency of the foreign buyer*. And these prices depend on the exchange rate. The lower the exchange rate, other things remaining the same, the lower are the prices of UK-produced goods and services to foreigners and the greater is the volume of UK exports. So if the exchange rate falls (and other influences remain the same), the quantity of pounds demanded in the foreign exchange market increases.

To see the exports effect at work, think about orders for the Rolls Royce Ardour turbine engine by the US navy. If the price of an engine is £300,000 and the exchange rate is $2.00 per pound, the price of the engine to the US Navy is $600,000. The navy decides that this price is too high. But if the exchange rate falls to $1.50 per pound and other things remain the same, the price of an engine falls to $450,000. The US Navy now decides to buy the engine and buys pounds in the foreign exchange market to pay for it.

Expected Profit Effect

The larger the expected profit from holding pounds, the greater is the quantity of pounds demanded in the foreign exchange market. But expected profit depends on the exchange rate. For a given expected future exchange rate, the lower the exchange rate today, the larger is the expected profit from buying pounds today and holding them, so the greater is the quantity of pounds demanded in the foreign exchange market today. Let's look at an example. Suppose that the Bank of New York Mellon expects the exchange rate to be $1.50 per pound at the end of the year. If today's exchange rate is also $1.50 per pound, BNY Mellon expects no profit from buying pounds sterling and holding them until the end of the year. But if today's exchange rate is $1.40 per pound and BNY Mellon buys pounds, it expects to sell those pounds at the end of the year for $1.50 per pound and make a profit of 10 cents per pound sterling.

The lower the exchange rate today, other things remaining the same, the greater is the expected profit from holding pounds and the greater is the quantity of pounds sterling demanded in the foreign exchange market today.

Demand Curve for Pounds Sterling

Figure 25.1 shows the demand curve for pounds sterling in the foreign exchange market. A change in the exchange rate, other things remaining the same, brings a change in the quantity of pounds demanded and a movement along the demand curve. The arrows show such movements.

We will look at the factors that change demand in the next section of this chapter. Before doing that, let's see what determines the supply of pounds.

Figure 25.1 The Demand for Pounds

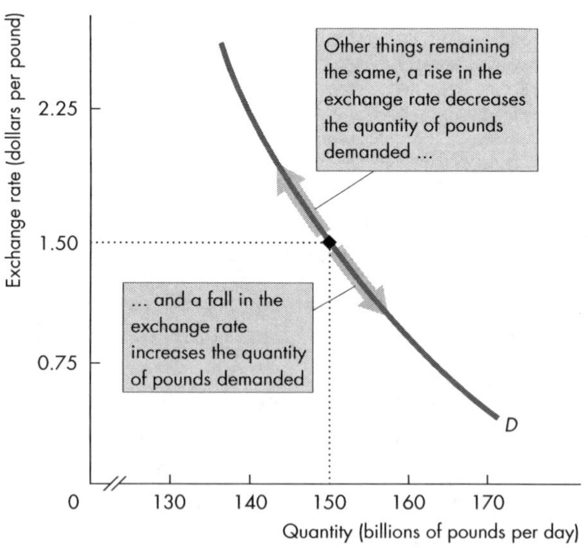

The quantity of pounds that people plan to buy depends on the exchange rate. Other things remaining the same, if the exchange rate rises, the quantity of pounds demanded decreases and there is a movement up along the demand curve for pounds. If the exchange rate falls, the quantity of pounds demanded increases and there is a movement down along the demand curve for pounds.

myeconlab Animation

Supply in the Foreign Exchange Market

People sell pounds and buy other currencies so that they can buy foreign-produced goods and services – UK imports. People also sell pounds and buy foreign currencies so that they can buy foreign assets such as bonds, stocks, businesses and real estate or so that they can hold part of their money in bank deposits denominated in a foreign currency. The quantity of pounds supplied in the foreign exchange market is the amount that traders plan to sell during a given time period at a given exchange rate. This quantity depends on many factors, but the main ones are:

1 The exchange rate
2 UK demand for imports
3 Interest rates in the UK and other countries
4 The expected future exchange rate

Let's look at the law of supply in the foreign exchange market – the relationship between the quantity of pounds supplied in the foreign exchange market and the exchange rate when the other three influences remain the same.

The Law of Supply of Foreign Exchange

Other things remaining the same, the higher the exchange rate, the greater is the quantity of pounds sterling supplied in the foreign exchange market.

The exchange rate influences the quantity of dollars supplied for two reasons:

- Imports effect
- Expected profit effect

Imports Effect

The larger the value of UK imports, the larger is the quantity of pounds sterling supplied in the foreign exchange market. But the value of UK imports depends on the prices of foreign-produced goods and services *expressed in pounds*. These prices depend on the exchange rate.

The higher the exchange rate, other things remaining the same, the lower are the prices of foreign-produced goods and services to residents in the UK and the greater is the volume of imports. So if the exchange rate rises (and other influences remain the same), the quantity of pounds supplied in the foreign exchange market increases.

Expected Profit Effect

This effect works just like that on the demand for pounds but in the opposite direction. For given expected future exchange rates, the higher the exchange rate of the pound today, other things remaining the same, the larger is the expected profit from selling pounds today and holding foreign currencies, so the greater is the quantity of pounds supplied.

Supply Curve of Pounds Sterling

Figure 25.2 shows the supply curve of pounds in the foreign exchange market. A change in the exchange rate, other things remaining the same, brings a change in the quantity of pounds supplied and a movement along the supply curve. The arrows show such movements.

Next we bring demand and supply together and determine equilibrium in the foreign exchange market.

Figure 25.2 The Supply of Pounds

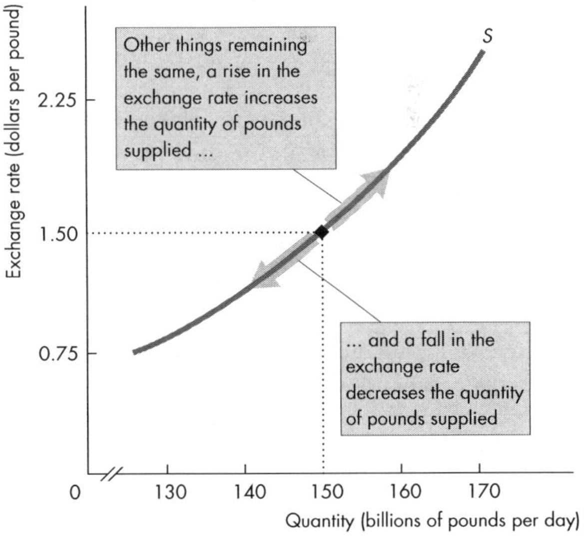

The quantity of pounds that people plan to sell depends on the exchange rate. Other things remaining the same, if the exchange rate rises, the quantity of pounds supplied increases and there is a movement up along the supply curve of pounds. If the exchange rate falls, the quantity of pounds supplied decreases and there is a movement down along the supply curve of pounds.

myeconlab Animation

Market Equilibrium

Equilibrium in the foreign exchange market depends on how the Bank of England, the ECB and other central banks operate. Here, we will study equilibrium when central banks keep out of this market. In a later section (on pp. 596–597), we examine the effects of alternative actions that the Bank of England or another central bank might take in the foreign exchange market.

Figure 25.3 shows the demand curve for pounds, *D*, from Figure 25.1 and the supply curve of pounds, *S*, from Figure 25.2, and the equilibrium exchange rate.

The exchange rate acts as a regulator of the quantities demanded and supplied. If the exchange rate is too high, there is a surplus – the quantity supplied exceeds the quantity demanded. For example, in Figure 25.3, if the exchange rate is $2.25 per pound, there is a surplus of pounds. If the exchange rate is too low, there is a shortage – the quantity supplied is less than the quantity demanded. For example, if the exchange rate is $0.75 per pound, there is a shortage of pounds.

At the equilibrium exchange rate, there is neither a shortage nor a surplus – the quantity supplied equals the quantity demanded. In Figure 25.3, the equilibrium exchange rate is $1.50 per pound. At this exchange rate, the quantity demanded and the quantity supplied are each £150 billion a day.

Figure 25.3 Equilibrium Exchange Rate

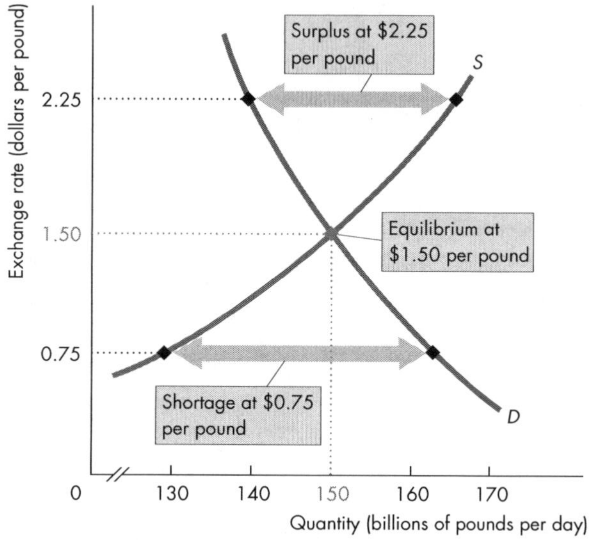

The demand curve for pounds is *D* and the supply curve is *S*. If the exchange rate is $2.25 per pound, there is a surplus of pounds and the exchange rate falls. If the exchange rate is $0.75 per pound, there is a shortage of pounds and the exchange rate rises. If the exchange rate is $1.50 per pound, there is neither a shortage nor a surplus of pounds and the exchange rate remains constant. The market is in equilibrium.

myeconlab Animation

The Powerful Pull of Equilibrium

The foreign exchange market is constantly pulled to its equilibrium by the forces of supply and demand. Foreign exchange traders are constantly looking for the best price they can get. If they are selling, they want the highest price available. If they are buying, they want the lowest price available. Information flows from trader to trader through the worldwide computer network, and the price adjusts minute by minute to keep buying plans and selling plans in balance. That is, the price adjusts minute by minute to keep the exchange rate at its equilibrium. Figure 25.3 shows how the exchange rate between the pound sterling and the US dollar is determined. The exchange rates between the pound and all other currencies are determined in a similar way. So are the exchange rates among the other currencies. But the exchange rates are tied together so that no profit can be made by buying one currency, selling it for a second one, and then buying back the first one. If such a profit were available, traders would spot it, demand and supply would change, and the exchange rates would snap into alignment.

Review Quiz

1. What are the influences on the demand for pounds in the foreign exchange market?
2. Provide an example of the exports effect on the demand for pounds.
3. What are the influences on the supply of pounds in the foreign exchange market?
4. Provide an example of the imports effect on the supply of pounds.
5. How is the equilibrium exchange rate determined?
6. What happens if there is a shortage or a surplus of pounds in the foreign exchange market?

You can work these questions in Study Plan 25.1 and get instant feedback. myeconlab

Exchange Rate Fluctuations

You've seen (in *Economics in Action* on p. 587) that the pound fluctuates a lot against the euro, the dollar and the yen. Changes in the demand for pounds or the supply of pounds bring these exchange rate fluctuations. We'll now look at the factors that make demand and supply change, starting with the demand side of the market.

Changes in the Demand for Pounds

The demand for pounds in the foreign exchange market changes when there is a change in:

- World demand for UK exports
- UK interest rate relative to the foreign interest rate
- The expected future exchange rate

World Demand for UK Exports

An increase in world demand for UK exports increases the demand for pounds. To see this effect, think about the sale of commercial air engines by Rolls Royce. An increase in demand for air travel in Australia sends Qantas on a global shopping spree to buy the Rolls Royce Trent 900 to power its expanding fleet of Super Airbuses. The demand for pounds now increases.

UK Interest Rate Relative to the Foreign Interest Rate

People and businesses buy financial assets to make a return. The higher the interest rate that people can make on UK assets compared with foreign assets, the more UK assets they buy.

What matters is not the level of the UK interest rate but the UK rate minus the foreign rate – a gap that is called the **UK interest rate differential**. If the UK interest rate rises and the foreign interest rate remains constant, the UK interest rate differential increases. The larger the UK interest rate differential, the greater is the demand for UK assets and the greater is the demand for pounds in the foreign exchange market.

The Expected Future Exchange Rate

For a given current exchange rate, other things remaining the same, a rise in the expected future exchange rate increases the profit that people expect to make by holding pounds and the demand for pounds increases today.

Figure 25.4 summarizes the influences on the demand for pounds. An increase in the demand for UK exports, a rise in the UK interest rate differential, or a rise in the expected future exchange rate increases the demand for pounds today and shifts the demand curve rightward from D_0 to D_1. A decrease in the demand for UK exports, a fall in the UK interest rate differential, or a fall in the expected future exchange rate decreases the demand for pounds today and shifts the demand curve leftward from D_0 to D_2.

Figure 25.4 Changes in the Demand for Pounds

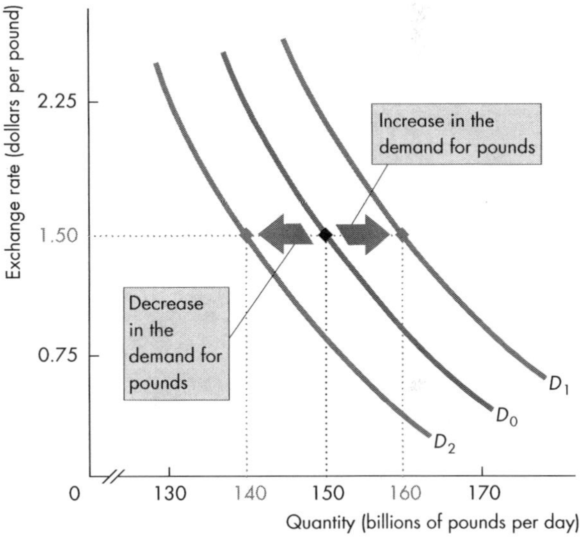

A change in any influence on the quantity of pounds that people plan to buy, other than the exchange rate, brings a change in the demand for pounds.

The demand for pounds

Increases if	*Decreases if*
◆ World demand for UK exports increases	◆ World demand for UK exports decreases
◆ The UK interest rate differential rises	◆ The UK interest rate differential falls
◆ The expected future exchange rate rises	◆ The expected future exchange rate falls

myeconlab Animation

Changes in the Supply of Pounds

The supply of pounds in the foreign exchange market changes when there is a change in:

- UK demand for imports
- UK interest rate differential
- The expected future exchange rate

UK Demand for Imports

An increase in the UK demand for imports increases the supply of pounds in the foreign exchange market. To see why, think about Tesco's purchase of DVD players. An increase in the demand for DVD players sends Tesco out on a global shopping spree. Tesco decides that Panasonic DVD players produced in Japan are the best buy, so it increases its purchases of these players. The supply of pounds now increases as Tesco goes to the foreign exchange market for Japanese yen to pay Panasonic.

UK Interest Rate Differential

The effect of the UK interest rate differential on the supply of pounds is the opposite of its effect on the demand for pounds. The larger the UK interest rate differential, the smaller is the supply of pounds in the foreign exchange market. With a higher UK interest rate differential, people decide to keep more of their funds in sterling assets and less in foreign currency assets. They buy a smaller quantity of foreign currency and sell a smaller quantity of pounds in the foreign exchange market. So, a rise in the UK interest rate, other things remaining the same, decreases the supply of pounds in the foreign exchange market.

The Expected Future Exchange Rate

For a given current exchange rate, other things remaining the same, a fall in the expected future exchange rate decreases the profit that can be made by holding pounds and decreases the quantity of pounds that people want to hold. To reduce their holdings of sterling assets, people must sell pounds. When they do so, the supply of pounds in the foreign exchange market increases.

Figure 25.5 summarizes the influences on the supply of pounds. If the supply of pounds decreases, the supply curve shifts leftward from S_0 to S_1. And if the supply of pounds increases, the supply curve shifts rightward from S_0 to S_2.

Figure 25.5 Changes in the Supply of Pounds

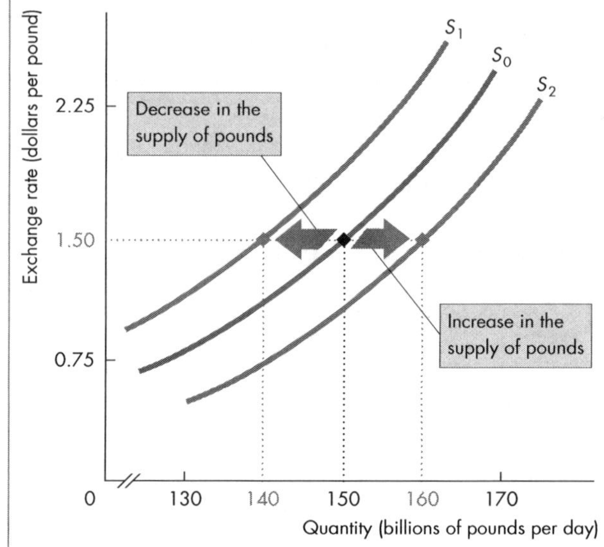

A change in any influence on the quantity of pounds that people plan to sell, other than the exchange rate, brings a change in the supply of pounds.

The supply of pounds

Increases if	*Decreases if*
UK demand for imports increases	UK demand for imports decreases
The UK interest rate differential falls	The UK interest rate differential rises
The expected future exchange rate falls	The expected future exchange rate rises

myeconlab Animation

Changes in the Exchange Rate

If the demand for pounds increases and the supply does not change, the exchange rate rises. If the demand for pounds decreases and the supply does not change, the exchange rate falls. Similarly, if the supply of pounds decreases and the demand does not change, the exchange rate rises. If the supply of pounds increases and the demand does not change, the exchange rate falls.

These predictions are exactly the same as those for any other market. Two episodes in the life of the pound illustrate these predictions.

ECONOMICS IN ACTION

The Rise and Fall of the Pound

The foreign exchange market is a striking example of a competitive market. The expectations of thousands of traders around the world influence this market minute-by-minute throughout the 24-hour global trading day.

Demand and supply rarely stand still and their fluctuations bring a fluctuating exchange rate. Two episodes in the life of the pound and yen illustrate these fluctuations: 2001–2007, when the pound appreciated and 2007–2009, when the pound depreciated.

An Appreciating Pound: 2001–2007

Between January 2001 and July 2007, the pound appreciated against the yen: it rose from 172 to 247 yen per pound. Part (a) of the figure provides an explanation for this appreciation.

In 2001, the demand and supply curves were those labelled D_{01} and S_{01}. The exchange rate was 172 yen per pound. During this period the UK was a good place to invest money. Property prices were rising and banks in the UK increasingly borrowed from foreign banks, particularly Japanese banks, in the global market for mortgage-backed securities. The Bank of England raised the *bank rate* from 3.5 per cent in 2003 to 5.75 per cent in July 2007 but interest rates in Japan barely changed. With the rise in the UK interest rate differential, funds flowed into the UK. Also, currency traders, anticipating this increased flow of funds into the UK expected the pound to appreciate against the yen. The demand for pounds increased, and the supply of pounds decreased.

In the figure, the demand curve shifted rightward from D_{01} to D_{07} and the supply curve shifted leftward from S_{01} to S_{07}. The exchange rate rose to 247 yen per pound. In the figure, the equilibrium quantity remained unchanged – an assumption.

A Depreciating Pound: 2007–2009

Between July 2007 and October 2009, the pound depreciated against the yen: it fell from 247 to 184 yen per pound. Part (b) of the figure provides a possible explanation for this depreciation. The demand and supply curves D_{07} and S_{07} are the same as in part (a).

From the third quarter of 2007 to the third quarter of 2009, the UK economy, along with the US and other developed economies, entered a severe financial crisis. Investment returns and property values fell sharply. The Bank of England cut the *bank rate*, but the Bank of Japan kept the interest rate in Japan unchanged. With a narrowing of the UK interest rate differential and a reversal of investment returns, funds flowed out of the UK. Also, currency traders expected the pound to depreciate against the yen. The demand for pounds decreased and the supply of pounds increased.

In part (b) of the figure, the demand curve shifted leftward from D_{07} to D_{09}, the supply curve shifted rightward from S_{07} to S_{09}, and the exchange rate fell to 184 yen per pound.

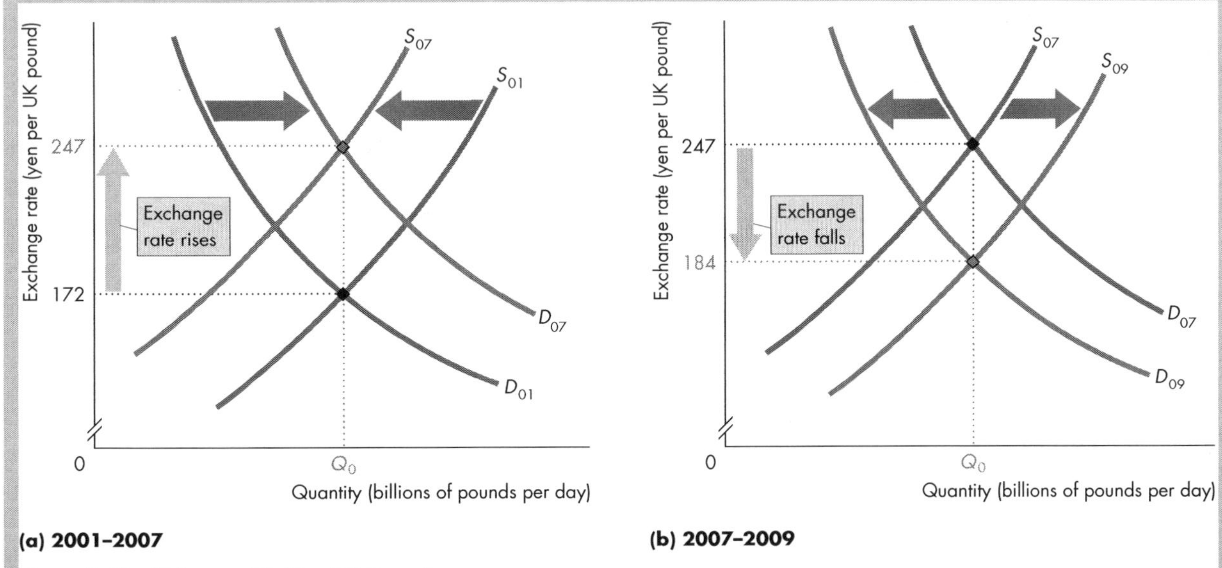

Figure 1 The Rising and Falling UK Pound

Fundamentals, Expectations and Arbitrage

Changes in the expected exchange rate change the actual exchange rate. But what makes the expected exchange rate change? The answer is new information about the *fundamental influences* on the exchange rate – the world demand for UK exports, UK demand for imports, and the UK interest rate relative to the foreign interest rate. Expectations about these variables change the exchange rate through their influence on the expected exchange rate, and the effect is instant.

To see why, suppose news breaks that the Bank of England will raise the interest rate next week. Traders now expect the demand for pounds to increase, the supply of pounds to decrease and the pound to appreciate. They expect to profit by buying pounds today and selling them next week for a higher price than they paid. The rise in the expected future value of the pound increases the demand for pounds today, decreases the supply of pounds today and raises the exchange rate. The exchange rate changes as soon as the news about a fundamental influence is received.

Profiting by trading in the foreign exchange market often involves arbitrage – the practice of buying in one market and selling for a higher price in another related market. Arbitrage ensures that the exchange rate is the same in New York, Tokyo, London and all other trading centres. It isn't possible to buy at a low price in London and sell for a higher price in New York. If it were possible, demand would increase in London and decrease in New York to make the prices equal.

Arbitrage also removes profit from borrowing in one currency and lending in another and buying goods in one currency and selling them in another. These arbitrage activities bring about:

- Interest rate parity
- Purchasing power parity

Interest Rate Parity

Suppose a bank deposit in pounds in London earns 5 per cent a year and a US dollar bank deposit in New York earns 3 per cent a year. In this situation, why does anyone deposit money in New York? Why doesn't all the money flow to London? The answer is because of exchange rate expectations. Suppose people expect the pound to depreciate by 2 per cent a year. This 2 per cent depreciation must be subtracted from the 5 per cent interest to obtain the net return of 3 per cent a year that an American can earn by depositing funds in London. The two returns are equal. This situation is one of **interest rate parity**, which means *equal rates of return.*

Adjusted for risk, interest rate parity always prevails. Funds move to get the highest return available. If for a few seconds a higher return is available in London than in New York, the demand for pounds increases and the pound appreciates until interest rate parity is restored.

Purchasing Power Parity

Suppose the price of a pair of Levi's jeans is £20 in London and $30 in New York. If the exchange rate is $1.50 per pound, the two monies have the same value. You can buy the jeans in London or New York for either £20 or $30 and it costs you the same in the two currencies.

The situation we've just described is called **purchasing power parity**, which *means equal value of money.* If purchasing power parity does not prevail, powerful arbitrage forces go to work.

Arbitrage Forces

To see these forces, suppose that the price of Levi's jeans in London rises to £30, but in New York, they remain at $30. The exchange rate remains at $1.50 per pound. In this case, a pair of jeans in New York still costs $30 or £20, but in London it costs £30 or $45. Money buys more in the US than in the UK. Money is not of equal value in the two countries.

If all (or most) prices have increased in the UK and not increased in the US, then people will generally expect that the value of the pound in the foreign exchange market must fall. In this situation, the exchange rate is expected to fall. The demand for pounds decreases, and the supply of pounds increases. The exchange rate falls, as expected. If the exchange rate falls to $1.00 per pound and there are no further price changes, purchasing power parity is restored. A pair of jeans that costs £30 in London also costs the equivalent of £30 ($30) in New York.

If prices rise in the US and other countries but remain constant in the UK, then people will expect the pound to appreciate. The demand for pounds increases, and the supply of pounds decreases. The exchange rate rises, as expected.

So far we've been looking at the forces that determine the *nominal* exchange rate – the amount of one money that another money buys. We're now going to study the *real* exchange rate.

The Real Exchange Rate

The **real exchange rate** is the relative price of UK-produced goods and services to foreign-produced goods and services. It is a measure of the quantity of the real GDP of other countries that a unit of UK real GDP buys.

The real US dollar exchange rate, *RER*, is

$$RER = (E \times P)/P^*$$

where E is the exchange rate (\$ per £), P is the UK price level, and P^* is the US price level.

To understand the real exchange rate, suppose that each country produces only one good and that the exchange rate E is \$1.50 per pound. The UK produces only bagpipes priced at £300 each, so P equals £300 and $E \times P$ equals \$450. The US produces only Stetson hats priced at \$100, so P^* equals \$100. Then the real pound exchange rate is

$$RER = (1.5 \times 300)/100 = 4.5 \text{ Stetson hats per bagpipe}$$

The Short Run

In the short run, if the nominal exchange rate changes, the real exchange rate also changes. The reason is that prices and the price levels in the UK and US don't change every time the exchange rate changes. Sticking with the bagpipes and Stetson hats example, if the pound appreciates to \$2.00 per pound and prices don't change, the real exchange rate rises to 6 Stetson hats per bagpipe. The price of a Stetson hat in the UK falls to £50 (\$100 ÷ \$2.00 per pound = £50).

Changes in the real exchange rate bring short-run changes in the quantity of imports demanded and the quantity of exports supplied.

The Long Run

In the long run, the situation is radically different: the nominal exchange rate and the price level are determined together and the real exchange rate does not change when the nominal exchange rate changes.

In the long run, demand and supply in the markets for goods and services determine prices. In the bagpipes and Stetson hats example, the world markets for bagpipes (they make them in Pakistan, India and Canada as well!) and Stetson hats determine their relative price. In our example the relative price is 4.5 hats per bagpipe. The same forces determine all relative prices and so determine nations' relative price levels. The quantity of money determines the price level and the exchange rate.

The Quantity Theory of Money Again

In the long run, if the pound appreciates prices do change. To see why, recall the quantity theory of money that you met in Chapter 24 (pp. 574–575).

In the long run, the quantity of money determines the price level. But the quantity theory of money applies to all countries, so the US quantity of money determines the US price level and the UK quantity of money determines the UK price level.

For a given real exchange rate, a change in the quantity of money brings a change in the price level *and* a change in the exchange rate.

Suppose that the quantity of money in the US doubles. The pound appreciates (the dollar depreciates) from \$1.50 per pound to \$3.00 per pound and all US prices double, so the price of a Stetson hat rises from \$100 to \$200. At the new US price and the new exchange rate, a Stetson hat in the UK still costs £66.67 (\$200 ÷ \$3.00 per pound or £66.67); and the real exchange rate remains at 4.5 Stetson hats per bagpipe.

If the US and the UK produced identical goods (if GDP in both countries consisted only of bagpipes), the real exchange rate in the long run would equal 1.

In reality, although there is overlap in what each country produces, UK real GDP is a different bundle of goods and services from US real GDP. So the relative price of US and UK real GDP – the real exchange rate – is not 1, and it changes over time.

The forces of demand and supply in the markets for the millions of goods and services that make up real GDP determine the relative price of US and UK real GDP, and changes in these forces change the real exchange rate.

Review Quiz

1. Why does the demand for pounds change?
2. Why does the supply of pounds change?
3. What makes the pound exchange rate change?
4. What is interest parity and what happens when this condition does not hold?
5. What is purchasing power parity and what happens when this condition does not hold?
6. What determines the real exchange rate and the nominal exchange rate in the short run?
7. What determines the real exchange rate and the nominal exchange rate in the long run?

You can work these questions in Study Plan 25.2 and get instant feedback. myeconlab

Exchange Rate Policy

Because the exchange rate is the price of a country's money in terms of another country's money, governments and central banks must have a policy towards the exchange rate. Three possible exchange rate policies are:

- Flexible exchange rate
- Fixed exchange rate
- Crawling peg

Flexible Exchange Rate

A **flexible exchange rate** is an exchange rate that is determined by demand and supply in the foreign exchange market with no direct intervention by the central bank.

Today, most countries, including the UK, operate a flexible exchange rate, and the foreign exchange market that we have studied so far in this chapter is an example of a flexible exchange rate regime.

But even a flexible exchange rate is influenced by central bank actions. If the Bank of England raises the UK interest rate and other countries keep their interest rates unchanged, the demand for pounds increases, the supply of pounds decreases, and the exchange rate rises. (Similarly, if the Bank of England lowers the UK interest rate, the demand for pounds decreases, the supply increases, and the exchange rate falls.)

In a flexible exchange rate regime, when the central bank changes the interest rate, its purpose is not usually to influence the exchange rate, but to achieve some other monetary policy objective. (We return to this topic at length in Chapter 31.)

Fixed Exchange Rate

A **fixed exchange rate** is an exchange rate that is determined by a decision of the government or the central bank and is achieved by central bank intervention in the foreign exchange market to block the unregulated forces of demand and supply.

The world economy operated a fixed exchange rate regime from the end of World War II to the early 1970s. China had a fixed exchange rate until recently. Hong Kong has had a fixed exchange rate for many years and continues with that policy today.

Active intervention in the foreign exchange market is required to achieve a fixed exchange rate. If the Bank of England wanted to fix the pound sterling exchange rate against the US dollar, the Bank of England would have to sell pounds to prevent the exchange rate from rising above the target value and buy pounds to prevent the exchange rate from falling below the target value.

There is no limit to the quantity of pounds that the Bank of England can *sell*. The Bank of England creates pounds and can create any quantity it chooses. But there is a limit to the quantity of pounds the Bank of England can *buy*. That limit is set by the foreign currency reserves held at the Bank of England because to buy pounds the Bank of England must sell foreign currency. Intervention to buy pounds stops when the foreign currency reserves run out.

Let's look at the foreign exchange interventions that the Bank of England can make.

Suppose the Bank of England wants the exchange rate to be steady at \$1.50. If the exchange rate rises above \$1.50, the Bank of England sells pounds. If the exchange rate falls below \$1.50, the Bank of England buys pounds. By these actions, the Bank of England keeps the exchange rate close to its target rate of \$1.50 per pound.

Figure 25.6 shows the Bank of England's intervention in the foreign exchange market. The supply of pounds is S and initially the demand for pounds is D_0. The equilibrium exchange rate is \$1.50 per pound. This exchange rate is also the Bank of England's target exchange rate, shown by the horizontal red line.

When the demand for pounds increases and the demand curve shifts rightward to D_1, the Bank of England sells £10 billion. This action prevents the exchange rate from rising. When the demand for pounds decreases and the demand curve shifts leftward to D_2, the Bank of England buys £10 billion. This action prevents the exchange rate from falling.

If the demand for pounds fluctuates between D_1 and D_2 and on average is D_0, the Bank of England can repeatedly intervene in the way we've just seen. Sometimes the Bank of England buys and sometimes it sells but, on average, it neither buys nor sells.

But suppose the demand for the pound *increases permanently* from D_0 to D_1. To maintain the exchange rate at \$1.50, the Bank of England must sell pounds and buy dollars, so foreign currency reserves would be increasing. At some point, the Bank of England would abandon the exchange rate of \$1.50 per pound and stop piling up foreign currency reserves.

Now suppose the demand for pounds *decreases permanently* from D_0 to D_2. In this situation, the Bank of England cannot maintain the exchange rate at \$1.50 per pound indefinitely. To hold the exchange rate at \$1.50,

Figure 25.6 Foreign Exchange Market Intervention

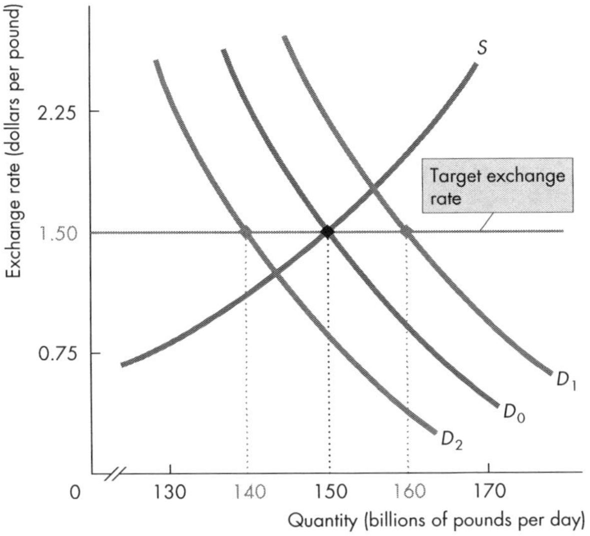

Initially, the demand for pounds is D_0, the supply of pounds is S, and the exchange rate is \$1.50 per pound. The Bank of England can intervene in the foreign exchange market to keep the exchange rate close to target (\$1.50 per pound in this example). If the demand for pounds increases and the demand curve shifts to D_1, the Bank sells pounds. If the demand for pounds decreases and the demand curve shifts to D_2, the Bank buys pounds. Persistent intervention on one side of the market cannot be sustained.

myeconlab Animation

ECONOMICS IN ACTION

Currency Wars

Brazil, Chile and China are three countries accused of manipulating their exchange rates to undervalue their currencies and make their exports cheap so they are able to take market share from other countries. (*Reading Between the Lines* on pp. 604–605 looks more closely at what Chile is doing.)

A country that manipulates its exchange rate in this way is using a fixed exchange rate or crawling peg policy and is buying foreign currency and selling its own currency to keep its price down.

A *currency war* breaks out when countries retaliate against exchange rate manipulators. So far, the world has avoided a currency war and it would take a retaliation from the US, the EU or Japan to start a big one.

What you've learned in this chapter tells you that currency manipulation is a short-run policy. Keeping the exchange rate low to lower export prices works as long as the low exchange rate doesn't bring higher import prices and a rise in wages and the overall price level. In the long run, that is exactly what happens. A policy of exchange rate manipulation can bring short-run gains at the expense of a higher price level in the long run.

A currency war is a self-defeating exercise that results in competitive depreciation and a general outbreak of inflation among the participating nations.

the Bank of England must buy pounds. When the Bank of England buys pounds in the foreign exchange market, it uses its foreign currency reserves. So the Bank of England's action decreases its foreign currency reserves. Eventually, the Bank of England would run out of foreign currency and would then have to abandon the target exchange rate of \$1.50.

Crawling Peg

A **crawling peg** is an exchange rate that follows a path determined by a decision of the government or the central bank and is achieved in a similar way to a fixed exchange rate by central bank intervention in the foreign exchange market. A crawling peg works like a fixed exchange rate except that the target value might change at fixed intervals or at random intervals. The peg seeks only to prevent large swings in the expected future exchange rate that change demand and supply and make the exchange rate fluctuate too wildly.

A crawling peg departs from the ideal if, as often happens with a fixed exchange rate, the target rate departs from the equilibrium exchange rate for too long. When this happens, the country either runs out of reserves or piles up reserves.

Review Quiz

1. What is a flexible exchange rate and how does it work?
2. What is a fixed exchange rate and how is its value fixed?
3. What is a crawling peg and how does it work?

You can work these questions in Study Plan 25.3 and get instant feedback. myeconlab

European Monetary Union

The European Monetary Union (EMU), formed on 1 January 1999, now consists of 17 member states of the EU that use the euro as their national currency. The UK is the only major member state to have remained outside the euro area. What is the UK missing and what is it gaining? Let's review the benefits and costs of the euro.

The Benefits of the Euro

A single currency in Europe has three benefits. It:

- Improves transparency and competition
- Decreases transactions costs
- Eliminates foreign exchange risk

Improves Transparency and Competition

A single currency provides a single unit of account so that prices are easily compared across the entire Eurozone. A country might gain a competitive advantage by becoming more efficient, but it cannot gain an advantage by artificially lowering the prices of its exports through a depreciation of its currency.

Decreases Transactions Costs

A single currency eliminates foreign exchange transactions costs – the costs of exchanging pesetas for francs at a bank or travel agent, such as commission charges or the margin between the buy and sell exchange rates we see posted in banks and currency exchanges. The removal of these costs benefits the consumer, who knows that a euro in France buys the same as a euro in Germany.

The total benefit from eliminating the transactions costs of currency exchange has been estimated at 0.3 to 0.4 per cent of EU GDP a year. For a country with an advanced banking system as in the UK, the EU Commission estimates that the benefits would be 0.1 per cent of GDP a year.

Eliminates Foreign Exchange Risk

With a single currency, exporters and importers no longer face foreign exchange risk. For example, Alpine Gardens, an Austrian garden company, has ordered a consignment of garden gnomes to be supplied by Britannia Gnomes Ltd, a Gloucester company, in three months' time. The contract and the price are set today, but payment will take place in three months' time. Alpine Gardens has to pay £50,000 in three months' time. To protect itself against an adverse change in the exchange rate, it buys £50,000 today in the forward market at today's exchange rate.

The reduction in exchange rate risk improves trade between EU countries. Cacharel, the French clothing designer, can source its material from Rome or Paris. On a strict exchange rate comparison, the Italian product is cheaper. But in the pre-euro days, the exchange rate between the French franc and Italian lira fluctuated unpredictably. Cacharel would not have wanted to be tied into a contract with the Italian supplier if the price in francs fluctuated with the exchange rate. Cacharel would have sourced the material from the more expensive French supplier because the price was guaranteed, but Cacharel had to charge its customers a higher price. Now, with the euro, a single currency eliminates this exchange rate risk. Cacharel can source its material from Rome, pay a lower price and pass the benefits of the lower price on to its customers. The lower price increases the quantity demanded of Cacharel clothing, which in turn increases the orders from Rome.

The removal of exchange risk means that many large companies are able to reduce their administration and financial management costs. They also no longer need to diversify their operations across borders and can consolidate them in one location.

If the euro had only benefits, a nation's choice would be simple, but the euro has costs too.

The Economic Costs of the Euro

A single currency in Europe has two costs:

- Loss of sovereignty
- Inability to respond to national shocks

Loss of Sovereignty

The pursuit of national economic goals requires policy instruments under the control of a national government. The EMU places all the instruments of monetary policy beyond the reach of national governments and a Stability and Growth Pact places strict limits on the use of fiscal policy and regional policy.

Common regional policy enables transfers to be made from Germany and France to Italy and Spain. But a political consensus must be found to sustain such transfers. In effect, a single currency implies a political union. A loss of monetary sovereignty implies a loss of political sovereignty.

Inability to Respond to National Shocks

Many, perhaps most, economic shocks that call for a monetary policy response are country-specific shocks or shocks that affect different countries in different ways.

For example, the dismantling of the Berlin Wall had a major impact on the German economy but barely any effect on the economies of Ireland and Portugal. Also, the shock had different effects on the two parts of Germany. East German workers were less productive and earned lower wage rates than their West German counterparts. Productivity and earnings differences induced a massive reallocation and relocation of jobs and people. A common monetary policy might stimulate the economy in the East and bring inflation to the West or keep inflation in check in the West and bring prolonged recession in the East.

An oil price increase is an example of a common shock that has different effects on different economies. In Germany, an oil importer, the price rise imparts a negative aggregate supply shock and creates a current account deficit. In the UK, an oil exporter, the price rise imparts a positive supply shock and creates a current account surplus. A common monetary policy might stimulate economic activity in Germany and bring inflation to the UK or hold inflation in check in the UK and bring stagnation in Germany.

A common monetary policy is inadequate to deal with the results of country-specific shocks.

The Optimum Currency Area

When there are benefits and costs, they must be weighed against each other and an optimum outcome found. Imagine a world in which the Welsh leek and Scottish thistle exchange for each other and for the English pound at exchange rates that fluctuate every day. The UK is almost certainly better off using one currency rather than three. Is Europe better off using the euro than 17 national currencies? And why stop at Europe! Would the world be better off with one currency rather than its 200-plus currencies?

To answer these questions, we need the concept of an **optimal currency area**, a geographical area that is better served by a single currency than by several currencies. Robert Mundell, an economics professor at Columbia University in New York City, won the Nobel Prize in 1999 for his work on this topic. Mundell claimed that the key factor required for an optimal currency area is free labour mobility either across regions or between jobs.

On this criterion, Scotland, Wales and England are better off with a single currency than they would be with an English pound, a 'Welsh leek' and a 'Scottish thistle'. No cultural or language barriers hamper the movement of labour. If a factory closes down in Merseyside and another opens in Clwyd, workers from Merseyside can travel to Wales to seek employment.

Lack of regional mobility is not a problem if there is mobility between jobs. For example, if Volkswagen closes a Polo production plant in Pamplona, Spain, and opens a new plant in Wolfsburg, Germany, we would not expect former Spanish car workers to migrate to Germany – although by current EU labour laws there is nothing stopping them from doing just that. If jobless car workers in Pamplona can easily retrain and find a new job in Spain, the absence of regional labour mobility doesn't weaken the case for a single currency.

A second criterion for an optimal currency area is that regions within the area face common economic shocks. It is claimed by some economists that economies with similar industrial structures and extensive trade with each other satisfy this criterion. And it is further claimed that the Eurozone countries have sufficiently similar industrial structures and sufficiently extensive trade links to meet this criterion.

Unlike the country-specific shocks that we've just considered, common shocks can be dealt with by a common monetary policy run by a common central bank. For example, if a rise in the price of oil affected all the countries in a monetary union in the same way, the central bank could react in a way that is appropriate for all the countries in the union.

Even if a country does not share a similar industrial structure and have extensive trade links with its neighbours, some argue that a single currency area will bring convergence to a common industrial structure and stimulate trade flows. For example, each major Canadian city is closer to a major US city than to other Canadian cities. But there is significantly more trade among Canadian cities (using one currency) than between the closer Canadian and US cities (using two currencies).

Review Quiz

1. What is the EMU?
2. What are the benefits of a single currency for Europe?
3. What are the costs of a single currency for Europe?
4. What is an optimal currency area?

You can work these questions in Study Plan 25.4 and get instant feedback.

myeconlab

Financing International Trade

You now know how the exchange rate is determined, but what is the effect of the exchange rate? How does currency depreciation or currency appreciation influence our international trade and payments? We're going to lay the foundation for addressing these questions by looking at the scale of international trading, borrowing, and lending and at the way in which we keep our records of international transactions. These records are called the *balance of payments accounts*.

Balance of Payments Accounts

A country's **balance of payments accounts** record its international trading and its borrowing and lending. There are three balance of payments accounts:

- Current account
- Capital and financial account
- Change in reserve assets

Current Account

The **current account** records the receipts from the sale of goods and services to foreigners, the payments for goods and services bought from foreigners, income and other transfers (such as foreign aid payments) received from and paid to foreigners. The large items in the current account are the receipts from the sale of goods and services to foreigners (exports) and the payments made for goods and services bought from foreigners (imports). Net income is the earnings from foreign financial assets such as bonds and shares, and net earnings of UK workers abroad and foreign workers in the UK. Net transfers – gifts to foreigners minus gifts from foreigners – are relatively small items.

Capital and Financial Account

The **capital and financial account** records all UK investments abroad and foreigners' investments in the UK. This account balance equals the amount that a country borrows from the rest of the world minus the amount that it lends to it.

Change in Reserve Assets

The **change in reserve assets** shows the net increase or decrease in a country's holdings of foreign currency reserves that comes about from the official financing of the difference between the current account and the capital and financial account balances. In practice, the change in reserve assets is an item in the capital account. It is itemized separately here so that you can see how the financing of the gap between the current account and the capital and financial account adds to or subtracts from reserve assets.

The Data in 2010

Table 25.1 shows the UK balance of payments accounts in 2010. Items in the current and capital and financial accounts with a positive sign provide the UK with foreign currency and items that have a minus sign cost the UK foreign currency. The table shows that UK imports of goods and services exceeded UK exports of goods and services in 2010 and that the current account balance was –£32 billion. How do we pay for our current account deficit? We pay by borrowing from abroad. The capital and financial account tells us by how much. We borrowed £525 billion but made loans of £513 billion, so our net foreign borrowing was £12 billion.

Some capital and current account transactions do not get recorded. These transactions include unidentified capital flows and illegal international trade such as that in illegal drugs and smuggling to evade tariffs or taxes.

Table 25.1

UK Balance of Payments Accounts in 2010

	(billions of pounds)
Current account	
Exports of goods and services	+423
Imports of goods and services	–467
Net income	+29
Net transfers	–17
Current account balance	–32
Capital and financial account	
Foreign investment in the UK	+525
UK investment abroad	–513
Capital and financial account balance	12
Balancing item	14
Change in reserve assets	
Increase(+)/Decrease(–) in the UK's official foreign currency reserves	+6

Source of data: Office for National Statistics, *UK Balance of Payments: The Pink Book*, 2010. Based on first three quarters of 2010.

ECONOMICS IN ACTION

Persistent Current Account Deficits

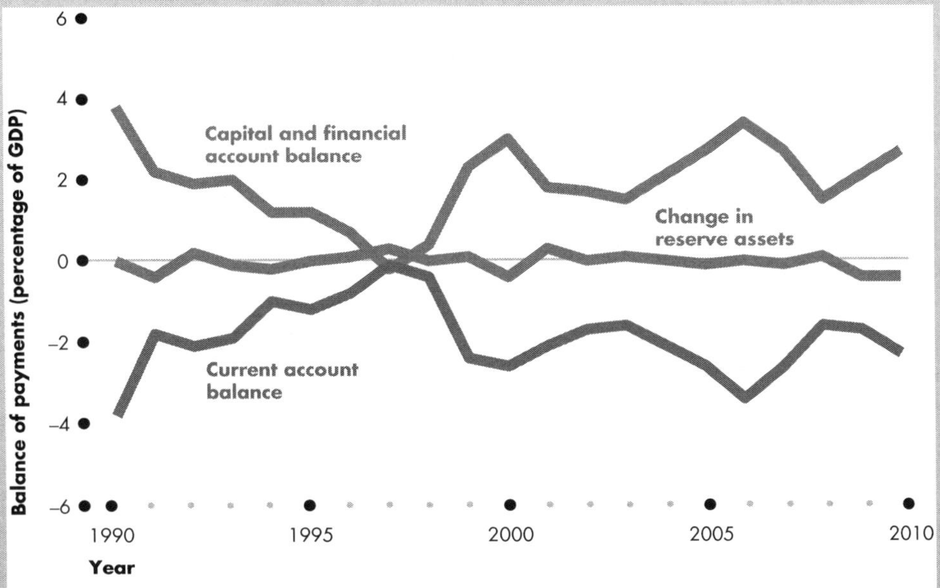

Figure 1 The UK Balance of Payments
Source of data: Office for National Statistics.

The numbers in Table 25.1 give a snapshot of the balance of payments accounts in 2010. The figure here puts that snapshot into a longer perspective by showing the balances over the period 1990 to 2010.

The UK has had a current account deficit every year. In 1997, the current account deficit got close to zero but not quite.

The capital and financial account balance is almost a mirror image of the current account deficit.

We call the net total of all these items the balancing item, which in 2010 was £14 billion.

Net borrowing from abroad minus the current account deficit is the balance that is financed from official UK reserves – the government's holdings of foreign currency. In 2010, those reserves changed by £6 billion.

The sum of the balances on the three balance of payments accounts equals zero.

To see more clearly what the nation's balance of payments accounts mean, think about your own balance of payments accounts. They are similar to the nation's accounts.

Individual Balance of Payments Accounts

An individual's current account records the income from supplying the services of factors of production and the expenditure on goods and services. Consider, for example, Joanne. She earned an income in 2010 of £25,000. Joanne has £10,000 worth of investments that earned her an income of £1,000. Joanne's current account shows an income of £26,000. Joanne spent £18,000 buying goods and services for consumption. She also bought a new studio apartment, which cost her £60,000. So Joanne's total expenditure was £78,000. The difference between her expenditure and income is £52,000 (£78,000 minus £26,000). This amount is Joanne's current account deficit.

To pay for expenditure of £52,000 in excess of her income, Joanne has either to use the money that she has in the bank or to take out a loan. In fact Joanne took a mortgage of £50,000 to help buy her house. This mortgage was the only borrowing that Joanne did, so her capital account surplus was £50,000. With a current account deficit of £52,000 and a capital account surplus of £50,000, Joanne was still £2,000 short. She got that £2,000 from her own bank account. Her cash holdings decreased by £2,000.

Joanne's income from her work and investments is analogous to a country's income from its exports. Her purchases of goods and services, including her purchase of a house, are analogous to a country's imports. Joanne's mortgage – borrowing from someone else – is analogous to a country's foreign borrowing. The change in her bank account is analogous to the change in the country's reserve assets.

Borrowers and Lenders, Debtors and Creditors

A country that is borrowing more from the rest of the world than it is lending to it is called a **net borrower**. Similarly, a **net lender** is a country that is lending more to the rest of the world than it is borrowing from it. A net borrower might be going deeper into debt or might simply be reducing its net assets held in the rest of the world. The total stock of foreign investment determines whether a country is a debtor or a creditor.

A **debtor nation** is a country that during its entire history has borrowed more from the rest of the world than it has lent to it. It has a stock of outstanding debt to the rest of the world that exceeds the stock of its own claims on the rest of the world. The UK is currently a debtor nation, but for a long time it was a creditor. A **creditor nation** is a country that has invested more in the rest of the world than other countries have invested in it. The largest creditor nation today is Japan.

Flows and Stocks

At the heart of the distinction between a net borrower and a debtor nation or a net lender and a creditor nation is the distinction between flows and stocks, which you have encountered many times in your study of macroeconomics.

Borrowing and lending are *flows* – amounts borrowed or lent per unit of time. Debts are *stocks* – amounts owed at a point in time. The flow of borrowing and lending changes the stock of debt. But the outstanding stock of debt depends mainly on past flows of borrowing and lending, not on the current period's flows. The current period's flows determine the change in the stock of debt outstanding.

During the 1960s and the 1970s, the UK current account periodically swung from surplus to deficit. When the current account was a surplus, the capital account was a deficit. On the whole the UK was a net lender to the rest of the world. It was not until the late 1980s that it became a significant net borrower.

The UK today is a small net debtor. But there are many countries that are debtor nations. The US is one. But the largest debtor nations are the capital-hungry developing countries. The international debt of these countries grew from less than one-third to more than one-half of their gross domestic product during the 1980s and created what was called the 'Third World debt crisis'.

Is Borrowing and Debt a Problem?

Does it matter if a country is a net borrower rather than a net lender? The answer to this question depends mainly on what the net borrower is doing with the borrowed money. If borrowed money is used to finance investment that in turn is generating economic growth and higher income, borrowing is not a problem. If the borrowed money is being used to finance consumption, then higher interest payments are being incurred and, as a consequence, consumption will eventually have to be reduced. In this case, the more the borrowing and the longer it goes on, the greater is the reduction in consumption that will eventually be necessary.

Current Account Balance

What determines the current account balance and the scale of a country's net foreign borrowing or lending? You've seen in Table 25.1 that the current account balance equals net exports plus two small items, net interest and net transfers. So net exports drives the current account balance. But what determines net exports?

To answer this question, we need to use the national income accounts. Table 25.2 will refresh your memory and summarize the necessary calculations for you. Part (a) lists the national income variables that are needed, with their symbols. Their values in the UK in 2010 are also shown.

Part (b) presents two key national income equations. First, equation (1) reminds us that GDP, Y, equals aggregate expenditure, which is the sum of consumption expenditure, C, investment, I, government expenditure on goods and services, G, and net exports (exports, X, minus imports, M). Equation (2) reminds us that aggregate income is used in three different ways. It can be consumed, saved or paid to the government in net taxes (taxes net of transfer payments). Equation (1) tells us how our expenditure generates our income. Equation (2) tells us how we dispose of that income.

Part (c) of the table looks at three balances – net exports, the government budget and the private sector. To get these balances, first subtract equation (2) from equation (1) in Table 25.2. The result is equation (3). By rearranging equation (3), we obtain a relationship for net exports that appears as equation (4) in the table.

Net exports, in equation (4), is made up of two components. The first is net taxes minus government expenditure and the second is saving minus investment. These items are the balances of the government and private

Table 25.2

Sector Balances in 2010

	Symbols and equations	Billions of pounds
(a) Variables		
Gross domestic product (GDP)	Y	1,448
Consumption expenditure	C	948
Investment	I	208
Government expenditure on goods and services	G	338
Exports	X	424
Imports	M	470
Saving	S	306
Net taxes	T	194
(b) Domestic Income and Expenditure		
Aggregate expenditure	(1) $Y = C + I + G + X - M$	
Uses of income	(2) $Y = C + S + T$	
(1) minus (2)	(3) $0 = I - S + G - T + X - M$	
(c) Surpluses and Deficits		
Net exports	(4) $X - M = (T - G) + (S - I)$ $= -144 + 98 = -46$	
Government budget	(5) $T - G = 194 - 338 = -144$	
Private sector	(6) $S - I = 306 - 208 = 98$	
(d) Financing Investment		
Investment is financed by the sum of:		
Private saving,	$S = 306$	
Net government saving and	$T - G = -144$	
Net foreign saving	$M - X = 46$	
That is:	(7) $I = S + (T - G) + (M - X)$ $= 208$	

Source of data: Office for National Statistics: Data are based on the first three quarters of 2010.

sectors. Net taxes minus government expenditure on goods and services is the *government's budget balance*. If that number is positive, the government's budget is a surplus and if the number is negative, it is a deficit.

The *private sector balance* is saving minus investment. If saving exceeds investment, the private sector has a surplus to lend to other sectors. If investment exceeds saving, the private sector has a deficit that has to be financed by borrowing from other sectors. As you can see from our calculations, the current account deficit is equal to the sum of the government's budget deficit and the private sector surplus. In the UK in 2010, the private sector had a balance of £98 billion and the government sector had a balance of –£144 billion. The government sector balance plus the private sector balance equals net exports of –£46 billion.

Part (d) of Table 25.2 shows how investment is financed. To increase investment, either private saving or the government surplus must increase, or net exports must decrease.

Where Is the Exchange Rate?

We haven't mentioned the exchange rate while discussing the balance of payments. Doesn't it play a role? The answer is that in the short run it does but in the long run it doesn't.

In the short run, a fall in the pound lowers the real exchange rate, which makes imports into the UK more costly and UK exports more competitive. A higher price of imported consumption goods and services might induce a decrease in consumption expenditure and an increase in saving. A higher price of imported capital goods might induce a decrease in investment. Other things remaining the same, an increase in saving or a decrease in investment decreases the private sector deficit and decreases the current account deficit.

But in the long run, a change in the nominal exchange rate leaves the real exchange rate unchanged and plays no role in influencing the current account balance.

Review Quiz

1. What are the transactions that we record in the balance of payments accounts?
2. Is the UK a net borrower or a net lender? Is it a debtor nation or a creditor nation?
3. How are the current account balance, the government sector balance and the private sector balance related?

You can work these questions in Study Plan 25.5 and get instant feedback. myeconlab

You have now completed your study of the foreign exchange market and the determination of the exchange rate and the balance of payments. You can round out this chapter in *Reading Between the Lines* on pp. 604–605, which looks at what Chile is doing in the foreign exchange market to try to boost its exports.

Reading Between the Lines

Intervention in the Foreign Exchange Market

The Financial Times, 4 January 2011

Chile Joins Currency War to Help Exporters

FT

Daniel Schweimler

Chile is set to become the latest country to join the 'global currency wars' on Tuesday after the central bank said it would spend up to $12bn this year to curb the peso's strength and so help exporters from one of Latin America's most open and best managed economies.

The move, announced late on Monday after the peso rose to nearly a three-year high against the dollar, took markets by surprise as Chile's central bank is known for its hands-off approach to its free-floating exchange rate.

The peso weakened by about 4 per cent on Tuesday as the news sunk in that the central bank would spend $50m a day from today selling pesos. Equivalent, in total, to 6 per cent of gross domestic product, the programme is the biggest intervention in Chile's history and only its fourth since 1999.

Felipe Larrain, Chile's finance minister, said: 'We are supporting domestic producers, our exporters, in the farm as well as industrial sectors who depend on exchange rates. We think it is a well targeted step that is going to have an effect on the exchange rate.'

Mexico is now the only big Latin American economy not seeking to weaken its currency via intervention, or by putting in place controls on capital inflows such as Brazil's 6 per cent tax on bond inflows. . . .

Some analysts fear that the surprise move by Chile could open the way for further unorthodox policies in other emerging markets.

Chile is expected to grow 6 per cent this year, boosted by exports of copper, which hit a record high of $9,754 a tonne on Tuesday, . . .

The Essence of the Story

- The Chilean peso has appreciated and is now at a three-year high against the US dollar.
- Worried that an appreciating peso would hurt exports of other goods and services, Chile's central bank is selling pesos and buying US dollars at the rate of $50 million a day.
- The Chilean central bank says it will spend up to $12 billion in selling pesos (6 per cent of Chile's GDP) in trying to stop the peso from appreciating.
- Other Latin American central banks are also intervening in the foreign exchange market to slow the appreciation of their currencies.

Economic Analysis

- Copper is one of Chile's main exports and an increase in the global demand for copper has increased the demand for Chilean pesos and increased Chile's *real* exchange rate.
- The central bank of Chile is manipulating the *nominal* exchange rate, but it can't manipulate the real exchange rate in the long run.
- Figure 1 shows the steady appreciation[1] of the peso that worries the Chilean central bank. It shows the depreciation on 4 January 2011 when the central bank announced it would spend $50 million per day to stop the appreciation.
- Figure 2 shows the market for the peso. In mid-December 2010, the demand curve for pesos was D_0 and the supply curve of pesos was S_0. The exchange rate was $2.11 per 1,000 peso (or 474 pesos per dollar).
- The increase in copper exports increased the demand for pesos and the demand curve shifted rightward from D_0 to D_1. The peso appreciated to $2.15 per 1,000 pesos (465 pesos per dollar).
- To stop the peso from appreciating too much, the central bank of Chile sells pesos and buys $50 million per day. This action increases the supply of pesos on the foreign exchange market from S_0 to S_1 and lowers the exchange rate to $2.04 per 1,000 pesos (490 pesos per dollar).
- The effect of this intervention will be temporary. Chile has a large current account surplus that brings a sustained high demand for pesos in the foreign exchange market. Figure 3 shows this surplus in 2010, which totalled $15 billion.
- The cental bank's foreign exchange market intervention will eventually increase the quantity of money in Chile, which will increase the price level and the real exchange rate.

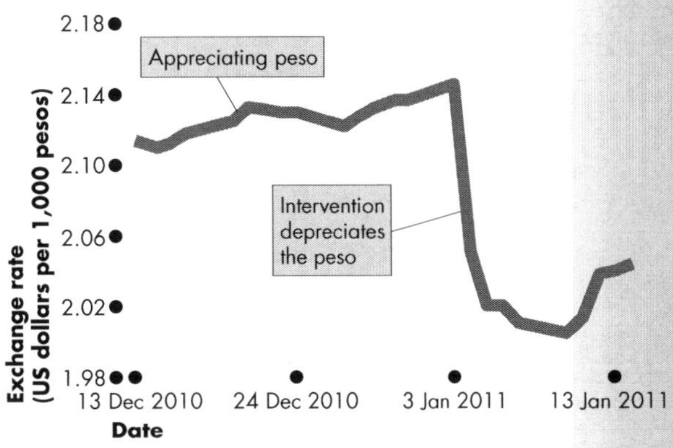

Figure 1 The Chilean peso exchange rate

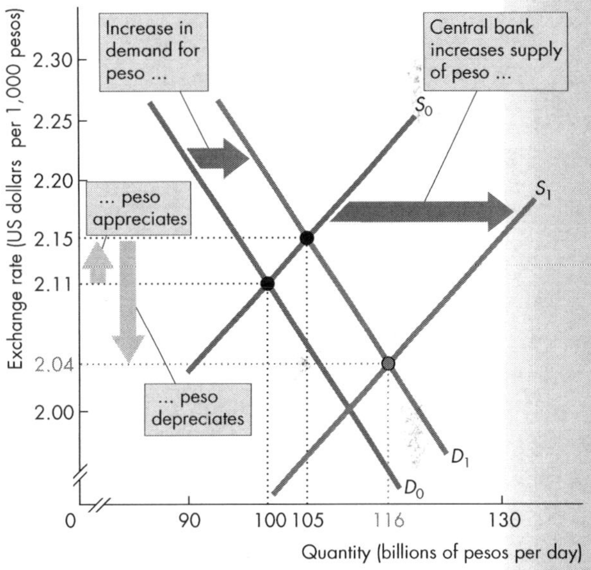

Figure 2 The foreign exchange market for Chilean peso

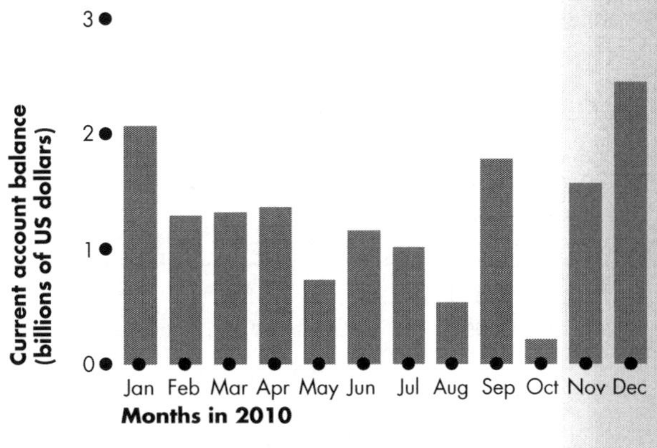

Figure 3 Chile's current account balance in 2010

[1] We express the price of the peso as US dollars per 1,000 pesos. For example, if 500 pesos buys US$1, the price of 1,000 pesos is $2.00.

SUMMARY

Key Points

The Foreign Exchange Market

- Foreign currency is obtained in exchange for domestic currency in the foreign exchange market.
- Demand and supply in the foreign exchange market determine the exchange rate.
- The higher the exchange rate, the smaller is the quantity of pounds demanded and the greater is the quantity of pounds supplied.
- The equilibrium exchange rate makes the quantity of pounds demanded equal the quantity of pounds supplied.

Working Problems 1 to 6 will give you a better understanding of the foreign exchange market.

Exchange Rate Fluctuations

- Changes in the world demand for UK exports, the UK interest rate differential, and the expected future exchange rate change the demand for pounds.
- Changes in UK demand for imports, the UK interest rate differential, and the expected future exchange rate change the supply of pounds.
- Exchange rate expectations are influenced by purchasing power parity and interest rate parity.
- In the long run, the nominal exchange rate is a monetary phenomenon and the real exchange rate is independent of the nominal exchange rate.

Working Problems 7 to 15 will give you a better understanding of exchange rate fluctuations.

Exchange Rate Policy

- An exchange rate can be flexible, fixed or on a crawling peg.
- To achieve a fixed or crawling exchange rate, a central bank must intervene in the foreign exchange market and either buy or sell foreign currency.

Working Problems 16 and 17 will give you a better understanding of exchange rate policy.

European Monetary Union

- The EMU is a group of 17 EU member states that use the euro as their national currency.
- The benefits of a single currency are improved transparency and competition, lower transactions costs and the elimination of exchange risk.
- The costs of a single currency are the loss of the ability to respond to a national economic shock and the loss of sovereignty.
- An optimal currency area is one for which the benefits outweigh the costs.

Working Problems 18 and 19 will give you a better understanding of the European Monetary Union.

Financing International Trade

- International trade, borrowing and lending are financed using foreign currency.
- A country's balance of payments accounts record its international transactions.
- The current account balance is similar to net exports and is determined by the government sector balance and the private sector balance.

Working Problems 20 and 21 will give you a better understanding of financing international trade.

Key Terms

Balance of payments accounts
Capital and financial account
Change in reserve assets
Crawling peg
Creditor nation
Current account
Debtor nation
Exchange rate
Fixed exchange rate
Flexible exchange rate
Foreign currency
Foreign exchange market
Interest rate parity
Net borrower
Net lender
Optimal currency area
Purchasing power parity
Real exchange rate
UK interest rate differential

STUDY PLAN PROBLEMS AND APPLICATIONS

myeconlab You can work Problems 1 to 21 in MyEconLab Chapter 25 Study Plan and get instant feedback.

The Foreign Exchange Market

(Study Plan 25.1)

Use the following data to work Problems 1 to 3.

The US dollar exchange rate decreased from 83.8 euro cents in January 2009 to 76.9 euro cents in January 2010, and it increased from \$0.89 Canadian in June 2009 to \$0.96 Canadian in June 2010.

1 Did the US dollar appreciate or depreciate against the euro? Did the US dollar appreciate or depreciate against the Canadian dollar?

2 What was the value of the Canadian dollar in terms of US dollars in June 2009 and June 2010? Did the Canadian dollar appreciate or depreciate against the US dollar over the year June 2009 to June 2010?

3 What was the value of one euro (100 euro cents) in terms of US dollars in January 2009 and January 2010? Did the euro appreciate or depreciate against the US dollar in 2009?

Use the following data to work Problems 4 to 6.

In January 2010, the exchange rate was 91 yen per US dollar. By September 2010, the exchange rate had fallen to 84 yen per US dollar.

4 Explain the exports effect of this change in the exchange rate.

5 Explain the imports effect of this change in the exchange rate.

6 Explain the expected profit effect of this change in the exchange rate.

Exchange Rate Fluctuations

(Study Plan 25.2)

7 On 3 August 2010, the US dollar was trading at 86 yen per US dollar on the foreign exchange market. On 13 September 2010, the US dollar was trading at 83 yen per US dollar.

a What events in the foreign exchange market might have brought this fall in the value of the US dollar?

b Did the events change the demand for US dollars, the supply of US dollars, or both demand and supply in the foreign exchange market?

8 Colombia is the world's biggest producer of roses. The global demand for roses increases and at the same time, the central bank in Colombia increases the interest rate. In the foreign exchange market for Columbian pesos, what happens to:

a The demand for pesos?

b The supply of pesos?

c The quantity of pesos demanded?

d The quantity of pesos supplied?

e The exchange rate of the peso against the US dollar?

9 If a euro deposit in a bank in Paris, France, earns interest of 4 per cent a year and a yen deposit in Tokyo, Japan, earns 0.5 per cent a year, other things remaining the same and adjusted for risk, what is the exchange rate expectation of the Japanese yen?

10 The UK pound is trading at 1.54 US dollars per UK pound. There is purchasing power parity at this exchange rate. The interest rate in the US is 2 per cent a year and the interest rate in the UK is 4 per cent a year.

a Calculate the UK interest rate differential.

b What is the UK pound expected to be worth in terms of US dollars one year from now?

c Which country more likely has the lower inflation rate? How can you tell?

11 Suppose that you can purchase a particular laptop from an online computer store for 827.12 euros or 477.25 pounds. The exchange rate is 1.4831 euros per pound. Does purchasing power parity prevail?

12 When the Chips Are Down

The *Economist* uses the price of a Big Mac to determine whether a currency is undervalued or overvalued. In July 2010, the price of a Big Mac was \$3.73 in New York, 13.2 yuan in Beijing, and 6.50 Swiss francs in Geneva. The exchange rates were 6.78 yuan per US dollar and 1.05 Swiss francs per US dollar.

Source: *The Economist*, 22 July 2010

a Was the yuan undervalued or overvalued relative to purchasing power parity?

b Was the Swiss franc undervalued or overvalued relative to purchasing power parity?

c Do you think the price of a Big Mac in different countries provides a valid test of purchasing power parity?

13 The Lesson: Buy Ruffles in Myanmar

A small bag of cheese-flavoured Ruffles potato chips is \$1.69 in Japan and only 8 cents in Myanmar. One hour at an Internet cafe costs \$0.62 in Vietnam, \$1.48 in China and \$3.40 in South Africa .

The Los Angeles Times, 23 April 2006

Do these prices indicate that purchasing power parity does not prevail? Why or why not?

14 The price level in the Eurozone is 112.4, the price level in the US is 109.1, and the nominal exchange rate was 80 euro cents per US dollar. What is the real exchange rate expressed as Eurozone real GDP per unit of US real GDP?

15 The US price level is 106.3, the Japanese price level is 95.4, and the real exchange rate is 103.6 Japanese real GDP per unit of US real GDP. What is the nominal exchange rate?

Exchange Rate Policy (Study Plan 25.3)

16 With the strengthening of the yen against the US dollar in 2010, Japan's central bank did not take any action. A leading Japanese politician has called on the central bank to take actions to weaken the yen, saying it will help exporters in the short run and have no long-run effects.

a What is Japan's current exchange rate policy?

b What does the politician want the exchange rate policy to be in the short run? Why would such a policy have no effect on the exchange rate in the long run?

17 **Double-talking the Dollar**

In the 1970s and 1980s, the US was constantly buying and selling foreign currencies to change the value of the dollar, but since 1995 it has made only a few transactions and since 2000 none at all. The foreign exchange market is so huge, trying to manipulate the dollar is largely futile. A currency's value reflects an economy's fundamentals: How well a country allocates resources, how productive its workers are, how it contains inflation, etc., but for years on end, currencies can move in directions that seem to have little to do with fundamentals. They overshoot their correct values, in part because nobody is ever sure exactly what those correct values are.

Source: *Time*, 5 May 2008

a How has US exchange rate policy evolved since the early 1970s?

b Explain why 'trying to manipulate the dollar is largely futile', especially in the long run.

c Explain why a currency can experience short-run fluctuations 'that seem to have little to do with fundamentals'. Illustrate with a graph.

European Monetary Union (Study Plan 25.4)

18 In the coalition accord following the 2010 General Election, the Conservative and Liberal Democrat parties agreed that 'Britain will not join or prepare to join the euro in this parliament'.

What are the costs of membership of the EMU that the UK avoids by retaining the pound sterling as its national currency? What are the benefits of membership that the UK is missing?

19 What are the benefits and costs that would arise if Wales left the pound sterling and established the 'Welsh leek' as its currency? Why might the balance of costs and benefits go against such a move?

Financing International Trade

(Study Plan 25.5)

20 The table gives some information about the UK international transactions in 2006.

Item	Billions of pounds
Imports of goods and services	424
Foreign investment in the UK	680
Exports of goods and services	370
UK investment abroad	656
Net interest income	23
Net transfers	–12

a Calculate the current account balance.

b Calculate the capital and financial account balance.

c Did UK reserves assets increase or decrease?

d Was the UK a net borrower or a net lender in 2006? Explain your answer.

21 **The US Debtor Nation**

The US is a debtor nation, and for most of the past 30 years it has been piling up large trade deficits. The current account has now reached a deficit of 6 per cent of GDP and must be financed by capital inflows. Foreigners must purchase large amounts of US assets, or the current account deficit cannot be financed.

Source: *Asia Times*, 28 September 2006

a Explain why a current account deficit 'must be financed by capital inflows'.

b Under what circumstances should the debtor nation status of the US be a concern?

ADDITIONAL PROBLEMS AND APPLICATIONS

myeconlab You can work these problems in MyEconLab if assigned by your lecturer.

The Foreign Exchange Market

22 Suppose that yesterday, the euro was trading on the foreign exchange market at 0.75 euros per US dollar and today the euro is trading at 0.78 euros per US dollar. Which of the two currencies (the euro or the US dollar) appreciated and which depreciated today?

23 Suppose that the exchange rate fell from 1.20 euros per pound to 1.16 euros per pound. What is the effect of this change on the quantity of euros that people plan to buy in the foreign exchange market?

24 Suppose that the exchange rate rose from 71 yen per US dollar to 100 yen per US dollar. What is the effect of this change on the quantity of US dollars that people plan to sell in the foreign exchange market?

25 Today's exchange rate between the yuan and the US dollar is 6.78 yuan per dollar and the central bank of China is buying US dollars in the foreign exchange market. If the central bank of China did not purchase US dollars would there be excess demand or excess supply of US dollars in the foreign exchange market? Would the exchange rate remain at 6.78 yuan per US dollar? If not, which currency would appreciate?

Exchange Rate Fluctuations

26 Yesterday, the current exchange rate was 0.95 US dollars per Canadian dollar and traders expected the exchange rate to remain unchanged for the next month. Today, with new information, traders now expect the exchange rate next month to rise to 1 US dollar per Canadian dollar. Explain how the revised expected future exchange rate influences the demand for Canadian dollars, or the supply of Canadian dollars, or both in the foreign exchange market.

27 On 1 January 2010, the exchange rate was 91 yen per US dollar. Over the year, the supply of US dollars increased and by January 2011, the exchange rate fell to 84 yen per US dollar. What happened to the quantity of US dollars that people planned to buy in the foreign exchange market?

Use the following news clip to work Problems 28 and 29.

Top US Real Estate Markets for Investment

Rahul Reddy has been investing in Australian real estate for the last two years. Now, with the Australian dollar growing in strength and the American housing market strained, he's got his eye on real estate in Florida and California. Encouraged by a weak US dollar and a belief in the resiliency of the US economy, investors are seeking investment properties and development opportunities in the US. Reddy says that the US is good for speculative higher-risk investments from our perspective because the strong Australian dollar will enable us to gain hold of real estate at prices we will probably not see for a long time. The US is an economic powerhouse that will recover, and if the exchange rate goes back to what it was a few years ago, investors will benefit.

Source: *Forbes*, 10 July 2008

28 Explain why foreigners are 'seeking investment properties and development opportunities in the US'.

29 Explain what would happen if the speculation made by Reddy became widespread. Would expectations become self-fulfilling?

Use the following information to work Problems 30 and 31.

Brazil's Overvalued Real

The Brazilian real has appreciated 33 per cent against the US dollar and has pushed up the price of a Big Mac in Sao Paulo to \$4.60, higher than the New York price of \$3.99. Despite Brazil's interest rate being at 8.75 per cent a year compared to the US interest rate at near zero, foreign funds flowing into Brazil surged in October.

Source: Bloomberg News, 27 October 2009

30 Does purchasing power parity hold? If not, does PPP predict that the Brazilian real will appreciate or depreciate against the US dollar? Explain.

31 Does interest rate parity hold? If not, why not? Will the Brazilian real appreciate further or depreciate against the US dollar if the US central bank raises the interest rate while the Brazilian interest rate remains at 8.75 per cent a year?

Exchange Rate Policy (Study Plan 25.3)

Use the following news clip to work Problems 32 to 35.

US Declines to Cite China as Currency Manipulator

The US has declined to cite China for manipulating its currency to gain unfair trade advantages against the US. America's growing trade deficit with China, which last year hit an all-time high of \$256.3 billion, is the largest deficit ever recorded with a single country. Chinese currency, the yuan, has risen in value by 18.4 per cent against the US dollar since the Chinese government loosened its currency system in July 2005. However, US manufacturers contend the yuan is still undervalued by as much as 40 per cent, making Chinese products more competitive in the US and US goods more expensive in China. China buys US dollar-denominated securities to maintain the value of the yuan in terms of the US dollar.

Source: MSN, 15 May 2008

32 What was the exchange rate policy adopted by China until July 2005? Explain how it worked. Draw a graph to illustrate your answer.

33 What was the exchange rate policy adopted by China after July 2005? Explain how it works.

34 Explain how fixed and crawling peg exchange rates can be used to manipulate trade balances in the short run, but not the long run.

35 Explain the long-run effect of China's current exchange rate policy.

36 **Aussie Dollar Hit by Interest Rate Talk**

The Australian dollar fell against the US dollar to its lowest value in the past two weeks. The CPI inflation rate was reported to be generally as expected but not high enough to justify previous expectations for an aggressive interest rate rise by Australia's central bank next week.

Source: Reuters, 28 October 2009

a What is Australia's exchange rate policy? Explain why expectations about the Australian interest rate lowered the value of the Australian dollar against the US dollar.

b To avoid the fall in the value of the Australian dollar against the US dollar, what action could the central bank of Australia have taken? Would such an action signal a change in Australia's exchange rate policy?

37 Japan's foreign exchange reserves have grown from $0.25 trillion in 2001 to $1.1 trillion in 2010. What has been Japan's exchange rate policy through these years?

European Monetary Union

38 The unemployment rate is much higher in Spain than in Germany. Does this fact mean that Spain would be better off leaving the euro and re-establishing the peseta as its national currency?

39 If the euro is a good idea, why isn't a single currency for the entire global economy an even better idea?

Financing International Trade

Use the following data to work Problems 40 to 42.The table gives some data about the UK economy in 2006.

Item	Billions of pounds
Consumption expenditure	827
Exports of goods and services	370
Government expenditure	288
Net taxes	278
Investment	229
Saving	185

40 Calculate the private sector balance.

41 Calculate the government sector balance.

42 Calculate net exports and show the relationship between the government sector balance and net exports.

Economics in the News

43 After you have studied *Reading Between the Lines* on pp. 604–605 answer the following questions.

a What does the Bank of Chile hope to achieve through its announced intervention in the foreign exchange market?

b What is the reason for the intervention?

c How will the announced intervention influence expectations?

d What will be the effects of the intervention in the short run and the long run?

44 **Gulf Countries Must Opt for Basket of Currencies**

Before 2008, the six countries of the Gulf Cooperation Council (GCC) had fixed exchange rates against the US dollar. Faced with a surge in inflation, they decided to establish the Gulf Monetary Union and common currency so that they could pursue a monetary policy independent of the US. The new currency would be pegged to a basket of currencies, comprising the US dollar, the Euro, the Japanese yen and the British pound. The exchange rate would be managed to tailor monetary policy to domestic conditions and withstand external shocks.

Source: *The Gulf Daily News*, 18 December 2008

a Explain why the GCC countries lacked independent monetary policy when their currencies were fixed to the US dollar.

b If the GCC countries had pursued an independent monetary policy and held their inflation steady, what would have happened to their exchange rates? Explain and illustrate.

c Why might a new common currency for the GCC countries linked to the US dollar, euro, yen and pound provide better insulation from US monetary policy?

d What would be the benefits arising from Gulf Monetary Union? What would be the costs of monetary union?

PART

8

Macroeconomic Fluctuations

Boom and Bust

To cure a disease and restore a patient to good health, doctors must first understand how the disease responds to different treatments. It also helps to understand the mechansims that operate to cause the disease.

Curing the economic ills of boom and bust is similar to curing our medical ills. We need to understand how the economy responds to the treatments we might prescribe to restore it to good health. We also need to understand the mechanisms that operate to cause a succession of boom and bust. The goal of the three chapters in this part is to explain what economists understand about these mechanisms.

Chapter 26 studies the *AS–AD* model, a model that explains what determines real GDP and the price level in the short run. The *AS–AD* model also enables us to see the ideas of the different schools of macroeconomic thought on the sources of aggregate fluctuations.

Chapter 27 explains the Keynesian aggregate expenditure model. This model provides the details on fluctuations in aggregate demand.

Chapter 28 looks at all the alternative theories of inflation and the business cycle and the short-run tradeoff between output and inflation (and between jobs and inflation).

Understanding Macroeconomic Fluctuations

During the Industrial Revolution, as technological change created new jobs and destroyed old ones, people began to wonder whether the economy could create enough jobs and sufficient demand to buy all the things that the new industrial economy could produce.

'No problem!' said John Baptiste Say. Writing in his 1803 book, *Traité d'économie politique* (*A Treatise on Political Economy*), he argues that production creates incomes that are sufficient to buy everything that is produced. This idea, put simply as 'supply creates its own demand', came to be known as *Say's Law*.

'A big problem!' said John Maynard Keynes. He turned Say's idea around and said it is demand that creates supply. Writing in his 1936 book, *The General Theory of Employment, Interest and Money*, he argued that aggregate production depends on what people are willing to buy. Production, said Keynes, depends on *effective* demand. Households, he noted, don't spend all their incomes on consumption. They save some of it. If businesses fail to spend on new capital (business investment) the amount that people save, aggregate demand will be less than aggregate supply and resources, particularly labour resources, will be unemployed and they could remain in that state indefinitely. According to Keynes, there are no automatic forces to restore full employment.

The aggregate supply–aggregate demand (*AS–AD*) model that you study in Chapter 26 combines the ideas of Say and Keynes. It is a model that translates Keynes' *General Theory* to explain how real GDP fluctuates around full employment. In this model, there is a mechanism that eventually restores full employment but it works slowly when resources are underemployed. At full employment, Say's Law operates and supply does create its own demand.

What you study in the next three chapters lays the foundation for the final part that investigates the role and power of fiscal policy and monetary policy to achieve inflation-free sustained growth of real GDP at full employment.

John Maynard Keynes, born in England in 1883, was one of the outstanding minds of the twentieth century. He represented Britain at the Versailles peace conference at the end of the First World War, was a master speculator on international financial markets (an activity he conducted from bed every morning and which made and lost him several fortunes) and played a prominent role in creating the International Monetary Fund.

He was a member of the Bloomsbury Group, a circle of outstanding artists and writers that included E. M. Forster, Bertrand Russell and Virginia Woolf.

Keynes was a controversial and quick-witted figure. A critic once complained that Keynes had changed his opinion on some matter, to which Keynes retorted: "When I discover I am wrong, I change my mind. What do you do?"

Keynes' book, *The General Theory of Employment, Interest and Money*, written during the Great Depression and published in 1936, revolutionized macroeconomics.

'The ideas of economists and political philosophers, both when they are right and when they are wrong, are more powerful than is commonly understood. Indeed the world is ruled by little else.'

JOHN MAYNARD KEYNES
The General Theory of Employment, Interest and Money

CHAPTER 26

Aggregate Supply and Aggregate Demand

After studying this chapter you will be able to:

- **Explain what determines aggregate supply**
- **Explain what determines aggregate demand**
- **Explain how real GDP and the price level are determined and what brings economic growth, inflation and the business cycle**
- **Describe the main schools of thought in macroeconomics**

The pace at which production grows and prices rise is uneven. Sometimes our economy is expanding and sometimes production and jobs shrink.

This chapter explains a model – the aggregate supply–aggregate demand model or *AS–AD* model – that represents the consensus view of macroeconomists about the forces that make our economy expand, that bring inflation and that cause business cycle fluctuations.

In *Reading Between the Lines* at the end of the chapter, we use the *AS–AD* model to interpret the course of real GDP and the price level in the German economy in 2010.

Aggregate Supply

The purpose of the aggregate supply–aggregate demand model that you study in this chapter is to explain how real GDP and the price level are determined and how they interact. The model uses similar ideas to those that you encountered in Chapter 3 when you learned how the quantity and price in a competitive market are determined. But the *aggregate* supply–*aggregate* demand model (*AS–AD* model) isn't just an application of the competitive market model. Some differences arise because the *AS–AD* model is a model of an imaginary market for the total of all the final goods and services. The quantity in this 'market' is real GDP and the price is the price level measured by the GDP deflator.

One thing that the *AS–AD* model shares with the competitive market model is that both distinguish between *supply* and the *quantity supplied*. We begin by explaining what we mean by the quantity of real GDP supplied.

Quantity Supplied and Supply

The *quantity of real GDP supplied* is the total quantity of goods and services, valued in constant base year (2006) pounds, that firms plan to produce during a given period. This quantity depends on the quantity of labour employed, the quantity of physical and human capital and the state of technology.

At any given time, the quantity of capital and the state of technology are fixed. They depend on decisions that were made in the past. The population is also fixed. But the quantity of labour is not fixed. It depends on decisions made by households and firms about the supply of and demand for labour.

The labour market can be in any one of three states: at full employment, above full employment, or below full employment. At full employment, the quantity of real GDP supplied is *potential GDP*, which depends on the full-employment quantity of labour (see Chapter 22, pp. 513–515). Over the business cycle, employment fluctuates around full employment and the quantity of real GDP supplied fluctuates around potential GDP.

Aggregate Supply Time Frames

Aggregate supply is the relationship between the quantity of real GDP supplied and the price level. This relationship is different in the long run than in the short run and to study aggregate supply, we distinguish between two time frames:

- Long-run aggregate supply
- Short-run aggregate supply

Long-run Aggregate Supply

Long-run aggregate supply is the relationship between the quantity of real GDP supplied and the price level when the money wage rate changes in step with the price level to maintain full employment. The quantity of real GDP supplied at full employment equals potential GDP and this quantity is the same regardless of the price level.

The *long-run aggregate supply curve* in Figure 26.1 illustrates long-run aggregate supply as the vertical line at potential GDP labelled *LAS*. Along the long-run aggregate supply curve, as the price level changes, the money wage rate also changes so the real wage rate remains at the full-employment equilibrium level and real GDP remains at potential GDP. The long-run aggregate supply curve is always vertical and is always located at potential GDP.

The long-run aggregate supply curve is vertical because potential GDP is independent of the price level. The reason for this independence is that a movement along the *LAS* curve is accompanied by a change in two sets of prices: the prices of goods and services – the price level – and the prices of the factors of production, most notably, the money wage rate. A 10 per cent increase in the prices of goods and services is matched by a 10 per cent increase in the money wage rate. Because the price level and the money wage rate change by the same percentage, the real wage rate remains unchanged at its full-employment equilibrium level. So when the price level changes and the real wage rate remains constant, employment remains constant and real GDP remains constant at potential GDP.

Production at a Pepsi Plant

You can see more clearly why real GDP is unchanged when all prices change by the same percentage by thinking about production decisions at a Pepsi bottling plant. How does the quantity of Pepsi supplied change if the price of Pepsi changes and the wage rate of the workers and prices of all the other resources used vary by the same percentage? The answer is that the quantity supplied doesn't change. The firm produces the quantity that maximizes profit. That quantity depends on the price of Pepsi relative to the cost of producing it. With no change in price relative to cost, production doesn't change.

Short-run Aggregate Supply

Short-run aggregate supply is the relationship between the quantity of real GDP supplied and the price level when the money wage rate, the prices of other resources and potential GDP remain constant. Figure 26.1 illustrates this relationship as the short-run aggregate supply curve *SAS* and the short-run aggregate supply schedule. Each point on the *SAS* curve corresponds to a row of the short-run aggregate supply schedule. For example, point *A* on the *SAS* curve and row *A* of the schedule tell us that if the price level is 100, the quantity of real GDP supplied is £1,200 billion. In the short run, a rise in the price level brings an increase in the quantity of real GDP supplied. The short-run aggregate supply curve slopes upward.

With a given money wage rate, there is one price level at which the real wage rate is at its full-employment equilibrium level. At this price level, the quantity of real GDP supplied equals potential GDP and the *SAS* curve intersects the *LAS* curve. In this example, that price level is 110. If the price level rises above 110, the quantity of real GDP supplied increases along the *SAS* curve and exceeds potential GDP; if the price level falls below 110, the quantity of real GDP supplied decreases along the *SAS* curve and is less than potential GDP.

Back at the Pepsi Plant

You can see why the short-run aggregate supply curve slopes upward by returning to the Pepsi bottling plant. If production increases, marginal cost rises and if production decreases, marginal cost falls (see Chapter 2, p. 35).

If the price of Pepsi rises with no change in the money wage rate and other costs, Pepsi can increase profit by increasing production. Pepsi is in business to maximize its profit, so it increases production.

Similarly, if the price of Pepsi falls while the money wage rate and other costs remain constant, Pepsi can avoid a loss by decreasing production. The lower price weakens the incentive to produce, so Pepsi decreases production.

And for the Economy

What's true for Pepsi bottlers is true for the producers of all goods and services. When all prices rise, the *price level* rises. If the price level rises and the money wage rate and other factor prices remain constant, all firms increase production and the quantity of real GDP supplied increases. A fall in the price level has the opposite effect and decreases the quantity of real GDP supplied.

Figure 26.1 Long-run and Short-run Aggregate Supply

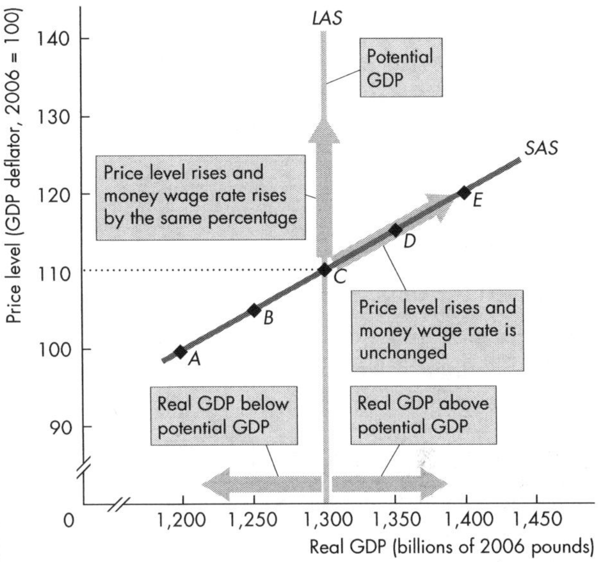

	Price level (GDP deflator)	Real GDP (billions of 2006 pounds)
A	100	1,200
B	105	1,250
C	110	1,300
D	115	1,350
E	120	1,400

In the long run, the quantity of real GDP supplied is potential GDP and the *LAS* curve is vertical at potential GDP. In the short-run, the quantity of real GDP supplied increases if the price level rises, while all other influences on supply plans remain the same.

The short-run aggregate supply curve, *SAS*, slopes upward. The short-run aggregate supply curve is based on the aggregate supply schedule in the table. Each point *A* to *E* on the curve corresponds to the row in the table identified by the same letter.

When the price level is 110, real GDP equals potential GDP (£1,300 billion). If the price level is greater than 110, real GDP exceeds potential GDP; if the price level is below 110, real GDP is less than potential GDP.

myeconlab Animation

Changes in Aggregate Supply

A change in the price level brings a change in the quantity of real GDP supplied, which is illustrated by a movement along the short-run aggregate supply curve. It does not change aggregate supply. Aggregate supply changes when an influence on production plans other than the price level changes. These other influences are changes in potential GDP and changes in the money wage rate. Let's begin by looking at a change in potential GDP.

Changes in Potential GDP

An increase in potential GDP increases both long-run aggregate supply and short-run aggregate supply. Figure 26.2 shows these effects.

Initially, the long-run aggregate supply curve is LAS_0 and the short-run aggregate supply curve is SAS_0. If potential GDP increases to £1,400 billion, long-run aggregate supply increases and the long-run aggregate supply curve shifts rightward to LAS_1. Short-run aggregate supply also increases, and the short-run aggregate supply curve shifts rightward to SAS_1. The two supply curves shift by the same amount only if the full-employment price level remains constant, which we will assume to be the case.

Potential GDP can increase for any of three reasons:

- An increase in the full-employment quantity of labour
- An increase in the quantity of capital
- An advance in technology

Let's look at these influences on potential GDP and the aggregate supply curves.

Figure 26.2 A Change in Potential GDP

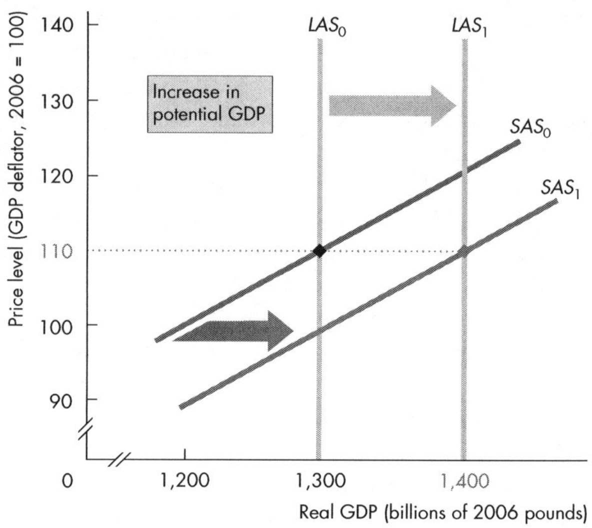

An increase in potential GDP increases both long-run aggregate supply and short-run aggregate supply. The long-run aggregate supply curve shifts rightward from LAS_0 to LAS_1 and the short-run aggregate supply curve shifts from SAS_0 to SAS_1.

myeconlab Animation

An Increase in the Full-employment Quantity of Labour

A Pepsi bottling plant that employs 100 workers bottles more Pepsi than an otherwise identical plant that employs 10 workers. The same is true for the economy as a whole. The larger the quantity of labour employed, the greater is real GDP.

Over time, real GDP increases because the labour force increases. But (with constant capital and technology) *potential* GDP increases only if the full-employment quantity of labour increases. Fluctuations in employment over the business cycle bring fluctuations in real GDP. But these changes in real GDP are fluctuations around potential GDP and long-run aggregate supply.

An Increase in the Quantity of Capital

A Pepsi bottling plant that has two production lines has more capital and produces more output than an otherwise identical plant that has one production line. For the economy, the larger the quantity of capital, the more productive is the workforce and the greater is its potential GDP. Potential GDP per person in capital-rich EU economies is vastly greater than that in capital-poor China and Russia.

Capital includes *human capital*. One bottling plant is managed by an economics graduate with an MBA and has a workforce with an average of 10 years of experience. This plant produces a much larger output than an otherwise identical plant that is managed by someone with no business training or experience and that has a young workforce that is new to bottling. The first plant has a greater amount of human capital than the second. For the economy as a whole, the larger the quantity of *human capital* – the skills that people have acquired in school and through on-the-job-training – the greater is potential GDP.

An Advance in Technology

A Pepsi bottling plant that has pre-computer age machines produces less than one that uses the latest robot technology. Technological change enables firms to produce more from any given amount of inputs. So even with fixed quantities of labour and capital, improvements in technology increase potential GDP.

Technological advances are by far the most important source of increased production over the past two centuries. Because of technological advances, one farmer in the UK today can feed 100 people and one auto worker can produce almost 14 cars and lorries in a year.

Let's now look at the effects of changes in the money wage rate and other resource prices.

Changes in the Money Wage Rate and Other Resource Prices

When the money wage rate or the money prices of other resources (such as the price of oil) change, short-run aggregate supply changes but long-run aggregate supply does not change.

Figure 26.3 shows the effect on aggregate supply of an increase in the money wage rate. Initially, the short-run aggregate supply curve is SAS_0. A rise in the money wage rate *decreases* short-run aggregate supply and shifts the short-run aggregate supply curve leftward to SAS_2.

The money wage rate (and other resource prices) affect short-run aggregate supply because they influence firms' costs. The higher the money wage rate, the higher are firms' costs and the smaller is the quantity that firms are willing to supply at each price level. So an increase in the money wage rate decreases short-run aggregate supply.

A change in the money wage rate does not change long-run aggregate supply because on the *LAS* curve, a change in the money wage rate is accompanied by an equal percentage change in the price level. With no change in *relative* prices, firms have no incentive to change production and real GDP remains constant at potential GDP. With no change in potential GDP, the long-run aggregate supply curve remains at *LAS*.

What Makes the Money Wage Rate Change?

The money wage rate can change for two reasons: departures from full employment and expectations about inflation. Unemployment above the natural rate puts downward pressure on the money wage rate, and unemployment below the natural rate puts upward pressure on the money wage rate. An expected increase in the inflation rate makes the money wage rate rise faster, and an expected decrease in the inflation rate slows the rate at which the money wage rate rises.

Figure 26.3 A Change in the Money Wage Rate

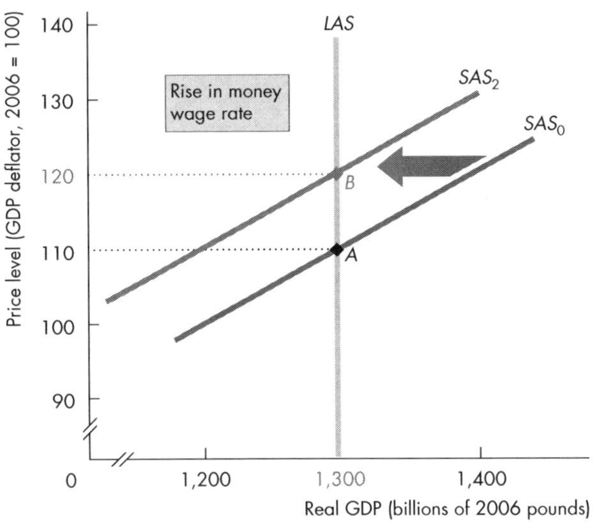

A rise in the money wage rate decreases short-run aggregate supply and shifts the short-run aggregate supply curve leftward from SAS_0 to SAS_2. A rise in the money wage rate does not change potential GDP, so the long-run aggregate supply curve does not shift.

myeconlab Animation

Review Quiz

1. If the price level and the money wage rate rise by the same percentage, what happens to the quantity of real GDP supplied? Along which aggregate supply curve does the economy move?
2. If the price level rises and the money wage rate remains constant, what happens to the quantity of real GDP supplied? Along which aggregate supply curve does the economy move?
3. If potential GDP increases, what happens to aggregate supply? Is there a shift of or a movement along the *LAS* curve? Does the *SAS* curve shift or is there a movenment along the *SAS* curve?
4. If the money wage rate rises and potential GDP remains the same, does the *LAS* curve or the *SAS* curve shift or is there a movement along the *LAS* curve or the *SAS* curve?

You can work these questions in Study Plan 26.1 and get instant feedback. myeconlab

Aggregate Demand

The quantity of real GDP demanded is the sum of real consumption expenditure (C), investment (I), government expenditure (G) and exports (X) minus imports (M). That is:

$$Y = C + I + G + X - M$$

The *quantity of real GDP demanded* is the total amount of final goods and services produced in the UK that people, businesses, governments and foreigners plan to buy.

These buying plans depend on many factors. The four main ones are:

1 The price level
2 Expectations
3 Fiscal policy and monetary policy
4 The world economy

We first focus on the relationship between the quantity of real GDP demanded and the price level. To study this relationship, we keep all other influences on buying plans the same and ask: How does the quantity of real GDP demanded vary as the price level varies?

Figure 26.4 Aggregate Demand

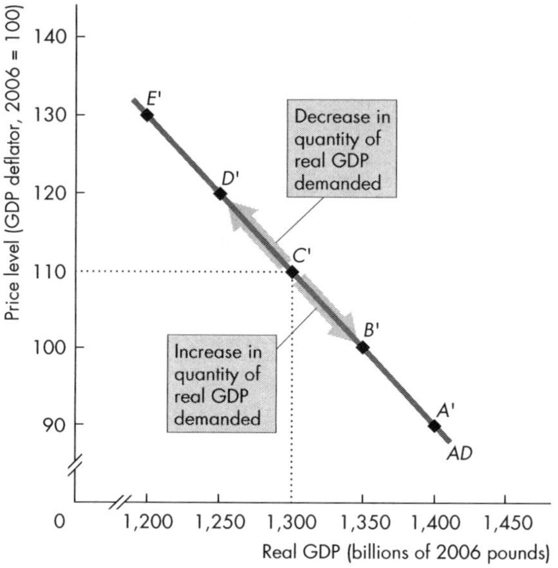

	Price level (GDP deflator)	Real GDP (billions of 2006 pounds)
A'	90	1,400
B'	100	1,350
C'	110	1,300
D'	120	1,250
E'	130	1,200

The aggregate demand curve (*AD*) shows the relationship between the quantity of real GDP demanded and the price level. The aggregate demand curve is based on the aggregate demand schedule in the table. Each point *A'* to *E'* on the curve corresponds to the row in the table identified by the same letter. For example, when the price level is 110, the quantity of real GDP demanded is £1,300 billion, shown by point *C'* in the figure.

A change in the price level with all other influences on aggregate buying plans remaining the same brings a change in the quantity of real GDP demanded and a movement along the *AD* curve.

myeconlab Animation

The Aggregate Demand Curve

Other things remaining the same, the higher the price level, the smaller is the quantity of real GDP demanded. This relationship between the quantity of real GDP demanded and the price level is called **aggregate demand**. Aggregate demand is described by an aggregate demand schedule and an aggregate demand curve.

Figure 26.4 shows an aggregate demand curve (*AD*) and an aggregate demand schedule. Each point on the *AD* curve corresponds to a row of the schedule. For example, point *C'* on the *AD* curve and row *C'* of the schedule tell us that if the price level is 110, the quantity of real GDP demanded is £1,300 billion.

The aggregate demand curve slopes downward for two reasons:

- Wealth effect
- Substitution effects

Wealth Effect

When the price level rises but other things remain the same, *real* wealth decreases. Real wealth is the amount of money in the bank, bonds, shares and other assets that people own, measured not in pounds but in terms of the goods and services that this money, bonds and shares will buy.

People save and hold money, bonds, shares and other assets for many reasons. One reason is to build up funds for education expenses. Another reason is to build up enough funds to meet possible medical or other big bills. But the biggest reason is to build up enough funds to provide a retirement income.

If the price level rises, real wealth decreases. People then try to restore their wealth. To do so, they must increase saving and, equivalently, decrease current consumption. Such a decrease in consumption is a decrease in aggregate demand.

Maria's Wealth Effect

You can see how the wealth effect works by thinking about Maria's buying plans. Maria lives in Moscow, Russia. She has worked hard all summer and saved 20,000 rubles (the ruble is the currency of Russia), which she plans to spend attending graduate school when she has finished her economics degree. So Maria's wealth is 20,000 rubles. Maria has a part-time job, and her income from this job pays her current expenses. The price level in Russia rises by 100 per cent, and now Maria needs 40,000 rubles to buy what 20,000 rubles once bought. To try to make up some of the fall in value of her savings, Maria saves even more and cuts her current spending to the bare minimum.

Substitution Effects

When the price level rises and other things remain the same, interest rates rise. The reason is related to the wealth effect that you've just studied. A rise in the price level decreases the real value of the money in people's pockets and bank accounts. With a smaller amount of real money around, banks can get a higher interest rate on loans. But faced with higher interest rates, people and businesses delay plans to buy new capital and consumer durable goods and cut back on spending.

This substitution effect involves changing the timing of capital consumer durable goods purchases and is called an *intertemporal* substitution effect – a substitution across time. Saving increases to increase future consumption.

To see this intertemporal substitution effect more clearly, think about your own plan to buy a new computer. At an interest rate of 5 per cent a year, you might borrow £1,000 and buy the new machine you've been researching. But at an interest rate of 10 per cent a year, you might decide that the payments would be too high. You don't abandon your plan to buy the computer, but you decide to delay your purchase.

A second substitution effect works through international prices. When the UK price level rises and other things remain the same, UK-made goods and services become more expensive relative to foreign-made goods and services. This change in *relative prices* encourages people to spend less on UK-made items and more on foreign-made items. For example, if the UK price level rises relative to the price level in France, fewer Vauxhall Vectras are sold in France and more Renaults are sold in the UK. Exports from the UK decrease, imports into the UK increase and the quantity of UK real GDP demanded decreases.

Maria's Substitution Effects

In Moscow, Maria makes some substitutions. She was planning to trade in her old motor scooter and get a new one. But with a higher price level and faced with higher interest rates, she decides to make her old scooter last one more year. Also, with the prices of Russian goods sharply increasing, Maria substitutes a low-cost dress made in Malaysia for the Russian-made dress she had originally planned to buy.

Changes in the Quantity of Real GDP Demanded

When the price level rises and other things remain the same, the quantity of real GDP demanded decreases – a movement up along the *AD* curve as shown by the arrow in Figure 26.4. When the price level falls and other things remain the same, the quantity of real GDP demanded increases – a movement down along the *AD* curve.

We've now seen how the quantity of real GDP demanded changes when the price level changes. How do other influences on buying plans affect aggregate demand?

Changes in Aggregate Demand

A change in any factor that influences buying plans other than the price level brings a change in aggregate demand. The main factors are:

- Expectations
- Fiscal policy and monetary policy
- The world economy

Expectations

An increase in expected future disposable income, other things remaining the same, increases the amount of consumption goods (especially items such as cars) that people plan to buy today and increases aggregate demand today.

An increase in the expected future inflation rate increases aggregate demand today because people decide to buy more goods and services at today's relatively lower prices. An increase in expected future profit increases the investment that firms plan to undertake today and increases aggregate demand today.

Fiscal Policy and Monetary Policy

The government's attempt to influence the economy by setting and changing taxes, making transfer payments and purchasing goods and services is called **fiscal policy**. A tax cut or an increase in transfer payments – for example, unemployment benefits or welfare payments – increases aggregate demand. Both of these influences operate by increasing households' *disposable* income. **Disposable income** is aggregate income minus taxes plus transfer payments. The greater the disposable income, the greater is the quantity of consumption goods and services that households plan to buy and the greater is aggregate demand.

Government expenditure on goods and services is one component of aggregate demand. So if the government spends more on hospitals, schools and motorways, aggregate demand increases.

Monetary policy consists of changes in interest rates and in the quantity of money in the economy. The quantity of money in the UK is determined by the Bank of England and the banks (in a process described in Chapter 24). An increase in the quantity of money increases aggregate demand.

To see why money affects aggregate demand, imagine that the Bank of England borrows the army's helicopters, loads them with millions of new £5 notes and sprinkles these notes like confetti across the nation. People gather the newly available money and plan to spend some of it. So the quantity of goods and services demanded increases. But people don't plan to spend all the new money. They save some of it and lend it to others through the banks. The interest rate falls, and with a lower interest rate, people plan to buy more consumer durables and firms plan to increase their investment.

The World Economy

Aggregate demand in each individual country is influenced by events in the world economy. The two main influences are changes in the foreign exchange rate and changes in world income. The *foreign exchange rate* is the amount of a foreign currency that you can

ECONOMICS IN ACTION

Fiscal Policy to Fight Recession

In 2008, as recession deepened, the world's two largest economies embarked on a massive fiscal stimulus. The US Congress cut taxes by $300 billion and increased government expenditure by $540 billion, totalling 6 per cent of US GDP. In China, government spending was increased by $200 billion or 5 per cent of GDP. The UK stimulus was 1.5 per cent of GDP.

The idea of these fiscal measures was to stimulate business investment and consumption expenditure and increase aggregate demand.

Monetary Policy to Fight Recession

In October 2008 and the months that followed, the central banks of the major Western economies, the US Federal Reserve, the European Central Bank, the Bank of Canada and the Bank of England, together cut their interest rates and took other measures to ease credit and encourage banks and other financial institutions to increase their lending.

Like the accompanying fiscal stimulus packages, the idea of these interest rate cuts and easier credit was to stimulate business investment and consumption expenditure and increase aggregate demand.

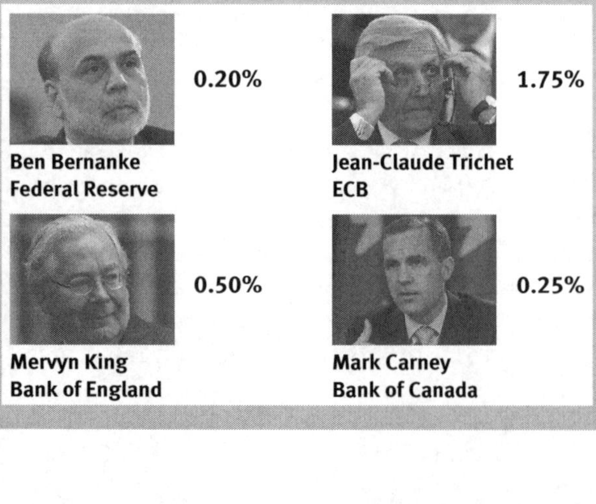

buy with a unit of domestic currency. Other things remaining the same, a rise in a country's foreign exchange rate decreases aggregate demand.

To see how the UK's foreign exchange rate influences aggregate demand in the UK, suppose that £1 is worth €1.10. A pair of Gucci shoes made in Italy costs €220 and an equivalent pair of Church's shoes made in England costs £190. In pounds, the Gucci shoes cost £200, so people around the world buy the cheaper Church's shoes from the UK.

Now suppose the exchange rate rises to €1.40 per pound. The Gucci shoes now cost £157.14 and are cheaper than the Church's shoes. People switch from Church's to Gucci shoes. As they make this switch, UK exports decrease, UK imports increase and aggregate demand in the UK decreases.

An increase in foreign income increases UK exports and increases UK aggregate demand – the aggregate demand for UK-produced goods and services. For example, an increase in income in the US, Japan and Germany increases the American, Japanese and German consumers' and producers' planned expenditures on UK-produced consumption goods and capital goods.

Figure 26.5 Changes in Aggregate Demand

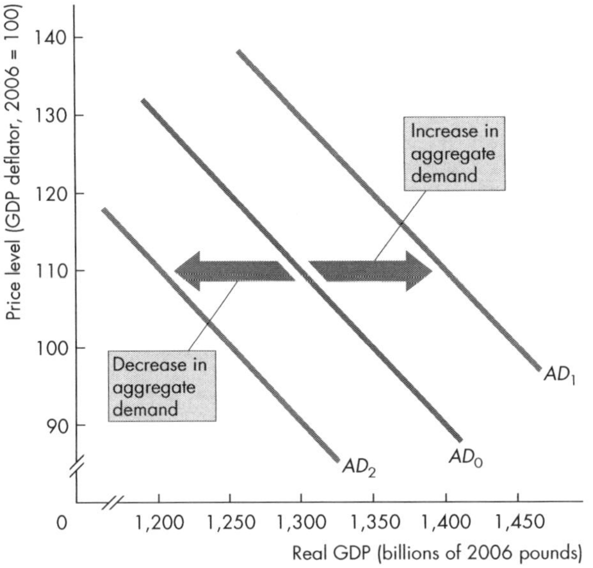

Aggregate demand

Decreases if:	*Increases if*:
◆ Expected future disposable income, inflation or profit decreases	◆ Expected future disposable income, inflation or profit increases
◆ Fiscal policy decreases government expenditure on goods and services, increases taxes or decreases transfer payments	◆ Fiscal policy increases government expenditure on goods and services, decreases taxes or increases transfer payments
◆ Monetary policy increases interest rates and decreases the quantity of money	◆ Monetary policy decreases interest rates and increases the quantity of money
◆ The foreign exchange rate increases or foreign income decreases	◆ The foreign exchange rate decreases or foreign income increases

myeconlab Animation

Shifts of the Aggregate Demand Curve

When aggregate demand changes, the aggregate demand curve shifts. Figure 26.5 shows two changes in aggregate demand and summarizes the factors that bring about such changes.

Aggregate demand increases and the aggregate demand curve shifts rightward from AD_0 to AD_1 when expected future disposable income, inflation or profit increases; government expenditure on goods and services increases; taxes are cut; transfer payments increase; the quantity of money increases and interest rates fall; the foreign exchange rate falls; or foreign income increases.

Aggregate demand decreases and the aggregate demand curve shifts leftward from AD_0 to AD_2 when expected future disposable income, inflation or profit decreases; government expenditure on goods and services decreases; taxes increase; transfer payments decrease; the quantity of money decreases and interest rates rise; the foreign exchange rate rises; or foreign income decreases.

Review Quiz

1. What does the aggregate demand curve show? What factors change and what factors remain the same when there is a movement along the aggregate demand curve?
2. Why does the aggregate demand curve slope downward?
3. How do changes in expectations, fiscal policy, monetary policy and the world economy change aggregate demand and the aggregate demand curve?

You can work these questions in Study Plan 26.2 and get instant feedback. myeconlab

Explaining Macroeconomic Trends and Fluctuations

The purpose of the *AS–AD* model is to explain changes in real GDP and the price level. The model's main purpose is to explain business cycle fluctuations in these variables. But the model also aids our understanding of economic growth and inflation trends. We begin by combining aggregate supply and aggregate demand to determine real GDP and the price level in equilibrium. Just as there are two time frames for aggregate supply, there are two time frames for macroeconomic equilibrium: a long-run equilibrium and a short-run equilibrium. We'll first look at short-run equilibrium.

Short-run Macroeconomic Equilibrium

The aggregate demand curve tells us the quantity of real GDP demanded at each price level, and the short-run aggregate supply curve tells us the quantity of real GDP supplied at each price level. **Short-run macroeconomic equilibrium** occurs when the quantity of real GDP demanded equals the short-run quantity of real GDP supplied at the point of intersection of the *AD* curve and the *SAS* curve. Figure 26.6 illustrates such an equilibrium at a price level of 110 and real GDP of £1,300 billion (point *C* and *C*').

To see why this position is the equilibrium, think about what happens if the price level is something other than 110. Suppose, for example, that the price level is 120 and that real GDP is £1,400 billion (at point *E* on the *SAS* curve). The quantity of real GDP demanded is less than £1,400 billion, so firms are unable to sell all their output. Unwanted inventories (stocks) pile up, and firms cut both production and prices. Production and prices are cut until firms can sell all their output. This situation occurs only when real GDP is £1,300 billion and the price level is 110.

Now suppose that the price level is 100 and real GDP is £1,200 billion (at point *A* on the *SAS* curve). The quantity of real GDP demanded exceeds £1,200 billion, so firms are unable to meet demand for their output. Inventories (stocks of finished but unsold items) decrease and customers clamour for more goods and services than firms are producing. So firms increase production and raise prices. Production and prices increase until firms can meet demand. This situation occurs only when real GDP is £1,300 billion and the price level is 110.

Figure 26.6 Short-run Macroeconomic Equilibrium

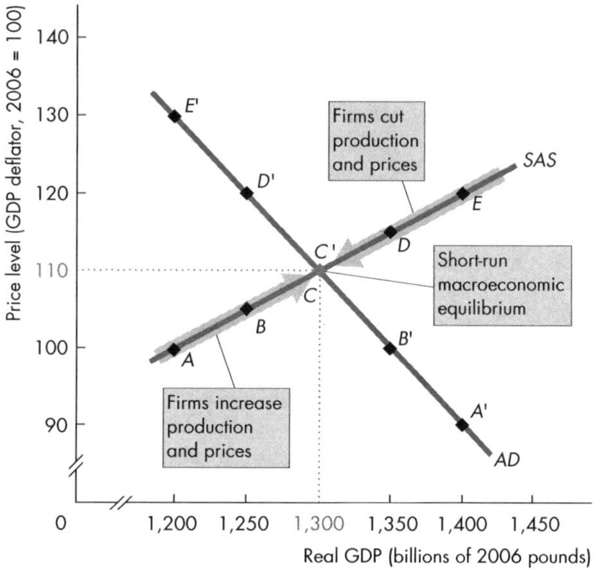

Short-run macroeconomic equilibrium occurs when real GDP demanded equals real GDP supplied – at the intersection of the aggregate demand curve (*AD*) and the short-run aggregate supply curve (*SAS*).

myeconlab Animation

In short-run macroeconomic equilibrium, the money wage rate is fixed. It does not adjust to bring full employment. So in the short run, real GDP can be greater than or less than potential GDP. But in the long run, the money wage rate does adjust and real GDP moves towards potential GDP. Let's look at the long-run equilibrium and see how we get there.

Long-run Macroeconomic Equilibrium

Long-run macroeconomic equilibrium occurs when real GDP equals potential GDP – equivalently, when the economy is on its *LAS* curve.

When the economy is away from long-run equilibrium, the money wage rate adjusts. If the money wage rate is too high, short-run equilibrium is below potential GDP and the unemployment rate is above the natural rate. With an excess supply of labour, the money wage rate falls. If the money wage rate is too low, short-run equilibrium is above potential GDP and the unemployment rate is below the natural rate. With an excess demand for labour, the money wage rate rises.

Figure 26.7 shows the long-run equilibrium and how it comes about. If the short-run aggregate supply curve is SAS_1, the money wage rate is too high to achieve full employment. A fall in the money wage rate shifts the *SAS* curve to *SAS** and brings full employment. If the short-run aggregate supply curve is SAS_2, the money wage rate is too low to achieve full employment. Now, a rise in the money wage rate shifts the *SAS* curve to *SAS** and brings full employment.

In long-run equilibrium, potential GDP determines real GDP and potential GDP and aggregate demand together determine the price level. The money wage rate adjusts to put the *SAS* curve through the long-run equilibrium point.

Let's now see how the *AS–AD* model helps us to understand economic growth and inflation.

Figure 26.7 Long-run Macroeconomic Equilibrium

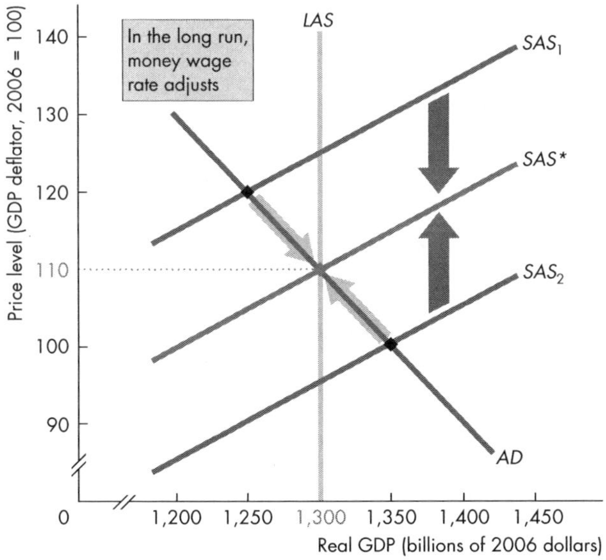

In long-run macroeconomic equilibrium, real GDP equals potential GDP. So long-run equilibrium occurs where the aggregate demand curve *AD* intersects the long-run aggregate supply curve *LAS*. In the long run, aggregate demand determines the price level and has no effect on real GDP. The money wage rate adjusts in the long run, so the *SAS* curve intersects the *LAS* curve at the long-run equilibrium price level.

myeconlab Animation

Economic Growth and Inflation in the *AS–AD* Model

Economic growth results from a growing labour force and increasing labour productivity, which together make potential GDP grow (Chapter 22, pp. 515–518). Inflation results from a growing quantity of money that outpaces the growth of potential GDP (Chapter 24, pp. 574–575).

The *AS–AD* model explains and illustrates economic growth and inflation. It explains economic growth as increasing long-run aggregate supply and it explains inflation as a persistent increase in aggregate demand at a faster pace than that of the increase in potential GDP.

ECONOMICS IN ACTION

UK Economic Growth and Inflation

The figure is a scatter diagram of UK real GDP and the price level. The graph has the same axes as those of the *AS–AD* model. Each dot represents a year between 1960 and 2010. The red dots are recession years. The pattern formed by the dots shows the combination of economic growth and inflation. Economic growth was fastest during the 1960s; inflation was fastest during the 1970s.

The *AS–AD* model interprets each dot as being at the intersection of the *SAS* and *AD* curves.

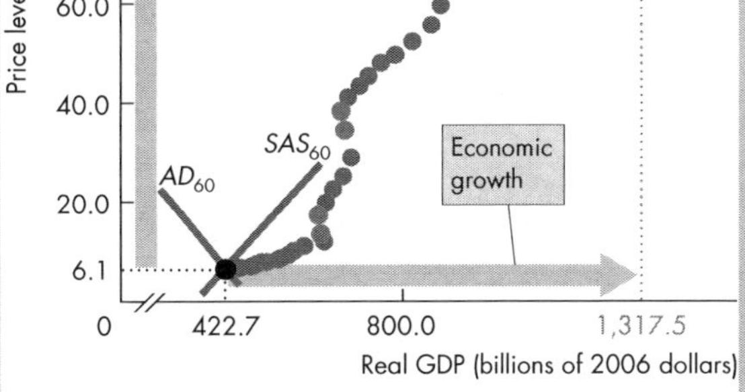

Figure 1 The Path of Real GDP and the Price Level

Source of data: Office for National Statistics

Figure 26.8 illustrates this explanation in terms of the shifting *LAS*, *SAS* and *AD* curves.

When the *LAS* curve shifts rightward from LAS_0 to LAS_1, potential GDP grows from £1,300 billion to £1,400 billion and in long-run equilibrium, real GDP also grows to £1,400 billion.

When the *AD* curve shifts rightward from AD_0 to AD_1, which is a growth of aggregate demand that outpaces the growth of potential GDP, the price level rises from 110 to 120.

If aggregate demand were to increase at the same pace as long-run aggregate supply, real GDP would grow with no inflation.

Our economy experiences periods of growth and inflation, like those shown in Figure 26.8, but it does not experience steady growth and steady inflation. Real GDP fluctuates around potential GDP in a business cycle. When we study the business cycle, we ignore economic growth and focus on the fluctuations around the trend. By doing so, we see the business cycle more clearly. Let's now see how the *AS–AD* model explains the business cycle.

Figure 26.8 Economic Growth and Inflation

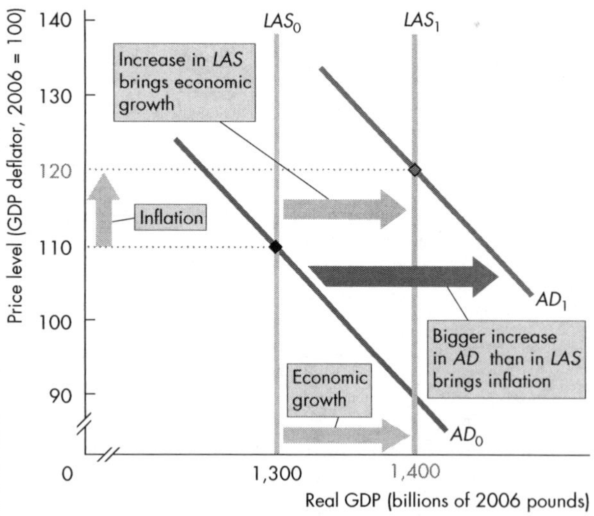

Economic growth is the persistent increase in potential GDP. Economic growth is shown as an ongoing rightward shift of the *LAS* curve. Inflation is the persistent rise in the price level. Inflation occurs when aggregate demand increases by more than the increase in long-run aggregate supply.

myeconlab Animation

The Business Cycle in the *AS–AD* Model

The business cycle occurs because aggregate demand and short-run aggregate supply fluctuate but the money wage rate does not adjust quickly enough to keep real GDP at potential GDP. Figure 26.9 shows three types of short-run equilibrium.

Figure 26.9(a) shows an above full-employment equilibrium. An **above full-employment equilibrium** is an equilibrium in which real GDP exceeds potential GDP. The gap between real GDP and potential GDP is the **output gap**. When real GDP exceeds potential GDP, the output gap is called an **inflationary gap**.

The above full-employment equilibrium shown in Figure 26.9(a) occurs where the aggregate demand curve AD_0 intersects the short-run aggregate supply

ECONOMICS IN ACTION

The UK Business Cycle

The UK economy had an inflationary gap in 2004 (at *A* in the figure), full employment in 2008 (at *B*) and a recessionary gap in 2009 (at *C*). The fluctuating output gap in the figure is the real-world version of Figure 26.9(d) and is generated by fluctuations in aggregate demand and short-run aggregate supply.

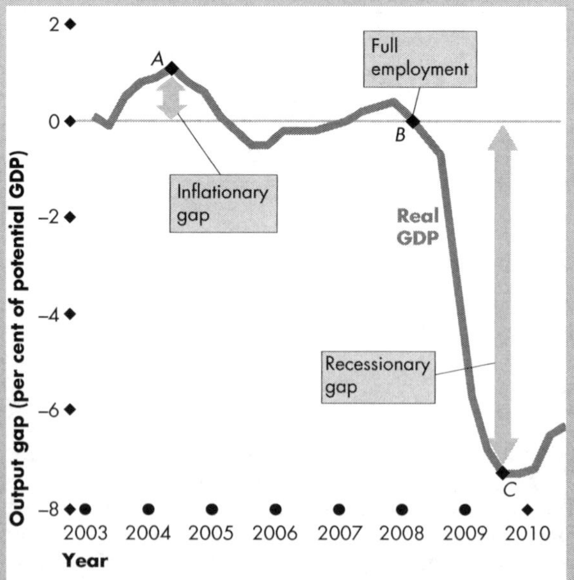

Figure 1 The UK Output Gap

Source of data: Office for National Statistics.

curve SAS_0 at a real GDP of £1,320 billion. There is an inflationary gap of £20 billion.

Figure 26.9(b) is an example of **full-employment equilibrium**, in which real GDP equals potential GDP. In this example, the equilibrium occurs where the aggregate demand curve AD_1 intersects the short-run aggregate supply curve SAS_1 at an actual and potential GDP of £1,300 billion.

In part (c), there is a below full-employment equilibrium. A **below full-employment equilibrium** is an equilibrium in which potential GDP exceeds real GDP. When potential GDP exceeds real GDP, the output gap is called a **recessionary gap**.

The below full-employment equilibrium shown in Figure 26.9(c) occurs where the aggregate demand curve AD_2 intersects the short-run aggregate supply curve SAS_2 at a real GDP of £1,280 billion with a recessionary gap of £20 billion.

The economy moves from one type of macroeconomic equilibrium to another as a result of fluctuations in aggregate demand and in short-run aggregate supply. These fluctuations produce fluctuations in real GDP. Figure 26.9(d) shows how real GDP fluctuates around potential GDP.

Let's now look at some of the sources of these fluctuations around potential GDP.

Figure 26.9 The Business Cycle

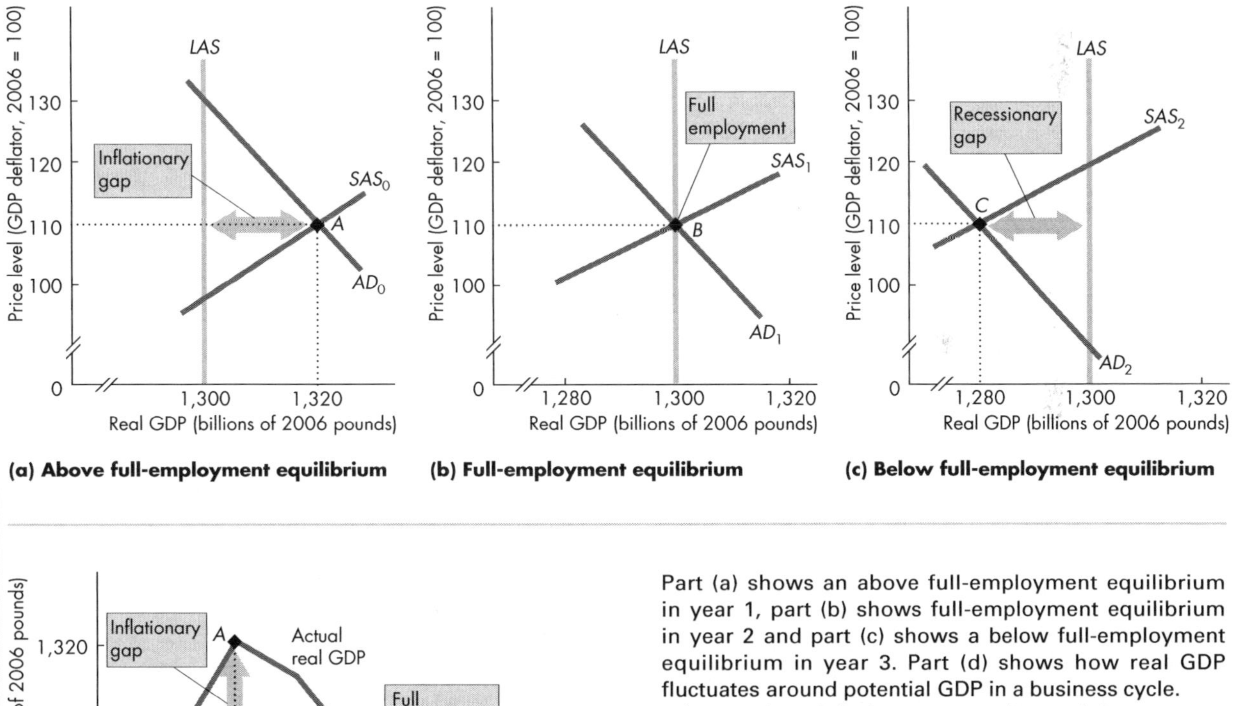

(a) Above full-employment equilibrium **(b) Full-employment equilibrium** **(c) Below full-employment equilibrium**

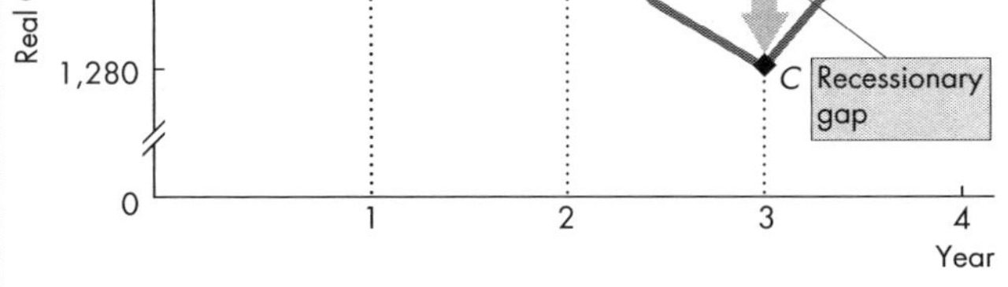

(d) Fluctuations in real GDP

Part (a) shows an above full-employment equilibrium in year 1, part (b) shows full-employment equilibrium in year 2 and part (c) shows a below full-employment equilibrium in year 3. Part (d) shows how real GDP fluctuates around potential GDP in a business cycle.

In year 1, an inflationary gap exists and the economy is at point *A*, in parts (a) and (d). In year 2, the economy is in full-employment equilibrium and the economy is at point *B* in parts (b) and (d). In year 3, a recessionary gap exists and the economy is at point *C* in parts (c) and (d).

myeconlab Animation

Fluctuations in Aggregate Demand

One reason real GDP fluctuates around potential GDP is that aggregate demand fluctuates. Let's see what happens when aggregate demand increases.

Figure 26.10(a) shows an economy at full employment. The aggregate demand curve is AD_0, the short-run aggregate supply curve is SAS_0 and the long-run aggregate supply curve is *LAS*. Real GDP equals potential GDP at £1,300 billion and the price level is 110.

Now suppose that the world economy expands and that the demand for UK-made goods increases in Japan, Canada and the US. The increase in UK exports increases aggregate demand and the aggregate demand curve shifts rightward from AD_0 to AD_1 in Figure 26.10(a).

Faced with an increase in demand, firms increase production and raise prices. Real GDP increases to £1,350 billion and the price level rises to 115. The economy is now in an above full-employment equilibrium. Real GDP exceeds potential GDP and there is an inflationary gap.

The increase in aggregate demand has increased the prices of all goods and services. Faced with higher prices, firms have increased their output rates. At this stage, prices of goods and services have increased but the money wage rate has not changed. (Recall that as we move along a short-run aggregate supply curve, the money wage rate is constant.)

Because the price level has increased and the money wage rate is unchanged, workers have experienced a fall in the buying power of their wages and firms' profits have increased. In these circumstances, workers demand higher wages and firms, anxious to maintain their employment and output levels, meet those demands. If firms do not raise the money wage rate, they will either lose workers or have to hire less productive ones.

As the money wage rate rises, the short-run aggregate supply curve begins to shift leftward. In Figure 26.10(b),

Figure 26.10 An Increase in Aggregate Demand

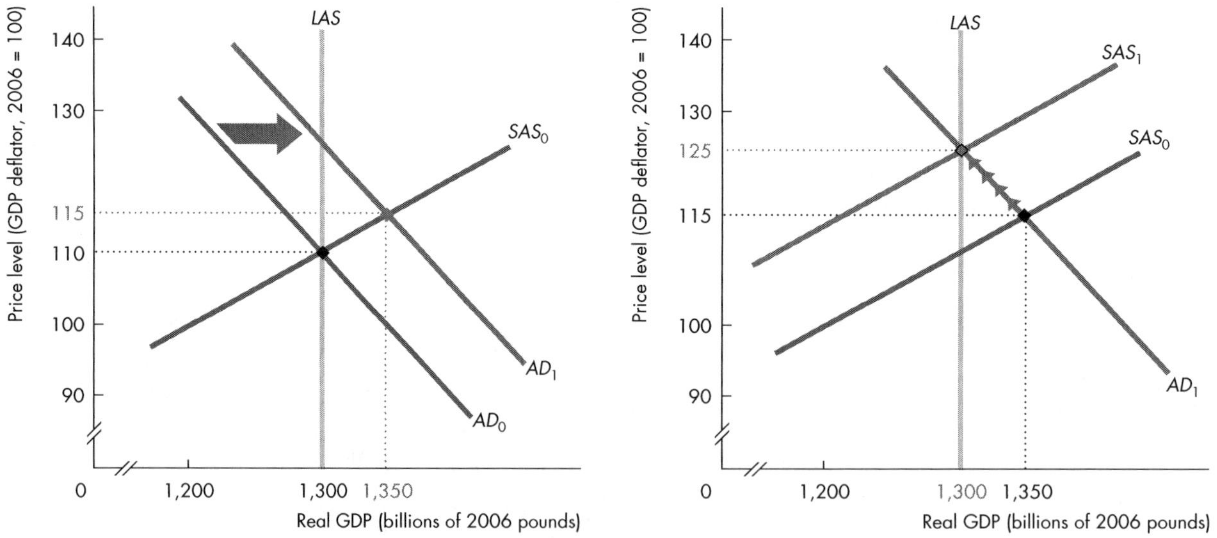

(a) Short-run effect

An increase in aggregate demand shifts the aggregate demand curve from AD_0 to AD_1. In the short run (part a), real GDP increases from £1,300 billion to £1,350 billion and the price level rises from 110 to 115. The economy has moved up along the *SAS* curve. In this situation, an inflationary gap exists.

(b) Long-run effect

In the long run (part b), with an inflationary gap, the money wage rate starts to rise. The short-run aggregate supply curve starts to shift leftward from SAS_0 to SAS_1. As the *SAS* curve shifts leftward, it intersects the aggregate demand curve AD_1 at higher price levels and real GDP decreases. Eventually, the price level rises to 125 and real GDP decreases to £1,300 billion – potential GDP.

myeconlab Animation

the short-run aggregate supply curve shifts from SAS_0 towards SAS_1. The rise in the money wage rate and the shift in the *SAS* curve produce a sequence of new equilibrium positions. Along the adjustment path, real GDP decreases and the price level rises. The economy moves up along its aggregate demand curve as the arrow heads show.

Eventually, the money wage rate rises by the same percentage as the price level. At this time, the aggregate demand curve AD_1 intersects SAS_1 at a new long-run equilibrium. The price level has risen to 125, and real GDP is back where it started, at potential GDP.

A decrease in aggregate demand has similar but opposite effects to those of an increase in aggregate demand. That is, a decrease in aggregate demand shifts the aggregate demand curve leftward. Real GDP decreases to less than potential GDP and a recessionary gap emerges. Firms cut prices. The lower price level increases the purchasing power of wages and increases firms' costs relative to their output prices because the money wage rate remains unchanged. Eventually, the money wage rate falls and the short-run aggregate supply curve shifts rightward. But the money wage rate changes slowly, so real GDP slowly returns to potential GDP and the price level falls slowly.

Let's now work out how real GDP and the price level change when aggregate supply changes.

Fluctuations in Aggregate Supply

Fluctuations in short-run aggregate supply can bring fluctuations in real GDP around potential GDP. Suppose that initially, real GDP equals potential GDP. Then there is a large but temporary rise in the price of oil. What happens to real GDP and the price level?

Figure 26.11 answers this question. The aggregate demand curve is AD_0, the short-run aggregate supply curve is SAS_0 and the long-run aggregate supply curve is *LAS*. Equilibrium real GDP is £1,300 billion, which equals potential GDP, and the price level is 110. Then the price of oil rises. Faced with higher energy and transportation costs, firms decrease production. Short-run aggregate supply decreases and the short-run aggregate supply curve shifts leftward to SAS_1. The price level rises to 120 and real GDP decreases to £1,250 billion.

Because real GDP decreases, the economy experiences recession. Because the price level increases, the economy experiences inflation. A combination of recession and inflation, called **stagflation**, actually occurred in the UK in the mid-1970s.

Figure 26.11 A Decrease in Aggregate Supply

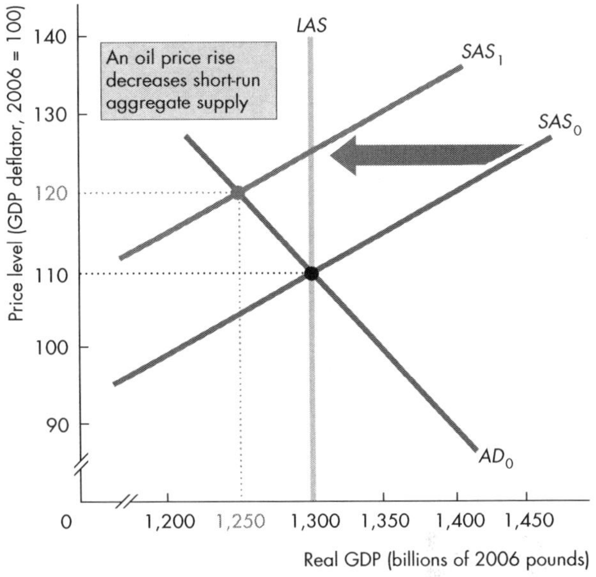

An increase in the price of oil decreases short-run aggregate supply and shifts the short-run aggregate supply curve leftward from SAS_0 to SAS_1. Real GDP decreases from £1,300 billion to £1,250 billion, and the price level increases from 110 to 120. The economy experiences both recession and inflation – a situation known as stagflation.

myeconlab Animation

Review Quiz

1. Does economic growth result from increases in aggregate demand, short-run aggregate supply or long-run aggregate supply?
2. Does inflation result from increases in aggregate demand, short-run aggregate supply or long-run aggregate supply?
3. Describe the three types of short-run macroeconomic equilibrium.
4. How do fluctuations in aggregate demand and short-run aggregate supply bring fluctuations in real GDP around potential GDP?

You can work these questions in Study Plan 26.3 and get instant feedback. myeconlab

We can use the *AS–AD* model to explain and illustrate the views of the alternative schools of thought in macroeconomics. That is your next task.

Macroeconomic Schools of Thought

Macroeconomics is an active field of research and much remains to be learned about the forces that make our economy grow, bring inflation and generate business cycles. There is a greater degree of consensus and certainty about economic growth and inflation trends – the longer term changes in real GDP and the price level – than there is about the business cycle – the short-term fluctuations in these variables. Here, we'll look only at differences of view about short-term fluctuations.

The *AS–AD* model that you've studied in this chapter provides a good foundation for understanding the range of views that macroeconomists hold about this topic. But what you will learn here is just a first glimpse at the scientific controversy and debate. We'll return to these issues at various later points in the text and deepen your appreciation of the alternative views.

Classification usually requires simplification. And classifying macroeconomists is no exception to this general rule. The classification that we'll use here is simple, but it is not misleading. We identify three macroeconomic schools of thought and examine the views of each group in turn. We examine:

- The classical view
- The Keynesian view
- The monetarist view

The Classical View

A **classical** macroeconomist believes that the economy is self-regulating and that it is always at full employment. The term 'classical' derives from the name of the founding school of economics that includes Adam Smith, David Ricardo and John Stuart Mill.

A **new classical** view is that business cycle fluctuations are the efficient responses of a well-functioning market economy that is bombarded by shocks that arise from the uneven pace of technological change.

The classical view can be understood in terms of beliefs about aggregate demand and aggregate supply.

Aggregate Demand Fluctuations

In the classical view, technological change is the most significant influence on both aggregate demand and aggregate supply. For this reason, classical macroeconomists don't use the *AS–AD* framework. But their views can be interpreted in this framework. A technological change that increases the productivity of capital brings an increase in aggregate demand because firms increase their expenditure on new plant and equipment. A technological change that lengthens the useful life of existing capital decreases the demand for new capital, which decreases aggregate demand.

Aggregate Supply Response

In the classical view, the money wage rate that lies behind the short-run aggregate supply curve is instantly and completely flexible. The money wage rate adjusts so quickly to maintain equilibrium in the labour market that real GDP always adjusts to equal potential GDP.

Potential GDP itself fluctuates for the same reasons that aggregate demand fluctuates: technological change. When the pace of technological change is rapid, potential GDP increases quickly and so does real GDP. When the pace of technological change slows, so does the growth rate of potential GDP.

Classical Policy

The classical view of policy emphasizes the potential for taxes to stunt incentives and create inefficiency. By minimizing the disincentive effects that taxes have, employment, investment and technological advance are at their efficient levels and the economy expands at an appropriate and rapid pace.

The Keynesian View

A **Keynesian** macroeconomist believes that left alone, the economy would rarely operate at full employment and that to achieve and maintain full employment, active help from fiscal policy and monetary policy is required. The term 'Keynesian' derives from the name of one of the twentieth century's most famous economists, John Maynard Keynes.

The Keynesian view is based on beliefs about the forces that determine aggregate demand and short-run aggregate supply.

Aggregate Demand Fluctuations

In the Keynesian view, *expectations* are the most significant influence on aggregate demand. And expectations are based on herd instinct or, what Keynes himself called 'animal spirits'. A wave of pessimism about future profit prospects can lead to a fall in aggregate demand and plunge the economy into recession.

Aggregate Supply Response

In the Keynesian view, the money wage rate that lies behind the short-run aggregate supply curve is extremely sticky downward. Basically, the money wage rate doesn't fall. So if there is a recessionary gap, there is no automatic mechanism for getting rid of it. If it were to happen, a fall in the money wage rate would increase short-run aggregate supply and restore full employment. But the money wage rate doesn't fall, so the economy remains stuck in recession.

A modern version of the Keynesian view known as the **new Keynesian** view holds that not only is the money wage rate sticky but that prices of goods and services are also sticky. With a sticky price level, the short-run aggregate supply curve is horizontal at a fixed price level.

Policy Response Needed

The Keynesian view calls for fiscal policy and monetary policy to actively offset the changes in aggregate demand that bring recession. By stimulating aggregate demand in a recession, full employment can be restored.

The Monetarist View

A **monetarist** is a macroeconomist who believes that the economy is self-regulating and that it will normally operate at full employment, provided that monetary policy is not erratic and that the pace of money growth is kept steady. The term 'monetarist' was coined by an outstanding twentieth century economist, Karl Brunner, to describe his own and Milton Friedman's views.

The monetarist view can be interpreted in terms of beliefs about the forces that determine aggregate demand and short-run aggregate supply.

Aggregate Demand Fluctuations

In the monetarist view, the *quantity of money* is the most significant influence on aggregate demand. And the quantity of money is determined by the Bank of England. If the Bank of England keeps money growing at a steady pace, aggregate demand fluctuations will be minimized and the economy will operate close to full employment. But if the Bank of England decreases the quantity of money or even just slows its growth rate too abruptly, the economy will go into recession. In the monetarist view, all recessions result from inappropriate monetary policy.

Aggregate Supply Response

The monetarist view of short-run aggregate supply is the same as the Keynesian view – the money wage rate is sticky. If the economy is in recession, it will take an unnecessarily long time for it to return unaided to full employment.

Monetarist Policy

The monetarist view of policy is the same as the classical view on fiscal policy. Taxes should be kept low to avoid disincentive effects that decrease potential GDP. Provided that the quantity of money is kept on a steady growth path, no active stabilization is needed to offset changes in aggregate demand.

The Way Ahead

You will encounter classical, Keynesian and monetarist views in the chapters that follow. In the next chapter, we study the classical model. Then we study the Keynesian model. From there, we study money and inflation and lay the foundation for a deeper look at the sources of macroeconomic fluctuations and economic growth. We finish with a close look at the fiscal policy and monetary policy that try to achieve faster growth, stable prices and a smoother cycle.

Review Quiz

1. What are the defining features of classical macroeconomics and what policies do classical macroeconomists recommend?
2. What are the defining features of Keynesian macroeconomics and what policies do Keynesian macroeconomists recommend?
3. What are the defining features of monetarist macroeconomics and what policies do monetarist macroeconomists recommend?

You can work these questions in Study Plan 26.4 and get instant feedback. myeconlab

To complete your study of the *AS–AD* model, take a look at the German economy in 2009–2010 through the eyes of this model in *Reading Between the Lines* on pp. 630–631.

Reading Between the Lines

Aggregate Supply and Aggregate Demand in Action

The Financial Times, 12 January 2011

Domestic Demand Spurs Growth in Germany

Ralph Atkins and Quentin Peel

Germany last year experienced its most dramatic economic turn round since the country's reunification. Gross domestic product expanded 3.6 per cent compared with the previous year – at least partly reversing a 4.7 per cent contraction in 2009, the federal statistical office in Wiesbaden reported on Wednesday.

The improvement in Europe's largest economy, led by a rebound in investment spending after its worst recession since the Second World War, provided welcome news for Eurozone policymakers – and also strengthened Germans' convictions that their focus on fiscal discipline is justified.

A surge in imports and modest pick-up in consumer spending, as well as the investment splurge, were cited by economists as evidence that domestic demand was increasingly driving growth – boosting the prospects that Germany's revival will have a knock-on effect in the Eurozone.

But despite Berlin's proclaimed fiscal prudence, the full effects of tightening measures implemented by Berlin have yet to be felt. Government spending rose 2.2 per cent last year, while the public sector deficit rose to 3.5 per cent of GDP.

Germany was . . . better placed than most European economies to benefit last year from rapid growth in countries such as China. . . . Hopes that the export and investment-led growth of 2010 will spark a rebound in consumer spending this year are based on the unexpectedly strong improvement in Germany's labour market.

Nevertheless, the composition of growth in 2010 left some observers sceptical about the speed with which Germany's export dependency is waning. Held back by weak car sales, consumer spending rose just 0.5 per cent last year. The proportion of their disposable incomes that Germans saved also rose.

The Essence of the Story

- During 2010 real GDP in Germany grew by 3.6 per cent.
- The rapid growth of GDP was led by growth in investment and exports.
- Consumer spending increased by only 0.5 per cent as Germans saved more.
- Germany is heavily dependent on exports for growth in demand.

Economic Analysis

- The quantity of real GDP demanded is the sum of real consumption, C, investment, I, government expenditure, G, and net exports, $X - M$:

$$Y = C + I + G + X - M$$

- The large increase in Germany's real GDP in 2010 resulted from an increase in aggregate demand that came mainly from investment and exports.
- Figure 1 shows the growth rates of consumption, investment and exports from the third quarter of 2008 to the fourth quarter of 2010.
- Figure 1 shows that the fluctuations in investment and exports are much larger than those in consumption. (The growth rate of real GDP is not shown but it lies between the three curves in the figure.)
- The rapid growth in Germany's exports, particularly those of engineering goods, resulted from a large increase in demand from China and other rapidly expanding economies in East Asia.
- A depreciation of the euro against the Chinese yuan and the US dollar also helped to boost Germany's exports.
- Germany's rapid real GDP growth decreased its recessionary gap.
- We estimate Germany's recessionary gap at the end of 2010 at 1 per cent of potential GDP.
- Figure 2 shows Germany's aggregate demand and aggregate supply curves in 2009 and 2010.
- The long-run aggregate supply curve is *LAS* and the short-run aggregate supply curve is *SAS*.
- In 2009, the aggregate demand curve was AD_0. Real GDP was €2,170 billion (in 2000 prices) and the price level was 109.

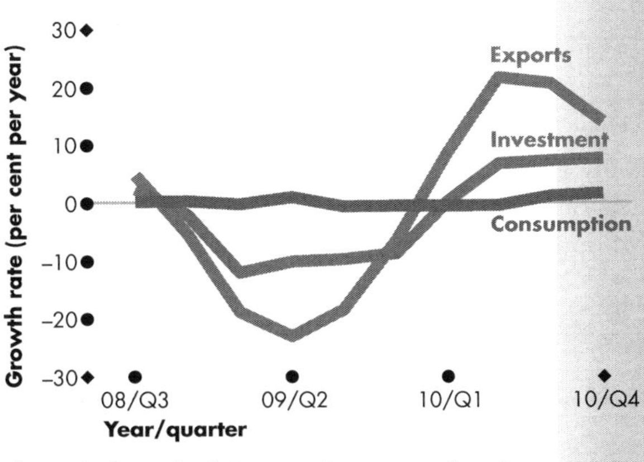

Figure 1 Growth of Germany's consumption, investment and exports

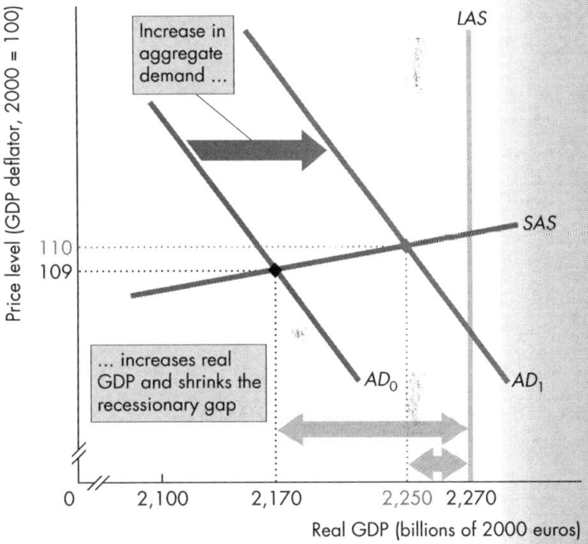

Figure 2 Germany's aggregate demand and aggregate supply

- In 2010, aggregate demand increased and the *AD* curve shifted rightward to AD_1. Real GDP increased to €2,250 billion and the recessionary gap closed to 1 per cent of potential GDP.
- The news article implies that Germany relies too much on exports and not enough on domestic consumption.
- That view is not correct. Germany has a comparative advantage in many engineering prodution activities, and Germany and its trading partners gain from international trade.

SUMMARY

Key Points

Aggregate Supply

- In the long run, the quantity of real GDP supplied is potential GDP.
- In the short run, a rise in the price level increases the quantity of real GDP supplied.
- A change in potential GDP changes both long-run and short-run aggregate supply. A change in the money wage rate or other resource prices changes only short-run aggregate supply.

Working Problems 1 to 3 will give you a better understanding of aggregate supply.

Aggregate Demand

- A rise in the price level decreases the quantity of real GDP demanded because of wealth and substitution effects.
- Changes in expectations, fiscal policy, monetary policy and the world economy change aggregate demand.

Working Problems 4 to 7 will give you a better understanding of aggregate demand.

Explaining Macroeconomic Trends and Fluctuations

- Aggregate demand and short-run aggregate supply determine real GDP and the price level.
- In the long run, real GDP equals potential GDP and aggregate demand determines the price level.
- Economic growth occurs because potential GDP increases and inflation occurs because aggregate demand grows more quickly than potential GDP.
- Business cycles occur because aggregate demand and aggregate supply fluctuate.

Working Problems 8 to 16 will give you a better understanding of macroeconomic trends and fluctuations

Macroeconomic Schools of Thought

- Classical economists believe that the economy is self-regulating and always at full employment.
- Keynesian economists believe that full employment can be achieved only with active policy.
- Monetarist economists believe that recessions result from inappropriate monetary policy.

Working Problems 17 to 19 will give you a better understanding of macroeconomic schools of thought.

Key Terms

Above full-employment equilibrium
Aggregate demand
Below full-employment equilibrium
Classical
Disposable income
Fiscal policy
Full-employment equilibrium
Inflationary gap
Keynesian
Long-run aggregate supply
Long-run macroeconomic equilibrium
Monetarist
Monetary policy
New classical
New Keynesian
Output gap
Recessionary gap
Short-run aggregate supply
Short-run macroeconomic equilibrium
Stagflation

STUDY PLAN PROBLEMS AND APPLICATIONS

myeconlab You can work Problems 1 to 19 in MyEconLab Chapter 26 Study Plan and get instant feedback.

Aggregate Supply (Study Plan 26.1)

1 Explain the influence of each of the following events on the quantity of real GDP supplied and aggregate supply in India and use a graph to illustrate.

- ◆ UK firms move their call handling, IT and data functions to India.
- ◆ Petrol prices rise.
- ◆ Wal-Mart and Starbucks open in India.
- ◆ Universities in India increase the number of engineering graduates.
- ◆ The money wage rate rises.
- ◆ The price level in India increases.

2 **Wages Could Hit Steepest Plunge in 18 Years**

A bad economy is starting to drag down wages for millions of workers. The average weekly wage has fallen 1.4% this year through September. Colorado will become the first state to lower its minimum wage since the federal minimum wage law was passed in 1938, when the state cuts its rate by 4 cents an hour.

Source: *USA Today*, 16 October 2009

Explain how the fall in the average weekly wage and the minimum wage will influence aggregate supply.

3 Chinese Premier Wen Jiabao has warned Japan that its companies operating in China should raise pay for their workers. Explain how a rise in wages in China will influence the quantity of real GDP supplied and aggregate supply in China.

Aggregate Demand (Study Plan 26.2)

4 South Africa trades with the UK. Explain the effect of each of the following events on South Africa's aggregate demand.

- ◆ The government of South Africa cuts income taxes.
- ◆ The UK experiences strong economic growth.
- ◆ South Africa sets new environmental standards that require power utilities to upgrade their production facilities.

5 The Bank of England cuts the quantity of money and all other things remain the same. Explain the effect of the cut in the quantity of money on aggregate demand in the short run.

6 Kenya trades with the UK. Explain the effect of each of the following events on the quantity of real GDP demanded and aggregate demand in Kenya.

- ◆ The UK goes into a recession.
- ◆ The price level in Kenya rises.
- ◆ Kenya increases the quantity of money.

7 **Durable Goods Orders Surge in May, New Home Sales Dip**

The US government announced that demand for durable goods rose 1.8 per cent, while sales of new homes dropped 0.6 per cent in May. US companies suffered a sharp drop in exports as other countries struggle with recession.

Source: *USA Today*, 24 June 2009

Explain how the items in the news clip influence US aggregate demand.

Explaining Macroeconomic Trends and Fluctuations (Study Plan 26.3)

Use the following graph to work Problems 8 to 10.

Initially, the short-run aggregate supply curve is SAS_0 and the aggregate demand curve is AD_0.

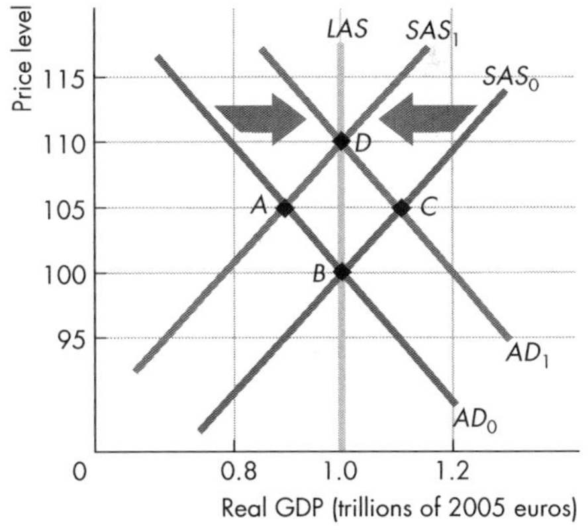

8 Some events change aggregate demand from AD_0 to AD_1. Describe two events that could have created this change in aggregate demand. What is the equilibrium after aggregate demand changed? If potential GDP is €1 trillion, the economy is at what type of macroeconomic equilibrium?

9 Some events change aggregate supply from SAS_0 to SAS_1. Describe two events that could have created this change in aggregate supply. What is the equilibrium after aggregate supply changed? If potential GDP is €1 trillion, does the economy have an inflationary gap, a recessionary gap or no output gap?

10 Some events change aggregate demand from AD_0 to AD_1 and aggregate supply from SAS_0 to SAS_1. What is the new macroeconomic equilibrium?

Use the following data to work Problems 11 to 13.

The following events have occurred in UK history:

- A deep recession hits the world economy.
- The world oil price rises sharply.
- UK businesses expect future profits to fall.

11 Explain for each event whether it changes short-run aggregate supply, long-run aggregate supply, aggregate demand or some combination of them.

12 Explain the separate effects of each event on UK real GDP and the price level, starting from a position of long-run equilibrium.

13 Explain the combined effects of these events on UK real GDP and the price level, starting from a position of long-run equilibrium.

Use the following data to work Problems 14 and 15.

The table shows the aggregate demand and short-run aggregate supply schedules of Mainland, a country in which potential GDP is €1,050 billion.

Price level	Real GDP demanded	Real GDP supplied in the short run
	(billions of 2005 euros)	
100	1,150	1,050
110	1,100	1,100
120	1,050	1,150
130	1,000	1,200
140	950	1,250
150	900	1,300
160	850	1,350

14 What is the short-run macroeconomic equilibrium real GDP and price level?

15 Does the country have an inflationary gap or a recessionary gap and what is its magnitude?

16 **Geithner Urges Action on Economy**

The US Treasury Secretary Timothy Geithner is reported as having said that the US can no longer rely on consumer spending to be the growth engine of recovery from recession. The government needs to sow the seeds for business investment and exports. 'We can't go back to a situation where we're depending on a near short-term boost in consumption to carry us forward,' he said.

Source: *The Wall Street Journal*, 12 September 2010

a Explain the effects of an increase in consumer spending on the short-run macroeconomic equilibrium.

b Explain the effects of an increase in business investment on the short-run macroeconomic equilibrium.

c Explain the effects of an increase in exports on the short-run macroeconomic equilibrium.

Macroeconomic Schools of Thought

(Study Plan 26.4)

17 Describe what a classical macroeconomist, a Keynesian, and a monetarist would want to do in response to each of the events listed in Problem 11.

18 **Adding Up the Cost of Obama's Agenda**

When campaigning, Barack Obama has made a long list of promises for new federal programmes costing tens of billions of dollars. Obama has said he would strengthen the nation's bridges and dams ($6 billion a year), extend health insurance to more people (part of a $65-billion-a-year health plan), develop cleaner energy sources ($15 billion a year), curb home foreclosures ($10 billion in one-time spending) and add $18 billion a year to education spending. In total a $50-billion plan to stimulate the economy through increased government spending. A different blueprint offered by McCain proposes relatively little new spending and tax cuts as a more effective means of solving problems.

Source: *Los Angeles Times*, 8 July 2008

a Based upon this news clip, explain what macroeconomic school of thought Barack Obama most likely follows.

b Based upon this news clip, explain what macroeconomic school of thought John McCain most likely follows.

19 Based upon the news clip in Problem 16, explain what macroeconomic school of thought US Treasury Secretary Timothy Geithner most likely follows.

ADDITIONAL PROBLEMS AND APPLICATIONS

myeconlab You can work these problems in MyEconLab if assigned by your lecturer.

Aggregate Supply

20 Explain for each event whether it changes the quantity of real GDP supplied, short-run aggregate supply, long-run aggregate supply or a combination of them.

- UK car producers switch to a new technology that raises productivity.
- Toyota and Honda build additional plants in the UK.
- The prices of car parts imported from China rise.
- Workers in UK car plants agree to a cut in the money wage rate.
- The UK price level rises.

Aggregate Demand

21 Explain for each event whether it changes the quantity of real GDP demanded or aggregate demand.

- UK car producers switch to a new technology that raises productivity.
- Toyota and Honda build new plants in Wales.
- The prices of car parts imported from China rise.
- Workers in UK car plants agree to a lower money wage rate.
- The UK price level rises.

22 **Inventories Surge**

The US Commerce Department reported that wholesale inventories rose 1.3 per cent in July, the best performance since July 2008. A major driver of the economy since late last year has been the restocking of depleted store shelves.

Source: Associated Press, 13 September 2010

Explain how a surge in inventories influences current aggregate demand.

23 **Low Spending Is Taking Toll on Economy**

The US Commerce Department reported that the economy continued to stagnate during the first three months of the year, with a sharp pullback in consumer spending the primary factor at play. Consumer spending fell for a broad range of goods and services, including cars, auto parts, furniture, food and recreation, reflecting a growing inclination toward thrift.

Source: *The New York Times*, 1 May 2008

Explain how a fall in consumer expenditure influences the quantity of real GDP demanded and aggregate demand.

Explaining Macroeconomic Trends and Fluctuations

Use the following information to work Problems 24 to 26.

The following events have occurred in UK history:

- The world economy goes into an expansion.
- UK businesses expect future profits to rise.
- The government increases its expenditure on goods and services in a time of war or increased international tension.

24 Explain for each event whether it changes short-run aggregate supply, long-run aggregate supply, aggregate demand or some combination of them.

25 Explain the separate effects of each event on UK real GDP and the price level, starting from a position of long-run equilibrium.

26 Explain the combined effects of these events on UK real GDP and the price level, starting from a position of long-run equilibrium.

Use the following data to work Problems 27 and 28.

In Japan, potential GDP is 600 trillion yen and the table shows the aggregate demand and short-run aggregate supply schedules.

Price level	Real GDP demanded	Real GDP supplied in the short run
	(billions of 2005 yen)	
75	600	400
85	550	450
95	500	500
105	450	550
115	400	600
125	350	650
135	300	700

27 **a** Draw a graph of the aggregate demand curve and the short-run aggregate supply curve.

b What is the short-run equilibrium real GDP and price level?

28 Does Japan have an inflationary gap or a recessionary gap and what is its magnitude?

Use the following information to work Problems 29 to 31.

Spending by Women Jumps

The magazine Women of China reported that Chinese women in big cities spent 63% of their income on consumer goods last year, up from a meager 26% in 2007. Clothing accounted for the biggest chunk of that spending, at nearly 30%, followed by digital products such as mobile phones and cameras (11%) and travel (10%). Chinese consumption as a whole grew faster than the overall economy in the first half of the year and is expected to reach 42% of GDP by 2020, up from the current 36%.

Source: *The Wall Street Journal*, 27 August 2010

29 Explain the effect of a rise in consumption expenditure on real GDP and the price level in the short run.

30 If the economy had been operating at a full-employment equilibrium,

a Describe the macroeconomic equilibrium after the rise in consumer spending.

b Explain and draw a graph to illustrate how the economy can adjust in the long run to restore a full-employment equilibrium.

31 Why do changes in consumer spending play a large role in the business cycle?

32 **It's Pinching Everyone**

The current inflationary process is a global phenomenon, but emerging and developing countries have been growing significantly faster than the rest of the world. Because there is no reason to believe that world production will rise miraculously at least in the immediate future, many people expect that prices will keep on rising. These expectations in turn exacerbate the inflationary process. Households buy more of non-perishable goods than they need for their immediate consumption because they expect prices to go up even further. What is worse is that traders withhold stocks from the market in the hope of being able to sell these at higher prices later on. In other words, expectations of higher prices become self-fulfilling.

Source: *The Times of India*, 24 June 2008

Explain and draw a graph to illustrate how inflation and inflation expectations 'become self-fulfilling'.

Macroeconomic Schools of Thought

33 **Should Congress Pass a New Stimulus Bill? No, Cut Taxes and Curb Spending Instead**

The first stimulus was not too meager, but it was the wrong policy prescription. Anybody who studies economic history would know that government spending doesn't produce long-term, sustainable growth, and jobs. The only sure way to perk up the job market is to cut taxes permanently and rein in public spending and excessive regulation.

Source: sgvtribune.com, 11 September 2010

Economists from which macroeconomic school of thought would recommend a second spending stimulus and which a permanent tax cut?

Economics in the News

34 After you have studied *Reading Between the Lines* on pp. 630–631, answer the following questions.

a Describe the growth of the German economy during 2010.

b Did Germany have a recessionary gap, an inflationary gap or full employment at the end of 2010?

c Use the *AS–AD* model to illustrate the German economy during 2010.

d Suppose that aggregate demand continues to expand rapidly through 2011 and that the ECB does not act strongly enough to dampen the expansion. Use the *AS–AD* model to illustrate the state of the German economy at the end of 2011. Indicate whether there is full employment, a recessionary gap or an inflationary gap.

e Suppose that aggregate demand continues to expand rapidly through 2011 but that the ECB acts strongly enough to halt the expansion. Use the *AS–AD* model to illustrate the state of the economy at the end of 2011. Indicate whether there is full employment, a recessionary gap or an inflationary gap.

CHAPTER 27

Expenditure Multipliers

After studying this chapter you will be able to:

- Explain how expenditure plans are determined
- Explain how equilibrium real GDP is determined when the price level is fixed
- Explain the expenditure multiplier when the price level is fixed
- Explain the relationship between aggregate expenditure and aggregate demand and explain the multiplier when the price level changes

Alicia Keys sings into a microphone in a barely audible whisper and through the magic of electronic amplification, her voice fills an auditorium. Sir Alan Sugar, entrepreneur, and his assistant are being driven along one of London's bumpy roads and thanks to the car's efficient shock absorbers, the assistant's notes are tapped into a BlackBerry without missing a keystroke.

Expenditure plans fluctuate like the volume of Alicia Keys' voice and the uneven surface of a London road. How does the economy react to those fluctuations? Does it behave like an amplifier or a shock absorber?

In *Reading Between the Lines* at the end of the chapter you will see the role played by fluctuations in consumption expenditure during 2009.

Fixed Prices and Expenditure Plans

In the Keynesian model that we study in this chapter, all the firms are like your grocery store: they set their prices and sell the quantities their customers are willing to buy. If they persistently sell a greater quantity than they plan to and are constantly running out of inventory, they eventually raise their prices. And if they persistently sell a smaller quantity than they plan to and have inventories piling up, they eventually cut their prices. But on any given day, their prices are fixed and the quantities they sell depend on demand, not supply.

Because each firm's prices are fixed, for the economy as a whole:

1 The *price level* is fixed and

2 *Aggregate demand* determines real GDP.

The Keynesian model explains fluctuations in aggregate demand at a fixed price level by identifying the forces that determine expenditure plans.

Expenditure Plans

Aggregate expenditure has four components: consumption expenditure, investment, government expenditure on goods and services and net exports (exports minus imports). These four components of aggregate expenditure sum to real GDP (see Chapter 20, pp. 461–462).

Aggregate planned expenditure is equal to the sum of the *planned* levels of consumption expenditure, investment, government expenditure on goods and services and exports minus imports. Two of these components of planned expenditure, consumption expenditure and imports, change when income changes and so they depend on real GDP.

A Two-Way Link Between Aggregate Expenditure and Real GDP

There is a two-way link between aggregate expenditure and real GDP. Other things remaining the same,

- An increase in real GDP increases aggregate expenditure and
- An increase in aggregate expenditure increases real GDP.

You are now going to study this two-way link starting with a review of the influences on consumption plans and saving plans.

Consumption and Saving Plans

Several factors influence consumption expenditure and saving plans. The more important ones are

1 Disposable income

2 Real interest rate

3 Wealth

4 Expected future income

Disposable income is aggregate income minus taxes plus transfer payments. Aggregate income equals real GDP, so disposable income depends on real GDP. To explore the two-way link between real GDP and planned consumption expenditure, we focus on the relationship between consumption expenditure and disposable income when the other three factors listed above are constant.

Consumption Expenditure and Saving

The table in Figure 27.1 lists the consumption expenditure and the saving that people plan at each level of disposable income. Households can only spend their disposable income on consumption or save it, so planned consumption expenditure plus planned saving always equals disposable income.

The relationship between consumption expenditure and disposable income, other things remaining the same, is called the **consumption function**. The relationship between saving and disposable income, other things remaining the same, is called the **saving function**.

Consumption Function

Figure 27.1(a) shows a consumption function. The y-axis measures consumption expenditure and the x-axis measures disposable income. Along the consumption function, the points labelled A to F correspond to the rows of the table. For example, point E shows that when disposable income is £800 billion, consumption expenditure is £750 billion. As disposable income increases, consumption expenditure also increases.

At point A on the consumption function, consumption expenditure is £150 billion even though disposable income is zero. This consumption expenditure is called autonomous consumption, and it is the amount of consumption expenditure that would take place in the short run even if people had no current income. Consumption expenditure in excess of this amount is called induced consumption, which is the consumption expenditure that is induced by an increase in disposable income.

45° Line

Figure 27.1(a) contains a 45° line, the height of which measures disposble income. At each point on this line, consumption expenditure equals disposable income. Between points *A* and *D*, consumption expenditure exceeds disposable income; between points *D* and *F* consumption expenditure is less than disposable income; and at point *D*, consumption expenditure equals disposable income.

Saving Function

Figure 27.1(b) shows a saving function. Again, the points *A* to *F* correspond to the rows of the table. For example, point *E* shows that when disposable income is £800 billion, saving is £50 billion. As disposable income increases, saving increases. Notice that when consumption expenditure exceeds disposable income in part (a), saving is negative in part (b). Negative saving is called *dissaving*.

Figure 27.1 Consumption Function and Saving Function

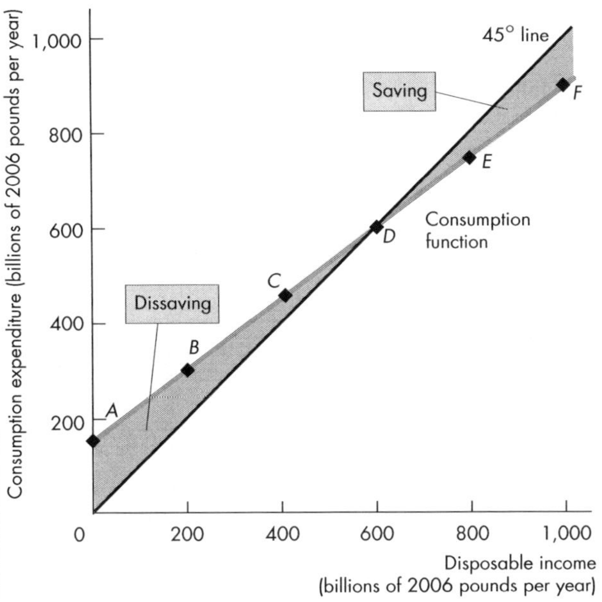

(a) Consumption function

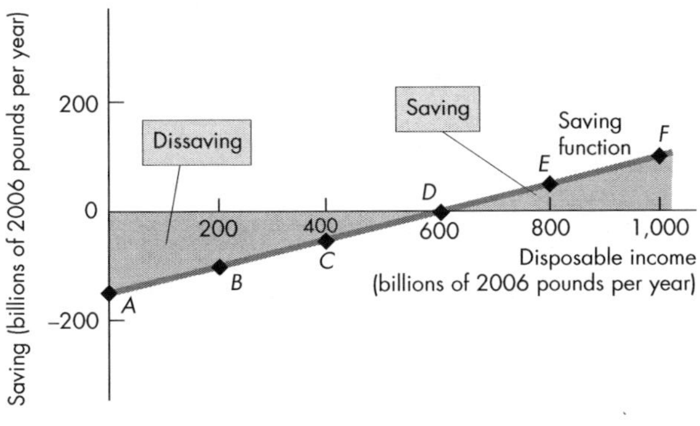

(b) Saving function

	Disposable income	Planned consumption expenditure	Planned saving
	(billions of 2006 pounds per year)		
A	0	150	−150
B	200	300	−100
C	400	450	−50
D	600	600	0
E	800	750	50
F	1,000	900	100

The table shows consumption expenditure and saving plans at various levels of disposable income. When disposable income is £800 (row *E*) planned consumption expenditure is £750 and planned saving is £50.

Part (a) of the figure shows the consumption function (the relationship between consumption expenditure and disposable income). The height of the consumption function measures consumption expenditure at each level of disposable income.

Part (b) shows the saving function (the relationship between saving and disposable income). The height of the saving function measures saving at each level of disposable income. Points *A* to *F* on the consumption and saving functions correspond to the rows in the table.

The height of the 45° line in part (a) measures disposable income. So along the 45° line, consumption expenditure equals disposable income. Consumption expenditure plus saving equals disposable income.

When the consumption function is above the 45° line, saving is negative (dissaving occurs). When the consumption function is below the 45° line, saving is positive. At the point where the consumption function intersects the 45° line, all disposable income is consumed and saving is zero.

myeconlab Animation

Marginal Propensities

The **marginal propensity to consume** (MPC) is the fraction of a *change* in disposable income that is consumed. It is calculated as the *change* in consumption expenditure (ΔC) divided by the *change* in disposable income (ΔYD) that brought it about. That is:

$$MPC = \frac{\Delta C}{\Delta YD}$$

In the table in Figure 27.1, when disposable income increases from £600 billion to £800 billion, consumption expenditure increases from £600 billion to £750 billion. The MPC is £150 billion divided by £200 billion, which equals 0.75.

The **marginal propensity to save** (MPS) is the fraction of a *change* in disposable income that is saved. It is calculated as the *change* in saving (ΔS) divided by the *change* in disposable income (ΔYD) that brought it about. That is:

$$MPS = \frac{\Delta S}{\Delta YD}$$

In the table in Figure 27.1, when disposable income increases by £200 billion, saving increases by £50 billion. The MPS is £50 billion divided by £200 billion, which equals 0.25.

Because an increase in disposable income is either spent on consumption or saved, the marginal propensity to consume plus the marginal propensity to save equals 1. You can see why by using the equation:

$$\Delta C + \Delta S = \Delta YD.$$

Divide both sides of the equation by the change in disposable income to obtain:

$$\frac{\Delta C}{\Delta YD} + \frac{\Delta S}{\Delta YD} = 1$$

$\Delta C/\Delta YD$ is the *marginal propensity to consume* (MPC) and $\Delta S/\Delta YD$ is the *marginal propensity to save* (MPS), so:

$$MPC + MPS = 1$$

Slopes and Marginal Propensities

The slope of the consumption function is the marginal propensity to consume and the slope of the saving function is the marginal propensity to save.

Figure 27.2(a) shows the MPC as the slope of the consumption function. A £200 billion increase in disposable income, shown as the base of the red triangle, brings a £150 billion increase in consumption expenditure, shown as the height of the red triangle. The slope of the consumption function is given by the formula 'slope equals rise over run' and is £150 billion divided by £200 billion, which equals 0.75 – the MPC.

Figure 27.2(b) shows the MPS as the slope of the saving function. A £200 billion increase in disposable income, the base of the red triangle, increases saving by £50 billion, the height of the triangle. The slope of the saving function is £50 billion divided by £200 billion, which equals 0.25 – the MPS is 0.25.

Figure 27.2 Marginal Propensities to Consume and Save

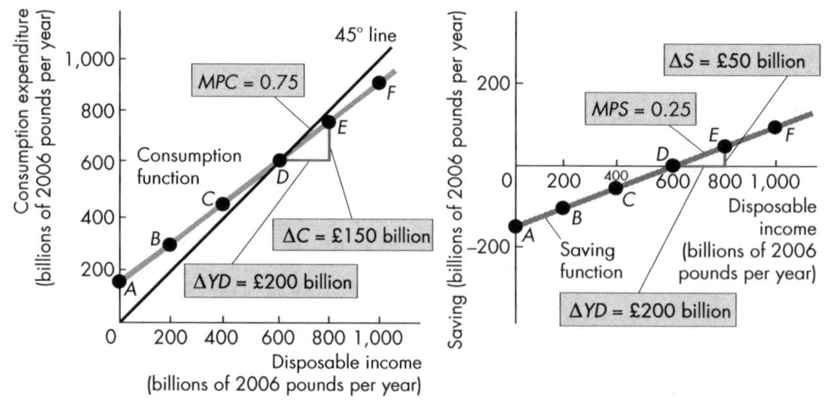

(a) Consumption function **(b) Saving function**

The *MPC* is equal to the change in consumption expenditure divided by the change in disposable income. It is measured by the slope of the consumption function. In part (a), the *MPC* is 0.75.

The marginal propensity to save, *MPS*, is equal to the change in saving divided by the change in disposable income. It is measured by the slope of the saving function. In part (b), the *MPS* is 0.25.

myeconlab Animation

ECONOMICS IN ACTION

The UK Consumption Function

Figure 1 shows the UK consumption function. Each blue dot represents consumption expenditure and disposable income for a particular year. (The dots are for the years 1970 to 2010 and the dots of eight of the years are identified.)

The line CF_{70} is an estimate of the UK consumption function in 1970, and the line CF_{10} is an estimate of the UK consumption function in 2010.

The slope of the consumption function in the figure is 0.8, which means that a £100 billion increase in disposable income brings an £80 billion increase in consumption expenditure. This slope is an estimate of the marginal propensity to consume and it is the middle of the range of values that economists have estimated for the marginal propensity to consume.

The consumption function shifts upward over time as other influences on consumption expenditure change. Of these other influences, the real interest rate and wealth fluctuate and so bring upward *and* downward shifts in the consumption function.

But rising expected future disposable income brings a steady upward shift in the consumption function. As the consumption function shifts upward, autonomous consumption expenditure increases.

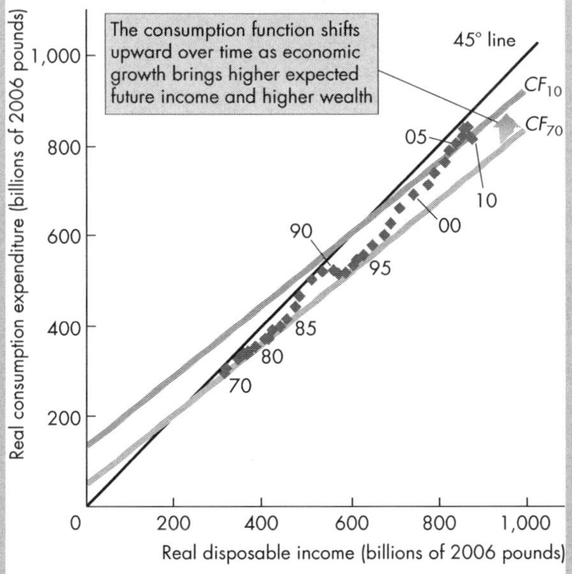

Figure 1 The UK Consumption Function

Source of data: Office for National Statistics.

Consumption and Real GDP

Consumption expenditure changes when disposable income changes and disposable income changes when real GDP changes. So consumption expenditure is a function of real GDP. An increase in real GDP increases disposable income, which increases consumption expenditure. We use this link between consumption expenditure and real GDP to determine equilibrium expenditure. But before we do so, we need to look at one other component of aggregate expenditure: imports. Like consumption expenditure, imports are influenced by real GDP.

Import Function

UK imports are determined by a number of factors, but in the short run with fixed prices, one factor dominates: UK real GDP. Other things remaining the same, the greater the UK real GDP, the larger is the quantity of UK imports. So an increase in UK real GDP brings an increase in UK imports.

The relationship between imports and real GDP is determined by the **marginal propensity to import** – the fraction of an increase in real GDP that is spent on imports. It is calculated as the change in imports divided by the change in real GDP that brought it about, other things remaining the same. For example, if a £100 billion increase in real GDP increases imports by £20 billion, the marginal propensity to import is 0.2.

Review Quiz

1. Which components of aggregate planned expenditure are influenced by real GDP?
2. Define and explain how we calculate the marginal propensity to consume and the marginal propensity to save.
3. How do we calculate the effects of real GDP on consumption expenditure and imports by using the marginal propensity to consume and the marginal propensity to import?

You can work these questions in Study Plan 27.1 and get instant feedback. myeconlab

Real GDP influences consumption expenditure and imports, which in turn influence real GDP. Your next task is to study the second piece of the two-way link between aggregate expenditure and real GDP and see how all the components of aggregate planned expenditure interact to determine real GDP.

Real GDP with a Fixed Price Level

You are now going to learn how expenditure plans determine real GDP when the price level is fixed. We begin by studying the relationship between aggregate planned expenditure and real GDP. We describe this relationship either by an aggregate expenditure schedule or by an aggregate expenditure curve. The *aggregate expenditure schedule* lists aggregate planned expenditure generated at each level of real GDP. The *aggregate expenditure curve* is a graph of the aggregate expenditure schedule.

Then we'll learn about the key distinction between *planned* expenditure and *actual* expenditure. And finally, we'll define and learn what determines equilibrium expenditure and real GDP.

Figure 27.3 Aggregate Expenditure

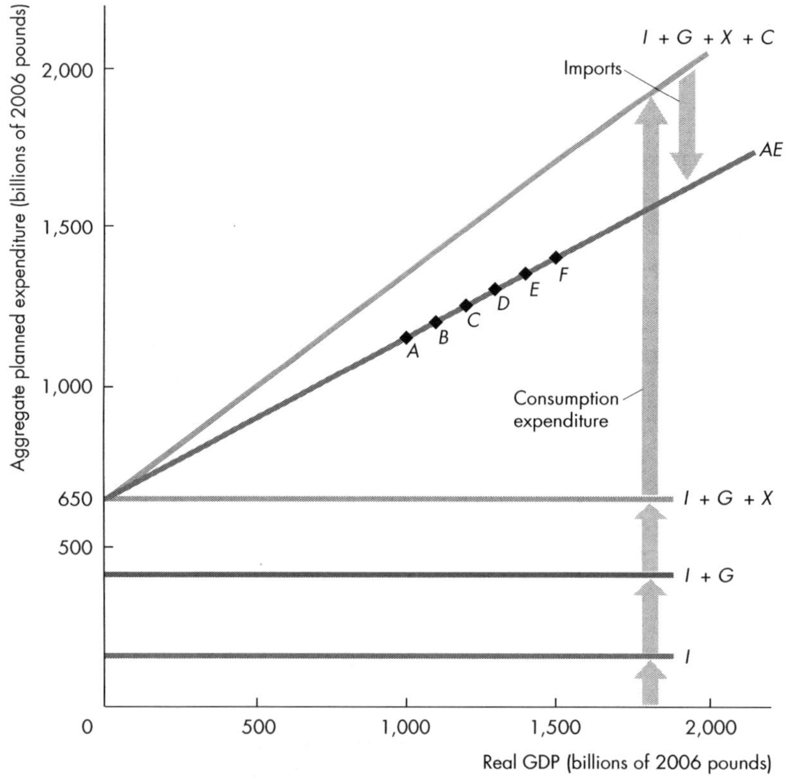

Aggregate planned expenditure is the sum of planned consumption expenditure, investment, government expenditure and exports minus imports. When real GDP is zero, aggregate planned expenditure is £650 billion. When real GDP is £1,000 billion, (row *A* of the table) planned consumption expenditure is £700 billion, planned investment is £150 billion, planned government expenditure is £260 billion, planned exports are £240 billion and planned imports are £200 billion, so aggregate planned expenditure is £1,150 billion.

The graph shows the relationship between the components of aggregate expenditure and real GDP. The green, blue and orange arrows show investment, government expenditure and exports – the expenditures that do not vary with real GDP. The red and purple arrows show consumption expenditure and imports – the expenditures that vary with real GDP. The red curve *AE* is the aggregate planned expenditure curve.

		Planned expenditure					
	Real GDP (*Y*)	Consumption expenditure (*C*)	Investment (*I*)	Government expenditure (*G*)	Exports (*X*)	Imports (*M*)	Aggregate planned expenditure ($AE = C + I + G + X - M$)
				(billions of 2006 pounds)			
	0	0	150	260	240	0	650
A	1,000	700	150	260	240	200	1,150
B	1,100	770	150	260	240	220	1,200
C	1,200	840	150	260	240	240	1,250
D	1,300	910	150	260	240	260	1,300
E	1,400	980	150	260	240	280	1,350
F	1,500	1,050	150	260	240	300	1,400

myeconlab Animation

Aggregate Planned Expenditure and Real GDP

The table in Figure 27.3 sets out an aggregate expenditure schedule together with the components of aggregate planned expenditure. To calculate aggregate planned expenditure at a given real GDP, we add the various components together. The first column of the table shows real GDP and the second column shows the consumption expenditure generated by each level of real GDP. A £1,000 billion increase in real GDP generates a £700 billion increase in consumption expenditure – the *MPC* is 0.7.

The next two columns show investment and government expenditure on goods and services. Investment depends on factors such as the real interest rate and the expected future profit. But at a given point in time, these factors generate a particular level of investment. Suppose this level of investment is £150 billion. Also, suppose that government expenditure on goods and services is £260 billion.

The next two columns show exports and imports. Exports are influenced by income in the rest of the world, prices of foreign-produced goods and services relative to the prices of similar UK-produced goods and services and foreign exchange rates. But exports are not directly affected by UK real GDP. In the table, exports appear as a constant £240 billion. In contrast, imports increase as real GDP increases. A £100 billion increase in real GDP generates a £20 billion increase in imports – the marginal propensity to import is 0.2.

The final column of the table shows aggregate planned expenditure – the sum of planned consumption expenditure, investment, government expenditure and exports minus imports.

Figure 27.3 plots an aggregate expenditure curve. Real GDP is shown on the x-axis and aggregate planned expenditure on the y-axis. The aggregate expenditure curve is the red line *AE*. Points *A* to *F* on this curve correspond to the rows of the table. The *AE* curve is a graph of aggregate planned expenditure (the last column) plotted against real GDP (the first column).

Figure 27.3 also shows the components of aggregate expenditure. The constant components – investment (I), government expenditure (G) and exports (X) – are shown by the vertical gaps between the horizontal lines. Consumption expenditure (C) is the vertical gap between the lines labelled $I + G + X + C$ and $I + G + X$.

To construct the *AE* curve, subtract imports (M) from the $I + G + X + C$ line. Aggregate expenditure is expenditure on UK-produced goods and services. But the components of aggregate expenditure, C, I and G include expenditure on imported goods and services. For example, if you buy a new mobile phone, your expenditure is part of consumption expenditure. But if the mobile phone is a Nokia made in Finland, your expenditure on it must be subtracted from consumption expenditure to find out how much is spent on goods and services produced in the UK – on UK real GDP. Money paid to Nokia for mobile phone imports from Finland does not add to aggregate expenditure in the UK.

Because imports are only a part of aggregate expenditure, when we subtract imports from the other components of aggregate expenditure, aggregate planned expenditure still increases as real GDP increases, as you can see in Figure 27.3.

Consumption expenditure minus imports, which varies with real GDP, is called **induced expenditure**. The sum of investment, government expenditure and exports, which does not vary with real GDP, is called **autonomous expenditure**. Consumption expenditure and imports can also have an autonomous component – a component that does not vary with real GDP. Another way of thinking about autonomous expenditure is that it would be the level of aggregate planned expenditure if real GDP were zero.

In Figure 27.3, autonomous expenditure is £650 billion – aggregate planned expenditure when real GDP is zero. For each £100 billion increase in real GDP, induced expenditure increases by £50 billion.

The aggregate expenditure curve summarizes the relationship between aggregate planned expenditure and real GDP. But what determines the point on the aggregate expenditure curve at which the economy operates? What determines *actual* aggregate expenditure?

Actual Expenditure, Planned Expenditure and Real GDP

Actual aggregate expenditure is always equal to real GDP, as we saw in Chapter 20 (p. 462). But aggregate *planned* expenditure does not necessarily equal actual aggregate expenditure and real GDP. How can actual expenditure and planned expenditure differ from each other? Why don't expenditure plans get implemented? The main reason is that firms might end up with greater inventories or with smaller inventories than planned. People carry out their consumption expenditure plans, the government implements its planned expenditure on goods and services and net exports are as planned. Firms carry out their plans to purchase new buildings, plant and equipment. But one component of investment is the increase in firms' inventories of goods. If aggregate planned expenditure is less than real GDP, firms don't sell all the goods and services they produce and they end up with more inventories than they had planned. They have unplanned inventories. If aggregate planned expenditure is greater than real GDP, firms sell more goods and services than they produce and inventories fall to below the level that firms had planned.

Equilibrium Expenditure

Equilibrium expenditure is the level of aggregate expenditure that occurs when aggregate *planned* expenditure equals real GDP. Equilibrium expenditure is a level of aggregate expenditure and real GDP at which everyone's spending plans are fulfilled. When the price level is fixed, equilibrium expenditure determines real GDP. When aggregate planned expenditure and actual aggregate expenditure are unequal, a process of convergence

Figure 27.4 Equilibrium Expenditure

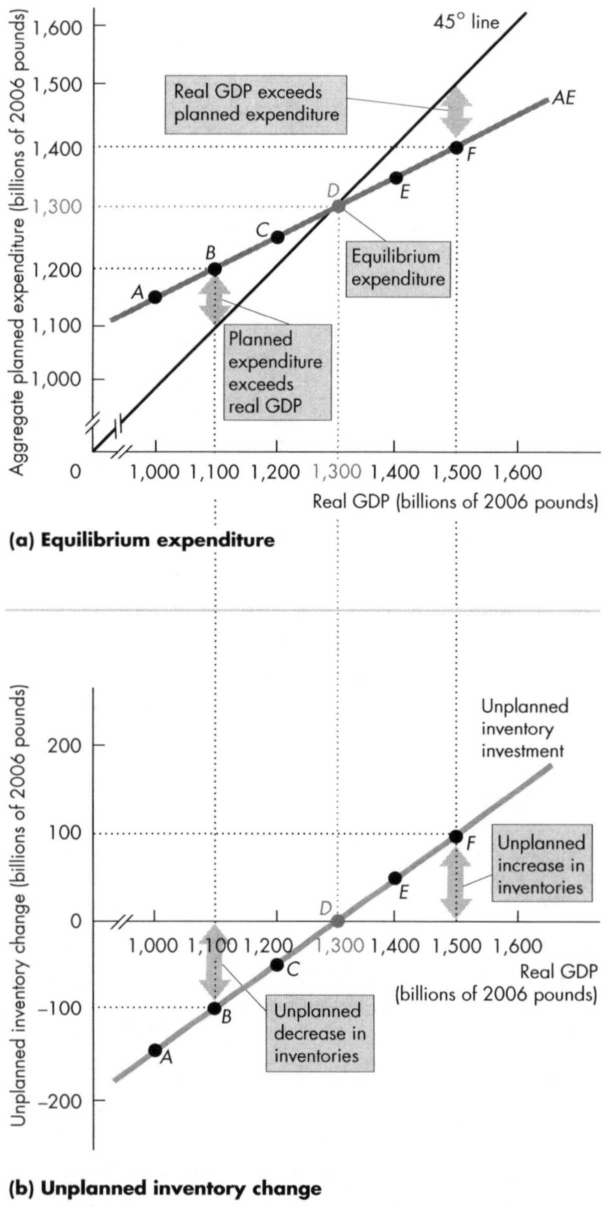

	Real GDP (*Y*)	Aggregate planned expenditure (*AE*)	Unplanned inventory change (*Y* – *AE*)
		(billions of 2006 pounds)	
A	1,000	1,150	–150
B	1,100	1,200	–100
C	1,200	1,250	–50
D	1,300	1,300	0
E	1,400	1,350	50
F	1,500	1,400	100

The table shows expenditure plans at different levels of real GDP. When real GDP is £1,300 billion, aggregate planned expenditure equals real GDP.

Part (a) of the figure illustrates equilibrium expenditure, which occurs when aggregate planned expenditure equals real GDP at the intersection of the 45° line and the *AE* curve. Part (b) of the figure shows the forces that bring about equilibrium expenditure.

When aggregate planned expenditure exceeds real GDP, firms' inventories decrease – for example, point *B* in both parts of the figure. Firms have an unplanned decrease in inventories, so they increase production. Real GDP increases.

When aggregate planned expenditure is less than real GDP, firms' inventories increase – for example, point *F* in both parts of the figure. Firms have an unplanned increase in inventories, so they decrease production. Real GDP decreases.

When aggregate planned expenditure equals real GDP, there are no unplanned inventory changes and real GDP remains constant at equilibrium expenditure.

myeconlab Animation

towards equilibrium expenditure occurs. And throughout this convergence process real GDP adjusts. Let's examine equilibrium expenditure and the process that brings it about.

Figure 27.4(a) illustrates equilibrium expenditure. The table sets out aggregate planned expenditure at various levels of real GDP. These values are plotted as points *A* through *F* along the *AE* curve. The 45° line shows all the points at which aggregate planned expenditure equals real GDP. So where the *AE* curve lies above the 45° line, aggregate planned expenditure exceeds real GDP; where the *AE* curve lies below the 45° line, aggregate planned expenditure is less than real GDP; and where the *AE* curve intersects the 45° line, aggregate planned expenditure equals real GDP. Point *D* illustrates equilibrium expenditure. At this point, real GDP is £1,300 billion.

Convergence to Equilibrium

What are the forces that move aggregate expenditure towards its equilibrium level? To answer this question, we must look at a situation in which aggregate expenditure is away from its equilibrium level. Suppose that in Figure 27.4, actual aggregate expenditure is £1,100 billion. But aggregate *planned* expenditure is £1,200 billion, point *B* in Figure 27.4(a). Aggregate planned expenditure exceeds *actual* expenditure. When people spend £1,200 billion and firms produce goods and services worth £1,100 billion, firms' inventories fall by £100 billion, point *B* in Figure 27.4(b). Because the change in inventories is part of investment, *actual* investment is £100 billion less than *planned* investment.

Real GDP doesn't remain at £1,100 billion for very long. Firms have inventory targets based on their sales. When inventories fall below target, firms increase production to restore inventories to their target levels. To increase inventories, firms hire additional labour and increase production.

Suppose that firms increase production in the next period by £100 billion. Real GDP increases by £100 billion to £1,200 billion. But again, aggregate planned expenditure exceeds real GDP. When real GDP is £1,200 billion, aggregate planned expenditure is £1,250 billion, point *C* in Figure 27.4(a). Again, inventories decrease, but this time by less than before. With real GDP of £1,200 billion and aggregate planned expenditure of £1,250 billion, inventories decrease by £50 billion, point *C* in Figure 27.4(b). Again, to restore inventories, firms hire additional labour and production increases; real GDP increases yet further.

The process that we have just described – planned expenditure exceeds real GDP, inventories (stocks) decrease and production increases to restore the inventories back to their target levels – ends when real GDP has reached £1,300 billion. At this real GDP, there is equilibrium expenditure. Unplanned inventory changes are zero. Firms do not change their production.

You can do a similar experiment to the one we've just done, but starting with a level of real GDP greater than equilibrium expenditure. In this case, planned expenditure is less than actual expenditure, inventories pile up and firms cut production. As before, real GDP keeps on changing (decreasing this time) until it reaches its equilibrium level of £1,300 billion.

This process of convergence to equilibrium is driven by changes in production and real GDP, not by changes in prices. Throughout the entire process the price level (and the price of every firm's output) remains fixed.

Review Quiz

1. Explain the relationship between aggregate planned expenditure and real GDP.
2. Distinguish between autonomous expenditure and induced expenditure.
3. What is the relationship between aggregate planned expenditure and real GDP at equilibrium expenditure?
4. What adjusts to achieve equilibrium expenditure?
5. If real GDP and aggregate expenditure are less than equilibrium expenditure, what happens to firms' inventories? How do firms change their production? What happens to real GDP?
6. If real GDP and aggregate expenditure are greater than equilibrium expenditure, what happens to firms' inventories? How do firms change their production? What happens to real GDP?

You can work these questions in Study Plan 27.2 and get instant feedback. myeconlab

We've learned that when the price level is fixed, real GDP is determined by equilibrium expenditure. And we have seen how unplanned changes in inventories and the production response they generate bring a convergence towards equilibrium expenditure. We're now going to study *changes* in equilibrium expenditure and discover an economic amplifier called the *multiplier*.

The Multiplier

Investment and exports can change for many reasons. A fall in the real interest rate might induce firms to increase their planned investment. A wave of innovation, such as occurred with the spread of multimedia computers in the 1990s, might increase expected future profits and lead firms to increase their planned investment. An economic boom in the US and Canada might lead to a large increase in their expenditure on UK-produced goods and services – UK exports. These are all examples of increases in autonomous expenditure in the UK.

When autonomous expenditure increases, aggregate expenditure increases and so do equilibrium expenditure and real GDP. But the increase in equilibrium expenditure and real GDP is *larger* than the change in autonomous expenditure. The **multiplier** is the amount by which a change in autonomous expenditure is magnified or multiplied to determine the change in equilibrium expenditure and real GDP.

To understand the basic idea of the multiplier, we'll work with an example economy in which there are no income taxes and no imports. So we'll first assume that these factors are absent. Then, when you understand the basic idea, we'll bring these factors back into play and see what difference they make to the multiplier.

The Basic Idea of the Multiplier

Suppose that investment increases. The additional expenditure by businesses means that aggregate expenditure and real GDP increase. The increase in real GDP increases disposable income, and with no income taxes, real GDP and disposable income increase by the same amount. The increase in disposable income brings an increase in consumption expenditure. And the increased consumption expenditure adds even more to aggregate expenditure. Real GDP and disposable income increase further, and so does consumption expenditure. The initial increase in investment brings an even bigger increase in aggregate expenditure because it induces an increase in consumption expenditure. The magnitude of the increase in aggregate expenditure that results from an increase in autonomous expenditure is determined by the *multiplier*.

The table in Figure 27.5 sets out aggregate planned expenditure. When real GDP is £1,200 billion, aggregate planned expenditure is £1,225 billion. For each £100 billion increase in real GDP, aggregate planned expenditure increases by £75 billion. This aggregate expenditure schedule is shown in the graph as the aggregate expenditure curve AE_0.

Initially, equilibrium expenditure is £1,300 billion. You can see this equilibrium in row *B* of the table, and in the graph where the curve AE_0 intersects the 45° line at the point marked *B*.

Now suppose that autonomous expenditure increases by £50 billion. What happens to equilibrium expenditure? You can see the answer in Figure 27.5. When this increase in autonomous expenditure is added to the original aggregate planned expenditure, aggregate planned expenditure increases by £50 billion at each level of real GDP. The new aggregate expenditure curve is AE_1. The new equilibrium expenditure, highlighted in the table (row *D'*), occurs where AE_1 intersects the 45° line and is £1,500 billion (point *D'*). At this point, aggregate planned expenditure equals real GDP. Equilibrium expenditure is £1,500 billion.

The Multiplier Effect

In Figure 27.5, the increase in autonomous expenditure of £50 billion increases equilibrium expenditure from £1,300 billion to £1,500 billion – an increase of £200 billion. That is, the change in autonomous expenditure leads, like Alicia Keys' electronic equipment, to an amplified change in equilibrium expenditure. This amplified change is the multiplier effect – equilibrium expenditure increases by more than the increase in autonomous expenditure. The multiplier is greater than 1.

Initially, when autonomous expenditure increases, aggregate planned expenditure exceeds real GDP. As a result, firm's inventories decrease. Firms respond by increasing production to restore their inventories to their target levels. As production increases, so does real GDP. With a higher level of real GDP, *induced expenditure* increases. So equilibrium expenditure increases by the sum of the initial increase in autonomous expenditure and the increase in induced expenditure. In this example, the initial increase in autonomous expenditure is £50 billion and induced expenditure increases by £150 billion, so equilibrium expenditure increases by £200 billion.

Although we have just analysed the effects of an *increase* in autonomous expenditure, the same analysis applies to a decrease in autonomous expenditure. If initially the aggregate expenditure curve is AE_1, equilibrium expenditure and real GDP are £1,500 billion. A decrease in autonomous expenditure of £50 billion shifts the aggregate expenditure curve downward by

Figure 27.5 The Multiplier

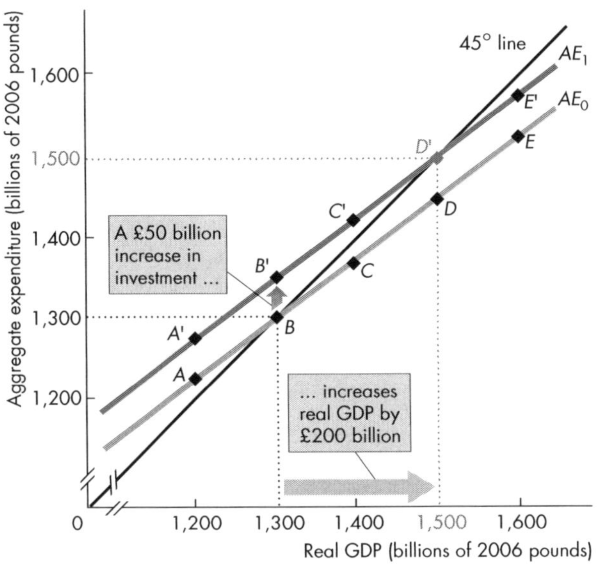

Real GDP (*Y*)	Aggregate planned expenditure: Original (AE_0)		New (AE_1)	
	(billions of 2006 pounds)			
1,200	*A*	1,225	*A'*	1,275
1,300	***B***	**1,300**	*B'*	1,350
1,400	*C*	1,375	*C'*	1,425
1,500	*D*	1,450	*D'*	**1,500**
1,600	*E*	1,525	*E'*	1,575

A £50 billion increase in autonomous expenditure shifts the *AE* curve upward by £50 billion from AE_0 to AE_1. Equilibrium expenditure increases by £200 billion from £1,300 billion to £1,500 billion. The increase in equilibrium expenditure is 4 times the increase in autonomous expenditure, so the multiplier is 4.

myeconlab Animation

£50 billion to AE_0. Equilibrium expenditure decreases from £1,500 billion to £1,300 billion. The decrease in equilibrium expenditure (£200 billion) is larger than the decrease in autonomous expenditure that brought it about (£50 billion).

Why Is the Multiplier Greater Than 1?

We've seen that equilibrium expenditure increases by more than the increase in autonomous expenditure. This makes the multiplier greater than 1. How come? Why does equilibrium expenditure increase by more than the increase in autonomous expenditure?

The multiplier is greater than 1 because of induced expenditure – an increase in autonomous expenditure *induces* further increases in expenditure. If Vodafone spends £10 million on a new telephone-video system, aggregate expenditure and real GDP immediately increase by £10 million. But that is not the end of the story. Electrical engineers and video-system designers now have more income and they spend part of the extra income on consumption goods and services.

Real GDP now increases by the initial £10 million plus the extra consumption expenditure induced by the £10 million increase in income. The producers of consumption goods and services now have increased incomes and they, in turn, spend part of the increase in their incomes on consumption goods and services. Additional income induces additional expenditure, which creates additional income.

The Size of the Multiplier

The economy is in a recession and now profit prospects start to look better. Firms are making plans for large increases in investment. The world economy is also heading towards expansion and exports are increasing. The question on everyone's lips is: how strong will the expansion be? This is a hard question to answer. But an important ingredient in the answer is working out the size of the multiplier.

The *multiplier* is the amount by which a change in autonomous expenditure is multiplied to determine the change in equilibrium expenditure that it generates. To calculate the multiplier, we divide the change in equilibrium expenditure by the change in autonomous expenditure. Let's calculate the multiplier for the example in Figure 27.5. Initially, equilibrium expenditure is £1,300 billion. Then autonomous expenditure increases by £50 billion and equilibrium expenditure increases by £200 billion to £1,500 billion. So:

$$\text{Multiplier} = \frac{\text{Change in equilibrium expenditure}}{\text{Change in autonomous expenditure}}$$

$$= \frac{£200 \text{ billion}}{£50 \text{ billion}} = 4$$

The Multiplier and the Slope of the *AE* Curve

The magnitude of the multiplier depends on the slope of the *AE* curve. In Figure 27.6, the *AE* curve in part (a) is steeper than the *AE* curve in part (b), and the multiplier is larger in part (a) than in part (b). To see why, let's do a calculation.

Aggregate expenditure and real GDP change because induced expenditure and autonomous expenditure change. The change in real GDP (ΔY) equals the change in induced expenditure (ΔN) plus the change in autonomous expenditure (ΔA). That is:

$$\Delta Y = \Delta N + \Delta A$$

But the change in induced expenditure is determined by the change in real GDP and the slope of the *AE* curve. To see why, begin with the fact that the slope of the *AE* curve equals the 'rise', ΔN, divided by the 'run', ΔY. That is:

$$\text{Slope of the } AE \text{ curve} = \Delta N \div \Delta Y$$

So:

$$\Delta N = \text{Slope of the } AE \text{ curve} \times \Delta Y$$

Now use this equation to replace ΔN in the first equation above to give:

$$\Delta Y = (\text{Slope of the } AE \text{ curve} \times \Delta Y) + \Delta A$$

Now, solve for ΔY as:

$$(1 - \text{Slope of the } AE \text{ curve}) \times \Delta Y = \Delta A$$

and rearrange to give:

$$\Delta Y = \frac{\Delta A}{1 - \text{Slope of the } AE \text{ curve}}$$

Finally, divide both sides of this equation by ΔA:

$$\text{Multiplier} = \frac{\Delta Y}{\Delta A} = \frac{1}{1 - \text{Slope of the } AE \text{ curve}}$$

Using the numbers for Figure 27.5, the slope of the *AE* curve is 0.75, so:

$$\text{Multiplier} = \frac{1}{1 - 0.75} = \frac{1}{0.25} = 4$$

When there are no income taxes and no imports, the slope of the *AE* curve equals the marginal propensity to consume (*MPC*). So the multiplier is:

$$\text{Multiplier} = \frac{1}{(1 - MPC)}$$

But (1 – *MPC*) equals *MPS*. So another formula for the multiplier is:

$$\text{Multiplier} = \frac{1}{MPS}$$

Because the marginal propensity to save (*MPS*) is a fraction – a number between 0 and 1 – the multiplier is greater than 1.

Figure 27.6 The Multiplier and the Slope of the AE Curve

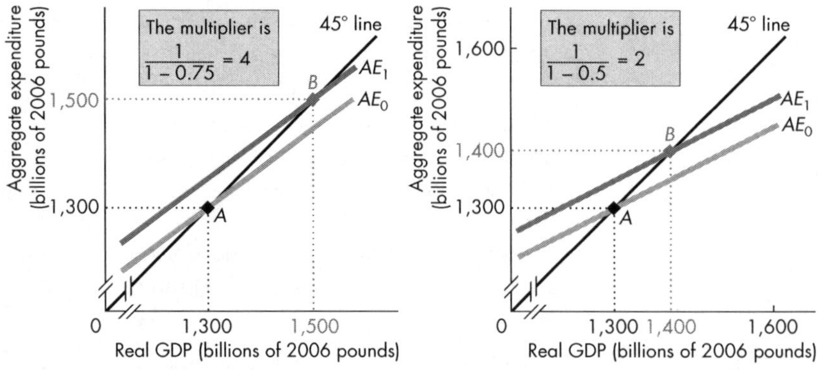

(a) Multiplier is 4

(b) Multiplier is 2

Imports and income taxes make the *AE* curve less steep and reduce the value of the multiplier. In part (a), with no imports and income taxes, the slope of the *AE* curve is 0.75 (the marginal propensity to consume) and the multiplier is 4.

But with imports and income taxes, the slope of the *AE* curve is less than the marginal propensity to consume. In part (b), the slope of the *AE* curve is 0.5. In this case, the multiplier is 2.

myeconlab Animation

Imports and Income Taxes

Imports and income taxes influence the size of the multiplier and make it smaller than it otherwise would be.

To see why, think about what happens following an increase in UK investment. An increase in investment increases real GDP, which in turn increases consumption expenditure in the UK. But part of this increase in consumption expenditure is expenditure on imported goods and services, not expenditure on UK-produced good and services. Only expenditure on goods and services produced in the UK increases UK real GDP. The larger the marginal propensity to import, the smaller is the change in UK real GDP.

Income taxes also make the multiplier smaller than it otherwise would be. Again, think about what happens following an increase in investment. An increase in investment increases real GDP. But because income taxes increase, disposable income increases by less than the increase in real GDP. Consequently, consumption expenditure increases by less than it would if taxes had not changed. The larger the income tax rate, the smaller is the change in disposable income and real GDP.

The marginal propensity to import and the marginal tax rate together with the marginal propensity to consume determine the multiplier. And their combined influence determines the slope of the *AE* curve.

Over time, changes in the marginal propensity to consume, the marginal propensity to import and the income tax rate change the value of the multiplier. These changes make the multiplier hard to predict. But they do not alter the fundamental fact that an initial change in autonomous expenditure leads to a magnified change in aggregate expenditure and real GDP.

The Mathematical Note on pp. 658–661 shows the effects of taxes, imports and the *MPC* on the multiplier.

The Multiplier Process

The multiplier effect isn't a one-shot, overnight event. It is a process that plays out over a few months. Figure 27.7 illustrates the multiplier process. In round 1, autonomous expenditure increases by £50 billion. At this time, real GDP increase by £50 billion (the green bar in round 1). This increase in real GDP increases induced expenditure in round 2. With the slope of the *AE* curve equal to 0.75, induced expenditure increases by 0.75 times the increase in real GDP, so the increase in real GDP of £50 billion induces a further increase in expenditure of £37.5 billion. This change in induced expenditure (the green bar in round 2), when added to the previous increase in expenditure (the blue bar in round 2), increases aggregate expenditure and real GDP by £87.5 billion. The round 2 increase in real GDP induces a round 3 increase in expenditure. The process repeats through successive rounds. Each increase in real GDP is 0.75 times the previous increase. The cumulative increase in real GDP gradually approaches £200 billion.

Figure 27.7 The Multiplier Process

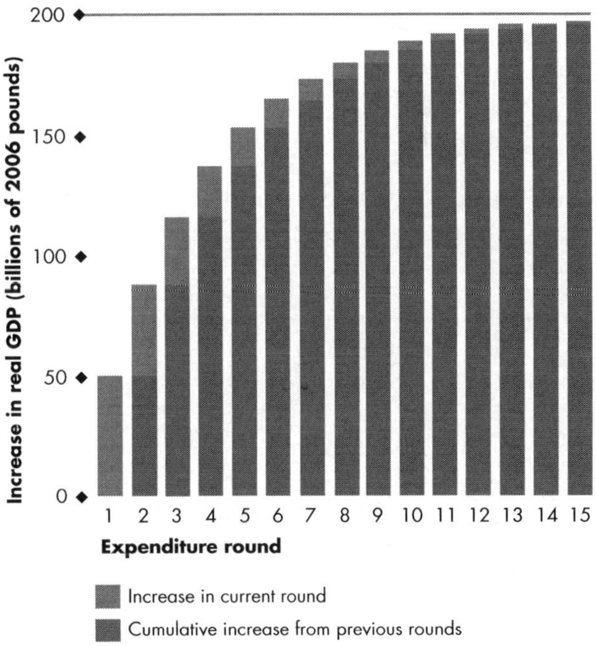

Autonomous expenditure increases by £50 billion. In round 1, real GDP increases by the same amount. With the slope of the *AE* curve equal to 0.75, each additional pound of real GDP induces an additional 0.75 of a pound of induced expenditure.

The round 1 increase in real GDP brings an increase in induced expenditure of £37.5 billion in round 2. At the end of round 2, real GDP has increased by £87.5 billion.

The extra £37.5 billion of real GDP in round 2 brings a further increase in induced expenditure of £28.1 billion in round 3. At the end of round 3, real GDP has increased to £115.6 billion.

This process continues with real GDP increasing by ever smaller amounts. When the process comes to an end, real GDP has increased by a total of £200 billion.

myeconlab Animation

ECONOMICS IN ACTION

The Multiplier in the Great Depression

The aggregate expenditure model and its multiplier were developed during the 1930s by John Maynard Keynes to understand the most traumatic event in economic history, the *Great Depression*.

In 1929, the global economies were booming. Real GDP had never been higher. By 1933, real GDP had fallen to 94 per cent of its 1929 level and unemployment had doubled from 1.25 million to 2.5 million.

Table 1 shows the GDP numbers and components of aggregate expenditure in 1929 and 1933.

Autonomous investment and exports fell sharply but autonomous consumption rose because a 14 per cent fall in the price level increased the real value of wealth. In all however, autonomous expenditure fell from \$17 billion to \$3 billion and exports fell by a large amount. Government expenditure held steady.

The figure uses the *AE* model to illustrate the Great Depression. In 1929, with autonomous expenditure of £10.7 billion, the *AE* curve was AE_{29}. Equilibrium expenditure and real GDP were £15.1 billion. By 1933, autonomous expenditure had fallen to £10.1 billion – a fall of £0.6 billion and the *AE* curve had shifted downward to AE_{33}. Equilibrium expenditure and real GDP had fallen to £14.2 billion.

The decrease in autonomous expenditure of £0.6 billion brought a decrease in real GDP of £0.9 billion. The multiplier was £0.9/£0.6 = 1.5. The slope of the *AE* curve is 0.33 – the fall in induced expenditure, £0.3 billion, divided by the fall in real GDP, £0.9 billion. The multiplier formula, 1/(1 – Slope of the *AE* curve), delivers a multiplier of 1.5.

Table 1

Components of Expenditure

	1929		1933	
	(billions of 1929 pounds)			
Induced consumption	8.4		7.9	
Induced imports	–4.0		–3.8	
Induced expenditure		4.4		4.1
Autonomous consumption	3.2		4.6	
Investment	1.9		1.1	
Government expenditure	1.8		1.9	
Exports	3.8		2.5	
Autonomous expenditure		10.7		10.1
GDP		**15.1**		**14.2**

Source of data: London & Cambridge Economic Service 1970.

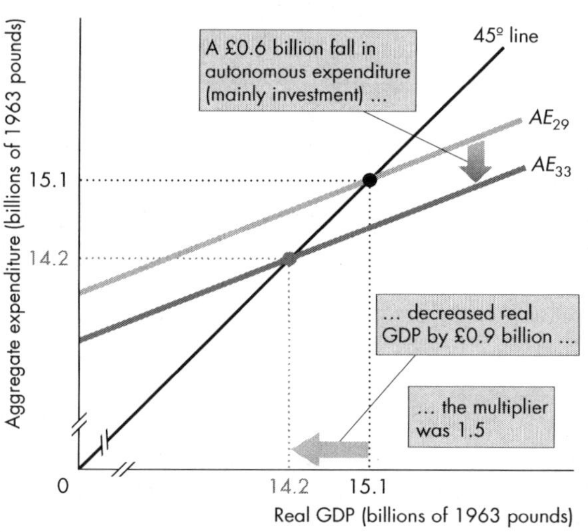

Figure 1 Aggregate Expenditure in the Great Depression

Business Cycle Turning Points

At business cycle turning points, the economy moves from expansion to recession or from recession to expansion. Economists understand these business cycle turning points like seismologists understand earthquakes. They know quite a lot about the forces and mechanisms that produce them, but they can't predict them. The forces that bring business cycle turning points are the swings in investment and exports. The multiplier is the mechanism that gives momentum to the economy's new direction.

Review Quiz

1. What is the multiplier? What does it determine? Why does it matter?
2. How do the marginal propensity to consume, the marginal propensity to import and the income tax rate influence the multiplier?
3. How do fluctuations in autonomous expenditure influence real GDP?

You can work these questions in Study Plan 27.3 and get instant feedback.

The Multiplier and the Price Level

We have just considered adjustments in spending that occur in the very short run when the price level is fixed. In this time frame, the economy's potholes, which are changes in investment and exports, are not smoothed by shock absorbers like those on the car travelling along a country road. Instead, they are amplified like Alicia Keys' voice. But these outcomes occur only when the price level is fixed. We now investigate what happens after a long enough time lapse for the price level to change.

Adjusting Quantities and Prices

When firms can't keep up with sales and their inventories fall below target, they increase production, but at some point they raise their prices. Similarly, when firms find unwanted inventories piling up, they decrease production, but eventually they cut their prices.

So far, we've studied the macroeconomic consequences of firms changing their production levels when their sales change, but we've not looked at the effects of price changes. When individual firms change their prices, the economy's price level changes.

To study the simultaneous determination of real GDP and the price level, we use the *aggregate supply–aggregate demand model*, which is explained in Chapter 26. But to understand how aggregate demand adjusts, we need to work out the connection between the aggregate supply–aggregate demand model and the equilibrium expenditure model that we've used in this chapter. The key to understanding the relationship between these two models is the distinction between the aggregate *expenditure* and aggregate *demand* and the related distinction between the *aggregate expenditure curve* and the *aggregate demand curve*.

Aggregate Expenditure and Aggregate Demand

The aggregate expenditure curve is the relationship between the aggregate planned expenditure and real GDP, when all other influences on aggregate planned expenditure remain the same. The aggregate demand curve is the relationship between the aggregate quantity of goods and services demanded and the price level, when all other influences on aggregate demand remain the same. Let's explore the links between these two relationships.

Deriving the Aggregate Demand Curve

When the price level changes, aggregate planned expenditure changes and the quantity of real GDP demanded changes. The aggregate demand curve slopes downward. Why?

There are two main reasons:

- Wealth effect
- Substitution effects

Wealth Effect

Other things remaining the same, the higher the price level, the smaller is the purchasing power of people's real wealth. For example, suppose you have £100 in the bank and the price level is 105. If the price level rises to 125, your £100 will buy fewer goods and services. You are less wealthy. With less wealth, you will probably want to spend a bit less and save a bit more. The higher the price level, other things remaining the same, the higher is saving and the lower is consumption expenditure and aggregate planned expenditure.

Substitution Effects

For a given expected future price level, a rise in the price level today makes current goods and services more expensive relative to future goods and services and results in a delay in purchases – an *intertemporal substitution.* A rise in the UK price level, other things remaining the same, makes UK-produced goods and services more expensive relative to foreign-produced goods and services. As a result, UK imports increase and UK exports decrease – an *international substitution.*

When the price level rises, each of these effects reduces aggregate planned expenditure at each level of real GDP. As a result, when the price level *rises*, the aggregate expenditure curve shifts *downward.* A fall in the price level has the opposite effect. When the price level *falls*, the aggregate expenditure curve shifts *upward.*

Figure 27.8(a) shows the shifts of the *AE* curve. When the price level is 105, the aggregate expenditure curve is AE_0, which intersects the 45° line at point *B*. Equilibrium expenditure is £1,300 billion. If the price level increases to 125, the aggregate expenditure curve shifts downward to AE_1, which intersects the 45° line at point *A*. Equilibrium expenditure decreases to £1,200 billion. If the price level decreases to 85, the aggregate

Figure 27.8 Equilibrium Expenditure and Aggregate Demand

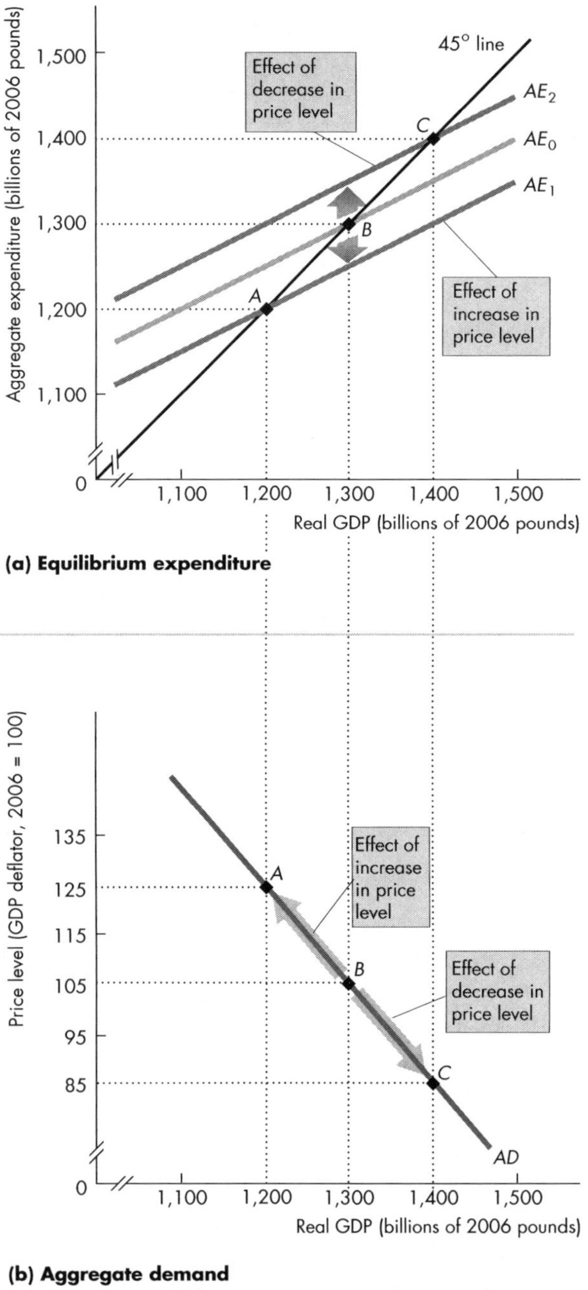

When the price level is 105, the *AE* curve is AE_0 and equilibrium expenditure is £1,300 billion at point *B*. When the price level rises to 125, the *AE* curve shifts downward to AE_1 and equilibrium expenditure is £1,200 billion at point *A*. When the price level falls to 85, the *AE* curve shifts upward to AE_2 and equilibrium expenditure is £1,400 billion at point *C*. Points *A*, *B* and *C* on the *AD* curve correspond to the equilibrium expenditure points *A*, *B* and *C*.

myeconlab Animation

expenditure curve shifts upward to AE_2, which intersects the 45° line at point *C*. Equilibrium expenditure increases to £1,400 billion.

We've just seen that when the price level changes, other things remaining the same, the aggregate expenditure curve shifts and the equilibrium expenditure changes. But when the price level changes, other things remaining the same, there is a movement along the aggregate demand curve.

Figure 27.8(b) shows the movements along the aggregate demand curve. At a price level of 105, the aggregate quantity of goods and services demanded is £1,300 billion – point *B* on the *AD* curve. If the price level rises to 125, the aggregate quantity of goods and services demanded decreases to £1,200 billion. There is a movement up along the aggregate demand curve to point *A*. If the price level falls to 85, the aggregate quantity of goods and services demanded increases to £1,400 billion. There is a movement down along the aggregate demand curve to point *C*.

Each point on the aggregate demand curve corresponds to a point of equilibrium expenditure. The equilibrium expenditure points *A*, *B* and *C* in Figure 27.8(a) correspond to the points *A*, *B* and *C* on the aggregate demand curve in Figure 27.8(b).

Changes in Aggregate Expenditure and Aggregate Demand

When any influence on aggregate planned expenditure other than the price level changes, both the aggregate expenditure curve and the aggregate demand curve shift. For example, an increase in investment or exports increases both aggregate planned expenditure and aggregate demand and shifts both the *AE* curve and the *AD* curve. Figure 27.9 illustrates the effect of such an increase.

Initially, the aggregate expenditure curve is AE_0 in part (a) and the aggregate demand curve is AD_0 in part (b). The price level is 105, real GDP is £1,300 billion and the economy is at point *A* in both parts of Figure 27.9.

Now suppose that investment increases by £100 billion. At a constant price level of 105, the aggregate expenditure curve shifts upward to AE_1. This curve intersects the 45° line at an equilibrium expenditure of £1,500 billion (point *B*). This equilibrium expenditure of £1,500 billion is the aggregate quantity of goods and services demanded at a price level of 105, as shown by point *B* in part (b). Point *B* lies on a new aggregate

Figure 27.9 A Change in Aggregate Demand

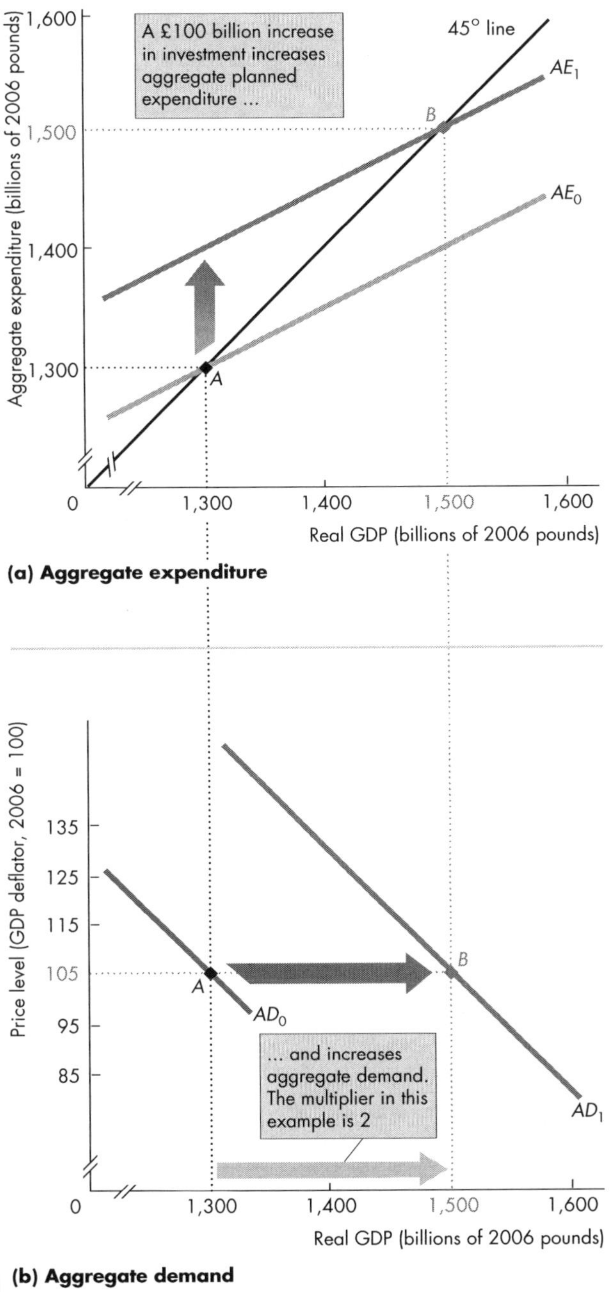

The price level is 105. When the aggregate expenditure curve is AE_0 in part (a), the aggregate demand curve is AD_0 in part (b). An increase in autonomous expenditure shifts the *AE* curve upward to AE_1. In the new equilibrium, real GDP is £1,500 billion (at point *B*). Because the quantity of real GDP demanded at a price level of 105 increases to £1,500 billion, the *AD* curve shifts rightward to AD_1.

myeconlab Animation

demand curve. The aggregate demand curve has shifted rightward to AD_1.

But how do we know by how much the *AD* curve shifts? The multiplier determines the answer. The larger the multiplier, the larger is the shift in the aggregate demand curve that results from a given change in autonomous expenditure. In this example, the multiplier is 2. A £100 billion increase in investment produces a £200 billion increase in the aggregate quantity of goods and services demanded at each price level. That is, a £100 billion increase in autonomous expenditure shifts the aggregate demand curve rightward by £200 billion.

A decrease in autonomous expenditure shifts the aggregate expenditure curve downward and shifts the aggregate demand curve leftward. You can see these effects by reversing the change that we've just described. If the economy is initially at point *B* on the aggregate expenditure curve AE_1 and on the aggregate demand curve AD_1, a decrease in autonomous expenditure shifts the aggregate expenditure curve downward to AE_0. The aggregate quantity of goods and services demanded decreases from £1,500 billion to £1,300 billion, and the aggregate demand curve shifts leftward to AD_0.

Let's summarize what we have just discovered:

If some factor other than a change in the price level increases autonomous expenditure, the *AE* curve shifts upward and the *AD* curve shifts rightward. The size of the *AD* curve shift equals the change in autonomous expenditure multiplied by the multiplier.

Equilibrium Real GDP and the Price Level

In Chapter 26, we learned that aggregate demand and short-run aggregate supply determine equilibrium real GDP and the price level. We've now put aggregate demand under a more powerful microscope and have discovered that a change in investment (or in any component of autonomous expenditure) changes aggregate demand and shifts the aggregate demand curve. The magnitude of the shift depends on the multiplier.

But whether a change in autonomous expenditure results ultimately in a change in real GDP, a change in the price level, or a combination of the two depends on aggregate supply. There are two time frames to consider: the short run and the long run. First we'll see what happens in the short run.

An Increase in Aggregate Demand in the Short Run

Figure 27.10 describes the economy. In part (a), the aggregate expenditure curve is AE_0 and equilibrium expenditure is £1,300 billion – point *A*. In part (b), aggregate demand is AD_0 and the short-run aggregate supply curve is *SAS*. (Chapter 26, pp. 615–617 explains the *SAS* curve.) Equilibrium is at point *A*, where the aggregate demand and short-run aggregate supply curves intersect. The price level is 105 and real GDP is £1,300 billion.

Now suppose that investment increases by £100 billion. With the price level fixed at 105, the aggregate expenditure curve shifts upward to AE_1. Equilibrium expenditure increases to £1,500 billion – point *B* in part (a). In part (b), the aggregate demand curve shifts rightward by £200 billion, from AD_0 to AD_1. How far the *AD* curve shifts is determined by the multiplier when the price level is fixed.

But with this new *AD* curve, the price level does not remain fixed. The price level rises and as it does so, the *AE* curve shifts downward. The short-run equilibrium occurs when the aggregate expenditure curve has shifted downward to AE_2 and the new aggregate demand curve, AD_1, intersects the short-run aggregate supply curve at point *C*. Real GDP is £1,430 billion and the price level is 118.

When the price level effects are taken into account, the increase in investment still has a multiplier effect on real GDP, but the multiplier effect is smaller than it would be if the price level were fixed. The steeper the slope of the *SAS* curve, the larger is the increase in the price level and the smaller is the multiplier effect on real GDP.

An Increase in Aggregate Demand in the Long Run

Figure 27.11 illustrates the effect of an increase in aggregate demand starting at full employment. Real GDP equals potential GDP, which is £1,300 billion. The long-run aggregate supply curve is *LAS*. Initially, the economy is at point *A* in part (a) and part (b).

Investment increases by £100 billion. The aggregate expenditure curve shifts upward to AE_1 and the aggregate demand curve shifts rightward to AD_1. With no change in the price level, the economy would move to point *B* and real GDP would increase to £1,500 billion. But in the short run, the price level rises to 118 and real GDP increases to £1,430 billion. With the higher price

Figure 27.10 The Multiplier in the Short Run

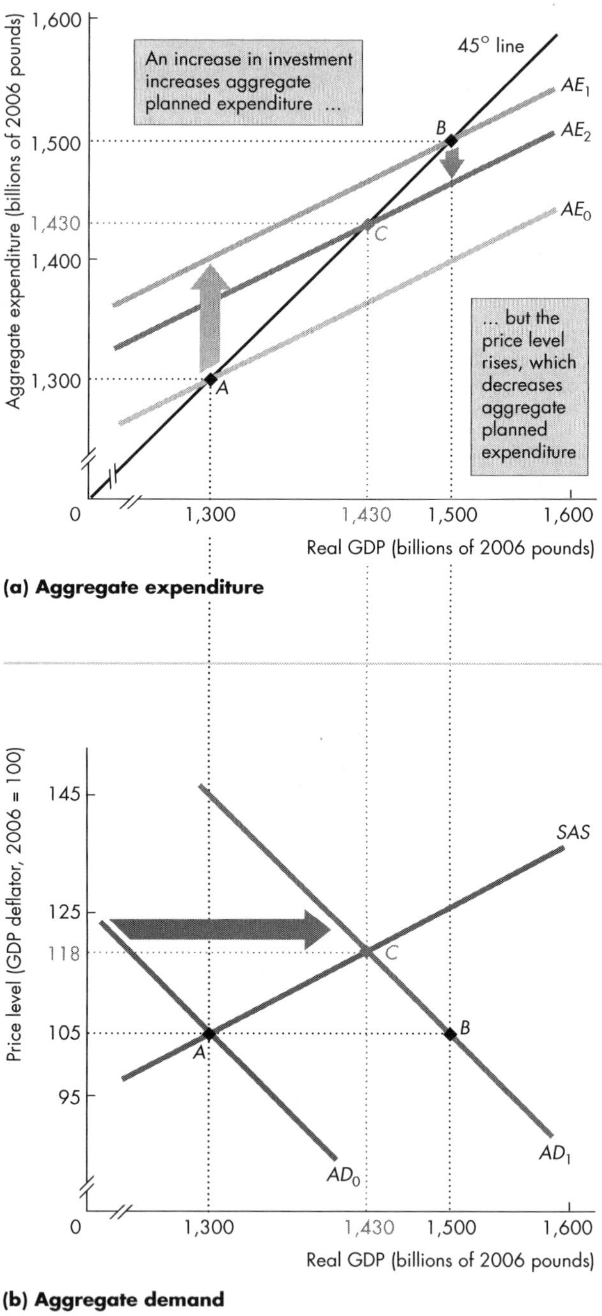

An increase in investment shifts the *AE* curve from AE_0 to AE_1 in part (a) and shifts the *AD* curve from AD_0 to AD_1 in part (b). The price level does not remain at 105 but rises, and the higher price level shifts the *AE* curve downward from AE_1 to AE_2. The economy moves to point *C*. In the short run, when prices are flexible, the multiplier is smaller than when the price level is fixed.

myeconlab Animation

Figure 27.11 The Multiplier in the Long Run

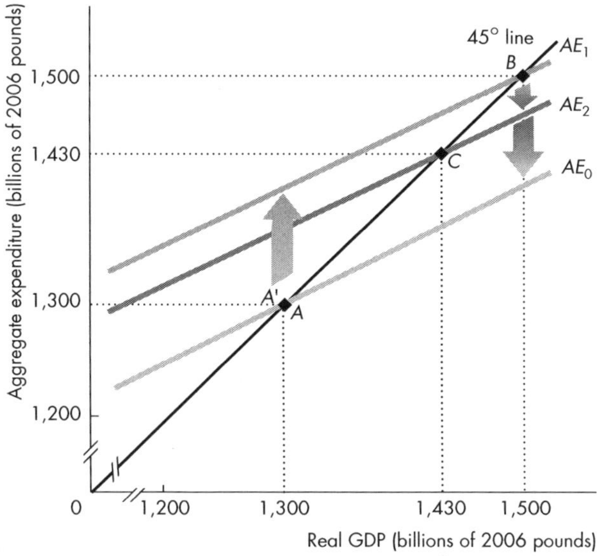

(a) Aggregate expenditure

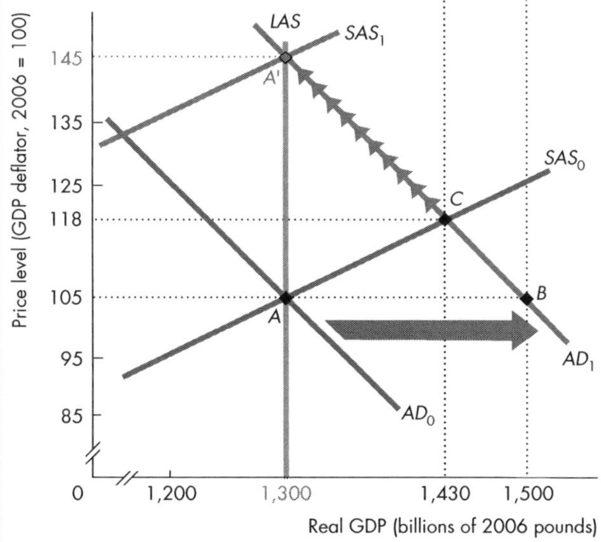

(b) Aggregate demand

Starting from point *A*, an increase in investment shifts the *AE* curve upward to AE_1 and shifts the *AD* curve rightward to AD_1. In the short run, the economy moves to point *C*. In the long run, the money wage rate rises, the *SAS* curve shifts to SAS_1, the price level rises, the *AE* curve shifts back to AE_0 and real GDP decreases. The economy moves to point *A'* and in the long run, the multiplier is zero.

myeconlab Animation

level, the aggregate expenditure curve shifts from AE_1 to AE_2. The economy is now in a short-run equilibrium at point *C*.

But real GDP now exceeds potential GDP. The workforce is more than fully employed, and in the long run shortages of labour increase the money wage rate. The higher money wage rate increases costs, which decreases short-run aggregate supply. The *SAS* curve begins to shift leftward towards SAS_1. The price level rises further and real GDP decreases. There is a movement along AD_1, and the *AE* curve shifts downward from AE_2 towards AE_0. When the money wage rate and the price level have increased by the same percentage, real GDP again equals potential GDP and the economy is at point *A'*. In the long run, the multiplier is zero.

Review Quiz

1. How does a change in the price level influence the *AE* curve and the *AD* curve?
2. If autonomous expenditure increases with no change in the price level, what happens to the *AE* curve and the *AD* curve? Which curve shifts by an amount determined by the multiplier? Explain why.
3. How does an increase in autonomous expenditure change real GDP in the short run? Does real GDP change by the same amount as the change in aggregate demand? Why or why not?
4. How does real GDP change in the long run when autonomous expenditure increases? Does real GDP change by the same amount as the change in aggregate demand? Why or why not?

You can work these questions in Study Plan 27.4 and get instant feedback. myeconlab

You are now ready to build on what you've learned about aggregate expenditure fluctuations. We'll study the business cycle and the roles of fiscal policy and monetary policy in smoothing the cycle while achieving price stability and sustained economic growth. In Chapter 28 we study the UK business cycle and inflation, and in Chapters 29 and 30 we study fiscal policy and monetary policy, respectively. But before you leave the current topic, *Reading Between the Lines* on pp. 656–657, looks at the effects of changes in the UK consumption function in the past few years.

Reading Between the Lines

Shifts in the UK Consumption Function

The Financial Times, 28 December 2010

Property Prices Link to Household Spending

FT

Norma Cohen

With house prices set for a modest decline over the coming year, economists are pondering a related question: what effect is this likely to have on patterns of household spending?

The question has been hotly debated, particularly as the house price boom came to a head – not only in Britain but in other economies, including the US, Spain and Ireland, where surging house prices accompanied falling savings rates and rising levels of consumer indebtedness.

Certainly, as prices fell in 2008–09, consumer spending fell sharply. Surveying the economy, economists John Campbell and Joao Cocco concluded that there was indeed a correlation between the wealth that many older households had accumulated in their homes and spending.

'It is tempting to attribute the correlation between house prices and consumption to a direct housing wealth effect: increasing house prices increases wealth, which in turn increases consumption,' they wrote. . . .

Similarly, according to John Muellbauer, a professor of economics at Oxford University who has studied housing and credit trends, suggesting that 'feel-good' factors produce a correlation between rising house prices and rising consumption is to miss the point.

The main reason that consumption rises with house prices is because of what he terms the 'collateral effect' – that is, as housing values rise, the value of collateral which can be used to back a loan rises too. As the value of that collateral falls, lenders, fearing losses, withdraw credit. That leads to economic shocks. . . .

The Essence of the Story

- The article asks if there is a link between house prices and consumer spending.
- When house prices soared in the UK, US, Spain and Ireland, the saving rate fell.
- House prices in the UK fell during 2008 and 2009.
- Consumer spending fell in the same period as the fall in house prices.

Economic Analysis

- A household's wealth consists of all the assets that it owns minus all the liabilities that it owes.
- A household's *real* wealth is its wealth in terms of the goods and services that it can buy and is wealth (nominal wealth) deflated by the price level.
- For a household that owns its home, the value of the home minus the outstanding balance owed on a mortgage is part of the household's wealth.
- A household's wealth can increase for either of two reasons: the household saves or the assets the household owns rise in value.
- In a household's wealth accumulation plan, it doesn't matter for which of these two reasons wealth increases.
- If a household's wealth increases because the value of its home has increased, the household has an incentive to increase consumption and save less out of its current disposable income.
- The increase in consumption expenditure shifts the consumption function upward.
- A fall in house prices, other things remaining the same, decreases wealth and provides the opposite incentive to decrease consumption expenditure and increase saving. The consumption function shifts downward.
- Figure 1 shows the annual rate of increase of house prices in the UK (HP inflation) and the growth in real consumption expenditure between 2007 and 2010.
- House prices fell during 2008 and 2009 as the annual increase in house prices became negative and wealth decreased.

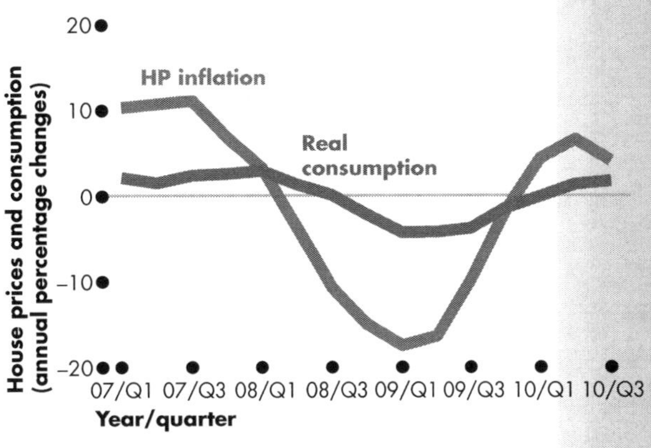

Figure 1 House prices and consumption expenditure

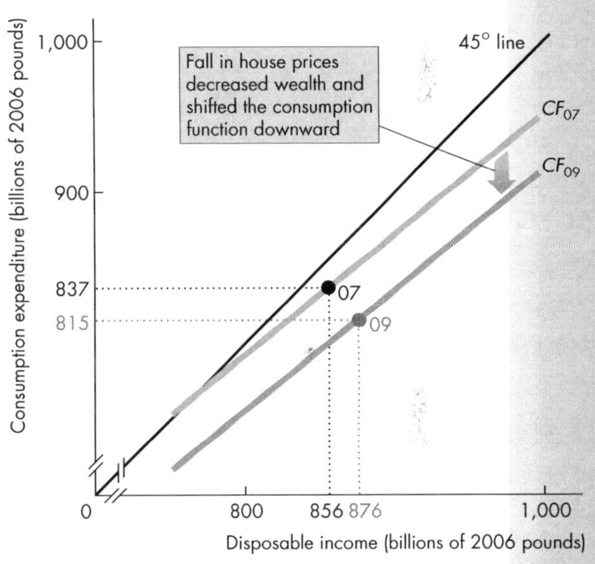

Figure 2 UK consumption functions in 2007 and 2009

- The figure also shows that in the third quarter of 2008 the annual growth in real consumer spending became negative, which means that real consumption expenditure fell over the same period as wealth declined.
- Figure 2 shows how the fall in the real value of wealth during 2008 and 2009 shifted the consumption function downward from CF_{07} to CF_{09}.

MATHEMATICAL NOTE

The Algebra of the Multiplier

This note explains the multiplier in greater detail. We begin by defining the symbols we need:

- Aggregate planned expenditure, AE
- Real GDP, Y
- Consumption expenditure, C
- Investment, I
- Government expenditure, G
- Exports, X
- Imports, M
- Net taxes, T
- Disposable income, YD
- Autonomous expenditure, A
- Autonomous consumption expenditure, a
- Autonomous taxes, T_a
- Marginal propensity to consume, b
- Marginal propensity to import, m
- Marginal tax rate, t

Aggregate Expenditure

Aggregate planned expenditure (AE) is the sum of planned consumption expenditure (C), investment (I), government expenditure (G) and exports (X) minus the planned amount of imports (M). That is:

$$AE = C + I + G + X - M$$

Consumption Function

Consumption expenditure (C) depends on disposable income (YD) and we write the consumption function as:

$$C = a + bYD$$

Disposable income (YD) equals real GDP minus net taxes ($Y - T$). So replacing YD with ($Y - T$), the consumption function becomes:

$$C = a + b(Y - T)$$

Net taxes equal autonomous taxes (that are independent of income), T_a, plus induced taxes (that vary with income), tY.

So we can write net taxes as

$$T = T_a + tY$$

Use this equation in the previous one to obtain:

$$C = a - bT_a + b(1 - t)Y$$

This equation describes consumption expenditure as a function of real GDP.

Import Function

Imports depend on real GDP and the import function is:

$$M = mY$$

Aggregate Expenditure Curve

Use the consumption function and the import function to replace C and M in the aggregate planned expenditure equation. That is:

$$AE = a - bT_a + b(1 - t)Y + I + G + X - mY$$

Collect the terms on the right-side of the equation that involve Y to obtain:

$$AE = [a - bT_a + I + G + X] + [b(1 - t) - m]Y$$

Autonomous expenditure (A) is $[a - bT_a + I + G + X]$ and the slope of the AE curve is $[b(1 - t) - m]$. So the equation for the AE curve, which is shown in Figure 1, is:

$$AE = A + [b(1 - t) - m]Y$$

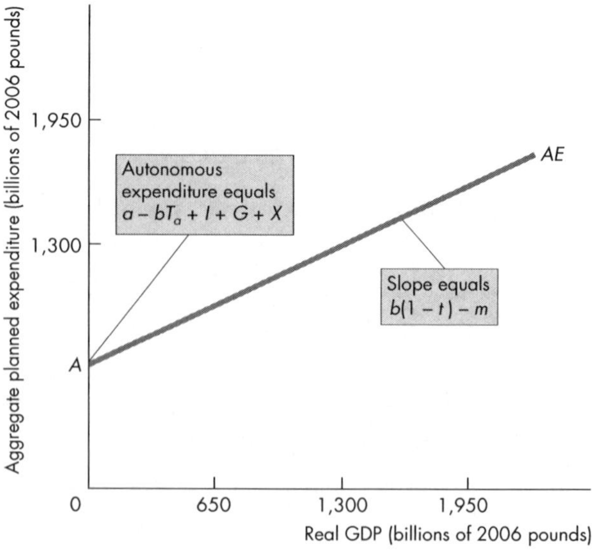

Figure 1 The *AE* Curve

Equilibrium Expenditure

Equilibrium expenditure occurs when aggregate planned expenditure (AE) equals real GDP (Y). That is:

$$AE = Y$$

In Figure 2, the scales of the x-axis (real GDP) and the y-axis (aggregate planned expenditure) are identical, so the 45° line shows the points at which aggregate planned expenditure equals real GDP. That is, along the 45° line, AE equals Y.

Figure 2 shows the point of equilibrium expenditure at the intersection of the AE curve and the 45° line.

To calculate equilibrium expenditure and real GDP, we solve the equations for the AE curve and the 45° line for the two unknown quantities AE and Y. So, starting with:

$$AE = A + [b(1 - t) - m]Y$$

$$AE = Y$$

replace AE with Y in the AE equation to obtain:

$$Y = A + [b(1 - t) - m]Y$$

The solution for Y is:

$$Y = \frac{1}{1 - [b(1 - t) - m]} A$$

The Multiplier

The *multiplier* equals the change in equilibrium expenditure and real GDP (Y) that results from a change in autonomous expenditure (A) divided by the change in autonomous expenditure. A change in autonomous expenditure (ΔA) changes equilibrium expenditure and real GDP (ΔY) by:

$$\Delta Y = \frac{1}{1 - [b(1 - t) - m]} \Delta A$$

$$\text{Multiplier} = \frac{1}{1 - [b(1 - t) - m]}$$

The size of the multiplier depends on the slope of the AE curve and the larger the slope, the larger is the multiplier. So the multiplier is larger:

1 The greater the marginal propensity to consume (b)
2 The smaller the marginal tax rate (t)
3 The smaller the marginal propensity to import (m)

An economy with no imports and no marginal taxes has $m = 0$ and $t = 0$. In this special case, the multiplier equals $1/(1 - b)$. If b is 0.75, the multiplier is 4 as shown in Figure 3.

In an economy with $b = 0.75$, $t = 0.2$ and $m = 0.1$, the multiplier is $1/[1 - 0.75(1 - 0.2) + 0.1]$, which equals 2.

Make up some more examples to show the effects of different values of b, t and m on the multiplier.

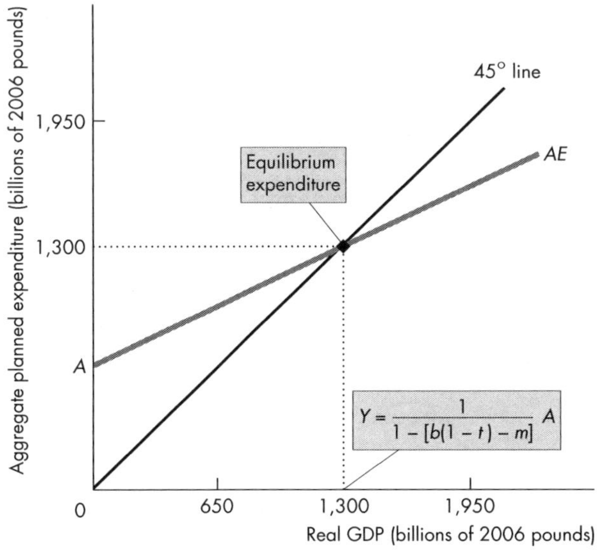

Figure 2 Equilibrium Expenditure

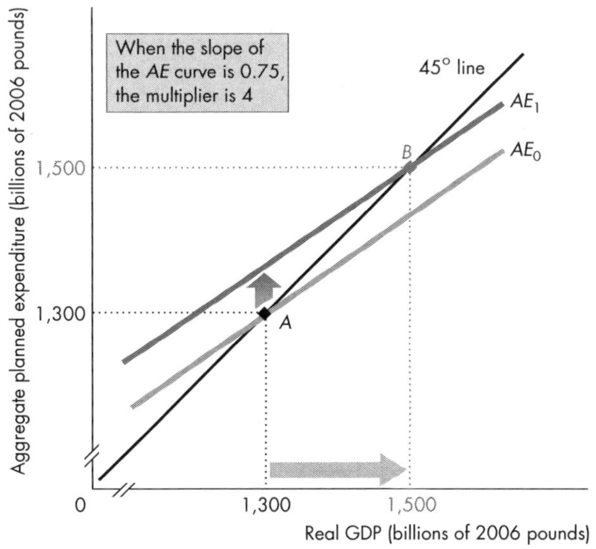

Figure 3 The Multiplier

Government Expenditure Multiplier

The **government expenditure multiplier** equals the change in equilibrium real GDP (Y) that results from a change in government expenditure (G) divided by the change in government expenditure. Because autonomous expenditure is equal to

$$A = a - bT_a + I + G + X$$

the change in autonomous expenditure equals the change in government expenditure. That is,

$$\Delta A = \Delta G$$

You can see from the solution for equilibrium expenditure Y that

$$\Delta Y = \frac{1}{1 - [b(1 - t) - m]} \Delta G$$

The government expenditure multiplier equals

$$\frac{1}{1 - [b(1 - t) - m]}$$

In an economy in which $t = 0$ and $m = 0$, the government expenditure multiplier is $1/(1 - b)$. With $b = 0.75$, the government expenditure multiplier is 4, as Figure 4 shows.

Make up some examples and use the above formula to show how b, m and t influence the government expenditure multiplier.

Autonomous Tax Multiplier

The **autonomous tax multiplier** equals the change in equilibrium expenditure (Y) that results from a change in autonomous taxes (T_a) divided by the change in autonomous taxes. Because autonomous expenditure is equal to

$$A = a - bT_a + I + G + X$$

the change in autonomous expenditure equals $-b$ multiplied by the change in autonomous taxes. That is,

$$\Delta A = -b\Delta T_a$$

You can see from the solution for equilibrium expenditure Y that

$$\Delta Y = \frac{-b}{1 - [b(1 - t) - m]} \Delta T_a$$

The autonomous tax multiplier equals

$$\frac{-b}{1 - [b(1 - t) - m]}$$

In an economy in which $t = 0$ and $m = 0$, the autonomous tax multiplier is $-b/(1 - b)$. In this special case, with $b = 0.75$, the autonomous tax multiplier equals -3, as Figure 5 shows.

Make up some examples and use the above formula to show how b, m and t influence the autonomous tax multiplier.

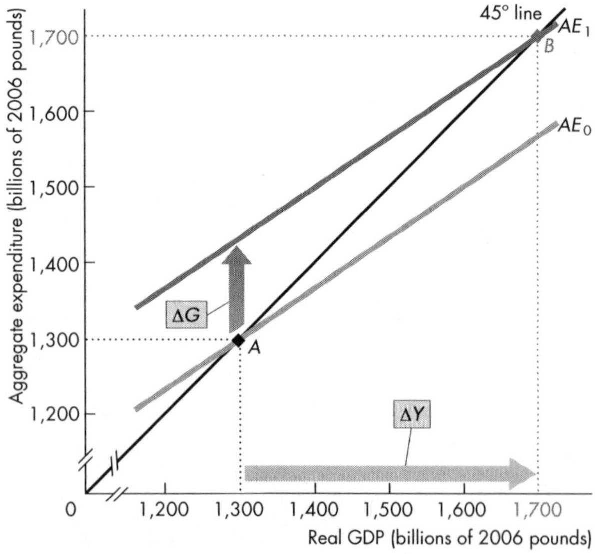

Figure 4 Government Expenditure Multiplier

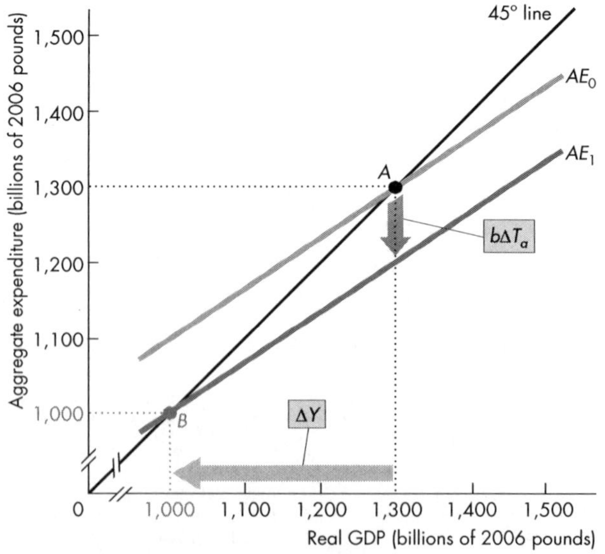

Figure 5 Autonomous Tax Multiplier

Balanced Budget Multiplier

The **balanced budget multiplier** equals the change in equilibrium expenditure (Y) that results from equal changes in government expenditure and autonomous taxes divided by the change in government expenditure. Because government expenditure and autonomous taxes change by the same amount, the budget balance does not change.

The change in equilibrium expenditure that results from the change in government expenditure is

$$\Delta Y = \frac{1}{1 - [b(1-t) - m]} \Delta G$$

And the change in equilibrium expenditure that results from the change in autonomous taxes is

$$\Delta Y = \frac{-b}{1 - [b(1-t) - m]} \Delta T_a$$

So the change in equilibrium expenditure resulting from the changes in government expenditure and autonomous taxes is

$$\Delta Y = \frac{1}{1 - [b(1-t) - m]} \Delta G + \frac{-b}{1 - [b(1-t) - m]} \Delta T_a$$

Notice that

$$\frac{1}{1 - [b(1-t) - m]}$$

is common to both terms on the right side. So we can rewrite the equation as

$$\Delta Y = \frac{-b}{1 - [b(1-t) - m]} (\Delta G - \Delta T_a)$$

The AE curve shifts upward by $\Delta G - b\Delta T_a$, as shown in Figure 6.

But the change in government expenditure equals the change in autonomous taxes. That is,

$$\Delta G = \Delta T_a$$

So we can write the equation as

$$\Delta Y = \frac{1-b}{1 - [b(1-t) - m]} \Delta G$$

The balanced budget multiplier equals

$$\frac{1-b}{1 - [b(1-t) - m]}$$

In an economy in which $t = 0$ and $m = 0$, the balanced budget multiplier is $(1 - b)/(1 - b)$, which equals 1, as Figure 6 shows.

Make up some examples and use the above formula to show how b, m and t influence the balanced budget multiplier.

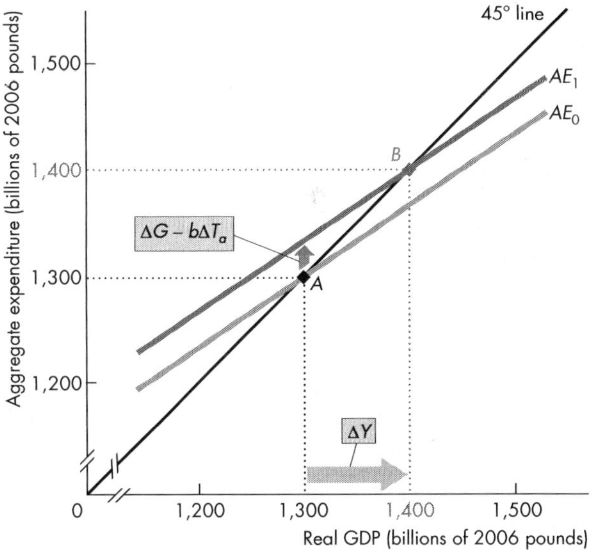

Figure 6 Balanced Budget Multiplier

SUMMARY

Key Points

Fixed Prices and Expenditure Plans

- When the price level is fixed, expenditure plans determine real GDP.
- Consumption expenditure is determined by disposable income, and the marginal propensity to consume (*MPC*) determines the change in consumption expenditure brought about by a change in disposable income. Real GDP is the main influence on disposable income.
- Imports are determined by real GDP, and the marginal propensity to import determines the change in imports brought about by a change in real GDP.

Working Problems 1 to 3 will give you a better understanding of fixed prices and expenditure plans.

Real GDP with a Fixed Price Level

- Aggregate *planned* expenditure depends on real GDP.
- Equilibrium expenditure occurs when aggregate planned expenditure equals actual expenditure and real GDP.

Working Problems 4 to 7 will give you a better understanding of real GDP with a fixed price level.

The Multiplier

- The multiplier is the magnified effect of a change in autonomous expenditure on equilibrium expenditure and real GDP.
- The multiplier is determined by the slope of the *AE* curve.
- The slope of the *AE* curve is influenced by the marginal propensity to consume, the marginal propensity to import and the income tax rate.

Working Problems 8 to 11 will give you a better understanding of the multiplier.

The Multiplier and the Price Level

- The aggregate demand curve is the relationship between the quantity of real GDP demanded and the price level, other things remaining the same.
- The aggregate expenditure curve is the relationship between aggregate planned expenditure and real GDP, other things remaining the same.
- At a given price level, there is a given aggregate expenditure curve. A change in the price level changes aggregate planned expenditure and shifts the aggregate expenditure curve. A change in the price level also creates a movement along the aggregate demand curve.
- A change in autonomous expenditure that is not caused by a change in the price level shifts the aggregate expenditure curve and shifts the aggregate demand curve. The magnitude of the shift of the aggregate demand curve depends on the multiplier and the change in autonomous expenditure.
- The multiplier decreases as the price level changes. The multiplier in the long run is zero.

Working Problems 12 to 21 will give you a better understanding of the multiplier and the price level.

Key Terms

Aggregate planned expenditure
Autonomous expenditure
Autonomous tax multiplier
Balance budget multiplier
Consumption function
Disposable income
Equilibrium expenditure
Government expenditure multiplier
Induced expenditure
Marginal propensity to consume
Marginal propensity to import
Marginal propensity to save
Multiplier
Saving function

STUDY PLAN PROBLEMS AND APPLICATIONS

myeconlab You can work Problems 1 to 22 in MyEconLab Chapter 27 Study Plan and get instant feedback.

Fixed Prices and Expenditure Plans

(Study Plan 27.1)

Use the following data to work Problems 1 and 2.

You are given the following information about the US economy.

Disposable income	Consumption expenditure
(trillions of dollars per year)	
3	3.4
4	4.2
5	5.0
6	5.8
7	6.6

1 Calculate the marginal propensity to consume.

2 Calculate saving at each level of disposable income and calculate the marginal propensity to save.

3 The US and China's Savings Problems

Last year China saved about half of its gross domestic product while the US saved only 13 per cent of its national income. The contrast is even starker at the household level – a personal saving rate in China of about 30 per cent of household income, compared with a US rate that dipped into negative territory last year (–0.4% of after-tax household income). Similar extremes show up in the consumption shares of the two economies.

Source: *Fortune*, 8 March 2006

Compare the *MPC* and *MPS* in the US and China. Why might they differ?

Real GDP with a Fixed Price Level

(Study Plan 27.2)

Use the figure in the next column to work Problems 4 and 5.

The figure illustrates the components of aggregate planned expenditure on Turtle Island. Turtle Island has no imports or exports, no incomes taxes and the price level is fixed.

4 Calculate autonomous expenditure and the marginal propensity to consume.

5 a What is aggregate planned expenditure when real GDP is €6 billion?

b If real GDP is €4 billion, what is happening to inventories?

c If real GDP is €6 billion, what is happening to inventories?

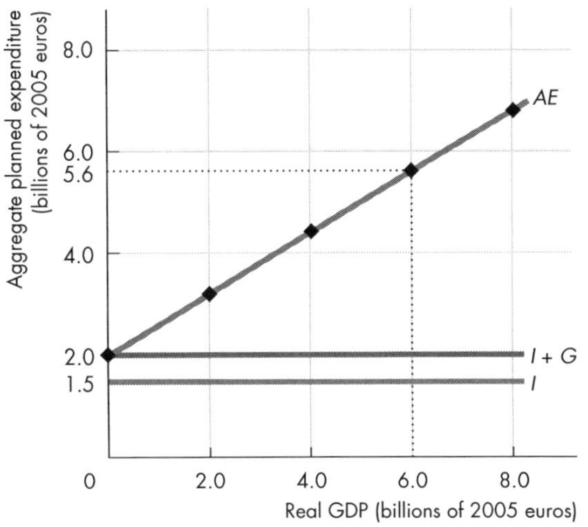

6 Explain the difference between induced consumption expenditure and autonomous consumption expenditure. Why isn't all consumption expenditure induced expenditure?

7 US Recovery?

In the second quarter, US businesses increased spending on equipment and software by 21.9 per cent, while a category that includes home building grew amid a rush by consumers to take advantage of tax credits for homes.

Source: *The Wall Street Journal*, 31 July 2010

Explain how an increase in business investment at a constant price level changes equilibrium expenditure.

The Multiplier (Study Plan 27.3)

Use the following data to work Problems 8 and 9.

An economy has a fixed price level, no imports and no income taxes. *MPC* is 0.80 and real GDP is £150 billion. Businesses increase investment by £5 billion.

8 Calculate the multiplier and the change in real GDP.

9 Calculate the new real GDP and explain why real GDP increases by more than £5 billion.

Use the following data to work Problems 10 and 11.

An economy has no imports and no income taxes. An increase in autonomous expenditure of £200 billion increases equilibrium expenditure by £800 billion.

10 Calculate the multiplier and the marginal propensity to consume.

11 What happens to the multiplier if an income tax is introduced?

The Multiplier and the Price Level

(Study Plan 27.4)

Use the following data to work Problems 12 to 16.

Suppose that the economy is at full employment, the price level is 100 and the multiplier is 2. Investment increases by £100 billion.

12 What is the change in equilibrium expenditure if the price level remains at 100?

13 **a** What is the immediate change in the quantity of real GDP demanded?

b In the short run, does real GDP increase by more than, less than or the same amount as the immediate change in the quantity of real GDP demanded?

14 In the short run, does the price level remain at 100? Explain why or why not.

15 **a** In the long run, does real GDP increase by more than, less than or the same amount as the immediate increase in the quantity of real GDP demanded?

b Explain how the price level changes in the long run.

16 Are the values of the multipliers in the short run and the long run larger or smaller than 2?

Use the following news clip to work Problems 17 and 18.

Cameron Wants Foreign Office to Make Export Drive a Priority

David Cameron vowed yesterday to put the Foreign Office in the vanguard of Britain's export drive, appointing a trade expert as its new permanent secretary and opening the door for business people to become ambassadors.

Source: *The Financial Times*, 22 July 2010

17 Will a £1 billion increase in UK exports increase aggregate expenditure by more than, less than or exactly £1 billion? Explain.

18 Explain and draw a graph to illustrate how an increase in exports will influence aggregate expenditure and aggregate demand in both the short run and the long run.

Use the following news clip to work Problems 19 to 21.

Working Poor More Pinched as Rich Cut Back

Cutbacks by the wealthy have a ripple effect across all consumer spending, said Michael P. Niemira, chief economist at the International Council of Shopping Centers. When shoppers splurge on $1,000 dinners and $300 limousine rides, that means fatter tips for the waiter and the driver. Sales clerks at upscale stores, who typically earn sales commissions, also depend on spending sprees of mink coats and jewelry.

Source: MSNBC, 28 January 2008

19 Explain and draw a graph to illustrate the process by which 'cutbacks by the wealthy have a ripple effect'.

20 Explain and draw a graph to illustrate how real GDP will be driven back to potential GDP in the long run.

21 Why is the multiplier only a short-run influence on real GDP?

Mathematical Note (Study Plan 27.MN)

22 You are given the following information about an economy: autonomous consumption expenditure is €50 billion, investment is €200 billion and government expenditure is €250 billion. The marginal propensity to consume is 0.7 and net taxes are €250 billion. Exports are €500 billion and imports are €450 billion. Assume that net taxes and imports are autonomous and the price level is fixed.

a What is the consumption function?

b What is the equation of the *AE* curve?

c Calculate equilibrium expenditure.

d Calculate the multiplier.

e If investment decreases to €150 billion, what is the change in equilibrium expenditure?

f Describe the process in part (e) that moves the economy to its new equilibrium expenditure.

ADDITIONAL PROBLEMS AND APPLICATIONS

myeconlab You can work these problems in MyEconLab if assigned by your lecturer.

Fixed Prices and Expenditure Plans

Use the following data to work Problems 23 and 24.

You are given the following information about the economy of Australia.

Disposable income	Saving
(billions of dollars per year)	
0	–5
100	20
200	45
300	70
400	95

23 Calculate the marginal propensity to save.

24 Calculate consumption at each level of disposable income. Calculate the marginal propensity to consume.

Use the following news clip to work Problems 25 to 27.

Americans $1.7 trillion Poorer

Americans saw their net worth decline by $1.7 trillion in the first quarter of 2008. Until then, net worth had been rising steadily since 2003. Michael Englund, senior economist with Action Economics said that the recent declines may not affect consumer spending. Americans have actually spent more in recent months – spending everything in their wallet and borrowing more. Household debt grew by 3.5 per cent with consumer credit rising at an annual rate of 5.75 per cent.

Source: CNN, 5 June 2008

25 Explain and draw a graph to illustrate how a decrease in household wealth theoretically influences the consumption function and saving function.

26 According to the news clip, how did consumption expenditure respond in the first quarter of 2008? What factors might explain why consumers' actual response differs from what the consumption function model predicts?

27 Draw a graph of a consumption function and show at what point consumers were actually operating in the first quarter. Explain your answer.

Real GDP with a Fixed Price Level

Use the following spreadsheet, which lists real GDP (*Y*) and the components of aggregate planned expenditure in billions of pounds, to work Problems 28 and 29.

	A	B	C	D	E	F	G
1		*Y*	*C*	*I*	*G*	*X*	*M*
2	*A*	100	110	50	60	60	15
3	*B*	200	170	50	60	60	30
4	*C*	300	230	50	60	60	45
5	*D*	400	290	50	60	60	60
6	*E*	500	350	50	60	60	75
7	*F*	600	410	50	60	60	90

28 Calculate autonomous expenditure. Calculate the marginal propensity to consume.

29 **a** What is aggregate planned expenditure when real GDP is £200 billion?

b If real GDP is £200 billion, explain the process that moves the economy towards equilibrium expenditure.

c If real GDP is £500 billion, explain the process that moves the economy towards equilibrium expenditure.

30 **UK Recovery Fears Remain Despite Growth**

Second quarter 2010 growth of the UK economy was at the fastest pace in 11 years. Despite this momentum, doubts remain over whether a strong recovery can be sustained. The two key components of demand that grew fastest were consumption expenditure and inventory investment. Inventory investment added 1 percentage point to growth and is at its highest since 1994.

With the effect of inventory investment likely to be short-lived and no other sources of stimulus, growth may slow.

Source: *The Financial Times*, 28 August 2010

Explain why a rise in inventories is associated with recovery and why the contribution of inventory investment to aggregate expenditure is likely to be short-lived.

The Multiplier

31 Darling's Risky Fiscal Stimulus

The government is taking a gamble. The Chancellor of the Exchequer is poised to unveil a short, sharp fiscal stimulus to boost consumption and stop the economy from sliding into a slump. The magnitude of the stimulus must be credible: something of the order of 1.5 per cent of gross domestic product.

Source: *The Financial Times*, 24 November 2008

If the slope of the *AE* curve in the UK is 0.6, calculate the immediate change in aggregate planned expenditure and the change in equilibrium expenditure if the price level doesn't change.

32 Cameron Bets On Northern Recipe For Growth

David Cameron has claimed that his 'northern alliance' with Nordic and Baltic states will become a driving force in 'the greenest region in the world' and 'avant-garde in delivering jobs and growth'. Mr Cameron announced that energy ministers would work on plans for an 'electricity super grid' to take green energy from one country to another and from offshore wind farms through sub-sea cables.

Source: *The Financial Times*, 21 January 2011

If, with high cyclical unemployment, the UK along with the Nordic and Baltic states spent £100 billion on green energy projects, how would equilibrium expenditure change, other things remaining the same?

The Multiplier and the Price Level

33 Stimulating Debate

Should the government hire people to bury banknotes down disused mineshafts, so that private firms can hire yet more people to dig them up again? Keynes said that there are circumstances in which government spending as wasteful as this could nevertheless be beneficial.

Source: *The Financial Times*, 30 October 2010

Explain and draw a graph to illustrate the effect of the activities described in the news clip on equilibrium expenditure, real GDP and the price level and contrast the outcomes for (i) an economy with considerable unemployment and (ii) an economy that is close to full employment.

Use the following news clip to work Problems 34 to 36.

Where Americans Will (and Won't) Cut Back

Consumer confidence has tumbled but even as consumers cut back on spending, there are some things they refuse to give up. Market research reports that Americans are demonstrating a strong reluctance to give up on everyday pleasures, but many are forced to prioritize and scale back some of their spending. Spending on dining out, out-of-the-home entertainment, clothes, vacations and buying lunch tend to be the first to be cut and many Americans are driving less and staying at home more. A whopping 50 per cent of Americans plan to buy an HD or flat-panel TV in the next year. Cable and satellite TV subscriptions are also way down the list on cutbacks. Despite the expense, another thing consumers refuse to go without completely is travel. Even in these tough times, 59 per cent of Americans plan to take a trip in the next six months.

Source: CNN, 16 July 2008

34 Which of the expenditures listed in the news clip are part of induced consumption expenditure and which are part of autonomous consumption expenditure? Explain why all consumption expenditure is not induced expenditure.

35 Explain and draw a graph to illustrate how declining consumer confidence influences aggregate expenditure and aggregate demand in the short-run.

36 Explain and draw a graph to illustrate the long-run effect on aggregate expenditure and aggregate demand of the decline in consumer confidence.

Economics in the News

37 After you have studied *Reading Between the Lines* on pp. 656–657 answer the following questions.

- **a** What happened to UK house prices during 2008 and 2009?
- **b** Why might a fall in house prices be associated with a fall in consumption, 'other things remaining the same'?
- **c** What happened to consumer spending in the UK in 2008 and 2009? Explain why.
- **d** What 'other things' could have happened in the economy that might have led to a different outcome?

38 The Biggest Risk to Growth

The biggest risk to growth in the UK is that the economies of its trading partners suffer badly, slowing demand for exports.

Source: *The Financial Times*, 11 November 2010

- **a** Does the decrease in UK exports bring a movement along the *AE* curve or a shift of the *AE* curve?
- **b** Suppose that UK exports decrease by £120 billion in 2011 and the multiplier is 1.5. If other things remain the same, what is the decrease in real GDP?
- **c** Suppose that the UK economy is at full employment in 2011 and exports increase by £120 billion. Will there still be a multiplier effect?

Mathematical Note

39 In an economy, autonomous spending is £20 billion and the slope of the *AE* curve is 0.6.

- **a** What is the equation of the *AE* curve?
- **b** Calculate equilibrium expenditure.
- **c** Calculate the multiplier if the price level is fixed.

CHAPTER

28

Inflation and Output Cycles

After studying this chapter you will be able to:

- **Explain how demand-pull and cost-push forces bring cycles in inflation and output**
- **Explain the short-run and long-run trade-off between inflation and unemployment**
- **Explain the main theories of the business cycle**

In the 1970s, Arthur M. Okun proposed what he called the 'misery index' – the sum of inflation and unemployment. Inflation and unemployment do make us miserable: inflation raises our cost of living and unemployment either takes our jobs or scares us into thinking that we might lose our jobs. Following the global financial crisis, both inflation and unemployment in the UK have risen and real income growth has fallen.

We want rapid income growth, low unemployment and low inflation, but can we have all three at the same time? Or do we face a trade-off among them? As this chapter explains, we face a trade-off in the short run but not in the long run. At the end of the chapter, in *Reading Between the Lines*, you will see how China is handling this short-run trade-off .

Inflation Cycles

In the long run, inflation is a monetary phenomenon. It occurs if the quantity of money grows faster than potential GDP. But in the short run, many factors can start an inflation, and real GDP and the price level interact. To study these interactions, we distinguish between two sources of inflation:

- Demand-pull inflation
- Cost-push inflation

Demand-pull Inflation

An inflation that results from an initial increase in aggregate demand is called **demand-pull inflation**. Demand-pull inflation can be kicked off by any of the factors that change aggregate demand. Examples are a cut in the interest rate, an increase in the quantity of money, an increase in government expenditure, a tax cut, an increase in exports, or an increase in investment stimulated by an increase in expected future profits.

Initial Effect of an Increase in Aggregate Demand

Suppose that last year the price level was 110 and both real GDP and potential GDP were £1,300 billion. Figure 28.1(a) illustrates this situation. The aggregate demand curve is AD_0, the short-run aggregate supply curve is SAS_0 and the long-run aggregate supply curve is *LAS*.

Now aggregate demand increases and the aggregate demand curve shifts rightward to AD_1. Such a situation arises if, for example, the Bank of England lowers the interest rate or exports increase.

With no change in potential GDP and with no change in the money wage rate, the long-run aggregate supply curve and the short-run aggregate supply curve remain at *LAS* and SAS_0, respectively.

The price level rises to 113 and real GDP increases above potential GDP to £1,350 billion. The economy experiences a 2.7 per cent rise in the price level (a price level of 113 compared with 110 in the previous year) and a rapid expansion of real GDP. Unemployment falls below its natural rate. The next step in the unfolding story is a rise in the money wage rate.

Figure 28.1 A Demand-pull Rise in the Price Level

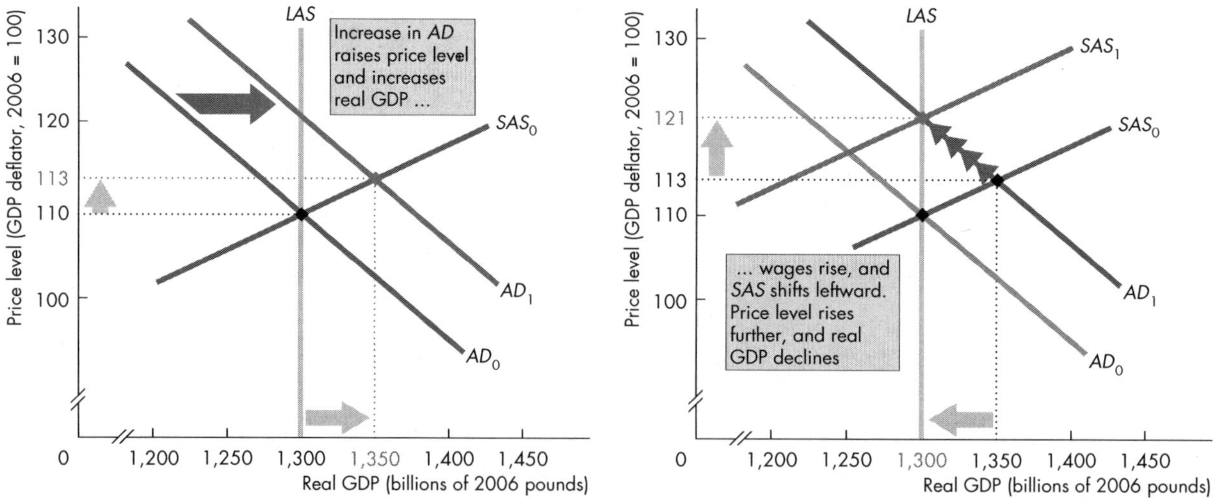

(a) Initial effect

(b) The money wage adjusts

In part (a), the aggregate demand curve is AD_0, the short-run aggregate supply curve is SAS_0 and the long-run aggregate supply curve is *LAS*. The price level is 110 and real GDP is £1,300 billion, which equals potential GDP. Aggregate demand increases to AD_1. The price level rises to 113 and real GDP increases to £1,350 billion.

In part (b), starting from above full employment, the money wage rate begins to rise and the short-run aggregate supply curve shifts leftward towards SAS_1. The price level rises further and real GDP returns to potential GDP.

myeconlab Animation

Money Wage Response

Real GDP cannot remain above potential GDP forever. With unemployment below its natural rate, there is a shortage of labour. In this situation, the money wage rate begins to rise. As the money wage rate rises, short-run aggregate supply starts to decrease and the *SAS* curve starts to shift leftward. The price level rises further and real GDP begins to decrease.

With no further change in aggregate demand – the aggregate demand curve remains at AD_1 – this process comes to an end when the short-run aggregate supply curve has shifted to SAS_1 in Figure 28.1(b). At this time, the price level has increased to 121 and real GDP has returned to potential GDP of £1,300 billion, the level from which it started.

A Demand-pull Inflation Process

The events that we've just studied bring *a one-time rise in the price level*, not inflation. For inflation to occur, aggregate demand must persistently increase.

The only way in which aggregate demand can persistently increase is if the quantity of money persistently increases. Suppose the government has a budget deficit that it finances by selling bonds. Also suppose that the Bank of England buys these bonds. When the Bank of England buys bonds, it creates more money. If the Bank of England responds continually to the budget deficit, aggregate demand increases year after year. The aggregate demand curve keeps shifting rightward. This persistent increase in aggregate demand puts continual upward pressure on the price level. The economy now experiences demand-pull inflation.

Figure 28.2 illustrates the process of demand-pull inflation. The starting point is the same as that shown in Figure 28.1. The aggregate demand curve is AD_0 and the short-run aggregate supply curve is SAS_0. Real GDP is £1,300 billion and the price level is 110. Aggregate demand increases, shifting the aggregate demand curve to AD_1. Real GDP increases to £1,350 billion and the price level rises to 113. The economy is at an above full-employment equilibrium. There is a shortage of labour and the money wage rate rises. The short-run aggregate supply curve shifts leftward to SAS_1. The price level rises to 121 and real GDP returns to potential GDP.

But the Bank of England increases the quantity of money again and aggregate demand continues to increase. The aggregate demand curve shifts rightward to AD_2. The price level rises further to 125 and real GDP again exceeds potential GDP at £1,350 billion. Yet

Figure 28.2 A Demand-pull Inflation Spiral

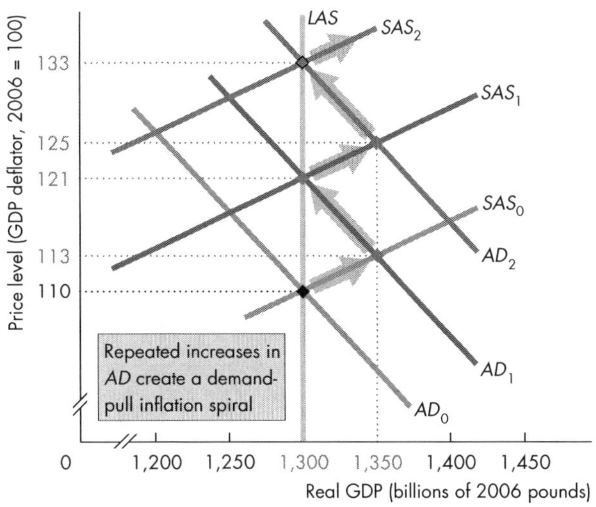

Each time the quantity of money increases, aggregate demand increases and the aggregate demand curve shifts rightward from AD_0 to AD_1 to AD_2 and so on.

Each time real GDP goes above potential GDP, the money wage rate rises and the short-run aggregate supply curve shifts leftward from SAS_0 to SAS_1 to SAS_2 and so on.

The price level rises from 110 to 113, 121, 125, 133 and so on. There is a perpetual demand-pull inflation. Real GDP fluctuates between £1,300 billion and £1,350 billion.

myeconlab Animation

again, the money wage rate rises and decreases short-run aggregate supply. The *SAS* curve shifts to SAS_2 and the price level rises further to 133. As the quantity of money continues to grow, aggregate demand increases and the price level rises in an ongoing demand-pull inflation process.

Demand-pull Inflation in Liverpool

You may better understand the inflation process that we've just described by considering what is going on in an individual part of the economy, such as a Liverpool soft drinks factory.

Initial Increase in Demand

Initially, when aggregate demand increases, the demand for soft drinks increases and the price of soft drinks rises. Faced with a higher price, the soft drinks factory works overtime and increases production. Conditions are good for workers in Liverpool and the soft drinks factory finds it hard to hang on to its best people. To do so it has to offer higher money wages. As money wages increase, so do the soft drinks factory's costs.

Aggregate Demand

What happens next depends on what happens to aggregate demand. If aggregate demand remains unchanged, the firm's costs are increasing but the price of soft drinks is not increasing as quickly as the factory's costs. Production is scaled back. Eventually, the money wage rate and costs increase by the same percentage as the price of soft drinks. In real terms, the soft drinks factory is in the same situation as it was initially – before the increase in aggregate demand. The soft drinks factory produces the same quantity of soft drinks and employs the same amount of labour as before the increase in aggregate demand.

But if aggregate demand continues to increase, so does the demand for soft drinks and the price of lemonade rises at the same rate as the money wage rate. The soft drinks factory continues to operate above full employment and there is a persistent shortage of labour. Prices and wages chase each other upward in an unending spiral.

Demand-pull Inflation in the UK

A demand-pull inflation like the one you've just studied occurred in the UK during the 1970s.

In 1972–1973, the government pursued an expansionary monetary and fiscal policy. Its goal was to lower the unemployment rate and boost the rate of economic growth. The aggregate demand curve shifted rightward, the price level increased quickly and real GDP moved above potential GDP. The money wage rate started to rise more quickly and the short-run aggregate supply curve shifted leftward.

The Bank of England responded with a further increase in the growth rate of the quantity of money. Aggregate demand increased even more quickly and a demand-pull inflation spiral unfolded.

By the mid-1970s, the inflation rate had reached more than 20 per cent a year. Contrary to the government's goal, the growth rate of real GDP didn't increase and the unemployment rate didn't decrease. On the contrary, the late 1970s were years of extremely high unemployment and slow real GDP growth.

You've seen how demand-pull inflation arises. Let's now see how an aggregate supply shock brings cost-push inflation.

Cost-push Inflation

An inflation that is kicked off by an increase in costs is called **cost-push inflation**. The two main sources of increases in costs are:

1 An increase in the money wage rate
2 An increase in the money prices of raw materials

At a given price level, the higher the cost of production, the smaller is the amount that firms are willing to produce. So if the money wage rate rises or if the prices of raw materials (for example, oil) rise, firms decrease their supply of goods and services. Aggregate supply decreases, and the short-run aggregate supply curve shifts leftward.[1]

Let's trace the effects of such a decrease in short-run aggregate supply on the price level and real GDP.

Initial Effect of a Decrease in Aggregate Supply

Suppose that last year the price level was 110 and real GDP was £1,300 billion. Potential real GDP was also £1,300 billion. Figure 28.3(a) illustrates this situation. The aggregate demand curve was AD_0, the short-run aggregate supply curve was SAS_0 and the long-run aggregate supply curve was *LAS*.

Now the world's oil producers form a price-fixing organization that strengthens their market power and increases the relative price of oil. They raise the price of oil, and this action decreases short-run aggregate supply. The short-run aggregate supply curve shifts leftward to SAS_1. The price level rises to 117 and real GDP decreases to £1,250 billion. The economy is at a below full-employment equilibrium and there is a recessionary gap.

The event that we've just described is a *one-time rise in the price level*. It is not inflation. In fact, a supply shock on its own cannot cause inflation. Something more must happen to enable a one-time supply shock, which causes a one-time rise in the price level, to be converted into a process of ongoing inflation. The quantity of money must persistently increase. Sometimes it does increase, as you will now see.

[1] Some cost-push forces, such as an increase in the price of oil accompanied by a decrease in the availability of oil, can also decrease long-run aggregate supply. We'll ignore such effects here and examine cost-push factors that change only short-run aggregate supply.

Figure 28.3 A Cost-push Rise in the Price Level

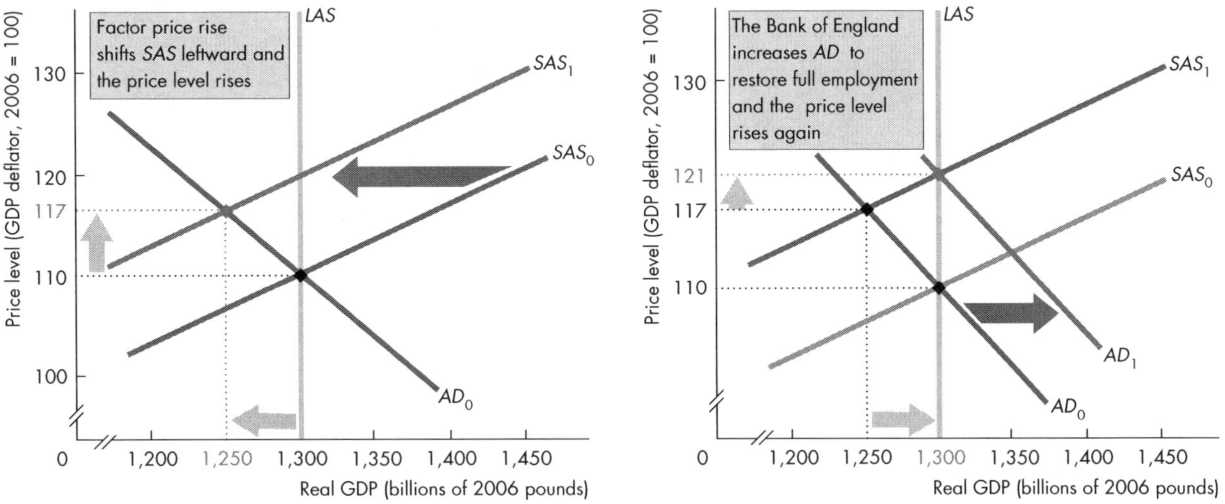

(a) Initial cost push

(b) The Bank of England responds

Initially, the aggregate demand curve is AD_0, the short-run aggregate supply curve is SAS_0 and the long-run aggregate supply curve is *LAS*. A decrease in aggregate supply shifts the short-run aggregate supply curve to SAS_1. The price level rises to 117 and real GDP decreases to £1,250 billion. The economy experiences a one-time rise in the price level.

In part (b), if the Bank responds by increasing aggregate demand to restore full employment, the aggregate demand curve shifts rightward to AD_1. The economy returns to full employment but the price level rises further to 121.

myeconlab Animation

Aggregate Demand Response

When real GDP decreases, unemployment rises above its natural rate. In such a situation, there is often an outcry of concern and a call for action to restore full employment. Suppose that the Bank of England cuts the interest rate and increases the quantity of money. Aggregate demand increases. In Figure 28.3(b), the aggregate demand curve shifts rightward to AD_1 and full employment is restored. But the price level rises further to 121.

A Cost-Push Inflation Process

The oil producers now see the prices of everything they buy increasing, so oil producers increase the price of oil again to restore its new high relative price. Figure 28.4 continues the story. The short-run aggregate supply curve now shifts to SAS_2. The price level rises and real GDP decreases.

The price level rises further, to 129, and real GDP decreases to £1,250 billion. Unemployment increases above its natural rate.

If the Bank of England responds yet again with an increase in the quantity of money, aggregate demand increases and the aggregate demand curve shifts to AD_2. The price level rises even higher – to 133 – and full employment is again restored. A cost-push inflation spiral results. The combination of a rising price level and falling real GDP is called **stagflation**.

You can see that the Bank of England has a dilemma. If it does not respond when producers raise the oil price, the economy remains below full employment. If it lowers the interest rate and increases the quantity of money to restore full employment, it invites another oil price hike that will call forth yet a further increase in the quantity of money.

If the Bank of England responds to each oil price hike by increasing the quantity of money, inflation will rage along at a rate decided by oil producers. But if it keeps the lid on money growth, the economy remains below full employment.

Figure 28.4 A Cost-push Inflation Spiral

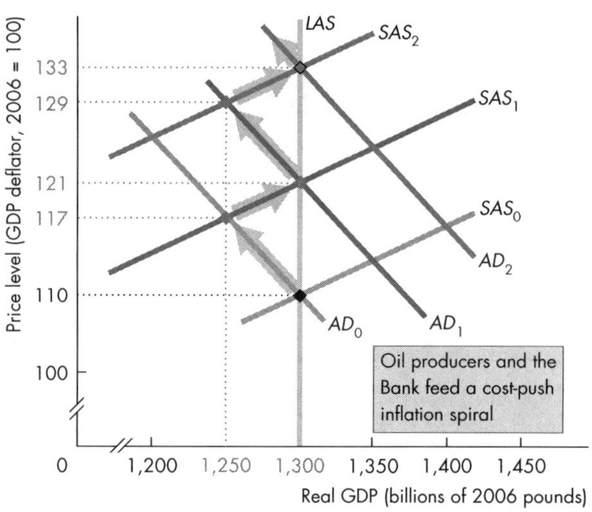

When a cost increase (for example, an increase in the world oil price) decreases short-run aggregate supply from SAS_0 to SAS_1, the price level rises to 117 and real GDP decreases to £1,250 billion. The central bank responds with an increase in the quantity of money that shifts the aggregate demand curve from AD_0 to AD_1. The price level rises again to 121 and real GDP returns to £1,300 billion. A further cost increase occurs, which shifts the short-run aggregate supply curve again, this time to SAS_2. Real GDP decreases again and the price level now rises to 129. The central bank responds again and the cost-push inflation spiral continues.

myeconlab Animation

Cost-push Inflation in Liverpool

What is going on in the Liverpool soft drinks factory when the economy is experiencing cost-push inflation?

When the oil price increases, so do the costs of producing soft drinks. These higher costs decrease the supply of soft drinks, increase the price and decrease the quantity produced. The factory lays off some workers.

This situation persists until either the Bank of England increases aggregate demand or the price of oil falls. If the Bank increases aggregate demand, the demand for soft drinks increases and so does the price. The higher price of soft drinks brings higher profits and the factory increases its production. It rehires the laid-off workers.

Cost-push Inflation in the UK

A cost-push inflation like the one you've just studied occurred in the UK during the 1970s. In 1974 the Organization of the Petroleum Exporting Countries (OPEC) raised the price of oil fourfold. The higher oil price decreased aggregate supply, which caused the price level to rise more quickly and real GDP to shrink. The Bank of England then faced a dilemma: would it increase the quantity of money and accommodate the cost-push forces or would it keep aggregate demand growth in check by limiting money growth?

In 1975, 1976 and 1977, the Bank of England repeatedly allowed the quantity of money to grow and inflation proceeded rapidly. In 1979 and 1980, OPEC was again able to push oil prices higher. On that occasion, the Bank of England decided not to respond to the oil price hike with an increase in the quantity of money. The result was a recession but also, eventually, a fall in inflation.

Expected Inflation

If inflation is expected, the fluctuations in real GDP that accompany demand-pull and cost-push inflation that you've just studied don't occur. Instead, inflation proceeds as it does in the long run, with real GDP equal to potential GDP and unemployment at its natural rate. Figure 28.5 explains why.

Suppose that last year the aggregate demand curve was AD_0, the aggregate supply curve was SAS_0 and the long-run aggregate supply curve was *LAS*. The price level was 110 and real GDP was £1,300 billion, which is also potential GDP.

To keep things as simple as possible, suppose that potential GDP does not change, so the *LAS* curve does not shift. Also suppose that aggregate demand *is expected to increase* to AD_1.

In anticipation of this increase in aggregate demand, the money wage rate rises and the short-run aggregate supply curve shifts leftward. If the money wage rate rises by the same percentage as the price level is expected to rise, the short-run aggregate supply curve for next year is SAS_1.

If aggregate demand turns out to be the same as expected, the aggregate demand curve is AD_1. The short-run aggregate supply curve, SAS_1, and AD_1 determine the actual price level at 121. Between last year and this year, the price level increased from 110 to 121 and the economy experienced an inflation rate equal to that expected. If this inflation is ongoing, aggregate demand increases (as expected) in the following year and the aggregate demand curve shifts to AD_2. The money wage rate rises to reflect the expected inflation and the short-run aggregate supply curve shifts to SAS_2. The price level rises, as expected, to 133.

Figure 28.5 Expected Inflation

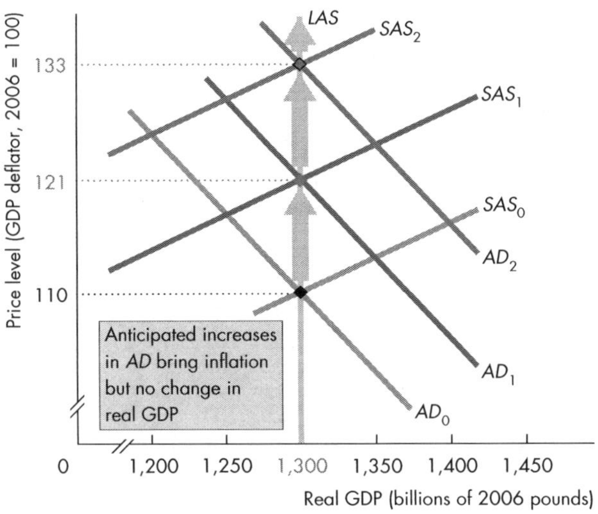

Potential real GDP is £1,300 billion. Last year, the aggregate demand curve was AD_0 and the short-run aggregate supply curve was SAS_0. The actual price level was the same as the expected price level – 110.

This year, aggregate demand is expected to increase to AD_1. The rational expectation of the price level changes from 110 to 121. As a result, the money wage rate rises and the short-run aggregate supply curve shifts to SAS_1.

If aggregate demand actually increases as expected, the actual aggregate demand curve AD_1 is the same as the expected aggregate demand curve. Real GDP is £1,300 billion and the actual price level is 121. The inflation is correctly expected.

Next year, the process continues with aggregate demand increasing as expected to AD_2 and the money wage rate rising to shift the short-run aggregate supply curve to SAS_2. Again, real GDP remains at £1,300 billion and the price level rises, as expected, to 133.

myeconlab Animation

What caused this inflation? The immediate answer is that because people expected inflation, the money wage rate increased and the price level increased. But the expectation was correct. Aggregate demand was expected to increase and it did increase. It is the actual and expected increase in aggregate demand that caused the inflation.

An expected inflation at full employment is exactly the process that the quantity theory of money predicts. To review the quantity theory of money, see Chapter 24, pp. 574–575.

This broader account of the inflation process and its short-run effects show why the quantity theory of money doesn't explain the fluctuations in inflation. The economy follows the course described in Figure 28.5, but as predicted by the quantity theory, only if aggregate demand growth is forecasted correctly.

Forecasting Inflation

To anticipate inflation, people must forecast it. Some economists who work for macroeconomic forecasting agencies, banks, insurance companies, trades unions and large companies specialize in inflation forecasting. The best forecast available is one that is based on all the relevant information and is called a **rational expectation**. A rational expectation is not necessarily a correct forecast. It is simply the best forecast with the information available. It will often turn out to be wrong, but no other forecast that could have been made with the information available could do better.

Inflation and the Business Cycle

When the inflation forecast is correct, the economy operates at full employment. If aggregate demand grows faster than expected, real GDP rises above potential GDP, the inflation rate exceeds its expected rate and the economy behaves like it does in a demand-pull inflation. If aggregate demand grows more slowly than expected, real GDP falls below potential GDP and the inflation rate slows.

Review Quiz

1. How does demand-pull inflation begin?
2. What must happen to create a demand-pull inflation spiral?
3. How does cost-push inflation begin?
4. What must happen to create a cost-push inflation spiral?
5. What is stagflation and why does cost-push inflation cause stagflation?
6. How does expected inflation occur?
7. How do the price level and real GDP change if the forecast of inflation is incorrect?

You can work these questions in Study Plan 28.1 and get instant feedback. myeconlab

Inflation and Unemployment: The Phillips Curve

Another way of studying inflation cycles focuses on the relationship and the short-run trade-off between inflation and unemployment, a relationship called the **Phillips curve** – so named because it was first suggested by New Zealand economist A.W. Phillips.

Why do we need another way of studying inflation? What is wrong with the *AS–AD* explanation of the fluctuations in inflation and real GDP? The first answer to both questions is that we often want to study changes in both the expected and actual inflation rates and for this purpose, the Phillips curve provides a simpler tool and clearer insights than the *AS–AD* model provides. The second answer to both questions is that we often want to study changes in the short-run trade-off between inflation and real economic activity (real GDP and unemployment) and again, the Phillips curve serves this purpose well.

To begin our explanation of the Phillips curve, we distinguish between two time frames (similar to the two aggregate supply time frames). We study

- The short-run Phillips curve
- The long-run Phillips curve

The Short-run Phillips Curve

The **short-run Phillips curve** shows the relationship between inflation and unemployment, holding constant:

1 The expected inflation rate
2 The natural unemployment rate

You've just seen in the previous section what determines the expected inflation rate. You learned about the natural unemployment rate and the factors that influence it in Chapter 21, pp. 489–490.

Figure 28.6 shows a short-run Phillips curve, *SRPC*. Suppose that the expected inflation rate is 10 per cent a year and the natural unemployment rate is 6 per cent, point *A*. A short-run Phillips curve passes through this point.

If inflation rises above its expected rate, the unemployment rate falls below its natural rate. This joint movement in the inflation rate and the unemployment rate is illustrated as a movement up the short-run Phillips curve from point *A* to point *B*. Similarly, if inflation falls below its expected rate, unemployment rises above the natural rate. In this case, there is movement down the short-run Phillips curve from point *A* to point *C*.

Figure 28.6 A Short-run Phillips Curve

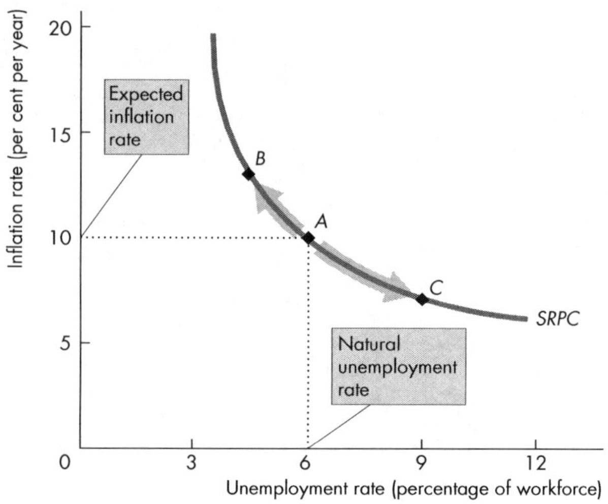

The short-run Phillips curve, *SRPC*, shows the relationship between the inflation rate and the unemployment rate at a given expected inflation rate and given natural unemployment rate. With an expected inflation rate of 10 per cent a year and a natural unemployment rate of 6 per cent, the short-run Phillips curve passes through point *A*.

An unexpected increase in aggregate demand lowers the unemployment rate and increases the inflation rate – a movement up the short-run Phillips curve to point *B*. An unexpected decrease in aggregate demand increases the unemployment rate and lowers the inflation rate – a movement down the short-run Phillips curve to point *C*.

myeconlab Animation

The Short-run Phillips Curve and the Short-run Aggregate Supply Curve

The short-run Phillips curve is like the short-run aggregate supply curve. A movement along the *SAS* curve that brings a higher price level and an increase in real GDP is equivalent to a movement along the short-run Phillips curve from *A* to *B* that brings an increase in the inflation rate and a decrease in the unemployment rate.

Similarly, a movement along the *SAS* curve that brings a lower price level and a decrease in real GDP is equivalent to a movement along the short-run Phillips curve from *A* to *C* that brings a decrease in the inflation rate and an increase in the unemployment rate.

The Long-run Phillips Curve

The **long-run Phillips curve** is a curve that shows the relationship between inflation and unemployment, when the actual inflation rate equals the expected inflation rate. The long-run Phillips curve is vertical at the natural unemployment rate. It is shown in Figure 28.7 as the vertical line *LRPC*.

The long-run Phillips curve tells us that any expected inflation rate is possible at the natural unemployment rate. This proposition is the same as the one you discovered in the *AS–AD* model, which predicts that when inflation is expected, real GDP equals potential GDP and unemployment is at its natural rate.

Changes in the Expected Inflation Rate

The short-run Phillips curve intersects the long-run Phillips curve at the expected inflation rate. A change in the expected inflation rate shifts the short-run Phillips curve but it does not shift the long-run Phillips curve.

In Figure 28.7, if the expected inflation rate is 10 per cent a year, the short-run Phillips curve is $SRPC_0$. If the expected inflation rate falls to 7 per cent a year, the short-run Phillips curve shifts downward to $SRPC_1$. The vertical distance by which the short-run Phillips curve shifts from point *A* to point *D* is equal to the change in the expected inflation rate. If the actual inflation rate also falls from 10 per cent to 7 per cent, there is a movement down the long-run Phillips curve from *A* to *D*. An increase in the expected inflation rate has the opposite effect to that shown in Figure 28.7.

The other source of a shift in the Phillips curve is a change in the natural unemployment rate.

Changes in the Natural Unemployment Rate

The natural unemployment rate changes for many reasons that are explained in Chapter 21, pp. 489–490. A change in the natural unemployment rate shifts both the short-run and the long-run Phillips curves. Figure 28.8 illustrates such effects. If the natural unemployment rate increases from 6 per cent to 9 per cent, the long-run

Figure 28.7 Short-run and Long-run Phillips Curves

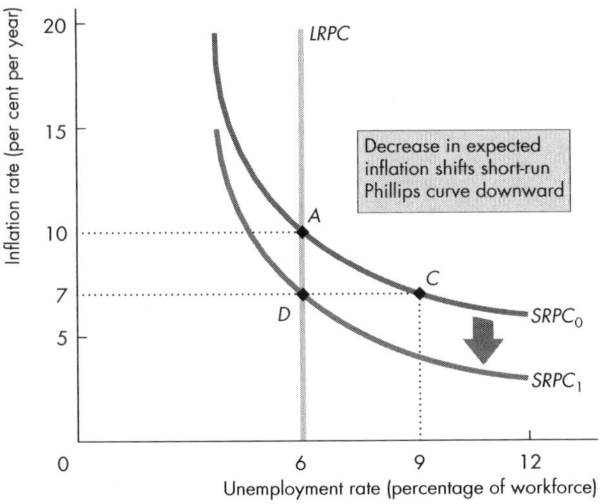

The long-run Phillips curve is *LRPC*, a vertical line at the natural unemployment rate. A fall in expected inflation shifts the short-run Phillips curve downward by the amount of the fall in the expected inflation rate.

For example, if the expected inflation rate falls from 10 per cent to 7 per cent a year, the short-run Phillips curve shifts downward from $SRPC_0$ to $SRPC_1$. The new short-run Phillips curve intersects the long-run Phillips curve at the new expected inflation rate – point *D*.

With the original expected inflation rate (10 per cent a year), an actual inflation rate of 7 per cent a year would occur at an unemployment rate of 9 per cent, at point *C*.

myeconlab Animation

Figure 28.8 A Change in the Natural Unemployment Rate

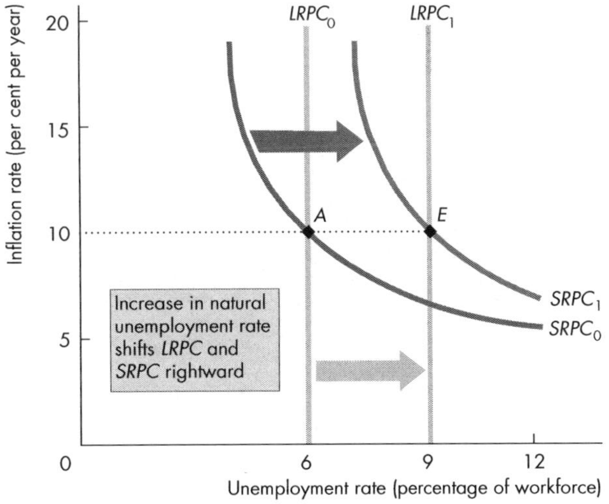

A change in the natural unemployment rate shifts both the short-run and long-run Phillips curves. Here the natural unemployment rate increases from 6 per cent to 9 per cent and the two Phillips curves shift rightward to $SRPC_1$ and $LRPC_1$. The new Phillips curves intersect at the expected inflation rate – point *E*.

myeconlab Animation

ECONOMICS IN ACTION

The Shifting Short-run Trade-off

When A.W. (Bill) Phillips first discovered the curve that bears his name, he was looking at data on wage inflation and unemployment between 1861 and 1957. It was hard to see the Phillips curve in the data. The scatter diagram of data covering almost 100 years was more like a snowstorm than a neat inverse relationship.

Figure 1(a) continues the story that Phillips began by showing a scatter diagram of the UK inflation rate and the unemployment rate from 1960 to 2010. Each dot represents the inflation rate and unemployment rate in a particular year. We certainly cannot see a Phillips curve similar to that shown in Figure 28.6.

But we can interpret the data in terms of a shifting short-run Phillips curve like those in Figures 28.7 and 28.8. Three short-run Phillips curves appear in Figure 1(b). During the 1960s the expected inflation rate was 2 per cent a year and the natural unemployment rate was 2 per cent at point *A*, so the short-run Phillips curve was $SRPC_0$. From the mid-1970s to the mid-1980s the expected inflation rate averaged 12.5 per cent a year and the natural unemployment rate averaged 8 per cent at point *B* so the short-run Phillips curve was $SRPC_1$. During the 1990s the expected inflation rate was 2.5 per cent a year and the natural unemployment rate was 5 per cent at point *C* so the short-run Phillips curve was $SRPC_2$.

All the points in the graph are on short-run Phillips curves that lie between those shown.

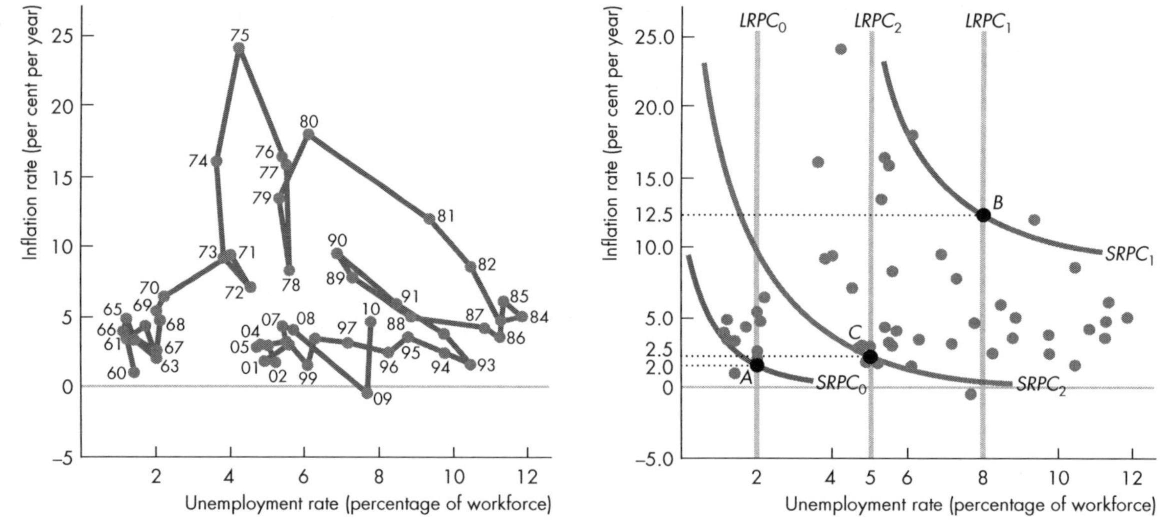

(a) Time sequence

(b) Shifting Phillips curves

Figure 1 Phillips Curves in the UK

Source of data: Office for National Statistics.

Phillips curve shifts from $LRPC_0$ to $LRPC_1$. If expected inflation is constant at 10 per cent a year, the short-run Phillips curve shifts from $SRPC_0$ to $SRPC_1$. Because the expected inflation rate is constant, the short-run Phillips curve $SRPC_1$ intersects the long-run curve $LRPC_1$ (point *E*) at the same inflation rate as that at which the short-run Phillips curve $SRPC_0$ intersects the long-run curve $LRPC_0$ (point *A*).

Changes in both the expected inflation rate and the natural unemployment rate have shifted the UK Phillips curve but the expected inflation rate has had the greater effect.

Review Quiz

1. How would you use the Phillips curve to illustrate an unexpected change in the inflation rate?
2. If the expected inflation rate increases by 10 percentage points, how would the short-run Phillips curve and long-run Phillips curve change?
3. If the natural unemployment rate increases, what happens to the short-run Phillips curve and the long-run Phillips curve?
4. Does the UK have a stable short-run Phillips curve? Explain why or why not.

You can work these questions in Study Plan 28.2 and get instant feedback.

The Business Cycle

The business cycle is easy to describe but hard to explain and business cycle theory remains unsettled and a source of controversy. We'll look at two approaches to understanding the business cycle:

- Mainstream business cycle theory
- Real business cycle theory

Mainstream Business Cycle Theory

The mainstream business cycle theory is that potential GDP grows at a steady rate while aggregate demand grows at a fluctuating rate. Because the money wage rate is sticky, if aggregate demand grows faster than potential GDP, real GDP moves above potential GDP and an inflationary gap emerges. And if aggregate demand grows slower than potential GDP, real GDP moves below potential GDP and a recessionary gap emerges. If aggregate demand decreases, real GDP also decreases in a recession.

Figure 28.9 illustrates this business cycle theory. Initially, actual and potential GDP are £1,000 billion. The long-run aggregate supply curve is LAS_0, the aggregate demand curve is AD_0 and the price level is 100. The economy is at full employment at point *A*.

An expansion occurs when potential GDP increases and the *LAS* curve shifts rightward to LAS_1. During an expansion, aggregate demand also increases, and usually by more than potential GDP, so the price level rises. Assume that in the current expansion, the price level is expected to rise to 110 and the money wage rate has been set based on that expectation. The short-run aggregate supply curve is SAS_1.

If aggregate demand increases to AD_1, real GDP increases to £1,300 billion, the new level of potential GDP, and the price level rises, as expected, to 110. The economy remains at full employment but now at point *B*.

If aggregate demand increases more slowly to AD_2, real GDP grows by less than potential GDP and the economy moves to point *C*, with real GDP at £1,250 billion and the price level at 107. Real GDP growth is slower and inflation is lower than expected.

If aggregate demand increases more quickly to AD_3, real GDP grows by more than potential GDP and the economy moves to point *D*, with real GDP at £1,350 billion and the price level at 113. Real GDP growth is faster and inflation is higher than expected.

Growth, inflation and the business cycle arise from the relentless increases in potential GDP, faster (on average) increases in aggregate demand and fluctuations in the pace of aggregate demand growth.

Figure 28.9 The Mainstream Business Cycle Theory

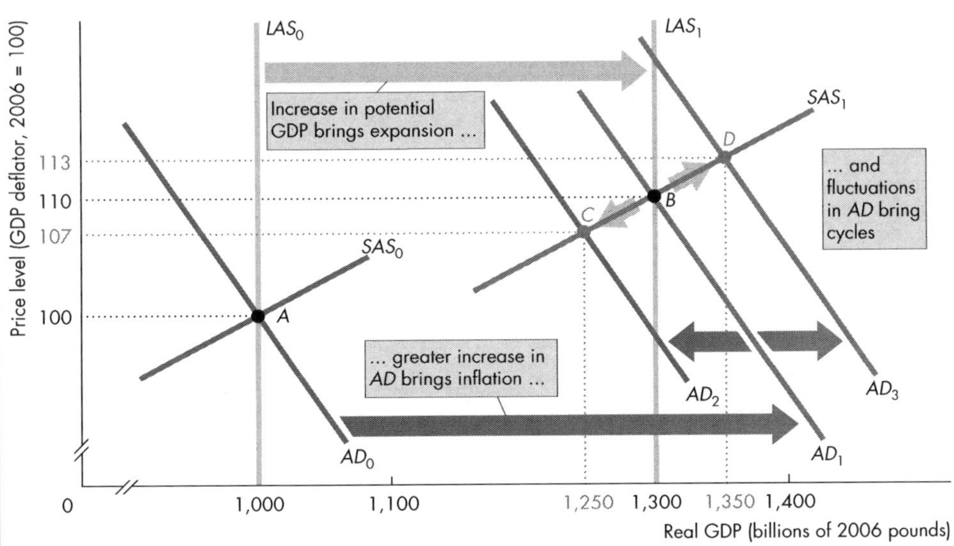

In a business cycle expansion, potential GDP increases and the *LAS* curve shifts rightward from LAS_0 to LAS_1. A greater than expected increase in aggregate demand brings inflation.

If the aggregate demand curve shifts to AD_1, the economy remains at full employment. If the aggregate demand curve shifts to AD_2, a recessionary gap arises. If the aggregate demand curve shifts to AD_3, an inflationary gap arises.

myeconlab Animation

This mainstream theory comes in a number of special forms that differ regarding the source of fluctuations in aggregate demand growth and the source of money wage stickiness.

Keynesian Cycle Theory

In **Keynesian cycle theory**, fluctuations in investment driven by fluctuations in business confidence – summarized by the phrase 'animal spirits' – are the main source of fluctuations in aggregate demand.

Monetarist Cycle Theory

In **monetarist cycle theory**, fluctuations in both investment and consumption expenditure, driven by fluctuations in the growth rate of the quantity of money, are the main source of fluctuations in aggregate demand.

Both the Keynesian and monetarist cycle theories simply assume that the money wage rate is rigid and don't explain that rigidity.

Two newer theories seek to explain money wage rate rigidity and to be more careful about working out its consequences.

New Classical Cycle Theory

In **new classical cycle theory**, the rational expectation of the price level, which is determined by potential GDP and *expected* aggregate demand, determines the money wage rate and the position of the *SAS* curve. In this theory, only unexpected fluctuations in aggregate demand bring fluctuations in real GDP around potential GDP.

New Keynesian Cycle Theory

The **new Keynesian cycle theory** emphasizes the fact that today's money wage rates were negotiated at many past dates, which means that past rational expectations of the current price level influence the money wage rate and the position of the *SAS* curve. In this theory, both unexpected and currently expected fluctuations in aggregate demand bring fluctuations in real GDP around potential GDP.

The mainstream cycle theories don't rule out the possibility that occasionally an aggregate supply shock might occur. An oil price rise, a widespread drought, a major hurricane, or another natural disaster could, for example, bring a recession. But supply shocks are not the normal source of fluctuations in the mainstream theories. In contrast, real business cycle theory puts supply shocks at centre stage.

Real Business Cycle Theory

The newest theory of the business cycle, known as **real business cycle theory** (or RBC theory), regards random fluctuations in productivity as the main source of economic fluctuations. These productivity fluctuations are assumed to result mainly from fluctuations in the pace of technological change, but they might also have other sources, such as international disturbances, climate fluctuations, or natural disasters. The origins of RBC theory can be traced to the rational expectations revolution set off by Robert E. Lucas, Jr., but the first demonstrations of the power of this theory were given by Edward Prescott and Finn Kydland and by John Long and Charles Plosser. Today, RBC theory is part of a broad research agenda called dynamic general equilibrium analysis, and hundreds of young macroeconomists do research on this topic.

We'll explore RBC theory by looking first at its impulse and then at the mechanism that converts that impulse into a cycle in real GDP.

The RBC Impulse

The impulse in RBC theory is the growth rate of productivity that results from technological change. RBC theorists believe this impulse to be generated mainly by the process of research and development that leads to the creation and use of new technologies.

To isolate the RBC theory impulse, economists measure the change in the combined productivity of capital and labour. Figure 28.10 shows the RBC impulse for the UK from 1971 to 2010. You can see that fluctuations in productivity growth are closely correlated with real GDP fluctuations.

The pace of technological change and productivity growth is not constant. Sometimes productivity growth speeds up, sometimes it slows and occasionally it even *falls* – labour and capital become less productive, on average. A period of rapid productivity growth brings a business cycle expansion, and a slowdown or fall in productivity triggers a recession (as it did in 2009).

It is easy to understand why technological change brings productivity growth. But how does technological change decrease productivity? All technological change eventually increases productivity. But if, initially, technological change makes a sufficient amount of existing capital – especially human capital – obsolete, productivity can temporarily fall. At such a time, more jobs are destroyed than created and more businesses fail than start up.

Figure 28.10 The Real Business Cycle Impulse

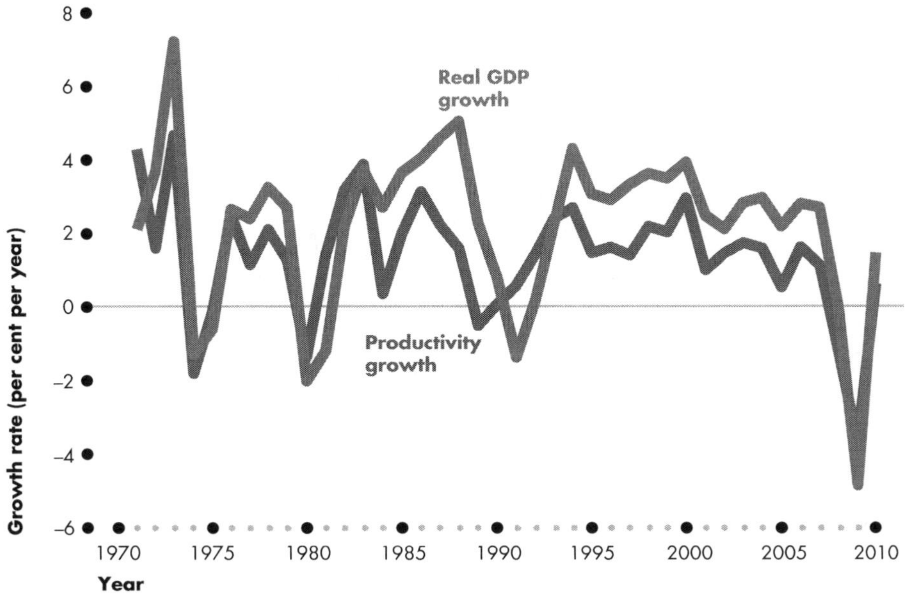

The real business cycle impulse is fluctuations in the growth rate of productivity that are caused by changes in technology. The fluctuations in productivity growth shown here are calculated by using growth accounting (the one-third rule) to remove the contribution of capital accumulation to productivity growth. Productivity fluctuations are correlated with real GDP fluctuations. Economists are not sure what the productivity variable actually measures or what causes it to fluctuate.

Sources of data: Office for National Statistics; and the authors' calculations.

myeconlab Animation

The RBC Mechanism

Two effects follow from a change in productivity that sparks an expansion or a contraction:

1 Investment demand changes
2 The demand for labour changes

We'll study these effects and their consequences during a recession. In an expansion, they work in the direction opposite to what is described here.

Technological change makes some existing capital obsolete and temporarily decreases productivity. Firms expect the future profits to fall and see their labour productivity falling. With lower profit expectations, they cut back their purchases of new capital, and with lower labour productivity, they plan to lay off some workers. So the initial effect of a temporary fall in productivity is a decrease in investment demand and a decrease in the demand for labour.

Figure 28.11 illustrates these two initial effects of a decrease in productivity. Part (a) shows the effects of a decrease in investment demand in the loanable funds market. The demand for loanable funds curve is *DLF* and the supply of loanable funds curve is *SLF* (both of which are explained in Chapter 23, pp. 540–544). Initially, the demand for loanable funds curve is DLF_0 and the equilibrium quantity of funds is £150 billion at a real interest rate of 6 per cent a year. A decrease in productivity decreases investment demand, and the demand for loanable funds curve shifts leftward from DLF_0 to DLF_1. The real interest rate falls to 4 per cent a year, and the equilibrium quantity of loanable funds decreases to £120 billion.

Figure 28.11(b) shows the demand for labour and supply of labour (which are explained in Chapter 22, pp. 513–514). Initially, the demand for labour curve is LD_0, the supply of labour curve is LS_0 and equilibrium employment is 50 billion hours a year at a real wage rate of £17.50 an hour. The decrease in productivity decreases the demand for labour, and the demand for labour curve shifts leftward from LD_0 to LD_1.

Before we can determine the new level of employment and real wage rate, we need to take a ripple effect into account – the key effect in RBC theory.

The Key Decision: When to Work?

According to RBC theory, people decide when to work by doing a cost–benefit calculation. They compare the return from working in the current period with the

Figure 28.11 The Loanable Funds and Labour Markets in a Real Business Cycle

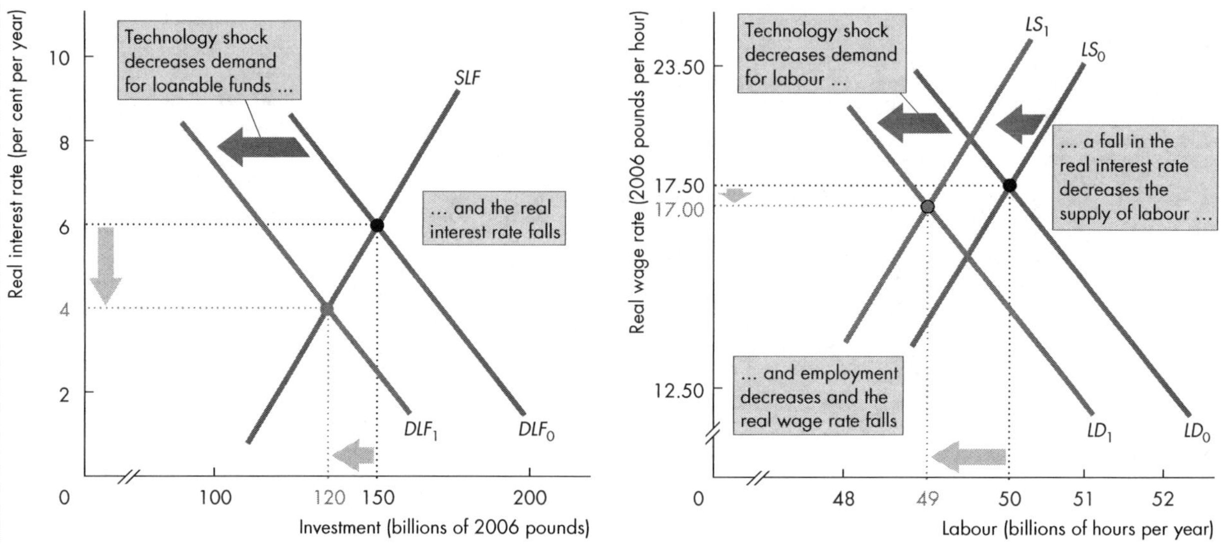

(a) Loanable funds and interest rate

(b) Labour and wage rate

In part (a), the supply of loanable funds *SLF* and initial demand for loanable funds DLF_0 determine the real interest rate at 6 per cent a year. In part (b), the initial demand for labour, LD_0 and supply of labour, LS_0, determine the real wage rate at £17.50 an hour and employment at 50 billion hours a year.

A technological change temporarily decreases productivity, which decreases both the demand for loanable funds and the demand for labour. The demand curves shift leftward to DLF_1 and LD_1 respectively.

In part (a), the real interest rate falls to 4 per cent a year. In part (b), the fall in the real interest rate decreases the supply of labour (the when-to-work decision) and the supply curve shifts leftward to LS_1. Employment decreases to 49 billion hours and the real wage rate falls to £17 an hour. A recession is under way.

myeconlab Animation

expected return from working in a later period. You make such a comparison every day at university. Suppose your goal in this course is to get an A. To achieve this goal, you work hard most of the time. But during the few days before the midterm and final exams, you work especially hard. Why? Because you believe that the return from studying close to the exam is greater than the return from studying when the exam is a long time away. So during the term, you take time off for the movies and other leisure pursuits, but at exam time, you study every evening and weekend.

RBC theory says that workers behave like you. They work fewer hours, sometimes zero hours, when the real wage rate is temporarily low, and they work more hours when the real wage rate is temporarily high. But to properly compare the current wage rate with the expected future wage rate, workers must use the real interest rate. If the real interest rate is 6 per cent a year, a real wage of £1 an hour earned this week will become £1.06 a year from now. If the real wage rate is expected to be £1.05 an hour next year, today's real wage of £1 looks good. By working longer hours now and shorter hours a year from now, a person can get a 1 per cent higher real wage. But suppose the real interest rate is 4 per cent a year. In this case, £1 earned now is worth £1.04 next year. Working fewer hours now and more next year is the way to get a 1 per cent higher real wage.

So the when-to-work decision depends on the real interest rate. The lower the real interest rate, other things remaining the same, the smaller is the supply of labour today. Many economists believe this *intertemporal substitution effect* to be of negligible size. RBC theorists believe that the effect is large, and it is the key feature of the RBC mechanism.

You saw in Figure 28.11(a) that the decrease in the demand for loanable funds lowers the real interest rate. This fall in the real interest rate lowers the return to current work and decreases the supply of labour.

In Figure 28.11(b), the labour supply curve shifts leftward to LS_1. The effect of the decrease in productivity on the demand for labour is larger than the effect of the fall in the real interest rate on the supply of labour. That is, the demand curve shifts farther leftward than does the supply curve. As a result, the real wage rate falls to £17 an hour and employment decreases to 49 billion hours. A recession has begun and is intensifying.

What Happened to Money?

The name *real* business cycle theory is no accident. It reflects the central prediction of the theory. Real things, not nominal or monetary things, cause the business cycle. If the quantity of money changes, aggregate demand changes. But if there is no real change – with no change in the use of resources and no change in potential GDP – the change in the quantity of money changes only the price level. In RBC theory, this outcome occurs because the aggregate supply curve is the *LAS* curve, which pins real GDP down at potential GDP, so when aggregate demand changes, only the price level changes.

Cycles and Growth

The shock that drives the business cycle of RBC theory is the same as the force that generates economic growth: technological change. On average, as technology advances, productivity grows; but as you saw in Figure 28.10, it grows at an uneven pace. Economic growth arises from the upward trend in productivity growth and, according to RBC theory, the mostly positive but occasionally negative higher frequency shocks to productivity bring the business cycle.

Criticisms of RBC Theory

The three main criticisms of RBC theory are that (1) the money wage rate is sticky, and to assume otherwise is at odds with a clear fact; (2) intertemporal substitution is too weak a force to account for large fluctuations in labour supply and employment with small real wage rate changes; and (3) productivity shocks are as likely to be caused by changes in aggregate demand as by technological change.

If aggregate demand fluctuations cause the fluctuations in productivity, then the traditional aggregate demand theories are needed to explain them. Fluctuations in productivity do not cause the business cycle but are caused by it!

Building on this theme, the critics point out that the so-called productivity fluctuations that growth accounting measures are correlated with changes in the growth rate of money and other indicators of changes in aggregate demand.

In Defence of RBC Theory

The defenders of RBC theory claim that the theory explains the macroeconomic facts about the business cycle and is consistent with the facts about economic growth. In effect, a single theory explains *both growth and the business cycle*. The growth accounting exercise that explains slowly changing trends also explains the more frequent business cycle swings.

Its defenders also claim that RBC theory is consistent with a wide range of *micro*economic evidence about labour supply decisions, labour demand and investment demand decisions and information on the distribution of income between labour and capital.

The strongest defence of RBC theory is not its detailed explanation of the cycle and growth but its method, the *dynamic general equilibrium* approach to studying the aggregate economy that is employed today by new classical and new Keynesian researchers as they continue to gain a better understanding of the economy.

Review Quiz

1. Explain the mainstream theory of the business cycle.
2. What are the four special forms of the mainstream theory of the business cycle and how do they differ?
3. According to RBC theory, what is the source of the business cycle? What is the role of fluctuations in the rate of technological change?
4. According to RBC theory, how does a fall in productivity growth influence investment demand, the market for loanable funds, the real interest rate, the demand for labour, the supply of labour, employment and the real wage rate?
5. What are the main criticisms of RBC theory and how do its supporters defend it?

You can work these questions in Study Plan 28.3 and get instant feedback. myeconlab

You can complete your study of inflation and economic fluctuations in *Reading Between the Lines* on pp. 682–683, which looks at inflationary pressures in China and the tough trade-off faced by that fast-changing economy.

Reading Between the Lines

China's Inflation–Growth Trade-off

The Financial Times, 21 November 2010

China's Twilight Economy Piles Pressure on Inflation Fight

FT

James Kynge

China has lambasted the US for its decision to launch another $600bn in monetary easing, fearing that this round of 'quantitative easing' may feed the flood of money rushing into mainland China from overseas. But while capital inflows are a problem for Beijing, there should be no doubt that China's swelling money supply and resurgent inflation are primarily 'Made in China'.

Bank lending . . . is looking increasingly likely to bust through the government's solemnly decreed 2010 target. . . . But more worrying . . . are the inflationary pressures springing from a subterranean world of informal finance. Although the size of China's underground financial system is uncertain, it is unlikely to be modest. . . .

Thus the total assets contained within China's twilight economy may well be in excess of Rmb6,000bn.

If this number is added to the 2010 official lending target of Rmb7,500bn, then it becomes clear that China's 2009 record lending splurge was no 'one-off' and may well be exceeded by this year's level.

It is pressures caused by such ballooning money supply, coupled with various structural influences inherent in the take-off of China's rural economy, that are the prime causes of inflation.

China knows that it cannot bring discipline to its huge, unregulated underground economy without sacrificing growth, and yet unless it grapples with the root causes of money supply, it may fail to tame inflation.

The Essence of the Story

- China's inflation rose throughout 2010.
- China criticizes the US for its policy of 'quantitative easing', which is flooding the world economy with money.
- Some of this money has gone to China and increased aggregate demand.
- Most of the increase in money in China comes from China's banks and its large informal banking system.

Economic Analysis

- China's inflation rate during 2010 was on an upward trend as you can see in Figure 1.
- Figure 2 shows the main source of the increase in inflation: a money growth rate that vastly exceeds the growth rate of real GDP.
- You can see in Figure 2 that the inflation rate and real GDP growth rate fluctuate in sympathy with the fluctuations in money growth but with a time lag.
- The news article notes that in addition to the growth of money there is a large growth in credit in the informal parts of China's economy.
- China is experiencing both demand-pull and cost-push inflation forces.
- Figure 3 illustrates these forces by showing what has been happening to China's aggregate demand and aggregate supply.
- In 2008, aggregate demand was AD_{08} and short-run aggregate supply was SAS_{08}. Real GDP was ¥26 trillion (in 2005 prices) and the price level was 120 (2005 = 100).
- In 2010, potential GDP was ¥31 trillion and the long-run aggregate supply curve was LAS_{10}.
- Between 2008 and 2010, the quantity of money increased, credit grew and a global expansion increased the demand for China's exports. Aggregate demand increased and the *AD* curve shifted rightward to AD_{10}.
- Commodity prices and the money wage rate increased, which decreased short-run aggregate supply and the *SAS* curve shifted leftward to SAS_{10}.
- To slow inflation, China must slow the money growth rate.
- This action will slow the rate of increase of aggregate demand and will temporarily slow the growth rate of real GDP.

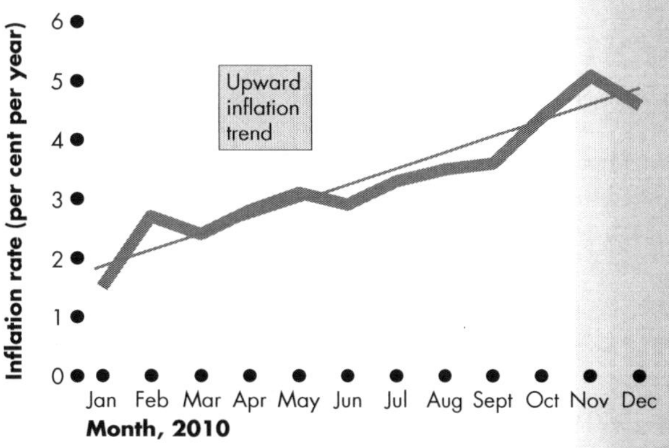

Figure 1 China's inflation in 2010

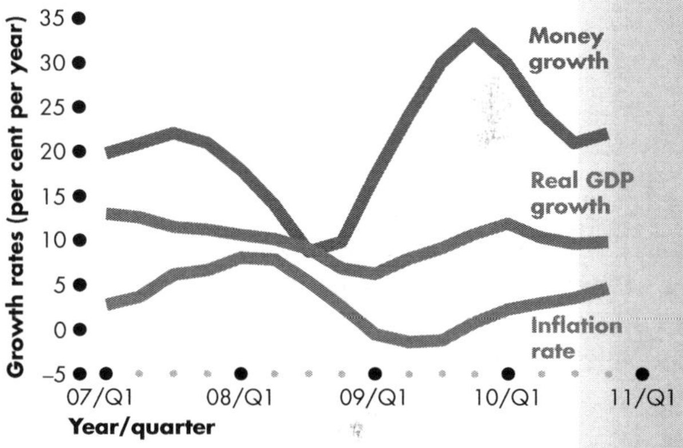

Figure 2 Money growth, real GDP growth and inflation

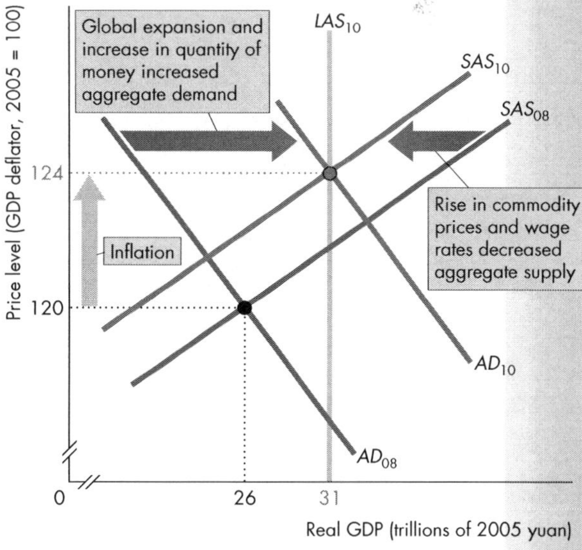

Figure 3 Changes in aggregate supply and aggregate demand

SUMMARY

Key Points

Inflation Cycles

- Demand-pull inflation is triggered by an increase in aggregate demand and fuelled by ongoing money growth. Real GDP cycles above full employment.
- Cost-push inflation is triggered by an increase in the money wage rate or raw material prices and is fuelled by ongoing money growth. Real GDP cycles below full employment in a stagflation.
- When the forecast of inflation is correct, real GDP remains at potential GDP.

Working Problems 1 to 11 will give you a better understanding of inflation cycles.

Inflation and Unemployment: The Phillips Curve

- The short-run Phillips curve shows the trade-off between inflation and unemployment when the expected inflation rate and the natural unemployment rate are constant.
- The long-run Phillips curve, which is vertical, shows that when the actual inflation rate equals the expected inflation rate, the unemployment rate equals the natural unemployment rate.

Working Problems 12 to 14 will give you a better understanding of inflation and unemployment: the Phillips curve.

The Business Cycle

- The mainstream business cycle theory explains the business cycle as fluctuations of real GDP around potential GDP and as arising from a steady expansion of potential GDP combined with an expansion of aggregate demand at a fluctuating rate.
- Real business cycle theory explains the business cycle as fluctuations of potential GDP, which arise from fluctuations in the influence of technological change on productivity growth.

Working Problem 15 will give you a better understanding of the business cycle.

Key Terms

Cost-push inflation
Demand-pull inflation
Keynesian cycle theory
Long-run Phillips curve
Monetarist cycle theory
New classical cycle theory
New Keynesian cycle theory
Phillips curve
Rational expectation
Real business cycle theory
Short-run Phillips curve
Stagflation

STUDY PLAN PROBLEMS AND APPLICATIONS

myeconlab You can work Problems 1 to 15 in MyEconLab Chapter 28 Study Plan and get instant feedback.

Inflation Cycles (Study Plan 28.1)

1 Pakistan: Is it Cost-Push Inflation?

With CPI already spiking 11.8 per cent for the first ten months of the fiscal year, the average CPI inflation for the same period last year stood at 22.35 per cent. Some economists insist the current bout of inflationary pressures is spawned by increasing prices of fuel, food, raw materials, transportation, construction materials, elimination of energy subsidies, etc as indicated by the spike in the wholesale price index (WPI), which rose 21.99 per cent in April from a year earlier.

Source: *Daily the Pak Banker*, 22 May 2010

Explain what type of inflation Pakistan is experiencing.

Use the following figure to work Problems 2, 3, 4 and 5. In each question, the economy starts out on the curves labelled AD_0 and SAS_0.

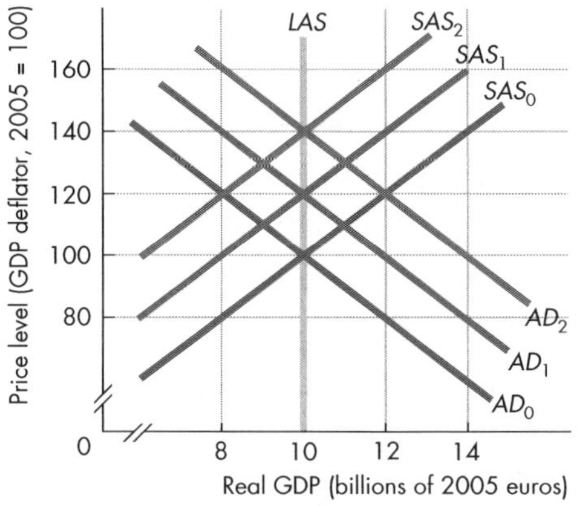

2 Some events occur and the economy experiences a demand-pull inflation.

a List the events that might cause a demand-pull inflation.

b Describe the initial effects of a demand-pull inflation.

c Describe what happens as a demand-pull inflation spiral proceeds.

3 Some events occur and the economy experiences a cost-push inflation.

a List the events that might cause a cost-push inflation.

b Describe the initial effects of a cost-push inflation.

c Describe what happens as a cost-push inflation spiral proceeds.

4 Some events occur and the economy is expected to experience inflation.

a List the events that might cause an expected inflation.

b Describe the initial effects of an expected inflation.

c Describe what happens as an expected inflation proceeds.

5 Suppose that people expect deflation (a falling price level), but aggregate demand remains at AD_0.

a What happens to the short-run and long-run aggregate supply curves? (Draw some new curves if you need to.)

b Describe the initial effects of an expected deflation.

c Describe what happens as it becomes obvious to everyone that the expected deflation is not going to occur.

Use the following news clip to work Problems 6 to 8.

Money's Too Loose to Mention

UK inflation at 3.7 per cent is above target and above forecasts. This inflation can't be blamed on temporary factors such as a rise in commodity prices or a tax increase, although these events did occur and will make inflation worse before it gets better. Rather, embedded inflation and inflation expectations seem to be rising and the UK now has higher inflation than any other developed economy.

Source: *The Financial Times*, 19 January 2011

6 Does the news clip describe a situation in which the UK is experiencing demand-pull inflation, cost-push inflation, or an expected inflation spiral? Explain.

7 Draw a graph to illustrate the effects of the temporary factors noted in the news clip.

8 Draw a graph to illustrate and explain how the UK might be experiencing an expected inflation spiral.

Use the following news clip to work Problems 9 to 11.

Tight Money Won't Slay Food, Energy Inflation

It's important to differentiate between a general increase in prices – a situation in which aggregate demand exceeds their aggregate supply – and a relative price shock. For example, a specific shock to energy prices can become generalized if producers are able to pass on the higher costs. So far, global competition has made that difficult for companies, while higher input costs have largely been neutralized by rising labour productivity. Since 2003, US core inflation has averaged less than 2 per cent a year in the 30 major economies. History also suggests the US central bank's gamble that slowing growth will shackle core inflation is a winning wager. The risk is that if US consumers don't believe price increases will slow, growing inflation expectations may become self-fulfilling.

Source: Bloomberg, 9 May 2008

9 **a** Explain the two types of inflation described in this news clip.

b Explain why 'rising labour productivity' can neutralize the effect on inflation of 'higher input costs'.

10 Explain how 'slowing growth' can reduce inflationary pressure.

11 Draw a graph to illustrate and explain how 'growing inflation expectations may become self-fulfilling'.

Inflation and Unemployment: The Phillips Curve (Study Plan 28.2)

12 **Iran Postpones Cutting Petrol Subsidies**

Inflation is about 10 per cent and the unemployment rate is about 14 per cent. Earlier this month Iran's main audit body slammed the government's plan to scrap petrol subsidies, warning that implementing such a reform might result in unrest. The government also intends to scrap subsidies on natural gas, which most Iranians use for cooking and heating, as well as electricity, but the new prices are still not known. However, in recent weeks some households have received electricity bills with nearly sevenfold price increases.

Source: AFP, 15 September 2010

a If Iran unexpectedly removes the subsidies and consumers don't know what the higher prices will be, draw a graph to show the most likely path of inflation and unemployment.

b If Iran removes the subsidies and announces the new prices so that consumers know what they are, draw a graph to show the most likely path of inflation and unemployment.

13 **Recession? Maybe. Depression? Get Real**

The unemployment rate during the Great Depression peaked at nearly 25 per cent in 1933, after an initial spike from 3 per cent in 1929 to nearly 8.7 per cent in 1930. The unemployment rate is just 5 per cent, only up from 4.5 per cent a year ago. Also during the Great Depression there was deflation, which is not happening today.

Source: CNN, 28 May 2008

a Can the inflation and unemployment trends during the Great Depression be explained by a movement along a short-run Phillips curve?

b Can the inflation and unemployment trends during 2008 be explained by a movement along a short-run Phillips curve?

14 **Inflation Report Press Conference**

Despite weak demand, inflation is above the 2 per cent target. The slack in the economy is likely to reduce inflationary pressure, but it is possible that rising import prices and commodity prices will push up inflation and inflation expectations.

Source: Bank of England, 10 November 2010

Explain this report in terms of shifts and movements along a short-run and long-run Phillips curve.

The Business Cycle (Study Plan 28.3)

15 **Debate on Causes of Joblessness Grows**

What is the cause of the high unemployment rate? One side says more government spending can reduce joblessness. The other says it's a structural problem – people who can't move to take new jobs because they are tied down to burdensome mortgages or firms that can't find workers with the requisite skills to fill job openings.

Source: *The Wall Street Journal*, 4 September 2010

Which business cycle theory would say that the rise in unemployment is cyclical? Which would say it is an increase in the natural rate? Why?

ADDITIONAL PROBLEMS AND APPLICATIONS

myeconlab You can work these problems in MyEconLab if assigned by your lecturer.

Inflation Cycles

Use the following news clip to work Problems 16 and 17.

Bernanke Sees No Repeat of '70s-Style Inflation

There is little indication today that a 1970s-style cost-push spiral is about to begin. Then, as now, a serious oil price shock occurred, but today's economy is more flexible in responding to difficulties, Bernanke said. Also, today the US Federal Reserve monitors inflation expectations. If people believe inflation will keep going up, they will change their behaviour in ways that aggravate inflation – thus, a self-fulfilling prophecy. In the 1970s, people demanded (and received) higher wages in anticipation of rapidly rising prices; hence, the cost-push spiral began. The inflation rate has averaged about 3.5 per cent over the past four quarters. That is 'significantly higher' than the Federal Reserve would like but much lower than the double-digit inflation rates of the mid-1970s and 1980, said Bernanke.

Source: *USA Today*, 4 June 2008

16 Draw a graph to illustrate and explain the inflation spiral that the US experienced in the 1970s.

17 **a** Explain the role that inflation expectations play in creating a self-fulfilling prophecy.

b Explain Bernanke's predictions about the impact of the 2008 oil price shock as compared to the 1970s shock.

Inflation and Unemployment: The Phillips Curve

Use the following information to work Problems 18 and 19.

The Reserve Bank of New Zealand (the central bank) signed an agreement with the New Zealand government in which the Bank agreed to maintain inflation inside a low target range. Failure to achieve the target would result in the governor of the Bank losing his job.

18 Explain how this arrangement might have influenced New Zealand's short-run Phillips curve.

19 Explain how this arrangement might have influenced New Zealand's long-run Phillips curve.

Use the following information and the figure in the next column to work Problems 20 and 21.

An economy has an unemployment rate of 4 per cent and an inflation rate of 5 per cent a year at point *A* in the figure. Some events occur that move the economy in a clockwise loop from *A* to *B* to *D* to *C* and back to *A*.

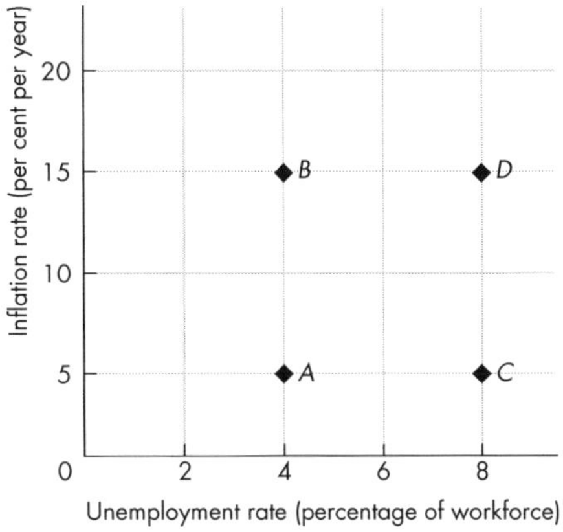

20 Describe the events that could create this sequence. Has the economy experienced demand-pull inflation, cost-push inflation, expected inflation, or none of these?

21 Draw in the figure the sequence of the economy's short-run and long-run Phillips curves.

Use the following news clip to work Problems 22 to 24.

Inflation in Brazil

Dilma Rouseff, Brazil's incoming president will face the challenge of consumer price inflation running well above the government's target of 4.5 per cent a year. Prices rose by 5.6 per cent in the 12 months to November and the rate is expected to reach 6 per cent by the year end. Price rises have spread to other sectors as the fast growth in Brazil's economy, expected to be about 7.5 per cent this year, puts pressure on supply.

Source: *The Financial Times*, 22 December 2010

22 Is Brazil experiencing demand-pull or cost-push inflation? Explain.

23 Draw a graph to illustrate the initial rise in the price level and the money wage rate response to a one-time rise in the price level.

24 Draw a graph to illustrate and explain how Brazil might experience an inflation spiral

Use the following information to work Problems 25 and 26.

Because the US Federal Reserve doubled the monetary base in 2008 and the government spent billions of dollars bailing out troubled banks, insurance companies and auto producers, some people are concerned that a serious upturn in the inflation rate will occur, not immediately but in a few years' time. At the same time, massive changes in the global economy might bring the need for structural change in the US.

25 Explain how the doubling of the monetary base and government bailouts might influence the short-run and long-run unemployment–inflation trade-offs. Will the influence come from changes in the expected inflation rate, the natural unemployment rate or both?

26 Explain how large-scale structural change might influence the short-run and long-run unemployment–inflation trade-offs. Will the influence come from changes in the expected inflation rate, the natural unemployment rate or both?

The Business Cycle

Use the following information to work Problems 27 to 29.

Suppose that the business cycle in the UK is best described by RBC theory and that a new technology increases productivity.

27 Draw a graph to show the effect of the new technology in the market for loanable funds.

28 Draw a graph to show the effect of the new technology in the labour market.

29 Explain the when-to-work decision when technology advances.

30 **Real Wages Fail to Match a Rise in Productivity**

For most of the last century, wages and productivity – the key measure of the economy's efficiency – have risen together, increasing rapidly through the 1950s and 1960s and far more slowly in the 1970s and 1980s. But in recent years, the productivity gains have continued while the pay increases have not kept up.

Source: *The New York Times*, 28 August 2006

Explain the relationship between wages and productivity in this news clip in terms of real business cycle theory.

Economics in the News

31 After you have studied *Reading Between the Lines* on pp. 682–683 answer the following questions.

- **a** Given the money growth rate in China, why isn't real GDP growing at a faster pace?
- **b** If the money growth rate in China remains at the levels of 2010, what do you expect to happen to inflation in 2011 and 2012?
- **c** Use the *AS–AD* model to describe the inflationary process in China.
- **d** What policies would you recommend to the Chinese government to reduce inflation? Explain why?

32 **Germany Leads Slowdown in Eurozone**

The pace of German economic growth has weakened 'markedly', but the reason is the weaker global prospects. Although German policymakers worry about the country's exposure to a fall in demand for its export goods, evidence is growing that the recovery is broadening with real wage rates rising and unemployment falling, which will lead into stronger consumer spending.

Source: *The Financial Times*, 23 September 2010

- **a** How does 'exposure to a fall in demand for its export goods' influence Germany's aggregate demand, aggregate supply, unemployment and inflation?
- **b** Use the *AS–AD* model to illustrate your answer to part (a).
- **c** Use the Phillips curve model to illustrate your answer to part (a).
- **d** What do you think the news clip means by 'the recovery is broadening with real wage rates rising and unemployment falling, which will lead into stronger consumer spending'?
- **e** Use the *AS–AD* model to illustrate your answer to part (d).
- **f** Use the Phillips curve model to illustrate your answer to part (d).

PART

9

Macroeconomic Policy

Trade-offs and Free Lunches

A policy trade-off arises if, in taking an action to achieve one goal, some other goal must be forgone. The Bank of England wants to avoid a rise in the inflation rate and a rise in the unemployment rate. But if the Bank raises the interest rate to curb inflation, it might increase unemployment. The Bank faces a short-run trade-off between inflation and unemployment.

A policy 'free lunch' arises if in taking actions to pursue one goal, some other (intended or unintended) goal is also achieved. The Bank of England wants to keep inflation in check and, at the same time, to boost the economic growth rate. If lower inflation brings greater certainty about the future and stimulates saving and investment, the Bank gets both lower inflation and faster real GDP growth. It enjoys a free lunch.

The two chapters in this part describe the institutional framework in which fiscal policy (Chapter 29) and monetary policy (Chapter 30) are made, describes the instruments of policy and analyses the effects of policy. This exploration of economic policy draws on almost everything that you learned in previous chapters.

These policy chapters serve as a capstone on your knowledge of macroeconomics and draw together all the strands in your study of the previous chapters.

Understanding Macroeconomic Policy

The central challenges of fiscal policy and monetary policy are to contribute to achieving the fastest possible sustainable growth rate of real GDP, to maintain a stable price level and to minimize the volatility of fluctuations of real GDP around potential GDP and of unemployment around the natural unemployment rate.

All fiscal policy and monetary policy actions work by influencing the incentives that people and businesses face. And these incentives can be influenced either in a well-understood and predictable manner or in a poorly understood and capricious or surprising manner.

Does it matter whether policy is predictable or a surprise?

Economists are in agreement that it does matter and that predictable policy actions do a better job than policy surprises.

A government that commits to a tax and spending regime that is sustainable and predictable and not subject to capricious change creates an environment in which self-interested decisions can best serve the social interest.

A central bank that adopts a well-understoood target, sets its policy instrument to achieve that target and explains its policy choices in the framework of its target delivers a better outcome for all the goals of macroeconomic policy than does a central bank that acts capriciously and surprises financial markets by its actions.

But there remains much debate about just what the targets of policy should be. Should fiscal policy be aimed at achieveing long-term growth and equity across the generations, or should it be aimed at the short-run stabilization objective of smoothing the cycles in economic activity? Should monetary policy be governed by an explicit inflation target, a money stock growth target or some implicit targets that might include stabilizing output and employment?

There are no settled answers to these questions.

Milton Friedman was born into a poor immigrant family in New York City in 1912. He was an undergraduate at Rutgers and a graduate student at Columbia University during the Great Depression. From 1977 until his death in 2006, Professor Friedman was a Senior Fellow at the Hoover Institution at Stanford University. But his reputation was built between 1946 and 1983, when he was a leading member of the 'Chicago School', an approach to economics developed at the University of Chicago and based on the views that free markets allocate resources efficiently and that stable and low money supply growth delivers macroeconomic stability.

Friedman has advanced our understanding of the forces that determine macroeconomic performance and clarified the effects of the quantity of money. For this work, he was awarded the 1977 Nobel Prize for Economic Science.

By reasoning from basic economic principles, Friedman (along with Edmund S. Phelps, the 2006 Economics Nobel Laureate) predicted that persistent demand stimulation would not increase output but would cause inflation.

When output growth slowed and inflation broke out in the 1970s, Friedman seemed like a prophet, and for a time his policy prescription, known as monetarism, was embraced around the world.

'Inflation is always and everywhere a monetary phenomenon.'

MILTON FRIEDMAN
The Counter-Revolution in Monetary Theory

CHAPTER

29

Fiscal Policy

After studying this chapter you will be able to:

- Describe the UK government's recent budgets
- Explain the supply-side effects of fiscal policy
- Explain how fiscal policy redistributes benefits and costs across generations
- Understand and explain fiscal stimulus in recession

Every spring, the Chancellor of the Exchequer presents his budget. In 2010, UK governments (central and local) spent 47 pence of every pound earned and had a budget deficit of £149 billion. Does a pound spent by the government have the same effects as a pound spent by someone else? What happens if governments spend more than they receive in receipts and run into debt? Does government debt damage economic growth and the well-being of future generations? How do taxes affect the economy?

You will find some of the answers in this chapter. And in *Reading Between the Lines* at the end of the chapter, you can see how the government of Ireland is using fiscal policy in an attempt to restore confidence in its debt and stimulate a flagging economy.

Government Budgets

A government's **budget** is an annual statement of projected outlays and receipts during the next year together with the laws and regulations that will support those outlays and receipts. The finance minister – the Chancellor of the Exchequer in the UK – presents the budget to Parliament in what is often a piece of political theatre and always a major media event.

A government's budget has three major purposes:

1 To state the scale and allocation of the government's outlays and its plans to finance its activities
2 To stabilize the economy
3 To encourage the economy's long-term growth and balanced regional development

Before the Second World War, the budget had only the first of these goals – to plan and finance the business of government.

But during the late 1940s and early 1950s, the budget began to assume its second purpose – stabilization of the economy.

In more recent years, the budget has assumed its third goal of helping to secure faster sustained economic growth and to seek balance across regions.

Today, the budget is the tool used by a government in pursuit of its fiscal policy. **Fiscal policy** is a government's use of its budget to achieve macroeconomic objectives such as full employment, sustained economic growth and price-level stability. It is the fiscal policy aspects of the budget that we focus on in this chapter.

Government budgets differ in size and detail, but they all have the same components. Here, we'll illustrate a government budget by looking at the UK.

Highlights of the UK Budget in 2010

Table 29.1 shows the main items in the UK government's budget. The numbers are projections for the fiscal year beginning in April 2010. The three main items in the budget are:

- Receipts
- Outlays
- Budget balance

Table 29.1

The Government Budget in 2010/11

Item			Projections (billions of pounds)
Receipts			**531**
Taxes on income and wealth		189	
Taxes on expenditure		186	
National Insurance contributions		97	
Other receipts and royalties		59	
Outlays			**695**
Expenditure on goods and services		388	
Health	107		
Education	59		
Law and order	22		
Defence	46		
Other	154		
Transfer payments		265	
Debt interest		42	
Budget balance (surplus +/deficit –)			**–164**

Source of data: HM Treasury, Budget 2010.

Receipts

Receipts come from four sources:

1 Taxes on income and wealth
2 Taxes on expenditure
3 National Insurance contributions
4 Other receipts and royalties

The largest source of revenue is *taxes on income and wealth*, which were projected to be £189 billion in 2010/11. These are the taxes paid by individuals on their incomes and wealth and the taxes paid by businesses on their profits.

The second largest source of revenue is *taxes on expenditure*, which in 2010/2011 were projected at £186 billion. These taxes include VAT and special duties and taxes on gambling, alcoholic drinks, petrol, luxury items and imported goods.

Third in size are *National Insurance contributions*, projected to be £97 billion in 2010/11. This revenue comes from contributions paid by workers and employers to fund the welfare and healthcare programmes.

Fourth in size are *other receipts and royalties*. This item includes oil royalties, stamp duties, car taxes, miscellaneous rents, dividends from abroad and profits from nationalized industries.

Outlays

Outlays are classified in three broad categories:

1 Expenditure on goods and services
2 Transfer payments
3 Debt interest

Expenditure on goods and services are by far the largest item at £388 billion in 2010/11.

Table 29.1 lists some of the larger components of these expenditures. Health (expenditure on the National Health Service) took £107 billion and education took another £59 billion. The provision of law and order and defence, the two traditional roles of government, took only £68 billion between them.

Transfer payments – £265 billion in 2010/11 – are payments to individuals, businesses, other levels of government and the rest of the world. These payments include National Insurance benefits, healthcare benefits, unemployment benefits, welfare supplements, grants to local authorities and aid to developing countries.

Debt interest, which in 2010/11 is projected to be £42 billion, is the interest on the government debt minus interest received by the government on its own investments.

The bottom line of the government budget is the balance – the surplus or deficit.

Budget Balance

The government's budget balance is equal to its receipts minus its outlays. That is:

Budget balance = Receipts – Outlays

If receipts exceed outlays, the government has a **budget surplus**. If outlays exceed receipts, the government has a **budget deficit**. If receipts equal outlays, the government has a **balanced budget**. In fiscal year 2010/11, with projected outlays of £695 billion and revenue of £531 billion, the projected government deficit is £164 billion.

How typical is the budget of 2010/11? Let's look at its recent history.

The Budget in Historical Perspective

Figure 29.1 shows the government's receipts, outlays and budget balance since fiscal year 1970/71. The figure expresses the receipts, outlays and the budget balance as percentages of GDP. Expressing them in this way lets us see how large government is relative to the size of the

Figure 29.1 UK Government Receipts, Outlays and Budget Balance

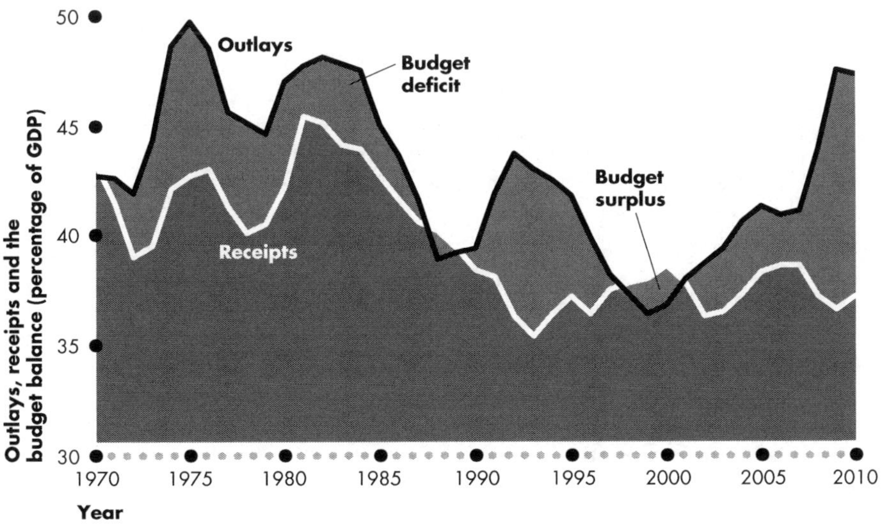

The figure records the UK government's receipts, outlays and budget deficit as percentages of GDP.

During the 1970s, the budget deficit became large and persisted well into the 1980s. A budget surplus appeared briefly in 1988, but income tax cuts and an increase in outlays turned the budget into a deficit again by 1990.

The budget returned to surplus at the end of the 1990s and in 2000 but for the rest of the 2000s, a large and growing deficit emerged.

Source of data: HM Treasury, *Budget 2010*.

myeconlab Animation

economy, and it helps us to study *changes* in the scale of government over time. You may think of these percentages of GDP as telling you how many pence of each pound that we earn get paid to and spent by the government.

Throughout most of this period there was a budget deficit. The deficit increases in recessions and decreases in expansions. The budget was in surplus only at the end of the 1980s and again in 1998 to 2000. The deficit was large during a deep recession of the early 1970s but the deficit has trended upwards and the largest deficit occurred during 2009 and 2010 when it exceeded 10 per cent of GDP.

Why did the government deficit grow so sharply in recent years? The immediate answer is that outlays increased and receipts decreased. But which components of outlays increased and which sources of receipts decreased? Let's look at receipts and outlays in a bit more detail.

Receipts

Figure 29.2 shows the components of receipts received by the government as a percentage of GDP, from 1988 to 2010. Government receipts as a percentage of GDP decreased sharply from 1988 to 1993. This decrease occurred because the 1990–1992 recession decreased tax revenues. Firms' profits fell, which lowered the taxes on business profits, and as the unemployment rate increased, the revenue from personal income taxes decreased.

Receipts trended upward from 1994 to 2000 as the economy settled into a long boom. They then settled to a plateau as the economy grew at a steady rate.

Receipts reached a peak in 2007 and then fell as the global recession took hold.

Outlays

Figure 29.3 shows the components of government outlays as percentages of GDP, between 1988 and 2010. Like receipts, outlays fluctuate over the business cycle. But unlike receipts, outlays have trended upwards. And the main source of increase is expenditure on goods and services, up from 20 per cent of GDP in 1990 to 27 per cent in 2010. Transfer payments have increased too, from 15 per cent of GDP in 1990 to 18 per cent in 2010.

Interest payment on government debt is a small component of government outlays. The amount of interest paid depends on the debt. In recent decades the ratio of debt to GDP fell so interest payments fell too. But in 2010 government debt jumped to become a large percentage of GDP and interest payments increased sharply.

Figure 29.2 UK Government Receipts

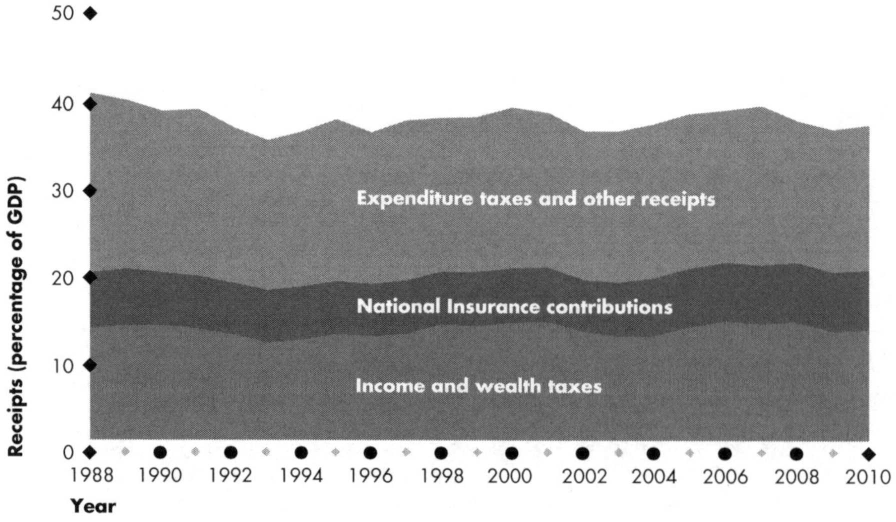

The figure shows the three components of government receipts: income and wealth taxes (including taxes on business profits), National Insurance contributions and expenditure taxes (including VAT).

Receipts from income and wealth fell during the recession of the early 1990s and 2008–2009.

Receipts increased during the strong expansion years from 1994 to 2001.

Source of data: HM Treasury, *Budget 2010*.

myeconlab Animation

Figure 29.3 UK Government Outlays

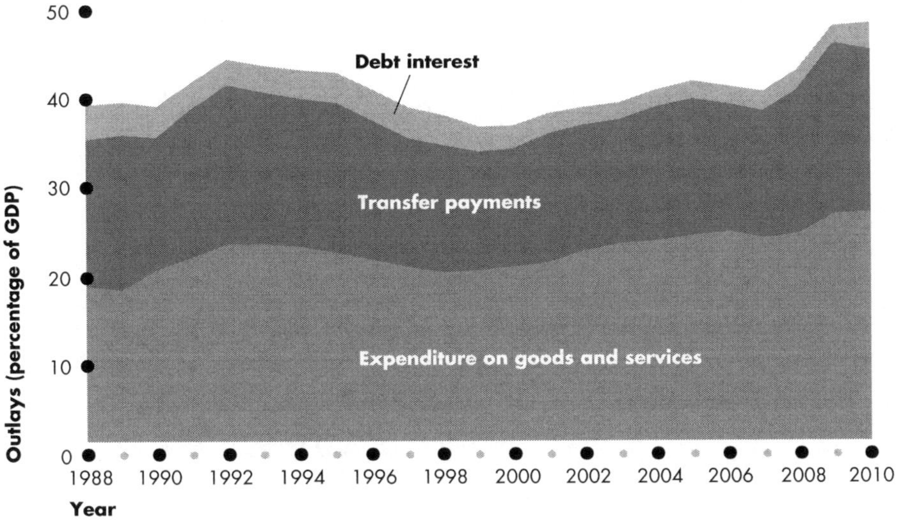

The figure shows three components of government outlays: expenditure on goods and services, transfer payments and debt interest.

Expenditure on goods and services has trended upward.

Transfer payments have also trended upward, but they are dominated by their cyclical changes.

Debt interest fell from 1996 to 2009 but then jumped in 2010.

Source of data: HM Treasury, *Budget 2010*.

myeconlab Animation

Deficit, Debt and Capital

Government debt is the total amount of borrowing by the government. It is the sum of past deficits minus the sum of past surpluses plus payments to buy assets minus receipts from the sale of assets.

A budget deficit or the purchase of assets increases government debt and a budget surplus or the sale of state-owned assets reduces government debt.

Figure 29.4 shows the history of UK government debt from 1975 to 2010. In 1975, the debt–GDP ratio was just under 60 per cent. The debt–GDP ratio fell during the next 15 years and fell especially sharply during the 1980s as the government sold off state-owned assets such as British Rail and British Telecom. The debt increased spectacularly during 2009 and 2010 when the budget went into deficit and the government bought a large public stake in two troubled banks: the RBS and Lloyds.

Like individual and business debt, government debt is incurred to buy assets. Governments own public assets such as roads, bridges, schools and universities, public libraries and defence equipment. But the value of UK government assets is only £400 billion, which falls well short of its total debt.

How do the UK deficit and debt compare with deficits and debts in other major economies and the EU?

Figure 29.4 UK Government Debt

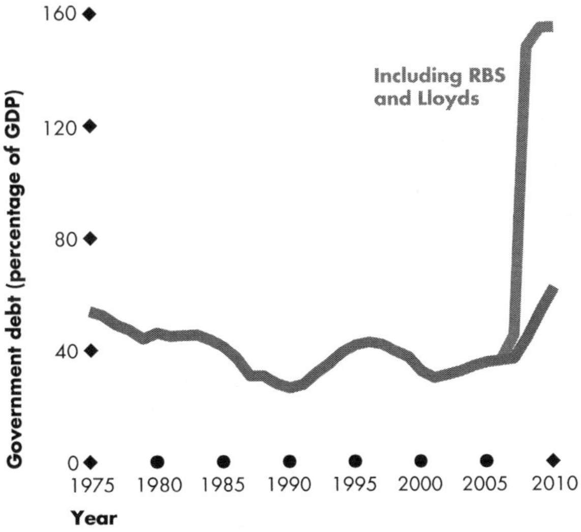

In 1975, UK government debt was 59 per cent of GDP. During the 1970s and 1980s the government reduced its debt by selling state assets such as British Rail and British Telecom. Government debt rose sharply after the 1990–1992 recession and fell from 1997 to 2002. In 2008–2010, a large budget deficit and the part-nationalisation of two banks, RBS and Lloyds, increased government debt astronomically.

Source of data: HM Treasury, *Budget 2010*.

myeconlab Animation

ECONOMICS IN ACTION

EU Government Budget Balances and Debts

The budget of each member state of the EU has similar categories of receipts and outlays to the UK budget. In addition to the national budgets, the Council of the EU draws up the EU budget, which the European Parliament approves.

The EU receives 89 per cent of its revenue from the member states and 11 per cent from EU tariffs on imports from non-member countries. Member states' contributions are based on VAT, which provides 13 per cent of revenue, and on gross national product, which produces 87 per cent of revenue. (A country's gross national product is equal to its gross domestic product plus net property income from the rest of the world.)

The total EU budget in 2010 was €141 billion – equivalent to less than 1 per cent of EU GDP. Figure 1 shows how the EU spends its resources. Structural measures – grants to weaker economic regions and expenditure on measures to improve competitiveness – take the largest slice at 45 per cent of total EU outlays. Agriculture – support for the Common Agricultural Policy (CAP) – and the environment take the next largest slice at 42 per cent of total EU outlays.

Despite its small size relative to GDP, the EU budget is hotly debated and contributes to economic life in many EU countries. For example, Ireland in the past has benefited from both the CAP and the EU structural programmes.

Most government revenue and outlays in the EU remain with the member states. The 27 members of the EU span a huge range of budgetary outcomes. Two aspects of these budgets are budget balances and government debt.

Figure 2 shows the budget balances of the 27 EU members in 2009. They range from a deficit of 15 per cent of GDP in Greece to 0.7 per cent in Luxembourg. The EU average is a deficit at 6.8 per cent of GDP. The UK has the third largest deficit.

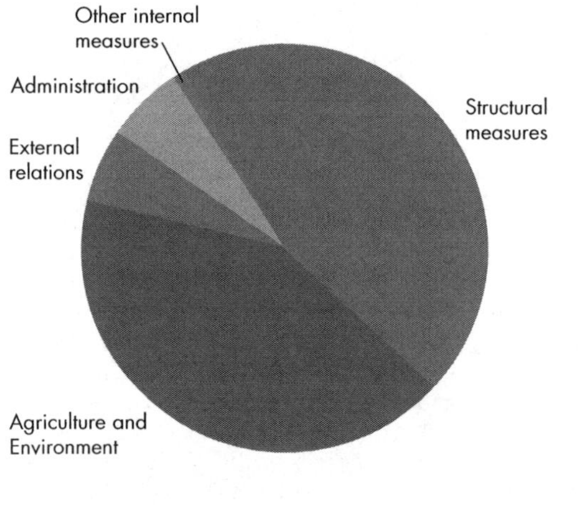

Figure 1 EU Budget Outlays 2009

Source of data for Figures 1, 2 and 3: Eurostat.

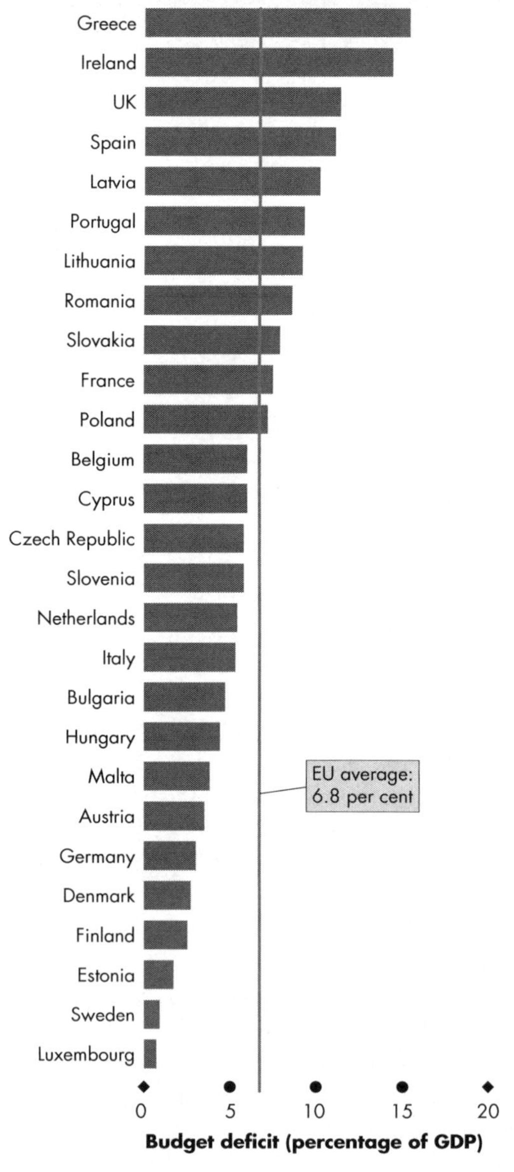

Figure 2 EU Budget Deficits in 2009

Figure 3 shows the EU government debt in 2009. It ranges from a high of 127 per cent of GDP in Greece to a low of 7 per cent in Estonia. The EU average debt is 74 per cent of GDP.

There is no significant correlation between debt and the budget balance. The UK has a budget deficit that is larger than the EU average and debt that is less than the EU average while Germany has a budget deficit that is below the EU average and debt equal to the EU average. Some EU countries with large debt such as Malta are running low deficits to bring the debt down, while others such as Greece have large deficits along with high debt–GDP ratios.

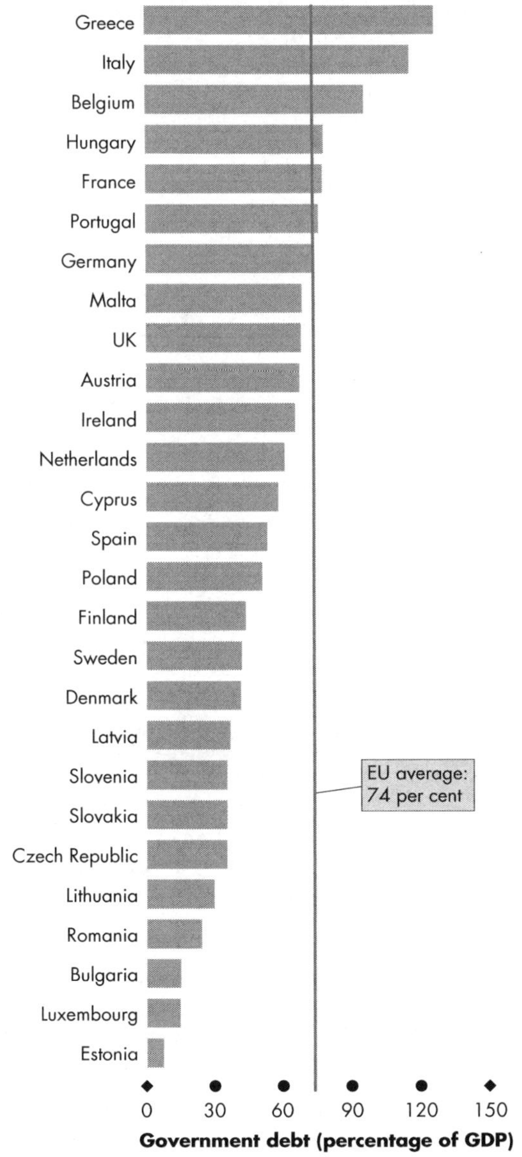

Figure 3 EU Government Debt in 2009

UK and EU Budget Balances and Debt in a Global Perspective

In *Economics in Action* (opposite), you can see that in 2009, the UK had a budget deficit of 11.4 per cent of GDP and the EU nations on average had a budget deficit of 6.8 per cent of EU GDP. How do these deficits compare with those in other advanced economies?

The answer is that the UK has one of the largest deficits and the EU average is in the middle of the pack. Only the US comes close to the UK with a deficit just below the UK's. Like the UK and US, Japan has a deficit greater than the EU's.

Among the countries that have smaller deficits than the EU average are the newly industrialized Asian economies (Hong Kong, Singapore, South Korea and Taiwan), Australia and Canada.

There is nothing inherently wrong with a government running a deficit, provided the resources are being used to add to the stock of social capital. There is also a case for a temporary government deficit to try to lift an economy from recession. We look more closely at using a deficit to stimulate the economy later in this chapter.

Review Quiz

1 What are the functions of a government's budget?
2 What are the goals of fiscal policy?
3 Describe the main sources of receipts and outlays in the budget of the UK government.
4 Under what circumstances does a government have a budget surplus?
5 Which members of the EU ran a budget deficit in 2009?
6 Which members of the EU had the largest debt levels in 2009?
7 Explain the connection between a government's budget deficit and its debt.

You can work these questions in Study Plan 29.1 and get instant feedback. myeconlab

Now that you know what the main components of the government's budget are, it is time to study the *effects* of fiscal policy. We'll begin by learning about the effects of taxes on employment, aggregate supply and potential GDP. Then we'll study the effects of budget deficits and see how fiscal policy brings redistribution across generations. Finally, we'll look at fiscal stimulus and see how it might be used to speed recovery from recession and stabilize the business cycle.

Supply-side Effects of Fiscal Policy

How do taxes on personal and corporate income affect real GDP and employment? The answer to these questions is controversial. Some economists, known as supply-siders, believe these effects to be large and an accumulating body of evidence suggests that they are correct. To see why these effects might be large, we'll begin with a refresher on how full employment and potential GDP are determined in the absence of taxes. Then we'll introduce an income tax and see how it changes the economic outcome.

Full Employment and Potential GDP

You learned in Chapter 22 (pp. 513–515) how the full-employment quantity of labour and potential GDP are determined. At full employment, the real wage rate adjusts to make the quantity of labour demanded equal the quantity supplied. Potential GDP is the real GDP that the full-employment quantity of labour produces.

Figure 29.5 illustrates a full-employment situation. In part (a), the demand for labour curve is *LD*, and the supply of labour curve is *LS*. At a real wage rate of £15 an hour and 50 billion hours of labour a year employed, the economy is at full employment.

In Figure 29.5(b), the production function is *PF*. When 50 billion hours of labour are employed, real GDP – which is also potential GDP – is £1,300 billion.

Let's now see how an income tax changes potential GDP.

The Effects of the Income Tax

The tax on labour income influences potential GDP and aggregate supply by changing the full-employment quantity of labour. The income tax weakens the incentive to work and drives a wedge between the take-home wage of workers and the cost of labour to firms. The result is a smaller quantity of labour and a lower potential GDP.

Graphical Analysis and Illustration

Figure 29.5 shows the outcome we've just described. In the labour market, the income tax has no effect on the demand for labour, which remains at *LD*. The reason is that the quantity of labour that firms plan to hire depends only on how productive labour is and what it costs – its real wage rate.

Figure 29.5 The Effects of the Income Tax on Aggregate Supply

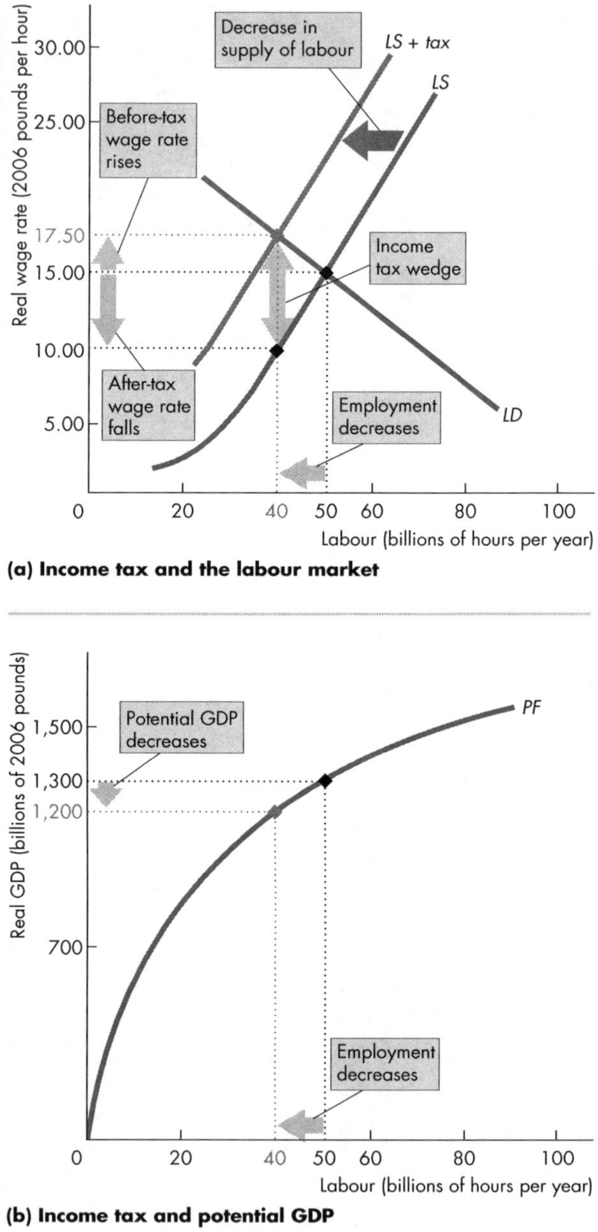

In part (a), with no income tax, the real wage rate is £15 an hour and employment is 50 billion hours. In part (b), potential GDP is £1,300 billion. An income tax shifts the supply of labour curve leftward to *LS* + *tax*. The before-tax wage rate rises to £17.50 an hour, the after-tax wage rate falls to £10 an hour, and the quantity of labour employed decreases to 40 billion hours. With less labour, potential GDP decreases to £1,200 billion.

myeconlab Animation

But the supply of labour does change. With no income tax, the real wage rate is £15 an hour and 50 billion hours of labour a year are employed. An income tax weakens the incentive to work and decreases the supply of labour. The reason is that for each pound of before-tax earnings, workers must pay the government an amount determined by the income tax code. So workers look at the after-tax wage rate when they decide how much labour to supply. An income tax shifts the supply curve leftward to *LS* + *tax*. The vertical distance between the *LS* curve and the *LS* + *tax* curve measures the amount of income tax. With the smaller supply of labour, the before-tax wage rate rises to £17.50 an hour but the after-tax wage rate falls to £10 an hour. The gap created between the before-tax and after-tax wage rates is called the **tax wedge**.

The new equilibrium quantity of labour employed is 40 billion hours a year – less than in the no-tax case. Because the full-employment quantity of labour decreases, so does potential GDP. And a decrease in potential GDP decreases aggregate supply.

In this example, the tax rate is high – £7.50 tax on a £17.50 wage rate is a tax rate of about 43 per cent. A lower tax rate would have a smaller effect on employment, which in turn would have a smaller effect on potential GDP.

An increase in the tax rate to above 43 per cent would decrease the supply of labour by more than the decrease shown in Figure 29.5. Equilibrium employment and potential GDP would also decrease still further. A tax cut would increase the supply of labour, increase equilibrium employment, and increase potential GDP.

Taxes on Expenditure and the Tax Wedge

The tax wedge that we've just considered is only a part of the wedge that affects labour-supply decisions. Taxes on consumption expenditure add to the wedge. The reason is that a tax on consumption raises the prices paid for consumption goods and services and is equivalent to a cut in the real wage rate.

The incentive to supply labour depends on the goods and services that an hour of labour can buy. The higher the taxes on goods and services and the lower the after-tax wage rate, the less is the incentive to supply labour. If the income tax rate is 25 per cent and the tax rate on consumption expenditure is 10 per cent, a pound earned buys only 65 pence worth of goods and services. The tax wedge is 35 per cent.

ECONOMICS IN ACTION

Some Real World Tax Wedges

Edward C. Prescott of Arizona State University, who shared the 2004 Nobel Prize for Economic Science, has estimated the tax wedges for a number of countries, among them the US, the UK and France.

The US Tax Wedge

The US tax wedge is a combination of 13 per cent tax on consumption and 32 per cent tax on incomes. The income tax component of the US tax wedge includes Social Security taxes and is the marginal tax rate – the tax rate paid on the marginal dollar earned.

France's Tax Wedge

Prescott estimates that in France, taxes on consumption are 33 per cent and taxes on incomes are 49 per cent.

The UK Tax Wedge

The estimates for the UK fall between those for the US and France. The figure shows these components of the tax wedges in the three countries.

Does the Tax Wedge Matter?

According to Prescott's estimates, the tax wedge has a powerful effect on employment and potential GDP. Potential GDP in France is 14 per cent below that of the US (per person), and the entire difference can be attributed to the difference in the tax wedge in the two countries.

Potential GDP in the UK is 41 per cent below that of the US (per person), and about a third of the difference arises from the different tax wedges. (The rest is due to different productivities.)

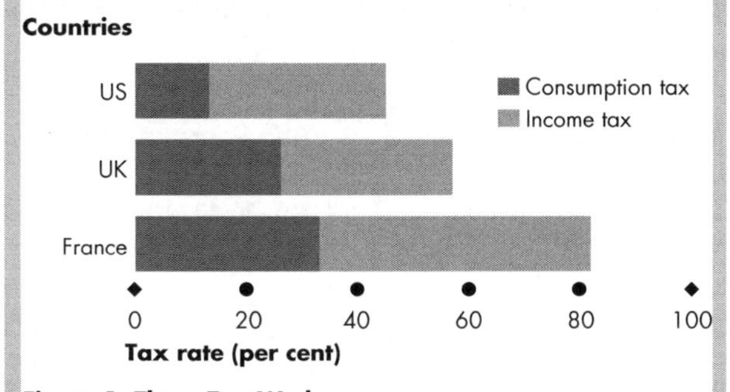

Figure 1 Three Tax Wedges

Source of data: Edward C. Prescott, *American Economic Review*, 2003.

Taxes and the Incentive to Save and Invest

A tax on interest income weakens the incentive to save and drives a wedge between the after-tax interest rate earned by savers and the interest rate paid by firms. These effects are analogous to those of a tax on labour income. But they are more serious for two reasons.

First, a tax on labour income lowers the quantity of labour employed and lowers potential GDP, while a tax on capital income lowers the quantity of saving and investment and slows the growth rate of real GDP.

Second, the true tax rate on interest income is much higher than that on labour income because of the way in which inflation and taxes on interest income interact. Let's examine this interaction.

Effect of Tax Rate on Real Interest Rate

The interest rate that influences investment and saving plans is the real after-tax interest rate. The real after-tax interest rate subtracts the income tax rate paid on interest income from the real interest rate. But the taxes depend on the nominal interest rate, not the real interest rate. So the higher the inflation rate, the higher is the true tax rate on interest income. Here is an example. Suppose the real interest rate is 4 per cent a year and the tax rate is 40 per cent.

If there is no inflation, the nominal interest rate equals the real interest rate. The tax on 4 per cent interest is 1.6 per cent (40 per cent of 4 per cent), so the real after-tax interest rate is 4 per cent minus 1.6 per cent, which equals 2.4 per cent.

If the inflation rate is 6 per cent a year, the nominal interest rate is 10 per cent. The tax on 10 per cent interest is 4 per cent (40 per cent of 10 per cent), so the real after-tax interest rate is 4 per cent minus 4 per cent, which equals zero. The true tax rate in this case is not 40 per cent but 100 per cent!

Effect of Income Tax on Saving and Investment

In Figure 29.6, initially there are no taxes. Also, the government has a balanced budget. The demand for loanable funds curve, which is also the investment demand curve, is *DLF*. The supply of loanable funds curve, which is also the saving supply curve, is *SLF*. The interest rate is 3 per cent a year, and the quantity of funds borrowed and lent is £200 billion a year.

A tax on interest income has no effect on the demand for loanable funds. The quantity of investment and borrowing that firms plan to undertake depends only on how productive capital is and what it costs – its real interest rate. But a tax on interest income weakens the incentive to save and lend and decreases the supply of loanable funds. For each pound of before-tax interest, savers must pay the government an amount determined by the tax code. So savers look at the after-tax real interest rate when they decide how much to save.

When a tax is imposed, saving decreases and the supply of loanable funds curve shifts leftward to *SLF* + *tax*. The amount of tax payable is measured by the vertical distance between the *SLF* curve and the *SLF* + *tax* curve. With this smaller supply of loanable funds, the interest rate rises to 4 per cent a year but the after-tax interest rate falls to 1 per cent a year. A tax wedge is driven between the interest rate and the after-tax interest rate, and the equilibrium quantity of loanable funds decreases. Saving and investment also decrease.

Figure 29.6 The Effects of a Tax on Capital Income

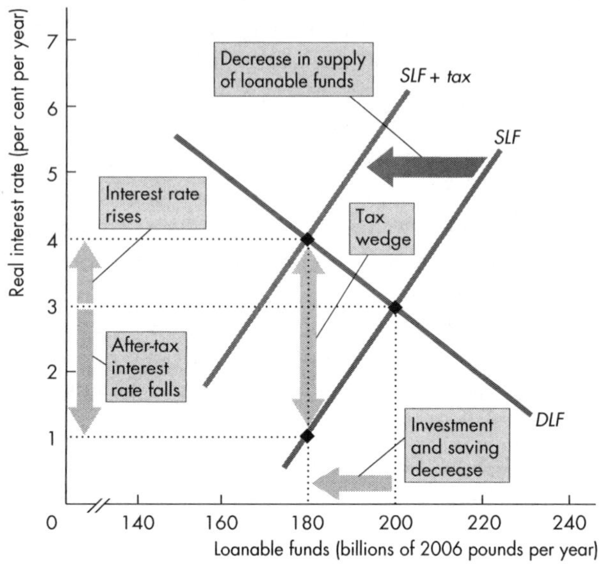

The demand for loanable funds and investment demand curve is *DLF*, and the supply of loanable funds and saving supply curve is *SLF*. With no income tax, the real interest rate is 3 per cent a year and investment is £200 billion. An income tax shifts the supply curve leftward to *SLF* + *tax*. The interest rate rises to 4 per cent a year, the after-tax interest rate falls to 1 per cent a year, and investment decreases to £180 billion. With less investment, the real GDP growth rate decreases.

myeconlab Animation

Tax Revenues and the Laffer Curve

An interesting consequence of the effect of taxes on employment and saving is that a higher tax rate does not always bring greater tax revenue. A higher tax rate brings in more revenue per pound earned. But because a higher tax rate decreases the number of pounds earned, two forces operate in opposite directions on the tax revenue collected.

The relationship between the tax rate and the amount of tax revenue collected is called the **Laffer curve**. The curve is so named because Arthur B. Laffer, a member of US President Ronald Reagan's Economic Policy Advisory Board, drew such a curve on a table napkin and launched the idea that tax cuts could increase tax revenue.

Figure 29.7 shows a Laffer curve. The tax rate is on the x-axis, and total tax revenue is on the y-axis. For tax rates below T^*, an increase in the tax rate increases tax revenue; at T^*, tax revenue is maximized; and a tax rate increase above T^* decreases tax revenue.

Most people think that the UK is on the upward-sloping part of the Laffer curve; so is the US. But France might be close to the maximum point or perhaps even beyond it.

Figure 29.7 A Laffer Curve

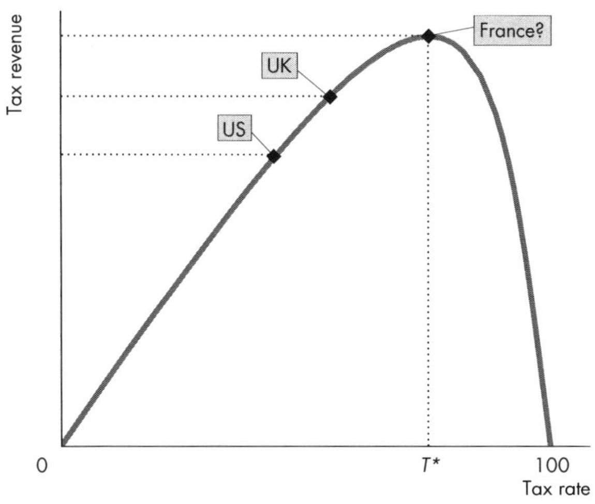

A Laffer curve shows the relationship between the tax rate and tax revenues. For tax rates below T^*, an increase in the tax rate increases tax revenue. At the tax rate T^*, tax revenue is maximized. For tax rates above T^*, an increase in the tax rate decreases tax revenue.

myeconlab Animation

The Supply-side Debate

Before 1980, few economists paid attention to the supply-side effects of taxes on employment and potential GDP. Then, when Ronald Reagan took office as president, a group of supply-siders began to argue the virtues of cutting taxes. Arthur Laffer was one of them. Laffer and his supporters were not held in high esteem among mainstream economists, but they were influential for a period. They correctly argued that tax cuts would increase employment and increase output. But they incorrectly argued that tax cuts would increase tax revenues and decrease the budget deficit. For this prediction to be correct, the US would have had to be on the 'wrong' side of the Laffer curve. Given that US tax rates are among the lowest in the industrial world, it is unlikely that this condition was met. And when the Reagan administration did cut taxes, the budget deficit increased, a fact that reinforces this view.

Supply-side economics became tarnished because of its association with Laffer and came to be called 'voodoo economics'. But mainstream economists, including Martin Feldstein, a Harvard professor who was Reagan's chief economic advisor, recognized the power of tax cuts as incentives but took the standard view that tax cuts without spending cuts would swell the budget deficit and bring serious further problems. This view is now widely accepted by economists of all political persuasions.

Review Quiz

1. How does a tax on labour income influence the equilibrium quantity of employment?
2. How does the tax wedge influence potential GDP?
3. Why are consumption taxes relevant for measuring the tax wedge?
4. Why are income taxes on capital income more powerful than those on labour income?
5. What is the Laffer curve and why is it unlikely that the UK is on the 'wrong' side of it?

You can work these questions in Study Plan 29.2 and get instant feedback. myeconlab

You now know how taxes influence potential GDP and saving and investment. Next we look at the generational effects of fiscal policy.

Generational Effects of Fiscal Policy

Is a budget deficit a burden on future generations? If it is, how will the burden be borne? And is the budget deficit the only burden on future generations? What about the deficit in the state pension fund? Does it matter who owns the bonds that the government sells to finance its deficit? What about the bonds owned by foreigners? Won't repaying those bonds impose a bigger burden than repaying bonds owned by UK residents?

To answer questions like these, we use a tool called **generational accounting** – an accounting system that measures the lifetime tax burden and benefits of each generation. This accounting system was developed by Alan Auerbach of the University of Pennsylvania and Laurence Kotlikoff of Boston University. Generational accounts for the UK have been prepared by Roberto Cardarelli and James Sefton of the National Institute of Economic and Social Research in London and Laurence Kotlikoff (reported in the *Economic Journal*, November 2000).

Generational Accounting and Present Value

Income taxes and National Insurance contributions are paid by people who have jobs. Pensions are paid to people after they retire. Healthcare benefits are also provided on a larger scale to older retired people. So to compare taxes and benefits, we must compare the value of taxes paid by people during their working years with the benefits received in their retirement years. To compare the value of an amount of money at one date with that at a later date, we use the concept of present value. A **present value** is an amount of money that, if invested today, will grow to equal a given future amount when the interest that it earns is taken into account. We can compare pounds today with pounds in 2030 or any other future year by using present values.

For example, if the interest rate is 5 per cent a year, £1,000 invested today will grow, with interest, to £11,467 after 50 years. So the present value (in 2010) of £11,467 in 2060 is £1,000.

By using present values, we can assess the magnitude of the government's debts to older citizens in the form of state pensions and medical benefits.

But the assumed interest rate and growth rate of taxes and benefits critically influence the answers we get. For example, at an interest rate of 3 per cent a year, the present value (in 2010) of £11,467 in 2060 is £2,616. The lower the interest rate, the greater is the present value of a given future amount.

Because there is uncertainty about the proper interest rate to use to calculate present values, plausible alternative numbers are used to estimate a range of present values.

Using generational accounting and present values, economists have studied the situation facing the governments arising from their pension and healthcare obligations, and they have found some time bombs!

The UK Welfare State and the Pensions Time Bomb

In 1942, as the Second World War was raging, William Beveridge (an economist and Director of the London School of Economics) envisaged a world in which the state provided social insurance that protected everyone from the five evils of 'want, disease, ignorance, squalor and idleness'. The *Beveridge Report* became the blueprint for the creation of the post-war welfare state, which provided universal pensions and health services as well as education and housing.

When state pensions and the National Health Service (NHS) were introduced, today's demographic situation was not foreseen. The age distribution of the UK population is dominated by a surge in the birth rate after the Second World War that created what is called the 'baby boom generation'. More than 12 million 'baby boomers' (almost 20 per cent of the population) are now retired or of retirement age. By 2033, more than 20 per cent of the population will have reached retirement age. Under today's arrangements, outlays on pensions and operating the NHS in 2033 will vastly exceed today's outlays. The obligation to make these outlays is a debt owed by the government and is just as real as the bonds that the government has issued to finance its budget deficits.

Fiscal Imbalance

To assess the government's obligations, economists use the concept of fiscal imbalance. **Fiscal imbalance** is the present value of the government's commitments to pay benefits minus the present value of its tax revenues. Fiscal imbalance is an attempt to measure the scale of the government's true liabilities – its true debt. The production of these accounts requires assumptions about future population trends, taxes, transfers and government expenditure, the initial value of government debt and the real rate of interest used in the present value discounting. The calculation of the fiscal imbalance is highly sensitive to these assumptions. For example, it matters very much whether pensions and unemployment benefits are linked to inflation or to earnings growth.

Estimates of UK and Other Fiscal Imbalances

On the assumption of strict control of government spending, Cardelli, Sefton and Kotlikoff reckon that the fiscal imbalance is 20 per cent of GDP. This figure is large but not an impossible one for the government to plan for. A more recent estimate is much less optimistic. Four economists at Freiburg University[1] estimate the UK's fiscal imbalance at a staggering 510 per cent of GDP. If this figure is correct, when added to the government's market debt in 2010, the total debt obligation of the UK government is 575 per cent of GDP – or £8.3 trillion (in 2010 prices).

Figure 29.8 shows the Freiburg economists' estimates of international fiscal imbalances for eight countries. The UK has the largest fiscal imbalance but the US, France and Germany also have sizeable fiscal imbalances.

Fiscal imbalance is an enormous obligation for many countries and it points to a catastrophic future. How can the UK government meet its pension and NHS obligations?

Figure 29.8 Fiscal Imbalances in Eight Economies

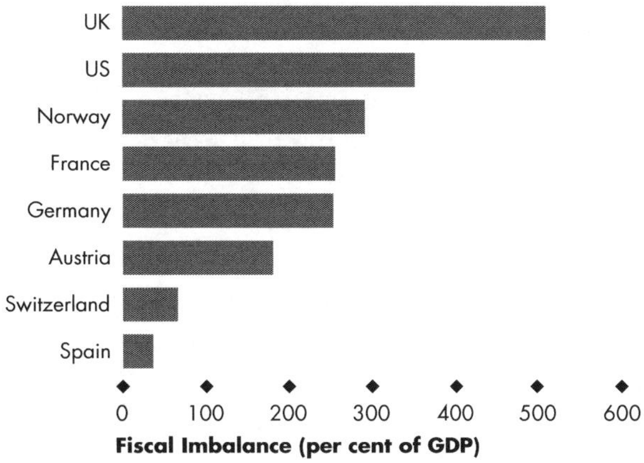

Fiscal imbalance is an enormous problem for many countries. On current tax and benefit rates, the UK government has a true debt of more than 5 years' GDP. The US government isn't far behind at almost 4 years' GDP. Even Norway and Germany, normally considered to have sound fiscal policies, owe almost 3 years' GDP to future citizens. Spain is at the other extreme with a fiscal imbalance of only a few months' GDP.

Source of data: Hagist, Moog, Raffelhüschen and Vatter (see footnote 1).

myeconlab Animation

Coping With Fiscal Imbalances

There are five possible ways of coping with the fiscal imbalances:

1 Raise income taxes
2 Raise National Insurance contributions
3 Cut government discretionary spending
4 Cut unemployment and other welfare state benefits
5 Raise the state pension age

None of these measures is painless or free from political controversy. By combining the five measures, the pain from each could be lessened, but it would still be severe.

Raising income taxes or raising National Insurance contributions would have damaging supply-side effects. Either action would lower potential GDP and the growth rate of real GDP and lower the well-being of future generations. Government discretionary spending is just about impossible to cut and doing so presents challenges for national security and public health and safety. This leaves cutting benefits as the only viable option.

There is one further way of meeting these obligations and that is to pay for them by printing money. But the consequence of this solution is a seriously high inflation rate (see Chapter 24, pp. 574–575).

Generational Imbalance

A fiscal imbalance must eventually be corrected and when it is, people either pay higher taxes or receive lower benefits. The concept of generational imbalance tells us who will pay. **Generational imbalance** is the division of the fiscal imbalance between the current and future generations, assuming that the current generation will enjoy the existing levels of taxes and benefits.

[1] Christian Hagist, Stefan Moog, Bernd Raffelhüschen and Johannes Vatter, "Public Debt and Demography – An International Comparison Using Generational Accounting", Cesifo DICE Report 4 2009.

The numbers produced by Cardarelli, Sefton and Kotlikoff (at the low end of the range of estimates) suggests that people born in 1972 (aged 25 in 1997) will pay 65 per cent more in taxes over their lifetime than those born in 1997.

Because the estimated fiscal imbalance is so large, it is not possible to predict how it will be resolved. But we can predict that the outcome will involve both lower benefits and higher taxes or paying bills with new money and creating inflation.

International Debt

You've seen that borrowing from the rest of the world is one source of loanable funds. What value of UK bonds are held abroad? Research by Adam Chester and Hann-Ju Ho of Lloyds-TSB suggests that 30 per cent or £284 billion of UK government bonds are held by foreign investors. This amount is well short of total UK foreign indebtedness because foreign investors own corporate bonds, shares and bank deposits.

The international debt of the UK is important because, when that debt is repaid, the UK will transfer real resources to the rest of the world. Instead of running a large net trade deficit, the UK will need a surplus of exports over imports. To make a surplus possible, UK saving must increase and consumption must decrease. Some tough choices lie ahead.

Review Quiz

1. What is a present value?
2. Distinguish between fiscal imbalance and generational imbalance.
3. How large was the estimated UK fiscal imbalance in 2010 and what is an indicator of how it divides between current and future generations?
4. What is the source of the UK fiscal imbalance and what are the painful choices that we face?
5. How much of UK government debt is held by the rest of the world?

You can work these questions in Study Plan 29.3 and get instant feedback. myeconlab

You now know how the supply-side effects of fiscal policy work and you've seen the shocking scale of fiscal imbalance. We conclude this chapter by looking at fiscal policy as a tool for fighting a recession.

Fiscal Stimulus

The 2008–2009 recession brought Keynesian macroeconomic ideas back into fashion and put a spotlight on **fiscal stimulus** – the use of fiscal policy to increase production and employment. But whether fiscal policy is truly stimulating, and if so, how stimulating, are questions that generate much discussion and disagreement. You're now going to explore these questions.

Fiscal stimulus can be either automatic or discretionary. A fiscal policy action that is triggered by the state of the economy with no action by government is called **automatic fiscal policy**. The increase in total unemployment benefits triggered by the massive rise in the unemployment rate through 2009 is an example of automatic fiscal policy.

A fiscal policy action initiated by government is called **discretionary fiscal policy**. It requires a change in a spending programme or in a tax law. A fiscal stimulus initiated by the Obama administration in the US in 2009 as a means of dealing with the recession is an example of discretionary fiscal policy.

Whether automatic or discretionary, an increase in government outlays or a decrease in government receipts can stimulate production and jobs. An increase in expenditure on goods and services directly increases aggregate expenditure. And an increase in transfer payments (such as unemployment benefits) or a decrease in tax revenues increases disposable income, which enables people to increase consumption expenditure. Lower taxes also strengthen the incentives to work and invest.

We'll begin by looking at automatic fiscal policy and the interaction between the business cycle and the budget balance.

Automatic Fiscal Policy and Cyclical and Structural Budget Balances

Two items in the government budget change automatically in response to the state of the economy. They are *tax revenues* and *means-tested spending*.

Automatic Changes in Tax Revenues

The tax laws that Parliament enacts don't legislate the number of pounds the government will raise. Rather they define the tax rates that people must pay. The number of pounds paid depend on tax rates and incomes. But incomes vary with real GDP, so tax revenues depend on real GDP. When real GDP increases in a business cycle expansion, wages and profits rise, so tax revenues from these incomes rise. When real GDP decreases in a recession, wages and profits fall, so tax revenues fall.

Means-tested Spending

The government creates programmes that pay benefits to qualified people and businesses. The spending on these programmes results in transfer payments that depend on the economic state of individual citizens and businesses. When the economy expands, unemployment falls, the number of people experiencing economic hardship decreases, so means-tested spending decreases. When the economy is in a recession, unemployment is high and the number of people experiencing economic hardship increases, so means-tested spending on unemployment benefits and food stamps increases.

Automatic Stimulus

Because government receipts fall and outlays increase in a recession, the budget provides automatic stimulus that helps to shrink the recessionary gap. Similarly, because receipts rise and outlays decrease in a boom, the budget provides automatic restraint to shrink an inflationary gap.

Cyclical and Structural Budget Balances

To identify the government budget deficit that arises from the business cycle, we distinguish between the **structural surplus or deficit**, which is the budget balance that would occur if the economy were at full employment, and the **cyclical surplus or deficit**, which is the actual budget balance *minus* the structural surplus or deficit.

Figure 29.9 illustrates these concepts. Outlays *decrease* as real GDP increases, so the outlays curve slopes downward; and receipts *increase* as real GDP increases, so the receipts curve slopes upward.

In Figure 29.9(a), potential GDP is £1,300 billion and if real GDP equals potential GDP, the government has a *balanced budget*. There is no structural surplus or deficit. But there might be a cyclical surplus or deficit. If real GDP is less than potential GDP at £1,200 billion, outlays exceed receipts and there is a *cyclical deficit*. If real GDP is greater than potential GDP at £1,400 billion, outlays are less than receipts and there is a *cyclical surplus*.

In Figure 29.9(b), if potential GDP equals £1,300 billion (line *B*), the structural balance is zero. But if potential

Figure 29.9 Cyclical and Structural Surpluses and Deficits

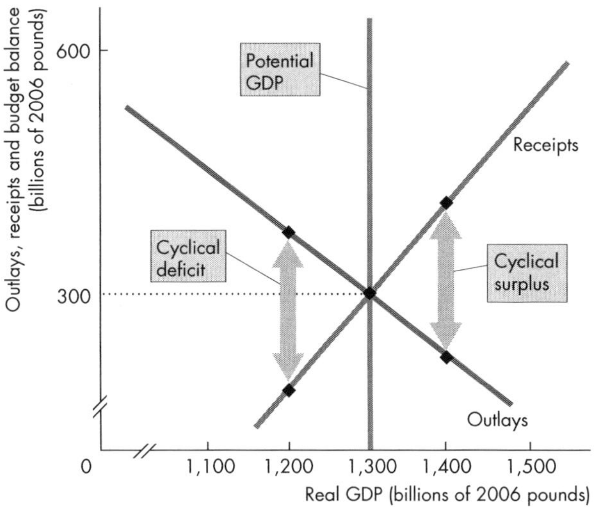

(a) Cyclical deficit and cyclical surplus

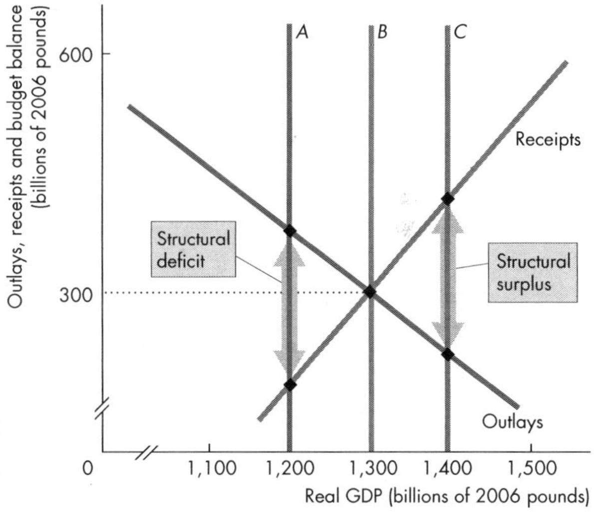

(b) Structural deficit and structural surplus

In part (a), potential GDP is £1,300 billion. When real GDP is less than potential GDP, the budget is in a cyclical deficit. When real GDP exceeds potential GDP, the budget is in a cyclical surplus. The government has a balanced budget when real GDP equals potential GDP.

In part (b), if potential GDP is £1,200 billion, there is a structural deficit and if potential GDP is £1,400 billion, there is a structural surplus. If potential GDP is £1,300 billion, the budget is in structural balance.

myeconlab Animation

GDP is £1,200 billion (line *A*), the government budget has a *structural deficit*. And if potential GDP is £1,400 billion (line *C*), the government budget has a *structural surplus*.

UK Structural Budget Balance

The UK budget deficit in 2010 was £131 billion. The recessionary gap (the gap between real GDP and potential GDP) was about 6 per cent of potential GDP. With a large recessionary gap, you would expect some of the deficit to be cyclical. But how much of the 2010 deficit was cyclical and how much was structural?

The International Monetary Fund estimates that the UK had a *structural deficit* of 7.6 per cent of potential GDP in 2010. Of the major developed economies, only the US is estimated to have a larger structural deficit than the UK.

Figure 29.10 shows the actual and cyclical deficits. The gap between the two shows the structural deficit. You can see that the cyclical deficit was small from 2004 to 2008. But it exploded in 2009 and 2010. When full employment returns, the cyclical deficit will vanish.

Figure 29.10 UK Cyclical and Structural Budget Balance

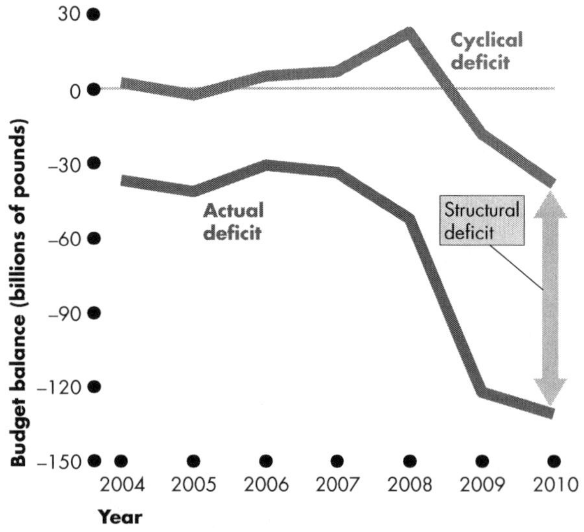

As real GDP shrank in the 2008–2009 recession, receipts fell, outlays increased, and the budget deficit increased. The cyclical deficit was small compared to the actual deficit; most of the 2010 deficit was structural.

Source of data: HM Treasury, *Budget 2010.*

myeconlab Animation

ECONOMICS IN ACTION

Fiscal Stimulus in the US Economy

In 2008, UK Prime Minister Gordon Brown called on all governments to cut taxes and increase spending to stimulate a flagging global economy. The world's largest economy came to Brown's party in grand style.

In February 2009 Barack Obama signed into law the American Recovery and Reinvestment Act at an economic forum he hosted in Denver. This act was the third and most ambitious in a series of stimulus packages aimed at increasing investment and consumer expenditure and leading to the creation of jobs.

The total package added $862 billion to the federal government's budget deficit: $288 billion from tax cuts and the rest from increased spending. The spending increases included payments to state and local governments ($144 billion), spending on infrastructure and science projects ($111 billion), programmes in healthcare ($59 billion), education and training ($53 billion), and energy ($43 billion).

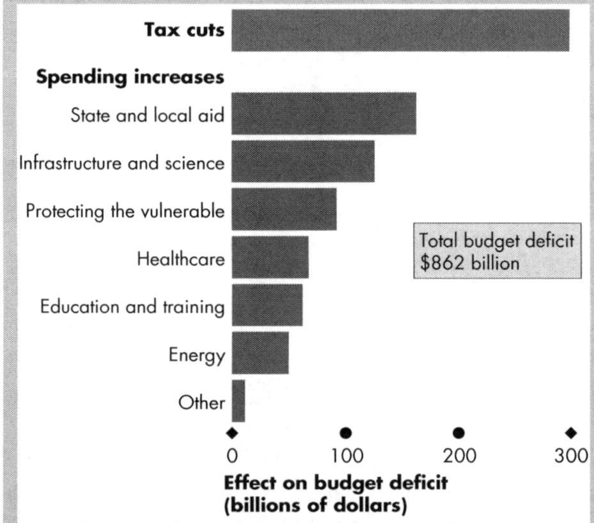

Figure 1 The Components of the 2009 Fiscal Stimulus Act

Obama signs the 2009 Fiscal Stimulus Act.

Discretionary Fiscal Stimulus

Most discussion of discretionary fiscal stimulus focuses on its effects on aggregate demand. But you've seen (on pp. 698–701) that taxes influence aggregate supply and that the balance of taxes and spending – the government budget deficit – can crowd out investment and slow the pace of economic growth. So discretionary fiscal stimulus has both supply-side and demand-side effects that end up determining its overall effectiveness.

We're going to begin our examination of discretionary fiscal stimulus by looking at its effects on aggregate demand.

Fiscal Stimulus and Aggregate Demand

An increase in government expenditure has a direct effect on aggregate demand. A tax cut influences aggregate demand by increasing disposable income and consumption expenditure. Both forms of fiscal stimulus have multiplier effects.

Let's look at the two main fiscal policy multipliers: the government expenditure and tax multipliers.

The **government expenditure multiplier** is the quantitative effect of a change in government expenditure on real GDP. Because government expenditure is a component of aggregate expenditure, an increase in government spending increases aggregate expenditure and real GDP. But does a £1 billion increase in government expenditure increase real GDP by £1 billion, or more than £1 billion, or less than £1 billion?

When an increase in government expenditure increases real GDP, incomes rise and the higher incomes bring an increase in consumption expenditure. If this were the only consequence of increased government expenditure, the government expenditure multiplier would be greater than 1.

But an increase in government expenditure increases government borrowing (or decreases government lending if there is a budget surplus) and raises the real interest rate. With a higher cost of borrowing, investment decreases, which partly offsets the increase in government spending. If this were the only consequence of increased government expenditure, the multiplier would be less than 1.

The actual multiplier depends on which of the above effects is stronger and the consensus is that the crowding-out effect is strong enough to make the government expenditure multiplier less than 1.

The **tax multiplier** is the quantitative effect of a change in taxes on real GDP. The demand-side effects of a tax cut are likely to be smaller than an equivalent increase in government expenditure. The reason is that a tax cut influences aggregate demand by increasing disposable income, only part of which gets spent. So the initial injection of expenditure from a £1 billion tax cut is less than a £1 billion.

A tax cut has similar crowding-out consequences to a spending increase. It increases government borrowing (or decreases government lending), raises the real interest rate and cuts investment.

The tax multiplier effect on aggregate demand depends on these two opposing effects and is probably quite small.

Figure 29.11 shows how fiscal stimulus is supposed to work if it is perfectly executed and has its desired effects.

Potential GDP is £1,400 billion and real GDP is below potential at £1,300 billion so the economy has a recessionary gap of £100 billion.

To restore full employment, the government passes a fiscal stimulus package. An increase in government

Figure 29.11 Expansionary Fiscal Policy

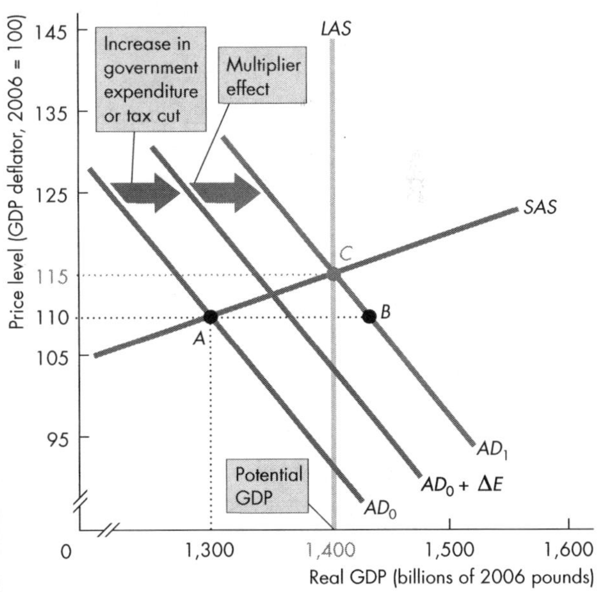

Potential GDP is £1,400 billion, real GDP is £1,300 billion, and there is a £100 billion recessionary gap. An increase in government expenditure and a tax cut increase aggregate expenditure by ΔE. The multiplier increases consumption expenditure. The *AD* curve shifts rightward to AD_1, the price level rises to 115, real GDP increases to £1,400 billion, and the recessionary gap is eliminated.

myeconlab Animation

expenditure and a tax cut increase aggregate expenditure by ΔE. If this were the only change in spending plans, the *AD* curve would shift rightward to become the curve labelled $AD_0 + \Delta E$ in Figure 29.11. But if fiscal stimulus sets off a multiplier process that increases consumption expenditure, and does not crowd out much investment expenditure, aggregate demand increases further and the *AD* curve shifts to AD_1.

With no change in the price level, the economy would move from point *A* to point *B* on AD_1. But the increase in aggregate demand brings a rise in the price level along the upward-sloping *SAS* curve and the economy moves to point *C*.

At point *C*, the economy returns to full employment and the recessionary gap is eliminated.

Fiscal Stimulus and Aggregate Supply

You've seen earlier in this chapter that taxes influence aggregate supply. A tax on labour income (on wages) drives a wedge between the cost of labour and the take-home pay of workers and lowers employment and output (p. 698). A tax on capital income (on interest) drives a wedge between the cost of borrowing and the return to lending and lowers saving and investment (p. 700). With less saving and investment, the real GDP growth rate slows.

These negative effects of taxes on real GDP and its growth rate and on employment mean that tax cuts increase real GDP and its growth rate and increase employment.

These supply-side effects of tax cuts occur along with the demand-side effects and are probably much larger than the demand-side effects and make the overall tax multiplier much larger than the government expenditure multiplier – see *Economics in Action.*

An increase in government expenditure financed by borrowing increases the demand for loanable funds. The real interest rate rises, which decreases investment and private saving. This cut in investment is the main reason why the government expenditure multiplier is so small and why a deficit-financed increase in government spending ends up making only a small contribution to job creation. And because government expenditure crowds out investment, it lowers future real GDP.

So a fiscal stimulus package that is heavy on tax cuts and light on government spending works. But an increase in government expenditure alone is not an effective way to stimulate production and create jobs.

The description of the effects of discretionary fiscal stimulus and its graphical illustration in Figure 29.11 makes it look easy: calculate the recessionary gap and the multipliers, change government expenditure and taxes, and eliminate the gap. In reality, getting the magnitude and the timing right is difficult.

Magnitude of Stimulus

Economists have diverging views about the size of the government expenditure and tax multipliers. This fact makes it impossible for government to determine the amount of stimulus needed to close a given output gap. Further, the actual output gap is not known and can only be estimated with error. For these two reasons, discretionary fiscal policy is risky.

ECONOMICS IN ACTION

How Big Are the Fiscal Stimulus Multipliers?

When the US government cut taxes by $300 billion and increased government expenditure by almost $500 billion, by how much did aggregate expenditure and real GDP change? How big were the fiscal policy multipliers? Was the government expenditure multiplier larger than the tax multiplier? These questions are about the multiplier effects on *equilibrium real GDP*, not just on aggregate demand.

President Obama's economic adviser, Christina Romer, a University of California, Berkeley, professor, expected the multiplier to be about 1.5. She was expecting the spending increase of $500 billion to go a long way towards closing the $1 trillion output gap in 2010.

Robert Barro, a professor at Harvard University, says this multiplier number is not in line with previous experience. Based on his calculations, an additional $500 billion of government spending would increase aggregate expenditure by only $250 billion because it would lower private spending in a crowding-out effect by $250 billion – the multiplier is 0.5.

Patrick Minford, a professor at Cardiff University, says that the government expenditure multiplier on real GDP is even smaller and is 0.35. He arrives at this number based on 30 years of research on the UK economy. Harald Uhlig, a professor at the University of Chicago, agrees with Minford's assessment of the multiplier and says this number also applies to the US.

If Minford and Uhlig are correct, a $500 billion increase in government spending increases aggregate expenditure by between $150 billion and $200 billion.

Time Lags

Discretionary fiscal stimulus actions are also seriously hampered by three time lags:

- Recognition lag
- Law-making lag
- Impact lag

Recognition Lag

The recognition lag is the time it takes to figure out that fiscal policy actions are needed. This process involves assessing the current state of the economy and forecasting its future state.

There is greater agreement about tax multipliers. Because tax cuts strengthen the incentive to work and to invest, they increase aggregate supply as well as aggregate demand.

These multipliers get bigger as more time elapses. Harald Uhlig says that after one year, the tax multiplier is 0.5 so that the $300 billion tax cut would increase real GDP by about $150 billion by early 2010. But with two years to respond, real GDP would be $600 billion higher – a multiplier of 2. And after three years, the tax multiplier builds up to more than 6. Patrick Minford's research on the UK economy supports the findings of Uhlig.

The implications of the work of Barro, Uhlig and Minford are that tax cuts are a powerful way to stimulate real GDP and employment but spending increases are not effective.

Christine Romer agrees that the economy hasn't performed in line with a multiplier of 1.5 but says other factors deteriorated and without the fiscal stimulus, the outcome would have been even worse.

Christina Romer 1.5

Robert Barro 0.5

Patrick Minford 0.35

Law-making Lag

The law-making lag is the time it takes to pass the laws needed to change taxes or spending. This process takes time because each MP has a different idea about what is the best tax or spending programme to change, so long debates and committee meetings are needed to reconcile conflicting views. The economy might benefit from fiscal stimulation today, but by the time the law has been passed, a different fiscal medicine might be needed.

Impact Lag

The impact lag is the time it takes from passing a tax or spending change to its effects on real GDP being felt. This lag depends partly on the speed with which government agencies can act and partly on the timing of changes in spending plans by households and businesses. These changes are spread out over a number of quarters and possibly a number of years.

Economic forecasting is steadily improving, but it remains inexact and subject to error. The range of uncertainty about the magnitudes of the government expenditure and tax multipliers make discretionary fiscal stimulus an imprecise tool for boosting production and jobs. Also the crowding-out consequences of fiscal stimulus raise serious questions about its effects on long-term economic growth.

Review Quiz

1. What is the distinction between automatic and discretionary fiscal policy?
2. How do taxes and means-tested spending programmes work as automatic stabilizers to dampen the business cycle?
3. How do we tell whether a budget deficit needs discretionary action to remove it?
4. How can the government use discretionary fiscal policy to stimulate the economy?
5. Why might fiscal stimulus crowd out investment?

You can work these questions in Study Plan 29.4 and get instant feedback. myeconlab

You've now seen the effects of fiscal policy, and *Reading Between the Lines* on pp. 710–711 applies what you've learned to the fiscal policy actions of the government of Ireland in the crisis of confidence that hit a number of EU economies in 2010.

Reading Between the Lines

Ireland's Fiscal Contraction

The Financial Times, 4 November 2010

Dublin Increases Budget Spending Cuts

FT

John Murray Brown and Alan Beattie

Ireland is facing budget cuts next month twice as savage as originally envisaged, as the embattled Fianna Fáil – led government seeks to reassure debt markets that its fiscal reduction plan is on track.

Officials said on Wednesday the December 7 budget would include a €6bn adjustment through cuts in public spending and tax increases, resulting in a deficit in 2011 of 9.25 – 9.5 per cent of gross domestic product.

This compares with 32 per cent this year, after including a one-off €30bn banks bail-out. . . .

The International Monetary Fund said Ireland's debt–GDP ratio in 2011 would be 21 percentage points higher than previously projected because of bailouts in the banking sector. Dublin on Thursday estimated that the debt would reach 105 per cent of GDP compared with 25 per cent before the crisis.

The fund calculated that Ireland's total financing needs in 2010 was the equivalent of 38.4 per cent of GDP.

Ireland's benchmark 10-year bond yields jumped to 7.67 per cent and the cost for Dublin to borrow compared with Germany, the Eurozone's biggest economy, also rose to a record 5.21 percentage points. . . .

The scale of next year's fiscal adjustment is twice the €3bn envisaged at the time of last year's budget and reflects the gloomier growth outlook where the government is now forecasting GDP to increase by 1.75 per cent next year, compared with a forecast of 3.3 per cent last December.

In 2010, growth is estimated at 0.25 per cent. The four-year plan to 2014 envisages savings of €15bn to bring the deficit below 3 per cent, the limit set for Eurozone members under the Maastricht treaty. . . .

The Essence of the Story

- Ireland has an unsustainably large government budget deficit.
- The government of Ireland is cutting expenditure and increasing taxes.
- The government's goal is to reduce the deficit from 32 per cent of GDP in 2010 to 3 per cent by 2014.

Economic Analysis

- The global financial crisis brought a banking crisis in Ireland, which the Irish government tackled by bailing out the banks.
- The bail-out drove the budget deficit and the debt–GDP ratio of the Irish government to levels never before experienced.
- Figure 1 shows the budget deficit and government debt as percentages of GDP in 2009 and 2010 and their projected values for 2011 and 2012 by a leading independent forecasting organization in Dublin.
- In 2010, the high deficits and debt increased the risk of default by the government of Ireland and drove the interest rate on its debt to more than 9 per cent a year.
- An increase in government spending that raises the interest rate crowds out private investment.
- The intent of the decrease in government spending and increase in taxes is to lower the default risk and lower the interest rate in Ireland.
- A fall in the interest rate will encourage private investment, which will eventually offset the fall in government spending.
- Figure 2 shows projected growth rates of government spending, private investment and real GDP for 2011 and 2012.
- Government spending is expected to fall, but private investment and real GDP are expected to increase.
- Figure 3 explains these changes. A fall in government spending decreases aggregate demand and shifts the *AD* curve leftward from AD_{10} to AD_{11}. Real GDP decreases.
- Eventually, the smaller deficit and debt diminishes the risk of default, the interest rate falls, and investment increases. The *AD* curve shifts rightward from AD_{11} to AD_{12}. Real GDP increases.

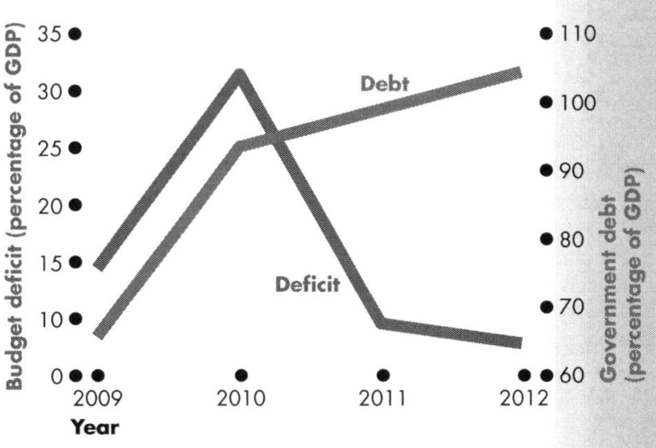

Figure 1 Ireland's government deficit and debt

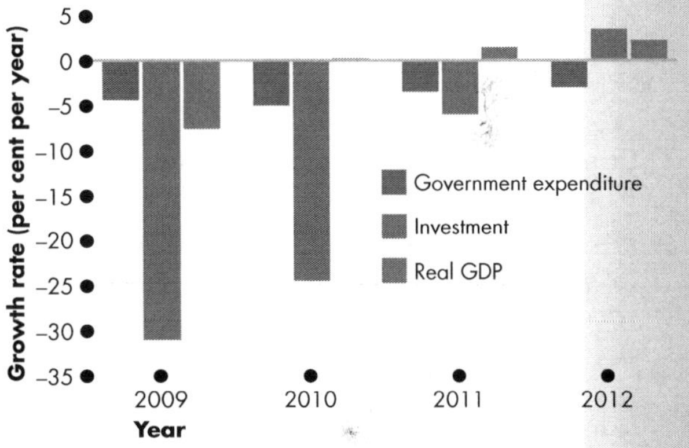

Figure 2 Past and projected growth rates

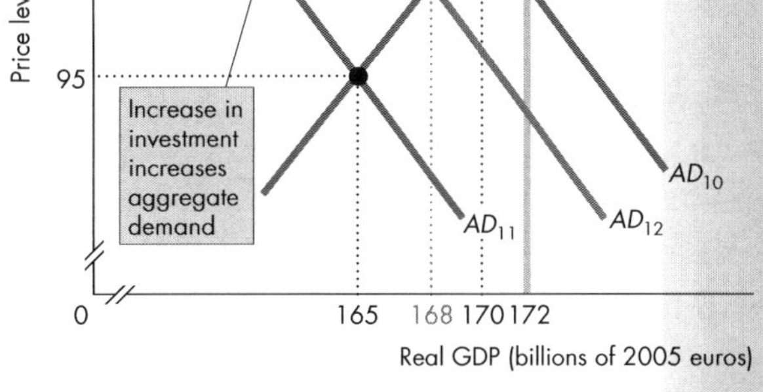

Figure 3 Ireland's aggregate supply and aggregate demand

SUMMARY

Key Points

Government Budgets

- The government budget finances the activities of the government and is used to conduct fiscal policy.
- Government receipts come from taxes on income and wealth, taxes on expenditure and National Insurance contributions.
- When government outlays exceed receipts, the government has a budget deficit.

Working Problems 1 to 3 will give you a better understanding of government budgets.

Supply-side Effects of Fiscal Policy

- Fiscal policy has supply-side effects because taxes weaken the incentive to work and decrease employment and potential GDP.
- Fiscal policy has supply-side effects because taxes weaken the incentive to save and invest, which lowers the growth rate of real GDP.
- The Laffer curve shows the relationship between the tax rate and the amount of tax revenue collected.

Working Problems 4 to 7 will give you a better understanding of the supply-side effects of fiscal policy.

Generational Effects of Fiscal Policy

- Generational accounting measures the lifetime tax burden and benefits of each generation.
- One study estimates the UK fiscal imbalance to be 510 per cent of the value of one year's production.
- Future generations will pay for 65 per cent of the benefits of the current generation.
- About 30 per cent of UK government debt is held by the rest of the world.

Working Problems 8 and 9 will give you a better understanding of the generational effects of fiscal policy.

Fiscal Stimulus

- Fiscal policy can be automatic or discretionary.
- Automatic fiscal policy might moderate the business cycle by stimulating demand in recession and restraining demand in a boom.
- Discretionary fiscal stimulus influences aggregate demand and aggregate supply.
- Discretionary changes in government expenditure or taxes have multiplier effects of uncertain magnitude but the tax multiplier is likely to be the larger one.
- Fiscal stimulus policies are hampered by uncertainty about multipliers and by time lags (law-making lags and the difficulty of correctly diagnosing and forecasting the state of the economy).

Working Problems 10 to 21 will give you a better understanding of fiscal stimulus.

Key Terms

Automatic fiscal policy
Balanced budget
Budget
Budget deficit
Budget surplus
Cyclical surplus or deficit
Discretionary fiscal policy
Fiscal imbalance
Fiscal policy
Fiscal stimulus
Generational accounting
Generational imbalance
Government debt
Government expenditure multiplier
Laffer curve
Present value
Structural surplus or deficit
Tax multiplier
Tax wedge

STUDY PLAN PROBLEMS AND APPLICATIONS

myeconlab You can work Problems 1 to 21 in MyEconLab Chapter 29 Study Plan and get instant feedback.

Government Budgets (Study Plan 29.1)

Use the following news clip to work Problems 1 and 2.

The Budget

George Osborne says he has little option but to push on with the harshest public spending cuts in living memory because a reversal would alarm the bond markets and plunge Britain into 'financial turmoil'. Responding to growing clamour for him to explore a 'plan B' for recovery, the chancellor insisted that there would be no weakening of the government's resolve in implementing austerity measures.

Source: *The Financial Times*, 30 January 2011

1 What is the UK government's plan for fiscal policy in the budget 2010?

2 What would be a 'plan B' for the government to adopt?

3 At the end of 2008, the government of China's debt was ¥4,700 billion. (¥ is yuan, the currency of China). In 2009, the government spent ¥6,000 billion and ended the year with a debt of ¥5,300 billion. How much did the government receive in tax revenue in 2009? How can you tell?

Supply-side Effects of Fiscal Policy

(Study Plan 29.2)

4 The government is considering raising the tax rate on labour income and asks you to report on the supply-side effects of such an action. Answer the following questions using appropriate graphs. You are being asked about *directions* of change, not exact magnitudes. What will happen to

a The supply of labour and why?

b The demand for labour and why?

c The equilibrium level of employment and why?

d The equilibrium before-tax wage rate and why?

e The equilibrium after-tax wage rate and why?

f Potential GDP?

5 What fiscal policy action might increase investment and speed economic growth? Explain how the policy action would work.

6 Suppose that instead of taxing *nominal* capital income, the government taxed real capital income. Use appropriate graphs to explain and illustrate the effect that this change would have on

a The tax rate on capital income.

b The supply of and demand for loanable funds.

c Investment and the real interest rate.

7 Suppose that in Sinoland, investment is £400 billion, saving is £400 billion, tax revenues are £500 billion, exports are £300 billion, and imports are £200 billion.

Calculate government expenditure and the government budget balance and explain the impact the government is exerting on investment: is the impact positive or negative?

Generational Effects of Fiscal Policy

(Study Plan 29.3)

8 The Office for Budget Responsibility projects that, under current policies, public debt will reach 233 per cent of GDP in 30 years and nearly 500 per cent in 50 years.

a What is a fiscal imbalance? How might the government reduce the fiscal imbalance?

b How would your answer to part (a) influence the generational imbalance?

9 **Increase in US Payroll Taxes Needed for Social Security**

US Social Security faces a $5.3 trillion shortfall over the next 75 years, but a congressional report says the massive gap could be erased by increasing payroll taxes paid by both employees and employers from 6.2 per cent to 7.3 per cent and by raising the retirement age to 70.

Source: *USA Today*, 21 May 2010

a Why is US Social Security facing a $5.3 trillion shortfall over the next 75 years?

b Explain how the suggestions in the news clip would reduce the shortfall.

c Would the suggestions in the news clip change the generational imbalance?

Fiscal Stimulus (Study Plan 29.4)

10 The economy is in a recession, and the recessionary gap is large.

a Describe the discretionary and automatic fiscal policy actions that might occur.

b Describe a discretionary fiscal stimulus package that could be used that would not bring an increase in the budget deficit.

c Explain the risks of discretionary fiscal policy in this situation.

Use the following news clip to work Problems 11 to 13.

Obama's Economic Recovery Plan

If the president is serious about focusing on jobs, a good start would be to freeze all tax rates and cut federal spending back to where it was before all the recent bailouts and stimulus spending.

Source: *USA Today*, 9 September 2010

11 What would be the effect on the budget deficit and real GDP of freezing tax rates and cutting government spending?

12 What would be the effect on jobs of freezing tax rates and cutting government spending?

13 If the government froze its current spending and instead cut taxes, what would be the effect on investment and jobs?

14 The economy is in a recession, the recessionary gap is large, and there is a budget deficit.

a Do we know whether the budget deficit is structural or cyclical? Explain your answer.

b Do we know whether automatic stabilizers are increasing or decreasing the output gap? Explain your answer.

c If a discretionary increase in government expenditure occurs, what happens to the structural deficit or surplus? Explain.

15 The research of economists Patrick Minford and Harald Uhlig suggests that tax cuts to stimulate the economy would pay for themselves in the long run.

a Explain what is meant by tax cuts paying for themselves. What does this statement imply about the tax multiplier?

b Why would tax cuts not pay for themselves?

Use the following news clip to work Problems 16 and 17.

Summers Calls for Infrastructure Spending

Larry Summers, the outgoing director of the White House National Economic Council, said the US must ramp up spending on domestic infrastructure to drive the economic recovery. He said that a combination of low borrowing costs, cheap building costs and high unemployment in the construction industry make this the ideal time to rebuild roads, bridges and airports.

Source: Ft.com, 7 October 2010

16 Is this infrastructure spending a fiscal stimulus? Would such spending be a discretionary or an automatic fiscal policy?

17 Explain how the rebuilding of roads, bridges and airports would drive the economic recovery.

Use the following news clip to work Problems 18 to 20.

Stimulus Debate Turns on Rebates

In 2008, as pressure built up on Washington to juice the economy, a one-time consumer rebate emerged as the likely centrepiece of a $150-billion stimulus programme. But who should actually get rebates? Everyone who pays income taxes? Or only lower- and middle-income households because they are more likely to spend more of their rebate than are higher-income households, spend it quickly, and every dollar spent on stimulus could generate a dollar in GDP?

Source: CNN, 22 January 2008

18 **a** Explain the intended effect of the $150 billion fiscal stimulus package. Draw a graph to illustrate the effect.

b Explain why the effect of this fiscal policy depends on who receives the tax rebates.

19 What would have a larger effect on aggregate demand: $150 billion worth of tax rebates or $150 billion worth of government spending?

20 Explain whether a stimulus package centred around a one-time consumer tax rebate is likely to have a small or a large supply-side effect.

21 Compare the impact on equilibrium real GDP of a same-sized decrease in taxes and increase in government expenditure.

ADDITIONAL PROBLEMS AND APPLICATIONS

myeconlab You can work these problems in MyEconLab if assigned by your lecturer.

Government Budgets

22 UK public sector net debt as a percentage of GDP in 2009/10 was 154.7 but excluding 'financial interventions' by the Bank of England, the net debt was 53.6 per cent of GDP.

Explain what accounts for this big difference in the two figures. What did the UK government do in 2008 to inflate the budget deficit and increase the debt–GDP ratio?

Supply-side Effects of Fiscal Policy

Use the following information to work Problems 23 and 24.

Suppose that in the UK, investment is £160 billion, saving is £140 billion, government expenditure on goods and services is £150 billion, exports are £200 billion and imports are £250 billion.

23 What is the amount of tax revenue? What is the government budget balance?

24 **a** Is the government's budget exerting a positive or negative impact on investment?

b What fiscal policy action might increase investment and speed economic growth? Explain how the policy action would work.

25 Suppose that capital income taxes are based (as they are in the UK and most countries) on nominal interest rates. And suppose that the inflation rate increases by 5 per cent. Use appropriate diagrams to explain and illustrate the effect that this change would have on

a The tax rate on capital income.

b The supply of loanable funds.

c The demand for loanable funds.

d Equilibrium investment.

e The equilibrium real interest rate.

Use the following news clip to work Problems 26 and 27.

Sir Richard Lambert, the outgoing head of the CBI, accused the government of failing to articulate a clear vision for economic growth. Commenting on the 50 per cent tax rate, he said that business investment in the UK will suffer if high paid individuals drifted elsewhere for tax reasons.

Source: *The Financial Times*, 25 January 2011

26 Why has the UK government raised the top rate of tax to 50 per cent?

27 What are the possible long-term consequences of such a tax rise on the supply-side of the economy, for tax revenues and the budget deficit?

Use the following news clip to work Problems 28 to 30.

Tax Hikes for Top Earners

750,000 more people will start to pay the 40% rate of tax as a result of forthcoming tax rises. However, 500,000 people will no longer be paying income tax because the point at which income tax starts to be paid will rise. The government has made the tax changes revenue neutral. The main gainers from the tax changes are lone parents and low income households.

Source: BBC, 31 January 2011

28 What do you think the term revenue neutral means?

29 Explain the potential demand-side effect of the tax changes.

30 Explain the potential supply-side effects of the tax changes.

Generational Effects of Fiscal Policy

31 **Push to Cut Deficit Collides With Politics as Usual**

So it goes in Campaign 2010 where cutting the deficit is a big issue but where support for doing some of the hard things to achieve that is running into politics as usual. Nowhere is that more apparent than in the debate – or lack thereof – on the nation's spending on big entitlement programs. According to the latest projections from the Congressional Budget Office, spending on the big three entitlement programs – Social Security, Medicare and Medicaid – is to rise by 70 per cent, 79 per cent, and 99 per cent, respectively, over the next 10 years.

Source: *The Wall Street Journal*, 5 October 2010

If politicians continue to avoid debating the projected increases in these three entitlement programmes, how do you think the fiscal imbalance will change? If Congress holds the budget deficit at $3.1 trillion, who will pay for the projected increases in expenditure?

Fiscal Stimulus

32 The economy is in a boom and the inflationary gap is large.

a Describe the discretionary and automatic fiscal policy actions that might occur.

b Describe a discretionary fiscal restraint package that could be used that would not produce serious negative supply-side effects.

c Explain the risks of discretionary fiscal policy in this situation.

33 The economy is growing slowly, the inflationary gap is large, and there is a budget deficit.

a Do we know whether the budget deficit is structural or cyclical? Explain your answer.

b Do we know whether automatic stabilizers are increasing or decreasing aggregate demand? Explain your answer.

c If a discretionary decrease in government expenditure occurs, what happens to the structural budget balance? Explain your answer.

Use the following news clip to work Problems 34 to 36.

Juicing the Economy Will Come at a Cost

The $150-billion stimulus plan will bump up the deficit, but not necessarily dollar for dollar. Here's why: if the stimulus works, the increased economic activity will generate federal tax revenue. But it isn't clear what the cost to the economy will be if a stimulus package comes too late – a real concern since legislation could get bogged down by politics.

Source: CNN, 23 January 2008

34 Explain why $150 billion of stimulus won't increase the budget deficit by $150 billion.

35 Is the budget deficit arising from the action described in the news clip structural or cyclical or a combination of the two? Explain.

36 Why might the stimulus package come 'too late'? What are the potential consequences of the stimulus package coming 'too late'?

Economics in the News

37 After you have studied *Reading Between the Lines* on pp. 710–711 answer the following questions.

a What policy is the Irish government following in dealing with its budget deficit and rising debt–GDP ratio?

b How does the Irish government plan to meet its target?

c What is the reason for the sharp rise in the budget deficit?

d What has happened to the Irish long-term bond rate as a result of the experience of high deficits and debt–GDP ratio?

e How has the recent history of high deficits and debt affected private investment?

f Why might a fiscal austerity programme lead to an expansion in private investment and reverse crowding out?

38 **US Financial Crisis Over? Not Really**

Economist Deepak Lal says the US financial crisis is not solved and contains the seeds of a more serious future crisis. For India and China, with no structural deficit, a temporary budget deficit above that resulting from automatic stabilizers makes sense. But it doesn't make sense for the US with its large structural deficit.

Source: rediff.com, 18 October 2010

More Fiscal Stimulus Needed

Economist Laura Tyson says there is a strong argument for more fiscal stimulus combined with a multi-year deficit reduction plan.

Source: marketwatch.com, 15 October 2010

a How has the business cycle influenced the US federal budget in the 2008–2009 recession?

b With which news clip opinion do you agree and why?

c Why might Laura Tyson favour a multi-year deficit reduction plan and would that address the concerns of Deepak Lal?

CHAPTER

30

Monetary Policy

After studying this chapter you will be able to:

- Describe the objectives and framework of UK monetary policy
- Explain how the Bank of England influences interest rates
- Explain the transmission channels through which the Bank of England influences inflation and real GDP
- Explain the Bank of England's extraordinary policy actions in 2008–2010

Every month, six eminent economists join the Governor and Deputy Governors of the Bank of England to analyse and deliberate on the state of the UK economy and to decide whether to change the interest rate. A similar meeting takes place each month in Frankfurt at the ECB. How do the Bank of England and ECB make their interest rate decisions? How do they get the interest rate to change? And how do a central bank's decisions influence the economy?

What special measures can a central bank take in a financial crisis like the one that engulfed the global economy in 2008?

This chapter explains monetary policy. And *Reading Between the Lines* at the end of the chapter looks at the Bank of England's policy dilemma at the beginning of 2011.

Monetary Policy Objectives and Framework

A nation's monetary policy objectives and the framework for setting and achieving them stem from the relationship between the central bank and government. Monetary policy making involves two activities:

1 Setting the policy objectives
2 Achieving the policy objectives

In a few countries, the central bank sets the objectives and decides how to achieve them. And in some countries, the government makes all the monetary policy decisions and tells the central bank what actions to take. But in most countries, including the UK, the government sets the monetary policy objectives and the central bank decides how to achieve them.

Here, we'll describe the objectives of UK monetary policy and the framework and assignment of responsibility for achieving those objectives.

Monetary Policy Objectives

The objectives of monetary policy are ultimately political and are determined by government. But they are pursued by the actions of the central bank. The Bank of England Act of 1998 sets out the objectives of UK monetary policy.

Bank of England Act 1998

The 1998 Bank of England Act sets out the Bank's monetary policy objectives as being:

(a) to maintain price stability, and
(b) subject to that, to support the economic policy of Her Majesty's Government, including its objectives for growth and employment.[1]

The Act also requires the Chancellor of the Exchequer to specify annually in writing:

(a) what price stability is to be taken to consist of, and
(b) what the economic policy of Her Majesty's Government is to be taken to be.[2]

One of the most important innovations in the 1998 Act is its establishment of the Monetary Policy Committee or MPC, an independent group of six experts who with the governor and two deputy governors make the monetary policy decisions. (See Chapter 24, p. 564 for more details on the composition of the MPC.)

Remit for the Monetary Policy Committee

The Chancellor renews and if necessary modifies the remit for the monetary policy committee at roughly annual intervals. This remit is stated in two parts corresponding to the two monetary policy objectives.

Price Stability Objective

The first part of the remit for the monetary policy committee is an operational definition of 'price stability'. Since the beginning of 2004, this objective has been specified as a target inflation rate of 2 per cent a year as measured by the 12-month increase in the Consumer Prices Index (CPI).

Although the inflation target is renewed annually, the intention is that inflation be locked in at a low and stable rate over the long term. To achieve long-term price stability, deviations from the inflation target in either direction that exceed 1 percentage point require the Governor of the Bank to write an open letter to the Chancellor explaining why the target has been missed and what steps will be taken to bring the inflation rate back to its target. And for every three months that the inflation rate misses its target by more than 1 percentage point, a further explanation must be provided.

Government Economic Policy Objectives

The government's economic policy objectives as they relate to monetary policy are to achieve high and stable levels of economic growth and employment.

Price stability is the key goal and a major contributor to achieving the other goals of government economic policy. Price stability provides the best available environment for households and firms to make the saving and investment decisions that bring economic growth. So price stability encourages the maximum sustainable growth rate of potential GDP.

But in the short run, the Bank of England faces a trade-off between inflation and economic growth and employment. Taking an action that is designed to lower the inflation rate and achieve stable prices might mean slowing the economic growth rate and lowering employment.

[1] Bank of England Act (1998) section 11.
[2] Bank of England Act (1998) section 12.

In both the primary objective of price stability and the consequential goal of high and stable growth and employment, monetary policy in the UK is similar to that in the rest of the EU (see *Economics in Action* on p. 720).

Actual Inflation and the Inflation Target

Figure 30.1 compares the CPI measure and target of 2 per cent a year since the beginning of 2004. January 2004 was the date the Bank of England was charged by the Chancellor of the Exchequer to switch from a target of 2.5 per cent a year inflation measured by the Retail Prices Index less mortgage interest payments (RPIX) to a target of 2 per cent a year measured by the Consumer Prices Index (CPI). During this period, the average rate of increase of the CPI was just above the target at 2.4 per cent a year.

The Bank of England was successful in keeping inflation within the target range of 1 per cent to 3 per cent a year for three years from the beginning of 2004. But during those years, the inflation rate moved from the bottom to the top of the target range. Inflation burst through the upper limit of the target range in March 2007. This event triggered an open letter from the Governor to the Chancellor as required by the Chancellor's remit for the Monetary Policy Committee. The 3 per cent a year upper bound was breached again from May 2008 to February 2009 and throughout 2010.

Rationale for an Inflation Target

Two main benefits flow from adopting an inflation target. The first is that the purpose of the Bank of England's policy actions are more clearly understood by financial market traders. A clearer understanding leads to fewer surprises and mistakes on the part of savers and investors.

The second benefit is that the target provides an anchor for expectations about future inflation. Firmly held expectations of low inflation make the short-run output–inflation (or unemployment–inflation) trade-off as favourable as possible – see Chapter 28, pp. 674–676. Also, firmly held (and correct) inflation expectations help individuals and firms to make better economic decisions, which in turn help to achieve a more efficient allocation of resources and a more stable economic growth rate.

Figure 30.1 Inflation Target and Outcomes

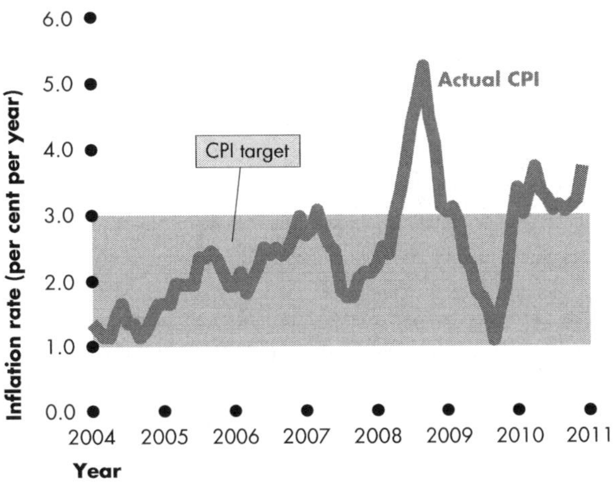

The MPC's inflation target is a range of 1 per cent to 3 per cent a year. Inflation was inside the target from 2004 until March 2007. From May 2008 to February 2009 and throughout 2010, inflation has been above the 3 per cent a year upper limit.

Source of data: Office for National Statistics.

myeconlab Animation

Controversy About Inflation Targeting

Not everyone agrees that the inflation targeting brings benefits. Critics argue that by focusing on inflation, the Bank of England sometimes permits the unemployment rate or real GDP growth rate to suffer.

The fear of these critics is that if the inflation rate begins to edge upward towards and perhaps beyond a full percentage point above target, the Bank of England might reign in aggregate demand and push the economy into recession. At the same time, the Bank might end up permitting the pound to rise on the foreign exchange market and making exports suffer.

One response of supporters of inflation targeting is that by keeping inflation low and stable, monetary policy makes its maximum possible contribution towards achieving full employment and sustained economic growth.

Another response is 'look at the growth and unemployment record'. From May 1997 when the Bank of England was made operationally independent and given the goal of price stability, until 2008, the UK economy was free from recession and had falling unemployment. Only when the entire global economy was reeling from financial crisis did the UK real GDP fall and unemployment begin to rise.

ECONOMICS IN ACTION

Monetary Policy in the Eurozone

The Eurozone is the 17 member states of the EU that use the euro as their currency. The European Central Bank (ECB), which was established in 1998, is the Eurozone's central bank.

The conduct of monetary policy in the Eurozone is very similar to that in the UK. In fact, today there has been a convergence of views on how monetary policy should be conducted and the central banks of most industrial countries pursue monetary policy using similar objectives, tools and decision-making frameworks.

The objectives of Eurozone monetary policy are laid out in Article 105 of the Treaty Establishing the European Community (the Treaty of Rome), which assigns overriding importance to price stability as the ECB's monetary policy goal. The Treaty also requires the ECB to support broader Community economic policies, which means supporting policies aimed at achieving sustained growth and high employment.

The ECB's Governing Council has defined price stability as 'a year-on-year increase in the Harmonised Index of Consumer Prices (HICP) for the euro area of . . . below, but close to, 2 per cent a year over the medium term.'

Like the Bank of England and most other central banks, the ECB recognizes 'that ensuring price stability is the most important contribution that monetary policy can make to achieve a favourable economic environment and a high level of employment'. In other words, price stability is the goal of monetary policy *because it contributes to the achievement of other economic objectives.*

Review Quiz

1 What are the objectives of monetary policy?
2 What is the rationale for setting an inflation target?
3 What is the Bank of England's record in achieving the inflation target?

You can work these questions in Study Plan 30.1 and get instant feedback. myeconlab

You now know the objective of monetary policy and the Bank of England's record in achieving it. You're now going to see how the Bank conducts monetary policy.

The Conduct of Monetary Policy

How does the Bank of England conduct its monetary policy? This question has two parts:

- What is the monetary policy instrument?
- How does the Bank make its monetary policy decisions?

The Monetary Policy Instrument

A **monetary policy instrument** is a variable that a central bank can directly control or closely target. The Bank of England must choose between two possible instruments: the monetary base or an interest rate.

The Bank's choice of monetary policy instrument is an interest rate. The Bank sets Bank Rate (also known as the Bank of England Base Rate), which is linked to the interest rate that banks earn on reserves and pay on borrowed reserves. The Bank then trades in the repo market to make the **repo rate** – the interest rate in the repo market – equal to Bank Rate. Banks can borrow and lend reserves in the repo market. A bank that is short of reserves and a bank that has excess reserves can use a repo to move the reserves from one bank to the other. The Bank of England also trades in the repo market.

Figure 30.2 shows the Bank Rate since January 2004. Bank Rate is normally changed in steps of a quarter of a percentage point.[3] The rate reached a peak of 5.75 per cent a year in 2007 and then fell in rapid succession in much greater steps than a quarter of a per cent to a low of 0.5 per cent a year in April 2009. The sharp fall in the Bank Rate was a coordinated attempt by the central banks of the developed world to deal with the credit crunch and the global financial crisis.

Between 2004 and 2007, Bank Rate was on a rising trend. The reason is that the inflation rate had moved up from below target to above target and by 2007 the inflation rate was pushing against the upper limit of a 3 per cent a year rate of increase of the CPI.

Since 2007, the Bank Rate has been lowered, first in short steps and then in rapid steps as the full scale of the economic crisis became apparent. During 2010 the inflation rate has been above the upper bound of 3 per cent a year but the rate of interest has remained at the historically low level of 0.5 per cent a year.

[3] When you read about interest changes in the press, you might encounter the term 25 basis points. A basis point is 100th of 1 per cent, so 25 basis points is 0.25 percentage points.

Figure 30.2 Bank Rate

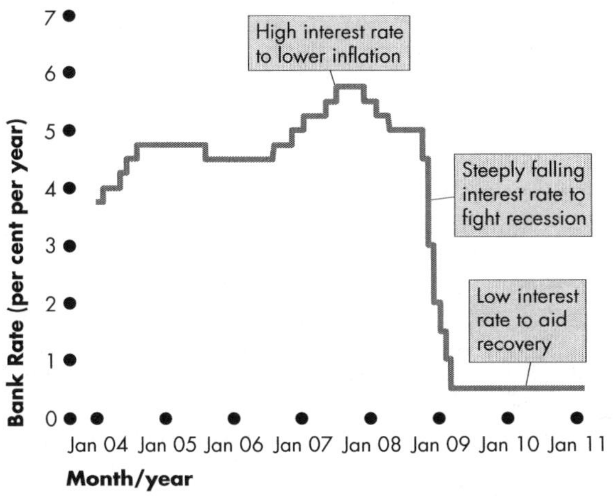

The Bank of England sets Bank Rate and then takes actions to ensure that the banking system is supplied with its desired level of reserves. When the inflation rate is above 2 per cent a year and the Bank wants to avoid going above target, it raises Bank Rate. When the inflation rate is below 2 per cent a year and the Bank wants to avoid going below target, it lowers Bank Rate.

Source of data: Bank of England.

myeconlab Animation

Figure 30.3 The Market for Bank Reserves

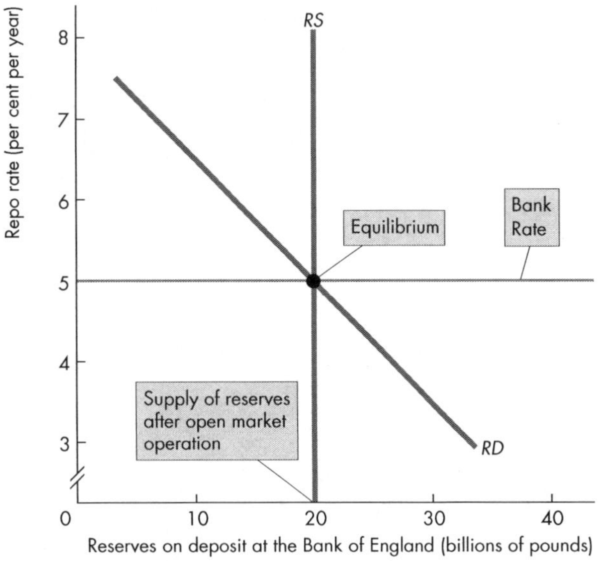

The demand curve for reserves is *RD*. The quantity of reserves demanded decreases as the repo rate rises because the repo rate is the opportunity cost of holding reserves. The supply curve of reserves is *RS*. The Bank of England uses open market operations to make the supply of reserves equal the quantity of reserves demanded (£20 billion in this case) at a repo rate equal to Bank Rate (5 per cent a year in this case).

myeconlab Animation

Having decided the appropriate level for Bank Rate, how does the Bank of England move the repo rate to its target level? The answer is by using open market operations (see Chapter 24, pp. 565–567) to adjust the quantity of monetary base.

To see how an open market operation changes the repo rate, we need to examine the repo market. The higher the repo rate, the greater is the quantity of overnight loans supplied on repurchase agreements and the smaller is the quantity of overnight loans demanded in the repo market. The equilibrium repo rate balances the quantities demanded and supplied.

An equivalent way of looking at the forces that determine the repo rate is to consider the demand for and supply of bank reserves. Banks hold reserves to meet their desired reserve ratio so that they can always make payments. But reserves are costly to hold. The alternative to holding reserves is to lend them in the repo market and earn the repo rate. The higher the repo rate, the higher is the opportunity cost of holding reserves and the greater is the incentive for banks to economize on the quantity of reserves held.

So the quantity of reserves demanded by banks depends on the repo rate. The higher the repo rate, other things remaining the same, the smaller is the quantity of reserves demanded.

Figure 30.3 illustrates the demand for bank reserves. The *x*-axis measures the quantity of reserves that banks hold on deposit at the Bank of England, and the *y*-axis measures the repo rate. The demand for reserves is the curve labelled *RD*.

The Bank's open market operations determine the supply of reserves shown by the supply curve *RS*. To decrease reserves, the Bank conducts an open market sale. To increase reserves, the Bank conducts an open market purchase.

Equilibrium in the market for bank reserves determines the repo rate where the quantity of reserves demanded by the commercial banks equals the quantity of reserves supplied by the Bank of England. By using open market operations, the Bank adjusts the supply of reserves to keep the repo rate equal to Bank Rate.

Next, we see how the Bank makes its policy decision.

ECONOMICS IN ACTION

Bank of England Decision Making

The MPC meets monthly to set the Bank Rate and throughout the month the committee gets an extensive briefing by the economists of the Bank of England where all the available industry, national and international data on economic performance, financial markets and inflation expectations are reviewed, discussed and weighed in a careful deliberative process.

The MPC meeting lasts two days and on the second day members explain their views as to what they think are the important factors in the economy and what they think the interest rate decision should be.

The Governor of the Bank then puts to the meeting the decision that he thinks will command a majority. Any member in a minority is asked to record what the interest rate should be and justify that decision formally in the minutes.

The interest rate decision is announced at 12 noon on the second day of the deliberations. After announcing a Bank Rate decision, the Bank engages in public communication to explain the reasons for the MPC's decision. The Bank of England's communication exercise is extremely thorough and includes a detailed and carefully researched *Inflation Report* and press conference with the Governor.

The Governor's press conference is recorded and a video placed on the Bank's website. (Take a look!)

The Bank of England's Decision-making Strategy

The Bank of England (along with most other central banks) follows a process that uses an *inflation targeting rule*. To implement its inflation targeting rule, the Bank must gather and process a large amount of information about the economy, the way it responds to shocks and the way it responds to policy. The Bank must then process all this data and come to a judgement about the best level at which to set Bank Rate.

The process begins with an exercise that uses a model of the UK economy that you can think of as a sophisticated version of the *AS–AD* model (see Chapter 26). The Bank's economists provide the MPC with a variety of forecasts and scenarios running two years into the future. Crucially the inflation rate is forecasted with probabilities assigned to each scenario so that the MPC is aware of the uncertainty and risks that surround any particular forecast.

Review Quiz

1. What is the Bank of England's monetary policy instrument?
2. What is the main influence on the MPC's interest rate decision?
3. What happens when the Bank of England buys or sells securities in the open market?
4. How is the repo rate determined?

You can work these questions in Study Plan 30.2 and get instant feedback.

Monetary Policy Transmission

You've seen that the Bank of England's goal is to keep the price level stable (keep the CPI inflation rate at 2 per cent a year) and to achieve maximum growth and employment (keep the output gap close to zero). And you've seen how the Bank can use its power to set Bank Rate at its desired level. We're now going to trace the events that follow a change in Bank Rate and see how those events lead to the ultimate policy goal. We'll begin with a quick overview of the transmission process and then look at each step a bit more closely.

Quick Overview

When the Bank of England lowers Bank Rate, other short-term interest rates and the exchange rate also fall. The quantity of money and the supply of loanable funds increase. The long-term real interest rate falls. The lower real interest rate increases consumption expenditure and investment. And the lower exchange rate makes UK exports cheaper and imports more costly. So net exports increase. Easier bank loans reinforce the effect of lower interest rates on aggregate expenditure. Aggregate demand increases, which increases real GDP and the price level relative to what they would have been. Real GDP growth and inflation speed up.

When the Bank raises Bank Rate, the sequence of events that we've just reviewed plays out but the effects are in the opposite directions.

Figure 30.4 provides a schematic summary of these ripple effects for both a cut (on the left) and a rise (on the right) in Bank Rate.

The ripple effects summarized in Figure 30.4 stretch out over a period of between one and two years but the time lags involved and the strength of each of the effects are never quite the same and are unpredictable.

The interest rate and exchange rate effects are immediate. They occur on the same day that the MPC announces its decision. Sometimes they even anticipate the decision. The effects on money and bank loans follow in a few weeks and run for a few months. Real long-term interest rates change quickly and often in anticipation of the short-term rate changes. Spending plans change and real GDP growth changes after about one year. And the inflation rate changes between one year and two years after the change in Bank Rate. But these time lags are especially hard to predict and can be longer or shorter.

We're going to look at each stage in the transmission process, starting with the interest rate effects.

Figure 30.4 The Ripple Effects of a Change in Bank Rate

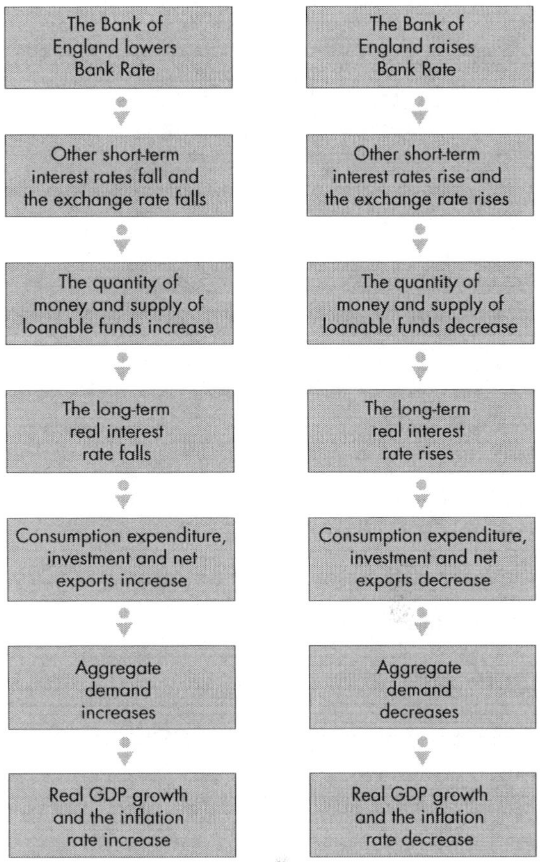

myeconlab Animation

Interest Rate Changes

The first effect of a monetary policy decision by the MPC is a change in Bank Rate. Other interest rates then change. Short-term interest rate effects occur quickly and predictably. Long-term interest rate effects occur more slowly and less predictably. Figure 30.5 shows the fluctuations in three interest rates: the repo rate, a short-term bill rate and a long-term bond rate.

Repo Rate

As soon as the MPC announces a new setting for Bank Rate, the Bank of England's bond dealers undertake the necessary open market operations to adjust reserves. There is little doubt about where the interest rate changes shown in Figure 30.5 are generated. They are driven by the Bank of England's monetary policy.

Figure 30.5 Three Interest Rates

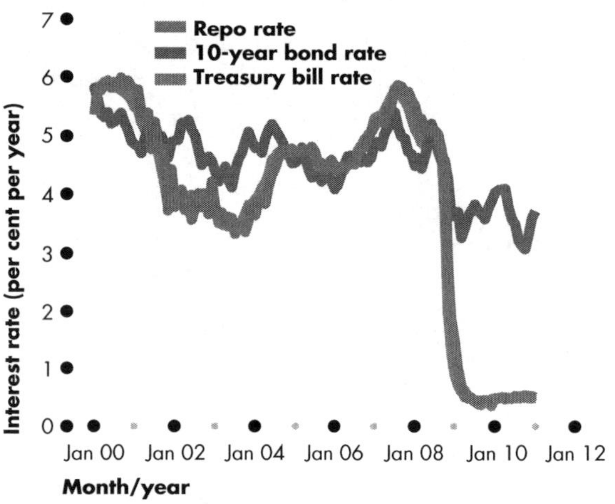

The short-term interest rates – repo rate and the short-term bill rate – move closely together. The long-term bond rate fluctuates less than the short-term rates but long-term and short-term interest rates move in the same general direction.

Source of data: Bank of England.

myeconlab Animation

The Short-term Bill Rate

The *short-term bill rate* is the interest rate paid by the UK government on 3-month Treasury bills. It is similar to the interest rate paid by UK businesses on short-term loans. Notice how closely the short-term bill rate follows the repo rate. The two rates are almost identical.

A powerful substitution effect keeps the 3-month Treasury bill rate and the repo rate close. Commercial banks have a choice about how to hold their short-term liquid assets. And an overnight loan to another bank is a close substitute for short-term securities such as 3-month Treasury bills. If the interest rate on the Treasury bill is higher than the repo rate, the quantity of overnight loans supplied decreases and the demand for Treasury bills increases. The price of a Treasury bill rises and the interest rate falls.

Similarly, if the interest rate on a Treasury bill is lower than the repo rate, the quantity of overnight loans supplied increases and the demand for Treasury bills decreases. The price of a Treasury bill falls, and the interest rate on Treasury bills rises.

When the interest rate on Treasury bills is close to the repo rate, there is no incentive for a bank to switch between making an overnight loan and buying Treasury bills. Both the Treasury bill market and the repo market are in equilibrium.

The Long-term Bond Rate

The *long-term bond rate* is the interest rate paid on bonds issued by large corporations. It is this interest rate that businesses pay on the loans that finance their purchase of new capital and that influences their investment decisions.

Two features of the long-term bond rate stand out: it does not track closely with the short-term rates, and it fluctuates less than the short-term rates so that in some years the long-term rate exceeds the short-term rate and in other years the gap is reversed.

A dominant effect on the long-term interest rate is the long-term expected inflation rate. In 1997, just before the Bank of England began inflation targeting, the expected inflation rate was high, so the long-term bond rate was also high, and much higher than the short-term rate. In an environment of uncertain long-term inflation, long-term loans are riskier than short-term loans. To provide the incentive that brings forth a supply of long-term loans, lenders must be compensated for the additional risk. Without compensation for the additional risk, only short-term loans would be supplied.

The long-term interest rate fluctuates less than the short-term rates because it is influenced by expectations about future short-term interest rates as well as current short-term interest rates. The alternative to borrowing or lending long term is to borrow or lend using a sequence of short-term securities. If the long-term interest rate exceeds the expected average of future short-term interest rates, people will lend long term and borrow short term. The long-term interest rate will fall. If the long-term interest rate is below the expected average of future short-term interest rates, people will borrow long term and lend short term. The long-term interest rate will rise.

These market forces keep the long-term interest rate close to the expected average of future short-term interest rates. And the expected average future short-term interest rate fluctuates less than the current short-term interest rate.

Exchange Rate Fluctuations

The exchange rate responds to changes in the interest rate in the UK relative to the interest rates in other countries – *the UK interest rate differential*. We explain this influence in Chapter 25 (see pp. 589–590).

When the Bank of England raises Bank Rate, the UK interest rate differential rises and, other things remaining the same, the pound appreciates. And when the Bank lowers Bank Rate, the UK interest rate differential falls and, other things remaining the same, the pound depreciates.

Many factors other than the UK interest rate differential influence the exchange rate, so when the Bank changes Bank Rate, the exchange rate does not usually change in exactly the way it would with other things remaining the same. So while monetary policy influences the exchange rate, many other factors also make the exchange rate change.

Money and Bank Loans

The quantity of money and bank loans change when the Bank of England changes Bank Rate. A rise in Bank Rate decreases the quantity of money and bank loans and a fall in Bank Rate increases the quantity of money and bank loans. These changes occur for two reasons: the quantity of money supplied by the banking system changes and the quantity of money demanded by households and firms changes.

You've seen that the Bank changes the quantity of bank reserves to keep the repo rate equal to Bank Rate. A change in the quantity of bank reserves changes the monetary base, which in turn changes the quantity of deposits and loans that the banking system can create. A rise in Bank Rate decreases reserves and decreases the quantity of deposits and bank loans created; and a fall in Bank Rate increases reserves and increases the quantity of deposits and bank loans created.

The quantity of money created by the banking system must be held by households and firms. The change in the interest rate changes the quantity of money demanded. A fall in the interest rate increases the quantity of money demanded and a rise in the interest rate decreases the quantity of money demanded.

A change in the quantity of money and the supply of bank loans directly affects consumption and investment plans. With more money and easier access to loans, consumers and firms spend more. With less money and loans harder to get, consumers and firms spend less.

The Long-term Real Interest Rate

Demand and supply in the market for loanable funds determine the long-term real interest rate, which equals the long-term nominal interest rate minus the expected inflation rate. The long-term real interest rate influences expenditure decisions.

In the long run, demand and supply in the loanable funds market depend only on real forces – on saving and investment decisions. But in the short run, when the price level is not fully flexible, the supply of loanable funds is influenced by the supply of bank loans. Changes in Bank Rate change the supply of bank loans, which changes the supply of loanable funds and changes the interest rate in the loanable funds market.

A fall in Bank Rate that increases the supply of bank loans increases the supply of loanable funds and lowers the equilibrium real interest rate. A rise in Bank Rate that decreases the supply of bank loans decreases the supply of loanable funds and raises the equilibrium real interest rate.

These changes in the real interest rate, along with the other factors we've just described, change expenditure plans.

Expenditure Plans

The ripple effects that follow a change in Bank Rate change three components of aggregate expenditure:

- Consumption expenditure
- Investment
- Net exports

Consumption Expenditure

Other things remaining the same, the lower the real interest rate, the greater is the amount of consumption expenditure and the smaller is the amount of saving.

Investment

Other things remaining the same, the lower the real interest rate, the greater is the amount of investment.

Net Exports

Other things remaining the same, the lower the interest rate, the lower is the exchange rate and the greater are exports and the smaller are imports.

So eventually, a cut in Bank Rate increases aggregate expenditure and a rise in Bank Rate curtails aggregate expenditure. These changes in aggregate expenditure plans change aggregate demand, real GDP and the price level.

Change in Aggregate Demand, Real GDP and the Price Level

The final link in the transmission chain is a change in aggregate demand and a resulting change in real GDP and the price level. By changing real GDP and the price level relative to what they would have been without a change in Bank Rate, the Bank influences its ultimate goals: the inflation rate and full employment.

The Bank Fights Recession

If inflation is low and real GDP is below potential GDP, the Bank takes actions that are designed to restore full employment. Figure 30.6 shows the effects of the Bank of England's actions, starting in the market for bank reserves and ending in the market for real GDP.

Market for Bank Reserves

In Figure 30.6(a), which shows the market for bank reserves, the MPC lowers Bank Rate from 5 per cent to 4 per cent a year. To keep the repo rate close to Bank Rate, the Bank of England buys securities and increases the supply of bank reserves from RS_0 to RS_1.

Money Market

With increased reserves, the banks create deposits by making loans and the supply of money increases. The short-term interest rate falls and the quantity of money demanded increases. In Figure 30.6(b), the increase in the supply of money shifts the supply of money curve from MS_0 to MS_1. The interest rate falls from 5 per cent to 4 per cent a year and the quantity of money increases from £1,400 billion to £1,500 billion. The interest rate in the money market and the repo rate are kept close to each other by the powerful substitution effect described on p. 724.

Loanable Funds Market

Banks create money by making loans. In the long run, an increase in the supply of bank loans is matched by a rise in the price level and the quantity of real loans is

Figure 30.6 The Bank of England Fights Recession

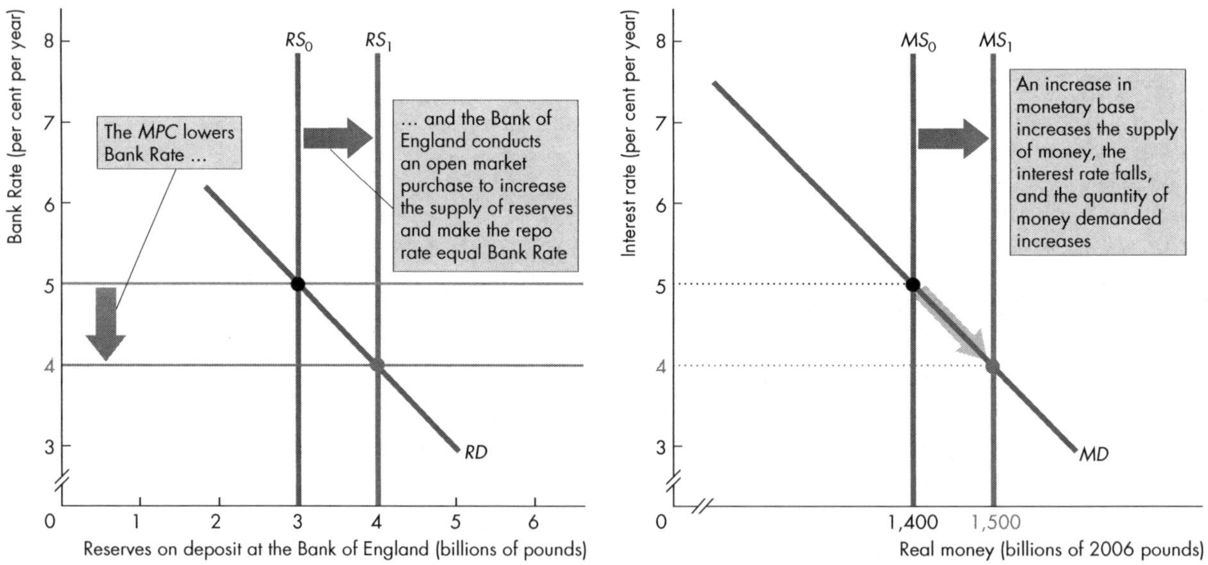

(a) The market for bank reserves

In part (a), the MPC lowers Bank Rate target from 5 per cent to 4 per cent a year. To make the repo rate equal to Bank Rate, the Bank of England buys securities in an open market operation and increases the supply of reserves from RS_0 to RS_1.

(b) Money market

In part (b), the increase in monetary base increases the supply of money from MS_0 to MS_1. The short-term interest rate falls and the quantity of money demanded increases. The short-term interest rate and Bank Rate change by similar amounts.

myeconlab Animation

unchanged. But in the short run, with a sticky price level, an increase in the supply of bank loans increases the supply of (real) loanable funds.

In Figure 30.6(c), the supply of loanable funds increases and the supply of loanable funds curve shifts rightward from SLF_0 to SLF_1. With the demand for loanable funds at *DLF*, the real interest rate falls from 6 per cent to 5.5 per cent a year. (Here, we assume a zero inflation rate so that the real interest rate equals the nominal interest rate.) The long-term interest rate changes by a smaller amount than the change in the short-term interest rate as described on p. 724.

The Market for Real GDP

Figure 30.6(d) shows aggregate demand and aggregate supply. Potential GDP is £1,300 billion, where *LAS* is located. The short-run aggregate supply curve is *SAS*, and initially, the aggregate demand curve is AD_0. Real GDP is £1,200 billion, which is less than potential GDP, so there is a recessionary gap. The Bank is reacting to this recessionary gap.

The increase in the supply of loans and the decrease in the real interest rate increase aggregate planned expenditure. (Not shown in the figure, a fall in the interest rate lowers the exchange rate, which increases net exports and also aggregate planned expenditure.) The increase in aggregate expenditure, ΔE, increases aggregate demand and also shifts the aggregate demand curve rightward to $AD_0 + \Delta E$. A multiplier process begins. The increase in expenditure increases income, which induces an increase in consumption expenditure. Aggregate demand increases further, and the aggregate demand curve eventually shifts rightward to AD_1.

The new equilibrium is at full employment. Real GDP is equal to potential GDP. The price level rises to 105 and then becomes stable at that level so after a one-time adjustment, there is price stability.

In this example, we have given the Bank a perfect hit at achieving full employment and keeping the price level stable. It is unlikely that the Bank would be able to achieve the precision of this example. A Bank Rate cut that is too little or too late leaves the economy in a recession and too big a cut sends inflation above target.

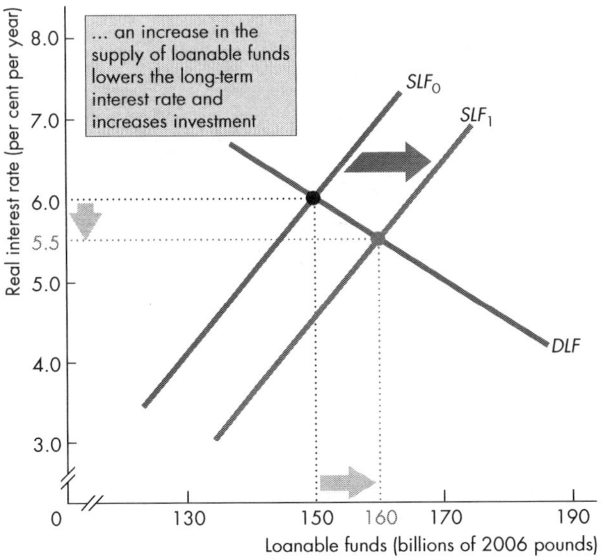

(c) The market for loanable funds

In part (c), an increase in the supply of bank loans increases the supply of loanable funds and shifts the supply of loanable funds curve from SLF_0 to SLF_1. The real interest rate falls and investment increases.

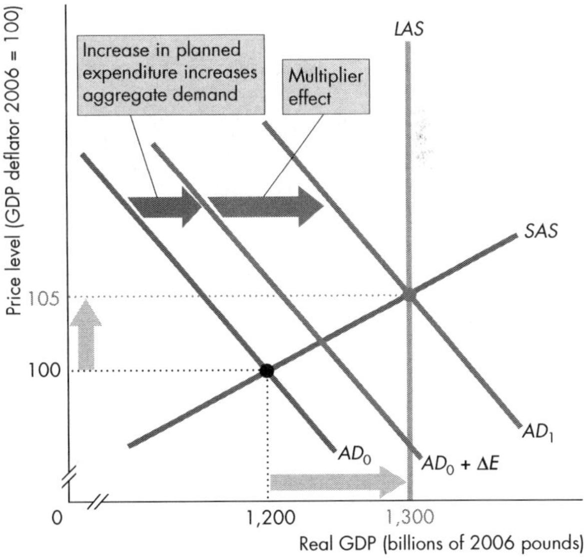

(d) Real GDP and the price level

In part (d), the increase in investment increases aggregate planned expenditure. The aggregate demand curve shifts to $AD_0 + \Delta E$ and eventually shifts rightward to AD_1. Real GDP increases to potential GDP and the price level rises.

The Bank Fights Inflation

If the inflation rate is too high and real GDP is above potential GDP, the Bank of England takes actions that are designed to lower the inflation rate and restore price stability. Figure 30.7 shows the effects of the Bank's actions starting in the market for reserves and ending in the market for real GDP.

Market for Bank Reserves

In Figure 30.7(a), which shows the market for bank reserves, the MPC raises Bank Rate from 5 per cent to 6 per cent a year. To keep the repo rate close to Bank Rate, the Bank sells securities and decreases the supply of reserves of the banking system from RS_0 to RS_1.

Money Market

With decreased reserves, the banks shrink deposits by decreasing loans and the supply of money decreases. The short-term interest rate rises and the quantity of money demanded decreases. In Figure 30.7(b), the supply of money decreases from MS_0 to MS_1, the interest rate rises from 5 per cent to 6 per cent a year and the quantity of money decreases from £1,400 billion to £1,300 billion.

Loanable Funds Market

With a decrease in reserves, banks must decrease the supply of loans. The supply of (real) loanable funds decreases, and the supply of loanable funds curve shifts leftward in Figure 30.7(c) from SLF_0 to SLF_1. With the demand for loanable funds at *DLF*, the real interest rate rises from 6 per cent to 6.5 per cent a year. (Again, we're assuming a zero inflation rate so that the real interest rate equals the nominal interest rate.)

The Market for Real GDP

Figure 30.7(d) shows aggregate demand and aggregate supply in the market for real GDP. Potential GDP and *LAS* are £1,300 billion. The short-run aggregate supply curve is *SAS* and initially, the aggregate demand is AD_0. Now, real GDP is £1,400 billion, which is greater than potential GDP, so there is an inflationary gap. The Bank is reacting to this inflationary gap.

Figure 30.7 The Bank of England Fights Inflation

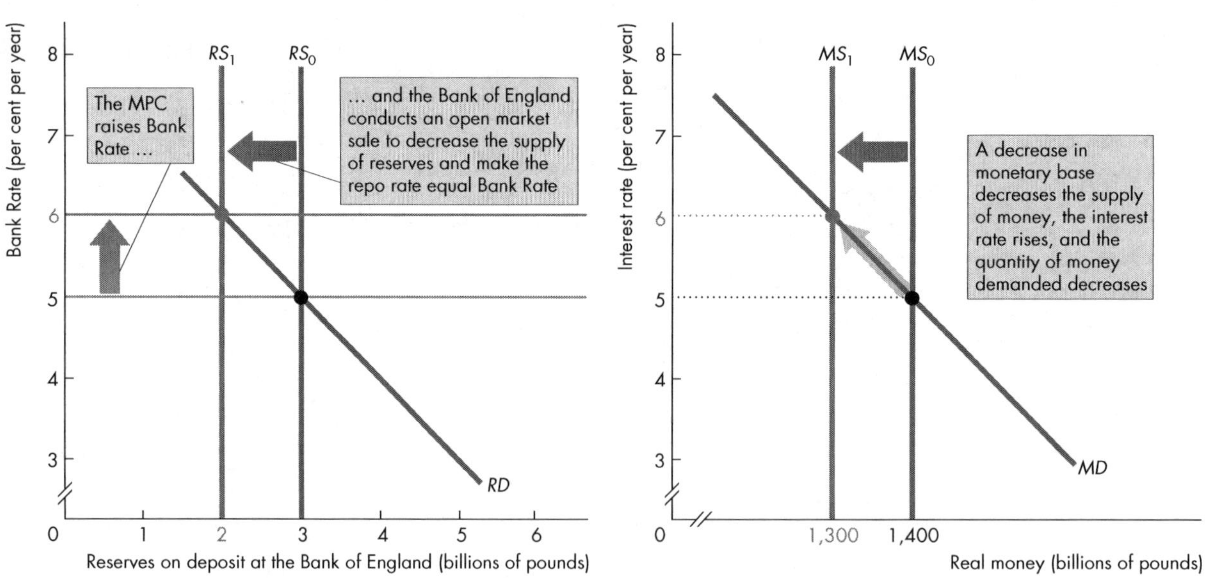

(a) The market for bank reserves

In part (a), the MPC raises Bank Rate from 5 per cent to 6 per cent. To make the repo rate equal to Bank Rate the Bank of England sells securities in an open market operation to decrease the supply of reserves from RS_0 to RS_1.

(b) Money market

In part (b), the supply of money decreases from MS_0 to MS_1, the short-term interest rate rises, and the quantity of money demanded decreases. The short-term interest rate and Bank Rate change by similar amounts.

myeconlab Animation

The decrease in the supply of bank loans, and the increase in the real interest rate decrease aggregate planned expenditure. (Not shown in the figures, a rise in the interest rate raises the exchange rate, which decreases net exports and also aggregate planned expenditure.)

The decrease in aggregate expenditure, ΔE, decreases aggregate demand and the aggregate demand curve shifts to $AD_0 - \Delta E$. A multiplier process begins. The decrease in expenditure decreases income, which induces a decrease in consumption expenditure. Aggregate demand decreases further, and the aggregate demand curve eventually shifts leftward to AD_1.

The economy returns to full employment. Real GDP is equal to potential GDP. The price level falls to 105 and then becomes stable at that level so after a one-time adjustment, there is price stability.

Again, in this example, we have given the Bank a perfect hit at achieving full employment and keeping the price level stable. If the Bank raised Bank Rate by too little or too late, the economy would have remained with an inflationary gap and the inflation rate would have moved above the target. And if the Bank raised Bank Rate by too much it would push the economy from inflation to recession.

Loose Links and Long and Variable Lags

The ripple effects of monetary policy that we've just analysed with the precision of an economic model are, in reality, very hard to predict and anticipate.

To achieve its inflation target and its additional mandate to support the government's economic policy of keeping real GDP growing at the maximum sustainable rate and maintaining full employment, the Bank needs a combination of good judgement and good luck.

Too large an interest rate cut can bring inflation, as it did during the 1970s. And too large an interest rate rise in an inflationary economy can create unemployment, as it did in 1981 and 1991.

Loose links in the chain that runs from Bank Rate to the ultimate policy goals make unwanted policy outcomes inevitable. And time lags that are both long and variable add to the Bank of England's challenges.

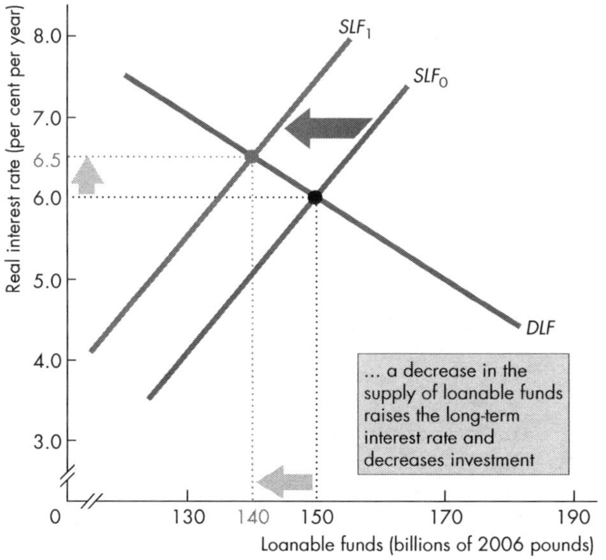

(c) The market for loanable funds

In part (c), a decrease in the supply of bank loans decreases the supply of loanable funds and shifts the supply of loanable funds curve from SLF_0 to SLF_1. The real interest rate rises and investment decreases.

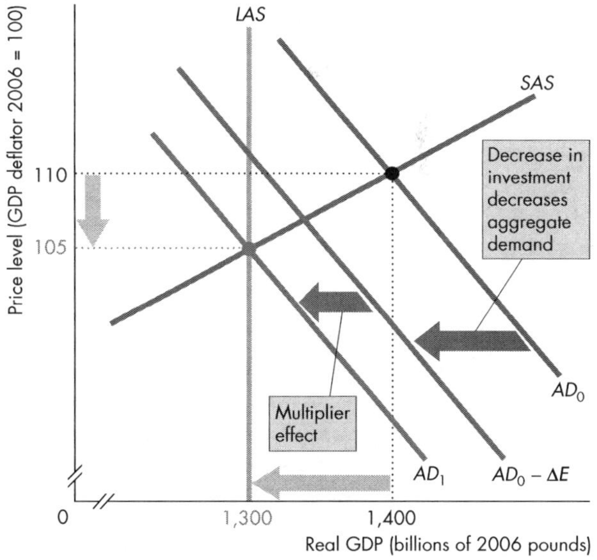

(d) Real GDP and the price level

In part (d), the decrease in investment decreases aggregate planned expenditure. The aggregate demand curve shifts to $AD_0 - \Delta E$ and eventually shifts leftward to AD_1. Real GDP decreases to potential GDP and the price level falls.

ECONOMICS IN ACTION

A Look at the Long and Variable Lag

You've studied the theory of monetary policy. Does it really work in the way we've described? It does, and Figure 1 provides some evidence to support this conclusion.

In Figure 1 the blue line shows Bank Rate that the Bank targets minus the long-term bond rate. You saw earlier (in Figure 30.5) that the short-term interest rates fluctuate more than the long-term rate. We can view the gap between the long-term bond rate and Bank Rate as a measure of how hard the Bank is trying to steer a change in course. When Bank Rate falls relative to the long-term bond rate, the Bank is cutting Bank Rate in an attempt to boost aggregate demand and stimulate real GDP growth. And when Bank Rate rises relative to the long-term bond rate, the Bank is raising Bank Rate in an attempt to decrease aggregate demand, restrain inflation and slow real GDP growth.

The red line in Figure 1 shows the real GDP growth rate one and a half years later.

You can see that when the MPC raises Bank Rate, the real GDP growth rate slows one and a half years later. And when the MPC lowers Bank Rate, the real GDP growth rate speeds up one and a half years later.

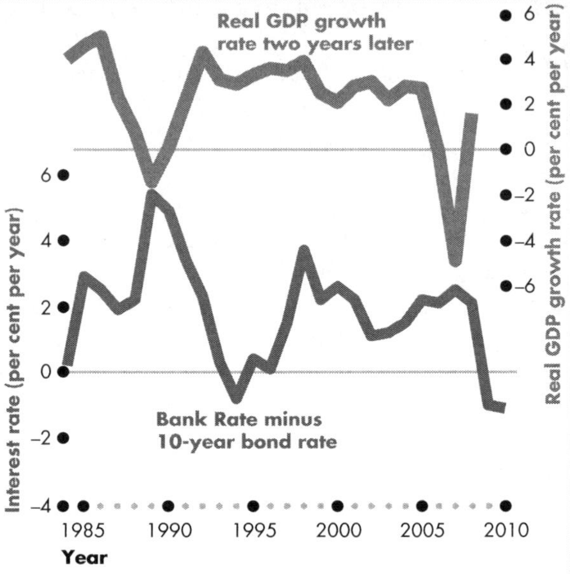

Figure 1 Interest Rates and Real GDP Growth

Sources of data: Bank of England and Office for National Statistics.

Not shown in this figure, with other things remaining the same, the inflation rate increases and decreases in line with the fluctuations in the real GDP growth rate. But the effects of an interest rate change on the inflation rate take even longer. Also, other influences on the inflation rate break the link between inflation and real GDP fluctuations.

Loose Link from Bank Rate to Spending

The real long-term interest rate that influences spending plans is linked only loosely to Bank Rate. Also, the response of the real long-term interest rate to a change in the nominal rate depends on how inflation expectations change. And the response of expenditure plans to changes in the real interest rate depends on many factors that make the response hard to predict.

Time Lags in the Adjustment Process

The Bank is especially handicapped by the fact that the monetary policy transmission process is long and drawn out. Also, the economy does not always respond in exactly the same way to a policy change. Further, many factors other than policy are constantly changing and bringing new situations to which policy must respond.

Review Quiz

1. Describe the channels by which monetary policy ripples through the economy and explain how each channel operates.
2. Do interest rates fluctuate in response to the Bank of England's actions?
3. How do the Bank of England's actions change the exchange rate?
4. How do the Bank of England's actions influence real GDP and how long does it take for real GDP to respond to the Bank's policy changes?
5. How do the Bank's actions influence the inflation rate and how long does it take for the inflation rate to respond to the Bank's policy changes?

You can work these questions in Study Plan 30.3 and get instant feedback. myeconlab

Extraordinary Monetary Stimulus

During the financial crisis and recession of 2008–2009, the Bank of England lowered the Bank Rate to 0.5 per cent a year. Bank Rate cannot fall much further, so what can the Bank do to stimulate the economy? The Bank of England has answered this question with some extraordinary policy actions. To understand those actions, we need to dig a bit into the anatomy of the financial crisis to which the Bank is responding. That's what we'll now do. We'll look at the key elements in the financial crisis and then look at the Bank's response.

The Key Elements of the Crisis

We can describe the crisis by identifying the events that changed the values of the assets and liabilities of banks and other financial institutions. Figure 30.8 shows the stylized balance sheet of a bank: deposits plus own capital equals reserves plus loans and securities (see Chapter 24, p. 562). Deposits and own capital are the banks' sources of funds (other borrowing is ignored here).

Deposits are the funds loaned to the bank by households and firms. A bank's *own capital* is the funds provided by its shareholders and includes the bank's undistributed profits (and losses). A bank's reserves are currency and its deposit at the Bank of England. A bank's loans and securities are the loans made by the bank and government bonds, private bonds, asset-backed bonds, and other securities that the bank holds.

Three main events can put a bank under stress:

1 A widespread fall in asset prices
2 A significant currency drain
3 A run on the bank

Figure 30.8 summarizes the problems that each event presents to a bank. A widespread fall in asset prices means that the bank suffers a capital loss. It must write down the value of its assets and the value of the bank's own capital decreases by the same amount as the fall in the value of its securities. If the fall in asset prices is large enough, the value of a bank's own capital might fall to zero, in which case the bank is insolvent. It fails.

A significant currency drain means that depositors withdraw funds and the bank loses reserves. This event puts the bank in a liquidity crisis. It is short of cash reserves.

A run on the bank occurs when depositors lose confidence in the bank and massive withdrawals of deposits occur. The bank loses reserves and must call in loans and sell off securities at unfavourable prices. Its own capital shrinks.

The red arrows in Figure 30.8 summarize the effects of these events and the problems they brought in the 2007–2008 financial crisis. A widespread fall in asset prices was triggered by the bursting of a house-price bubble in the US that saw house prices switch from rapidly rising to falling. With falling house prices, sub-prime mortgage defaults occurred and the prices of mortgage-backed securities and derivatives whose values are based on these securities began to fall. Many of these mortgage backed securities were being held by banks and financial institutions around the world.

People with money market mutual fund deposits began to withdraw them, which created a fear of a massive withdrawal of these funds analagous to a bank run like the one experienced by Northern Rock.

With low reserves and even lower own capital, banks, in turn, called in loans. A lot of these loans were to other banks in the money market. The loanable funds market and money market dried up.

Because the loanable funds market is global, the same problems quickly spread to other economies, and foreign exchange markets became highly volatile.

Hard-to-get loans, market volatility and increased uncertainty transmitted the financial and monetary crisis to real expenditure decisions.

Figure 30.8 The Ingredients of a Financial and Banking Crisis

Event	Deposits	+ Own capital	= Reserves	+ Loans and securities	*Problem*
Widespread fall in asset prices		▼		▼	Solvency
Currency drain	▼		▼		Liquidity
Run on bank	▼	▼	▼	▼	Liquidity and solvency

The Policy Actions

Policy actions in response to the financial crisis on both sides of the Atlantic dribbled out over a period of more than a year. Here, we'll focus on the UK policy actions, which may be placed under four broad headings:

- Interest rate cuts
- Bank bailouts
- Quantitative easing
- Macro-prudential regulation

Interest Rate Cuts

The Bank of England's first and natural response to the 2007 financial crisis was to lower Bank Rate. But it acted slowly at first. In August 2007 when the initial shocks were felt, Bank Rate was at a relatively high 5.75 per cent. The Bank was more concerned about the risk that inflation would burst through the 3 per cent upper bound of its target than it was about the risk of recession so the Bank Rate cuts were timid: down to 5.5 per cent in December, 5.25 per cent in February 2008, and 5 per cent in April 2008.

It wasn't until the crisis deepened with massive bank failures in the US and tottering UK banks that interest rates fell steeply. But starting in October 2008, the fall was steep, down to 0.5 per cent by March 2009.

Bank Bailouts

The first signs that the financial crisis might be serious and need an extraordinary policy response was the run on Northern Rock. At first, the Bank of England hesitated to act. But in September 2007, it extended a deposit insurance guarantee to Northern Rock's depositors and provided emergency loans to the bank.

The serious risk of bank failure and massive bailouts didn't come until a year later, in October 2008, when the biggest banks, RBS, Lloyds TSB and HBOS were on the brink of collapse.

The policy response to this situation blurs the distinction between monetary policy and fiscal policy for it was the UK government, not the Bank of England, that made the bold moves. The government forced a merger between Lloyds and HBOS and injected £37 billion into RBS and the enlarged Lloyds TSB. These banks were now partly owned by the taxpayer – 60 per cent in the case of RBS and 40 per cent in the case of Lloyds.

The other two large commercial banks, Barclays and HSBC, raised additional capital without government help.

The bailed out RBS and Lloyds turned out to need a further injection of public funds in November 2009 when they received a further £31 billion. This injection of funds took the taxpayer stake in RBS to 84 per cent, making it virtually a nationalized firm.

The goal of these massive and unusual injections of public funds into large commercial banks was designed to ensure that the banks didn't fail. Failure would have had a ripple effect (a tsunami effect is perhaps a better metaphor) through the entire national and global financial system and would have brought an enormous crash in the quantity of money (bank deposits) in the UK economy.

Quantitative Easing

The Bank of England launched a programme of quantitative easing in March 2009. **Quantitative easing (QE)** occurs when the Bank of England creates an increase in the monetary base by buying government bonds and high grade corporate bonds in the open market. The sellers of these bonds might be commercial banks but they also are pension funds and insurance companies. The Bank set aside £200 billion for QE purchases.

You can see that QE is a type of *open market operation*. In normal times, the Bank of England performs open market operations by buying repurchase agreements, *repos*, and UK Treasury Bills. These open market operations (see p. 721) supply the quantity of reserves that enable the Bank of England to keep short-term interest rates close to Bank Rate.

With the large interest rate cuts after October 2008, open market operations were used on a massive scale to keep the banks well supplied with reserves. This action lowered bank holdings of securities and increased their reserves.

The Bank of England's QE open market operations take place in the market for loanable funds. With short-term interest rates as low as they can go, the goal of QE is to increase the monetary base and lower long-term interest rates.

The idea is that QE would make the banks flush with excess reserves, which they would lend to firms and households. The quantity of money would increase and asset prices would rise. With easier access to credit and greater wealth from higher asset prices, consumption expenditure and investment would increase aggregate demand and real GDP would grow more quickly.

Did QE succeed in achieving its goals? The final verdict is not yet in but a first look at the effects of QE is not encouraging.

QE did not lower long-term interest rates (although it might have prevented them from rising) and it did not bring a large increase in bank lending and the quantity of money.

Interest rates on long-term bonds had fallen from around 5 per cent in mid-2008 to around 3.25 per cent in March 2009 when QE began. From March 2009 to end 2010, interest rates on long-term bonds had no visible trend or change.

The commercial banks reserves swelled but rather than increasing loans to firms and households, the banks have sat on their excess reserves. Consumers have been using any spare cash to pay off debt (repay loans to the banks).

The overall outcome is that the monetary base has risen but the quantity of money has not. Figure 30.9 shows the growth of the M4 definition of money and the money multiplier. Both fell dramatically during 2009 and remained low during 2010.

Supporters of QE say that without it the recession would be even worse and if there is a fault it is that the Bank of England has been too timid and should have employed QE on a larger scale.

Figure 30.9 QE, M4 Growth and the Money Multiplier

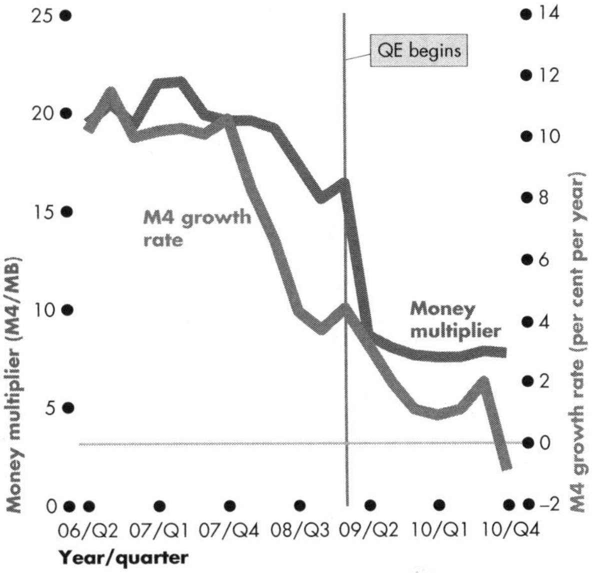

Before the Bank of England embarked on its QE policy, the money multiplier was falling and the growth rate of M4 was slowing. After QE began, the money multiplier crashed as the commercial banks sat on their excess reserves and M4 growth slowed even further as people paid off existing bank loans.

Source of data: Bank of England.

myeconlab Animation

Macro-prudential Regulation

Macro-prudential regulation is regulation of the monetary financial institutions and other financial institutions and financial markets to lower the risk of crisis and failure of these institutions and markets.

We briefly described how monetary financial institutions are regulated in Chapter 24 (see p. 562). The key components of this regulation are the assignment of responsibility for oversight and monitoring of financial institutions and markets and rules governing the liquidity and scale of own funds for financial institutions.

UK macro-prudential regulation is evolving and will change over the next few years as the Bank of England plays an enhanced role along with the Treasury and the Financial Services Authority.

A debate will be ongoing about what it means for a bank to be 'too big to fail' and whether large banks should be broken up into smaller banks.

A further ongoing debate will consider the appropriate scale and cyclical characteristics of commercial banks'own funds and the appropriate composition of a bank's assets and liabilities.

While all the extraordinary measures evolve and respond to the changing situation, the Bank of England will need to keep a firm grip on its main policy objective: its inflation target.

Review Quiz

1. What are the three main ingredients of a financial and banking crisis?
2. What policy actions have the Bank of England and the UK government taken in response to the financial and banking crisis?
3. What is QE and what is the key idea in using it?
4. Did QE work?

You can work these questions in Study Plan 30.3 and get instant feedback. myeconlab

To complete your study of monetary policy, take a look at *Reading Between the Lines* on pp. 734–735 and see how the Bank of England faced a monetary policy dilemma in 2011.

Reading Between the Lines

Monetary Policy Dilemma

The Financial Times, 1 February 2011

Conflicting Data Paint Picture of Two-speed Economy

FT

Norma Cohen

Conflicting data have presented a picture of a two-speed economy that is likely to sharpen the dilemma the Bank of England's policy setters face at their monthly meeting next week.

Output from the UK manufacturing sector surged to a record high in January according to a closely watched survey, with readings for new orders showing a particularly sharp rise. Offsetting that positive finding were new data showing that lending to businesses and households was very weak in December, coupled with news that the National House price survey showed a 0.1 per cent decline in January from a month earlier. . . .

The Markit/CIPS survey for the purchasing managers' index rose to 62 in January from 58.7 in December, the highest reading since the survey was created in 1992.

Underscoring the growth message – given the historical link between expansion and rising prices – the survey also flashed a danger signal on inflation. Input prices – the cost of goods the manufacturers need to assemble their products – registered their highest reading on record. Markit, which compiles the index said average purchase prices had risen at the steepest pace in the survey's history. . . .

In any case, offsetting the strong message from the manufacturing survey, were new data from the Bank showing that lending to private non-financial companies contracted again in December, that approvals for loans to buy homes fell to a 21 month low and that a key measure of money supply is contracting. . . .

Over all, the data suggest very sluggish lending to the household sector. The rate at which total net lending to households is growing, looked at over the previous six month or 12 month periods, is the slowest since the Bank began keeping records in 1988. On these measures net lending is expanding at rates of 0.4 and 0.7 per cent.

The Essence of the Story

- A survey of purchasing managers in the manufacturing sector indicates a fast recovering UK economy.
- Bank lending to businesses is weak and new mortgage loans and house prices have fallen.
- Other data suggest a build up of inflationary pressure with input prices rising rapidly.
- With conflicting information about different parts of the economy, the recovery remains fragile.

Economic Analysis

- The UK economy is sending conflicting signals that make it difficult to read the true strength of the recovery.
- Figure 1 shows the strong expansion of manufacturing output throughout 2010. This signal suggests a strong recovery.
- Inflationary pressure has been building up with input prices of the production industries rising at double-digit rates and CPI inflation is above the upper bound of the inflation target (see Figure 30.1, p. 719).
- Inflation expectations are also increasing. Figure 2 shows that inflation is expected to hit 4 per cent a year in 2011 and to be close to 3 per cent per year in five years.
- Both the manufacturing output and inflation data suggest a strong recovery that requires a a rise in Bank Rate and a reversal of quantitative easing (QE) to bring the inflation rate back into the target range.
- Other indicators point in the opposite direction. Figure 3 shows the rate of growth of bank lending to businesses and households, which fell throughout 2010.
- The dilemma for the Bank of England is whether it should raise Bank Rate to choke off rising inflation expectations or keep Bank Rate low and anticipate that a weakening recovery will remove the inflationary pressures.
- If the recovery really is fragile, raising Bank Rate might stop the recovery and send the economy into a double dip recession.
- If the recovery really is strong, not raising Bank Rate risks a permanent rise in the expected inflation rate, which will be costly to lower in the future.
- Making the wrong decision will increase the volatility of real GDP growth and inflation and delay the recovery. The outcome could be higher inflation or lower real GDP growth.

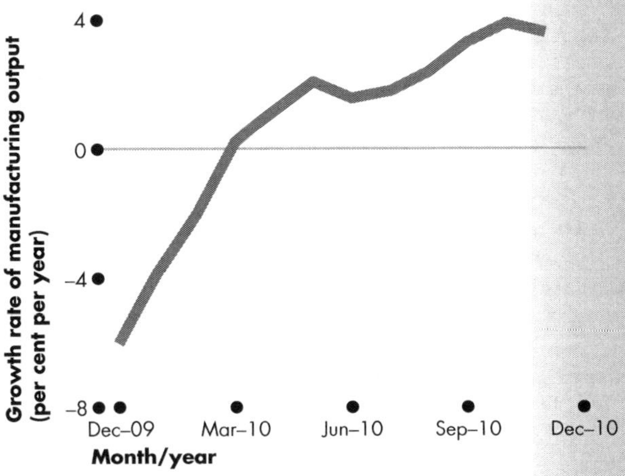

Figure 1 Growth rate of manufacturing output

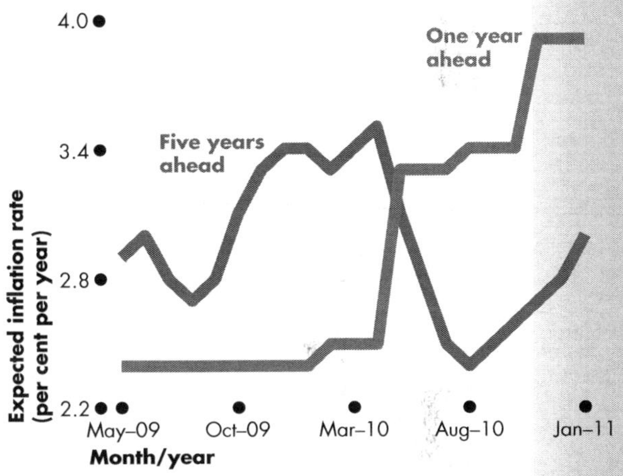

Figure 2 Inflation expectations

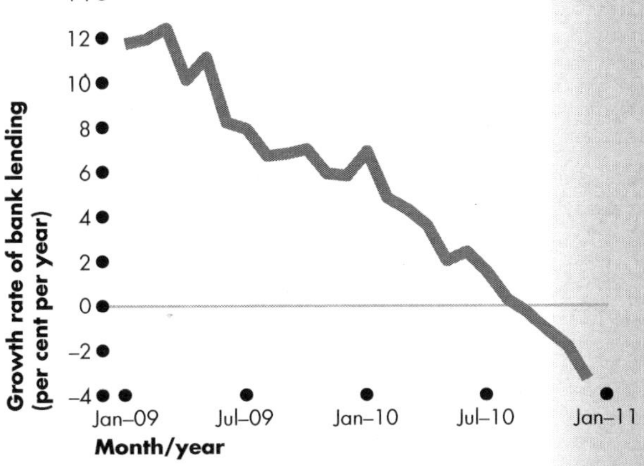

Figure 3 Growth of bank lending

SUMMARY

Key Points

Monetary Policy Objectives and Framework

- The Bank of England Act 1998 requires the Bank to use monetary policy to achieve stable prices and to support the government's economic policies of high and stable economic growth and employment.
- Each year, the Chancellor of the Exchequer specifies the Bank's remit in terms of a numerical target for the inflation rate.
- Since 2004, the Bank has been required to achieve an inflation rate measured by the CPI of 2 per cent a year.

Working Problems 1 to 5 will give you a better understanding of monetary policy objectives and framework.

The Conduct of Monetary Policy

- The Bank's monetary policy instrument is Bank Rate.
- The Bank's Monetary Policy Committee (MPC) sets Bank Rate and announces any change at roughly monthly intervals.
- The Bank pushes the repo rate close to Bank Rate by using open market operations.
- By buying or selling securities in the open market, the Bank is able to change bank reserves and change the repo rate.

Working Problems 6 to 10 will give you a better understanding of the conduct of monetary policy.

Monetary Policy Transmission

- A change in Bank Rate changes other interest rates, the exchange rate, the quantity of money and loans, aggregate demand and eventually real GDP and the price level.
- A change in Bank Rate changes real GDP a year to 18 months later and changes the inflation rate with an even longer time lag.

Working Problems 11 to 20 will give you a better understanding of monetary policy transmission.

Extraordinary Monetary Stimulus

- A financial crisis has three ingredients: a widespread fall in asset prices, a currency drain and a run on banks.
- The Bank of England and Treasury responded to the financial crisis with four groups of measures: steep interest rate cuts, bank bailouts, quantitative easing and macro-prudential regulation.

Working Problems 21 to 26 will give you a better understanding of extraordinary monetary stimulus.

Key Terms

Macro-prudential regulation
Monetary policy instrument
Quantitative easing (QE)
Repo rate

STUDY PLAN PROBLEMS AND APPLICATIONS

myeconlab You can work Problems 1 to 26 in MyEconLab Chapter 30 Study Plan and get instant feedback.

Monetary Policy Objectives and Framework (Study Plan 30.1)

1 'Unemployment is a more serious economic problem than inflation and it should be the focus of the Bank of England's monetary policy.' Evaluate this statement and explain why the Bank's primary policy goal is price stability and not full employment.

2 'Because the CPI inflation rate includes the prices of food and fuel, which are volatile and influenced by global demand and supply, the Bank of England should strip these items from the index that it targets.' Explain why the Bank of England is required to target the CPI inflation rate.

3 'Monetary policy is too important to be left to the MPC. The government should be responsible for it.' How is responsibility for monetary policy allocated among the MPC, Parliament, and the government?

4 **Mervyn King Gives Warning over UK Public Deficit**

Mervyn King says the government must cut the public deficit.

Source: BBC, 20 January 2010

a Does the governor of the Bank of England have either authority or responsibility for the UK government budget deficit?

b How might a government budget deficit complicate the Bank's monetary policy? [Hint: Think about the effects of a deficit on interest rates.]

c How might the Bank's monetary policy complicate Parliament's deficit cutting? [Hint: Think about the effects of monetary policy on interest rates.]

5 **Inflation: Surging Fuel Costs Push CPI to 3.4 per cent**

At 3.4 per cent, consumer price inflation (CPI) is now way above the Bank of England's government-set target of 2 per cent, the highest since January and one of the steepest rates in Europe.

Source: *The Guardian*, 20 April 2010

a What does this news clip imply about the MPC's interest rate decisions?

b How can the 3.4 per cent inflation rate be reconciled with the Bank of England's obligations under the 1998 Bank of England Act?

The Conduct of Monetary Policy (Study Plan 30.2)

6 What are the two possible monetary policy instruments, which one does the Bank of England use, and how has its value behaved since 2004?

7 How does the Bank of England hit its repo rate target? Illustrate your answer with an appropriate graph.

8 What does the Bank of England do to determine whether Bank Rate should be raised, lowered or left unchanged?

Use the following news clip to work Problems 9 and 10.

Bank of England's Trade-off

When the Bank of England's MPC meets on Thursday, it will be shaping up for its first three-way vote, amid an intensifying debate on the trade-off between apparent signs of inflation and indications that the economy is sinking into stagnation.

Source: *The Financial Times*, 6 October 2010

9 Explain the dilemma faced by the Bank of England in October 2010.

10 **a** Why might the MPC have decided to cut Bank Rate in the months following the October 2010 meeting?

b Why might the MPC have decided to raise Bank Rate in the months following the October 2010 meeting?

Monetary Policy Transmission (Study Plan 30.3)

11 What are the roles of Bank Rate and the long-term interest rate in the monetary policy transmission process?

12 **a** Is it the long-term nominal interest rate or the long-term real interest rate that influences spending decisions? Explain why.

b How does the market determine the long-term nominal interest rate and why doesn't it move as much as the short-term rates?

Use the following news clip to work Problems 13 and 14.

The Pound's Sharp Fall

Masahiro Sakane, chairman of Komatsu, the Japanese maker of construction and mining equipment, says the company's plant in north-east England will benefit from the pound's sharp fall against the euro.

Source: *The Financial Times*, 5 March 2010

13 How does a lower sterling exchange rate influence monetary policy transmission?

14 Would a fall in the exchange rate mainly influence unemployment or inflation?

Use the following news clip to work Problems 15 to 17.

Economists Growth Forecasts

Economic recovery and job creation in the UK over the next few years will depend on growth in business investment.

Source: *The Financial Times*, 29 December 2010

15 Explain the effects of the Bank of England's low interest rates on business investment. Draw a graph to illustrate your explanation.

16 Explain the effects of business investment on aggregate demand. Would you expect it to have a multiplier effect? Why or why not?

17 What actions might the Bank of England take to stimulate business investment further?

Use the following news clip to work Problems 18 to 20.

Shrinking Economy Shock

The UK economy shrank in the final quarter of 2010, a shock contraction that casts doubt on the strength of growth in the industrialised world and the wisdom of early fiscal tightening.

Source: *The Financial Times*, 25 January 2011

18 If real GDP continues to shrink, what would most likely happen to the output gap and unemployment in 2011?

19 **a** What actions that the Bank of England had taken in 2009 and 2010 would you expect to influence UK real GDP growth in 2011? Explain how those policy actions would transmit to real GDP.

b Draw a graph of aggregate demand and aggregate supply to illustrate your answer to part (a).

20 What further actions might the Bank of England take in 2011 to influence the real GDP growth rate in 2011? [Remember the time lags in the operation of monetary policy.]

Extraordinary Monetary Stimulus

(Study Plan 30.4)

Use the following news clip to work Problems 21 to 23.

UK Pound Weakens on QE Bets

The pound fell to the weakest level in almost seven months against the euro as mortgage approvals dropped to the least since March 2009, heightening speculation that the Bank of England may soon be pressed into quantitative easing.

Source: fxnonstop.com, 25 October 2010

21 What is the connection between actions that the Bank of England might take and the foreign exchange value of the pound?

22 What is the significance of falling mortgage approvals? How does that suggest further QE?

23 Why might the Bank contemplate further QE? What are the arguments for and against further quantitative easing at the beginning of 2011?

24 Suppose that the UK government had not bailed out RBS and Lloyds and instead had allowed them to fail.

a How would the failure have changed the quantity of money and interest rates?

b How would real GDP and the inflation rate have been different?

25 Suppose that the Bank of England had raised Bank Rate in 2010 as the inflation rate moved above the 3 per cent upper bound.

a How would the repo rate have differed from its actual path?

b How would real GDP and the inflation rate have been different?

26 **Prospects Rise for US Federal Reserve Easing Policy**

William Dudley, president of the New York Fed, raised the prospect of the Fed becoming more explicit about its inflation goal to 'help anchor inflation expectations at the desired rate.'

Source: ft.com, 1 October 2010

a Why might inflation targeting be especially important in a financial crisis?

b How does 'anchor[ing] inflation expectations at the desired rate' help to make QE work better?

ADDITIONAL PROBLEMS AND APPLICATIONS

myeconlab You can work these problems in MyEconLab if assigned by your lecturer.

Monetary Policy Objectives and Framework

Use the following information to work Problems 27 to 29.

The statutory role of the Bank of England is to maintain price stability, and subject to that, to support the economic policy of Her Majesty's Government, including its objectives for growth and employment.

27 Explain the harmony among these goals in the long run.

28 Explain the conflict among these goals in the short run.

29 Based on the performance of UK inflation and unemployment in 2010, which of the Bank's goals appears to have taken priority?

30 The deep 2008–2009 recession and the overshoot of inflation above the upper bound of the target suggests that the inflation target should be raised. Do you agree? Why or why not?

31 Suppose the Chancellor of the Exchequer decided to strip the Bank of England of its operational independence to meet a government specified inflation target and gave Cabinet the task of deciding interest rate changes. How would you expect the policy choices to change? Which arrangement would most likely provide price stability?

32 The European Central Bank (ECB) targets the Eurozone inflation rate to make it remain below but close to 2 per cent a year. To pursue this goal, the ECB sets the official ECB interest rate but pays close attention to the growth rate of the quantity of money.

a Compare and contrast the policy objectives of the ECB and the Bank of England.

b Compare and contrast the policy strategies of the ECB and the Bank of England.

Use the following news clip to work problems 33 and 34.

Government borrowing rose from £17.4 billion a year ago to £23.3 billion in November the highest total for a single month since records began in 1993, and much higher than the £17 billion that economists had predicted.

Source: *The Financial Times*, 21 December 2010

33 How would the government deficit change in 2011 and 2012 if the Bank of England raised interest rates?

34 How would the government deficit change in 2011 and 2012 if the Bank of England did not raise the rate of interest and the value of sterling depreciated sharply?

The Conduct of Monetary Policy

35 Looking at Bank Rate since 2000, identify periods during which, with the benefit of hindsight, the rate might have been kept too low. Identify periods during which it might have been too high.

36 Explain the dilemma that rising inflation and weakening growth poses for the Bank of England.

37 Why might the Bank of England decide to lower interest rates when inflation is rising and growth is weakening?

38 Why might the Bank of England decide to raise interest rates when inflation is rising and growth is weakening?

Monetary Policy Transmission

Use the following information to work problems 39 to 41.

From 2008 to 2010 the rate of interest on UK 10-year maturity bonds fell from 4.6 per cent a year to 3.6 per cent a year. During the same period, the Bank Rate fell from 4.7 per cent a year to 0.5 per cent a year.

39 What role does the long-term real interest rate play in the monetary policy transmission process?

40 How does the Bank Rate influence the long-term real interest rate?

41 What do you think happened to inflation expectations between 2008 and 2010 and why?

Use the following information to do problems 42 and 43.

Financial markets predict a 95 per cent or more certainty that rates will rise by a quarter of a percentage point in June, October and January over 2011 and 2012, leaping from 0.5 per cent to 1.25 per cent.

Source: *The Financial Times*, 24 January 2011

42 How do expectations of the future of the interest rate influence the exchange rate?

43 How does monetary policy influence the exchange rate?

44 **Dollar Tumbles to 15-year Low Against Yen**

The dollar tumbled to a fresh 15-year low on persistent fears over the US economic outlook.

Source: yahoo.com, 7 October 2010

a How do 'fears over the US economic outlook' influence the exchange rate between the US dollar and the UK pound?

b How does US monetary policy influence the exchange rate between the US dollar and the UK pound?

c How does US monetary policy influence the UK economy?

Use the following news clip to work Problems 45 and 46.

Top Economist says America Could Plunge into Recession

Robert Shiller, Professor of Economics at Yale University, predicted that there was a very real possibility that the US would be plunged into a Japan-style slump, with house prices declining for years.

Source: timesonline.co.uk, 31 December 2007

45 What challenge do falling house prices pose for the conduct of monetary policy? How could monetary policy prevent house prices from falling?

46 Describe the time lags in the response of output and inflation to monetary policy actions designed to respond to falling house prices.

Use the following news clip to work Problems 47 and 48.

Greenspan Says Economy Strong

The US central bank chairman, Alan Greenspan, said inflation was low, consumer spending had held up well through the downturn, housing-market strength was likely to continue, and businesses appeared to have unloaded their glut of inventories, setting the stage for a rebound in production.

Source: cnn.com, July 16, 2002

47 What monetary policy actions would you expect to have created the situation described by Alan Greenspan?

48 What monetary policy actions would you expect a central bank to take in the situation described by Alan Greenspan?

Extraordinary Monetary Stimulus

49 Between August 2007 when the global financial crisis started and April 2008, Bank Rate was cut from 5.75 per cent to 5 per cent. Only when the shockwaves intensified in October 2008 did the Bank of England respond with extraordinary rate cuts, dropping Bank Rate to 0.5 per cent by March 2009.

a Why was the Bank of England so timid in its initial interest rate cuts in the first year of the global financial crisis?

b How would you expect the massive rate cuts between October 2008 and March 2009 to influence real GDP and the inflation rate in 2009, 2010 and 2011? Describe the transmission mechanisms and the time lags.

50 Explain how bailing out troubled banks and taking them into public ownership avoids the risk of a serious collapse of aggregate demand. Does the government borrowing to buy the troubled banks have any effect on aggregate demand?

51 Explain the key differences between QE and normal open market operations.

52 What are the three ingredients of a financial and banking crisis and how do the four extraordinary monetary policy actions address each of them?

53 The UK economy suffered a shock contraction in real GDP in the fourth quarter of 2010. Shadow chancellor Ed Balls said the figures were a matter of 'great concern' and due largely to the speed and scope of the coalition government's deficit reduction programme.

Source: BBC, 24 January 2011

a If the Bank of England had expected the economy to weaken in the fourth quarter, what policy actions might it have taken differently from what it did take?

b Describe the time lags in the response of output to the policy actions you have prescribed.

Economics in the News

54 After you have studied *Reading Between the Lines* on pp. 734–735 answer the following questions.

a Why does the Bank of England face a dilemma in setting monetary policy?

b What would be the short-term and long-term consequences of delaying a rise in the interest rate if inflation turned out to remain above the upper bound of the target throughout 2011?

c What would be the short-term and long-term consequences of raising interest rates immediately if the UK economy was weak during 2011?

d What is the role of expectations in determining what the Bank of England monetary policy should be in the current period?

55 The governor of the Bank of England Mervyn King said that inflation could reach 5 per cent a year within a few months and that this was of more concern than the surprise drop in GDP in the fourth quarter of 2010.

Source: *The Daily Telegraph*, 15 February 2011

a What was the Bank of England's monetary policy throughout 2010?

b Given the Governor's comments, what would you expect the Bank of England's monetary policy to be in 2011?